Teacher's Edition

¡Ya verás! GOLD
Nivel 1

John R. Gutiérrez
The Pennsylvania State University

Harry L. Rosser
Boston College

Marta Rosso-O'Laughlin
Tufts University

HH **Heinle & Heinle Publishers**
An International Thomson Publishing Company
ITP Boston, MA • 02116 • U.S.A.

Visit us on the Internet **http://yaveras.heinle.com**

The publication of the *¡Ya verás! Gold*, **Nivel 1**, Teacher's Edition was directed by the members of the Heinle & Heinle School Publishing Team.

Team Leader: Vincent Duggan
Publisher: Denise St. Jean
Production Services Coordinator: Mary McKeon
Market Development Director: Pamela Warren

Also participating in the publication of this program were:

Assistant Editor: Sonja Regelman
Manufacturing Coordinator: Wendy Kilborn
Development, Design, Composition: Hispanex Inc.
Cover Art: Mark Schroder
Cover: Rotunda Design

Manufactured in the United States of America

ISBN 0-8384-8428-X (Teacher's Edition)

Library of Congress Catalog Card Number:

10 9 8 7 6 5 4 3 2

Contents

◆

Welcome to ¡Ya verás! *Gold* • • • • • • • • • • • • • • **4**

The *¡Ya verás! Gold* Textbooks 5
The *¡Ya verás! Gold* Program Components 6
Philosophy and Goals 8

¡Ya verás! *Gold, Nivel 1* • • • • • • • • • • • • • • • • **9**

The Student Text 9
The Teacher's Edition 13
The Components 14

Teaching with ¡Ya verás! *Gold, Nivel 1* • • • • • • • • • • • **18**

General Teaching Suggestions 18
Working with Native Spanish Speakers 20
Planning the School Year on Varied Schedules 22
Sample Lesson Plans 23

Pedagogical Considerations • • • • • • • • • • • • • • • • • • • **25**

Critical Thinking Skills 25
Cooperative Learning 25
Pair Work and Group Work 26
Assessment 28
Teacher Behaviors 31
¡Ya verás! Gold and The Multiple Intelligences 33
¡Ya verás! Gold and *The Standards for Foreign Language Learning* 35

The ¡Ya verás! *Gold* Program Scope and Sequence • • • • **36**

Scope and Sequence of *Nivel 1* 36
Scope and Sequence of *Nivel 2* 40
Scope and Sequence of *Nivel 3* 44

Welcome to
¡Ya verás! Gold!

The program that makes it easy for you and your students to shine!

* Students accomplish more with its accessible organization and manageable chapter format.

* Standards-based textbook sections and time-saving correlations to the Five Cs in the Teacher's Edition make it easy to address the Foreign Language Standards.

* Complete technology options, including video, CD-ROM, writing assistant software, Internet activities, and real-time chat rooms, create exciting links to the Spanish-speaking world.

* Skill-based strategies, process writing, Multiple Intelligences correlations and teaching tips, suggestions and components for Spanish-speaking students—and more!—empower every student to succeed.

The ¡Ya verás! Gold Textbooks

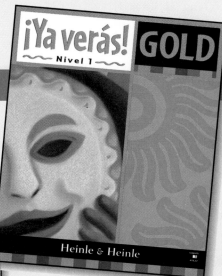

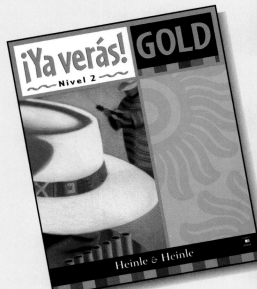

The *¡Ya verás! Gold* Program Components

Nivel 1

Print/Media Components

- TEACHER'S EDITION
- WORKBOOK
- LABORATORY MANUAL
- TEACHER'S EDITION OF THE WORKBOOK/LAB MANUAL
- LABORATORY PROGRAM CASSETTES/CDS
  For use with the Laboratory Manual
- TEXTBOOK CASSETTES/CDS
  For pronunciation, textbook-related listening activities, and recordings of selected in-text readings
- TAPESCRIPT
  Transcripts of the Laboratory Program and Textbook Cassettes/CDs
- MIDDLE SCHOOL GUIDE
  Teaching suggestions, **Etapa** activities, and **Nivel A** to **Nivel B** bridging activities
- WORKBOOK FOR SPANISH-SPEAKING STUDENTS

- ANSWER KEY TO THE WORKBOOK FOR SPANISH-SPEAKING STUDENTS
- OVERHEAD TRANSPARENCIES
- TEACHER'S RESOURCE BOOK
  Placement test for Spanish-speaking students, unit grammar review masters, activity masters for textbook-related listening and oral work, and an optional Preliminary Chapter for level 1
- LESSON PLAN BOOK
  Plans for traditional and block schedules
- TESTING PROGRAM
  Quizzes, tests, exams, portfolio assessments, oral assessments
- TESTING CASSETTES/CDS
  For use with the Testing Program
- VIDEOSCRIPT AND VIDEO ACTIVITIES
- VIDEO GUIDE

Technology Components

- VIDEO PROGRAM
  Chapter-level and unit-level modules
- *MUNDOS HISPANOS 1* DUAL PLATFORM CD-ROM
- PRACTICE SOFTWARE FOR WINDOWS AND MACINTOSH
- *ATAJO* WRITING ASSISTANT FOR WINDOWS AND MACINTOSH
- COMPUTERIZED TESTING PROGRAM FOR WINDOWS WITH TEACHER'S GUIDE
- COMPUTERIZED TESTING PROGRAMS FOR MACINTOSH WITH TEACHER'S GUIDE
- *¡YA VERÁS!* WEB SITE
  Chapter-level and unit-level Internet activities
- *PUEBLOLINDO* VIRTUAL INTERACTIVE COMMUNITY
  Real-time chat rooms free-of-charge to users of Heinle & Heinle Spanish materials, text-specific activities for individuals and pairs/small groups, and Teacher's Manual

Nivel 2

Print/Media Components

- TEACHER'S EDITION
- WORKBOOK
- LABORATORY MANUAL
- TEACHER'S EDITION OF THE WORKBOOK/LAB MANUAL
- LABORATORY PROGRAM CASSETTES/CDS
- TEXTBOOK CASSETTES/CDS
- TAPESCRIPT
- WORKBOOK FOR SPANISH-SPEAKING STUDENTS
- ANSWER KEY TO THE WORKBOOK FOR SPANISH-SPEAKING STUDENTS
- OVERHEAD TRANSPARENCIES
- TEACHER'S RESOURCE BOOK
- LESSON PLAN BOOK
- TESTING PROGRAM
- TESTING CASSETTES/CDS
- VIDEO GUIDE

Technology Components

- VIDEO PROGRAM
- *MUNDOS HISPANOS 2* DUAL PLATFORM CD-ROM
- PRACTICE SOFTWARE FOR WINDOWS AND MACINTOSH
- *ATAJO* WRITING ASSISTANT FOR WINDOWS AND MACINTOSH
- COMPUTERIZED TESTING PROGRAM FOR WINDOWS WITH TEACHER'S GUIDE
- COMPUTERIZED TESTING PROGRAM FOR MACINTOSH WITH TEACHER'S GUIDE
- *¡YA VERÁS! GOLD* WEB SITE
- *PUEBLOLINDO* VIRTUAL INTERACTIVE COMMUNITY

Nivel 3

Print/Media Components

- TEACHER'S EDITION
- WORKBOOK
- LABORATORY MANUAL
- TEACHER'S EDITION OF THE WORKBOOK/LAB MANUAL
- LABORATORY PROGRAM CASSETTES/CDS
- TEXTBOOK CASSETTE/CDS
- TAPESCRIPT
- WORKBOOK FOR SPANISH-SPEAKING STUDENTS

- ANSWER KEY TO THE WORKBOOK FOR SPANISH-SPEAKING STUDENTS
- OVERHEAD TRANSPARENCIES
- TEACHER'S RESOURCE BOOK
- LESSON PLAN BOOK
- TESTING PROGRAM
- TESTING CASSETTES/CDS
- VIDEO GUIDE

Technology Components

- VIDEO PROGRAM
  Unit-level modules
- PRACTICE SOFTWARE FOR WINDOWS AND MACINTOSH
- *ATAJO* WRITING ASSISTANT FOR WINDOWS AND MACINTOSH
- COMPUTERIZED TESTING PROGRAM FOR WINDOWS WITH TEACHER'S GUIDE
- COMPUTERIZED TESTING PROGRAM FOR MACINTOSH WITH TEACHER'S GUIDE
- *¡YA VERÁS! GOLD* WEB SITE
- *PUEBLOLINDO* VIRTUAL INTERACTIVE COMMUNITY

For Middle School Students

- STUDENT TEXTS, *NIVEL A* AND *NIVEL B*
- WORKBOOKS, *NIVEL A* AND *NIVEL B*
- MIDDLE SCHOOL GUIDE
  Teaching suggestions, **Etapa** activities, and **Nivel A** to **Nivel B** bridging activities

Philosophy and Goals

¡Ya verás! Gold is a communicative, integrated learning system grounded in the principles of the American Council on the Teaching of Foreign Languages (ACTFL) *Proficiency Guidelines*. The program also responds to the most recent challenges and opportunities experienced by modern language educators. These include a diverse, heterogeneous student population, multiple course schedules, increased emphasis on student-centered instruction, alternative assessment options, rapidly changing and growing technology, and the increasing impact of the *Standards for Foreign Language Learning: Preparing for the 21st Century* on curriculum requirements, course content, classroom objectives, and teaching practices.

Principles of the *¡Ya verás! Gold* Program

¡Ya verás! Gold is based on a number of principles and assumptions:

- The principles of the ACTFL *Proficiency Guidelines* can serve effectively as the underpinnings of a communicative approach in which students learn to function as accurately as possible within contexts and in situations they are most likely to encounter either in a Spanish-speaking country or with Spanish speakers in the United States.

- The *Standards for Foreign Language Learning* of the 1990s encompass the principles of the Proficiency Guidelines of the 1980s and properly go beyond them to provide modern language professionals with a broader, informed view of what students should know and be able to do.

- The four skills—listening, speaking, reading, and writing—and culture can and should reinforce one another in an ever-widening spiral.

- Language learning materials should assist teachers in making the transition to standards-oriented instruction by incorporating the Five Cs of the *Standards for Foreign Language Learning*—Communication, Cultures, Connections, Comparisons, and Communities.

- Contexts should be selected according to the frequency with which they occur in real life so that students can readily relate to them.

- Student-student and student-teacher interaction should be based on tasks that simulate real-world situations.

- It is possible for students to use the language creatively from the outset and, therefore, free expression can and should be encouraged on a regular basis.

- Everyday spoken Spanish does not include every vocabulary item and grammatical structure in the Spanish language. Thus, language-learning materials should emphasize the elements most frequently used by native speakers in daily life.

- Grammar is a means for effective communication. It should therefore not be presented for its own sake but for its role in transmitting spoken and/or written messages as accurately as possible.

- Trial and error are a necessary part of the language-acquisition process.

- Because assimilation requires sufficient time and practice, it demands frequent, consistent recycling as students progress through materials.

- Language-learning materials and teaching techniques should be student-centered and accommodate the varied ways in which students learn, acknowledging both the Multiple Intelligences and learning styles.

- Language learning materials need to be flexible and offer extensive resources—both print- and technology-based—to meet students' and teachers' diverse needs.

- The goal of teaching is to make students independent users of Spanish.

Classroom Implications

- What students "can do" is the primary focus of instruction oriented to the development of functional proficiency. Grammar, pronunciation, syntax, and cultural aspects of language study are viewed as tools used to accomplish functional tasks. In *¡Ya verás! Gold*, students are made aware of the task at hand and the functions that are needed to carry it out. Tasks are placed in a context that is culturally realistic, as well as meaningful and interesting for students.

- For students to become proficient speakers of another language, they need time to engage in communicative oral activities. The more time students spend in pair and group work, the more oral practice each of them will have. *¡Ya verás! Gold* has been built around a progression of carefully planned and well-timed paired and small-group activities, ranging from controlled to meaningful to open ended.

- Since the curriculum in a proficiency-oriented program is spiral, rather than linear, the scope and sequence of *¡Ya verás! Gold* is based on the premise that for students to be able to use what they are learning, the curriculum cannot treat each topic or structure during only one segment of the course. Instead, it must return again and again to the same functions, the same contexts, and the same structures, each time reinforcing what has gone before while introducing new elements.

- The development of language proficiency can be enhanced by activities that integrate the skills, that is, in which work in one skill can serve as stimulus material to activities in another skill. *¡Ya verás! Gold* develops all four language skills as well as culture, and in keeping with its real-life focus, provides realistic, multi-faceted activities in which students implement a cross-section of skills within a given context.

The Student Text

The *¡Ya verás! Gold, Nivel 1*, student text consists of six units. Each unit contains three chapters, which are further divided into brief, manageable lessons called **etapas**. Each chapter ends with an **En línea** Internet-based feature, a **Vocabulario** section that lists all active word and expressions and an **Encuentros culturales** reading. Each unit concludes with a multi-faceted **¡Sigamos adelante!** section. If you wish to begin your classes without the textbook, an optional Preliminary Chapter is provided in the Teacher's Resource Book.

Perhaps the most important aspect of *¡Ya verás! Gold* are the **etapas**, which serve as built-in lesson plans designed for completion in two 50-minute classes or in one 90-minute block. Students succeed by working with manageable amounts of vocabulary and grammar backed up with plenty of meaningful and communicative activities. The **etapas** are also unique in that, in addition to new material, each contains a review of the previous **etapa** and a final review of the **etapa** itself.

Every **etapa** contains the vocabulary, functions, and grammar necessary to its sub-theme. These, in turn, contribute to the functions and contexts of the chapter, which, in turn, illustrate the larger context of the unit. Articulation within units and across units is thus assured through the interplay and integration of functions, contexts, and accuracy features, as laid out in the scope and sequence of the *¡Ya verás! Gold* Program at the end of this Teacher's Guide.

The Unit Opener

Each unit begins with a two-page spread that sets the scene for the unit's three chapters. Objectives expressed in functional terms, as well as the titles of the chapters and their **etapas**, are listed. Photographs illustrate the unit's overarching theme. The **¿Qué ves?** section poses a series of questions that gets students to examine the photographs, drawing them into the theme and building their background knowledge and anticipation.

The Chapter Opener

The chapter opening page spotlights the aspect of the unit theme that will be addressed throughout the chapter. Chapter-specific objectives are provided in functional terms and a captioned photo or other illustration brings the chapter theme to life.

The Etapa Sections

Preparación

The **Preparación** section focuses students on the **etapa** theme through questions that build background and/or prior knowledge and engage them in thinking critically about the upcoming content.

Etapa Opener

Through a variety of formats—dialogues, monologues, third-person narratives, captioned drawings and photo collages, and authentic and simulated documents—the **etapa** opener introduces vocabulary central to the **etapa's** theme. Simultaneously, it virtually always activates targeted language functions and previews grammatical structures to be presented in the **etapa**. The **etapa** opener is largely supported by an overhead transparency and, whenever appropriate, is recorded on the Textbook Cassettes/CDs.

¡Te toca a ti!

The **¡Te toca a ti!** exercises and activities practice the new vocabulary presented in the **etapa** opener, in most cases moving students from controlled responses to open-ended use of the language. Among the many activity types featured are sentence completions, directed conversations, visually-cued activities, realia-based tasks, personal questions, diverse pair work and small group work, full-class circulating activities, situations, role-plays, surveys, and interviews accompanied by grids that students are to complete.

Comentarios CULTURALES

The **Comentarios culturales** expand the development of the **etapa's** theme, describing the practices, perspectives, and products of Spanish-speakers and Hispanic cultures throughout the Spanish-speaking world. Where appropriate, comparisons are drawn between the culture in which students operate in the United States and the cultures of Spanish-speakers to develop further their awareness of both cultures. The **Comentarios culturales** sections appear on a floating basis within an **etapa** in order to capitalize on cultural references as they arise.

PRONUNCIACIÓN

The pronunciation sections appear strategically, explaining the basics of the Spanish sound system as they relate to the vocabulary students are learning. Points covered include the Spanish alphabet, the vowels, vowel combinations, consonants such as **d, g, n, ñ, l, ll, r,** and **rr,** sounds such as **/k/, /b/,** and **/s/,** and the **jota.**

The explanations bring out the differences and similarities between the Spanish and English sound systems, thereby helping students to understand the nature of both languages. In addition, they always move from symbol to sound so that students are given the tools to pronounce the sounds in new words as they proceed through the textbook.

Each **Pronunciación** section is reinforced by a **Práctica** exercise, permitting immediate practice of the point presented. The pronunciation explanation and **Práctica** exercise are both recorded on the Textbook Cassettes/CDs.

Repaso

Unique to *¡Ya verás! Gold,* the **Repaso** activities build students' confidence with consistent recycling of vocabulary, grammatical structures, and language functions presented in previous **etapas.** Systematically integrated, the **Repaso** activities allow students to revisit previously seen language five or six times in every chapter in both familiar and new contexts. The activities take on a wide range of types—from visually-based to pair and small-group work.

ESTRUCTURA

Each **Estructura** section presents a new grammatical structure from a communicative perspective—that is, the grammar point is tied logically to the theme and context(s) of the **etapa** and to the tasks that students are expected to carry out. The explanations are written in English throughout so that students may use them independently for study and reference at home or in class. Wherever applicable, the new structures, in tandem with their model sentences, are compared and contrasted with English to allow students to discover linguistic and grammatical patterns and to foster awareness of the similarities and differences between the ways both languages express ideas and concepts.

NOTA GRAMATICAL

Where applicable, the **Nota gramatical** sections follow up **Estructura** sections, calling out refinements or closely related subpoints.

PALABRAS ÚTILES

The **Palabras útiles** sections present lexical points and uses of vocabulary items and/or phrases directly related to the main **Estructura** sections.

Aquí practicamos

The **Aquí practicamos** sections provide a series of exercises and activities that reinforce the explanations and language presented in the preceding **Estructura, Nota gramatical,** and/or **Palabras útiles** sections. The practice sets largely move students from mechanical or controlled responses to bridging, meaningful activities to open-ended, communicative tasks, focusing on the use of new language while also re-entering some previously presented vocabulary, grammar, and functions. The **Aquí practicamos** sections offer the same wide range of activity types as the **¡Te toca a ti!** sections.

Aquí escuchamos

The **Aquí escuchamos** listening section revolves around a conversation or monologue, recorded on the Textbook Cassettes/CDs but not printed in the student text, that incorporates the vocabulary, structures, and language function(s) of the **etapa.** Students are given full support for working with the listening passage through an initial scene-setting line followed by pre-, while-, and post-listening stages. Whenever these activities require writing on the part of students, an activity master is provided in the Teacher's Resource Book.

Antes de escuchar prepares students for the listening passage by concentrating on its theme and context with brief tasks that elicit background and/or prior knowledge and that engage students' critical thinking and anticipatory skills. **A escuchar** features varied activities such as checking off words or expressions heard, filling in grids with key ideas, identifying speakers, and completing cloze sentences to focus students' listening as they hear the conversation or monologue. Finally, **Después de escuchar** checks students' overall comprehension of what they heard.

In the listening passages, students are exposed to a wide range of native speaker voices and accents. Together with the Textbook Cassettes/CDs and the Activity Masters in the Teacher's Resource Book, the **Aquí escuchamos** sections help develop students' listening skills and build overall listening comprehension.

?¿Qué crees?

These short multiple-choice questions appear periodically in the margins of the student text, presenting interesting factoids about the Spanish-speaking world as they relate to the **etapa's** theme and contexts. The answers to the questions are found on the following page of the student text.

¡ADELANTE!

The **¡Adelante!** activities draw together the language presented throughout the entire **etapa**, recycling vocabulary, grammatical structures, and language functions as they foster creative use of Spanish and self-expression. Each section contains a capstone activity for speaking and another for writing. Among the speaking activities are cued conversations, situations, role-plays, interviews, surveys, and descriptions of drawings. Writing tasks include generating lists, postcards, notes, short letters, schedules/calendars, brief directed paragraphs, picture strip stories, posters, and illustration-based descriptions. The diversity of the activities is matched by the variety of ways in which students may carry them out— individually, with a partner, in small groups, or by circulating among the full class.

Because the **¡Adelante!** section occurs at the end of each **etapa**, students experience closure of chunks of related language and dynamic, engaging communicative interactions regularly and consistently.

The End-of-Chapter Sections

EN LÍNEA

Located at the end of the last **¡Adelante!** section in each chapter, **En línea** signals the availability of an Internet activity on the *¡Ya verás!* Web site. These activities not only reinforce the chapter's theme, language, and cultural points, they motivate students with their high-interest, youth-oriented topics and feature a complete series of support exercises and activities. Very importantly, the activities take students to linked Web sites throughout the Spanish-speaking world, creating connections through which students experience Spanish and the distinctive viewpoints of Spanish-speaking people directly. When students return to the *¡Ya verás!* Web site to complete the activities, they are led to process the information gathered and to apply it to real-life situations and themselves.

VOCABULARIO

The **Vocabulario** section provides a list of the active vocabulary presented in the **etapas** of each chapter. The listings are organized by language functions, contexts/themes, and general vocabulary under parts of speech. English equivalents are not provided so that students can use the section for reviewing before chapter tests, unit exams, and/or oral assessments you may wish to administer.

ENCUENTROS CULTURALES

The main source of reading instruction in *¡Ya verás! Gold*, each **Encuentros culturales** section spotlights a topic spun off from the chapter's theme. The reading selections expose students to varied text types with an emphasis on authentic passages and documents, providing linguistically and culturally rich input. Because the selections are from or cover diverse locations around the Spanish-speaking world, they also represent additional links to the distinctive viewpoints of Spanish speakers and their cultural practices, perspectives, and products.

The **Antes de leer** pre-reading section prepares students for the text, developing reading strategies and providing broad initial work with the selection. Marginal boxes list the strategies, such as activating background and/or prior knowledge, skimming, scanning, and examining format for content clues, to heighten students' consciousness that reading skills can be transferred from English to Spanish and/or acquired and used to improve their reading in both languages.

The **Guía para la lectura** section highlights receptive vocabulary and cultural information key to students' understanding of the selection. Comprehension of main ideas and important details is checked through a variety of formats in the **Después de leer** section. The final item in these activities homes in on students' personalized reactions to what they read and asks them to apply the reading to their own lives.

Conversemos un rato

The **Conversemos un rato** communicative activities are the oral performance points to which all of the materials in the unit's three chapters lead. By bringing together vocabulary, grammar, cultural points, and language functions presented across all three chapters, they provide opportunities for students to demonstrate the language they know, in which contexts, and with what degree of accuracy.

The activities are done in pairs or small groups. Instructions are given primarily in English to avoid giving away key structures and vocabulary and to encourage students to use a variety of ways to express themselves. Using English in the direction lines also approximates real-life situations in which students might find themselves in Spanish-speaking communities in the United States or in Spanish-speaking countries. For example, if they were to enter a store in Guadalajara, Mexico their reason for being there would exist in their minds in English.

Taller de escritores

The **Taller de escritores** section is devoted to developing students' writing skills using a process-oriented approach. As students work with the writing assignments, which involve real-life, meaningful tasks, they are taken through a series of activities laid out in four distinct steps—reflection or pre-writing, first draft, peer editing, and final draft. The culminating fifth step provides options for "publication," evaluation, or the placement of the final writing product in students' portfolios.

The writing strategy focused on in each **Taller de escritores** section is listed for students in a marginal box. As is the case with the marginal reading strategies boxes, the intent is to impress upon students that they can improve their writing skills through specific techniques.

Conexión con...

The **Conexión con...** sections link students' study of Spanish to content from other disciplines such as mathematics, sociology, and geography. Carefully chosen for their relationship to the unit's theme, the selections broaden students' learning experiences and expand their information base through familiar and relevant subject matter.

The **Para empezar** section sets the scene for the material, activates prior and/or background knowledge, and encourages the use of critical thinking skills. Follow-up comprehension and interactive activities elicit students reactions and ask students to apply the information in various ways—individually, in pairs, in small groups, or as a class.

Vistas

Each **Vistas** section spotlights from one to four Spanish-speaking countries or areas of significant Hispanic influence and presence in the United States. Photographs draw students into the locations. Students gain an overview of each place from listings of the capital and principal cities, population figures, geographical statistics, languages spoken, and currencies used. The **Vistas** sections are arranged so that by the end of *¡Ya verás! Gold*, **Nivel 3**, students will have "visited" the twenty Spanish-speaking countries around the world, as well as eight American states.

EXPLORA

The **Explora** feature concludes each **Vistas** section, informing students that they can learn more about the spotlighted locations by visiting the **Nuestros vecinos** page on the *¡Ya verás!* Web site. Here, students will find a list of linked URLs to which they can connect for additional information and direct experiences with the targeted places. By tapping these technology-based resources, students gain new vehicles for practicing their language skills and for enriching their knowledge of contemporary culture and everyday life in the target locations. And because students get to choose among the URLs, they can experience the motivation and empowerment that comes from controlling the direction their explorations take.

En la comunidad

The **En la comunidad** sections address directly the "C" of Communities of the *Standards for Foreign Language Learning*. Each section begins with a monologue by an individual who shares how knowing Spanish benefits his/her professional life, underscoring the valuable role students' study of Spanish can play in the careers on which they eventually embark. The featured individuals, whose jobs are related to the unit theme, represent varied walks of life, and, like most of your students, are non-native Spanish speakers.

Follow-up **¡Ahora te toca a ti!** activities then propel students beyond the classroom with easily executed, manageable tasks that get them using their knowledge of Spanish in their community and/or investigating its presence. If you and your students live in a community where Spanish and its influence is a rare commodity, an option related to the selected career is also provided for your use.

The Teacher's Edition

The Teacher's Edition is your principle teaching resource for *¡Ya verás! Gold, Nivel 1*. In addition to this Teacher's Guide, it contains a wealth of information designed to save you time as you use the student text and its components. Multi-faceted marginal annotations also provide on-the-spot support where you need it at its point of use.

Marginal Support Boxes and Annotations

- Highly visible, at-a-glance Unit, Chapter, and **Etapa** Support Materials boxes with correlations and specific references to all applicable program components

- Component-specific icons with correlations and specific references at point-of-use

- Chapter Objectives broken out by functions, contexts, accuracy, and pronunciation

- Clear Teach/Model and Practice/Apply markers throughout each **etapa** and **¡Sigamos adelante!** section

- Unit, chapter, and **etapa** warm-ups and wrap-ups

- Setting the Context information

- A Multiple Intelligences correlation box for every **etapa** and every part of each **¡Sigamos adelante!** section

- A *Standards for Foreign Language Learning* correlation box for every **etapa** and every part of each **¡Sigamos adelante!** section

- Focus on Culture and Spanish for Spanish Speakers boxes with suggestions, and other useful information

- Individual Needs boxes with tips for more-prepared and less-prepared students

- FYI annotations that highlight miscellaneous information and reminders about additional resources

- References to each chapter's Improvised Conversation or Monologue and its corresponding Textbook Activity Master

- Annotations for virtually every activity and section of each **etapa**, chapter, and **¡Sigamos adelante!** section with icons pinpointing the skills (for example, listening or critical thinking) and the dynamics (for instance, pair work or cooperative learning)

- Suggestions for addressing the Multiple Intelligences and learning styles over and above the materials in the student text

- Suggestions spun off from student text materials for increased implementation of the *Standards for Foreign Language Learning*

Samples of the Varied Tips Provided in the Teacher Annotations

- **ANSWERS**
- **PRESENTATION**
- **EXPANSION**
- **SUGGESTION**
- **FYI**
- **VARIATION**
- **POSSIBLE ANSWERS**
- **VOCABULARY EXPANSION**

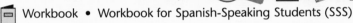

Component Icons

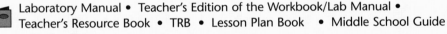

- Workbook • Workbook for Spanish-Speaking Students (SSS)

- Laboratory Manual • Teacher's Edition of the Workbook/Lab Manual • Teacher's Resource Book • TRB • Lesson Plan Book • Middle School Guide • Testing Program

- Laboratory Program Cassettes/CDs • Textbook Cassettes/CDs • Testing Cassettes/CDs

- Tapescript

- Video Guide • Video Program

- *Mundos hispanos 1* CD-ROM

- Practice Software • Computerized Testing Programs

- *Atajo* Writing Assistant

- Overhead Transparencies

Skill Icons

- Critical Thinking
- Listening

- Writing
- Speaking

Special Purpose Icons

- Cooperative Learning
- Pair Work
- Group Work
- Role Play

- Internet
- Multiple Intelligences
- *Standards for Foreign Language Learning*

The Components

The Workbook provides extensive and varied contextualized writing activities that reinforce the vocabulary, grammatical structures, and language functions presented in each **etapa**. Two resources included to help students use the workbook independently of the student text are the **Vocabulario** list found at the end of each chapter in the student text and **Repaso** recaps of in-text grammar explanations.

A Planning Strategy worksheet, containing personalized questions set in the context of the unit theme, opens each unit to get students anticipating and thinking critically about what they will study.

An **Aquí leemos** section closes each unit with authentic documents or texts followed by comprehension checks, a logic and/or word game, and a directed writing assignment. The workbook contains numerous art- and realia-based activities. Several writing assignments are corrrelated via icons to the *Atajo* Writing Assistant Software.

 LABORATORY MANUAL

The Laboratory Manual contains contextualized listening-and-speaking, listening-and-reading, and listening-and-writing activities for each chapter to be done in conjunction with the Laboratory Program Cassettes/CDs. Listening discrimination and pronunciation exercises are also included. The activities are based on a variety of features such as grids, charts, check-off lists, drawings, authentic documents, and simulated realia.

Special end-of-chapter activities revolve around the continuing story of a group of Hispanic teenagers from Mexico, Puerto Rico, Colombia, Spain, and the United States who run a fictional worldwide radio network, **Radio futuro**. At the end of each unit, a series of **Ya llegamos** activities recycles and recombines language presented across the units' chapters.

 TEACHER'S EDITION OF THE WORKBOOK/LAB MANUAL

This is the combined Workbook and Lab Manual with overprinted answers to all activities.

 LABORATORY PROGRAM CASSETTES/CDS

This set of twelve cassettes or ten CDs contains the recordings to be used in conjunction with the chapter-level and unit-level listening activities in the Laboratory Manual. They offer a variety of native speaker voices from around the Spanish-speaking world.

 TEXTBOOK CASSETTES/CDS

The Textbook Cassettes/CDs are for use with the student textbook. They move sequentially through the **etapas**, providing recordings of the majority of **etapa** openers, the **Pronunciación** explanations and their accompanying **Práctica** exercises, and the **Aquí escuchamos** listening passages. The final recording for each chapter is a semi-scripted improvised conversation or monologue centered around the chapter theme and its functions, vocabulary, and structures. Not printed in the student text, each improvised conversation and monologue is referenced in the Teacher's Edition along with its accompanying Textbook Activity Master.

The recorded **etapa** openers represent the types of speech that people listen to in real-life situations, for example conversations, monologues, and narratives. Materials that are clearly reading-based, such as illustration captions and authentic documents, are not included. The Textbook Cassettes/CDs feature the voices of various native-speakers, including diverse accents, recorded with attention to clarity and manageable rates of speech.

 TAPESCRIPT

This contains complete transcripts of the Laboratory Program Cassettes/CDs and the Textbook Cassettes/CDs.

MIDDLE SCHOOL GUIDE

The Middle School Guide provides practical suggestions for working with middle school students, as well as age-appropriate, **etapa**-level activities for the eighteen chapters of the student text. Bridging activities that review the principle language functions, vocabulary, and grammatical structures of *¡Ya verás! Gold*, *Nivel A* for students who are beginning *Nivel B* are also included.

 WORKBOOK FOR SPANISH-SPEAKING STUDENTS

The Workbook for Spanish-Speaking Students contains materials tailored to the needs of Spanish speakers who are enrolled in classes with non-native Spanish learners. At the beginning of each chapter, a reading, supported by pre- and post-reading and Spanish glosses, previews grammatical and other points in context. The **Sonidos y palabras** section treats sounds and homophones that pose difficulties to Spanish speakers. **Nuestro idioma** focuses on problematic grammatical structures, regional usage, language variation, and false cognates. Both sections are fully reinforced by practice activities.

Each chapter ends with **¡Adelante!** speaking and writing activities that recycle language covered throughout the chapter. A unit-level **¡Sigamos adelante!** section with **Conversemos un rato** oral activities and a process-oriented **Taller de escritores** writing section additionally synthesizes the language taught across three chapters. Throughout the workbook, the themes and content presented are closely related to those in the corresponding chapters and units of the student textbook. This is to make the work of Spanish-speaking students a cohesive, easy-to-manage part of *¡Ya verás! Gold* and all of your classes.

 ANSWER KEY TO THE WORKBOOK FOR SPANISH-SPEAKING STUDENTS

This answer key contains the answers to all activities in the workbook with discrete responses.

 OVERHEAD TRANSPARENCIES

These full color visuals feature maps of the Spanish-speaking world and reproductions of drawings, photographs, and authentic documents from the student text for use with sections and activities in the student text.

 TEACHER'S RESOURCE BOOK

The Teacher's Resource Book (TRB) provides several important tools: unit-level masters with summaries of grammar explanations and additional practice sets, activity masters for use with the **etapa**-level **Aquí escuchamos** sections and the chapter-level improvised conversations/ monologues, and worksheets for use with oral textbook activities that require completing grids or other forms of writing.

The Teacher's Resource Book also contains the Placement Test for Spanish-Speaking Students. This important diagnostic tool consists of listening, speaking, reading, and writing assessments with scoring rubrics and administration guidelines.

 LESSON PLAN BOOK

This valuable resource saves preparation time with lesson plans for each **etapa** and **¡Sigamos adelante!**, organized in warm-up, presentation, review, recycling, and assessment segments. Also included are warm-up-to-assessment sequences for end-of-chapter materials. Suggestions for fifty-minute class periods and ninety-minute block schedules are provided, as well as sample plans for the 4 x 4 and AB blocks.

TESTING PROGRAM

The Testing Program includes **etapa** quizzes, chapter tests, unit exams, and a final exam that check listening, reading, and writing skills, as well as grammar, vocabulary, and culture, in contexts mirroring the textbook themes and language functions. Oral assessments are provided for all chapters and units. The Testing Program begins with Portfolio Assessment and ends with a Teacher's Guide containing complete answer keys, scoring guides, the scripts for all listening sections, and grading rubrics for the oral assessments.

TESTING CASSETTES/CDS

These cassettes and CDs contain recordings of the listening comprehension sections included in the Testing Program for each **etapa** quiz, chapter test, unit test, and final exam. All materials were recorded for clarity and appropriate rates of speech and with the voices of many different native Spanish speakers.

VIDEO GUIDE

The first part of the Video Guide features the complete transcript of the chapter- and unit-level modules of the Video Program. The second part consists of pre-viewing activities and manageable, realistic viewing and post-viewing activities tailored to students' language abilities.

 VIDEO PROGRAM

The *¡Ya verás!* Gold, *Nivel 1* Video Program brings authentic input and the Spanish-speaking world into the classroom with a module for each textbook chapter and unit. The chapter modules feature engaging dramatic scenes and interviews with native speakers from diverse age groups and walks of life that recycle and expand on the theme and language presented in the student text. In conjunction with the worksheets in the Video Guide, carefully crafted, on-screen instruction and strategies empower students to work successfully with the scripted and authentic footage.

The unit-level **Vistas** modules zoom in on a country or city in the United States showcased in the corresponding **Vistas** section in the student text. The captivating images enable students to experience directly everyday life, cities, towns, monuments, and breathtaking geographical panoramas throughout the Hispanic world. The accompanying specially-scripted narratives purposely reuse and reinforce previously taught vocabulary and grammar to heighten students' enjoyment of and success with the segments.

 MUNDOS HISPANOS 1 CD-ROM

This dual platform, interactive multimedia program provides richly textured and culturally loaded chapter-by-chapter vocabulary, grammar, listening, and reading segments with full pedagogical support. Chapter-specific writing tasks are carried out by easy access to the *Atajo* Writing Assistant program which is fully incorporated into each of the three program CDs. Engaging and fun **Pasatiempos** activities that integrate language skills and cultural knowledge conclude every chapter. User-friendly exploration and navigation aids—a bilingual dictionary, vocabulary/grammar/pronunciation assistants, a program map, and a general help guide—are always available with a click of a button.

PRACTICE SOFTWARE

Available in Windows and Macintosh versions, this software includes mechanical and controlled practice of grammar and vocabulary for each chapter. The software can benefit students who need more time with language concepts. It may also be useful for students who have missed classes and require make-up work.

Esta ciudad, enclavada sobre un promontorio y rodeada por el Tajo, ha sido declarada[1] Monumento Nacional con todos sus palacios,[2] iglesias, puentes[3] y arrabales.[4] Posee muestras[5] inapreciables del arte árabe, mudéjar,[6] judío[7] y cristiano. Toledo representa el clásico cruce de culturas y es la síntesis más brillante de la historia y del arte españoles.

Lugares de interés
- Catedral gótica (siglo XIII)
- El Greco (Catedral, Museo del Greco, Santo Tomé, Museo de San Vicente, Santo Domingo el Antiguo, Capilla de San José)
- Sinagoga del Tránsito
- Santa María la Blanca
- Mezquita[8] del Cristo de la Luz
- Hospital de Santa Cruz
- Hospital de Afuera
- Alcázar, en reconstrucción

Toledo
CIUDAD DE MÚLTIPLES CULTURAS

ATAJO WRITING ASSISTANT

This award-winning software for Windows and Macintosh is a complete student-centered support system for the development of writing skills in Spanish that combines a powerful word processor with databases of language reference materials. As students write and edit their work in one on-screen window, they can call up multiple windows containing information customized to their specific writing needs.

The easy-to-access, extensive databases include a bilingual dictionary of 10,000 entries, recordings of the dictionary entries and contextualized examples of their usage, a Spanish spell-check, a verb conjugator of over 500,000 verb forms, a grammar reference, an index of language functions, and groupings of thematically-organized vocabulary.

Atajo is ideal for use with every **¡Adelante!** writing activity in the student text and with all workbook activities accompanied by the *Atajo* icon. Teacher annotations also conveniently correlate each in-text **Taller de escritores** section to *Atajo*, including specific references to its index of language functions, vocabulary database, and reference grammar.

 ## COMPUTERIZED TESTING PROGRAMS

Available in Windows and Macintosh versions, the computerized testing programs offer a bank of testing items that can be used in addition to or in place of the printed Testing Program. The bank may be customized by modifying existing items, adding new items, and randomly selecting among these items to create as many versions of quizzes, tests, or exams as desired. The accompanying Teacher's Guide describes hardware requirements, installation procedures, and easy-to-implement instructions.

 ## ¡YA VERÁS! *GOLD* WEB SITE

Located on the Internet at yaveras.heinle.com, the *¡Ya verás!* Web Site features exciting and dynamic materials for you and your students. The **Para profesores** page supplies program-related information plus suggestions for using the Internet in Spanish classroom. The **Información** page makes available a glossary of common Spanish Internet terms, tips about searching for Spanish sites, and other resources that will help you and your students navigate the net successfully in Spanish. The **¡Tienes que verlo!** page lists "cool sites" from around the Hispanic world, all of which are in Spanish.

Very importantly, the Web site contains two pages that expressly reinforce the chapters and units in *¡Ya verás! Gold, Nivel 1*. Activities complementing each chapter's theme and language are found on the **Actividades** page. Truly interactive, these contextualized activities give students detailed instructions about the series of tasks to be performed, emphasizing specific information that students are to find at linked Web sites around the Spanish-speaking world. As students surf the net visiting the sites, they gather the information and return to the *¡Ya verás!* Web site to enter it in the worksheets. Each set of tasks then ends with a personalized, communicative activity that students carry out with a partner, in a small group, or by circulating among the full class.

The **Nuestros vecinos** page is an extension of the **Vistas** sections in each unit's **¡Sigamos adelante!** section. Links to sites for all twenty Spanish-speaking countries and the United States take students to every corner of the Hispanic world.

PUEBLOLINDO VIRTUAL INTERACTIVE COMMUNITY

For the first time with any Spanish textbook program, your students can communicate in real-time with both native Spanish speakers and other students of Spanish in an Hispanic cyber town, complete with all the sights and sounds of Spanish-speaking cultures.

Available on the Internet at www.PuebloLindo.heinle.com, *PuebloLindo* is a virtual interactive community (VIC) with multiple locations designed as chat rooms. Students can take a cab to the **Avenida Central** to meet up with friends or attend a **tertulia** in the **Escuela de lenguas**. They can visit diverse locations like the **Oficina de Turismo**, the **Restaurante La Amistad**, and the **Casa de Cambio** where they engage in real-world tasks as they meet and talk to others.

Free-of-charge to users of Heinle & Heinle Spanish materials, *PuebloLindo* also provides paired, small-group, and individual activities specific to *¡Ya verás! Gold*. A Teacher's Manual contains helpful materials such as a complete description of the VIC and an explanation of the pedagogy and successful technological precedents on which it is based.

Teaching with ¡Ya verás! Gold, Nivel 1

General Teaching Suggestions

You may find it helpful to refer to earlier sections in this Teacher's Guide for descriptions of the textbook sections mentioned here. Because the special features and annotations in the Teacher's Editions provide extensive, detailed teaching support for each section and activities, this section covers general tips and techniques.

The *Etapas*

It is important to keep in mind both the completeness and the flexibility inherent in the **etapas**. Because of their rich, yet efficient construction, you may choose to proceed through them in a linear fashion, without having to reorganize the material or worry about such questions as variety, the recycling of material, or pacing. On the other hand, you may also decide to skip certain parts and return to them as review mechanisms after having begun a subsequent **etapa**. For example, you might treat the **Aquí escuchamos** section in this fashion, or you might choose to have students work on only the oral activity in an **¡Adelante!** section, reserving the writing activity for homework or for in-class work as you administer oral assessments to individual students. Instead of pausing to do the **Repaso** activities where they occur, you might occasionally opt to use them as warm-ups or bell ringers. A key part of the **etapa** structure is that it affords you both a built-in linear lesson plan that you may follow sequentially and a tool you can shape to your own preferences and time constraints.

Estructura, Nota gramatical, and Palabras útiles

In general, these sections can be presented either inductively or deductively. It is recommended, however, that, whenever possible, an inductive approach be used. In either case, it is beneficial to have students close their books so that they pay close attention to your examples and explanations. You might also want to make grammatical presentations in simplified, telegraphic-style Spanish, punctuated by examples.

The deductive approach is most appropriate for grammar points that do not merit prolonged class time, are particularly simple, have an exact equivalent in English, or do not lend themselves readily to an inductive presentation. Examples of this type of grammatical structure are demonstrative adjectives (**este, esta, ese, esa**) and the interrogative adjective **cuánto** and its various forms. Rather than devoting valuable class time to lengthy presentations, such grammatical topics are best dealt with as efficiently as possible to leave more time for practice. The following are examples of inductive and deductive approaches to presenting the preterite.

The Inductive Approach (from example to rule)

- Put some drawings on the board or use a transparency that shows a person going through a series of actions done on a typical day.
- Have students say what the person does typically, using the present tense.
- Put the previous day's date on the board to signal **ayer**.
- Redo each action, using the preterite.
- Go through the actions again and have students repeat each item.
- Use yourself and the first person singular to transform each item.
- Have students individually use the first person to go through the actions again.
- End your presentation with a short, concise explanation about the formation.
- Return to the drawings and have students redo the sequence of actions using different pronouns.

The Deductive Approach (from rule to example)

- Put several examples of the preterite on the board or on a transparency.
- Explain the rules of formation in simple terms using the examples.
- Elicit uses of the preterite through personalized questions and answers.

Textbook Exercises and Activities

While the teaching annotations in the Teacher's Edition provide numerous suggestions for using the practice materials in the student text, it may be worthwhile to point out that many of exercises and activities can be used with books closed, as well as open, or with a combination of closed and open books. Having students practice vocabulary and grammar with books closed can bring a welcome change of pace to the classroom that can be either teacher-centered or student-centered wherever appropriate.

In addition, controlled exercises and activities can be carried out in an interesting fashion by having students work in pairs so that one partner's book remains opened and the other's is closed. Students can run through the entire activity this way and then switch roles, as well as open and closed books, and go through the activity once again. This gives each student the opportunity to give and receive the cues or to ask and answer the questions. A variation on this technique is to have students do the same, but one student has the book open and the other closed for the odd-numbered items. They then switch to do the even-numbered items.

Encuentros culturales

These cultural readings may be used in varied ways. You can have students read them silently in class or have them read only the first paragraph silently and then proceed to having selected students read each subsequent paragraph aloud. You might also read aloud to students, emphasizing key points and using your voice and gestures to increase the immediacy and meaning of the selections. Timed reading can also be used for either entire readings or parts of them. When using this technique, tell students that they have a specific time period in which they are to read as much of the selection and/or paragraph(s) as possible to try to get the main ideas. Timed reading can help students improve both their focus on meaning and their reading speed.

Homework Options

The *¡Ya verás! Gold* components provide many materials that can be used for homework, such as the Workbook, the Workbook for Spanish-Speaking Students, the Unit Grammar Review masters, the video activities, the Internet activities, and *PuebloLindo*, but many teachers like to know that the student text can also be a source of homework assignments. While every textbook section can be assigned for study purposes in preparation for subsequent in-class work, following are some suggestions for homework based on specific sections.

- **Preparación:** Have students read and answer the questions in writing.

- **¡Te toca a ti!** and **Aquí practicamos:** Assign selected activities in their entirety, only the even- or odd-numbered items, or the first half of an activity.

- **Comentarios culturales:** Have students read the cultural notes and prepare comprehension checks of main ideas in various formats—true/false, multiple choice, matching, and simple questions. As students progress in their studies, these could be written in Spanish.

- **Estructuras, Nota gramatical,** and **Palabras útiles:** Assign for study as part of students' preparation for in-class participation during the next class.

- **¡Adelante!:** The oral activities can assigned for oral preparation in anticipation of the next class meeting. The writing activities can be done as homework, and any participation needed by a partner or other classmates can then take place in class.

- **Encuentros culturales:** These can be read and the comprehension checks done in writing. It is a good idea, however, to guide students through the pre-reading materials in class before assigning the remainder of the sections as homework.

- **Conversemos un rato:** As with the oral **¡Adelante!** activities, students can go over these activities on their own and make notes of words and expressions to use when doing them in class with other students.

- **Taller de escritores:** Both the **Primer borrador** and **Versión final** sections are appropriate for work outside of the classroom.

- **Conexión con…:** Students could complete the **Para empezar** section, read the selection, and do any comprehension or extension activities that do not require the involvement of a partner or other students.

- **En la comunidad:** Give students a time frame such as one or two weeks in which to carry out the **¡Ahora te toca a ti!** community-based activities and to prepare the report-back materials.

Working with Native Spanish Speakers

In the best of all possible worlds, schools would have two Spanish language tracks—one for monolingual speakers of English and another for native speakers of Spanish. The reality, as teachers nationwide know, is that many schools typically enroll native speakers in the same language classes as non-native learners of Spanish. What can you do if you find yourself in this situation? Although *¡Ya verás! Gold* was created to teach Spanish as a foreign language to non-native speakers of Spanish, it includes, as described earlier in this Teacher's Guide, three resources designed to address the special needs of Hispanic students who may be enrolled in your classes: The Placement Test for Spanish-Speaking Students, the Workbook for Spanish-Speaking Students along with its Answer Key, and distinctively boxed Spanish for Spanish Speakers marginal annotations throughout the Teacher's Editions.

Who are Native Speakers?

Native Spanish speakers is a broad term used to refer to the full spectrum of Hispanic students who have either grown up in or immigrated to the United States. Some of these students may well have learned to speak and understand Spanish at home, but may have never received formal instruction in reading or writing. Others may have learned to understand Spanish from hearing it used in their homes or immediate environments by family, family friends, and people in their communities, but have not cultivated their own speaking, reading or writing abilities. Some may be able to understand, speak, and read Spanish, but have not developed writing skills. Still others may have had very limited exposure to Spanish in their homes, depending on their families' attitudes toward maintaining the language and the number of generations the family has been in the United States. In addition, although there are areas in the United States where Hispanics of the same geographical origin have settled and continue to live over generations, it is not uncommon for other areas to be populated by Spanish-speakers from diverse heritages and from locations where different varieties of Spanish are used. Clearly, native speakers of Spanish are far from uniform in either the linguistic skills or the regional varieties of the language they bring to the classroom.

What do Native Speakers Bring to the Classroom?

The first order of business is to capitalize on the linguistic skills these students already bring to the classroom. If students already speak and comprehend Spanish, but lack competencies in reading and writing, they will need instruction in those skills. One focus should be teaching students how Spanish is expressed in the written mode. Contrary to general belief, Spanish is not as phonetic as people think—it is not written just the way it sounds. While it may be more phonetic than English or French, it is far from what linguists would term a phonetic language. For example, the sound of /k/ can be written with a number of symbols: **qu (que, queso)**; **c** before **a, o, u (casa, cosa, cuna)**; and even with the letter **k (kilo, kimono)**. As Spanish-speaking students take their first steps toward becoming literate in Spanish, they need to devote some attention to spelling. The following chart shows some of the more problematic sound/symbol correlations they need to master.

Problematic Sound/Symbol Correlations

b	**v**	**z + a**	**z + o**
z + u	**c + e**	**c + i**	**s + any vowel**
h	**x**	**ll**	**y**
g + e	**g + i**	**j**	

Another area that can be addressed to improve literacy is reading instruction. *¡Ya verás! Gold* incorporates a number of reading activities that reflect the latest research in this area. Hispanic students in modern language classes generally already read English, for they have most likely been educated in American schools. (Students who are not yet literate in English should be in ESL classes rather than modern language classes.) However, as reading research has shown, the transfer of reading skills from one language to another is far from automatic. Because students need support when learning to read any language, special attention should be paid to having Spanish-speaking students go through all of the activities that accompany the readings in *¡Ya verás! Gold*.

What about "Standard" Spanish?

Although many Hispanic students already speak Spanish, it may not be the variety of language that is taught in the typical classroom. In sociolinguistic terms, people in this group are termed "diglossic". This means that while one language is used for all formal or what are termed "high" functions, another is used in all informal or "low" functions. Among many Hispanics in the United States, English is generally considered appropriate for formal exchanges (political rallies, business meetings, announcements, sermons, lectures, classrooms, etc.), and Spanish is used in informal situations within the home and among other members of the speech community. Because of this, many Spanish-speaking students have seldom had the opportunity to hear Spanish as it is used for the high or formal functions of the language, except perhaps for radio and television where available. Having had few models for the high or formal register of the language, their skills in this aspect of Spanish have remained underdeveloped. In light of this, it is important that part of the classroom learning of these students involves becoming aware of varied language registers and getting acquainted with formal and academic Spanish.

Most Spanish-speaking students can expand their range of functions in Spanish. The Spanish that they speak is not wrong. The only mistake they may make is to use the particular variety of Spanish they know in an inappropriate social situation. However, many people, including members of the Spanish teaching profession, often refer to what these students speak as "dialect," a term that can convey connotations of substandard, even defective. In fact, any variety of a language is technically a dialect, even the educated standard. Again, drawing from the field of sociolinguistics, everyone speaks a dialect. The tremendous concern over "correct" speech is explicable only when the social functions of dialects are considered, even though it can be shown that no dialect is inherently better or worse than another. It is necessary for students to be able to command educated varieties of speech if they wish to be able to hold certain kinds of jobs. However, any attempt to teach a standard dialect to a nonstandard speaker needs to take into account the social reasons that explain why people speak the way they do.

With regard to listening, most students, even those whose families have been in the United States for three or four generations and who may have weak speaking skills, will be able to understand spoken Spanish. What they need to work on is exposure to the variety of ways that Spanish is spoken. As all Spanish teachers know, there are a number of ways to speak Spanish correctly. A Spaniard does not sound like a Chilean, nor a Bolivian like a Mexican, nor a Puerto Rican like an Argentine. The listening activities of the *¡Ya verás! Gold* student texts, textbook cassettes/CDs, laboratory programs, videos, and CD-ROMs have been created with this in mind. Spanish-speaking students hear the language as it is spoken in many parts of the Spanish-speaking world. This not only exposes them to a wide range of language varieties and registers; it also validates for them the very existence of language variation and instills them with pride in the richness of their heritage language.

Finally, since Spanish-speaking students are not beginning from ground zero, it is up to you, as teachers, to meet them where they are and take them as far as you can. Always endeavor to be sensitive to how they express themselves, for while it may be inappropriate to use certain vocabulary words and expressions in the classroom, it may be completely appropriate to do so within their speech community. Rather than "fixing" how they speak and write Spanish, it is up to you to capitalize on the linguistic strengths they bring to your classroom and help them increase their range of linguistic functions.

Planning the School Year on Varied Schedules

Completing the Textbook

¡*Ya verás! Gold, Nivel 1* is intended to be completed in one school year. If you do not finish the textbook because of factors particular to your school and classes or lack of familiarity with the materials during the first two years of using the program, this should not be a major source of concern to you. It is important to know that ¡*Ya verás! Gold, Nivel 2* begins with a complete review of the major language functions, vocabulary, and grammatical structures presented throughout level 1 in three preliminary chapters called **Capítulos preliminares A, B,** and **C.** Further, ongoing, consistent recycling and re-entry of language is a hallmark of the level 2 textbook and its accompanying ancillaries. For teachers who wish to have a sense of a reasonable stopping point in ¡*Ya verás! Gold, Nivel 1*, it is recommended that you complete **Unidad 5,** so that students will have been exposed to the present tense, the preterite, and the future with **ir a** + infinitive.

The following general suggestions for planning the school year using ¡*Ya verás! Gold, Nivel 1* are based on the core material in the textbook. If you choose to try out some or all of the options and additional activities suggested in the teacher annotations, you will want to keep pacing in mind. There are many inviting suggestions from which to choose; however, attempting to do everything, particularly during your first year of using the program, could keep you from completing the textbook in one year.

¡Ya verás! Gold, Nivel 1 and Schools with Fifty-Minute Class Periods

School/Class-Related Activities and Textbook Sections	Number of Days
Total class days	180
Administration and school events	15
Testing	24
Optional preliminary chapter (3 **etapas**)	6
The first chapter of each unit (3 **etapas** each)	36
The second and third chapters of each unit (2 **etapas** each)	48
The **Encuentros culturales** sections (1½ days each)	27
The **¡Sigamos adelante!** sections (4 days each)	24

¡Ya verás! Gold, Nivel 1 and Schools on Block Scheduling

School/Class-Related Activities and Textbook Sections	Number of Blocks
Assumed number of total blocks	90
Administration and school events	9-11
Testing	12-13
Optional preliminary chapter (3 **etapas**)	3
The first chapter of each unit (3 **etapas** each)	18
The second and third chapters of each unit (2 **etapas** each)	24
The **Encuentros culturales** sections	9
The **¡Sigamos adelante!** sections	13-14

Sample Lesson Plans

The following lesson plans are abbreviated versions of the lesson plans you will find in the Lesson Plan Book. The full-length versions contain complete correlations to ancillary materials such as cassettes/CDs and transparencies, as well as alternative and expanded activities. The following samples are provided for a 50-minute class period and a 90-minute block. These lesson plans are not meant to be definitive or prescriptive. Many options exist for using *¡Ya verás! Gold, Nivel 1* effectively and creatively in the classroom. Clearly, no one lesson plan can respond to the wide range of class schedules, the diversity of students and teachers, and the curriculum guidelines and needs of all districts and schools. For additional information and model lesson plans, refer to the *¡Ya verás! Gold, Nivel 1,* Lesson Plan Book.

50-minute Class Period

Day 1

Warm-up	Choose one of the following warm-up activities to introduce the students to basic expressions in Spanish: the *Planning Strategy* from the *Workbook*, p.1, the Preliminary Chapter of the *Teacher's Resource Book* pp. 1-8, or the **Los nombres españoles** activity in the *Middle School Teacher's Guide*, p.1.	5 minutes
Etapa **Presentation**	Present the introductory dialogues and photos in the *Student Edition*, p. 3. Use *Transparency 8* to focus on specific items. Pair up students to role-play the mini-dialogues. Present the **saludos, despedidas** and **respuestas** in the *Student Edition*, p. 4. Have students practice the new expressions by completing Activities A & B.	10 minutes
Pronunciation	Play the recording of the alphabet and of the **Práctica**, Activity C, from the Textbook Cassettes/CDs. Have students spell words from the **Práctica**, as well as their first and last names.	10-15 minutes
Grammatical Structures	Introduce the information in the **Estructura** on *Student Edition* p. 6 to present the verb **gustar** followed by an infinitive. have students practice this structure by completing Activity D in pairs.	15-20 minutes

Day 2

Review/ Warm-up	Review by quickly repeating Activity A **(Saludos)** and Activity E **(¿Muchísimo o muy poco?).**	10 minutes
Vocabulary in Context	Introduce the adverbs **mucho** and **poco** from the **Palabras útiles**, *Student Edition* p. 7. Activity E can be done orally or as a written assignment.	5 minutes
Listening Practice	Hand out the **Aquí escuchamos** Textbook Activity Master, TRB p. 60. Have students suggest expressions as indicated in **Antes de escuchar**, *Student Edition*, p. 7. Then play the audio materials for **Aquí escuchamos** twice. Have students answer the questions under **Después de escuchar** on the activity master, then ask volunteers to read their answers aloud.	10 minutes
Etapa **Synthesis**	Model the **¡Mucho gusto!** activity on *Student Edition* p. 8, then have students write out and role-play their dialogues in groups of three. Have students write postcards for the **Una Postal** activity on the same page.	15-20 minutes
HOMEWORK	Have students complete the activities on pp. 3-5 in the *Workbook*.	

90-minute Class Period

Day 1

Warm-up	Choose one of the following warm-up activities to introduce to the students to basic expressions in Spanish: the Planning Strategy from the Workbook, p. 1, the Preliminary Chapter of the Teacher's Resource Book pp. 1-8, or the **Los nombres españoles** activity in the Middle School Teacher's Guide, p. 1.	5 minutes
Etapa **Presentation**	Present the introductory dialogues and photos in the Student Edition, p. 3. Use Transparency 8 to focus on specific items. Pair up students to role-play the mini-dialogues. Present the **saludos, despedidas** and **respuestas** in the Student Edition, p. 4. Have students practice the new expressions by completing Activities A & B.	10 minutes
Pronunciation	Play the recording of the alphabet and of the **Práctica**, Activity C, from the Textbook Cassettes/CDs. Have students spell words from the **Práctica**, as well as their first and last names.	10-15 minutes
Review/ Warm-up	Review by quickly repeating Activity A **(Saludos)** and Activity E **(¿Muchísimo o muy poco?)**.	15-20 minutes
Grammatical Structures	Introduce the information in the **Estructura** on Student Edition p. 6 to present the verb **gustar** followed by an infinitive. Have students practice this structure by completing Activity D in pairs.	5 minutes
Vocabulary in Context	Introduce the adverbs **mucho** and **poco** from the **Palabra útiles**, Student Edition p. 7. Activity E can be done orally or as a written assignment.	5 minutes
Listening Practice	Hand out the **Aquí escuchamos** Textbook Activity Master, TRB p. 60. Have students suggest expressions as indicated in **Antes de escuchar**, Student Edition, p. 7. Then play the audio materials for **Aquí escuchamos** twice. Have students answer the questions under **Después de escuchar** on the activity master, then ask volunteers to read their answers aloud.	10 minutes
Etapa **Synthesis**	Model the **¡Mucho gusto!** activity on Student Edition p. 8, then have students write out and role-play their dialogues in groups of three. Have students write postcards for the **Una Postal** activity on the same page(This can also be done for homework).	15-20 minutes
HOMEWORK	Have students complete the activities on pp. 3-5 in the Workbook.	

Pedagogical Considerations

Because *¡Ya verás! Gold* provides a proficiency-oriented, integrated approach to teaching and learning Spanish, implementing it fully creates a lively classroom environment characterized by frequent student-centered interaction and performance-based dynamics. While many teachers nationwide are experienced in this approach and use it creatively during each class period, less-experienced teachers and those new to this approach naturally raise questions about various pedagogical considerations closely allied to it. These descriptions and their guidelines are intended to answer many of those questions.

Critical Thinking Skills

In order to thrive in a rapidly changing world, students need to be able to think independently and analytically, synthesize large amounts of information, and make appropriate judgments. Teaching students to think critically is an ongoing process in which students and teachers work together to become more aware of their cognitive processes. The modern language classroom, with its emphasis on linguistic discovery and cultural enrichment, is an ideal place for developing critical thinking skills.

Critical thinking may be considered a multi-step process in which students bring a number of skills to bear on an issue or problem. The following critical thinking skills are developed in *¡Ya verás! Gold* and highlighted in the Teacher's Editions with special icons and distinct teaching suggestions.

Analysis/Prediction

- **Analyzing:** Examining something from every angle to see what it is and how it works
- **Activating prior knowledge:** Using what one already knows in order in order to understand something better
- **Making hypotheses:** Making predictions or hypotheses about a problem or issue

Synthesis

- **Categorizing:** Organizing information into groups with similar qualities or attributes
- **Comparing and contrasting:** Looking for similarities and differences between ideas, people, places, and things
- **Drawing inferences:** Guessing logical explanations or reasons for choices, actions, and events
- **Synthesizing:** Pulling together ideas and pieces of information in order to form a logical whole

Evaluation/Personalization

- **Evaluating:** Determining worth, weighing strengths, and weaknesses
- **Determining preferences:** Making personal value judgments
- **Prioritizing:** Rating precedence in order of importance or urgency
- **Creating:** Producing an original work based on what one has learned and value judgments that one has made

Cooperative Learning

Cooperative learning is an effective tool on which modern language teachers can draw in the classroom. Its principles dovetail in many ways with the development of language and critical thinking skills, the acknowledgment of varied student learning styles and abilities, and the use of language for the purposeful communication of messages and ideas. Cooperative learning is based on the idea that students can learn effectively from one another in small-group interactions if their work is carefully detailed and assigned with specific information about the goal, the process, the timing, and the reporting of the results of their tasks. It is important to recognize that in order for an activity to be considered true cooperative learning, it must call for an outcome, such as a group product or decision, resulting from initial individual input and then a final negotiated consensus developed by all members of the team.

The elements of cooperative learning are integral to *¡Ya verás! Gold*. They are embodied in its small-group activities, particularly those activities marked with the cooperative learning icon in the margins of the Teacher's Editions, as well as the additional annotations identified with the same icon.

The following principles are central to cooperative learning:

- Positive interdependence, or the sense that students need each other in order to complete the group's tasks, is essential. Establishing mutual goals such as having the group members receive the same grade or earn the same bonus points contributes to this. Other ways include sharing the same materials—one sheet of paper, one pencil, the same props—and assigning defined roles—such as the recorder, the encourager, the reader, and the reporter or performer(s).

- Face-to-face interaction for the purpose of completing a task fosters important, meaningful exchanges among students as they work together to achieve their goal. For example, they need to ask and answer questions, give and receive explanations, elaborate, and summarize, all of which engages them in real-world communication.

- A group's work is not successful unless each member either learns the material or helps with and understands the task. This promotes individual accountability, but also reduced dependence on the teacher and increased linguistic independence.

- Social skills such as negotiation, compromise, decision making, and trust needed for the effective collaboration with others both in and beyond the classroom are an integral part of the process. Such skills are introduced and reinforced in the groups' interactions, creating a positive social atmosphere in which students learn to work with others and to accept the contributions that they can make to their learning.

- It is important to bring the group work to closure by group processing or some form of debriefing. Among the different forms this may take are the acting out of a role-play by the entire group, the performance of two group members, the reporting of one group member, and the sharing of information by individuals during a full-class reporting session.

Clearly, these elements of cooperative learning are consonant with many aspects of modern language teaching and learning. Still other benefits can derive from using cooperative learning in the classroom. Students are exposed to multiple points of view and ways of expression. They have the opportunity to manipulate language in ways that are most suitable to them. They are given a chance to raise language issues that are of interest to them and that might not surface in teacher-directed activities. By working with others in a supportive way, their anxiety level can be lowered and their confidence bolstered. In addition, you, as teachers, can circulate throughout the classroom, observing students, assisting them when necessary, and sensitizing yourself to their progress, needs, and interests.

Pair Work and Group Work

It is strongly recommended that you take three simple steps before you use a new, unfamiliar "structure" with students: 1) read through all of the directions, 2) gather any necessary materials, and 3) practice carrying out the activity, including saying the directions aloud. When you become familiar with the "structures," you will discover that they are not only simple and predictable, but that the results are very rewarding.

Putting Students into Pairs and Groups

Throughout the school year it is important to vary pair and group compositions so that students can interact regularly with different classmates. The optimal sizes are 2, 3 or 4 students, depending on what students are to do in the activity. With larger groups, some students tend to dominate while others may participate marginally or not at all.

Various pair and group combinations can be made: 1) more-prepared students with less-prepared students, 2) groups of more-prepared students, 3) groups of less-prepared students, and 3) random selection of students without concern for weaknesses and strengths. If you decide to pair or group students according to strengths and weaknesses, it is best to plan this ahead of time. Such on-the-spot, unplanned group selection can take valuable class time away from doing the activities themselves. Another time-saving measure is assigning students to partners or groups for a specified period of time such as three weeks, a marking period, or for the duration of a chapter. At the end of the time period, they then change partners or become part of a new group.

Here are some ways that you might wish to use to have students form groups:

- As students enter the classroom, they take a number or a colored piece of paper out of a bowl or box. All students with the same number or color form a group.

- Students count off in Spanish from 1 to 3 or from 1 to 4, depending on the nature of the activity. Groups can be formed from like numbers, for example, all of the 1s, or in numerical order, for instance, 1–3 or 1–4. The same can be done with the letters A, B, C, and D or, if you prefer, A, B, C, and Ch.

- Students turn to the classmates sitting next to and behind them.

- The students at each set of three or four seats in a row comprise a group.

- If students are given the option to work on different activities, they can group themselves according to the activity that interests them the most.

Implementing Pair Work and Group Work Successfully

Many teachers nationwide enjoy success with pair and group work by implementing the following guidelines.

Establishing Rules

- To save time and to minimize milling around and socializing, settle on a signal that lets students know that they are to get with their partner or their group. Signals that might be used include clapping your hands once or twice, ringing a bell, blowing a whistle, or flicking the classroom lights.

- Insist that students use Spanish, and make encouraging and helping each other part of their pair and group work responsibilities. Establish a system by which students call upon you for help only as a final recourse if communication between and among them becomes well and truly stuck.

- Place a time limit on each activity, announce it to students and/or write it on the board, and stick to it in order to help keep students on task. You could set a timer or the beeper on a travel alarm clock.

- At the end of each activity, signal clearly that it is time to stop. Many teachers simply use the same signal for indicating that students are to form pairs or groups.

Providing Guidance

- Before students break into pairs or groups, go through the directions with students to clarify the task. If the textbook also provides a model, it is a good idea to go through it, even to the point of acting it out in front of the class with another student or students. This increases the clarity of what students are to accomplish and provides input and useful linguistic suggestions. The most successful pair and group interactions are clearly defined so that, once students are with their partner or in their group, they know what to do.

- Teach students expressions, phrases, and sentences for asking for/giving information, requesting/giving clarification, hesitating, and paraphrasing so that they can help and support each other during their interactions. Additionally, give them ways to ask you for help in Spanish that they can use when they raise their hands.

- Be a monitor, circulating among pairs and groups to see that each student has the opportunity to contribute to the activity and that no one is sitting on the sidelines while others do the work. Also, act as a facilitator, responding to students questions when they arise and helping them get the interaction functioning once again. These behaviors have other benefits. For example, students understand that you place importance on pair and group work and that their conduct and participation matter. You can also take notes of common errors, examples of language used well by individuals, and positive behaviors.

Implementing Reporting and Debriefing

- Take the time to debrief pair and group work. Some of the ways of doing this are pointed out under Cooperative Learning earlier in this section of the Teacher's Guide.

- Periodically, use the reporting-back stage of group work as a way to assign grades for different students on different days.

- Discuss with students any notes you took as you circulated around the classroom, telling them about common errors, exemplary language samples, and positive behaviors. You could also point out some of the alternate structures or vocabulary they could have used in the activity. This type of discussion can raise cultural questions, language considerations, and communicative strategies that integrate and expand on what students did in their groups.

Assessment

¡Ya verás! Gold provides you with multiple options for evaluating and assessing students' progress. As described earlier in this Teacher's Guide, the program's assessment resources are made up of the Testing Program, including oral tests and portfolio assessment, the Testing Cassettes/CDs, the Computerized Testing Programs, and the Placement Test for Spanish-Speaking Students. The *¡Ya verás! Gold, Nivel 3,* Testing Program also contains a composition for each chapter, mirroring the systematic writing strand integrated into that student text and its workbook.

The *¡Ya verás! Gold* Testing Programs and Prochievement Testing

The quizzes, chapter tests, unit exams, and final exams in the *¡Ya verás! Gold* Testing Programs can best be described as prochievement testing instruments, or achievement tests with a proficiency-orientation. A definition used by ACTFL in its Programs for Language Professionals is the fusion of proficiency and achievement testing that provides a more holistic way of assessing how well specific learned tasks are performed than customary discrete-item tests. Like achievement tests, the materials in the *¡Ya verás! Gold* Testing Programs are text-specific, measuring what students have learned in the **etapas**, chapters, and units. Like proficiency tests, they are contextualized, providing real-life situations in which students demonstrate how well they use their language skills to fulfill communicative goals. In short, the *¡Ya verás! Gold* Testing Programs are based on the premise of "testing what and how one teaches." They assume a consistency between teaching/learning and the assessment of students' progress.

¡Ya verás! Gold and the Oral Proficiency Interview

The Oral Proficiency Interview (OPI) is a face-to face test that assesses an individual's speaking ability in a foreign or second language. The interview can last from five to thirty minutes, depending on the interviewee's level of language use. The resulting speech sample is rated on a scale from Novice (the ability to communicate minimally with learned materials) through Intermediate, Advanced, and Superior levels (the ability to participate effectively in most formal and informal conversations on practical, social, professional, and abstract topics and to support opinions and hypothesize using native-like discourse strategies). Low, Mid and High ratings distinguish among performances within the Novice and Intermediate levels; the Advanced level is divided into Advanced and Advanced-Plus.

Some states require the administration of the Oral Proficiency Interview at the end of the third year of instruction at the secondary school level, with the expectation that students should score in the low- to mid-Intermediate range. A less staff-intensive alternative test called the Simulated Oral Proficiency Interview (SOPI) is also sometimes used. The SOPI does not require a live interview, but rather provides a list of questions to which the interviewee responds on tape.

It is important to recognize that administering the OPI or the SOPI requires the intensive training of interviewers/ raters and their subsequent attendance at refresher courses so that the reliability and validity of these tests are safeguarded and maintained. Without this training, giving these tests should not be attempted. In addition, the OPI and/or the SOPI are meant to be administered relatively infrequently, for example, after a year or more of language study. They are not designed for use in assigning classroom grades to students.

The emphasis on real-life, task-based use of language in the OPI has several ramifications for students. If they have been learning Spanish from a somewhat traditional, grammar-based program, the OPI could offer some difficulty. *¡Ya verás! Gold* provides several regular features that are well suited to preparing students for the OPI. The **¡Adelante!** and **Conversemos un rato** cumulative oral activities are particularly useful because of their realistic, open-ended situations that recycle and spiral previously studied language functions, grammatical structures, and vocabulary. Moreover, the *¡Ya verás! Gold* Testing Programs are prochievement-based so that students are always evaluated on what they can do, not simply on their mastery of discrete aspects of the language. After studying Spanish with *¡Ya verás! Gold, Niveles 1-3*, students will have received ample support for taking the OPI.

Assessing Speaking and Writing

Certain materials in the *¡Ya verás! Gold* student texts and workbooks are suitable for use in assessing students' speaking and writing performance. For speaking, you can use the oral activities in the **¡Adelante!** and **Conversemos un rato** sections. For writing, you can draw on the **¡Adelante!** writing activities, the **Taller de escritores** process-writing sections, and the activities in the workbook preceded by the *Atajo* icon.

It is recommended that, when you evaluate speaking and writing tasks, you grade them holistically as many teachers nationwide already do with great success. Doing so acknowledges students' abilities to communicate messages and content, not just their use of vocabulary and grammatical structures. It also can save valuable time, particularly if done in conjunction with a rubric. Rubrics rely on criterion-referenced scoring that holds speaking and writing samples accountable to the criteria itself and not to other samples. You may want to use or modify the following rubric to facilitate your grading work. For more information about holistic grading and rubrics, see the Introductions to the *¡Ya verás! Gold* Testing Programs.

5 or A Very good to excellent command of the language. Very few errors of syntax. Wide range of vocabulary, including idiomatic usage. High level of fluency. Appropriate cultural behaviors and/or concepts. Exceeded the assigned task.

4 or B Good command of the language. Few errors of syntax. Above-average range of vocabulary. Good idiomatic usage and little awkwardness of expression. Good fluency. Mostly appropriate cultural behaviors and/or concepts. Met the assigned task and made some attempts to go beyond it.

3 or C Comprehensible expression. Some serious errors of syntax and some successful self-correction. Some fluency, but hesitant. Moderate range of vocabulary and idiomatic usage. Some appropriate cultural behaviors and/or concepts. Met the assigned task, but did not attempt to go beyond it.

2 or D Poor command of the language. Limited fluency. Narrow range of vocabulary and of idiomatic usage. Frequent recourse to English and structures that force interpretation of meaning. Inappropriate cultural behaviors and/or concepts or little-to-no recognition of them. Did not meet the assigned task.

1 or F Unacceptable from almost every point of view. Language not comprehensible or English principally used. Did not accomplish the task.

Using Portfolios

A portfolio is any collection of student work. Most often, it is a folder containing some of the better work a student has produced. Instructionally, a portfolio allows students to examine the work they have produced, to select special pieces of work, and to reflect on what they have learned and how they learned it. In other words, a portfolio is a collection of work that exhibits a student's efforts and progress.

The contents of a portfolio can be as varied as your and your students' imaginations. In addition to samples of writing work, individual students might prepare an audiocassette with a first-person monologue or a third-person narrative. To showcase both listening and speaking skills, pairs or small groups could videotape a role-play, an interview, or a mock talk show. Projects can be placed in a portfolio, as well as journal entries, print outs of Internet activities, and the results of students' experiences with Spanish beyond the classroom. Some teachers also encourage students to include written quizzes, tests, or exams on which they experienced particular success or progress.

The portfolio assessment piece found at the beginning of the *¡Ya verás! Gold* Testing Programs describes the role portfolios play in language learning and the portfolio process. It also provides student Activity Rating and Reflection Sheets, as well as teaching instructions and suggestions for each unit.

The oral activities in the **¡Adelante!** and **Conversemos un rato** sections of the student texts can serve as the basis of oral pieces to include in students' portfolios. Good sources of writing pieces are the **¡Adelante!** writing activities, the **Taller de escritores** process-writing sections, and the activities in the workbooks preceded by the *Atajo* icon. The **¡Ahora te toca a ti!** activities of the **En la comunidad** sections and the Internet activities on the *¡Ya verás!* Web site can be used for both oral and written samples of students' experiences and contacts with Spanish outside of the classroom.

The purpose of a portfolio is to record student growth over time, allowing students to think about what they have learned and how they have learned it. Throughout the process, students gain a sense of pride and confidence in their abilities. The portfolio also provides a record of student achievement for teachers, parents, and other audiences. In this way, the portfolio becomes a window through which student learning and performance can be viewed.

Teacher Behaviors

Correction Strategies

It is recommended that error correction be handled in such a way that students construe it as helping them to communicate more accurately and effectively. In short, error correction can and should be a confidence builder.

- Don't underestimate the power of praise and pointing out what students did well. In fact, accentuating the positive aspects of students' work before moving to correction can be very motivating and effective.

- When students are engaged in mechanical, controlled, or directed exercises, you might want to apply correction systematically to provide immediate feedback so students can work on their linguistic accuracy.

- It is recommended that you make every effort not to interrupt students to call attention to errors when they are working in pairs or small groups, when they are performing an activity for the class, or when they are interacting meaningfully with you. Instead, reserve correction until such interactions are completed, perhaps initiating additional controlled practice by the whole class to correct common errors you noticed. An added benefit to this is that, at this point, it is not necessary to single out the students who made the original errors. Students may retain anonymity, yet benefit from becoming aware of their mistakes and from seeing, hearing, and practicing appropriate and correct language.

Speech Behaviors

- Rather than slow down your speech rate artificially in your efforts to help students understand, try to use a normal rate of speech at all times. Hearing Spanish spoken in this way will help students develop their listening comprehension skills and will prepare them for Spanish spoken by native speakers beyond the classroom. It would be a disservice to students to have them encounter Spanish outside of the class only to find the rate of speech overwhelming or to lead them to expect that native speakers will "slow down" for their benefit.

- Make efforts to limit or eliminate "teacher talk" such as saying *muy bien, de acuerdo*, or *bien* after student answers or statements. While such rejoinders are often used as positive feedback, they are typically evaluative of grammatical accuracy and rarely responsive to the messages students conveyed. In communicative situations when students say something meaningful and/or personalized, it is recommended that you respond to the message naturally as you would if the exchange were taking place outside of the modern language classroom in "real life." This shows students that they were understood, and it underscores that what they said matters. You might use phrases like *¿Es verdad?*, *¡No me digas!*, *¿En serio?*, and *¡Qué interesante!* and proceed to ask follow-up questions to keep the conversational ball rolling for a few minutes. The added advantage of natural speech is that students gradually learn the many expressions you use and will eventually incorporate them into their own use of the language.

- It is best to avoid automatically repeating what you ask or say to students in Spanish. Constant repetition underestimates students' ability to understand the first time. It also hinders the development of listening comprehension skills because, as students become accustomed to the repetition and come to expect it, they learn not to listen the first time something is said. Repetition should be used if students have truly not understood the first time, in which case the statement should probably be rephrased. For these occasions, teaching students sentences and phrases for asking for clarification or repetition, such as *Perdón* and *No comprendí*, early on is a helpful strategy.

- It is also recommended not to repeat systematically what students say. Because such repetition is often used as a correction strategy, it can become a behavior pattern even when no correction is needed. Again, reacting to students' content as you would in real life is advisable. For example, if a student volunteered *"El fin de semana pasado fui a una fiesta,"* you might respond by saying *"Ah, qué bien. ¿Fuiste a una fiesta? ¿Y qué tal la fiesta?"*

- Try to let students finish what they are trying to say even when they hesitate, pause, or grope for words. This, too, can happen when they engage in everyday interactions outside of the classroom. To help them with these situations when they arise, you might teach them hesitation markers such as **este...** to use as they give themselves time to think. If, however, it is clear that communication has stalled completely, it is appropriate and useful for you to help out.

Body Language

- Moving around the entire classroom, instead of remaining in the front of the room, helps to maintain the energy level of the class and the interest of students.

- When addressing individual students, it is a good idea to move physically within their conversational range to indicate your interest in what they have to say and to underscore the "realness" of the communication. Although this may be strategically more difficult in large classes, aisles or clusters of seats can be created to reduce the space between the teacher and individual students.

- Establishing and maintaining eye contact with the student with whom you are interacting is important. As teachers, it is sometimes easy to become preoccupied with the next question you are going to ask the next student or the next step in your lesson plan. Almost imperceptibly, this can lead you to abandon eye contact with a student before the communication has been completed, thereby devaluing it and placing it overtly in the light of artificial, classroom talk rather than the true exchange of information.

- Research has shown that eye-level interaction is less threatening and has a positive impact on student performance. Since students are frequently seated and you, as teacher, are usually standing, it is reasonable that students may feel hovered over or looked down on physically. This could be alleviated if you placed some empty seats in different parts of the room where you can sit down, as needed, and address students in that part of the room.

Silence

- It takes the mind approximately three seconds to process a question. Given this fact, it is important to give students enough time to think of a response, allowing for enough silence in which it can be formulated. Interfering too quickly, for example, by repeating the question successively in different ways, inhibits thinking and is likely to be very frustrating for students.

- Being sensitive to silences that are constructive and those that become uncomfortable is a valuable teaching skill. Only when the discomfort stage sets in should students be helped out. This can be done by reformulating the question, by supplying a response that you would make and then repeating the question, or by directing the question to other students and returning later to the silent student to see if she/he is then able to respond.

MULTIPLE INTELLIGENCES

¡Ya verás! *Gold* and The Multiple Intelligences

The Theory of Multiple Intelligences

When cognitive scientist and psychologist, Professor Howard Gardner, published his Theory of Multiple Intelligences in his seminal book, *Frames of Mind* in 1985, he was gratifyingly surprised by the enthusiasm with which numerous educators embraced it. Over recent years, educators' interest in the theory has increased. As most teachers nationwide know, it is currently being used in disciplines across the curriculum, including modern languages.

For teachers not familiar with Gardner's theory, it may prove helpful to keep a few basic principles in mind. According to Gardner, all intelligences have equal claim to priority, that is, no one intelligence holds more value or importance than another. Moreover, everyone possesses all of the intelligences to some extent, but individuals differ in the degree of skill and the nature of their combination. While people have strong proclivities to one or more of the intelligences, they can develop and strengthen others. Finally, as Gardner himself has stressed, it is important to recognize that the point of the Theory of Multiple Intelligences is not that everything should be taught seven or eight ways. ("Eight ways" refers to the recent addition of naturalistic intelligence to the theory. According to Gardner, this intelligence designates the ability to recognize and classify plants, minerals, and animals; it may also include the ability to recognize cultural artifacts such as cars and sneakers.)

The Multiple Intelligences

LINGUISTIC

The capacity to use language—one's native language and perhaps other languages—to express what's on one's mind and to understand other people

Associated careers: poet, writer, orator, lawyer

Associated activities: conducting interviews; telling stories; debating; writing poems, myths, legends, new articles, etc.; creating a talk show; playing word games

LOGICAL-MATHEMATICAL

As the name implies, logical ability and mathematical ability, as well as scientific ability

Associated careers: mathematician, logician, scientist

Associated activities: manipulating numbers and quantities; understanding underlying principles; describing patterns; designing and conducting experiments; making up analogies and syllogisms; creating and applying formulas; calculating; working with logic puzzles

SPATIAL

The ability to form a mental model of a spatial world and to be able to maneuver and operate using that model

Associated careers: sailor, engineer, surgeon, sculptor, painter, chess master, architect

Associated activities: making charts, maps, clusters and graphs; creating slide shows, videos, and photo albums; illustrating, drawing, sketching, and painting; sculpting; doodling

MUSICAL

The ability to think in music, to be able to hear patterns, recognize them, remember them, and perhaps manipulate them

Associated careers: musician; music teacher; instrument maker; composer; conductor

Associated activities: singing; rapping; giving a presentation with musical accompaniment; indicating rhythmical patterns; making a musical instrument and using it to demonstrate a concept or to illustrate a topic

BODILY-KINESTHETIC

The ability to solve problems or to fashion products using one's whole body, or parts of the body

Associated careers: athlete; dancer; actor; choreographer; mechanic; craftsperson; physical therapist

Associated activities: building and constructing; bringing in materials and props to demonstrate a concept or to explain a topic; miming; using puppets; creating movement or a sequence of movement

INTERPERSONAL

The ability to understand other people: what motivates them, how they work, how to work cooperatively with them

Associated careers: teacher, counselor, social worker, salesperson, politician

Associated activities: leading discussions and interactions; teaching others; intentionally using social skills to learn about something and from others; participating in service projects; engaging in pair and group work

INTRAPERSONAL

The capacity to form an accurate model of oneself and to be able to use that model to operate effectively in life

Associated careers: not applicable

Associated activities: setting and pursuing goals; planning; writing journal entries; creating and reflecting on a portfolio; assessing work independently; personalizing; prioritizing and making choices

Learning Styles and the Multiple Intelligences

Dating from 1927 with the work of Carl Jung, learning-style theory has its roots in the field of psychoanalysis. Learning styles focus on the differences in how individuals absorb information, think about it, and evaluate it. In other words, according to researchers in this field, learning styles look closely at the process of learning while the Multiple Intelligences center on the content and products of learning. Gardner, on the other hand, has stated that learning styles are claims about ways in which individuals approach everything they do and thus are very different from multiple intelligences.

Despite the differences of opinion between proponents of learning styles and advocates of multiple intelligences, these two areas of research are complimentary in many ways.

- Both can be used as compasses for working with individual students.
- Both provide choices to students.
- Both acknowledge that individuals have multiple facets and that these can change and/or grow as students continue to learn.
- Both can be drawn on for assessment purposes and alternatives.
- Both are evolving areas of research, advancing seriously the understanding of the learner and how people learn.
- Both celebrate and respect diversity.

The Multiple Intelligences, Learning Styles, and ¡Ya verás! Gold

Throughout the **¡Ya verás!** Gold Teacher's Editions, you will find a boxed feature entitled Multiple Intelligences for every **etapa** and every part of each **¡Sigamos adelante!** section. These boxes correlate the "classic" seven intelligences to sections and activities in the student text. Recognizing that numerous modern language teachers are also concerned and familiar with certain learning styles, the rubrics used for the spatial and musical intelligences are expanded to include visual and auditory, respectively. You will also find annotations throughout the Teacher's Editions marked by the Multiple Intelligences-Learning Styles icons. These teaching tips and suggestions provide additional ways of incorporating these exciting learning resources into your classes.

The Standards

¡Ya verás! Gold and The Standards for Foreign Language Learning

Published in 1996 under the auspices of the National Standards in Foreign Language Education Project whose original collaborators include ACTFL, the American Association of Teachers of French, the American Association of Teachers of German, and American Association of Teachers of Spanish and Portuguese, the *Standards for Foreign Language Learning: Preparing for the 21st Century* stand as the new framework for the teaching and learning of communication skills in modern languages. Since their release, the Standards have galvanized the profession, re-energizing it and exerting a powerful influence on curricular guidelines nationwide.

¡Ya verás! *Gold* was created with the Standards firmly in mind. Teachers nationwide familiar with the program will recognize that the pedagogical underpinnings of the program have been in harmony with the Standards since its inception. They will also see that textbook sections like **Conexión con…, En línea, Vistas, Explora,** and **En la comunidad**, in combination with the boxed Standards correlations and other annotations with the Standards icon found throughout the Teacher's Editions, are specially written and integrated to help teachers implement easily and effortlessly innovations brought to the profession by the Standards.

Heinle & Heinle, the publisher of ***¡Ya verás!*** *Gold*, is also proud to be the exclusive publisher of the *Standards for Foreign Language Leaning* training video, worktext, and poster in cooperation with ACTFL. As the specialized publisher of ESL and modern languages, Heinle & Heinle is enthusiastically committed to its ongoing partnership with both modern language teachers and their professional organizations.

Standards for Foreign Language Learning

COMMUNICATION

Communicate in Languages Other Than English

Standard 1.1: Students engage in conversations, provide and obtain information, express feelings and emotions, and exchange opinions.

Standard 1.2: Students understand and interpret written and spoken language on a variety of topics.

Standard 1.3: Students present information, concepts, and ideas to an audience of listeners or readers on a variety of topics.

CULTURES

Gain Knowledge and Understanding of Other Cultures

Standard 2.1: Students demonstrate an understanding of the relationship between the practices and perspectives of the culture studied.

Standard 2.2: Students demonstrate an understanding of the products and perspectives of the culture studied.

CONNECTIONS

Connect with Other Disciplines and Acquire Information

Standard 3.1: Students reinforce and further their knowledge of other disciplines through the foreign language.

Standard 3.2: Students acquire information and recognize the distinctive viewpoints that are only available through the foreign language and its cultures.

COMPARISONS

Develop Insight into the Nature of Language and Culture

Standard 4.1: Students demonstrate understanding of the nature of language through comparisons of the language studied and their own.

Standard 4.2: Students demonstrate understanding of the concept of culture through comparisons of the language studied and their own.

COMMUNITIES

Participate in Multilingual Communities at Home and Around the World

Standard 5.1: Students use the language both within and beyond the school setting.

Standard 5.2: Students show evidence of becoming life-long learners by using the language for personal enjoyment and enrichment.

Scope and Sequence of *Nivel 1*

UNIT	FUNCTIONS	CONTEXTS	ACCURACY

1
Vamos a tomar algo
	Ordering food and drink
	Greeting, introducing, and saying goodbye
	Expressing likes and dislikes
	Asking and answering yes and no questions
	Finding out information about people
		Café
		Tapas bars
		Mexican restaurants
			The verb **gustar** + infinitive
			  Expressing likes and dislikes
			Gender of nouns
			Indefinite articles
			Subject pronouns
			Present tense of regular **-ar** verbs
			  Expressing frequency
			Asking and answering yes/no and tag
			  questions
			Conjugated verbs followed by infinitives
			Present tense of **ser**
			Names of countries
			Adjectives of nationality
			Nouns for professions

2 *¡Vamos a conocernos!*	Identifying personal belongings Obtaining information about other people Talking about preferences Talking about one's family	School Home Various settings	Definite articles Possession with **de** Possessive adjectives (first and second person) Numbers from 0 to 20 **Hay** + noun **Gustar (me gustan/te gustan)** Review of **ser** + **de** for possession **-Er** and **-ir** verbs Present tense of the verb **tener** **Tener que** + inifinitive Questions with **dónde, cuántos, cuántas,** **quién, qué**, and **por qué** **Ser** + descriptive adjectives

3
¿Dónde y a qué hora?
	Identifying public buildings and places in a
	  city
	Asking for and giving directions
	Getting people to do something
	Talking about leisure-time activities
	Making plans
	Telling and asking for the time
		Cities and towns
		Festivals
			Present tense of the verbs **ir, querer,**
			  preferir, estar, venir
			The contraction **al**
			Expressions of frequency
			Numbers from 20 to 100
			Expressions with **tener**
			The preposition **de**
			The contraction **del**
			Commands with **Ud.** and **Uds.**
			Irregular command forms
			Telling time
			Estar + adjectives of condition
			Possessive adjectives (third person)

CULTURE	PRONUNCIATION	READING STRATEGIES	WRITING STRATEGY	SPOTLIGHTED LOCATIONS
Greetings and leave-takings **Abrazos** Cafés Meals and snack-times **Tapas** Formal and informal greetings Puerto Rican cuisine Differing terms for food between Latin America and Spain The plantain in Caribbean cuisine	The Spanish alphabet The vowels **a, e, i, o, u**	Examining format for content clues Recognizing cognates Scanning for specific information Skimming for the gist Using the title and photos, artwork, and illustrations to predict content and/or meaning	List writing	Puerto Rico
Hispanic music Hispanic last names Family in the Hispanic world Bike riding in Latin America Social life among Latin American teens Immigration patterns of South America	The consonants **p, t, d**, and **b** The sound of **/k/**	Activating background and/or prior knowledge Recognizing cognates Scanning for specific information Using photos, artwork, and illustrations to predict content and/or meaning	List writing	Ecuador Chile Honduras
The typical city in the Spanish-speaking world Telephone expressions Stores and their names Addresses and telephone numbers The Spanish language in the world Town celebrations Little Havana, Florida Central American ecotourism Festivals in Latin America	Pronunciation The consonants **g, j, m, n**, and **ñ** The sound of **/s/**	Activating background and/or prior knowledge Examining format for content clues Scanning for specific information Using the title and photos to predict content and/or meaning	Group brainstorming using clusters	Little Havana Florida Costa Rica

Scope and Sequence of *Nivel 1*

UNIT	FUNCTIONS	CONTEXTS	ACCURACY
4 *Vamos al centro*	Making plans to go downtown Identifying what to do in town Talking about when and how to go downtown Taking subways and taxis Making and accepting invitations Expressing wishes and desires	Cities and towns Subway stations	The immediate future: **Ir a** + infinitive **Tener ganas de** + infinitive The days of the week Present tense of **hacer** and **poder** Adverbs used for expressing present and future time Talking about the future with **pensar** Numbers 100 to 1,000,000 Discussing plans with **esperar** and **querer** + infinitive
5 *Tu tiempo libre*	Talking about past events and activities Situating activities in the past Talking about actions in the past, present, and future	Leisure-time activities Sports	Preterite of regular **-ar, -er, -ir** verbs Preterite of the irregular verbs **hacer, ir, andar, estar,** and **tener** Adverbs, prepositions, and other expressions used to designate the past **Hace** and **hace que** Preterite of verbs ending in **-gar** and **-car** Expressions used to talk about a series of actions Present progressive tense Past, present, and future time
6 *Vamos de compras*	Making purchases and choices Expressing quantity Asking for prices Comparing things	Various shops (music, stationery, sporting goods, clothing, and shoes)	The verb **gustar** (presented with all indirect object pronouns) Affirmative and negative familiar commands Demonstrative adjectives and pronouns Expressions of quantity The interrogative words **cuál/cuáles** Expressions of comparison Expressing equality

CULTURE	PRONUNCIATION	READING STRATEGIES	WRITING STRATEGY	SPOTLIGHTED LOCATIONS
El Prado The metro in Madrid Tickets for public transportation **La puerta del sol** plaza, Madrid Latino musicians Transportation in Latin America Getting to Iguazú	The consonants **h, ch, ll**	Activating background and/or prior knowledge Scanning for specific information Skimming for the gist Using photos to predict content and/or meaning Using the title to predict content and/or meaning	Individual brainstorming using clusters	Iguazú Argentina Mexico
Leisure times of youth in the Spanish-speaking world Surfing in Uruguay and El Salvador Roberto Clemente		Activating background and/or prior knowledge Examining format for content clues Recognizing cognates Scanning for specific information Using photos to predict content and/or meaning Using the title to predict content and/or meaning	Making an outline	Uruguay El Salvador California Florida
Open-air markets Tropical fruits and vegetables Shoes sizes in Spain and Latin America Quinceañera **Centro Sambil** (mall) in Caracas, Venezuela Guatemalan weaving and clothing	The consonants **r, rr, f**, and **l**	Activating background and/or prior knowledge Examining format for content clues Recognizing cognates Scanning for specific information Skimming for the gist Using photos to predict content and/or meaning Using the title to predict content and/or meaning Using the title and photos to predict content and/or meaning	Asking who?, what?, and why?	Guatemala Venezuela New Mexico Arizona El Salvador

Scope and Sequence of Nivel 2

UNIT	FUNCTIONS	CONTEXTS	ACCURACY
Capítulos preliminares	**Capítulos preliminares A, B,** and **C** provide a review of the major language functions, grammatical structures, and vocabulary covered in **¡Ya verás!** Gold, **Nivel 1.**		
1 *Descripciones*	Describing the weather Understanding weather reports and meteorological maps Describing objects Describing people	Vacation sites Weather reports Various sayings relevant to interactions with family and friends	Weather expressions with **hacer, estar, hay** Weather expressions with **llover, lloviznar, nevar,** and **tronar** The months of the year, dates, and seasons Stem-changing verbs The verb **saber** Agreement of adjectives Plural forms of adjectives Position of adjectives The verb **conocer** The personal **a** **Ser para** + pronouns The shortened adjectives **buen, mal,** and **gran**
2 *Vamos a instalarnos*	Obtaining and paying for a hotel room Understanding classified ads Understanding brochures related to lodging Describing one's lodging Telling time using the 24-hour clock Describing furniture and items in a room	Tourist guidebooks Airline and train schedules Classified ads Hotels Apartments and houses	Ordinal numbers Preterite of **dormir** The verbs **salir** and **llegar** (present and preterite) Time expressions, parts of an hour The 24-hour clock The verbs **decir** and **poner** (present and preterite) Expressions with **decir**

CULTURE	PRONUNCIATION	READING STRATEGIES	WRITING STRATEGY	SPOTLIGHTED LOCATIONS
Climate in Latin American countries Siestas Temperatures in Spain and Latin America Hurricanes Latin American film-making Yangui/Latino stereotypes	The vowel combinations **ia, ie, io,** and **ua**	Activating background and/or prior knowledge Recognizing cognates Scanning for specific information Using the title to predict content and/or meaning	Making an outline	New York Illinois
Youth hostels and inexpensive youth-oriented lodging Spanish words for building floors Family stays in exchange programs Apartments in Spanish-speaking cities **Paradores** in Puerto Rico Lifestyles in Costa Rica Machu Picchu, Perú	The vowel combinations **ue, uo, ui,** and **ai**	Activating background and/or prior knowledge Examining format for content clues Skimming for the gist Using the title to predict content and/or meaning	List writing	Puerto Rico Costa Rica Peru

UNIT	FUNCTIONS	CONTEXTS	ACCURACY
3 *Nuestro día*	Describing daily routines and vacation activities Issuing invitations for leisure-time activities Organizing and coordinating plans Giving advice and suggestions	Home, school, towns, and cities Vacation sites Advertisements Schedules and listings of movies, plays, and television Party invitations	Present tense of reflexive verbs **Ud.** and **Uds.** command forms of reflexive verbs **Tú** command forms of reflexive verbs Direct object pronouns Position of double object pronouns The immediate future with reflexive verbs Reflexive versus non-reflexive verbs Pronouns with commands
4 *La salud*	Taking about parts of the body and physical complaints Talking about past routines and habitual activities Describing illnesses and complaints Suggesting medical remedies Giving and getting advice on health-related topics Describing dietary and sleeping habits	School Various leisure-time settings Pharmacies Doctor's offices Diets and sleep routines	Formation and uses of the imperfect Imperfect of **ver, ser,** and **ir** Preterite of reflexive verbs The verb **doler** Indirect object pronouns The verb **dar** The verb **pedir** The time expressions **desde cuándo, desde (que), cuánto tiempo hace,** and **hace (que)**
5 *Aventura y deporte*	Understanding short descriptions Talking about the recent past Describing places and events in the past	Sports Leisure-time activities	Preterite of high frequency irregular verbs: **conducir, traer, decir, poder, saber, poner, leer, caer(se), creer, ver,** and **oír** Various meanings of the verb **ponerse** Using the imperfect and the preterite to talk about past actions, descriptions, and interrupted actions Imperfect and preterite: Changes of meaning and summary of uses

CULTURE	PRONUNCIATION	READING STRATEGIES	WRITING STRATEGY	SPOTLIGHTED LOCATIONS
Attitudes toward time in Spanish-speaking cultures Courtesy in the Spanish language Movie-going **La quinceañera** History of chocolate and its current popularity **Telenovelas** Work projects in the Dominican Republic	The vowel combinations **ei, oi, eu,** and **au**	Activating background and/or prior knowledge Recognizing cognates Skimming for the gist Using the title and format to predict content and/or meaning	List writing	Dominican Republic Bolivia
Pharmacies in the Spanish-speaking world Meters and kilograms Latin American attitudes toward food and body image Medicine in the Hispanic world **Mi jardín,** a poem about health		Reading Strategies Activating background and/or prior knowledge Recognizing cognates Skimming for the gist Using photos, artwork, and illustrations to predict content and/or meaning Using the title to predict content and/or meaning	Free-writing	Spain
Quecha riddles and rhymes Hispanic women in sports Latinos in popular sports		Activating background and/or prior knowledge Recognizing cognates Scanning for specific information Skimming for the gist Using the title to predict content and/or meaning	Focusing on who?, what?, when?, where?, and why?	Argentina Cuba

Scope and Sequence of *Nivel 3*

UNIT	FUNCTIONS	CONTEXTS/TOPICS	ACCURACY
Capítulo preliminar	The **Capítulo preliminar** provides a review of the major language functions, grammatical structures, and vocabulary covered in **¡Ya verás!** *Gold*, **Nivel 2**.		
1 *La ropa y la comida*	Purchasing clothing and shoes Asking for information Commenting on clothing and food Making meal and restaurant plans Understanding menus and recipes Ordering and paying for food	Department stores, clothing stores, and shoe stores Restaurants	Double object pronouns: indirect object pronouns **me, te, nos, le,** and **les** with direct object pronouns Position of object pronouns with infinitives and present participles Position of object pronouns with commands **Gustar** and verbs like **gustar** Impersonal **se** **Estar** + adjectives to describe states or conditions Adding emphasis to a description Negative and affirmative expressions
2 *¡Vamos de viaje!*	Organizing trips Using the telephone Talking about means of transportation Making travel arrangements Understanding road maps	Airports, train stations, bus terminals, and road and highway travel Travel in various Spanish-speaking countries	The future tense The future tense of irregular verbs Special uses of the future tense Prepositions of place: **a, en, de, por, para, entre, hasta, hacia, cerca de,** and **lejos de** The prepositions **antes de** and **después de** Prepositional pronouns The present perfect Irregular past participles The past perfect

CULTURE	PRONUNCIATION	READING STRATEGIES	WRITING STRATEGY	SPOTLIGHTED LOCATIONS
Clothing and fashion Madrid's weekly guide to culture **Xitomatl** Chilis Clothing as an expression of self among Latin American youths Attitudes towards food in the Hispanic world Latin American cuisine		Examining format for content clues Recognizing cognates Scanning for specific information Using context to guess meaning Using the title to predict content and/or meaning Using the title and photos to predict content and/or meaning	List writing	Guatemala
Trains in Spain Telephone numbers Train schedules and calendars **Los ángeles verdes** Taxis in Mexico City The telephone throughout Latin America The Mexican subway system Roberto José Guerrero, Colombian race car driver		Activating background and/or prior knowledge Examining format for content clues Recognizing cognates Scanning for specific information Skimming for the gist Using the title and photos to predict content and/or meaning	Making an outline	Uruguay Paraguay Colombia

Scope and Sequence of *Nivel 3*

UNIT	FUNCTIONS	CONTEXTS/TOPICS	ACCURACY
3 *El arte y la música en el mundo hispano*	Offering opinions Discussing abstract topics such as art and music Expressing emotions Expressing wishes, preferences	Mexican muralism Frida Kahlo Picasso, Miró, and Dalí Picasso's **Guernica** **Molas** in traditional Cuna Indian folk art Painted carts of Sarchí, Costa Rica Mexican masks **Santero** figurines of New Mexico History of **La bamba** **El tango** **Mariachi** music **El flamenco**	The subjunctive mood The subjunctive with **ojalá que** The subjunctive of verbs with spelling changes The subjunctive of **dar, estar, haber, ir, saber,** and **ser** The subjunctive of reflexive verbs The subjunctive with expressions of will The subjunctive for conveying emotions and reactions The subjunctive of verbs that end in **-cer** and **-cir** Expressions to convey an emotion or a reaction
4 *El mundo de las letras*	Understanding and discussing diverse text types Expressing doubt, uncertainty, and improbability Talking about conditions contrary to fact Supporting an opinion	**Fotonovelas** Camilo José Cela and the Nobel Prize for Literature Magazines in Argentina Octavio Paz's **El pájaro** Mayan legends Profile of Miguel de Cervantes The Afro-Hispanic influence on contemporary Spanish-language Literature of the Caribbean Excerpt from Alejo Carpentier's **El reino de este mundo** Luis Pales Matos' **Danza negra** Magical realism in Spanish-language literature Excerpt from Gabriel García Márquez's **Cien años de soledad** Samples of Enrique Anderson Imbert's **casos** Excerpt from Julio Cortázar's **El esbozo de un sueño** Excerpt from Isabel Allende's **La casa de los espíritus** Excerpt from Laura Esquivel's **Como agua para chocolate**	The subjunctive to express unreality, uncertainty, and doubt **Creer** and **no creer** with the subjunctive The subjunctive with indefinite, nonexistant, or imaginary antecedents The subjunctive with the conjunctions **en caso de, sin que, con tal que, antes de que, para que,** and **a menos de** The subjunctive and indicative with **cuando** and **aunque** The conditional The conditonal of **decir, haber, hacer, poder, poner, querer, saber, salir, tener,** and **venir** Special uses of the conditional tense The imperfect subjunctive and actions in the past The imperfect subjunctive and **si** clauses The indicative and **si** clauses The imperfect subjunctive and the sequence of tenses The subjunctive with the conjunctions **en caso de, sin que, con tal que, autes de que, para que,** and **a menos de** The subjunctive and indicative with **cuando** and **aunque**

CULTURE	PRONUNCIATION	READING STRATEGIES	WRITING STRATEGY	SPOTLIGHTED LOCATIONS
The lyrics of *La bamba* The lyrics of *Los laureles*		Activating background and/or prior knowledge Scanning for specific information Using context to guess meaning Using the title and photos to predict content and/or meaning	Automatic writing	Colorado Texas
The Hispanic population of the United States The popularity of Don Quijote		Activating background and/or prior knowledge Identifying the main idea Recognizing cognates Scanning for specific information Skimming for the gist Using context to guess meaning Using the title to predict content and/or meaning Using the title and photos and/or illustrations to predict content and/or meaning	Free-writing	Nicaragua Panama

¡Ya verás! GOLD

Nivel 1

John R. Gutiérrez

The Pennsylvania State University

Harry L. Rosser

Boston College

Marta Rosso-O'Laughlin

Tufts University

HH **Heinle & Heinle Publishers**

An International Thomson Publishing Company

ITP   Boston, MA • 02116 • U.S.A.

Visit us on the Internet **http://yaveras.heinle.com**

The publication of *¡Ya verás! Gold, Nivel 1*, was directed by the members
of the Heinle & Heinle School Publishing Team.

Team Leader: Vincent Duggan
Publisher: Denise St. Jean
Production Services Coordinator: Mary McKeon
Market Development Director: Pamela Warren

Also participating in the publication of this program were:
Assistant Editor: Sonja Regelman
Manufacturing Coordinator: Wendy Kilborn
Development, Design and Composition: Hispanex Inc.
Cover Art: Mark Schroder
Cover: Rotunda Design

Manufactured in the United States of America

ISBN 0-8384-8554-5 (student text)

10 9 8 7 6 5 4 3 2 1

To the Student

You are about to begin an exciting and valuable experience. Learning a new language will open up cultures other than your own: different ways of living, thinking, and seeing. In fact, there is an old Spanish proverb that underscores the importance of knowing another language. It states: *El que sabe dos lenguas vale por dos*—the person who speaks two languages is worth two people.

Today the Spanish language is spoken all over the world by more than 300 million people. Many of you will one day have the opportunity to visit a Spanish-speaking country. Your experience will be all the richer if you can enter into the cultures of those countries and interact with their people. However, even if you don't get to spend time in one of those countries, Spanish is very much alive right here in this country, for it is spoken every day by millions of Americans!

Do you already know some Spanish speakers in your community or have you ever been exposed to elements of Hispanic culture? Perhaps you have sampled some Mexican food or turned on the television to find a Spanish news broadcast. Perhaps you have listened to the music of Gloria Estefan or Rubén Blades or maybe seen a movie in Spanish with English subtitles. The possibilities are endless.

Once you begin to use the Spanish language in class, you will discover that you can interact with Spanish speakers or your classmates and teacher right away. Knowing that of over 80,000 words found in the Spanish language, the average Spanish speaker uses only about 800 on a daily basis might help to persuade you of this! Therefore, the most important task ahead of you is not to accumulate a large quantity of knowledge about Spanish grammar and vocabulary but rather to use what you learn as effectively and creatively as you can.

Communicating in a foreign language means understanding what others say and transmitting your messages in ways that avoid misunderstandings. As you learn to do this, you will find that making errors is part of language learning. Think of mistakes as positive steps toward effective communication. They don't hold you back; they advance you in your efforts.

Learning a language takes practice, but it's an enriching experience that can bring you a lot of pleasure and satisfaction. We hope your experience with *¡Ya verás! Gold, Nivel 1*, is both rewarding and enjoyable!

iii

Acknowledgments

Creating a secondary program is a long and complicated process which involves the dedication and hard work of a number of people. First of all, we express our heartfelt thanks to the Secondary School Publishing Team at Heinle & Heinle for its diligent work on *¡Ya verás! Gold* and to Hispanex of Boston, MA for the many contributions its staff made to the program. We thank Kenneth Holman who created the textbooks' initial interior design and the designers at Hispanex who refined and created it.

Our thanks also go to Charles Heinle for his special interest and support and to Jeannette Bragger and Donald Rice, authors of *On y va!* We thank Jessie Carduner, Charles Grove, and Paul D. Toth for their contributions to the interdisciplinary sections in the student textbook. We also express our appreciation to the people who worked on the fine set of supporting materials available with the *¡Ya verás! Gold*, level 1, program: Greg Harris, Workbook; Chris McIntyre and Jill Welch, Teacher's Edition; Joe Wieczorek, Laboratory Program; Kristen Warner, Testing Program; Susan Malik, Middle School Activities and Teacher's Guide; Sharon Brown, Practice Software; and Frank Domínguez, Ana Martínez-Lage, and Jeff Morgenstein, the *Mundos hispanos 1* multimedia program.

Finally, a very special word of acknowledgment goes to our children:
— To Mía and Stevan who are always on their daddy's mind and whose cultural heritage is ever present throughout *¡Ya verás! Gold.*
— To Susan, Elizabeth, and Rebecca Rosser, whose enthusiasm and increasing interest in Spanish inspired their father to take part in this endeavor.

John R. Gutiérrez and Harry L. Rosser

The publisher and authors wish to thank the following teachers who pilot-tested the ¡Ya verás!, Second Edition, program. Their use of the program in their classes provided us with invaluable suggestions and contributed important insights to the creation of ¡Ya verás! Gold.

Nola Baysore
Muncy JHS
Muncy, PA

Barbara Connell
Cape Elizabeth Middle School
Cape Elizabeth, ME

Frank Droney
Susan Digiandomenico
Wellesley Middle School
Wellesley, MA

Michael Dock
Shikellamy HS
Sunbury, PA

Jane Flood Clare
Somers HS
Lincolndale, NY

Nancy McMahon
Somers Middle School
Lincolndale, NY

Rebecca Gurnish
Ellet HS
Akron, OH

Peter Haggerty
Wellesley HS
Wellesley, MA

José M. Díaz
Hunter College HS
New York, NY

Claude Hawkins
Flora Mazzucco
Jerie Milici
Elena Fienga
Bohdan Kodiak
Greenwich HS
Greenwich, CT

Wally Lishkoff
Tomás Travieso
Carver Middle School
Miami, FL

Manuel M. Manderine
Canton McKinley HS
Canton, OH

Grace Angel Marion
South JHS
Lawrence, KS

Jean Barrett
St. Ignatius HS
Cleveland, OH

Gary Osman
McFarland HS
McFarland, WI

Deborah Decker
Honeoye Falls-Lima HS
Honeoye Falls, NY

Carrie Piepho
Arden JHS
Sacramento, CA

Rhonda Barley
Marshall JHS
Marshall, VA

Germana Shirmer
W. Springfield HS
Springfield, VA

John Boehner
Gibson City HS
Gibson City, IL

Margaret J. Hutchison
John H. Linton JHS
Penn Hills, PA

Edward G. Stafford
St. Andrew's-Sewanee School
St. Andrew's, TN

Irene Prendergast
Wayzata East JHS
Plymouth, MN

Tony DeLuca
Cranston West HS
Cranston, RI

Joe Wild-Crea
Wayzata Senior High School
Plymouth, MN

Katy Armagost
Manhattan HS
Manhattan, KS

William Lanza
Osbourn Park HS
Manassas, VA

Linda Kelley
Hopkinton HS
Contoocook, NH

John LeCuyer
Belleville HS West
Belleville, IL

Sue Bell
South Boston HS
Boston, MA

Wayne Murri
Mountain Crest HS
Hyrum, UT

Barbara Flynn
Summerfield Waldorf School
Santa Rosa, CA

The publisher and authors wish to thank the following people who reviewed the manuscript for the *¡Ya verás!*, Second Edition, program. Their comments were invaluable to its development and of great assistance in the creation of *¡Ya verás! Gold*.

High School Reviewers

Georgio Arias, Juan De León, Luís Martínez (McAllen ISD, McAllen, TX); **Katy Armagost** (Mt. Vernon High School, Mt. Vernon, WA); **Yolanda Bejar, Graciela Delgado, Bárbara V. Méndez, Mary Alice Mora** (El Paso ISD, El Paso, TX); **Linda Bigler** (Thomas Jefferson High School, Alexandria, VA); **John Boehner** (Gibson City High School, Gibson City, IL); **Kathleen Carroll** (Edinburgh ISD, Edinburgh, TX); **Louanne Grimes** (Richardson ISD, Richardson, TX); **Greg Harris** (Clay High School, South Bend, IN); **Diane Henderson** (Houston ISD, Houston, TX); **Maydell Jenks** (Katy ISD, Katy, TX); **Bartley Kirst** (Ironwood High School, Glendale, AZ); **Mala Levine** (St. Margaret's Episcopal School, San Juan Capistrano, CA); **Manuel Manderine** (Canton McKinley Sr. High School, Canton, OH); **Laura Martin** (Cleveland State University, Cleveland, OH); **Luis Millán** (Edina High School, Minneapolis, MN); **David Moffett, Karen Petmeckey, Pat Rossett, Nereida Zimic** (Austin ISD, Austin, TX); **Jeff Morgenstein** (Hudson High School, Hudson, FL); **Rosana Pérez, Jody Spoor** (Northside ISD, San Antonio, TX); **Susan Polansky** (Carnegie Mellon University, Pittsburgh, PA); **Alva Salinas** (San Antonio ISD, San Antonio, TX); **Patsy Shafchuk** (Hudson High School, Hudson, FL); **Terry A. Shafer** (Worthington Kilbourne High School, West Worthington, OH); **Courtenay Suárez** (Montwood High School, Socorro ISD, El Paso, TX); **Alvino Téllez, Jr.** (Edgewood ISD, San Antonio, TX); **Kristen Warner** (Piper High School, Sunrise, FL); **Nancy Wrobel** (Champlin Park High School, Champlin, MN)

Middle School Reviewers

Larry Ling (Hunter College High School, New York, NY); **Susan Malik** (West Springfield High School, Springfield, VA); **Yvette Parks** (Norwood Junior High School, Norwood, MA)

Contenido

¡Bienvenidos al mundo hispánico!   xvi

Mapas   xvii

UNIDAD 1   *Vamos a tomar algo*   1

CAPÍTULO 1   *Vamos al café* • • • • • • • • • • • • • • • • 2

PRIMERA ETAPA   3
¡Hola! ¿Qué tal?

- **Comentarios culturales** Saludos y despedidas
- **Pronunciación** The Spanish alphabet
- **Estructura** Expressing likes and dislikes: **Gustar** + activities (**me, te**)
- **Palabras útiles** Expressing likes and dislikes
- **Aquí escuchamos** "Hola y adiós"
- **Adelante**

SEGUNDA ETAPA   9
¡Un refresco, por favor!

- **Pronunciación** The vowel a
- **Estructura** The indefinite articles **un, unos, una, unas**
- **Comentarios culturales** Los cafés
- **Aquí escuchamos** "En un café"
- **Adelante**

TERCERA ETAPA   15
¡Vamos a comer algo!

- **Pronunciación:** The vowel **e**
- **Estructura** The present tense of regular **-ar** verbs—first and second persons
- **Palabras útiles** Expressing frequency
- **Comentarios culturales** Las comidas
- **Aquí escuchamos** "¡A comer!"
- **Adelante**
- **En línea**

Vocabulario • 22
Encuentros culturales Mesón del pirata • • • • • • • • • • • • • • • • • • 24

CAPÍTULO 2   *¡Vamos a un bar de tapas!* • • • • • • • • • • 26

PRIMERA ETAPA   27
Las tapas españolas

- **Pronunciación** The vowel **i**
- **Comentarios culturales** Las tapas
- **Estructura** The present tense of regular **-ar** verbs—third person
- **Palabras útiles** Asking and answering yes/no questions
- **Aquí escuchamos** "En un bar de tapas"
- **Adelante**

SEGUNDA ETAPA   36
¡Buenos días!... ¡Hasta luego!

- **Comentarios culturales** Saludos informales y formales
- **Pronunciación** The vowel **o**
- **Estructura** The conjugated verb followed by an infinitive
- **Aquí escuchamos** "El señor y la señora Jiménez"
- **Adelante**
- **En línea**

Vocabulario • 43
Encuentros culturales Así los decimos • • • • • • • • • • • • • • • • • • 44

CAPÍTULO 3 · ¿Te gusta la comida mexicana? · · · · · · · 46

PRIMERA ETAPA 47
¡Vamos a un restaurante!

- **Pronunciación** The vowel **u**
- **Estructura** The present tense of the verb **ser**
- **Palabras útiles** Names of countries
- **Aquí escuchamos** "En un restaurante mexicano"
- **Adelante**

SEGUNDA ETAPA 56
¡Qué comida más rica!

- **Estructura** Adjectives of nationality
- **Nota gramatical** Nouns of profession
- **Aquí escuchamos** "Descripción personal"
- **Adelante**
- **En línea**

Vocabulario · 63
Encuentros culturales ¡Qué delicioso! · · · · · · · · · · · · · · · · · · · 65

¡Sigamos adelante!

Conversemos un rato · · · · · · · · · · · · · · · · · · · 67
Taller de escritores Writing photo captions · · · · · · · · · · · · · · · · · 68
Conexión con las ciencias La merienda y la nutrición · · · · · · · · · · · 70
Vistas de los países hispanos Puerto Rico · · · · · · · · · · 72
En la comunidad ¡Bienvenidos a Randy's Diner! · · · · · · · · · · · · · · · 73

UNIDAD 2 *Vamos a conocernos* 75

CAPÍTULO 4 · ¿De quién es? · · · · · · · · · · · · · · · · · · · 76

PRIMERA ETAPA 77
¿Qué llevas a la escuela?

- **Pronunciación** The consonant **p**
- **Estructura** The definite article
- **Nota grammatical** Expressing possession with **de**
- **Aquí escuchamos** "¿Qué llevas a la escuela?"
- **Adelante**

SEGUNDA ETAPA 84
¿Qué hay en tu cuarto?

- **Pronunciación** The consonant **t**
- **Palabra útiles** Numbers from **0** to **20**
- **Palabras útiles** **Hay** + noun
- **Aquí escuchamos** "¿Qué hay en tu cuarto?"
- **Adelante**

TERCERA ETAPA 90
En mi casa

- **Pronunciación:** The sound of /**k**/
- **Estructura** Possessive adjectives: first and second persons
- **Aquí escuchamos** "¿Dónde vives?"
- **Adelante**
- **En línea**

Vocabulario · 99
Encuentros culturales "Caballo de acero" · · · · · · · · · · · · · · · · 100

CAPÍTULO 5

Me gusta mucho... • • • • • • • • • • • **102**

PRIMERA ETAPA   103
Mis gustos

- **Estructura** The verb **gustar**
- **Pronunciación** The consonant **d**
- **Estructura** **ser** + **de** for possession
- **Aquí escuchamos** "Mis gustos"
- **Adelante**

SEGUNDA ETAPA   112
¿Qué te gusta más?

- **Pronunciación** The consonant **d** (continued)
- **Estructura** The present tense of **-er** + **-ir** verbs
- **Aquí escuchamos** "¿Qué te gusta más?"
- **Adelante**
- **En línea**

Vocabulario • **120**
Encuentros culturales La agenda de Mabel • • • • • • • • • • • • **121**

CAPÍTULO 6

¡Ésta es mi familia! • • • • • • • • • • **123**

PRIMERA ETAPA   124
Yo vivo con...

- **Comentarios culturales** Los apellidos
- **Pronunciación** The sound of **/b/**
- **Estructura** The verb **tener**
- **Palabras útiles** **Tener que** + infinitive
- **Aquí escuchamos** "Mi familia"
- **Adelante**

SEGUNDA ETAPA   132
Tengo una familia grande

- **Pronunciación** The sound of **/b/** (continued)
- **Comentarios culturales** La familia
- **Estructura** Information questions with **dónde, cuántos(as), quién, qué, por qué**
- **Estructura** Descriptive adjectives
- **Aquí escuchamos** "La familia de Isabel"
- **Adelante**
- **En línea**

Vocabulario • **143**
Encuentros culturales Un árbol ecuatoriano • • • • • • • • • • • • **144**

¡Sigamos adelante!

Conversemos un rato • **146**
Taller de escritores Writing a paragraph • • • • • • • • • • • • • • • **147**
Conexión con la sociología La familia en nuestra sociedad • • • • • • • **148**
Vistas de los países hispanos Ecuador, Chile, Honduras • • • • • • • • **150**
En la comunidad ¡Programa tu carrera! • • • • • • • • • • • • • • • • **153**

UNIDAD 3 ¿Dónde y a qué hora? 154

CAPÍTULO 7   ¿Adónde vamos? •••••••••••• 156

PRIMERA ETAPA   157
Los edificios públicos

- **Comentarios culturales** La ciudad típica
- **Pronunciación** The consonant **g**
- **Estructura** The verb **ir** and the contraction **al**
- **Palabras útiles** Expressions of frequency
- **Aquí escuchamos** "El autobús"
- **Adelante**

SEGUNDA ETAPA   164
¿Quieres ir al cine?

- **Comentarios culturales** El teléfono
- **Pronunciación** The consonant **g** (continued)
- **Estructura** The verbs **querer** and **preferir**
- **Aquí escuchamos** "En el centro"
- **Adelante**

TERCERA ETAPA   173
Las tiendas

- **Comentarios culturales** Las tiendas
- **Pronunciación:** The sound of Spanish **j**
- **Comentarios culturales** Las direcciones y los teléfonos
- **Palabras útiles** Numbers from **20** to **100**
- **Palabras útiles** Expressing frequency
- **Aquí escuchamos** "Números"
- **Adelante**
- **En línea**

Vocabulario ••••••••••••••••••••••••••••• **181**
Encuentros culturales La Pequeña Habana **182**

CAPÍTULO 8   ¿Dónde está...? •••••••••••• 184

PRIMERA ETAPA   185
¿Está lejos de aquí?

- **Pronunciación** The sound of **/s/**
- **Nota gramatical** The preposition **de** and the definite article **el**
- **Estructura** The verb **estar**
- **Aquí escuchamos** "No estamos lejos"
- **Adelante**

SEGUNDA ETAPA   193
¿Cómo llego a...?

- **Comentarios culturales** El español en el mundo
- **Pronunciación** The sound of **/s/** (continued)
- **Estructura** The imperative with **Ud.** and **Uds.**
- **Aquí escuchamos** "Está cerca de aquí"
- **Adelante**
- **En línea**

Vocabulario ••••••••••••••••••••••••••••••• **200**
Encuentros culturales El centro colonial de Quito •••••••••••• **201**

CAPÍTULO 9 · *¡La fiesta del pueblo!* · · · · · · · · · · · **203**

PRIMERA ETAPA   **204**
¿A qué hora son los bailes folklóricos?

- **Comentarios culturales** La fiesta del pueblo
- **Pronunciación** The consonants **m** and **n**
- **Estructura** Telling time
- **Palabras útiles** Questions about time
- **Estructura** The verb **venir**
- **Aquí escuchamos** "La hora"
- **Adelante**

SEGUNDA ETAPA   **212**
¿Cómo están Uds.?

- **Pronunciación** The consonant **ñ**
- **Estructura** Estar + adjectives of condition
- **Estructura** Possessive adjectives: third person
- **Aquí escuchamos** "¿Cómo están?"
- **Adelante**
- **En línea**

Vocabulario · **219**
Encuentros culturales Los muchos colores de júbilo · · · · · · · · · · · · **220**

¡Sigamos adelante!

Conversemos un rato · **222**
Taller de escritores Writing a persuasive description · · · · · · · · · · · · **223**
Conexión con la geografía Los husos horarios · · · · · · · · · · · · · · **224**
Vistas de los países hispanos Costa Rica · · · · · · · · · · · · · · · **226**
En la comunidad Paul Kearney: En caso de una emergencia · · · · · · · · **227**

UNIDAD 4 *Vamos al centro*   **229**

CAPÍTULO 10 · *¿Quieres ir al centro?* · · · · · · · · · · · **230**

PRIMERA ETAPA   **231**
¿Para qué?

- **Pronunciación** The consonant **h**
- **Estructura** The immediate future: ir a + infinitive
- **Palabras útiles Tener ganas +** infinitive
- **Aquí escuchamos** "¿Quieres ir al centro?"
- **Adelante**

SEGUNDA ETAPA   **241**
¿Cuándo vamos?

- **Estructura** The days of the week
- **Estructura** The verb **hacer**
- **Aquí escuchamos** "¿Cuándo vamos?"
- **Adelante**

TERCERA ETAPA   **248**
¿Cómo prefieres ir, en coche o a pie?

- **Estructura** The verb **poder**
- **Aquí escuchamos** "¿Puedes ir conmigo?"
- **Adelante**
- **En línea**

Vocabulario · · · · · · · · · · · · **254**
Encuentros culturales Estrellas de la música latina · · · · · · · · **255**

Contenido   **xi**

CAPÍTULO 11

Vamos a tomar el metro · · · · · · · · · · **257**

PRIMERA ETAPA   **258**
¿En qué dirección?

- **Pronunciación** The consonant **ch**
- **Comentarios culturales** El metro
- **Estructura** Adverbs for the present and future
- **Aquí escuchamos** "¿Tomamos el metro?
- **Adelante**

SEGUNDA ETAPA   **266**
En la taquilla

- **Estructura** Adjectives of nationality
- **Comentarios culturales** Billetes para el transporte público
- **Estructura** The verb **pensar** and **pensar** + infinitive
- **Aquí escuchamos** "¿Qué piensan hacer?"
- **Adelante**
- **En línea**

Vocabulario · **272**
Encuentros culturales Viaje por latinoamérica · · · · · · · · · · · · · · · **273**

CAPÍTULO 12

¿Cómo vamos? · · · · · · · · · · · · · · · · **275**

PRIMERA ETAPA   **276**
¡Vamos a tomar un taxi!

- **Pronunciación** The consonant **ll**
- **Comentarios culturales** La Puerta del Sol en Madrid
- **Palabras útiles** Numbers from **100** to **1,000,000**
- **Aquí escuchamos** "¡Taxi, taxi!"
- **Adelante**

SEGUNDA ETAPA   **283**
En la agencia de viajes

- **Estructura** **Esperar** + infinitive, expressions for discussing plans
- **Aquí escuchamos** "Vamos de viaje"
- **Adelante**
- **En línea**

Vocabulario · **288**
Encuentros culturales Explora el "Agua Grande" · · · · · · · · · · · · · **289**

¡Sigamos adelante!

Conversemos un rato · **291**
Taller de escritores Writing a letter · **292**
Conexión con la biblioteconomía Clasificación de la Biblioteca del Congreso · **294**
Vistas de los países hispanos México · · · · · · · · · · · · · · · · · · · **296**
En la comunidad Caryl Feinstein—preparada para el siglo xx · · · · · · · **297**

UNIDAD 5 *Tu tiempo libre* 298

CAPÍTULO 13   *Los pasatiempos* • • • • • • • • • • • • • • 300

PRIMERA ETAPA   301
¿Qué te gusta hacer?

- **Estructura** Preterite tense of **-ar** verbs
- **Estructura** The preterite of the verb **hacer**
- **Aquí escuchamos** "¿Qué te gusta hacer?
- **Adelante**

SEGUNDA ETAPA   310
¿Adónde fuiste?

- **Estructura** The preterite of the verb **ir**
- **Estructura** Preterite tense of **-er** and **-ir** verbs
- **Aquí escuchamos** "¿Qué hiciste anoche?"
- **Adelante**

TERCERA ETAPA   318
Una semana típica

- **Estructura** Adverbs, prepositions, and other expressions used to designate the past
- **Estructura** Preterite tense of the verbs **andar, estar** and **tener**
- **Aquí escuchamos** "¿Qué hiciste este fin de semana?"
- **Adelante**
- **En línea**

Vocabulario • 325
Encuentros culturales Tu tiempo libre • • • • • • • • • • • • • • • • 326

CAPÍTULO 14   *Actividades deportivas* • • • • • • • • • • • • 328

PRIMERA ETAPA   329
Los deportes

- **Estructura** **Hace** and **Hace que** for expressing how long ago something occurred
- **Estructura** The preterite of verbs ending in **-gar**
- **Aquí escuchamos** "Los deportes"
- **Adelante**

SEGUNDA ETAPA   338
Deportes de verano

- **Estructura** The preterite of verbs ending in **-car**
- **Palabras útiles** Expressions used to talk about a series of actions
- **Aquí escuchamos** "¡Qué bien lo pasaste!"
- **Adelante**
- **En línea**

Vocabulario • • • • • • • • • • • 347
Encuentros culturales • • 348
   Una página de "surfing" latinoamericano

CAPÍTULO 15 · *Dos deportes populares* · · · · · · · · · · **350**

PRIMERA ETAPA 351
El béisbol

- **Estructura** The present progressive
- **Aquí escuchamos** "¿Vienes a la fiesta?"
- **Adelante**

SEGUNDA ETAPA 358
El tenis

- **Estructura** Past, present, and future time
- **Aquí escuchamos** "¿Para qué vas al centro?"
- **Adelante**
- **En línea**

Vocabulario · **366**
Encuentros culturales Un héroe de Puerto Rico · · · · · · · · · · · · · **367**

¡Sigamos Adelante!

Conversemos un rato · **369**
Taller de escritores Writing a report · · · · · · · · · · · · · · · **370**
Conexión con las ciencias Los ejercicios aérobicos y la utilización de energía · **372**
 Vistas de los países hispanos California and Florida · · · · · · · · · · **374**
En la comunidad Se buscan estrellas de béisbol · · · · · · · · · · · · · **375**

UNIDAD 6 *Vamos de compras* 376

CAPÍTULO 16 *Vamos al centro comercial* · · · · · · · · · · **378**

PRIMERA ETAPA 379
En la tienda de música

- **Pronunciación** The consonant **r**
- **Estructura** The verbs **gustar** and **encantar**
- **Aquí escuchamos** "Me gusta la música"
- **Adelante**

SEGUNDA ETAPA 384
En la papelería

- **Pronunciación** The consonant **rr**
- **Estructura** The imperative with **tú**: affirmative familiar commands
- **Aquí escuchamos** "Para mi computadora"
- **Adelante**

TERCERA ETAPA 390
La tienda de deportes

- **Estructura** The imperative with **tú**: negative familiar commands
- **Aquí escuchamos** "El tenista"
- **Adelante**
- **En línea**

Vocabulario · **395**
Encuentros culturales Ritos importantes para los jóvenes hispanohablantes · **396**

Txiv

CAPÍTULO 17 — *¿Cuánto cuesta...?* • • • • • • • • • • • • 398

PRIMERA ETAPA 399
Día de feria

- **Comentarios culturales** Los mercados al aire libre
- **Pronunciación** The consonant **f**
- **Estructura** Demonstrative adjectives
- **Palabras útiles** Expressions of specific quantity
- **Aquí escuchamos** "De compras en el mercado"
- **Adelante**

SEGUNDA ETAPA 408
En el supermercado

- **Comentarios culturales** Las frutas y los vegetales tropicales
- **Estructura** The interrogative words **cuál** and **cuáles**
- **Nota gramatical** Demonstrative pronouns
- **Aquí escuchamos** "Por favor compra..."
- **Adelante**

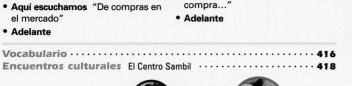

Vocabulario • 416
Encuentros culturales El Centro Sambil • • • • • • • • • • • • • 418

CAPÍTULO 18 — *¿Qué quieres comprar?* • • • • • • • • • • 420

PRIMERA ETAPA 421
Tienda "La Alta Moda"

- **Pronunciación** The consonant **l**
- **Estructura** Expressions of comparison
- **Aquí escuchamos** "¿Más o menos?"
- **Adelante**

SEGUNDA ETAPA 428
Zapatería "El Tacón"

- **Estructura** Expressing equality
- **Comentarios culturales** Tallas internacionales
- **Aquí escuchamos** "¿De qué talla?"
- **Adelante**
- **En línea**

Vocabulario • 435
Encuentros culturales Los trajes de Guatemala • • • • • • • • • • • 436

¡Sigamos adelante!

Conversemos un rato • 438
Taller de escritores Writing a composition • • • • • • • • • • • • • 439
Conexión con la economía: El tipo de cambio • • • • • • • • • • • • 440
Vistas de los países hispanos Venezuela, El Salvador, New Mexico and Arizona • 442
En la comunidad Yolanda Miller: representante de tus derechos • • • • • 445

Contenido **XV**

¡Bienvenidos al mundo hispánico!

Did you know that Spanish is spoken by more than 360 million people around the world and that is the third most widely spoken language after Chinese and English? In fact, Spanish, which originated in a tiny corner of Castile, Spain, is the principal language of 20 countries. After English, it is also the most commonly spoken language in the United States, boasting more than 22 million speakers! These simple facts, however, only hint at the vibrant diversity of the Spanish language and the rich tapestry of Hispanic cultures.

Like many languages, Spanish has been shaped by geography. The Spanish spoken by the Chileans living in the shadows of the snow-capped Andes has evolved differently from that of the Argentines herding cattle on the vast grass-filled plains known as the pampas. Even within a country as small as the Dominican Republic, the way Spanish sounds in the capital city of Santo Domingo differs from the way it is spoken in rural areas.

In many places, Spanish was also shaped by the cultures and languages of the indigenous peoples who lived there long before the arrival of Spanish-speakers—for example, the Maya of Mexico's Yucatan peninsula and Guatemala, and the Guaranis of Paraguay. Just as the United States is a "melting pot" of many cultures, the Spanish-speaking world represents a dynamic linguistic and cultural mosaic. ¡Bienvenidos al mundo hispánico! You are about to embark on a fascinating journey!

Te toca a ti

Examine the maps in your textbook to find the following information.

1. The twenty Spanish-speaking countries
2. The name of the river that separates Mexico from the United States
3. The only country in Central America that is not considered a Spanish-speaking country
4. The number and names of the countries in South America where Spanish is not the principal language
5. The Spanish-speaking island in the Caribbean that is part of the United States
6. A Spanish-speaking country in Africa

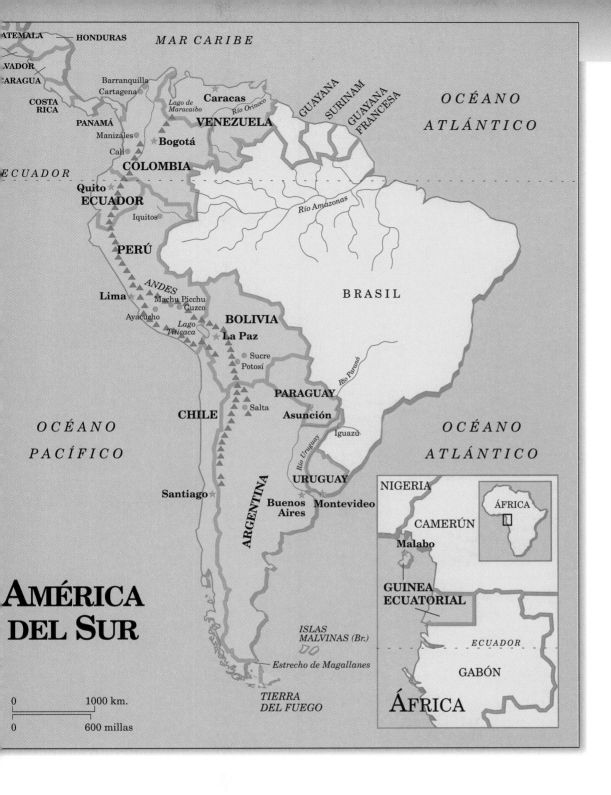

MAR CARIBE

ATEMALA — HONDURAS

VADOR

ARAGUA

COSTA
RICA

PANAMÁ

Barranquilla
Cartagena

Manizales

Cali

ECUADOR

Lago de
Maracaibo

Caracas

Río Orinoco

VENEZUELA

Bogotá

COLOMBIA

Quito
ECUADOR

Iquitos

PERÚ

ANDES

Lima

Machu Picchu
Cuzco

Ayacucho

Lago
Titicaca

BOLIVIA

La Paz

Sucre

Potosí

CHILE

Salta

PARAGUAY

Asunción

Santiago

ARGENTINA

Río Uruguay

Iguazú

URUGUAY

**Buenos
Aires**

Montevideo

GUAYANA
SURINAM
GUAYANA
FRANCESA

OCÉANO
ATLÁNTICO

Río Amazonas

BRASIL

Río Paraná

OCÉANO
PACÍFICO

OCÉANO
ATLÁNTICO

AMÉRICA
DEL SUR

ISLAS
MALVINAS (Br.)

Estrecho de Magallanes

TIERRA
DEL FUEGO

0   1000 km.

0   600 millas

NIGERIA

CAMERÚN

ÁFRICA

Malabo

**GUINEA
ECUATORIAL**

ECUADOR

GABÓN

ÁFRICA

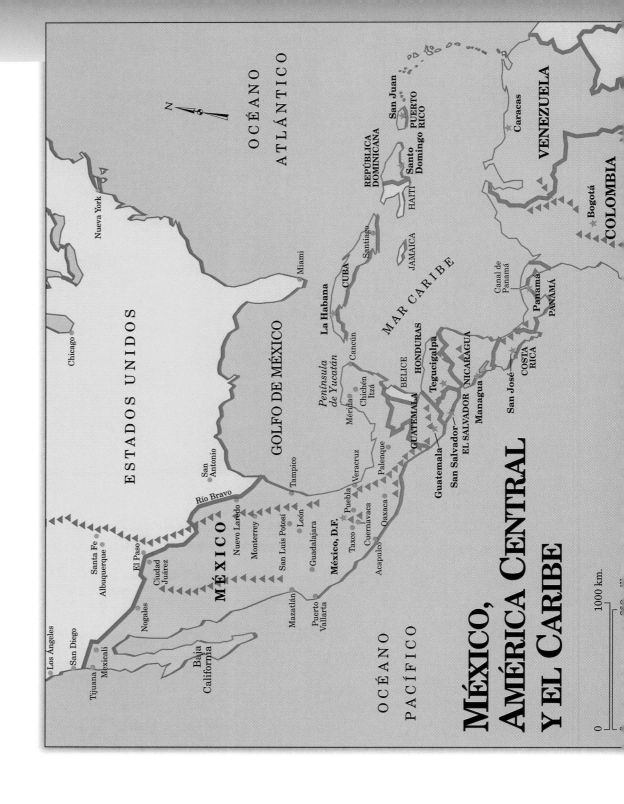

México, América Central y el Caribe

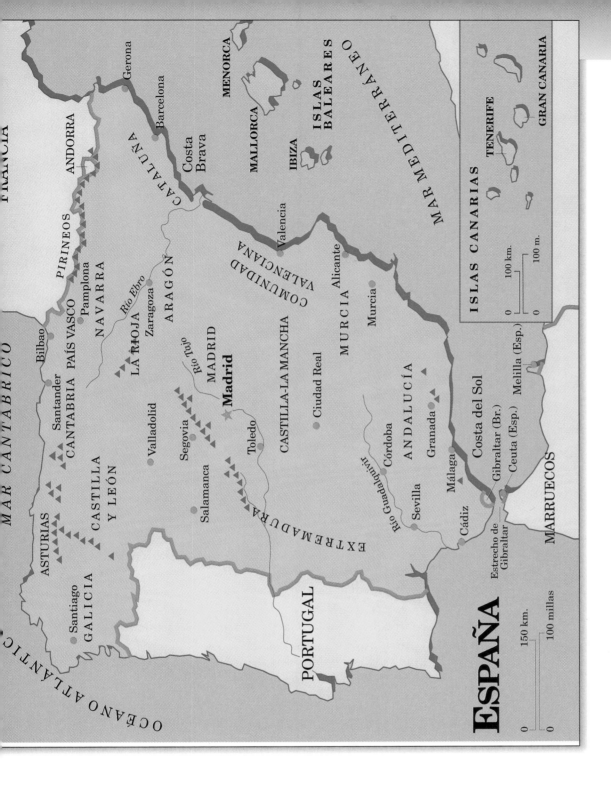

ESPAÑA

UNIDAD 1

Setting the Context

Each unit of Nivel 1 of *¡Ya verás! Gold* features a young person from a Spanish-speaking country; once they have been introduced, these people reappear from time to time in the activities.

The young native Spanish speaker featured in Unit 1 is Miguel Palacios from Spain. Since the over-arching task of Unit 1 is ordering food and drink, Miguel and the other characters are seen in a variety of places where young people go for refreshments or to eat. Chapter 1 is centered around the café; Chapter 2 around a **tapas** bar; and Chapter 3 around Mexican restaurants. Two of the end-of-chapter readings, **Encuentros culturales**, extend the unit theme to other Spanish-speaking countries. Chapter 1 features a restaurant in Puerto Rico; and Chapter 3 features Caribbean cuisine. Chapter 2 features Spanish cognates, including words for several different kinds of food.

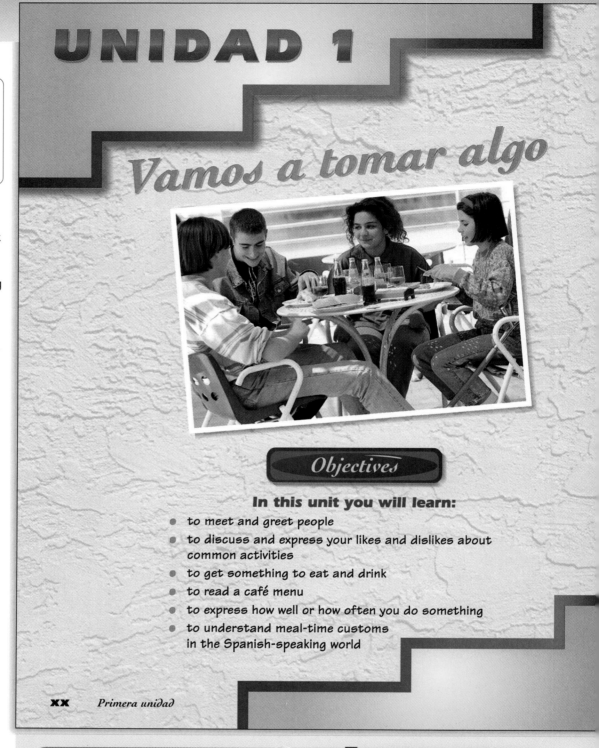

UNIDAD 1

Vamos a tomar algo

Objectives

In this unit you will learn:

- to meet and greet people
- to discuss and express your likes and dislikes about common activities
- to get something to eat and drink
- to read a café menu
- to express how well or how often you do something
- to understand meal-time customs in the Spanish-speaking world

xx *Primera unidad*

Unit Support Materials

- Workbook: **Aquí leemos** pp. 34-36
- Lab Manual: **Ya llegamos** pp. 21-22
- Lab Program: Cassette Side B; CD 10, Tracks 1-3
- Tapescript: Lab Program pp. 28-30
- TRB: Unit Grammar Review Masters: pp. 13-15; Answer Key pp. 50
- Lesson Plan Book: **¡Sigamos adelante!** p. 18
- Workbook for Spanish-speaking Students: pp. 19-20
- Testing Program: Unit Test pp. 33-38; Answer Key & Testing Cassettes/CDs Tapescript pp. T14-T15;

- Oral Assessment pp. T16; Portfolio Assessment pp. Piv-Pvi
- Testing Cassettes: Cassette Side A
- Computerized Testing Program: Windows™; Macintosh®
- Atajo Writing Assistant Software: Student Text pp. 68-69
- Video Program: Cassette 1, 26:43-29:30
- Video Guide: Videoscript pp. 15-16; Activities p. 95
- Internet Explorations: Student Text p. 72

¿Qué ves?

- Where are the people in these photographs?
- What are they doing?
- What kinds of beverages are they having?
- Where do you like to go for something to eat or drink?

The Planning Strategy is a brief warm-up to each unit of the text. It appears on the first Workbook page of each unit and is designed to give students a general overview of the language functions, themes and topics to be covered in the entire unit.

You can assign the Planning Strategy for Unit 1 as homework or you can do it in class. If you do it in class, verify that everyone knows what a **café** is; then proceed to search for American "equivalents," such as fast-food restaurants. To help students become aware of the use of "formulaic" expressions in English, have them role play some of the items. Have two or three sets of students play the scene, then ask the class to identify the different formulaic expressions used in each situation.

Linguistic Comparisons 4.1
Cultural Comparisons 4.2

Vamos al café
Primera etapa: ¡Hola! ¿Qué tal?
Segunda etapa: ¡Un refresco, por favor!
Tercera etapa: ¡Vamos a comer algo!

¡Vamos a un bar de tapas!
Primera etapa: Las tapas españolas
Segunda etapa: ¡Buenos días!... ¡Hasta luego!

¿Te gusta la comida mexicana?
Primera etapa: ¡Vamos a un restaurante
Segunda etapa: ¡Qué comida más rica!

1

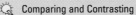

Spanish for Spanish Speakers

Personalize

Have Spanish speakers mention, in Spanish, what they see in the photographs. Ask them about beverages they themselves drink that are different from those depicted in the photos.

Cultural Comparisons 4.2

Focus on Culture

Examining the photos

Have students study the photos of Miguel Palacios and his friends. Ask them to compare the way people in the photos are dressed with the way they themselves are dressed. What are the similarities? What are the differences?

Comparing and Contrasting

Cultural Practices and Perspectives 2.1
Cultural Comparisons 4.2

CAPÍTULO 1

OBJECTIVES

Functions
- Ordering food and drink
- Greeting, introducing, and saying good-bye to friends
- Expressing likes and dislikes
- Asking and answering yes and no questions

Context
- **Café**

Accuracy
- The verb **gustar** + infinitive
- Expressing likes and dislikes
- Gender of nouns
- Indefinite articles
- Subject pronouns
- Present tense of regular **-ar** verbs
- Expressing frequency

Pronunciation
- The Spanish alphabet
- The vowel **a**
- The vowel **e**

Preliminary Support Materials

A preliminary chapter is available in the Teacher's Resource Book as an option for starting *¡Ya verás! Gold*, Nivel 1. Its three **etapas** present **Me llamo...**, first names in Spanish, basic greetings, colors, seasons, days of the week, weather expressions, classroom expressions, numbers 1-30, and telling time. Total Physical Response (TPR) is used extensively in the third **etapa** as a teaching technique. If you prefer, you may begin immediately with Chapter 1 because all the topics presented in the preliminary chapter are covered elsewhere in *¡Ya verás! Gold*

- Overhead Transparencies: 1, 1a, 2, 3, 3a, 4, 4a, 5, 5a, 6, 6a, 7
- Middle School Activities: p. 1

Vamos al café

—Yo quisiera un refresco.
—Entonces, vamos al café.

Objectives

- ordering food and drink
- greeting, introducing, and leavetaking with friends
- expressing likes and dislikes
- asking and answering yes/no questions

2 *Primera unidad* Vamos a tomar algo

Chapter Support Materials

- Lab Manual: pp. 3-8
- Lab Program: Cassette, Side A; CD 1, Tracks 1-8
- TRB: Textbook Activity Masters: pp. 60-63
- Textbook Cassettes/CDs: Cassette 1, Side A; CD 1, Tracks 1-12
- Tapescript: Lab Program pp. 1-7; Textbook Cassttes/CDs p. 188
- Middle School Activities: pp. 2-5
- TRB: Placement Test for Spanish-speaking Students: pp. 9-12
- Workbook for Spanish-speaking Students: pp. 1-6
- Answer Key to SSS Workbook: pp. 1-2
- Practice Software: Windows™; Macintosh®
- Testing Program: Chapter Test pp. 9-13; Answer Key & Testing Cassettes Tapescript pp. T4, T5; Oral Assessment p. T5
- Testing Cassettes: Cassette Side A
- Computerized Testing Program: Windows™; Macintosh®
- Video Program: Cassette 1, 00:00-7:58
- Video Guide: Videoscript pp. 3-6; Activities pp. 85-86
- **Mundos hispanos 1**
- Internet Activities: Student Text p. 21

PRIMERA ETAPA

Preparación

- What do you think these teenagers are saying to each other as they meet on the street or in a public place?
- What gestures are they making?
- When you introduce a friend to someone, what do you usually do?
- What are some expressions that you use in English when you meet people?
- What do you say when you are about to leave?

¡Hola! ¿Qué tal?

Alba:	**Buenos días**, Teresa.
Teresa:	Buenos días, Alba. **¿Cómo estás?**
Alba:	**Muy bien, gracias. ¿Y tú?**
Teresa:	**Más o menos.**

Laura:	**¡Hola**, Anita! **¿Qué tal?**
Anita:	Muy bien, Laura. ¿Y tú?
Laura:	**Bien**, gracias. Anita, **te presento a** Juan. Juan, Anita.
Anita:	¡Hola!
Juan:	**Mucho gusto.**

Buenos días *Good morning*   **¿Cómo estás?** *How are you?*   **Muy bien, gracias.** *Very well, thank you.*
¿Y tú? *And you?*   **Más o menos.** *So-so.*   **Hola** *Hello*   **¿Qué tal?** *How are you? How is it going?*
Bien *Well, fine*   **te presento a...** *let me introduce you to...*   **Mucho gusto.** *Nice to meet you.*

Capítulo 1 Vamos al café   **3**

TEACH/MODEL

¡Hola! ¿Qué tal?

PRESENTATION

 TRANSPARENCIES 8

TEXTBOOK CASSETTE/CD CASSETTE 1, SIDE A; CD 1, TRACK 1

TAPESCRIPT PP. 186-187

With books closed, show the overhead transparency of the photographs on page 3 as you play the recordings of the mini-dialogues. After students have heard the recordings, read them aloud to the class, having students repeat first as a whole class, then in groups, and then individually. Then divide the class into pairs and groups of three in which each student plays the role of a character in one of the dialogues in order to practice reading and acting out the exchanges. After five minutes of practice, call on some pairs and groups to act out the dialogues for the class, reminding them to use appropriate gestures. Then present the greetings, good-byes, and their responses on page 4 and have students resume working with their partners or group members to vary the mini-dialogues. After several minutes of practice, ask for volunteers to present their new exchanges to the class.

 Auditory-Musical
Visual-Spatial

Interpretive Communication 1.2
Presentational Communication 1.3

Etapa Support Materials

- Workbook: pp. 3-5
- TRB: Textbook Activity Masters: p. 60
- Textbook Cassettes/CDs: Cassette 1, Side A; CD 1 Track 1
- Tapescript: Textbook Cassettes/CDs pp.186-187
- Overhead Transparency: 8
- Middle School Activities: pp. 4, 6, 7

- Lesson Plan Book: pp. 1-2
- Testing Program: Quiz pp. 1-2; Answer Key & Testing Cassettes/CDs Tapescript pp. T1
- Testing Cassettes: Cassette Side A
- Computerized Testing Program: Windows™; Macintosh®
- Atajo Writing Assistant Software: Student Text p. 8

¡Hola! ¿Qué tal?

VOCABULARY EXPANSION

You may want to introduce these additional expressions for saying good-bye by writing them on the board or on an overhead transparency and modeling them for students: **Hasta mañana, Hasta pronto,** and **Hasta la vista.** You might also introduce **Igualmente,** which is presented as active vocabulary in Chapter 2, as a response to **Mucho gusto.**

PRACTICE / APPLY

A. Saludos

SUGGESTION

Have students do this activity as a whole class in a chain. To begin, have one student direct the first item, **¡Hola!**, to the student on his (her) right. This student responds and then directs the second activity item to the student on his (her) right. Continue in this fashion until all activity items have been completed. Ask students to include their classmates' names with the activity items (**¡Hola, María!**). Also, to encourage students to pay attention, change the direction of the chain at unpredictable intervals.

POSSIBLE ANSWERS

1. ¡Hola!/Buenos días.
2. Buenos días./¡Hola!
3. Muy bien, gracias./Regular.
4. Bien, ¿y tú?
5. Buenas tardes.
6. Más o menos./Bastante bien./ Regular.
7. Buenas noches.
8. Nada/No pasa nada.
9. Bastante bien./Muy bien

B. ¡Hola! ¿Qué tal?

SUGGESTION

Encourage students to incorporate appropriate body language as described in **Comentarios culturales** on page 5 into their role-plays.

Interpersonal Communication 1.1
Cultural Practices and Perspectives 2.1

¡Hola!   ¿Cómo estás?   ¿Qué tal?   Hasta luego.

Saludos *(Greetings)*

Buenos días.
Buenas tardes. *Good afternoon.*
Buenas noches. *Good evening. Good night.*
¡Hola!
¿Cómo estás?
¿Cómo te va? *How's it going?*
¿Qué hay? *What's new?*
¿Qué pasa? *What's going on?*
¿Qué tal?

Respuestas *(Answers)*

Buenos días.
Buenas tardes.
Buenas noches.
¡Hola!
Bien, gracias. ¿Y tú?
Muy bien, gracias. ¿Y tú?
Más o menos. ¿Y tú?
Regular. *OK.*
Bastante bien. *Pretty good.*

Despedidas *(Farewells)*

Adiós. *Good-bye.*
Hasta luego. *See you later.*
Nos vemos. *See you.*

Respuestas

Adiós.
¡Chao! *Bye!*

¡Te toca a ti!

A. Saludos Answer these greetings appropriately.

1. ¡Hola!
2. Buenos días.
3. ¿Cómo estás?
4. ¿Qué tal?
5. Buenas tardes.
6. ¿Cómo te va?
7. Buenas noches.
8. ¿Qué pasa?
9. ¿Qué hay?

B. ¡Hola! ¿Qué tal? You are talking to a new Spanish-speaking student in the hallway of your school. A friend of yours approaches and you greet each other. You introduce the new student. Then you all say good-bye to each other. Working in groups of three, act out the situation. Follow the model.

MODELO

Tú:	*¡Hola! ¿Qué tal?*
Amigo(a):	*Bien, gracias, ¿y tú?*
Tú:	*Bien, gracias. Te presento a Marilú.*
Amigo(a):	*¡Hola!*
Marilú:	*Mucho gusto.*
Tú:	*Hasta luego.*
Amigo(a):	*Nos vemos.*
Marilú:	*Adiós.*

4   *Primera unidad* Vamos a tomar algo

MULTIPLE INTELLIGENCES

- Linguistic: All activities
- Logical-Mathematical: D, E
- Bodily-Kinesthetic: B
- Auditory-Musical: **Pronunciación,** C, **Aquí escuchamos**
- Interpersonal: A, **¡Mucho gusto!, Comentarios culturales**
- Intrapersonal: **Una postal**

The Standards

- Interpersonal Communication 1.1: A, D
- Interpretive Communication 1.2: A, D, **Aquí escuchamos, Adelante** activities
- Presentational Communication 1.3: B
- Cultural Practices and Perspectives 2.1: **Comentarios culturales**
- Cultural Products and Perspectives 2.2: **Comentarios culturales**
- Linguistic Comparisons 4.1: **Palabras útiles**
- Cultural Comparisons 4.2: **Comentarios culturales**

Comentarios CULTURALES

Saludos y despedidas

The body language that accompanies greetings and good-byes in Hispanic cultures is somewhat different from North American customs. In both situations, it is customary for Spanish-speaking men to shake hands formally or even exchange an **abrazo;** a brief embrace with a pat or two on the back. Among women, the custom is to kiss each other: on both cheeks in Spain and on only one cheek in Latin America. When a young man and woman who know each other meet, they generally kiss on one or both cheeks. Older people will usually shake hands unless they know each other well. When Spanish speakers of any age greet each other or engage in conversation, they generally stand closer to each other than do speakers of English.

PRONUNCIACIÓN THE SPANISH ALPHABET

A good place to start your study of Spanish pronunciation is with the alphabet. Listed below are the letters of the Spanish alphabet along with their names.

a	a	j	jota	r	ere
b	be	k	ka	rr	erre
c	ce	l	ele	s	ese
ch	che[1]	ll	elle[1]	t	te
d	de	m	eme	u	u
e	e	n	ene	v	ve
f	efe	ñ	eñe	w	doble ve
g	ge	o	o	x	equis
h	hache	p	pe	y	i griega
i	i	q	cu	z	zeta

[1] When looking up words in Spanish dictionaries and publications with alphabetical listings such as telephone directories, entries beginning with **ñ** are listed separately, following those beginning with **n.** Entries for **ch** and **ll** also used to be listed separately. For simplicity and to make Spanish more computer compatible internationally, the Association of Spanish Language Academies voted in 1994 to eliminate separate alphabetical lists for **ch** and **ll.** Such entries are now listed under **c** and **l,** respectively.

Capítulo 1 Vamos al café **5**

Práctica C

EXPANSION

For additional practice using the Spanish alphabet, have students spell their first names and their last names. You might also have them spell words and section titles on the opening pages of Unit 1 and Chapter 1, as well as those located throughout this **etapa**.

TEACH/MODEL

Estructura

PRESENTATION

Introduce **me gusta/te gusta** as vocabulary items without going into their construction. If you have Spanish-speaking students in your class, ask them simple questions such as **¿Te gusta escuchar música rock?**, and have them answer in complete sentences: **Sí, me gusta escuchar... .** If there are no Spanish-speaking students, make simple statements about yourself. Have students repeat them, first as a whole class, then in groups, and then individually. Examples: **Me gusta hablar español. Me gusta escuchar música rock. Me gusta bailar.** Use gestures, body language, and pantomiming where possible. Then ask questions that are likely to elicit affirmative answers from your students. Example: **Me gusta escuchar música rock. ¿Te gusta escuchar música rock?**, etc.

PRACTICE/APPLY

D. ¿Qué te gusta?

SUGGESTION

Begin by directing students to ask each other the questions in the activity (**María, pregúntale a Juan el número uno.**). Then, pair up students and have them do the activity again with their partners for additional practice. Answers will vary, but will all follow one of two formats: **Sí, me gusta...** or **No, no me gusta... .**

Presentational Communication 1.3

Práctica

C. Spell the following words using the Spanish alphabet.

1. pan	5. aceitunas	9. mermelada	13. jamón
2. refresco	6. bocadillo	10. calamares	14. pastel
3. mantequilla	7. naranja	11. sándwich	15. tortilla
4. leche	8. limón	12. desayuno	

ESTRUCTURA

The verb **gustar** + infinitive

—Me gusta bailar.   *I like to dance.*
—¿Te gusta cantar?   *Do you like to sing?*
—No me gusta cantar; **me gusta** escuchar música.   *I don't like to sing; I like to listen to music.*

—¿Te gusta hablar español?   *Do you like to speak Spanish?*
—Sí, pero **no me gusta** estudiar y practicar.   *Yes, but I don't like to study and practice.*

1. To express in Spanish certain activities that you like or do not like to do, you can use the construction **gustar** + infinitive.

2. An infinitive is the simple form of a verb. It is not conjugated, that is, it shows no subject or number (singular or plural). For example, in English *to introduce* is an infinitive, while *introduces* is a conjugated form of the verb. Note that the Spanish infinitives in the preceding sentences all end in **-ar**.

Aquí practicamos

D. ¿Qué (What) te gusta? Answer the following questions, according to the model.

> MODELO   ¿Te gusta estudiar?
> *Sí, me gusta estudiar.* o: *No, no me gusta estudiar.*

1. ¿Te gusta bailar?
2. ¿Te gusta hablar español en clase?
3. ¿Te gusta cantar ópera?
4. ¿Te gusta practicar el español?
5. ¿Te gusta estudiar matemáticas? ¿historia?
6. ¿Te gusta escuchar música rock? ¿clásica?

6 *Primera unidad* Vamos a tomar algo

☀ Spanish for Spanish Speakers

Recognizing Customs

Ask Spanish speakers if they recognize some of the customs and behaviors that are mentioned in the **Comentarios culturales**. Find out if they know about or have experienced other variations of them.

Cultural Practices and Perspectives 2.1

Problematic Spelling Combinations

Point out words in **Práctica C** that have spelling combinations that are problematic for Spanish speakers. For example, **qu** and **ll** in **mantequilla**, the **c** in **aceitunas**, the **ll** in **bocadillo** and **tortilla**, and the **j** in **naranja** and **jamón**. For a more detailed explanation of these problematic spelling combinations, refer to the preface of this Teacher's Edition.

Linguistic

PALABRAS ÚTILES

Expressing likes and dislikes

Here are some words that can be used to express whether you like something very much or just a little. These words are called *adverbs*. They are used after the verb **gustar.**

mucho	*a lot*	**poco**	*a little*
muchísimo	*very much*	**muy poco**	*very little*

Me gusta **mucho** bailar. — *I like dancing a lot.*
Me gusta **muy poco** escuchar música clásica. — *I like listening to classical music very little.*

Aquí practicamos

E. ¿Muchísimo o muy poco? Say how much or how little you like these activities. Follow the model.

MODELO cantar
Me gusta mucho cantar. o: *Me gusta muy poco cantar.*

1. bailar
2. hablar en clase
3. hablar español
4. escuchar música rock
5. escuchar música clásica
6. estudiar
7. cantar

Aquí escuchamos

¡Hola y adiós! *Some friends run into each other on the street.*

Antes de escuchar Think of some of the common expressions, questions, and responses typically used in Spanish when meeting friends or acquaintances.

A escuchar Listen twice to the two exchanges between friends before answering the questions about them on your activity master.

Después de escuchar Answer the following questions based on what you heard.

Conversación 1
1. What are the names of the two people in the conversation?
2. What does the boy respond when asked how he is?
3. Do the two people already know each other? How do you know?
4. What expression do they both use when they say good-bye?

Conversación 2
1. In general, what time of day is it when the people meet?
2 What country is one of the speakers from?
3. Who makes a reference at the end to someone's family?

Spanish for Spanish Speakers

Writing Practice
Have Spanish speakers do Activity E as a writing activity. Encourage them to exchange their writing with a classmate and engage in peer-editing.
Linguistic

Listening in Context
Although most Spanish-speakers understand spoken Spanish, through this **Aquí escuchamos** section, you can introduce them to "listening in context." Have them listen for and write down any new vocabulary words that they hear in the dialogues.
Auditory-Musical

TEACH/MODEL

Palabras útiles

PRESENTATION
Introduce these adverbs by making statements with which students are likely to agree. Emphasize the adverbs with the tone of your voice and use hand gestures. Examples: **Me gusta mucho escuchar música. Me gusta poco estudiar.**, etc. Then ask simple questions such as **¿Te gusta mucho escuchar música?**

Auditory-Musical
Linguistic

PRACTICE/APPLY

E. ¿Muchísimo o muy poco?

SUGGESTION
Have one student close his (her) textbook and have the other student keep it open. The student with the open textbook then asks a **¿Te gusta...?** question for each of the activity items. His (her) partner answers each question, using an adverb from **Palabras útiles.**

Interpersonal Communication 1.1

TEACH/MODEL

Aquí escuchamos

PRESENTATION

TEXTBOOK CASSETTE/CD CASSETTE 1, SIDE A; CD 1, TRACKS 1-2

TAPESCRIPT PP. 186-187

TRB: ACTIVITY MASTER, P. 60

Call students' attention to the scene-setting line that precedes **Antes de escuchar** to help them anticipate what they will hear. To help students focus their listening, go over the questions in **Después de escuchar** before you play the **A escuchar** conversations. Play the conversations twice, having the students simply listen the first time, and having them take notes on their activity master as they listen for the second time.

Auditory-Musical
Interpretive Communication 1.2

PRACTICE/APPLY

Después de escuchar

ANSWERS

Conversación 1
1. María Elena, Carlos
2. Bastante bien, gracias.
3. Yes, they know each other's names and need no introductions.
4. Hasta luego.

Conversación 2
1. morning
2. Puerto Rico
3. José Manuel

ETAPA SYNTHESIS

¡Mucho gusto!

SUGGESTION

 First do one or two model dialogues as a class. Then have students work in groups of three and write out their own dialogues. After they finish writing, tell them to practice the dialogues orally three times, playing different roles and using different greetings each time. When the time limit is up, have volunteers present their dialogues to the class.

 Interpersonal Communication 1.1
Presentational Communication 1.3

Una postal

FYI

 ATAJO WRITING ASSISTANT SOFTWARE

You might want to have students use this software program when doing this activity.

Additional Practice and Recycling

FYI

WORKBOOK, PP. 3-5

For recycling and additional practice of the vocabulary, structures, and language functions presented throughout this **etapa,** you can assign the workbook activities as in-class work and/or homework. Answers to the activities are overprinted on each page of the Teacher's Edition of the Workbook.

T8 Unit 1, Chapter 1

¡ADELANTE!

 ¡Mucho gusto! You and a friend are sitting in a café when another friend arrives. 1) Greet the arriving friend. 2) Introduce him (her) to your other friend. 3) Discuss which refreshments on the menu you each like. 4) One of the two friends who have just met should ask the other a question about his (her) likes or dislikes. (**¿Te gusta escuchar música rock?**) 5) The other one should respond. (**Sí, me gusta escuchar música rock. Me gusta cantar también.**) 6) Finally, after finishing your drink you get up and say good-bye to your two friends.

 Una postal Write a postcard to a friend. Make sure it includes a greeting, a list of three things you like to do, a question about your friend's likes or dislikes, and a farewell.

Perú

☀ Spanish for Spanish Speakers

Developing Writing Skills

Always have Spanish speakers complete the writing activities in the **¡Adelante!** sections. While many students may already have some level of oral and listening comprehension skills in Spanish, their writing abilities may not be as well developed. **Una postal** provides a good opportunity to begin building basic literacy skills in Spanish. Have students engage in peer-editing as well.

Additional Etapa Resources

Refer to the **Etapa** Support Materials list on the opening page of this **etapa** for detailed cross-references to these assessment options.

SEGUNDA ETAPA

Preparación

- What beverages can you order at a restaurant or a café?
- Think about what you drink at different times during the day. What do you normally drink at breakfast time? At lunch? In the evening?
- When you are really thirsty, what do you most like to drink?

¡Un refresco, por favor!

Two girls at a café want to have a drink (un refresco).

María:	Pst, camarero.
Camarero:	Sí, señorita, ¿qué desea tomar?
María:	Una limonada, por favor.
Camarero:	Y usted, señorita, ¿qué desea?
Yolanda:	Yo quisiera un licuado de banana, por favor.

A few seconds later...

Camarero:	Aquí tienen ustedes. Una limonada y un licuado de banana.
María:	Muchas gracias, señor.
Camarero:	De nada.

camarero *waiter*   señorita *miss*   ¿qué desea tomar? *what do you want to drink?*   Una limonada *A lemonade*
Yo quisiera *I would like*   un licuado *a milkshake*   Aquí tienen ustedes. *Here you are.*   Muchas gracias *Thank you very much*   señor *sir*   De nada. *You're welcome.*

Capítulo 1 Vamos al café   **9**

TEACH/MODEL

¡Un refresco, por favor!
PRESENTATION

 TRANSPARENCIES 8

 TEXTBOOK CASSETTE/CD CASSETTE 1, SIDE A; CD 1, TRACK 6

 TAPESCRIPT P. 187

First explain the scene, then act it out playing the customers and the waiter. Have students listen to the Textbook Cassette/CD and repeat both parts. Or, read each line and have students repeat, first as a whole class, then in groups, and then in pairs. Treat **quisiera** as a vocabulary item.

Introduce the vocabulary with the transparency or while students look at the pictures in the book. Have them repeat the items while looking at the pictures.

Next, play the role of the waiter and have students get your attention to order hot or cold drinks, either using the transparency or the pictures in the book. Ask **¿Qué desea tomar?** randomly to elicit the names of different beverages. After practicing the names of beverages, ask for volunteers to act out the mini-dialogue with their books closed.

 Auditory-Musical

Interpretive Communication 1.2

VOCABULARY EXPANSION
You might want to introduce **mesero/mesera** as other words for waiter/waitress.

Etapa Support Materials

- Workbook: pp. 6, 7
- TRB: Textbook Activity Masters: p. 61
- Textbook Cassettes/CDs: Cassette 1, Side A
- Tapescript: Textbook Cassettes/CDs p. 187
- Overhead Transparencies: 9, 10, 10a, 11, 11a
- Lesson Plan Book: pp. 3-4

- Testing Program: Quiz pp. 3-5; Answer Key & Testing Cassettes Tapescript p. T2
- Testing Cassettes: Cassette Side A
- Computerized Testing Program: Windows™; Macintosh®
- Atajo Writing Assistant Software: Student Text p. 14

VOCABULARY EXPANSION

In most of the Spanish-speaking world, **café** or **cafecito** is a demi-tasse of strong black coffee. **Café con leche** is half strong black coffee and half hot milk; **chocolate** is hot milk with cocoa. In Spain and Mexico, **plátano** is used for banana, and in Puerto Rico and other parts of the Caribbean, **guineo** is the preferred word. **Granadina** is grenadine, a nonalcoholic red syrup made from pomegranates, often mixed with mineral water and served with a wedge of lemon or lime. **Licuado** (also known as **batido**) is a drink made by combining either milk or water with fresh fruit and sugar in a blender, and **refresco** is any soft drink.

 Linguistic Comparisons 4.1

PRACTICE/APPLY

A. En el café

SUGGESTIONS

 Have students work with their partners, alternating the roles of waiter and client. Do the activity with the whole class by having one student play the role of waiter and asking a student seated across the aisle what he (she) wishes. Continue until all students have played both roles.

Individual Needs

Less-prepared Students
Less-prepared students could benefit from a further review of vocabulary in Activity A. Use the transparency of hot and cold drinks with the overlay, and have the students close their books while you point to choices.

More-prepared Students
More-prepared students can practice longer dialogues in which they meet at a **café**, introduce friends, and then order refreshments.

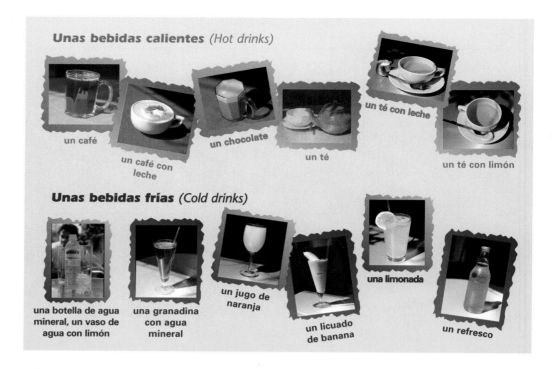

Unas bebidas calientes (Hot drinks)

un café
un café con leche
un chocolate
un té
un té con leche
un té con limón

Unas bebidas frías (Cold drinks)

una botella de agua mineral, un vaso de agua con limón
una granadina con agua mineral
un jugo de naranja
un licuado de banana
una limonada
un refresco

¡Te toca a ti!

A. En el café You are in a café. A classmate will play the role of the waiter (waitress). When he (she) asks what you want, order the following drinks. Follow the model.

> **MODELO**　un café con leche
> Camarero(a):　*¿Qué desea, señorita (señor)?*
> Tú:　*Un café con leche, por favor.*

1. un refresco
2. un té con limón
3. una botella de agua
4. un chocolate
5. un licuado de banana
6. una granadina con agua mineral
7. una limonada
8. un café
9. un vaso de agua con limón
10. un jugo de naranja
11. un té con leche
12. un té

☀ Spanish for Spanish Speakers

Drink Variations

Ask Spanish speakers for variations of the **bebidas**. They may know how to pronounce the names of these drinks, but may never have seen them written. Help them with the spelling of the variations by writing them on the board or overhead. It may be helpful to focus on the words with difficult spelling combinations, such as the **ll** in **botella**, the **j** of **jugo**, the **c** of **licuado**, and the **v** of **vaso**.

MULTIPLE INTELLIGENCES

- Linguistic: All activities
- Logical-Mathematical: A
- Auditory-Musical: **Pronunciación**, D, **Aquí escuchamos**
- Interpersonal: **¡Un refresco, por favor!**, C, E, G, **¿Qué desean tomar?**, **A mí me gusta**

B. Camarero(a), por favor

Get the waiter's (waitress's) attention and order the drink of your choice. A classmate will play the role of the waiter (waitress). Follow the model.

MODELO

Tú:	*Pst, camarero(a).*
Camarero(a):	*Sí, señor (señorita), ¿qué desea tomar?*
Tú:	*Un licuado de banana, por favor.*

C. Aquí tienen

Play the role of the waiter (waitress) or one of two students at a café. Each student orders a drink, but the waiter (waitress) forgets who ordered what. Work in groups of three. Follow the model.

MODELO

Camarero(a):	*¿Qué desean tomar?*
Estudiante 1:	*Una granadina con soda, por favor.*
Camarero(a):	*¿Y Ud., señor (señorita)?*
Estudiante 2:	*Yo quisiera un refresco, por favor.*
Camarero(a):	*Aquí tienen. Un refresco para Ud....*
Estudiante 1:	*No, señor(ita), una granadina.*
Camarero(a):	*¡Ah, perdón (sorry)! Una granadina para Ud., y un refresco para Ud.*
Estudiante 2:	*Sí, gracias.*
Camarero(a):	*De nada.*

PRONUNCIACIÓN THE VOWEL a

The sound of the vowel **a** in Spanish is pronounced like the *a* of the English word *father* except that the sound is shorter in Spanish.

Práctica

D. Listen and repeat as your teacher models the following words.

1. hola	5. tapas	9. calamares
2. va	6. canta	10. cacahuetes
3. pan	7. habla	
4. patatas	8. hasta	

Repaso

E. Hola, te presento a... The Spanish Club has organized a meeting so that new members can get to know each other. Select a partner and introduce yourself and your partner to three people.

Capítulo 1 Vamos al café **11**

B. Camarero(a), por favor
SUGGESTION

 Play the waiter (waitress) yourself or have more-prepared students do so. Have each student in the class get your attention and order a drink. No order may be repeated until all drinks have been mentioned. If your students have already learned the numbers in the **Etapas preliminares** in the Teacher's Resource Book, ask them to keep track of the orders and do a summary at the end: **tres limonadas, dos licuados de banana, cinco refrescos**, etc.

Synthesizing

C. Aquí tienen
VARIATION

 Have students work in groups of three and write out a different dialogue following the model. Then have groups volunteer to act out the dialogues for the class. They may use the photos on page 10 for reference.

Presentational Communication 1.3

EXPANSION

During these early stages of instruction when conversation is limited, or later in the year for review, students can play a game of charades to practice verbs.

  Visual-Spatial

TEACH/MODEL

Pronunciación
PRESENTATION

TEXTBOOK CASSETTE/CD CASSETTE 1, SIDE A; CD 1, TRACK 7

TAPESCRIPT P. 187

Point out that the Spanish **a** sounds like the English *ah* sound but more tense or clipped. Then have students listen to the explanation for **a** on the Textbook Cassette/CD. The speaker will model the correct pronunciation of the words in **Práctica D**. Have students follow along in their texts and repeat after each word.

Auditory-Musical

The Standards

- Interpersonal Communication 1.1: A, B, **Adelante** activities
- Interpretive Communication 1.2: A, B, F, **Aquí escuchamos**
- Presentational Communication 1.3: B, E, C, **Adelante** activities
- Connections with Distinctive Viewpoints 3.2: G, **Comentarios culturales**
- Linguistic Comparisons 4.1: P, **Estructura**

Spanish for Spanish Speakers

Práctica D

Have the Spanish speakers focus on the **h** of **hola, habla, hasta,** and **cacahuetes** and the **v** of **va**. Have them try to come up with other words that contain the letters **h** and **v** and encourage them to practice writing them.

Linguistic Comparisons 4.1

E. Hola, te presento a...

SUGGESTION

Pairs of students may circulate around the whole class or you may divide students into groups of six or more.

Estructura

PRESENTATION

Pointing to students, say **un estudiante** or **una estudiante**, stressing the indefinite article with your voice each time. Then continue by saying some of the drinks learned. For example: **Deseo una granadina, no un refresco.** After students understand the use of **un** with masculine nouns and **una** with feminine nouns, point out the plural forms **unos** and **unas**.

F. ¿Un o unos? ¿Una o unas?

ANSWERS

1. un	**2.** unas
3. un	**4.** un
5. unos	**6.** un

G. Yo quisiera... ¿Y tú?

ANSWERS

1. Yo quisiera un chocolate. ¿Y tú?/Un refresco.
2. Yo quisiera un té. ¿Y tú?/Una limonada.
3. Yo quisiera un vaso de agua mineral. ¿Y tú?/Un jugo.
4. Yo quisiera una granadina con agua mineral. ¿Y tú?/Un café.
5. Yo quisiera un licuado de banana. ¿Y tú?/Un chocolate.
6. Yo quisiera un té con leche. ¿Y tú?/Un té con limón.

EXPANSION

With books closed, read each drink listed in Activities F and G in the singular and without the articles. Have one student repeat the item with the correct indefinite article and then have the next student give the item in its plural form with its corresponding article.

ESTRUCTURA

Gender of nouns and the indefinite articles

	Singular		Plural	
Masculine	**un refresco**	*a soft drink*	**unos refrescos**	*some soft drinks*
Feminine	**una botella**	*a bottle*	**unas botellas**	*some bottles*

1. Almost every noun in Spanish has a grammatical gender; that is, it is either masculine or feminine. Most nouns that end in **–o** are masculine (**un jugo**), and most nouns that end in **–a** are feminine (**una granadina**). In general, nouns that refer to male people or animals are masculine (**un señor**), and nouns that refer to female people or animals are feminine (**una señorita**). However, other words, like **té** and **café**, do not fall into these categories, so you should learn the gender of nouns as you learn their meanings.

2. In Spanish, the indefinite article has four forms. The form used depends on the noun's gender and on whether it is singular or plural. Masculine singular nouns use **un** *(a, an)*; feminine nouns use **una** *(a, an)*; masculine plural nouns use **unos** *(some)*; and feminine plural nouns use **unas** *(some)*. Note that if a noun is plural in Spanish, it usually ends with an **–s** whether it is masculine or feminine.

Aquí practicamos

F. **¿Un o unos? ¿Una o unas?** Add the correct indefinite article to these nouns. Follow the model.

> **MODELO** botella de agua mineral
> *una botella de agua mineral*

1. jugo de naranja	4. vaso de agua
2. botellas de agua mineral	5. refrescos
3. té	6. café con leche

G. **Yo quisiera... ¿Y tú?** You and a friend are deciding what to have to drink. Express what you want to order and then ask your friend what she (he) would like. Follow the model.

> **MODELO** té / café con leche
> **Tú:** *Yo quisiera un té, ¿y tú?*
> **Amigo(a):** *Un café con leche.*

1. chocolate / refresco	4. granadina con agua mineral / café
2. té / limonada	5. licuado de banana / chocolate
3. vaso de agua mineral / jugo	6. té con leche / té con limón

---

Spanish for Spanish Speakers

Informal and Formal Spanish

Remember that most Spanish speakers already have a command of a variety of Spanish that is used in informal, very familiar contexts. This situation is a fairly informal one, but have the students focus on using vocabulary that may be new for them. Emphasize that it may be necessary to use such vocabulary when talking to speakers who are from other parts of the Spanish-speaking world. Accept how the students say it the first time. What they have said may be totally appropriate in their speech community. This is a good place to have them focus on the differences between how they may say something in their speech community and how the book is teaching them to express this. Your main objective should be to expand the range of real-world contexts in which these students can use Spanish.

Comentarios CULTURALES

Los cafés

In the Spanish-speaking world, young and old people enjoy meeting at cafés for a drink and a snack at different times during the day. In many neighborhoods of a town or city one can find cafés, each with its own particular clientele and atmosphere. In a café near a school or university, for example, it is possible to see groups of students sitting at tables discussing their studies and politics or just laughing and chatting with friends. Older people may prefer sitting in a quieter café where they can listen to music while they read the newspaper, play cards or dominoes, or simply relax watching the passersby. In the summertime, tables are often set outside for the enjoyment of the customers.

Aquí escuchamos

En un café *Clara and her friends are having something to drink at a café.*

Antes de escuchar Based on the information you have learned in this chapter, answer the following questions.

1. What are some beverages you expect Clara and her friends will order?
2. What do you say to order something in Spanish?

 A escuchar Listen to the conversation that Clara and her friends have with the waiter at the café, paying special attention to what each young person orders.

Después de escuchar On your activity master, circle the items Clara and her friends ordered.

agua mineral	licuado	té
café	limonada	
leche	refresco	

Capítulo 1 Vamos al café **13**

Comentarios culturales

SUGGESTION

Ask students to think of a café located in their neighborhood and have them talk about the customs, activities, and behavior of its clientele. Then ask them to compare and contrast the culture of cafés they know with that of the café mentioned here.

 Cultural Comparisons 4.2

TEACH/MODEL

Aquí escuchamos

PRESENTATION

	TEXTBOOK CASSETTE/CD CASSETTE 1, SIDE A; CD 1, TRACK 8
	TAPESCRIPT P. 187
	TRB: ACTIVITY MASTER, P. 61

Call students' attention to the scene-setting line that precedes **Antes de escuchar** in order to set the context of listening activity and to help students anticipate what they will hear. Have students brainstorm the language asked about in **Antes de escuchar**, and write their ideas on the board or on an overhead transparency. Then, to help students focus their listening, go over the questions in **Después de escuchar** before you play the **A escuchar** conversations.

Interpretive Communication 1.2

PRACTICE/APPLY

Antes de escuchar

ANSWERS

1. limonada, café, agua mineral
2. yo quisiera un/una…

Después de escuchar

ANSWERS

una limonada
un café
una botella de agua mineral

ETAPA SYNTHESIS

¿Qué desean tomar?
SUGGESTION

You may wish to have more-prepared students in the class model this before students work with their classmates. Then divide the class into groups of four. Have students do the conversation several times, allowing each group member to play a different part. Insist that students vary the drinks they order, or even change their orders: **"Una limonada—no, un chocolate, por favor."**

 Auditory-Musical

A mí me gusta...
FYI

 ATAJO WRITING ASSISTANT SOFTWARE

You might want to have students use this software program when doing this activity.

Additional Practice and Recycling
FYI

📁 WORKBOOK, PP. 6, 7

For recycling and additional practice of the vocabulary, structures, and language functions presented throughout this **etapa**, you can assign the workbook activities as in-class work and/or homework. Answers to the activities are overprinted on each page of the Teacher's Edition of the Workbook.

¡ADELANTE!

 ¿Qué desean tomar? You and two friends are in a café. Decide what each person will order, call the waiter (waitress), and place your order. Work in groups of four and follow the model.

MODELO

Tú:	*¿Qué desean tomar?*
Amigo(a) 1:	*Yo quisiera una limonada.*
Amigo(a) 2:	*Un café para mí (for me).*
Tú:	*Pst, camarero(a).*
Camarero(a):	*Sí, señorita (señor), ¿qué desean?*
Tú:	*Una limonada, un café y un té con limón, por favor.*
Camarero(a):	*Muy bien, señorita (señor).*

 A mí me gusta... Get together with a classmate to do the following.

1. Make your own separate lists of six different beverages ranked in the order of your personal preferences.
2. Exchange lists and compare your preferences.
3. Identify three beverages that both of you like, adding to your original lists if necessary.

Café El Parnaso
Calle Mayor 27
Bahía Blanca, Argentina
(831-6517)

un café con leche	1.00
un café con leche	1.00
una limonada	1.50
un chocolate caliente	1.75

☀ Spanish for Spanish Speakers

Building Writing Skills

Have Spanish speakers fully carry out the **A mí me gusta** activity. Remember, while many of them already speak and understand spoken Spanish, they may not know how to write the language. This is a good place to continue building basic literacy skills in Spanish. Have them pay special attention to the spelling of the vocabulary that has been introduced in this **etapa**, especially those words that may have problematic spelling combinations. This is also a good place to have them engage in peer-editing. Have them look at the written work of a partner and focus on the spelling.

Additional Etapa Resources

Refer to the **Etapa** Support Materials list on the opening page of this **etapa** for detailed cross-references to these assessment options.

TERCERA ETAPA

Preparación

- What are some of the things you can order for breakfast in a restaurant?
- What is your favorite breakfast food?
- What do you generally like to eat for lunch?
- What do you have for a snack now and then?

¡Vamos a comer algo!

un bocadillo

un croissant *(Spain)*

un pan dulce

un pastel de fresas

una rebanada de pan

mermelada

mantequilla

un pan tostado

un desayuno

un sándwich de jamón y queso

*Two friends (**amigas**), Ana and Clara, are at a café.*

Ana: Quisiera tomar un café. ¿Y tú?
Clara: Yo quisiera **comer algo.**
Ana: En **este** café **tienen** bocadillos, sándwiches y pasteles.
Clara: **Pues, voy a comer** un pastel, mm... **con** un café con leche.
Ana: Y para mí un sándwich de jamón y queso.

un bocadillo: *a sandwich made with a French roll; may have different fillings, such as cheese, ham, sausage, an omelette, etc.; most common in Spain.*
un pan dulce: *any kind of sweet roll, cinnamon roll, danish, etc.; usually eaten with hot chocolate; this expression is commonly used in Mexico.*

comer algo *to eat something*   **este** *this*   **tienen** *they have*   **Pues** *Then*   **voy a comer** *I'm going to eat*   **con** *with*

Capítulo 1 Vamos al café   **15**

¡Vamos a comer algo!
PRESENTATION

 TRANSPARENCIES 12 AND 12A

 TEXTBOOK CASSETTE/CD CASSETTE 1, SIDE A; CD 1, TRACK 9

 TAPESCRIPT P. 188

With books closed, show students the transparency without the overlay. Have them repeat the items and order breakfast. Then repeat the process for lunch, adding the overlay if necessary. With books still closed, have students listen to the Textbook Cassette/CD. Then read each line of the dialogue again, having them repeat first as a whole class, then in groups, and then in pairs or individually.

 Interpretive Communication 1.2

Etapa Support Materials

- Workbook: pp. 8-12
- TRB: Textbook Activity Masters: pp. 62, 63
- Textbook Cassettes/CDs: Cassette 1, Side A

- Tapescript: Textbook Cassttes/CDs p. 188
- Overhead Transparencies: 12, 12a
- Middle School Activities: pp. 8-10
- Lesson Plan Book: pp. 5-6

- Testing Program: Quiz p. 6; Answer Key & Testing Cassettes Tapescript p. T3
- Testing Cassettes: Cassette Side A
- Computerized Testing Program: Windows™; Macintosh®
- Atajo Writing Assistant Software: Student Text p. 21

PRACTICE/APPLY

A. ¿Vas a comer algo?

SUGGESTION

Have students vary their answers using **yo quisiera** or **yo voy a comer**. Do the activity as a whole class using the **pregúntale** format: **María, pregúntale a Juan el número uno**, etc.

B. El desayuno

SUGGESTION

Have students work in groups of three or four, ordering several different meals and taking turns playing the waiter. Have volunteers present their dialogues to the class.

🌐 Presentational Communication 1.3

Individual Needs

More and Less-prepared Students
Assign students to groups of three or four, mixing more- and less-prepared students in each group. Have students prepare a longer dialogue together, with the number of lines varying among the students according to their preparedness. Have them pretend to meet after class at a local restaurant, greet each other, introduce new students, talk about what they like, and order snacks and drinks.

TEACH/MODEL

Pronunciación

PRESENTATION

 TEXTBOOK CASSETTE/CD CASSETTE 1, SIDE A; CD 1, TRACK 10

 TAPESCRIPT P. 188

Point out that the Spanish **e** sounds more tense or clipped than the English *-ay* sound. Then have students listen to the explanation for **e** on the Textbook Cassette/CD. The speaker will model the correct pronunciation of the words in the **Práctica C**. Have students follow along in their texts and repeat after each word.

🔊 Auditory-Musical

T16 Unit 1, Chapter 1

¡Te toca a ti!

A. ¿Vas (Are you going) a comer algo? You and a friend are at a snack bar. Decide what snack you will each have from the suggested items. Follow the model.

> **MODELO** un sándwich de queso / un sándwich de jamón
> **Tú:** ¿Vas a comer algo?
> **Amigo(a):** Yo quisiera un sándwich de queso.
> **Tú:** Yo voy a comer un sándwich de jamón.

1. un bocadillo de jamón / un bocadillo de queso
2. un pastel de fresas / un pastel de banana
3. un croissant / un pan dulce
4. un sándwich de queso / un sándwich de jamón y queso
5. un pan tostado / una rebanada de pan
6. un licuado de banana / un pan con mantequilla
7. un pan con mermelada / un pan dulce
8. un sándwich de jamón / un sándwich de queso

B. El desayuno You are having breakfast in a café in Condado, Puerto Rico. What would you like to order from the waiter (waitress)? Work with a partner and follow the model.

> **MODELO** **Camarero(a):** ¿Qué desea, señor (señorita)?
> **Tú:** Un café y un pan tostado, por favor.

PRONUNCIACIÓN THE VOWEL e

The sound of the vowel **e** in Spanish is pronounced like the *e* of the English word *bet* except that the sound is shorter in Spanish.

Práctica

C. Listen and repeat as your teacher models the following words.

1. que	5. café	9. es
2. leche	6. tres	10. ese
3. Pepe	7. nene	
4. este	8. té	

Focus on Culture

More About Food
Point out that a typical breakfast consists of a cup of **café con leche** and a piece of bread or toast with butter and/or jam. Discuss the difference between an American sandwich and a **bocadillo** (**torta** in Mexico). Bread for this kind of sandwich is baked fresh two or three times a day in all parts of the Hispanic world.

🌐 Cultural Comparisons 4.1

MULTIPLE INTELLIGENCES

- Linguistic: All activities
- Logical-Mathematical: A, E
- Auditory-Musical: **Pronunciación C, Aquí escuchamos**
- Interpersonal: B, D, G, I, **La merienda, ¿Qué vamos a comer?**
- Intrapersonal: **Palabras útiles, H**

Repaso

D. Después de clase (After class)
You are meeting a friend in a nearby café. She (he) arrives with a person that you have never met before. 1) Greet your friend. 2) She (he) introduces you to the new person, and the three of you sit down for a drink. 3) The waiter (waitress) comes and takes your orders. While you wait, 4) you ask the new person what things she (he) likes to do. Work in groups of four, assigning one role to each person.

ESTRUCTURA

Subject pronouns and the present tense of regular –ar verbs: First and second persons

Subject Pronouns

Singular		Plural	
yo	I	nosotros	we (masculine)
tú	you (informal)	nosotras	we (feminine)
usted	you (formal)	vosotros(as)	you (informal)
		ustedes	you

1. **Tú** is used to address a friend, a child, a family member, or anyone with whom you are on a first-name basis. **Usted** (abbreviated **Ud.**) is used with older people, teachers, or anyone that you do not know very well. In general, the use of **usted** indicates a respectful or formal relationship.

2. **Nosotras** is used to refer to a group of all women; **nosotros** refers to a group of males and females or a group of all males.

3. **Vosotros(as)** is used as the plural of **tú** only in Spain. **Ustedes** (abbreviated **Uds.**) is used as the plural of both **usted** and **tú** throughout Latin America.

Present tense of regular –ar verbs: First and second persons

Subject Pronoun	Verb Ending	Conjugated form of the verb **tomar**
yo	–o	tom**o**
tú	–as	tom**as**
usted	–a	tom**a**
nosotros (as)	–amos	tom**amos**
vosotros (as)	–áis	tom**áis**
ustedes	–an	tom**an**

Capítulo 1 Vamos al café **17**

 PRACTICE / APPLY

D. Después de clase
SUGGESTION

 Explain the activity and allow groups five minutes to prepare. Then have two or three groups present their versions in front of the class.

Individual Needs

More-prepared Students
Encourage students who presented a longer dialogue in Activity B to resolve a problem—such as receiving the wrong order—this time in their dialogue.

 Interpersonal Communication 1.1

TEACH / MODEL

Estructura
FYI
Only first- and second-person forms are presented here in order to allow students to practice talking to each other before referring to other people. This way they can concentrate on the interplay between **tú/Ud.** and **yo/Uds./nosotros.** The third-person form is presented in Chapter 2.

PRESENTATION
Using gestures, establish the difference between the different pronouns: **yo, tú, nosotros,** and **ustedes.** Then, using gestures and verbs used earlier in the infinitive with **gustar,** form simple sentences and have students repeat them. Say a few sentences in the **yo** form, continue with a few in the **tú** form, and then with the **ustedes** and **nosotros** forms. Use cognates and pantomime as much as possible. Suggestions: **Yo canto en las fiestas. Yo bailo en las fiestas. Tú escuchas música moderna. Tú estudias español.** Explain the difference between **tú** and **usted** and give the plural forms of each one. Point out the abbreviations **Ud.** and **Uds.**

 Auditory-Musical Bodily-Kinesthetic

PRESENTATION (CONTINUED)

While **vosotros(as)** and its forms are included in grammar explanations, they are not practiced in textbook activities for active use, nor are they evaluated in the Testing Program. For those teachers who wish students to have some practice writing **vosotros(as)** and its forms, occasional items are included in the Workbook. For purposes of recognition and awareness, point out **vosotros(as)** and its forms. Explain that its use is widespread in Spain, but that the **ustedes** form is more common worldwide and will be used in class.

Make simple statements and then ask students related questions that are likely to elicit affirmative answers. For example: **Yo escucho la radio. ¿Tú escuchas la radio?** Then, using gestures, continue with the plural forms. **Nosotros hablamos español. ¿Uds. hablan español?** Use the verbs on this page and as many cognates and gestures as possible. Once enough students have responded correctly, write the verb endings on the board and continue asking questions.

Point out to students that in Spanish, subject pronouns are frequently omitted because it is easy to tell what the subject is from the verb ending.

VARIATION

Try a **pregúntale** activity here. To make it easier for students, point to the correct form on the chalkboard when they are asking or responding to the questions. Example: **María, pregúntale a Juan si estudia español.**

PRACTICE / APPLY

E. Todos cantan

SUGGESTIONS

 Have the students work in pairs. You may also want to have students write out the responses for practice. Then have them edit their partner's work for mistakes in spelling or verb endings.

🔺 Linguistic

ESTRUCTURA (continued)

4. The infinitives of Spanish verbs end in **–ar, –er,** or **–ir.** Verbs consist of two parts: a stem (**tom–** for the **–ar** verb **tomar**), which carries the meaning, and an ending, which indicates the subject or person the verb refers to (**–as** for **tú**), as well as the tense. In Spanish, verb endings are very important because each one must agree in person (first, second, or third) and number (singular or plural) with its subject.

5. To conjugate any regular **–ar** verb, drop the **–ar** and replace it with the ending that corresponds to the subject. In addition to **tomar,** you already know some other regular **–ar** verbs: **bailar, cantar, desear, escuchar, estudiar, hablar,** and **practicar.** Two new verbs are **trabajar** *(to work)* and **viajar** *(to travel).*

6. The Spanish present tense has three English equivalents. When a statement is made negative in the present tense by adding **no** in front of the conjugated form of the verb, there are two English equivalents.

Yo canto en el café.	*I sing at the café. I am singing at the café.*
Nosotros no bailamos aquí.	*We are not dancing here. We do not dance here.*

Aquí practicamos

E. Todos (Everyone) cantan Replace the subjects in italics and make the necessary changes in the verbs. Follow the model.

> **MODELO** Yo bailo mucho. (tú / usted / nosotros / ustedes)
> > *Tú bailas mucho.*
> *Usted baila mucho.*
> *Nosotros bailamos mucho.*
> *Ustedes bailan mucho.*

1. *Tú* cantas en el café. (usted / yo / nosotros / ustedes)
2. *Nosotros* practicamos en la clase. (tú / usted / yo / ustedes)
3. *Usted* habla español. (ustedes / yo / nosotras / tú)
4. *Yo* viajo a Guatemala. (tú / usted / nosotros / ustedes)
5. *Ustedes* estudian mucho. (yo / tú / usted / nosotras)
6. *Nosotras* escuchamos música. (tú / yo / usted / ustedes)

F. ¡Muy bien! Say whether you do or do not do the following activities. Follow the model.

> **MODELO** bailar bien
> *Yo no bailo bien.* o: *Yo bailo bien.*

1. cantar muy bien
2. hablar mucho
3. practicar el piano
4. trabajar mucho
5. escuchar música rock
6. hablar en clase
7. estudiar poco
8. viajar a Paraguay

PALABRAS ÚTILES

Expressing frequency

You can use the following words and phrases to express how well or how often you do something.

bien	*well*	todos los días	*every day*
muy bien	*very well*	siempre	*always*
mal	*poorly*	a veces	*sometimes*

Aquí practicamos

G. Hablo español todos los días Say how well or how often you engage in the following activities. Follow the model.

> **MODELO** estudiar
> *Yo estudio todos los días.*

1. hablar español
2. bailar
3. cantar en clase
4. estudiar
5. escuchar música popular
6. trabajar

H. Preguntas personales (Personal questions)
Answer the following questions. Follow the model.

> **MODELO** ¿Cantas bien?
> *No, canto mal.* o: *Sí, canto bien.*

1. ¿Bailas mucho?
2. ¿Trabajas después de *(after)* clase?
3. ¿Hablas español muy bien?
4. ¿Estudias mucho o poco?
5. ¿Practicas el tenis?
6. ¿Escuchas música popular? ¿rock? ¿clásica?
7. ¿Cantas todos los días?
8. ¿Viajas todos los días a Nueva York?

Capítulo 1 Vamos al café **19**

 Spanish for Spanish Speakers

Palabras útiles

Although it is not used in formal or written Spanish, native speakers may, in their speech communities, use the word **bien** followed by an adjective or adverb to mean *quite* or *very*, for example **bien tarde** (*quite late*) or **bien rico** (*very tasty*).

See if students know other adverbial phrases expressing *how often*, such as **todo el tiempo, nunca, de vez en cuando**. Have them use these phrases in sentences. Encourage peer editing.

 Linguistic Comparisons 4.1

F. ¡Muy bien!
SUGGESTION

Have students ask their partners questions with the cues provided. Encourage them to add different adverbs to vary their answers.

ANSWERS
1. Yo (no) canto muy bien.
2. ...hablo mucho.
3. ...practico el piano.
4. ...trabajo mucho.
5. ...escucho música rock.
6. ...hablo en clase.
7. ...estudio poco.
8. ...viajo a España.

TEACH/MODEL

Palabras útiles
PRESENTATION

Review adverbs from the previous **etapa** by asking simple questions: **¿Estudias mucho o poco? ¿Viajan Uds. mucho o poco?** Then create sentences with the new adverbs. Have students repeat first as a whole class, then in groups, and then individually: **Yo hablo español bien. Yo hablo ruso mal.**

Activating Prior Knowledge

PRACTICE/APPLY

G. Hablo español todos los días
ANSWERS
1. Yo hablo español...
2. Yo bailo...
3. Yo canto en clase...
4. Yo estudio...
5. Yo escucho música popular...
6. Yo trabajo...

H. Preguntas personales
VARIATION

Divide the class into two teams and send a student from each team to the board. Read a question from the activity and tell them to write their answer as quickly and accurately as possible. The faster, more accurate team gets a point. If the answers are incorrect, students may hand off to another member of their team.

I. Mi amigo(a) y yo

Individual Needs

More-prepared Students
Sit in front of the class and have more-prepared students *interview* you about your typical week for the school newspaper, asking you questions with the **Ud.** form based on the various activities they have been practicing. This allows them to be creative at the same time that it reinforces the **Ud./yo** format.

Interpersonal Communication 1.1

Aquí escuchamos

 TEXTBOOK CASSETTE/CD CASSETTE 1, SIDE A; CD 1, TRACK 11

 TAPESCRIPT P. 188

 TRB: ACTIVITY MASTER, P. 62

Antes de escuchar
ANSWERS
1. sándwich, bocadillo, pastel, croissant, pan dulce, pan tostado
2. ¿Qué desea, señor (señorita)?

Después de escuchar
ANSWERS
sándwich
pan dulce
café
pastel

I. Mi amigo(a) y yo   Talk with a classmate about what you each do in a typical week. Then compare these activities with what your parents do. Using -ar verbs that you know, think of at least three pairs of examples. Follow the models.

MODELOS

| Tú: | *Mi amigo y yo estudiamos mucho.* |
| Amiga(o): | *Y nuestros padres trabajan mucho.* |

| Amiga(o): | *Yo escucho música rock.* |
| Tú: | *Y mi madre escucha música clásica.* |

Comentarios CULTURALES

Las comidas

In Spanish-speaking countries, there are often cafés near schools and universities where students meet before or after class. It is common to have a snack at mid-morning and at mid-afternoon, because lunch and dinner are frequently served late. Lunch is the largest meal of the day in many countries, including Colombia, and it is often served later than in the U.S. Traditionally, people would return home from work for a long lunch, although this custom is now changing. People who take long lunches usually start their work day earlier in the morning and finish later in the evening than is common in the U.S. Dinner may be served as late as 10:00 P.M. in some countries, such as Spain.

Aquí escuchamos

¡A comer!   *Luis and his friends are having a bite to eat at a café.*

Antes de escuchar   Based on what you have learned about food in this chapter, answer the following questions.

1. What are some of the things you expect Luis and his friends to order?
2. What question does a waiter (waitress) usually ask when first taking an order?

 A escuchar   Listen to the conversation Luis and his friends have with the waitress, paying special attention to what each person orders.

Después de escuchar   On your activity master, put a check mark next to each item that Luis and his friends ordered.

| ___ agua mineral | ___ croissant | ___ pan dulce | ___ pastel |
| ___ bocadillo | ___ jugo | ___ pan tostado | ___ sándwich |

Focus on Culture

Comentarios culturales

In Spanish-speaking countries, the typical breakfast (**desayuno**) consists of **café con leche** and **pan**, with butter and/or jam and sometimes cheese. A mid-morning snack or brunch (called the **almuerzo** in Mexico) is eaten between 10:30 and 12:00. People usually eat regional snacks or have **licuados** at this time. The main meal of the day is generally eaten between 1:30 and 3:30, and it is called the **comida** (Spain and Mexico) or **almuerzo** (South America and the Caribbean). There is usually a late afternoon snack between 5:00 and 6:00 called the **merienda** (called **once** in Chile), which usually consists of coffee or tea and pastry or regional sweets. Supper (**cena**) is normally a light meal of leftovers or regional foods, and perhaps a dessert such as fruit, cheese, **flan**, or **arroz con leche**.

Connections with Distinctive Viewpoints 3.2

¡ADELANTE!

 La merienda (Snack time) You go to a café at mid-morning for a snack and run into a classmate whom you don't know very well.

1. Greet each other.
2. Order something to eat.
3. While waiting for your food, ask each other questions to get acquainted. You can find out if the other person likes to travel, dance, and sing. Ask how well and how frequently he (she) does these activities. Finally, ask if he (she) works, how often, and if he (she) likes to work or not.

 ¿Qué vamos a tomar? With a classmate, write a list of your favorite beverages.

1. Make your own separate lists of six different beverages ranked in the order of your personal preferences.
2. Exchange lists and compare your preferences.
3. Identify three beverages that both of you like, adding to your original lists if necessary.

EN LÍNEA

Connect with the Spanish-speaking world!
Access the *¡Ya verás! Gold* home page for
Internet activities related to this chapter.

http://yaveras.heinle.com

Capítulo 1 Vamos al café **21**

La merienda
SUGGESTION

 You play the waiter and first do one or two dialogues as a class. Then have students work with their partners. You may want them to write out their scripts and then practice them several times, varying their answers each time. Then have your Spanish-speaking students or other volunteers present their dialogues to the class.

¿Qué vamos a comer?
FYI

 ATAJO WRITING ASSISTANT SOFTWARE

You might want to have students use this software program when doing this activity.

Additional Practice and Recycling
FYI

 WORKBOOK, PP. 8-12

For recycling and additional practice of the vocabulary, structures, and language functions presented throughout this **etapa**, you can assign the workbook activities as in-class work and/or homework. Answers to the activities are overprinted on each page of the Teacher's Edition of the Workbook.

Individual Needs

Less-prepared Students
Less-prepared students could play the part of the waiter for **La merienda**, writing their questions on a pad of paper, until they are comfortable with more extensive dialogue.

Additional Etapa Resources

Refer to the **Etapa** Support Materials list on the opening page of this **etapa** for detailed cross-references to these assessment options.

☀ Spanish for Spanish Speakers

Meal Customs

Ask students about their eating habits in the United States. Encourage them to share any customs that they or their relatives may maintain from the country where their family originated. You may want to ask some students to make brief presentations to the class about their mealtime customs that might be different.

Presentational Communication 1.3
Cultural Practices and Perspectives 2.1

CHAPTER WRAP-UP

Vocabulario

FYI

The **Vocabulario** includes vocabulary that students have used in the chapter's activities. These words and expressions are found again in the comprehensive Glossary at the back of the book, along with other vocabulary found in the readings and realia. English translations are not included in the **Vocabulario**. This allows students to distinguish the words they know from those they do not remember.

VOCABULARY GAME

You may want to play **El juego de las categorías** as a wrap-up activity for practicing the vocabulary. You name a category (**saludos, respuestas, bebidas, comidas, adverbios, verbos,** etc.); with books closed, students write as many items as they can remember for each category. Give points for the most answers.

VARIATION

Students write words beginning with a certain letter. (For this chapter, **b**, **d**, **e**, **c**, and **t** are particularly good.) Give a spelling dictation at this time to reinforce the sounds of the Spanish alphabet.

Have students make a list of the masculine nouns and another of the feminine nouns, including the articles.

Categorizing

VOCABULARIO

The Vocabulario *section consists of the new words and expressions presented in the chapter. When reviewing or studying for a test, you can go through the list to see if you know the meaning of each item. In the glossary at the end of the book, you can check the words you do not remember.*

Para charlar

Para saludar

Buenos días.
Buenas tardes.
Buenas noches.
¡Hola!
¿Cómo estás?
¿Cómo te va?
¿Qué hay?
¿Qué pasa?
¿Qué tal?

Para contestar

Buenos días.
Buenas tardes.
Buenas noches.
¡Hola!
Bien, gracias. ¿Y tú?
Muy bien, gracias.
Bastante bien.
Más o menos.
Regular.

Para despedirse

Adiós.
Chao.
Hasta luego.
Nos vemos.

Para presentar

Te presento a…

Para contestar

Mucho gusto.
¡Hola!

Para expresar gustos

Me gusta…
Te gusta…
No me gusta…
No te gusta…

Para hablar en un restaurante

¿Qué desea tomar?
¿Qué desean tomar?
Yo quisiera…
¿Y Ud.?
Voy a comer…
Para mí…
Aquí tienen ustedes.
por favor
Vamos al café.
Vamos a tomar algo.

Spanish for Spanish Speakers

Keeping a Vocabulary Notebook

Ask Spanish-speaking students to start a notebook with a section for lists of words such as **Palabras con ll**, **Palabras con v**, **Palabras con b**. Have them create another section entitled **Así lo digo yo** where they list words and expressions that they already know and variations to what has been presented in class. Have them start their notebooks by entering words and expressions from this vocabulary list in the two sections.

 Categorizing
Creating

 Linguistic

 Interpretive Communication 1.2

Temas y contextos

Bebidas

una botella de agua
  mineral
un café
un café con leche
un chocolate
una granadina (con
  agua mineral, con
  soda)
un jugo de naranja
un licuado de
  banana
una limonada
un refresco
un té
un té con leche
un té con limón
un vaso de agua
  (con limón)

Comidas

un bocadillo
un croissant
un desayuno
mantequilla
mermelada
un pan dulce
un pan tostado
un pastel de fresas
una rebanada de
  pan
un sándwich de
  jamón y queso

Vocabulario general

Sustantivos

un(a) amigo(a)
abrazo
un(a) camarero(a)
el español
una merienda
la música
un señor
una señorita

Pronombres

yo
tú
usted (Ud.)
nosotros(as)
ustedes (Uds.)

Verbos

bailar
cantar
comer
desear
escuchar
estudiar
gustar
hablar
practicar
tomar
trabajar
viajar

Adverbios

a veces
bien
después de
mal
muchísimo
mucho
muy
muy bien
muy poco
poco
siempre
todos los días

Otras palabras
(words) **y
expresiones**

algo
caliente
con
De nada.
este
frío(a)
Muchas gracias.
no
perdón
pues
sí
un(a)
unos(as)

Additional Chapter Resources

Refer to the Chapter Support Materials list on the opening page of this chapter for detailed cross-references to *¡Ya verás! Gold*'s student-centered technology components and various assessment options.

Improvised Conversation

PRESENTATION

 TEXTBOOK CASSETTE/CD CASSETTE 1, SIDE A; CD 1, TRACK 12

 TAPESCRIPT P. 190

 TRB: ACTIVITY MASTER, P. 63

 Have students listen to this conversation in which two people are placing orders at a café. Refer to the Teacher's Resource Book for the corresponding activity master.

 Interpretive Communication 1.2

Listening Skills Development

FYI

 LAB MANUAL, PP. 3-8

 LAB CASSETTE SIDE A, CD 1, TRACKS 1-8

 TAPESCRIPT: LAB PROGRAM, PP. 1-7

It is now appropriate to work through the lab manual activities and their accompanying recordings in class or in the language laboratory. These materials provide reinforcement of the pronunciation points, vocabulary, structures, and language functions presented throughout the **etapas** and continue the development of listening comprehension skills provided in the **Aquí escuchamos** sections and the Improvised Conversation.

Resources for Spanish-speaking Students

FYI

 WORKBOOK FOR SPANISH-SPEAKING STUDENTS, PP. 1-6

 ANSWER KEY TO SSS WORKBOOK PP. 1-2

Activities specially written to meet the needs of Spanish-speaking students are available in this workbook for the reinforcement and extension of the topics and language presented in this chapter.

Mesón del Pirata

SUGGESTION

Discuss a Spanish menu. What strategies might you use to figure out unfamiliar words? Emphasize that it is unusual for a non-native speaker of Spanish to recognize every item on a menu. Encourage them to make intelligent guesses based on:
1. cognates (**restaurante, aventura**) or
2. context (the general categories, such as **platos típicos**).

 Linguistic Comparisons 4.1

PRACTICE/APPLY

Antes de leer

POSSIBLE ANSWERS

1. an advertisement for a restaurant; for the public
2. viejo San Juan
3. exquisitas, puertorriqueñas, chef, especialidades, incomparables

SUGGESTION

Have students talk about what comes to mind when they hear the word *chef*. What is the difference between a *chef* and a *cook*? What do your students know about Puerto Rican food?

 Activating Prior Knowledge

Mesón del Pirata

Antes de leer

Reading Strategies
- Examining format for content clues
- Skimming for the gist
- Scanning for specific information
- Recognizing cognates

1. Study the format of the following document. Can you tell what type of document it is? For whom is it intended?

2. Skim the very top part of the document. Can you guess where the restaurant is located?

3. Scan the middle of the document and find at least five cognates (words spelled similarly in English and Spanish that have the same meaning). Then, guess what type of restaurant is being described.

Restaurante

Mesón del Pirata
¡Donde comer es una aventura!

★ *Situado en el viejo San Juan* ★

Calle del Cristo 137
Tel 258-9553 • Fax 258-9221

Tenemos las más exquisitas comidas puertorriqueñas de toda la isla. Nuestro chef, Don Tico, ha sido aclamado como el mejor chef de comida criolla de San Juan. Nuestras especialidades criollas son incomparables.

•••••••••••••••• PLATOS TÍPICOS ••••••••••••••••

tostones con mariscos • tostones rellenos con mariscos • queso frito del país • arafritas de plátano • surullitos de maíz rellenos con	queso • quesitos fritos • fricasé de conejo • filete relleno con chorizos • arroz con pollo • asopao de pollo

---

☀ Spanish for Spanish Speakers

Summarizing

Have students go through all of the activities that accompany the readings in this program. Then they can summarize the readings in Spanish for extra writing practice. They might also keep a list of new vocabulary they find in the readings, especially food vocabulary, to include in their Vocabulary Notebook.

Guía para la lectura

1. Here are some words and expressions to keep in mind as you read.

Tenemos	*We have*
ha sido aclamado como	*Has been acclaimed, praised as*
el mejor	*the best*

2. **La comida criolla** is the term used in a number of Latin American countries to describe prepared food that is considered typical or national. In Puerto Rico **comida criolla** is similar to Spanish food but with Puerto Rican ingredients and spices.

Después de leer

1. Why do you think the restaurant chose the name *Mesón del Pirata*?

2. Where is the restaurant located?

3. Which of the following statements accurately describes the foods that are served at the restaurant? More than one statement may be correct.

   ☐ Mostly American dishes are served.
   ☐ The restaurant claims to have an entertaining and lively atmosphere.
   ☐ The restaurant specializes in Puerto Rican dishes.
   ☐ The chef is well-known and has been recognized as one of the best.
   ☐ Dancing and live music are offered.

4. Would you like to go to the restaurant? Why or why not?

Capítulo 1 Vamos al café **25**

Spanish for Spanish Speakers

Food Recognition

Ask Spanish Speakers if they recognize any of the food items listed at the bottom of the advertisement. Then have them describe the food they know to the other students in the class. You can also review the pronunciation of **ll** in the words **rellenos, pollo,** and **rellena**.

Interpersonal Communication 1.1

Después de leer

POSSIBLE ANSWERS

1. Eating there is an adventure; because it looks like a pirate's den.
2. Calle del Cristo, 137 in San Juan, Puerto Rico
3. 3rd and 4th statements
4. Answers will vary.

CAPÍTULO 2

OBJECTIVES

Functions
- Ordering food and drink
- Greeting, introducing, and saying good-bye

Context
- **Tapas** bars

Accuracy
- Subject pronouns
- Present tense of regular **-ar** verbs
- Asking and answering yes/no and tag questions
- Conjugated verbs followed by infinitives

Pronunciation
- The vowel **i**
- The vowel **o**

CHAPTER WARM-UP

Setting the Context

In preparation for their learning about foods and how to order them, have students study the photo on this page. Do they know what type of establishment this is? Which foods do they recognize? Where might students go in their community to get a snack? Have them talk about these places—the people who go there, the kinds of food that can be ordered, the atmosphere, and the unwritten rules of etiquette governing the way people interact there.

¡Vamos a un bar de tapas!

El bar de tapas es muy popular en España.

Objetives

- ordering something to eat
- greeting, introducing, and saying good-bye

26 *Primera unidad* Vamos a tomar algo

Chapter Support Materials

- Lab Manual: pp. 9-13
- Lab Program: Cassette Side B; CD 1, Tracks 9-16
- TRB: Textbook Activity Masters: pp. 64-68
- Textbook Cassettes/CDs: Cassette 1, Side A; CD 1, Track 18
- Tapescript: Lab Program pp. 8-19; Textbook Cassettes/CDs p. 190
- Middle School Activities: pp. 11-14
- Workbook for Spanish-speaking Students: pp. 7-12
- Answer Key to SSS Workbook: pp. 2-4
- Practice Software: Windows™; Macintosh®

- Testing Program: Chapter Test pp. 19-22; Answer Key & Testing Cassettes Tapescript pp. T8, T9; Oral Assessment pp. T9
- Testing Cassettes: Cassette Side A
- Computerized Testing Program: Windows™; Macintosh®
- Video Program: Cassette 1, 8:08-16:43
- Video Guide: Videoscript pp. 7-11; Activities pp. 87-89
- **Mundos hispanos 1**
- Internet Activities: Student Text p. 42

PRIMERA ETAPA

Preparación

- As you noticed in Chapter 1, people eat different kinds of food when it is time for a snack. Here are some typical snacks from Spain, called **tapas.**

- Try to identify the different **tapas** in the picture. Do you recognize any of them?

- Have you ever had a **tapa?** Would you like to try this kind of snack? Why or why not?

Las tapas españolas

Aquí hay (Here are) *algunas tapas españolas típicas.*

aceitunas   **cacahuetes**   **calamares**

pan con chorizo   **patatas bravas**   **queso**

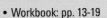

tortilla (de patatas)

patatas bravas: *cooked potatoes diced and served with a spicy sauce*

tortilla (de patatas): *a thick Spanish omelette made with eggs, potatoes, and onions; served in small bite-sized pieces*

Capítulo 2 ¡Vamos a un bar de tapas! **27**

TEACH/MODEL

Las tapas españolas

PRESENTATION

Tell students that, as they saw in Chapter 1, there are different kinds of food people eat when it is time for a snack. In the picture they will see some typical snacks from Spain. Ask them to try to identify the different **tapas** in the picture. Do they recognize any of them? Have they ever had a **tapa?** Would they like to try this kind of snack? Why or why not? Do we have anything similar to a **tapas** bar in the United States?

 Cultural Comparisons 4.2

SUGGESTION

TRANSPARENCIES 13 AND 13A

Begin with a brief planning strategy, asking students what they eat after school if they are hungry. Then introduce the **tapas** with the transparency or point them out in the text. Ask simple questions that students will recognize: **¿Te gustan los cacahuetes? ¿Te gusta el queso?** Then explain what the other foods are: **chorizo** is a spicy sausage similar in taste to pepperoni, but softer in texture. **Calamares** (squid) are served in many ways (marinated, in sauces, deep-fried, etc.) and are very popular. Point out that the **tortilla** in the picture—which is made of potatoes, eggs, onions, etc.—is called **tortilla española** to distinguish it from the **tortilla** that in Mexico and Central America is a thin pancake. Explain that the latter **tortillas** can be made of flour (**harina**) or corn (**maíz**). Corn **tortillas** can be made of various types of corn: blue, yellow, white.

VOCABULARY EXPANSION

Cacahuetes (or **cacahuates**) is the word used for peanuts in Spain, Mexico, and Central America; **maní** is used in South America and the Caribbean. **Patata** is the word used for potato in Spain; **papa** is used in the Americas.

Linguistic Comparisons 4.1

Etapa Support Materials

- Workbook: pp. 13-19
- TRB: Textbook Activity Masters: pp. 64, 65
- Textbook Cassettes/CDs: Cassette 1, Side A; CD 1, Track 13
- Tapescript: Textbook Cassettes/CDs p. 189
- Overhead Transparencies: 13, 13a
- Middle School Activities: p. 15
- Lesson Plan Book: pp. 8-9

- Testing Program: Quiz pp. 14-16; Answer Key & Testing Program Tapescript p. T6
- Testing Cassettes: Cassette Side A
- Computerized Testing Program: Windows™; Macintosh®
- Atajo Writing Assistant Software: Student Text p. 35

A. ¡Camarero(a), más aceitunas, por favor!

ANSWERS

All answers will follow the same format:
Camarero(a), más _____ , por favor.

B. Pasa las patatas, por favor.

ANSWERS

All answers will follow the same format:
No, pasa _____ , por favor.

VARIATION

 Have students ask their partners questions with the foods using **o**. Example: **¿Deseas la tortilla o las patatas?**

Determining Preferences

C. ¡Qué hambre!

SUGGESTION

Tell students to use foods and drinks that others in their group have not already chosen.

Individual Needs

More-prepared Students
Students could play the waiter (waitress) and give other students suggestions of what to order:
¿Desean comer _____ o _____?

TEACH/MODEL

Pronunciación

PRESENTATION

 TEXTBOOK CASSETTE/CD CASSETTE 1, SIDE A; CD 1, TRACK 13

 TAPESCRIPT P. 189

Point out that the Spanish **i** is more tense and clipped than the English long **e** sound. Contrast the English word *see* and the Spanish word **sí**. Other examples: *dee*/**di**; *me*/**mi**; *tea*/**ti**; *knee*/**ni**.

Then have students listen to the explanation for the vowel **i** on the Textbook Cassette/CD.

Auditory-Musical

 Linguistic Comparisons 4.1

¡Te toca a ti!

A. ¡Camarero(a), más (more) aceitunas, por favor! You are in a **bar de tapas** with your friends, and you want to order more **tapas.** Ask the waiter (waitress) to bring you some. Follow the model.

> **MODELO** aceitunas
> *Camarero(a), más aceitunas, por favor.*

1. cacahuetes
2. tortilla
3. patatas bravas
4. aceitunas
5. pan con chorizo
6. queso
7. calamares

B. Pasa (Pass) las patatas, por favor. Your friend offers you some **tapas,** but the ones that you want to eat are too far away from you. Ask your friend to pass them to you. Work in pairs and follow the model.

> **MODELO** Amigo(a): ¿Deseas la tortilla? (las patatas)
> Tú: *No, pasa las patatas, por favor.*

1. ¿Deseas los cacahuetes? (las aceitunas)
2. ¿Deseas el queso? (el chorizo)
3. ¿Deseas la tortilla de patatas? (el pan)
4. ¿Deseas los calamares? (la tortilla)
5. ¿Deseas las aceitunas? (el queso)
6. ¿Deseas el chorizo? (las patatas bravas)
7. ¿Deseas el pan? (los calamares)

C. ¡Qué hambre! (I'm starving!) You are very hungry and want something more to eat than **tapas.** What do you order? Work in groups of four. One person is the waiter (waitress) and the others are customers. Take turns ordering something to eat. Use some of the vocabulary that you already know from Chapter 1. Follow the model.

> **MODELO** Camarero(a): ¿Qué desean comer?
> Tú: Yo quisiera un sándwich de jamón y queso.

 PRONUNCIACIÓN THE VOWEL **i**

The sound of the vowel **i** in Spanish is pronounced like the *ee* of the English word *beet*, except it is shorter in Spanish.

28 *Primera unidad* Vamos a tomar algo

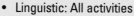 MULTIPLE INTELLIGENCES

- Linguistic: All activities
- Logical-Mathematical: A, B, H
- Visual-Spatial: **Estructura**
- Auditory-Musical: **Pronunciación**, D, I, J, **Aquí escuchamos**
- Interpersonal: F, K, **Chismes, Más actividades**
- Intrapersonal: C, E

 The Standards

- Interpersonal Communication 1.1: A, B, C, F, **Chismes**
- Interpretive Communication 1.2: A, C, **Aquí escuchamos**
- Presentational Communication 1.3: E, K, **Más actividades**
- Cultural Practices and Perspectives 2.1: **Comentarios culturales**
- Cultural Products and Perspectives 2.2: **Las tapas españolas, Comentarios culturales**
- Linguistic Comparisons 4.1: **Pronunciación, Palabras útiles**

Práctica

D. Listen and repeat as your teacher models the following words for you.

1. sí	4. allí	7. hija	10. tiza
2. mi	5. y	8. mochila	11. Lili
3. silla	6. mira	9. ti	12. libro

Comentarios CULTURALES

Las tapas

In Spain, one of the most popular meeting places for friends is the **bar de tapas.** Spaniards commonly stop in these places after work or before dinner for a snack and something to drink. These snacks are called **tapas** and include such things as peanuts, olives, cheese, and bite-sized pieces of **tortilla española.** Sometimes these **tapas** are provided at no charge with each beverage order. The menu also includes more substantial food, such as **bocadillos** and different kinds of fried fish. **La Chuleta** is one of the better-known **tapas** bars in Madrid.

Repaso

E. Mis actividades Say whether or not you do the following activities. If you do them, say how often or how well. Follow the model.

> **MODELO** cantar
> *Yo no canto muy bien.*

1. trabajar	4. cantar	7. hablar español
2. escuchar música	5. hablar inglés	8. estudiar matemáticas
3. viajar	6. bailar	

❓¿Qué crees?

In Spain, a typical breakfast would be:

a) bacon and eggs
b) coffee and toast
c) pancakes with hot syrup

respuesta 🖙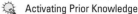

F. Una conversación en un café You meet two friends at a café for a snack. 1) One of you should make introductions. 2) Then place your order. While waiting for the waiter (waitress) to bring your food and beverages, 3) ask each other questions about the things you like to do. On a signal from your teacher, 4) end your conversation and say good-bye.

Capítulo 2 ¡Vamos a un bar de tapas!   **29**

Estructura

PRESENTATION

Begin by doing a quick oral drill on third-person subject pronouns. Repeat the gestures you used previously to explain **yo**, **tú**, **ustedes**, and **nosotros**. Then establish references for **él**, **ella**, **ellos**, and **ellas**. Substitute pronouns for proper names, pointing to different members of the class: **Alicia—ella, José—él, María y Ana—ellas, Juan y Jorge—ellos**, etc. Point out that a large group of females with only one male would still be substituted with the pronoun **ellos**.

SUGGESTION

Then ask simple **tú** questions, such as **¿Cantas bien? ¿Estudias mucho?** Summarize using third-person forms, as in **María canta bien. Ella canta bien.**, etc. Continue with **ustedes** questions: **¿Viajan mucho o poco? ¿Hablan español bien?** Point to two or three students as you direct these questions and then have one answer as a spokesperson for the others: **Viajamos poco. No hablamos español bien.**, etc. Then summarize: **Alicia y Jorge viajan poco. Ellos viajan poco.**, etc.

Activating Prior Knowledge

ESTRUCTURA

Subject pronouns and the present tense of regular -ar verbs: Third person

¿Miguel? Él **viaja** mucho.

¿Anita? Ella **habla** español muy bien.

¿Jaime y Tomás? Ellos **cantan** bien.

¿Paquita y Laura?
Ellas no **estudian** mucho.

¿Juan y Clara? Ellos **bailan**.

Tú and Usted

The uses of **tú** and **usted** in familiar and formal contexts varies in different Spanish-speaking countries. In Colombia, for example, it is common to always use the **usted** forms, including between mothers and their children and among other close relatives. In most countries the **usted** form is used as a courtesy towards older people, who may give a younger person permission to address them with **tú** forms as they get to know them. In some countries, such as Argentina and Costa Rica, the informal form of address is **vos** instead of **tú**, and its verb conjugations are different.

Linguistic Comparisons 4.1

ESTRUCTURA (continued)

Subject Pronouns

Singular		Plural	
él	*he*	**ellos**	*they* (masculine)
ella	*she*	**ellas**	*they* (feminine)

1. **Ellas** is used to refer to groups of females; **ellos** refers to groups of males or groups of males and females.

Present Tense of Regular *-ar* Verbs

Subject Pronoun	Verb Ending	Conjugated form of the verb **trabajar**
él	**–a**	trabaj**a**
ella	**–a**	trabaj**a**
ellos	**–an**	trabaj**an**
ellas	**–an**	trabaj**an**

2. To form the present tense of any regular **-ar** verb in the third person, add to the stem the verb ending that corresponds to the subject. Remember that the stem is found by dropping the **-ar** from the infinitive (**trabaj-** for the **-ar** verb **trabajar**).

3. The endings for **él** and **ella** are the same as these used for **usted**, and the ones for **ellos** and **ellas** are the same as those used for **ustedes**.

4. Some additional **-ar** verbs and expressions that you should learn are **ganar dinero** *(to earn money)*, **mirar** *(to look at, to watch)*, and **tocar** *(to touch, to play a musical instrument)*.

5. In Spanish, since verb endings indicate the subject, subject pronouns are frequently omitted.

Escuchas música clásica.	*You listen to classical music.*
Hablan español.	*They speak Spanish.*

6. Subject pronouns are, however, used with conjugated verb forms for emphasis or clarification.

Usted toma un café y **yo tomo** un té.	*You are having a coffee and I am having a tea.*

Capítulo 2 ¡Vamos a un bar de tapas!   **31**

Estructura

SUGGESTION

Write the third-person subject pronouns and verb forms on the board. Then make up sentences and have students repeat first as a whole class, then in groups, and then individually. Examples: **José desea un café. Ana y Luisa estudian mucho. Los profesores trabajan mucho.** Continue by having students change sentences from the singular to the plural. Suggestions: **Ella baila muy bien. (Ellas bailan muy bien.) Él mira la televisión mucho. (Ellos miran la televisión mucho.)**

TEACH/MODEL

PRESENTATION

Point out that the verb endings for **Ud.** and **Uds.** forms are the same as those of third-person forms. The origin of **Ud.** is **Vd.**, an abbreviation for **Vuestra Merced**, a term that was used in addressing royalty or the aristocracy. It is now used formally to show respect, although the degree of formalilty varies from country to country. Have students repeat sentences using the **Ud.** and **Uds.** forms. Examples: **Ud. viaja mucho. Uds. hablan español.** Then have students change sentences from the singular to the plural. Suggestions: **Ud. desea un refresco. (Uds. desean un refresco.) Ud. estudia inglés. (Uds. estudian inglés.)**

PRACTICE/APPLY

After students have practiced third-person endings sufficiently, review the first and second person again by asking simple questions. Then have them change simple statements from the singular to the plural. Remind them that the most commonly used plural for the **tú** form is the **Uds.** form.

G. Las actividades

SUGGESTION

Students who learn better by listening could benefit from a guessing game. Describe a member of the class: **Esta persona canta en el coro y practica la música todos los días.** Students can guess who is being described. Then say the entire sentence: **Clara canta en el coro. Clara practica la música todos los días.**

🔺🔺 Auditory-Musical

VARIATION

You can personalize this activity by having students use people they know as the subjects for these sentences. Provide a list of examples on the board: **Mis padres, mi hermano(a), mis amigos(as), mi familia y yo, mis amigos y yo.** Write on the board any new vocabulary that you introduce for this purpose.

H. Mis amigos colombianos

SUGGESTION

Do this first as a **pregúntale** activity to make sure that students substitute the subject pronouns correctly. Then have students ask their partners the questions for extra practice. Point out that one of the purposes of this activity is to practice the subject pronouns.

ANSWERS

1. No, él baila muchísimo.
2. No, ellas estudian mucho.
3. No, ella trabaja a veces.
4. No, ellos cantan mal.
5. No, ellos escuchan música clásica a veces.
6. No, ella gana muy poco.

VARIATION

Students could repeat the activity and add information in order to review the use of **gustar: No, Jack baila muchísimo. Le gusta mucho bailar.** Tell students to use **le** to replace a singular subject and **les** to replace a plural subject in their statements.

🔺🔺 Linguistic

Aquí practicamos

G. Las actividades Describe the activities that the people in the left-hand column are doing by forming sentences with phrases from the other two columns.

A	B	C
ellos	cantar	en un café
yo	hablar	una limonada
Juan y Alicia	trabajar	en clase
nosotras	escuchar	inglés
Carlos	mirar	dinero
Patricia y yo	bailar	música clásica
ustedes	tomar	todos los días
tú	viajar	en casa
ellos	desear	patatas bravas
el señor Suárez	estudiar	a San Salvador
el (la) profesor(a)	practicar	la televisión
mis hermanos	necesitar	

H. Mis amigos colombianos (My Colombian friends) Your Colombian friends have some questions for you and your classmates. Answer their questions using subject pronouns and the expressions in parentheses. Follow the model.

> **MODELO**   **Amigo(a):** ¿John habla español mal? (muy bien)
>   **Tú:** No, *él habla español muy bien.*

1. ¿Jack baila muy poco? (muchísimo)
2. ¿Nancy y Kay estudian poco? (mucho)
3. ¿Helen trabaja todos los días? (a veces)
4. ¿Julie y Tom cantan bien? (mal)
5. ¿Ed y Andy escuchan música clásica todos los días? (a veces)
6. ¿Lisa gana mucho? (muy poco)

32   *Primera unidad* Vamos a tomar algo

☀ Spanish for Spanish Speakers

Vocabulary Expansion

Have Spanish speakers think of other **-ar** verbs not listed in the Activity G. Ask them to work with a partner to combine lists and determine if they are familiar with the verbs their partner chose. Encourage them to practice writing and saying new verbs.

🔺🔺 Linguistic

PALABRAS ÚTILES

Asking and answering yes/no questions

—¿**Tú estudias** mucho?   *Do you study a lot?*
—**Sí, yo estudio** mucho.   *Yes, I study a lot.*

—¿**Hablan ustedes** francés?   *Do you speak French?*
—**No, nosotros no hablamos** francés.   *No, we don't speak French.*

—**Ellos trabajan** mucho, ¿**no**?   *They work a lot, don't they?*
—**Sí, ellos trabajan** mucho.   *Yes, they work a lot.*

—**Ella no toca** la guitarra, ¿**verdad**?   *She doesn't play the guitar, does she?*
—**No, ella no toca** la **guitarra**.   *No, she doesn't play the guitar.*

1. There are three basic ways to ask these kinds of questions in Spanish.
   • Make your voice rise at the end of a group of words: ¿**Usted baila bien?**
   • Invert the order of the subject and verb: ¿**Practican ellas** español en clase?
   • Add the words ¿**no**? or ¿**verdad**? after the statement. In such questions, ¿**no**? and ¿**verdad**? are equivalents of expressions like *don't you?, aren't you,? isn't he (she)?* at the end of English sentences. Note that ¿**no**? or ¿**verdad**? can be used at the end of an affirmative statement, but only ¿**verdad**? is used at the end of a negative statement.

Nosotras cantamos bien, ¿**no**?   *We sing well, don't we?*

Tú **no ganas** mucho dinero, ¿**verdad**?   *You don't earn much money, do you?*

2. To answer these kinds of questions negatively, place **no** before the conjugated verb.

Yo **no viajo** mucho.   *I do not travel a lot.*

Aquí practicamos

I. **¿Usted desea un café?** Change each statement to a question by making your voice rise at the end of the sentence.

1. Usted desea un café.
2. Tú miras mucho la TV.
3. Román trabaja poco.
4. La señorita Ruiz gana mucho dinero.
5. Ustedes estudian mucho.
6. Ester toca el piano.
7. Nosotros viajamos a Ecuador.
8. Ellos cantan bien.

Capítulo 2 ¡Vamos a un bar de tapas!   **33**

J. ¿Verdad?

SUGGESTION

Do as a whole-class activity by having one student read the statement and another change it. Example: **María, lee el número uno, y Juan, cámbialo.** Students will quickly become accustomed to different commands and formats. By doing the activity as a class, you can see if students understand how to use the tag endings.

 Presentational Communication 1.1

ANSWERS

Answers will vary, but the tag ending used in items 4 and 7 should be ¿verdad?

K. Hagan preguntas

SUGGESTIONS

 TRB: ACTIVITY MASTER, P. 64

Have students format their reports as follows: 1) Tell how you asked the question. 2) List the people who answered affirmatively. 3) Summarize the responses using a subject pronoun. Example: **Cantas muy bien, ¿no? Juan, Jaime, Ana y Luisa: Ellos cantan muy bien.** Have students also include their own responses to the questions when they present their reports. Some of their statements will use **nosotros** as the subject. Remind students to use **tú** when they address classmates and **usted** when addressing their teacher.

 Presentational Communication 1.3

J. ¿Verdad? Now use ¿no? or ¿verdad? to change the following statements into questions.

1. Paquita habla bien el alemán *(German)*.
2. Ana y Rosa cantan muy mal.
3. Tú hablas español en el laboratorio.
4. Ella no estudia mucho.
5. Ellos trabajan poco.
6. Ustedes toman té.
7. Usted no gana mucho dinero.
8. Reynaldo toca el violín todos los días.

K. Hagan preguntas (Ask questions) You want to find as many people as you can who participate in the following activities. Ask your classmates and your teacher questions based on the model. On your activity master, keep track of who answers **sí** by writing their names in the blanks beside each activity. Be prepared to report the results of your poll.

MODELO hablar francés
Tú hablas francés, ¿verdad? o:
¿Señor (Señorita), habla usted francés?

1. cantar muy bien				
2. viajar mucho				
3. estudiar poco				
4. estudiar todos los días				
5. no tomar té				
6. hablar español en casa				
7. tocar un instrumento				
8. mirar la TV mucho				
9. trabajar a veces				
10. escuchar música clásica				
11. practicar el tenis				

  **Spanish for Spanish Speakers**

Spoken Spanish

Ask Spanish speakers to listen to the Spanish used in the **Aquí escuchamos** recording and to compare it to the Spanish they use in their communities. Encourage student to focus, for example, on the consonant **s**: Does it sound similar to the *s* in English? Is it barely audible (as is often the case in Spanish spoken in the Caribbean)?

Is it similar to the *th* sound in English? How does it contrast with their spoken Spanish? You might want to have the rest of the class participate in this activity.

☼ Comparing and Contrasting
🔺 Auditory-Musical
⊛ Linguistic Comparisons 4.1

Aquí escuchamos

En un bar de tapas *Beatriz, Linda, and Cristina are at a tapas bar. It's 1:30 in the afternoon.*

Antes de escuchar Think about vocabulary you might hear in the conversation.

 A escuchar As you listen to the conversation, put a check mark on your activity master next to each of the following words every time you hear it.

__aceitunas	__pan con chorizo
__agua mineral	__refresco
__calamares	__tortilla de patatas

Después de escuchar On your activity master, indicate which food items each girl ordered. Be aware that Beatriz speaks first, then Linda, then Cristina.

	1. Beatriz	2. Linda	3. Cristina
a. agua mineral			
b. tortilla			
c. calamares			
d. pan con chorizo			
e. refresco			

¡ADELANTE!

 Chismes (Gossip) Your friend knows the new student in the class better than you do. Invite your friend to have a snack so you can ask some questions. Find out if the new student is a good singer and dancer, if she travels a great deal, if she watches TV a lot, if she works, etc. Order something to eat and drink as well.

 Más actividades Working with a partner, ask each other questions in Spanish. Use them to write nine sentences describing nine different activities. Include three that you both do on a regular basis, three that only you do regularly, and three that your partner does regularly. Your first three sentences should begin with **Nosotros...**, the next three should begin with **Yo...**, and the last three will have your partner's name as the subject. Be prepared to report all the information to the class.

Capítulo 2 ¡Vamos a un bar de tapas! **35**

Aquí escuchamos

	TEXTBOOK CASSETTE/CD CASSETTE 1, SIDE A; CD 1, TRACK 14
	TAPESCRIPT P. 189
	TRB: ACTIVITY MASTER, P. 65

Después de escuchar

ANSWERS

Beatriz: b, e (tortilla, refresco)
Linda: c, e (calamares, refresco)
Cristina: a, e (agua mineral, pan con chorizo)

 ETAPA SYNTHESIS

Chismes

SUGGESTION

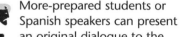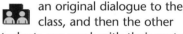 More-prepared students or Spanish speakers can present an original dialogue to the class, and then the other students can work with their partners to make up dialogues of their own.

 Presentational Communication 1.3

Más actividades

FYI

ATAJO WRITING ASSISTANT SOFTWARE

You might want to have students use this software program when doing this activity.

Additional Practice and Recycling

FYI

WORKBOOK, PP. 13-19

For recycling and additional practice of the vocabulary, structures, and language functions presented throughout this **etapa**, you can assign the workbook activities as in-class work and/or homework. Answers to the activities are overprinted on each page of the Teacher's Edition of the Workbook.

Additional Etapa Resources

Refer to the **Etapa** Support Materials list on the opening page of this **etapa** for detailed cross-references to these assessment options.

 Spanish for Spanish Speakers

Imagining Future Activities

Have Spanish-speaking students with more extensive vocabularies imagine themselves doing the **Más actividades** writing activity in ten or fifteen years, comparing their activities as adults.

 Comparing and Contrasting

TEACH/MODEL

¡Buenos días! ... ¡Hasta luego!

PRESENTATION

 TRANSPARENCIES 14

TEXTBOOK CASSETTE/CD CASSETTE 1, SIDE A; CD 1, TRACK 15

TAPESCRIPT P. 189

 First review the greetings and introductions from Chapter 1 (**¡Hola! ¿Qué tal? ¿Cómo estás? ¿Cómo te va? Te presento a...**) by walking around the room and shaking hands as students answer. Then present the dialogue by using the Textbook Cassette/CD and the transparency or by reading the dialogue and having students repeat, first as a whole class, then in groups, and then individually. Then have your Spanish-speaking students or other volunteers act out the scene with their books closed.

Interpretive Communication 1.2

VOCABULARY EXPANSION

Point out to students that when speaking about a man or a woman, Spanish speakers often use the words **el señor** and **la señora**, rather than the literal translations **el hombre** or **la mujer**. For example, it would be more common to say **La señora baila muy bien**, rather than **La mujer baila muy bien**. Also point out that unlike in English, the articles **el** and **la** are used before the titles **señor** and **señora** when the terms are used within a sentence, but that they are not used when referring to the person directly. For example: **Hablamos con el señor y la señora Ramírez**, but **Sr. Ramírez, ¿qué desea?** You might want to mention the terms **don** and **doña**, which may be used as a respectful yet familiar form of address with the first name of an older person with whom one is well acquainted: **Doña Carmen, Don Luis**, etc.

Linguistic Comparisons 4.1

SEGUNDA ETAPA

Preparación

- In Spanish-speaking cultures, certain courtesies are generally observed between people who meet for the first time. A certain degree of respectful formality by a younger person toward an older person is usually expected.

- How would you address a person who is older than you, or someone you haven't met before or don't know very well?

- How would you expect an older person who doesn't know you very well to address you in a public place?

- When people meet on the street and introductions are in order, who should take the responsibility to make them, as a courtesy?

¡Buenos días! ... ¡Hasta luego!

*At the café, Lucas Pereda and his friend Jaime Torres run into two friends of Lucas' parents, **el señor** and **la señora** García.*

el señor *Mr.*   la señora *Mrs.*

36   *Primera unidad* Vamos a tomar algo

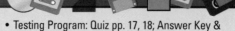
Etapa Support Materials

- Workbook: pp. 20-24
- TRB: Textbook Activity Masters: pp. 66-68
- Textbook Cassettes/CDs: Cassette 1, Side A; CD 1, Track 15
- Tapescript: Textbook Cassettes/CDs pp. 189-190
- Overhead Transparency: 14
- Middle School Activities: pp. 16-19
- Lesson Plan Book: pp. 10-11

- Testing Program: Quiz pp. 17, 18; Answer Key & Testing Cassettes Tapescript p. T7
- Testing Cassettes: Cassette Side A
- Computerized Testing Program: Windows™; Macintosh®
- Atajo Writing Assistant Software: Student Text p. 42

Sr. y Sra. García:	Buenos días, Lucas.
Lucas:	¡Oh! Buenos días, señor García. Buenos días, señora. **¿Cómo están ustedes?**
Sra. García:	Muy bien, gracias. ¿Y tú?
Lucas:	**Estoy** muy bien, gracias. **Quisiera presentarles a mi amigo** Jaime Torres. El señor y la señora García.
Sr. y Sra. García:	Mucho gusto, Jaime.
Jaime:	**Encantado,** señora. Mucho gusto, señor.
Sr. García:	**¿Van a** tomar un café?
Lucas:	No, **acabamos de** tomar unos refrescos.
Sr. García:	¡Ah! Pues, hasta luego. **Saludos a tus padres.**
Lucas:	Gracias.
Lucas y Jaime:	Adiós, señor, señora.
Sr. y Sra. García:	Adiós.

Saludos	**Presentaciones** (Introductions)
Buenos días.	Quisiera presentarle(s) a...
¿Cómo están ustedes?	Encantado(a).
¿Cómo está usted?	Mucho gusto.
(Estoy) Bien, gracias. ¿Y Ud.?	Igualmente. *Likewise.*

¿Cómo están ustedes? How are you? **Estoy** *I am* **Quisiera presentarles a mi amigo** *I would like to introduce you to my friend* **Encantado** *Delighted* **Van a** *Are you going to* **acabamos de** *we've just finished* **Saludos a tus padres.** *Greetings to your parents.*

Comentarios CULTURALES

Saludos informales y formales

When greeting people and making introductions, different expressions denote different degrees of formality or informality: **¡Hola!, ¿Qué tal?, ¿Cómo estás?, ¿Cómo te va?, Te presento a...** are used informally with people you know well and with peers. **¿Cómo está usted?, ¿Cómo están ustedes?, Quisiera presentarles(le) a...** are more formal and are used with older people or people you do not know very well. It is not uncommon for older people or superiors to speak informally to a younger person who addresses them as **usted,** as you saw in the conversation between Lucas, Jaime, and **el señor** and **la señora** García.

Capítulo 2 ¡Vamos a un bar de tapas! **37**

PRESENTATION (CONTINUED)
When practicing greetings and introductions, you will probably wish to have students use **tú** when talking among themselves, and **Ud.** when speaking to you. Take this opportunity to stress the importance of recognizing and respecting levels of language. With the help of students, make the following lists on the board: expressions and gestures that go along with **tú**, with **Ud.**, and with both **tú** and **Ud.** Some expressions will include the words **tú** or **Ud.** (**¿Cómo está Ud.? ¿Cómo estás tú?**, etc.) and others will not (**¿Qué tal? ¿Cómo te va?**).

Linguistic Comparisons 4.1

VARIATION
For more practice with the formal expressions, designate several students to play *older people*. You might want to give each *older person* a prop (hat, briefcase) that signals his (her) new identity.

VOCABULARY EXPANSION
Explain that when someone has been introduced to you and says either **Encantado/Encantada** or **Mucho gusto**, an appropriate response would be **Igualmente**. Mention other expressions, such as **Tanto gusto. El gusto es mío. ¿Cómo le va?** (formal version of **¿Cómo te va?**)

Linguistic

☀ Spanish for Spanish Speakers

Greeting Variations

Ask Spanish speakers for variations they might have heard of the formal and informal **saludos**, **presentaciones** and **despedidas** that are introduced in the dialogue and the **Comentarios culturales**. Help students with the spelling of these variations by writing them on the board or overhead. If you have mentioned the terms **don** and **doña**, ask Spanish speakers if they have heard that form of address and with what person this form was used.

Linguistic Comparisons 4.1

PRACTICE/APPLY

A. ¿Qué respondes?

SUGGESTION

Review other greetings, introductions, and good-byes from Chapter 1, addressing the students randomly.

 Activating Prior Knowledge

B. Buenos días, señor (señora, señorita)

EXPANSION

Expand the activity by choosing several students to play the role of *older persons*, giving them the opportunity to switch levels of language as they work their way around the class.

TEACH/MODEL

Pronunciación

PRESENTATION

 TEXTBOOK CASSETTE/CD CASSETTE 1, SIDE A; CD 1, TRACK 16

 TAPESCRIPT P. 189

Continue to emphasize the clipped nature of the Spanish vowels. Contrast the sound of the English word *no* and that of the Spanish word **no**. Other examples: *low*/**lo**; *tow*/**to**; *sew*/**so**; *poe*/**po**.

Then have students listen to the explanation for the vowel **o** on the Textbook Cassette/CD. The speaker will model the correct pronunciation of the words in **Práctica C**. Have students follow along and repeat after each word.

Auditory-Musical

Linguistic Comparisons 4.1

PRACTICE/APPLY

D. Escuchen bien

ANSWERS

Answers will follow the model, substituting the cues.

T38 Unit 1, Chapter 2

¡Te toca a ti!

A. ¿Qué respondes? (How do you answer?)

Respond to each question or statement with an appropriate expression. Address the person in parentheses by name. Follow the model.

> **MODELO** Buenos días, Alberto. (Sr. Pérez)
> *Buenos días, señor Pérez.*

1. ¿Cómo estás, Adela? (Sr. Carrillo)
2. ¡Hola, Lourdes! (Sra. Ramírez)
3. Quisiera presentarle a mi amigo Pepe. (Sra. Ruiz)
4. ¿Cómo están ustedes, señores? (Margarita)
5. Mucho gusto, Raquel. (Sra. Castillo)

B. Buenos días, señor (señora, señorita)
Greet and shake hands with your teacher, introduce a classmate to him (her), and then say good-bye.

PRONUNCIACIÓN   THE VOWEL o

The sound of the vowel **o** in Spanish is pronounced like the *o* in the English word *open*, except it is much shorter in Spanish.

Práctica

C. Listen and repeat as your teacher models the following words.

1. ojo	4. chorizo	7. jugo	10. vaso
2. con	5. año	8. política	11. nosotros
3. algo	6. como	9. por	12. disco

Repaso

D. Escuchen bien (Listen carefully) Play the roles of the following students and enact their conversation according to the model. Anita asks Marcos a question. After Marcos answers, Claudia asks Ada what he said, and Ada tells her.

> **MODELO** hablar inglés
> **Anita:** *Marcos, ¿tú hablas inglés?*
> **Marcos:** *No, yo no hablo inglés.*
> **Claudia:** *Ada, ¿habla inglés Marcos?*
> **Ada:** *No, él no habla inglés.*

38 *Primera unidad* Vamos a tomar algo

 MULTIPLE INTELLIGENCES

- Linguistic: All activities
- Logical-Mathematical: A, F, H
- Bodily-Kinesthetic: B, D, **Buenos días señor (señora)**
- Auditory-Musical: **Pronunciación C, Aquí escuchamos**
- Interpersonal: E
- Intrapersonal: G, **Preferencias**

 The Standards

- Interpersonal Communication 1.1: A, B, D, E, F, **Adelante** activities
- Interpretive Communication 1.2: A, E, **Aquí escuchamos**
- Presentational Communication 1.3: J
- Cultural Practices and Perspectives 2.1: **Comentarios culturales**
- Linguistic Comparisons: **Pronunciación**
- Cultural Comparisons 4.2: I

1. tocar la guitarra
2. bailar muy bien
3. viajar a Bolivia
4. tomar café con leche todos los días
5. mirar mucho la TV
6. estudiar francés *(French)*
7. cantar muy mal
8. trabajar muchísimo

E. Mi amigo(a) In pairs, 1) ask your partner questions to gather information about him (her). 2) Then, create a profile of the two of you on your activity master. Put an X under each activity that each of you does well or often. 3) Prepare to report on your similarities and differences. Follow the model.

	hablar	estudiar	cantar	bailar	viajar	trabajar	tocar
yo							
mi amigo(a)							

 MODELO

Tú:	*Carmencita, cantas bien, ¿verdad?*
Carmencita:	*Sí, canto bien.*
Tú:	*Mi amiga Carmencita canta bien.*
	Yo no canto bien, pero bailo muy bien.

ESTRUCTURA

The conjugated verb followed by the infinitive

¿**Deseas trabajar**?   *Do you want to work?*

Ellas no **necesitan estudiar** mucho.   *They don't need to study a lot.*

1. When two verbs are used with each other, the first verb is conjugated to agree with the subject and the second verb remains in the infinitive form. This construction occurs frequently with some verbs and expressions you already know: **desear** and **yo quisiera**. It also occurs with **acabar de** *(to have just done something)*, **necesitar** *(to need)*, and **tú quisieras** *(you would like)*.

2. To make this construction negative, place **no** in front of the conjugated verb form.

3. To confirm an affirmative statement someone has just said, use the word **también** *(also, too)* after the infinitive. For a negative statement, use **tampoco** *(neither, either)*.

—Deseo bailar.   *I want to dance.*
—Deseo bailar **también**.   *I want to dance too.*

—No deseo estudiar.   *I don't want to study.*
—No deseo estudiar **tampoco**.   *I don't want to study either.*

Capítulo 2 ¡Vamos a un bar de tapas!   **39**

 Spanish for Spanish Speakers

Problematic Spellings
Point out to the students the **j** of **ojo** and **jugo**; the **z** of **chorizo**; the **v** of **vaso**. Have them come up with other words using **j**, **z**, and **v**, and practice writing these words in their Vocabulary Notebook.

🔺🔺 Linguistic

E. Mi amigo(a)
SUGGESTION

 TRB: ACTIVITY MASTER, P. 66

 After the students have created their profiles on the activity master, have pairs regroup by four or six to report the similarities and differences recorded on their grids.

🔧 Comparing and Contrasting

⊛ Interpersonal Communication 1.1

TEACH/MODEL

Estructura
PRESENTATION
Remember that the word **quisieras** is introduced here as a vocabulary item. There is no need to explain tense or mood at this point. You can introduce this structure by asking simple questions with verbs learned in Chapter 1. ¿**Te gusta bailar?** ¿**Quisieras bailar?** ¿**Deseas bailar?** Continue with statements and have students repeat. Examples: **Me gusta hablar español. Uds. desean hablar español bien. Yo quisiera hablar francés también.**, etc. Then write a few sentences on the board to show two-verb combinations. Point out the conjugated verbs and the infinitive forms. Explain that only the first verb is conjugated. Point out that this structure is parallel to the English structure in sentences such as *I want to do that, You wish to dance, They need to work*, etc.

Practice a few sentences with **acabar de**. Explain that it is an idiomatic expression and that they should not try to translate it. Examples: **Nosotros acabamos de practicar los verbos. El profesor García acaba de viajar a Venezuela.**, etc.

⊛ Linguistic Comparisons 4.1

PRACTICE / APPLY

F. ¿Quisieras tú...?

SUGGESTION

 Have students work with partners. Encourage them to be creative in their answers and to try to practice vocabulary that they have learned thus far. Remind them that the purpose of this activity is to practice **quisiera** and that they should use it in all of their questions and answers.

✎ Activating Prior Knowledge

G. ¿Deseas o necesitas?

SUGGESTION

📓 TRB: ACTIVITY MASTER, P. 67

Answers will vary but will all contain the **yo** form of the verbs. Partners' responses will all contain a **también** in affirmative statements and a **tampoco** in negative statements, according to the model. Have the pairs regroup by four or six to report the similarities and differences recorded on their activity master.

✎ Comparing and Contrasting

◎ Interpersonal Communication 1.1

Aquí practicamos

F. ¿Quisieras tú...? At a party, you try to impress a boy (girl) whom you like by asking in Spanish if he (she) would like to do certain things. Use the following expressions to form your questions. He (she) can answer affirmatively or negatively. Follow the model.

> **MODELO**   comer algo *(something)*
>   Tú: *¿Quisieras comer algo?*
>   Amigo(a):   *Sí, quisiera comer unas patatas bravas.* o: *No, quisiera bailar.*

1. bailar
2. cantar
3. escuchar música española *(Spanish)*
4. tomar algo
5. hablar español
6. comer unas tapas

G. ¿Deseas o necesitas? On your activity master, indicate whether you want or need to do the following activities. Mark your answers by writing **sí** or **no** in each space. Then see if your classmate wants or needs to do the same things as you. If your classmate gives the **same sí** response as you, he (she) should add **también** to the answer on the activity master. If your classmate gives the same **no** response as you, he (she) should add **tampoco**. Look at the models for examples. Be prepared to report 1) one activity you both want to do, 2) one you both need to do, 3) one that neither one of you wants to do, and 4) one that neither of you needs to do.

> **MODELOS**   Gathering information:
>   estudiar
>   Tú: *Necesito estudiar.*
>   Compañero(a):   *Yo necesito estudiar también.* o: *No deseo estudiar.*
>
>   Tú: *No necesito estudiar.*
>   Compañero(a):   *Yo sí necesito estudiar.* o: *Yo no necesito estudiar tampoco.*
>
> **MODELO**   Reporting: *Mi amiga Ana y yo deseamos viajar a Sudamérica. Necesitamos ganar dinero. No deseamos trabajar mucho. No necesitamos gastar mucho.*

40   *Primera unidad* Vamos a tomar algo

	Yo necesito	Yo deseo	Mi amigo(a) necesita	Mi amigo(a) desea
viajar a Sudamérica (South America)				
hablar español				
tomar un refresco				
trabajar mucho				
tocar el piano				
mirar la TV				
estudiar mucho				
ganar mucho dinero				

H. Consejos (Pieces of advice)

Your mother (**mamá**) tells you what you need to do. Tell her that you have already done everything she mentions. Follow the model.

MODELO   estudiar matemáticas

> **Mamá:** *Necesitas estudiar matemáticas.*
> **Tú:** *Pero (But) acabo de estudiar matemáticas.*

1. estudiar inglés
2. trabajar mucho
3. comer bien
4. hablar en español
5. ganar dinero
6. practicar el piano

H. Consejos

SUGGESTION

  Have students do the activity with their partners or do as a whole class activity by having one student give the mother's statement and another give the student's reply. Example: **Juan, ¿qué dice mamá? María, ¿qué dice el estudiante?**

Presentational Communication 1.3

ANSWERS

1. Necesitas estudiar inglés.
Pero acabo de estudiar inglés.
2. Necesitas trabajar mucho.
Pero acabo de trabajar mucho.
3. Necesitas comer bien.
Pero acabo de comer bien.
4. Necesitas hablar en español.
Pero acabo de hablar en español.
5. Necesitas ganar dinero.
Pero acabo de ganar dinero.
6. Necesitas practicar el piano.
Pero acabo de practicar el piano.

Focus on Culture

Reviewing Cultural Practices

To recap cultural practices, perspectives, and products, ask students what they remember about Spanish **tapas** and other foods discussed in this chapter. Also ask them what they remember about meal times discussed in Chapter 1. Have them compare Spanish eating habits to their own.

Cultural Practices and Perspectives 2.1
Cultural Products and Perspectives 2.2
Cultural Comparisons 4.2

Aquí escuchamos

 TEXTBOOK CASSETTE/CD CASSETTE 1, SIDE A; CD 1, TRACK 17

 TAPESCRIPT P. 190

Después de escuchar

ANSWERS

1. Alicia. She is speaking to someone older.
2. Sr. and Sra. Jiménez; because Alicia is younger.
3. They decide to go to a café.
4. **Mucho gusto, gracias**

ETAPA SYNTHESIS

Buenos días, señor (señora)

SUGGESTION

 Let your Spanish-speaking students model the conversation before having students do the activity in groups of three.

Preferencias

FYI

 ATAJO WRITING ASSISTANT SOFTWARE

Have students use this software program when doing this activity.

Additional Practice and Recycling

FYI

 WORKBOOK, PP. 20-24

For recycling and additional practice of the vocabulary, structures, and language functions presented throughout this **etapa**, assign the workbook activities as in-class work/homework. Answers to the activities are overprinted on each page of the Teacher's Edition of the Workbook.

Aquí escuchamos

El señor y la señora Jiménez *Alicia and her friend Reynaldo meet some friends of her parents in the park.*

Antes de escuchar Think of some of the set formal and informal phrases you know in Spanish for greetings, introductions, and farewells (page 37).

 A escuchar Listen twice to the conversation, and pay particular attention to the formal and informal phrases Alicia, Reynaldo, and **señor** and **señora** Jiménez use.

Después de escuchar Answer the following questions about the conversation you just heard.

1. Who uses the more formal **usted** forms in the conversation? Why is this so?
2. Who uses the more informal **tú** forms? Why?
3. What do the two couples decide to do?
4. What are some of the set courtesy phrases that you hear more than once in the conversation?

¡ADELANTE!

 Buenos días, señor (señora) While walking with a friend, you run into a Venezuelan colleague of your parents, Sr. (Sra.) Ruiz. Introduce your friend to him (her). Sr. (Sra.) Ruiz will ask the two of you about what you like to do.

 Preferencias Write six different things that you prefer doing as opposed to other activities. Follow the model.

MODELO *No deseo mirar la televisión, pero deseo escuchar música.*

EN LÍNEA

Connect with the Spanish-speaking world! Access the *¡Ya verás! Gold* home page for Internet activities related to this chapter.

http://yaveras.heinle.com

42 *Primera unidad* Vamos a tomar algo

Additional Etapa Resources

Refer to the **Etapa** Support Materials list on the opening page of this **etapa** for detailed cross-references to these assessment options.

VOCABULARIO

Para charlar

Para saludar

¿Cómo está Ud.?
¿Cómo están Uds.?
Buenos días.
Saludos a tus
  padres.

Para contestar

Bien, gracias. ¿Y
  Ud.?
Estoy bien, gracias.
Muy bien, gracias.

Para presentar

Quisiera presentar-
  le(les) a…

Para contestar

Encantado(a).
Igualmente.

Temas y contextos

Tapas españolas

unas aceitunas
unos cacahuetes
unos calamares
chorizo
pan
unas patatas bravas
queso
una tortilla (de patatas)

Vocabulario general

Pronombres

él
ella
ellos
ellas

Verbos

acabar de
ganar
mirar
necesitar
pasar
tocar

Otras palabras y expresiones

mi amigo(a)
aquí hay
dinero
español(a)
mamá
más
¿no?
pero
preguntas
presentación
¡Qué hambre!
¿Quisieras…?
el señor
la señora
Sudamérica
también
tampoco
Van a…?
¿verdad?

Capítulo 2 ¡Vamos a un bar de tapas! **43**

CHAPTER WRAP-UP

Improvised Conversation

 TEXTBOOK CASSETTE/CD CASSETTE 1, SIDE A; CD 1, TRACK 18

 TAPESCRIPT P. 190

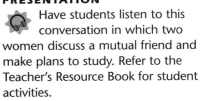 TRB: ACTIVITY MASTER, P. 68

PRESENTATION

Have students listen to this conversation in which two women discuss a mutual friend and make plans to study. Refer to the Teacher's Resource Book for student activities.

Interpretive Communication 1.2

EXPANSION

Write the words **química**, **biología**, and **física** on the board. Guide students to guess the meaning of the word **química** based on these new cognates.

Linguistic Comparisons 4.1

Listening Skills Development

FYI

 LAB MANUAL PP. 9-13

 LAB CASSETTE SIDE B, CD 1, TRACKS 9-16

 TAPESCRIPT: LAB PROGRAM PP. 8-19

It is now appropriate to work through the lab manual activities and their accompanying recordings in class or in the language laboratory.

Resources for Spanish-speaking Students

FYI

 WORKBOOK FOR SPANISH-SPEAKING STUDENTS: PP. 7-12

 ANSWER KEY TO SSS WORKBOOK PP. 2-4

Activities specially written to meet the needs of Spanish-speaking students are available in this workbook for the reinforcement and extension of the topics and language presented in this chapter.

Additional Chapter Resources

Refer to the Chapter Support Materials list on the opening page of this chapter for detailed cross-references to ¡*Ya verás! Gold*'s student-centered technology components and various assessment options.

☀ Spanish for Spanish Speakers

Keeping a Vocabulary Notebook

Remind Spanish-speaking students to add words and expressions from this vocabulary section to the problematic spelling combination categories and personal new vocabulary lists they started in their notebooks in Chapter 1. Reinforce that they should continue to do this each time a chapter in the textbook is completed.

PRACTICE/APPLY

Así lo decimos
Antes de leer
POSSIBLE ANSWERS

1. Cognates include: diferentes, personas, frecuentemente, expresiones, referirse
2. Alphabetized list, such as a dictionary, glossary, or thesaurus
3. attractive: handsome, cute, good-looking;
   crazy: insane, foolish, silly;
   money: cash, currency, dough

ENCUENTROS CULTURALES

Así lo decimos

Antes de leer

Reading Strategies
- Examining format for content clues
- Scanning for specific information
- Recognizing cognates

1. The Spanish paragraph below contains several cognates. Scan the paragraph for cognates and identify their meanings.

2. Glance at the boxed list below. Based on the way the information is organized, can you guess what kind of list it is?

3. In this reading you will see several synonyms in Spanish for the words *attractive*, *crazy*, and *money*, among others. Can you think of synonyms for these words in English? Name some of the synonyms and explain in which situation each one would be used.

El español se habla en muchos países diferentes. Las personas que hablan español pueden comprenderse unas a otras, pero frecuentemente usan palabras o expresiones diferentes para referirse a las mismas cosas. Aquí hay unas palabras que las personas usan en diferentes países.

Attractive	Atractivo, guapo, mono, ser una monada, estar bueno
Avocado	Aguacate, palta
Banana	Plátano, banana, banano, guineo
Bean	Ejote, frijol, habichuela, haba, judía
Bus	Autobús, camión, guagua, omnibús
Car	Automóvil, carro, coche, máquina
Crazy	Loco, chiflado, chalado, ido, pirado, tocado
Drinking straw	Paja de sorber, pajita, pajilla, popote, sorbeto
Gossip	Chisme, cotorreo, cháchara, parloteo
Grapefruit	Pomelo, toronja
Kite	Cometa, papalote, chiringa, barrilete, birlocha, milocha, volantín
Money	Dinero, plata, buenamoza, chavos, duros, pasta, pelas
Orange *(fruit)*	Naranja, china
Peach	Durazno, melocotón
Peas	Guisantes, arvejas
Pineapple	Ananás, piña
Shrimp	Camarón, gamba, esquila, quisquilla
Suitcase	Maleta, valija
Trunk *(car)*	Baúl, cajuela, maletero, portaequipajes

Guía para la lectura

Here are some words and expressions to keep in mind as you read.

se habla	*is spoken*
pueden	*can*
comprenderse unas a otras	*understand each other*
las mismas cosas	*the same things*

Después de leer

1. Why do you think there are many ways of saying the same thing in Spanish?

2. Can people from different Spanish-speaking countries understand each other? Why do you think that is?

3. Find out the countries in which some of the synonyms listed are used. You can use dictionaries, ask Spanish-speaking classmates or friends, or interview your teacher.

Los nombres para las frutas varían mucho de país a país

Aquí se venden judías... ¿O son habichuelas?... ¿O son ejotes?...

Capítulo 2 ¡Vamos a un bar de tapas! **45**

Después de leer

POSSIBLE ANSWERS

1. Answers will vary.

2. Yes, despite regional expressions and vocabulary, the basic Spanish language (structures, vocabulary, etc.) is used in most Spanish-speaking countries.

3. Some examples are:
   Avocado: Aguacate (Puerto Rico), palta (South America)
   Banana: Plátano (Spain), guineo (Caribbean)
   Bean: Frijol (Mexico), habichuela (Puerto Rico), haba (Spain), judía (Spain)
   Car: Automóvil (South America), carro (Puerto Rico), coche (Spain)
   Grapefruit: Pomelo (Spain, South America), toronja (Puerto Rico)
   Orange: Naranja (Spain, South America), china (Caribbean)

CAPÍTULO 3

OBJECTIVES

Functions
- Ordering food and drink
- Finding out information about people

Context
- Mexican restaurants

Accuracy
- Present tense of **ser**
- Names of countries
- Adjectives of nationality
- Nouns for professions

Pronunciation
- The vowel **u**

CHAPTER WARM-UP

Setting the Context

In preparation for their learning about ordering food and drink, have students study the photo on this page. Ask if they have ever bought any fast food from a street vendor, such as at a hot dog stand or a booth at a county fair. Have they ever eaten fast food at a Mexican restaurant? Do they recognize the food in the photo?

CORNERS GAME
Have the four corners of the classroom represent popular types of restaurants, for example: pizza, Mexican, hamburger, barbecue, diner, etc.

Have students indicate their restaurant preferences by going to the corresponding corner. Each group should list in English the reasons for their choice in the form of single-phrase characteristics, such as price, service, quality of food, atmosphere, etc. Write the types of restaurants on the board and under each one list the reasons from each group.

Select the four most frequently named reasons and designate each corner of the classroom to represent one of these four. Have students select the one reason they feel is most important for choosing a restaurant by going to the corresponding corner.

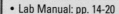 Determining Preferences

¿Te gusta la comida mexicana?

—Quisiera comer algo.
—¿Te gusta la comida mexicana?

Objectives

- ordering something to eat
- finding out information about people

46 *Primera unidad* Vamos a tomar algo

Chapter Support Materials

- Lab Manual: pp. 14-20
- Lab Program: Cassette Side A; CD 2, Tracks 1-8
- TRB: Textbook Activity Masters: pp. 69-71
- Textbook Cassettes/CDs: Cassette 1, Side A; CD 1, Track 24
- Tapescript: Lab Program pp. 18-27; Textbook Cassettes/CDs pp. 191-192
- Middle School Activities: pp. 20-24
- Workbook for Spanish-speaking Students: pp. 13-18
- Answer Key to SSS Workbook pp. 5-7

- Practice Software: Windows™; Macintosh®
- Testing Program: Chapter Test pp. 28-31; Answer Key & Testing Cassettes Tapescript pp. T11, T12; Oral Assessment p. T12
- Testing Cassettes: Cassette Side A
- Computerized Testing Program: Windows™; Macintosh®
- Video Program: Cassette 1, 16:25-26:33
- Video Guide: Videoscript pp. 12-14; Activities pp. 91-93
- **Mundos hispanos 1**
- Internet Activities: Student Text p. 62

PRIMERA ETAPA

Preparación

- Before you start working on this **etapa,** think about what you already know about Mexican food. You may already be familiar with some of the dishes you are going to learn about in this **etapa.** Make a list of all the Mexican dishes you know.

- Now think of several features that describe or characterize this kind of food; for example, colors, spices, vegetables, meats, the kinds of dishes and utensils used for serving and eating them, etc.

¡Vamos a un restaurante!

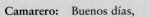

Rafael y Pablo **están** (are) en un restaurante en México.

Camarero:	Buenos días, señores. ¿Qué van a pedir?
Rafael:	Yo quisiera comer un **taco de pollo** con **frijoles.**
Pablo:	Para mí, una **enchilada de carne** con **arroz.**
Camarero:	¿Y para tomar?
Rafael:	Un vaso de agua con limón.
Camarero:	¿Y para Ud., señor?
Pablo:	Una limonada, **bien** fría, por favor.
Camarero:	Muy bien.

¿Qué van a pedir? *What will you have?*   **taco de pollo** *chicken taco*   **frijoles** *beans*   **enchilada de carne** *meat enchilada*
arroz *rice*   **bien** *very*

Capítulo 3 ¿Te gusta la comida mexicana?   **47**

Etapa Support Materials

- Workbook: pp. 25-28
- TRB: Textbook Activity Masters: p. 69
- Textbook Cassettes/CDs: Cassette 1, Side A; CD 1, Track 19
- Tapescript: Textbook Cassettes/CDs pp. 190-191
- Overhead Transparencies: 15-18
- Lesson Plan Book: pp. 13-14

- Testing Program: Quiz pp. 23-25; Answer Key & Testing Cassettes Tapescript p. T10
- Testing Cassettes: Cassette Side A
- Computerized Testing Program: Windows™; Macintosh®
- Atajo Writing Assistant Software: Student Text p. 55

TEACH/MODEL

¡Vamos a un restaurante!

PRESENTATION

TRANSPARENCIES 15

TEXTBOOK CASSETTE/CD CASSETTE 1, SIDE A; CD 1, TRACK 19

TAPESCRIPT P. 190

Ask students to make a list of all the Mexican dishes they know. Have them think of several features of this kind of food, for example: colors, spices, meats, and kinds of dishes and utensils used for serving and eating them.

Play the recording of the short dialogue on the Textbook Cassette/ CD. Afterwards ask what happened and what was ordered. Use the transparency of Mexican food to introduce the food items mentioned in the dialogue and on page 46.

FYI

Note that **están** is lexical only in the scene-setting line. The verb **estar** will be presented fully in Chapter 8. Point out to students that in spoken Spanish, **bien** may be used to mean *very*: **bien fría** means *very cold*, and **bien caliente** means *very hot*.

Interpretive Communication 1.2

VOCABULARY EXPANSION

Introduce additional Mexican food items such as **guacamole**, **tostadas** (crisp flat tortillas with toppings such as beans, lettuce, onions, cheese, chicken, and salsa), **huevos rancheros** (eggs served on a corn tortilla and topped with a spicy tomato sauce), **pollo con mole** (chicken served in a sauce made up of over 20 ingredients, including chocolate and chile), and **quesadillas** (tortillas with cheese inside folded over and fried, served with hot sauce). Mention that Mexican and tex-mex food are different, although they share a common heritage. Some of these items have a Mexican version and a tex-mex version. **Burritos** (flour tortilla with beans and cheese) are an exclusively tex-mex dish and are not usually served in Mexico.

Cultural Products and Perspectives 2.2

PRACTICE / APPLY

A. ¿Qué va a pedir?

SUGGESTION

TRANSPARENCY 16

Use the transparency of Mexican food to introduce the food items mentioned in this dialogue.

VARIATION

Play the waiter yourself. Have students get your attention and order something. No orders may be repeated until all items have been chosen. Or have students work with their partners asking each other questions until they have practiced all of the food items shown.

 Bodily-Kinesthetic

 Presentational Communication 1.3

---

enchilada: *soft corn* **tortilla** *filled with cheese, meat, or chicken, and served with hot sauce*

frijoles: *pinto or black beans cooked until tender; may be served mashed, most often as a side dish*

taco: *a corn tortilla filled with meat, chicken, or other fillings, and topped with lettuce, tomato, grated cheese, and sauce*

tortilla: *made of corn meal and shaped like a pancake; in Mexico, the* **tortilla** *is served with most meals and takes the place of bread*

¡Te toca a ti!

A. ¿Qué va a pedir? You are in a Mexican restaurant. Look at the pictures and decide what you are going to order based on the cues. A classmate will play the role of waiter (waitress). Follow the model.

MODELO enchilada de queso
Camarero(a): *¿Qué va a pedir?*
Tú: *Yo quisiera comer una enchilada de queso.*
Camarero(a): *Muy bien.*

1. enchilada de carne

2. enchilada de queso

3. tacos de pollo

4. tacos de carne

5. arroz con frijoles

6. frijoles

Spanish for Spanish Speakers

Vocabulary Expansion

Ask Spanish speakers if they know of other dishes that contain similar ingredients as those mentioned in Activity A (such as **arroz con pollo**) or other words for the same items (such as **habichuelas**, the word used in Puerto Rico for **frijoles**). Spanish-speaking countries often have different words for the same items, just as in English-speaking countries.

Linguistic Comparisons 4.1

MULTIPLE INTELLIGENCES

- Linguistic: All activities
- Logical-Mathematical: B
- Visual-Spatial: A, C, **Estructura**, G
- Bodily-Kinesthetic: E
- Auditory-Musical: **Pronunciación**, D, G, **Aquí escuchamos**
- Interpersonal: F, H, **Intercambio**
- Intrapersonal: **Mis actividades**

B. ¿En España o en México? Do you think these people are in Spain or in Mexico? Decide based on the food they are eating.

1. A mí me gusta mucho comer tapas con un refresco.
2. Yo quisiera un bocadillo de jamón, por favor.
3. Para mí una enchilada de carne con salsa, por favor.
4. Yo voy a tomar un chocolate.
5. Voy a comer un sándwich de jamón y queso.
6. Yo deseo un taco de pollo con frijoles.

C. ¿Vamos (Are we going) a comer algo? When asked this question, the people pictured below all answered **sí,** but they all wanted different things. Match each statement with the appropriate drawing.

1.

2.

3.

4.

a. Yo quisiera comer unas tapas y tomar algo bien frío.
b. A mí me gusta la comida mexicana... Mm..., ¡tacos y frijoles con arroz!
c. Yo deseo un café con leche y un sándwich.
d. Nosotros deseamos unos licuados de fresas con unos bocadillos.

Capítulo 3 ¿Te gusta la comida mexicana? **49**

TEACH/MODEL

Pronunciación

PRESENTATION

 TEXTBOOK CASSETTE/CD CASSETTE 1, SIDE A; CD 1, TRACK 20

TAPESCRIPT P. 190

Continue to emphasize the tense, clipped nature of the Spanish vowels. Contrast the difference between the *u* of the English word *rule* and the **u** of the Spanish word **su**. Stress the fact that the **u** in Spanish can never be pronounced like the *you* sound in many English words. Write *university* and **universidad** on the board and say each word so that students can hear the difference. Follow with **Cuba**, pronouncing it in both languages.

Then have students listen to the explanation for the vowel **u** on the Textbook Cassette/CD. The speaker will model the correct pronunciation of the words in **Práctica D**. Have students follow along in their texts and repeat after each word.

Auditory-Musical

Linguistic Comparisons 4.1

PRACTICE/APPLY

E. ¡Hola! ¿Que tal?

VARIATION

 Assign each item to a different group of students, setting a time limit. Tell them to use body language and to vary their responses as much as possible. Then have each pair (or group of three) present their mini-dialogue to the class. Have the class listen for mistakes in formal/informal language and correct them after each presentation.

Bodily-Kinesthetic

Presentational Communication 1.3

PRONUNCIACIÓN THE VOWEL u

The sound of the vowel **u** in Spanish is pronounced like the **u** of the English word *rule*, except it is shorter in Spanish.

Práctica

D. Listen and repeat as your teacher models the following words.

1. tú
2. lunes
3. Perú
4. un
5. gusta
6. saludos
7. Cuba
8. mucho
9. jugo
10. música

Repaso

E. ¡Hola! ¿Qué tal? With classmates, play the roles of the people depicted in each of the following situations. Pay attention to the level of language—whether it should be formal or informal according to the situation. Follow the model.

Silvia   Cristina

MODELO		
	Silvia:	*¡Hola, Cristina!*
	Cristina:	*¡Hola! ¿Qué tal, Silvia?*
	Silvia:	*Muy bien. ¿Y tú?*
	Cristina:	*Mm… más o menos.*

1. Sr. González   Srta. Díaz   2. Enrique   Antonio   3. Héctor   Teresa   Samuel

50 *Primera unidad* Vamos a tomar algo

Focus on Culture

Roots of Mexican Cuisine

Point out that much of Mexican cuisine dates back to pre-Columbian times. Corn, beans, and chile peppers have been an important part of the Native American diet for thousands of years. The Aztecs and other native peoples made chile sauce with tomatoes, onions, and chile peppers to flavor their foods. **Molcajetes** (grinding stones) used to grind corn to make tortillas have been discovered at many ruins that pre-date Aztec and Mayan history. **Mole** was a very popular sauce with the Aztecs and other indigenous peoples. **Atole**, a hot drink made of sweetened corn meal and water, was also a favorite of early native Mexicans, and is still popular today.

Connections with Other Disciplines 3.1

4. Amalia   Clara   Sra. Rivas

5. Aldo   Luis

6. Sra.   Gerardo
Mendoza

F. **¿Te gusta bailar?**
SUGGESTIONS

TRB: ACTIVITY MASTER, P. 69

Have students use the chart on their activity master to survey three classmates. Have them keep track of the answers on the activity master, so they can report back to the class. Be sure to set a time limit for this and all other full-class activities.

Presentational Communication 1.3

F. **¿Te gusta bailar?**   For each activity listed, survey three classmates. Ask them whether they like the activity. Keep track of their answers on your activity master, writing their names in the appropriate columns. Follow the model.

> **MODELO**   bailar
>> **Tú:** *Luisa, ¿te gusta bailar?*
>> **Luisa:** *Sí, me gusta mucho bailar. o: Sí, yo bailo mucho.*
>>
>> **Tú:** *Tomás, ¿te gusta bailar?*
>> **Tomás:** *No, me gusta muy poco bailar. o: No, yo bailo muy poco.*
>>
>> **Tú:** *Rafael, ¿te gusta bailar?*
>> **Rafael:** *No, me gusta poco bailar.*

	muy poco	poco	mucho	muchísimo
bailar	Tomás	Rafael	Luisa	
cantar				
estudiar				
hablar español				
tomar café				
mirar la TV				
viajar				
trabajar en clase				
ganar dinero				

Capítulo 3 ¿Te gusta la comida mexicana?   **51**

Estructura

FYI

Please note that the expression **Allí están** is lexical only at this point. The verb **estar** will be presented for active use in Chapter 8. Start out by telling students that they are going to learn a new verb that does not follow the pattern that they have studied so far.

PRESENTATION

 TRANSPARENCY 18

Engage in a conversation with students about where you are from and where they are from. For example: **Yo soy de Houston, Texas. Yo no soy de Michigan. ¿Y tú? ¿Tú eres de Texas también?** Then summarize the student's answer. **Él/ella es de ____.** Continue asking questions and when two students come from the same place, say **Ellos/ellas son de ____.** To practice the **nosotros** form, refer to a well-known person. **Yo soy de Texas y el senador X es de Texas también. El senador y yo somos de Texas. Nosotros somos de Texas.** When all the forms have been established, write the conjugations on the board. Make up sentences and have students repeat them first together, and then individually. Present **¿De dónde + ser?** by making simple statements about people whose origin students are likely to know. For example: **Yo soy de Ohio. El senador X es de Ohio. El presidente no es de Ohio. ¿De dónde es el presidente? ¿De dónde es ____?**, etc.

Practice the negative form by giving more sentences and having students change them to the negative. Remind them that to do so, they should use **no** before the verb.

You could also show students the transparency of the map. Mention famous Latinos and ask where they are from. **¿De dónde es Gabriela Sabatini?** After mentioning the origins of several using the **Es de ____** form, question students about them again to see if they remember.

 Connections with Other Disciplines 3.1

ESTRUCTURA

The present tense of the verb *ser*

Pablo: ¡Hola! **Yo soy** Pablo Hernández. Y tú, ¿quién *(who)* **eres?**
Tomás: **Yo soy** Tomás García.

Pablo: ¿De dónde **eres,** Tomás?
Tomás: **Soy** de Bogotá, Colombia. ¿Y tú?
Pablo: **Yo soy** de Lima, Perú.

Pablo: ¡Mira! Allí están *(There are)* Luisa y Raquel.
Tomás: ¿También **son** de Lima?

Luisa: No, **nosotras somos** de los Estados Unidos.
Raquel: Sí, **somos** de Miami.

ser *(to be)*			
yo	**soy**	nosotros(as)	**somos**
tú	**eres**	vosotros(as)	**sois**
él		ellos	
ella	**es**	ellas	**son**
Ud.		Uds.	

1. Some important Spanish verbs like the verb **ser** are irregular. This means that they do not follow a regular conjugation pattern, so you need to memorize their forms.

2. To ask where someone or something is from, use the expression **¿de dónde + ser?** To express place of origin, use **ser + de** followed by the name of a country or city.

—¿De dónde son Uds?   *Where are you from?*
—Somos de Bolivia.   *We are from Bolivia.*

☀ Spanish for Spanish Speakers

Dialect Variations

Most Spanish speakers will already know the forms of the verb **ser**. A common dialectal variation involves the **nosotros** form: some Spanish speakers will use the form **semos** instead of **somos**.

🌐 Linguistic Comparisons 4.1

PALABRAS ÚTILES

Names of countries

Here are the names of places and countries in the world where Spanish is spoken, as well as the names of some other countries.

Países de habla hispana (Spanish-speaking countries)

(la) Argentina	Honduras
Bolivia	México
Chile	Nicaragua
Colombia	Panamá
Costa Rica	(el) Paraguay
Cuba	(el) Perú
(el) Ecuador	Puerto Rico
El Salvador	(la) República Dominicana
España	(el) Uruguay
Guatemala	Venezuela

Otros países

Alemania *Germany*	Inglaterra *England*
(el) Canadá	Italia
(la) China	(el) Japón
(los) Estados Unidos	Rusia
Francia	Vietnam

The Spanish term for the United States (los **Estados Unidos**) is often abbreviated **los EE.UU.** *(the U.S.).*

Aquí practicamos

G. Ellos no son de los Estados Unidos Even though a great number of Spanish-speaking people live in the United States, many were not born here. When you ask them if they are from the U.S., they tell you where they are from originally. Using the cues, ask and answer questions with a partner according to the model.

> **MODELO** Julia / Cuba
> **Tú:** *Julia, ¿eres de los Estados Unidos?*
> **Julia:** *No, no soy de los Estados Unidos. Soy de Cuba.*

1. Jorge / Guatemala	5. Daniel / Paraguay
2. Patricia / Ecuador	6. Luisa / Bolivia
3. Ángela / Argentina	7. Francisco / Venezuela
4. Mercedes / Colombia	

Capítulo 3 ¿Te gusta la comida mexicana? **53**

Palabras útiles

VOCABULARY EXPANSION
You may want to add other countries to the list, such as **Austria, Bélgica, Camboya, Corea, Dinamarca, Egipto, Escocia, Finlandia, Grecia, Holanda, India, Irak, Irán, Israel, Noruega, Portugal, Suecia, Suiza,** and **Turquía.**

G. Ellos no son de los Estados Unidos

 TRANSPARENCY 18

ANSWERS
1. Jorge, ¿eres de los Estados Unidos? No, no soy de los Estados Unidos. Soy de Guatemala.

Answers 2-7 will follow the same format.

☀ Spanish for Spanish Speakers

Telling Birthplaces
Have students ask Spanish speakers if they are from the United States. Spanish speakers should answer **Sí, soy de los Estados Unidos.** or **No, no soy de los Estados Unidos. Soy de _____,** according to their countries of origin.

Focus on Culture

The Spanish-Speaking World
If you haven't done **Etapas C** and **D** of the **Etapas preliminares** in the Teacher's Resource Book, take this time to discuss the Spanish-speaking world (capital cities, geographical diversity, etc.). Use the transparencies or have students look at the maps on pp. xvii, xviii, and xix. If you have already done this, review capitals and other cultural information.

 Connections with Other Disciplines 3.1

H. ¿De dónde eres?

SUGGESTION

If more than one student in the group is from the same state, have the student reporting practice using various forms of **ser**: **Anita y James son de Nueva York, Duane es de Indiana, y yo soy de Nuevo México.**

Aquí escuchamos

TEXTBOOK CASSETTE/CD CASSETTE 1, SIDE A; CD 1, TRACK 21

TAPESCRIPT P. 191

Antes de escuchar

ANSWERS
1. **tacos** and **enchiladas**
2. *Answers may vary.*

Después de escuchar

ANSWERS
1. late morning or lunchtime
2. **un refresco** or **una limonada**
3. no
4. yes
5. Costa Rican, Spanish

H. ¿De dónde eres?
Find out where five of your classmates were born. Then be prepared to report the results to the class. Follow the model.

MODELO		
	Tú:	*Anita, ¿de dónde eres?*
	Anita:	*Soy de Nueva York.*
	Tú:	*Anita es de Nueva York.*

Aquí escuchamos

En un restaurante mexicano *Carolina and her friends are at a Mexican restaurant.*

Antes de escuchar Think about vocabulary you might hear in the conversation at the restaurant. Then, answer the following questions.

1. What do people often eat for lunch or dinner in Mexico?
2. What Mexican dishes would you order if you were with Carolina and her friends?

A escuchar Listen twice to the conversation, and pay attention to what is ordered and to what the friends reveal about themselves.

Después de escuchar Answer the following questions based on what you heard.

1. At approximately what time of day does the conversation take place?
2. Name one of the drinks you heard ordered.
3. Does Pepe order anything to eat or drink?
4. Does Pepe like hot and spicy food?
5. What nationalities are represented in the group of friends?

Focus on Culture

Tex-Mex and Mexican Food

Much of the food served at Mexican restaurants in the United States are really North American inventions. The typical ground beef **taco** at fast-food restaurants would surprise most Mexicans, for whom a **taco** is anything you roll up inside a soft corn tortilla (except ground beef). Traditional Mexican **tacos** are usually served with chopped onion and cilantro and with a choice of sauces. **Flautas** are rolled and fried and are usually served with sour cream, crumbled fresh white cheese, shredded lettuce, and hot sauce.

Cultural Products and Perspectives 2.2

¡ADELANTE!

 Intercambio (Exchange) Ask a classmate the following questions. After answering them, he (she) will ask you the same set of questions.

1. ¿De dónde eres tú?
2. ¿Quisieras viajar a México?
3. ¿Te gusta la comida mexicana?
4. ¿Deseas comer en un restaurante mexicano?
5. ¿Qué quisieras comer?

 Mis actividades Write a list of six different activities that you like to do. Be prepared to report them back to the class.

Capítulo 3 ¿Te gusta la comida mexicana? **55**

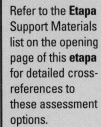
 Spanish for Spanish Speakers

Expanding Range of Contexts

In the **Intercambio** activity, have students focus on using vocabulary that may be new for them. Emphasize that it may be necessary to use such vocabulary when talking to speakers who are from other parts of the Spanish-speaking world. This is a good place to have them focus on the differences between how they say something in their speech community and how the book is teaching them to express this, validating both.

Connections with Distinctive Viewpoints 3.2

 ETAPA SYNTHESIS

Intercambio

SUGGESTION

 Have students work in pairs asking each other questions. Then have them report back to the class by asking questions randomly. **María, ¿de dónde es tu compañero/compañera?**, etc.

Individual Needs

Less-prepared Students
Students can underline the verbs in each question and then determine what is being asked before attempting to answer. You may also wish to provide question and answer cards that they can read and match prior to doing the activity orally.

 Logical-Mathematical

Mis actividades

FYI

ATAJO WRITING ASSISTANT SOFTWARE

You might want to have students use this software program when doing this activity.

SUGGESTION

Have students categorize their activities. For example, what do they like to do after school? What do they like to do to celebrate their birthdays?

 Categorizing

Additional Practice and Recycling

FYI

WORKBOOK, PP. 25-28

For recycling and additional practice of the vocabulary, structures, and language functions presented throughout this **etapa**, you can assign the workbook activities as in-class work and/or homework. Answers to the activities are overprinted on each page of the Teacher's Edition of the Workbook.

¡Qué comida más rica!

PRESENTATION

 TRANSPARENCIES 19

TEXTBOOK CASSETTE/CD CASSETTE 1, SIDE A; CD 1, TRACK 22

TAPESCRIPT P. 191

 Use the dialogue as a listening comprehension activity, playing the recording from the Textbook Cassette/CD. If possible, show the transparency of the menu for **Restaurante la Estancia**. Then ask students what the people are eating in the photo on this page.

Auditory- Musical

VARIATION

Read the dialogue, having students repeat first as a whole class, then in groups, and then individually. Then point out the adjectives used to describe food. Introduce new vocabulary, such as **delicioso**, **¡Qué picante!**, and **Es riquísima** and write these expressions on the board. Mention different foods and have students comment using the expressions.

Interpretive Communication 1.2

SEGUNDA ETAPA

- Can you describe the difference between an **enchilada** and a **taco?**
- Do you like **salsa de chile?** Do you prefer **salsa** that is hot, medium, or mild?
- Have you ever had **flan** for dessert? If so, do you like it? Why or why not?

¡Qué comida más rica!

Sara y Carlos van a pedir comida mexicana.

Sara: Mm... ¡Qué comida más rica! ¿Qué es?
Señora: Son enchiladas con **salsa de chile.**
Carlos: ¡Ay!... **¡Qué picante!** No me gusta. Es muy picante para mí.
Señor: **Aquí hay otra** enchilada que no es picante.
Carlos: Mm... ¡Sí! **¡Ésta** es **riquísima!**
Sara: Carlos, el **flan** es delicioso también.
Carlos: Sí. ¡Qué **bueno!**
Sara: Me gusta mucho la comida mexicana. Es muy diferente de la comida **norteamericana.**

chile: *a pepper ranging from mild to very hot; used to make sauces*

flan: *common dessert in Hispanic countries; baked custard topped with caramel sauce*

¡Qué comida más rica! *What delicious food!* Qué *What* salsa de chile *hot pepper sauce* ¡Qué picante! *How hot (spicy)!* Aquí hay otra *Here is another* Ésta *This one* riquísima *delicious* flan *custard* bueno *good* norteamericana *from the U.S.*

Etapa Support Materials

- Workbook: pp. 29-33
- TRB: Textbook Activity Masters: pp. 70, 71
- Textbook Cassettes/CDs

- Tapescript: Textbook Cassettes/CDs
- Overhead Transparency: 19
- Middle School Activities: pp. 25-29
- Lesson Plan Book

- Testing Program: Quiz pp. 26, 27; Answer Key & Testing Cassettes Tapescript pp. T10, T11
- Testing Cassettes: Cassette Side A
- Computerized Testing Program: Windows™; Macintosh®
- Atajo Writing Assistant Software: Student Text p. 62

¡Te toca a ti!

A. ¿Qué tal es? (What is it like?) Complete and rewrite the sentences according to your food preferences. If the noun is masculine, use the ending **-o** for the adjective; if it is feminine, use the ending **-a**. Follow the model.

> **MODELO** *El flan es* delicioso.

1. _____ riquísimo(a).
2. _____ rico(a).
3. _____ malo(a) *(bad)*.
4. _____ horrible.
5. _____ bueno(a).
6. _____ picante.

B. ¿Cómo (How) son? What is your opinion of the following foods? Tell what you think about each one. Follow the model.

> **MODELO** un taco con salsa
> *Un taco con salsa es muy picante. No me gusta.*

1. una hamburguesa
2. un pastel de fresas
3. una enchilada de queso
4. un croissant
5. un flan
6. un bocadillo de jamón

Repaso ♻

C. ¿De dónde son estas comidas? Ask a classmate where these foods come from. He (she) should answer accordingly. Follow the model.

> **MODELO** la salsa de chile
> **Tú:** *¿De dónde es la salsa de chile?*
> **Compañero(a):** *Es de México.*

1. las enchiladas
2. la tortilla de patatas
3. el croissant
4. las hamburguesas
5. las patatas bravas

ESTRUCTURA

Adjectives of nationality and noun-adjective agreement

País	Adjetivo	País	Adjetivo
Alemania	alemán (alemana)	Chile	chileno(a)
Argentina	argentino(a)	China	chino(a)
Bolivia	boliviano(a)	Colombia	colombiano(a)
Canadá	canadiense	Costa Rica	costarricense

Capítulo 3 ¿Te gusta la comida mexicana? **57**

Focus on Culture

Street Markets

Have students study the photo on page 56. Explain that the food stand is at a street market (called **tianguis** in Mexico). At these markets people buy and sell everything from household goods to clothing to food, and they are set up every week on the same day and in the same place.

🌐 Cultural Practices and Perspectives 2.1

PRACTICE / APPLY

A. ¿Qué tal es?
VARIATION

Have students use a chart to describe how they feel about the food items below. Create a chart with the following headings on the top row: **picante, riquísimo(a), rico(a), bueno(a), malo(a), horrible**.

List the following items in the first column: **una hamburguesa, un pastel de fresas, una enchilada de queso, un licuado de banana, un croissant, un flan, un bocadillo de jamón** and **un taco de pollo**. Ask the class for their opinions and mark their answers with an X under the appropriate adjective.

🔆 Categorizing
Evaluating

B. ¿Cómo son?
VARIATION

Do as a **pregúntale** activity (**María, pregúntale a Juan si le gusta...**) or have students work with partners, asking questions with **¿Te gusta... ?** Make sure that they follow the model. You may want to do a couple as a whole class before they work in pairs.

C. ¿De dónde son estas comidas?
SUGGESTIONS

Have students work in pairs or do as a whole class activity using the **pregúntale** format. Point out that if the food item is plural, they must use **¿De dónde son... ?** You may want to do a couple of questions as a whole class first.

🔍 Activating Prior Knowledge

ANSWERS

1. ¿De dónde son las enchiladas?
   Son de México.
2. ¿De dónde es la tortilla de patatas?
   Es de España.
3. ¿De dónde es el croissant?
   Es de España (Francia).
4. ¿De dónde son las hamburguesas?
   Son de los Estados Unidos.
5. ¿De dónde son las patatas bravas?
   Son de España.

Estructura

PRESENTATION

Ask yes/no questions with adjectives of nationality as you show pictures of famous foreign people. Or make statements mentioning the nationalities of famous people (both male and female) that students are likely to know, and have students repeat. Stress the endings in these statements to emphasize the differences in masculine and feminine forms.

Then introduce the adjectives of nationality that appear in point two. Write them on the board in two groups, masculine and feminine. Point out that, in Spanish, adjectives of nationality are not capitalized. Then point out the differences in spelling between forms, such as adding an -**a** and dropping the accent.

◣◢ Visual-Spatial

VOCABULARY EXPANSION

Tell students that the use of an article with certain countries is becoming optional. Some countries such as **(la) Argentina, (el) Canadá, (la) China, (el) Ecuador, (los) Estados Unidos, (el) Japón (el) Paraguay, (el) Perú,** and **(el) Uruguay** may or may not take an article. Mention additonal adjectives of nationality: **camboyano, coreano, filipino, haitiano, laosiano, samoano** (all with four forms like **cubano** and **peruano**); **tailandés** (with four forms like **inglés** or **francés**); **israelí, iraquí, iraní** (all with only two forms like **iraní, iraníes**); **vietnamita** (with only two forms: **vietnamita** for masculine or feminine singular and **vietnamitas** for the plural). Students do not need to learn all of these additional adjectives of nationality for production. They should be encouraged to choose those that are most related to their personal family situations and their community.

ESTRUCTURA (CONTINUED)

País	Adjetivo	País	Adjetivo
Cuba	cubano(a)	Nicaragua	nicaragüense
Ecuador	ecuatoriano(a)	Panamá	panameño(a)
El Salvador	salvadoreño(a)	Paraguay	paraguayo(a)
España	español(a)	Perú	peruano(a)
Estados Unidos	estadounidense	Puerto Rico	puertorriqueño(a)
Francia	francés (francesa)	la República Dominicana	dominicano(a)
Guatemala	guatemalteco(a)		
Honduras	hondureño(a)	Rusia	ruso(a)
Inglaterra	inglés (inglesa)	Uruguay	uruguayo(a)
Italia	italiano(a)	Venezuela	venezolano(a)
Japón	japonés (japonesa)	Vietnam	vietnamita
México	mexicano(a)		

In Spanish, adjectives agree in gender (masculine or feminine) and number (singular and plural) with the person or thing to which they refer.

1. Adjectives that end in -**o** are masculine. Change the -**o** to -**a** to obtain the feminine form.

Él es **argentino.**   Ella es **argentina.**

2. Singular adjectives that end in a consonant (-**l, -n, -s**) form the feminine by adding an -**a**. Note that, if there is a written accent on the final vowel of the masculine singular adjective, it is dropped in the feminine singular form.

Él es **español.**   Ella es **española.**
Él es **alemán.**   Ella es **alemana.**
Él es **japonés.**   Ella es **japonesa.**

3. Some adjectives have identical masculine and feminine forms.

Él es **estadounidense.**   Ella es **estadounidense.**
Él es **vietnamita.**   Ella es **vietnamita.**

4. To form the plural of adjectives that end in a vowel, simply add -s to the masculine or feminine singular forms. If the singular form ends in a consonant, add -es for masculine adjectives and -as for feminine adjectives.

Ellos son **mexicanos.**   Ellas son **mexicanas.**
Ellos son **españoles.**   Ellas son **españolas.**
Ellos son **canadienses.**   Ellas son **canadienses.**

5. All inhabitants of North, Central, and South America live in the Americas (**las Américas**) and are, thus, Americans (**americanos**). Therefore, to express that someone or something is from the United States, use either **estadounidense** or **norteamericano(a)**.

 The Standards

- Interpersonal Communication 1.1: B, C, D, E, G
- Interpretive Communication 1.2: A, F
- Presentational Communication 1.3: **Mini-descripción**
- Cultural Products and Perspectives 2.2: **¡Qué comida más rica!**, C, H
- Connections with Distinctive Viewpoints 3.2: B, **En la feria de la comida**
- Cultural Comparisons 4.2: C

Focus on Culture

Americano

Point out that the term **americano** is often synonymous with citizens of the United States, but it is sometimes offensive to people outside the United States, since all inhabitants of North, Central, or South America are **americanos**. Thus, **norteamericano** is the best word to refer to people from the United States.

 Cultural Practices and Perspectives 2.1

Aquí practicamos

D. ¿Y David? Answer the questions according to the model. In the first four items, the first person is female and the second is male.

> **MODELO**   Alicia es venezolana. ¿Y Alberto?
> *Él es venezolano también.*

1. Gladis es colombiana. ¿Y Fernando?
2. Ester es cubana. ¿Y José?
3. Adelita es peruana. ¿Y Pepito?
4. Marilú es española. ¿Y Paco?

In the next four items, the first person is male and the second person is female.

> **MODELO**   Pancho es boliviano. ¿Y Marta?
> *Ella es boliviana también.*

5. Luis es costarricense. ¿Y Clara?
6. Pedro es argentino. ¿Y Luisa?
7. Miguel es panameño. ¿Y Teresa?
8. Tomás es puertorriqueño. ¿Y Elena?

E. Las nacionalidades You are with a group of young people from all over the world. Find out their nationalities by making the assumptions indicated, asking a friend, and then correcting your mistakes. Follow the model.

> **MODELO**   Margarita — argentina / Nueva York
> **Tú:**   ¿Margarita es argentina?
> **Amiga(o):**   No, ella es de Nueva York.
> **Tú:**   Ah, ella es estadounidense entonces (then).
> **Amiga(o):**   Claro, es estadounidense.

1. Lin-Tao (m.) — japonés / Pekín
2. Sofía — mexicana / Roma
3. Jean-Pierre — francés / Quebec
4. Jill — canadiense / Londres
5. Hilda y Lorena — colombianas / Berlín
6. Olga y Nicolás — venezolanos / Moscú

Capítulo 3 ¿Te gusta la comida mexicana?   **59**

PRACTICE/APPLY

D. ¿Y David?

SUGGESTIONS

Have students work in pairs following the model carefully. Make sure that they substitute the names with subject pronouns when responding. You could also do this activity with the whole class by having one student read each item and having another respond. Example: **Juan, lee el número uno. María, contesta.**

ANSWERS

1. Él es colombiano también.
2. Él es cubano también.
3. Él es peruano también.
4. Él es español también.
5. Ella es costarricense también.
6. Ella es argentina también.
7. Ella es panameña también.
8. Ella es puertorriqueña también.

E. Las nacionalidades

ANSWERS

1. ¿Lin-Tao es japonés? No, él es de Pekín. Ah, él es chino entonces. Claro, es chino.
2. ¿Sofía es mexicana? No, ella es de Roma. ...es italiana... .
3. ¿Jean-Pierre es francés? No, él es de Quebec. ...es canadiense... .
4. ¿Jill es canadiense? No, ella es de Londres. ...es inglesa... .
5. ¿Hilda y Lorena son colombianas? No, ellas son de Berlín. ...son alemanas... .
6. ¿Olga y Nicolás son venezolanos? No, ellos son de Moscú. ...son rusos... .

VARIATION

Test students' knowledge of Latin American and Spanish capitals by saying statements such as **Soy de Tegucigalpa** and having them guess, **¿Es usted de Honduras? Sí, soy hondureño.**

Connections with Other Disciplines 3.1

☀ Spanish for Spanish Speakers

Problematic Spellings

Have students focus on the spelling of those words with any problematic combinations. For example, point out the **rr, c,** and **s** in **costarricense; v** in **boliviano; cu** in **ecuatoriano; h** in **hondureño; güe** in **nicaragüense; y** in **paraguayo** and **uruguayo; rr** and **qu** in **puertorriqueño; z** in **venezolano.**

 Linguistic

Focus on Culture

Puerto Rico

Remind students that Puerto Ricans are citizens of the United States and are able to enter and leave the country without passports or visas. Puerto Rico is a commonwealth of the U.S., uses the same currency, and is subject to federal laws. However, Puerto Ricans cannot vote in U.S. elections unless they establish their residency on the mainland.

Cultural Comparisons 4.2

Nota gramatical

PRESENTATION

Make statements with the cognates among the new vocabulary words, stressing with your voice the difference between the masculine and feminine forms. Bring in pictures of people in different identifiable occupations and have students repeat sentences about them. Have students repeat the names of occupations listed in the first point. Make statements using the masculine form and have students change them to the feminine. Continue this procedure with points two, three, and four. Have students look at the photographs on page 60. Ask them: What do you think are the professions of these two people? Why do you think that? Have them list logical possibilities among the words they have just learned and provide supporting reasons.

🔍 Drawing Inferences

VOCABULARY EXPANSION

Mention other nouns for professions, such as **actor, actriz, asistente social** (**trabajador/trabajadora social** in some countries), **carpintero/carpintera, científico/científica, consejero/consejera, electricista, empleado/empleada, fotógrafo/fotógrafa, gerente, jefe, programador/programadora, psicólogo/psicóloga, vendedor/vendedora.** Write these occupations on the board and ask students about their parents' occupations: **Mi mamá es enfermera. ¿Tú mamá es enfermera también?** or **¿Qué es tu mamá/papá?** You may also want to mention some words for workplaces, such as **escuela, oficina, hospital, fábrica** (factory). Ask students to mention some occupations for each workplace.

🔗 Interpretive Communication 1.2

NOTA GRAMATICAL

Nouns for professions

Most nouns that refer to work or occupation follow the same patterns as adjectives of nationality.

1. If the masculine ends in -o, the feminine form changes -o to -a.

Él es **abogado** *(lawyer)*.	Ella es **abogada**.
Él es **secretario** *(secretary)*.	Ella es **secretaria**.
Él es **ingeniero** *(engineer)*.	Ella es **ingeniera**.
Él es **enfermero** *(nurse)*.	Ella es **enfermera**.
Él es **médico** *(doctor)*.	Ella es **médica**.

2. Nouns that end in the consonant -r form the feminine by adding -a to the end of the word.

Él es **contador** *(accountant)*.	Ella es **contadora**.

3. Nouns that end in the vowel -e, as well as those that end in -ista, have the same masculine and feminine forms.

Él es **estudiante**.	Ella es **estudiante**.
Él es **periodista** *(journalist)*.	Ella es **periodista**.

4. Nouns for professions form their plural in the same way as the adjectives of nationality. Add -s to the masculine or feminine singular form if the noun ends in a vowel. If the singular form ends in a consonant, add -es or -as.

Ellos son **abogados**.	Ellas son **abogadas**.
Ellos son **estudiantes**.	Ellas son **estudiantes**.
Ellos son **profesores**.	Ellas son **profesoras**.

Aquí practicamos

F. ¿El señor Martínez? Él es... You and a friend are attending a function with your parents. You point out to your friend various acquaintances of your parents and state their professions. Follow the models.

MODELOS   Sr. Martínez / abogado
               ¿El señor Martínez? Él es abogado.

               Sr. y Sra. Martínez / ingeniero
               ¿El señor y la señora Martínez? Ellos son ingenieros.

1. Sr. y Sra. Herrera / médico
2. Sr. Pérez / profesor
3. Sr. y Sra. López / abogado
4. Sra. Quintana / secretario
5. Sra. Dávila / ingeniero
6. Sr. y Sra. Valdés / profesor
7. Patricio / estudiante de universidad
8. Sra. González / contador
9. Roberta / estudiante de colegio
10. Sr. y Sra. Chávez / periodista

G. Yo quisiera ser abogado(a) From the following list, choose several careers or jobs that you would like and several that you would not like. Which of these careers or jobs would you most like to have? Which of these careers or jobs would you not want to have? Follow the model to answer these questions.

MODELO   *Yo quisiera ser médico(a), pero no quisiera ser abogado(a).*

periodista	hombre (mujer) de negocios	médico(a)
dentista	(*businessman, businesswoman*)	ingeniero(a)
profesor(a)	abogado(a)	enfermero(a)
secretario(a)	camarero(a)	contador(a)

Aquí escuchamos

Descripción personal *María Victoria Rodríguez, a Mexican-American, introduces herself.*

Antes de escuchar Based on what you have learned in this **etapa**, think about the sort of information that you might hear in a personal description.

 A escuchar Listen twice to the description before answering the true-or-false questions about it on your activity master.

? ¿Qué crees?

Approximately how many people of Spanish-speaking origin are there in the United States?

a) fewer than 10 million
b) 15 million
c) more than 20 million

respuesta 🖙

☀ **Spanish for Spanish Speakers**

Adjective Variations

Ask Spanish speakers what adjectives they could use to describe the food items that they have tried. Ask them for variations. Help them with the spelling of the variations they provide. Point out to them that **riquísimo** is spelled with a **qu** and **hay** with an **h**.

☀ **Spanish for Spanish Speakers**

Expansion

For Activity G, have Spanish speakers come up with questions based on the selected professions, such as: **¿Qué profesiones son las más populares? ¿Cuáles requieren más educación? ¿Para qué profesiones es necesario viajar?** The rest of the class should repeat the question, and then answer.

🔎 Determining Preferences
🌐 Interpretive Communication 1.2

PRACTICE / APPLY

F. ¿El señor Martínez? Él es...

SUGGESTIONS

Have students work in pairs, following the model. Emphasize the use of the definite article **el** or **la** before the titles **señor** and **señora**. Mention that when saying *Mr. and Mrs.* in Spanish (**el Sr. y la Sra.**), Spanish speakers may use an abbreviated version: **los Sres. García (los señores García).** Give them that option when they complete the activity. They should be able to say **los Sres.** in number 1, 3, 6, and 10. Also, remind students that when an adjective refers to a pair or a group of males and females, it takes on the same form as the masculine plural.

ANSWERS

1. ¿El Sr. y la Sra. Herrera? Ellos son médicos.
2. ¿El Sr. Pérez? Él es profesor.
3. ¿El Sr. y la Sra López? Ellos son abogados.
4. ¿La Sra. Quintana? Ella es secretaria.
5. ¿La Sra. Dávila? Ella es ingeniera.
6. ¿El Sr. y la Sra. Valdés? Ellos son profesores.
7. ¿Patricio? Él es estudiante de universidad.
8. ¿La Sra. González? Ella es contadora.
9. ¿Roberta? Ella es estudiante de colegio.
10. ¿El Sr. y la Sra. Chávez? Ellos son periodistas.

G. Yo quisera ser abogado(a)

EXPANSION

Have students get into groups of six or eight and answer the question, **¿Qué quisieras ser?** The group recorder keeps a tally of the professions mentioned. Then have another student from each group report which professions were selected by their group and by whom: **Billy quisiera ser abogado; Ana y Bryan quisieran ser médicos.** Record on the board each profession and put a mark beside it each time it is selected.

🔎 Comparing and Contrasting
Determining Preferences
Evaluating

Aquí escuchamos

  TEXTBOOK CASSETTE/CD CASSETTE 1, SIDE A; CD 1, TRACK 23

  TAPESCRIPT P. 191

  TRB: ACTIVITY MASTER, P. 70

Después de escuchar
ANSWERS
1. False, she is from San Antonio, Texas.
2. True
3. True
4. True
5. False, she wants to study to be a lawyer and hopes to become a politician.
6. True

ETAPA SYNTHESIS

En la feria de la comida
SUGGESTION
Before beginning the activity, review by listing various countries, nationalities, and descriptions of food from those countries.

Mini-descripción
FYI

  ATAJO WRITING ASSISTANT SOFTWARE

You might want to have students use this software program when doing this activity.

EXPANSION
Have students make illustrations or collect photos to accompany their descriptions, and then compile them for inclusion in a classroom newsletter.

Additional Practice and Recycling
FYI

 WORKBOOK, PP. 29-33

For recycling and additional practice of the vocabulary, structures, and language functions presented throughout this **etapa**, you can assign the workbook activities as in-class work and/or homework. Answers to the activities are overprinted on each page of the Teacher's Edition of the Workbook.

Después de escuchar On your activity master, indicate whether the following statements are true or false. If a statement is false, provide the correct information in English.

1. María Victoria is from New Mexico.
2. María Victoria's parents are originally from Mexico.
3. Playing the guitar is one of María Victoria's favorite activities.
4. Studying is an important part of María Victoria's routine.
5. Someday María Victoria would like to be an actress.
6. María Victoria is concerned about the needs of other people.

 c

¡ADELANTE!

 En la feria de la comida You and a friend are at an international food fair.

1. You each name three foods that you wish to sample, describing each one. Choose foods from two different countries.
2. Each of you then describes someone from another country who is at the fair, telling the person's name, nationality, profession, and two interesting things that the person likes to do. Follow the model.

MODELO   *Allí está Juan. Él es cubano. Él es fotógrafo. Juan canta y baila bien.*

Mini-descripción Interview an adult. Write four to six sentences in Spanish describing her (him). Include basic information about the person, such as her (his) interests, activities, and profession. Be prepared to report back to the class on what you learned about this person.

EN LÍNEA
Connect with the Spanish-speaking world! Access the *¡Ya verás! Gold* home page for Internet activities related to this chapter.

http://yaveras.heinle.com

☀ Spanish for Spanish Speakers

Peer Editing

In the **Adelante** activities, have students pay special attention to the spelling of the vocabulary that has been introduced in this **etapa**, especially those words that may have problematic spelling combinations. This is a good place to have Spanish-speaking students engage in peer-editing. Have them look at the written work of a partner and correct spelling errors.

Additional Etapa Resources

Refer to the **Etapa** Support Materials list on the opening page of this **etapa** for detailed cross-references to these assessment options.

VOCABULARIO

VOCABULARIO

Para charlar   Temas y contextos

Para comentar sobre la comida

bueno
malo(a)
¡Qué comida más rica!
¡Qué picante!
riquísimo(a)

Las nacionalidades

alemán (alemana)
argentino(a)
boliviano(a)
canadiense
chileno(a)
chino(a)
colombiano(a)
costarricense
cubano(a)
dominicano(a)
ecuatoriano(a)
español(a)
estadounidense
francés (francesa)
guatemalteco(a)
hondureño(a)
inglés (inglesa)
italiano(a)
japonés (japonesa)
mexicano(a)
nicaragüense
norteamericano(a)
panameño(a)
paraguayo(a)
peruano(a)
puertorriqueño(a)
ruso(a)
salvadoreño(a)
uruguayo(a)
venezolano(a)
vietnamita

Los países

Alemania
Argentina
Bolivia
Canadá
Chile
China
Colombia
Costa Rica
Cuba
Ecuador
El Salvador
España
(los) Estados Unidos
Francia
Guatemala
Honduras
Inglaterra
Italia
Japón
México
Nicaragua
Panamá
Paraguay
Perú
Puerto Rico
la República Dominicana
Rusia
Uruguay
Venezuela
Vietnam

Capítulo 3 ¿Te gusta la comida mexicana?   **63**

Additional Chapter Resources

Refer to the Chapter Support Materials list on the opening page of this chapter for detailed cross-references to *¡Ya verás! Gold*'s student-centered technology components and various assessment options.

CHAPTER WRAP-UP

Vocabulario

PRESENTATION
Review the adjectives by mentioning different foods and having students describe them.

SUGGESTIONS
Collect or have students bring in a set of photos from magazines and newspapers of people of various occupations.

1) Show each photo to the class and have students try to guess the occupation depicted.

2) Divide the class into groups of four. Each student shows a photo and the group tries to guess the occupation.

3) Then, create new groups in which students present the *new* photos to a different set of classmates.

 Making Hypotheses

COUNTRIES AND NATIONALITIES GAME
With books closed, name a country and have students write down the corresponding adjective of nationality. Give points for each correct answer. You could divide the class into teams. Each team member must answer when it is his (her) turn and if this person cannot give the correct answer, then the other team has the opportunity to do so.

TEAM CHARADES GAME
Have the vocabulary words indicating occupation written out on individual cards. Put all the cards into a hat or box. Divide the class into teams of four. Place the teams in different parts of the room, so that teammates can communicate with each other without other teams overhearing. Ask one member from each team to pull a card from the hat or box. Each team should plan a charade representing the occupation they have drawn, and to present the charade to the other teams so they can try to guess their word.

VOCABULARIO

Listening Skills Development

FYI

 LAB MANUAL, PP. 14-20

 LAB CASSETTE SIDE A, CD 2, TRACKS 1-8

TAPESCRIPT: LAB PROGRAM PP. 18-27

It is now appropriate to work through the lab manual activities and their accompanying recordings in class or in the language laboratory. These materials provide reinforcement of the pronunciation points, vocabulary, structures, and language functions presented throughout the **etapas** and continue the development of listening comprehension skills provided in the **Aquí escuchamos** sections and the Improvised Conversation.

Improvised Conversation

PRESENTATION

 TEXTBOOK CASSETTE/CD CASSETTE 1, SIDE A; CD 1, TRACK 24

 TAPESCRIPT PP. 191-192

 TRB: ACTIVITY MASTER, P. 71

Have students listen to this conversation in which three people try to decide on a restaurant. Refer to the TRB for student activities.

Resources for Spanish-speaking Students

FYI

 WORKBOOK FOR SPANISH-SPEAKING STUDENTS: PP. 13-18

 ANSWER KEY TO SSS WORKBOOK PP. 5-7

Activities specially written to meet the needs of Spanish-speaking students are available in this workbook for the reinforcement and extension of the topics and language presented in this chapter.

Vocabulario continued

Temas y contextos	Vocabulario general
La comida mexicana	**Verbos**
arroz	ser
carne	
chile	**Otras palabras y expresiones**
una enchilada	Allí está(n)…
flan	Aquí hay otro(a)…
unos frijoles	bien
una hamburguesa	bienvenidos(as)
pollo	cómo
salsa (de chile)	¿De dónde es (eres)?
un taco	ésta
una tortilla	está(n)
	intercambio
Las profesiones	¡Mira!
un(a) abogado(a)	¿Qué tal es?
un(a) contador(a)	¿Qué es?
un(a) dentista	¿Qué va(n) a pedir?
un(a) enfermero(a)	¿quién?
un(a) estudiante	ser de
un hombre (una mujer) de negocios	vamos
un(a) ingeniero(a)	
un(a) médico(a)	
un(a) periodista	
un(a) profesor(a)	
un(a) secretario(a)	

64 *Primera unidad* Vamos a tomar algo

 Spanish for Spanish Speakers

Keeping a Vocabulary Notebook
Remind Spanish-speaking students to add words and expressions from this vocabulary section to the problematic spelling combination categories and personal new vocabulary lists they started in their notebooks in Chapter 1. Reinforce that they should continue to do this each time a chapter in the textbook is completed.

ENCUENTROS CULTURALES

¡Qué delicioso!

Antes de leer

1. Look at the title above. Then look at the photos and the document on page 66. Based on these things, what do you expect the reading to be about?

2. Briefly skim the first paragraph of the reading. What kind of food do you think the reading is about?

3. This reading mentions dishes eaten in Cuba, Puerto Rico, the Dominican Republic, and Colombia. Look at a map of Latin America and locate each place.

> **Reading Strategies**
> - Using the title to predict content
> - Using photos, artwork and illustrations to predict content
> - Skimming for the gist

Para los españoles y los mexicanos, el plátano es lo mismo que la banana. Pero en la región del Caribe, el plátano es una fruta con una textura, tamaño y sabor muy diferente. También es un aspecto muy importante de la cultura. Muchas familias, especialmente las familias en áreas rurales, tienen un árbol de plátano en el patio de su casa.

Hay muchas maneras de preparar el plátano. Como parte de una fiesta internacional, un grupo de estudiantes en una escuela secundaria de Providence, Rhode Island celebra la comida criolla con unos platos que contienen plátano. En su mesa hay platos de Cuba, de Puerto Rico, de Colombia y de la República Dominicana. El menú para la fiesta está en la página 66.

Capítulo 3 ¿Te gusta la comida mexicana? **65**

PRACTICE/APPLY

¡Qué delicioso!
Antes de leer
ANSWERS
1. food, bananas, plantains
2. el plátano

Focus on Culture

The plantain

The plantain, a staple of the Caribbean diet, is used in its green form (**plátano verde**) and in its ripe form (**plátano maduro**). They can be prepared in a variety of ways: fried, cooked, mashed, mixed with other ingredients, as a side dish, dessert, snack or part of a main meal.

Cultural Products and Perspectives 2.2

La cocina criolla

SUGGESTION
Remind students that **cocina criolla** is used in many parts of Latin America to refer to food that is typical of a region. Ask students what kinds of foods might be typical of their region or country of origin.

Después de leer

ANSWERS
Answers will vary.

LA COCINA CRIOLLA

- **Los platanutres**
  como papitas, pero de plátano verde

- **Los tostones**
  plátanos fritos, como *french fries*

- **El piñón**
  un plato como lasaña, pero se usa plátano maduro en vez de pasta

- **El mofongo**
  después de cocinar el plátano verde, se le muele con tocino y especias

- **Los pasteles, o pastelones**
  como tamales pero se rellena la hoja del plátano con papas, plátano, carne y/o queso

- **Plátano con frijoles**
  una combinación rica de plátano, frijoles y tomate

- **Plátanos con salsa de caramelo**
  un plato dulce; se cocina plátano maduro en mantequilla, jugo de naranja y azúcar. Se sirve con helado de vainilla.

Guía para la lectura

1. Here are some words and expressions to keep in mind as you read.

plátano	*plantain*	**papitas**	*potato chips*
mismo	*same*	**se muele**	*it is ground*
tamaño	*size*	**tocino**	*bacon*
sabor	*taste*	**se rellena**	*one fills*
maneras	*ways*	**se cocina**	*one cooks*
platos	*dishes*	**azúcar**	*sugar*
mesa	*table*	**helado**	*ice cream*

2. **Papas** is the word for potatoes in Latin America. In Spain, they are called **patatas.**

Después de leer

1. Do you know anyone who prepares foods that include **plátano**? If so, compare and contrast these foods with those on the menu.

2. Which of the dishes mentioned on the menu sounds the most appetizing to you? Explain why.

3. If you were planning an international party for your school, what kinds of foods would you include? Explain your choices.

66 *Primera unidad* Vamos a tomar algo

Conversemos un rato

A. En el café Role-play the following situations with three other classmates.

1. You are in Puerto Rico on an exchange program in order to improve your Spanish. You run into a friend you've met at your daily language classes.

   a. Greet your friend and invite him (her) to join you at a nearby café.

   b. As you stroll to the café, talk about how things are going.

   c. At the café, interact with the waiter (waitress) to order something to eat and drink.

   d. Introduce your friend to another friend who arrives at the café.

2. With the same classmates, reenact your café conversation, but this time extend it so that you and your two friends get to know each other better.

   a. Find out what your newly arrived friend wants to eat and/or drink and place the order with the waiter (waitress).

   b. As your friends ask each other about their nationalities and origins, listen and try to encourage the conversation.

   c. Find out what languages all three of you are studying or know how to speak.

B. ¡Vamos a comer algo! You are with a group of friends chatting in a mall on a Saturday evening. With three or four classmates, role-play the following discussion about where you want to eat.

1. All members of the group suggest a place where they would like to go. Each suggestion should be supported by details that make the choice appealing.

2. As each person makes a suggestion, you and your friends react by indicating what you like and dislike about the place and its menu.

3. Reach an agreement with your friends about where the group will go.

67

¡Sigamos adelante! Resource

FYI

LESSON PLAN BOOK P. 18

You might find it helpful to refer to the Lesson Plan Book before you and your students begin the end-of-unit materials.

PRACTICE / APPLY

A. En el café

SUGGESTION

 You can have students use the list of foods in the advertisement of **Mesón del Pirata** on page 26 or the **cocina criolla** discussed on pages 65-66.

B. ¡Vamos a comer algo!

VARIATION

 Have students role-play the same situation but as members of the same family rather than as a group of friends.

 Presentational Communication 1.3

MULTIPLE INTELLIGENCES

- Auditory-Musical
- Bodily-Kinesthetic
- Interpersonal

The Standards

- Presentational Communication 1.3

Spanish for Spanish Speakers

Informal Situations

The situations in these activities are informal, but have the students focus on using vocabulary that may be new to them. Have them pay close attention to the differences between how they say something in their speech community and how the book is teaching them to express it.

 Activating Prior Knowledge

 Linguistic Comparisons 4.1

TEACH/MODEL

Taller de escritores Resource

FYI

 ATAJO WRITING ASSISTANT SOFTWARE

You might want to have students use this software program when writing the first draft and final version of their writing assignment. Tell them that the following language references in **Atajo** are directly related to and will be helpful to their work.

Phrases: Appreciating food; Describing objects; Expressing an opinion

Vocabulary: Food: Bread, cereals, cheeses, drinks, fish & seafood, fruits, legumes & vegetables, meat, nuts & dried fruit, pastry, spices, seasoning

Grammar: Articles: Indefinite **un**, **una**; Verbs: Present, Use of **gustar**, Use of **ser**

PRACTICE/APPLY

A. Reflexión

SUGGESTION

Remind students to refer for help in writing to the **Vocabulario** list at the end of each chapter, as well as to the **Estructura** and **Nota gramatical** sections in the **etapas**.

EXPANSION

With the whole class brainstorm a list of words and ideas to express feelings about food. Then have students look at the list to determine which of these words they know how to say in Spanish.

Linguistic

Taller de escritores

Writing extended picture captions

Como un pastel o un croissant todos los días. Son deliciosos, especialmente con chocolate o café con leche.

Writing Strategy
• List writing

A. Reflexión

You are going to increase your writing skills in Spanish by writing extended picture captions. Begin by drawing four illustrations or selecting four photos from magazines. Your art/selections should depict food you like and dislike. As you look at each food item, on a separate sheet of paper, write as many key words or phrases in Spanish as you can think of to express your feelings about the food.

MULTIPLE INTELLIGENCES

• Linguistic
• Interpersonal
• Visual-Spatial

*Deseo un sándwich de jamón.
No me gusta comer comida
dulce. Quisiera agua mineral
con el sándwich.*

B. Primer borrador Keeping in mind that the readers of your captions will be your classmates and teacher, write three to four related sentences for each picture you drew or selected. Refer back to Chapters 1-3 for vocabulary.

C. Revisión con un(a) compañero(a) Exchange papers with a classmate. Read each other's work and comment on it, based on the questions below.

1. What do you like best about your classmate's first draft?
2. What part do you find the clearest?
3. What part do you find the most interesting?
4. Does the first draft keep the audience in mind?
5. Does the writing reflect the task assigned?
6. Does the first draft raise questions that, if answered, you think would make the writing clearer, more interesting, or more complete?

D. Versión final At home, revise your first draft, incorporating changes based on the feedback from your classmate. Revise content and check your grammar, spelling, punctuation, and accent marks. Bring your final draft to class.

E. Carpeta After you turn in your art with captions, your teacher may choose to place it in your portfolio, display it on a bulletin board, or use it to evaluate your progress.

¡Sigamos adelante!   **69**

B. Primer borrador
SUGGESTION
Have students discuss why it is important to keep the audience in mind when writing captions.

 Evaluating

C. Revisión con un(a) compañero(a)
SUGGESTION
Model a peer review with the whole class by showing some sample captions on a transparency and answering the six revision questions together. Remind students to start their feedback with something positive and to include some constructive suggestions to improve the captions.

D. Versión final
SUGGESTION
Make students aware that they do not have to incorporate all the suggestions given by their classmates, but rather take the ideas or corrections that they feel would improve the content and expression of the message.

E. Carpeta
SUGGESTION
Point out to students that, as they keep adding samples of their written work to their **carpeta** (portfolio), they will be able to see the progress in their writing in Spanish.

The Standards

- Interpretive Communication 1.2
- Presentational Communication 1.3

Para empezar

VARIATION

Have students work in groups of three to complete this activity within a ten-minute time limit. Copy the following information on the board or an overhead transparency. Ask one student in each group to take one of these roles: 1) the "asker," who poses the questions **¿Dónde/Cuándo te gusta merendar?** to the other group members, and 2) the "presenter," who must be prepared to provide a report on the result of the group's findings to you or to the class.

¿Dónde te gusta merendar?
  En casa
  En la cocina _____
  Enfrente de la televisión _____
  En el sofá _____
  En mi cama _____
  ¿ ? _____
En la escuela
  En la clase de español _____
  En el patio de la escuela _____
  En el autobús _____
  En los pasillos _____

¿Cuándo te gusta merendar?
Por la mañana _____
Por la tarde _____
Por la noche _____
Todo el día _____
Antes de dormir _____
Después de hacer ejercicios _____
¿ ? _____

Determining Preferences

Conexión con las ciencias

Las meriendas y la buena nutrición

Para empezar Reading about science in Spanish is not as difficult as you might think. English and Spanish have many cognates. These are words that are spelled similarly in both languages and share the same meaning. For example, **nutrición, minerales**, and **proteínas** are cognates of *nutrition, minerals*, and *proteins*, respectively. Looking purposely for cognates will help you understand more easily what you read.

Thinking about the title of a reading will also improve your reading skills. Based on the title, what do you think this reading is about? Can you predict what the author will say about the topic? What words might be important to know when reading about this topic?

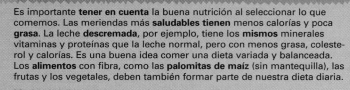

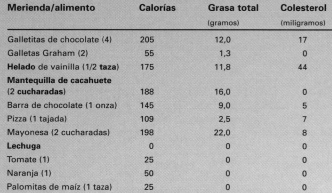

Es importante **tener en cuenta** la buena nutrición al seleccionar lo que comemos. Las meriendas más **saludables tienen** menos calorías y poca **grasa**. La leche **descremada**, por ejemplo, tiene los **mismos** minerales vitaminas y proteínas que la leche normal, pero con menos grasa, colesterol y calorías. Es una buena idea comer una dieta variada y balanceada. Los **alimentos** con fibra, como las **palomitas de maíz** (sin mantequilla), las frutas y los vegetales, deben también formar parte de nuestra dieta diaria.

Merienda/alimento	Calorías	Grasa total (gramos)	Colesterol (miligramos)
Galletitas de chocolate (4)	205	12,0	17
Galletas Graham (2)	55	1,3	0
Helado de vainilla (1/2 **taza**)	175	11,8	44
Mantequilla de cacahuete (2 **cucharadas**)	188	16,0	0
Barra de chocolate (1 onza)	145	9,0	5
Pizza (1 tajada)	109	2,5	7
Mayonesa (2 cucharadas)	198	22,0	8
Lechuga	0	0	0
Tomate (1)	25	0	0
Naranja (1)	50	0	0
Palomitas de maíz (1 taza)	25	0	0

tener en cuenta *to take into account* saludables *healthy, nutritious* tienen *have* grasa *fat*
descremada *skimmed* mismos *same* alimentos *food* palomitas de maíz *popcorn*
helado *ice cream* taza *cup* mantequilla de cacahuete *peanut butter* cucharadas *tablespoons*
lechuga *lettuce*

70 *Primera unidad* Vamos a tomar algo

 The Standards

- Interpersonal Communication 1.1
- Connections with Other Disciplines 3.1

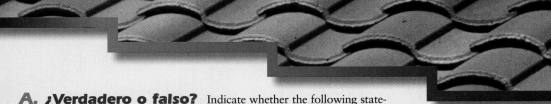

A. ¿Verdadero o falso?
Indicate whether the following statements are true (**verdadero**) or false (**falso**), based on what you read.

1. La lechuga y el tomate son alimentos que tienen fibra.
2. La mayonesa es un alimento muy saludable porque tiene poca grasa y pocas calorías.
3. Es una buena idea tomar helado todos los días.
4. Es importante tener una dieta variada y balanceada.
5. Las palomitas de maíz con mantequilla son más saludables que las palomitas sin mantequilla.
6. La leche descremada tiene las mismas proteínas que la leche normal.

B. Las meriendas
Work with a partner and the chart to complete the activities below.

1. First, rank the snacks in the chart from most nutritious (a), to least nutritious (h), based on the information provided in the reading. Then, tell your partner about your rankings in Spanish. Use the following model as a guide.

> **MODELO** *La mantequilla de cacahuete no tiene mucho colesterol, pero sí tiene mucha fibra. Para mí, es a.*

2. Now rank the snacks from the one you think has the best taste (sabor) (a) to the one you think has the worst taste (h). Then, explain your rankings to your partner. Use the following models as a guide.

> **MODELOS** *¡Qué delicioso! Como galletitas Graham todos los días. Para mí, son a.*
>
> *No me gusta comer uvas. Son horribles. Para mí, son h.*

Meriendas

	Nutrición		Sabor	
	Yo	Mi compañero(a)	Yo	Mi compañero(a)
4 galletitas Graham	___	___	___	___
un sándwich de mantequilla de cacahuete	___	___	___	___
una taza de palomitas de maíz	___	___	___	___
una pizza de tomate y queso	___	___	___	___
helado de vainilla	___	___	___	___
15 uvas	___	___	___	___
4 galletitas de chocolate	___	___	___	___
un bocadillo de jamón y queso	___	___	___	___

¡Sigamos adelante! **71**

A. ¿Verdadero o falso
ANSWERS
1. verdadero
2. falso
3. falso
4. verdadero
5. falso
6. verdadero

B. Las meriendas
POSSIBLE ANSWERS
1. **a.** 15 uvas
   b. una taza de palomitas de maíz
   c. un bocadillo de jamón y queso
   d. 4 galletitas Graham
   e. una pizza con tomate y queso
   f. un sándwich de mantequilla de maní
   g. 4 galletitas de chocolate
   h. helado de vainilla
2. Answers will vary

VARIATION

 Have students ask their partners the following questions about several of the foods listed in the chart.
1. **¿Con qué frecuencia comes _____?** Possible answers: **nunca, casi nunca, a veces, con frecuencia, todos los días**
2. **¿Tiene mucha grasa _____?**
3. **¿Cuántas calorías contiene _____?**
4. **¿Es muy saludable _____? ¿Por qué (no)?**

 Analyzing
 Interpersonal

EXPANSION

For a five-day period, at home and in school, have students read the packaging labels on their snack foods provided by manufacturers and record quantities of nutrients on a chart like the one on page 70.

 Analyzing
 Categorizing
 Evaluating

MULTIPLE INTELLIGENCES

• Logical-Mathematical

TEACH/MODEL

Puerto Rico

PRESENTATION

Explain that Puerto Rico is a commonwealth (or free associated state) of the United States. Puerto Ricans may consider themselves Puerto Ricans first, but they are also United States citizens so they do not need passports or visas to enter or leave this country. They use the same currency, postal service, and other social services. Puerto Ricans enlist in the United States military, they have a non-voting representative in Congress; they do not pay federal income taxes, and they do not participate in the presidential elections.

Cultural Comparisons 4.2

PRACTICE/APPLY

EXPANSION

Ask students to compare and contrast Puerto Rico with the United States based on what they learned in the first unit or on previous knowledge. What is different? How are some things the same? Do they see any signs of American influence in Puerto Rico? Are there any signs of Puerto Rican influence in the United States?

Comparing and Contrasting

Vistas
de los países hispanos

Puerto Rico

Capital: San Juan

Ciudades principales: Bayamón, Ponce, Carolina, Caguas, Mayagüez

Población: 3.500.000

Idiomas: español

Área territorial: 9.104 km²

Clima: moderado, temperatura promedio es de 24° C

Moneda: dólar

moderado *moderate*   promedio *average*

EXPLORA

Find out more about Puerto Rico! Access the **Nuestros vecinos** page on the *¡Ya verás! Gold* web site for a list of URLs.

http://yaveras.heinle.com/vecinos.htm

72   *Primera unidad* Vamos a tomar algo

MULTIPLE INTELLIGENCES

• Visual-Spatial

The Standards

• Connections with Distinctive Viewpoints 3.2

Focus on Culture

The Puerto Rican Flag

The Puerto Rican flag, which resembles Cuba's flag, was adopted in 1895 during the revolutionary struggles against Spanish colonial domination. It was officially recognized in 1852 and now flies alongside the United States flag.

Connections with Distinctive Viewpoints 3.2

En la comunidad

Using Spanish in your Community

Spanish is more than just words you study. It connects you to millions of people in the U.S. and in other countries. Whether you hear it in the mall, in your favorite sitcom, need it for work, or for travel, it can prove more useful than you ever imagined. As you will learn throughout these sections, Spanish is a rich, colorful thread that links culture to culture and helps you get ahead in the world of work.

¡Bienvenidos a Randy's Diner!

"When I started this business, I never dreamed I'd learn Spanish. Back then, there were hardly any Spanish-speakers in St. Paul. Today, most of my customers speak Spanish. I've expanded my menu to suit their tastes. This year I'm even taking a Spanish class at the University of Minnesota so that I can communicate better with my new neighbors and customers. So if you'd like to try a delicious **licuado,** a tasty **churro,** or some **huevos revueltos,** you've come to the right place. **¡Estamos aquí para servirles!**"

¡Ahora te toca a ti!

In your community, choose a restaurant that serves typical food from Latin America or Spain. With a classmate, visit the restaurant and order your meal in Spanish. Before going, review food vocabulary listed in the **Vocabulario** section at the end of Chapters 1-3. After your visit, in Spanish, write or make an audio recording of a description of your meal.

If there are no Hispanic restaurants in your community, imagine that you own one similar to Randy's. With a classmate, name your restaurant. Then, research Spanish and Latin American dishes. Decide which to include on your menu and be prepared to explain your choices. Present your restaurant and menu to the class. Your classmates will discuss your menu in Spanish, ask you questions about it, and vote on the dish they find most appealing.

huevos revueltos *scrambled eggs*
churros *sweet, fried-dough pastries*

¡Sigamos adelante! **73**

UNIDAD 2

Setting the Context

Unit 2 features Carmen Candelaria, a young high school student from Mexico. The general theme of the unit is getting to know someone. Chapter 4 deals with some of the material aspects of a young person's life (school supplies, housing, and transportation). Chapter 5 concentrates on activities, likes, and dislikes. Chapter 6 focuses on the family. By the end of this unit, students will be able to create simple Spanish-language self-portraits.

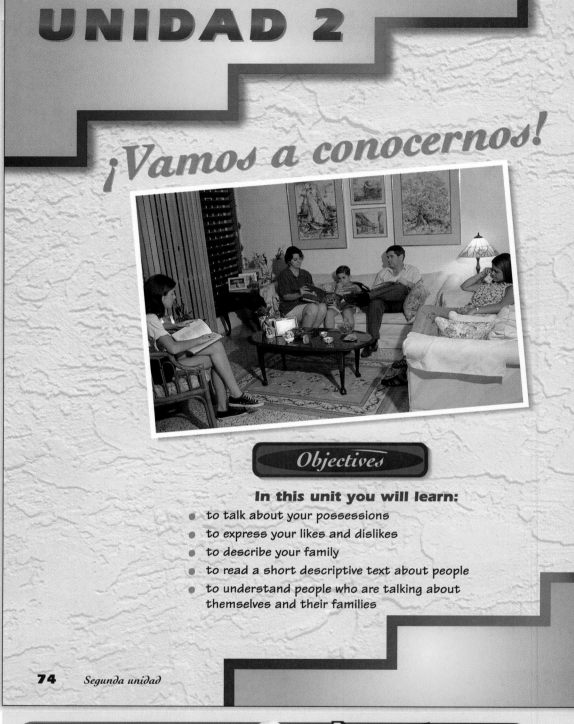

UNIDAD 2

¡Vamos a conocernos!

Objectives

In this unit you will learn:

- to talk about your possessions
- to express your likes and dislikes
- to describe your family
- to read a short descriptive text about people
- to understand people who are talking about themselves and their families

74 *Segunda unidad*

Unit Support Materials

- Workbook: **Aquí leemos** pp. 77-80
- Lab Manual: **Ya llegamos** pp. 41, 42
- Lab Program: Cassette Side B; CD 10, Tracks 4-7
- Tapescript: Lab Program pp. 61-64
- TRB: Unit Grammar Review Masters: pp. 16-23; Answer Key pp. 51-53
- Lesson Plan Book: **¡Sigamos adelante!** p. 36
- Workbook for Spanish-Speaking Students: pp. 39, 40
- Testing Program: Unit Test pp. 65-71; Answer Key & Testing Cassettes Tapescript pp. T27, T28;

Oral Assessment pp. T28; Portfolio Assessment pp. Pvii-Px
- Testing Cassettes: Cassette Side B
- Computerized Testing Program: Windows™; Macintosh®
- Atajo Writing Assistant Software: Student Text p. 147; Workbook p. 77
- Video Program: Cassette 1, 53:55-57:16
- Video Guide: Videoscript pp. 29-30; Activities pp. 105-106
- Internet Explorations: Student Text pp. 150-152

¿Qué ves?

- Where are the people in these photographs?
- Who are they with?
- What are they doing?

UNIT WARM-UP

Planning Strategy

 WORKBOOK, P. 37

If you do not assign the Planning Strategy (Workbook, page 37) for homework or if students have difficulty coming up with English expressions, you might try asking several students to role play each of the situations: you can ask someone to introduce herself (himself) to another student; you can have two or three students describe their families; you can ask several students whether they like sports, rock music, or modern art, and how they feel about skiing, eating at fast-food restaurants, studying, etc. After each response, point out the expressions used and then ask the class to suggest other possibilities.

¿De quién es?

Primera etapa: ¿Qué llevas a la escuela?
Segunda etapa: ¿Qué hay en tu casa?
Tercera etapa: En nuestra casa

Me gusta mucho...

Primera etapa: Mis gustos
Segunda etapa: ¿Qué te gusta más?

Ésta es mi familia

Primera etapa: Yo vivo con...
Segunda etapa: Tengo una familia grande

75

OBJECTIVES

Functions
- Identifying personal belongings
- Obtaining information about other people

Contexts
- School
- Home

Accuracy
- Definite articles
- Possession with **de**
- Possessive adjectives (first and second person)
- Numbers from 0 to 20
- **Hay +** noun

Pronunciation
- The consonant **p**
- The consonant **t**
- The sound of **/k/**

CHAPTER WARM-UP

Setting the Context

CD CP In preparation for their learning about identifying personal belongings, have students form teams of four. Divide each team into pairs. Explain that each pair will compare their school supplies to see what they have, how many supplies they have in common, and how many are different.

One student in each pair should then present the pair's similarities and differences with the other pair on their team. The other student in each pair will summarize the similarities and differences between the two pairs.

Ask a representative from each team to summarize their similarities and differences for the class. Then ask if any student would like to try to make a general summary of all the teams' similarities and differences.

Comparing and Contrasting

CAPÍTULO 4

¿De quién es?

—¿Cuántos discos compactos tienes?
—Tengo veinte. Éste es mi favorito.

Objectives

- identifying personal belongings
- obtaining information about other people

Chapter Support Materials

- Lab Manual: pp. 23-29
- Lab Program: Cassette Side A; CD 2, Tracks 9-17
- TRB: Textbook Activity Masters: pp. 72-76
- Textbook Cassettes/CDs: Cassette 1, Side A; CD 1, Track 31
- Tapescript: Lab Program pp. 31-40; Textbook Cassettes/CDs p. 193
- Middle School Activities: pp. 30-33
- Placement Test for Spanish-speaking Students
- Workbook for Spanish-Speaking Students: pp. 21-26
- Answer Key to SSS Workbook pp. 7-9
- Practice Software: Windows™; Macintosh®
- Testing Program: Chapter Test pp. 46-48; Answer Key & Testing Cassettes Tapescript p. T19; Oral Assessment p. T20
- Testing Cassettes: Cassette Side B
- Computerized Testing Program: Windows™; Macintosh®
- Video Program: Cassette 1, 29:35-40:00
- Video Guide: Videoscript pp. 17-21; Activities pp. 97-98
- **Mundos hispanos 1**
- Internet Activities: Student Text p. 98

PRIMERA ETAPA

Preparación

- As you get ready to begin this **etapa,** think about the items you take to school. Make a list of at least five items that you usually take to school.

- In this **etapa** you will also learn to say that something belongs to someone else. If you have borrowed a calculator from a friend, how would you say, in English, whose calculator it is?

¿Qué llevas a la escuela?

Me llamo *Elena.* **Llevo** *muchas* **cosas** *a la escuela.*

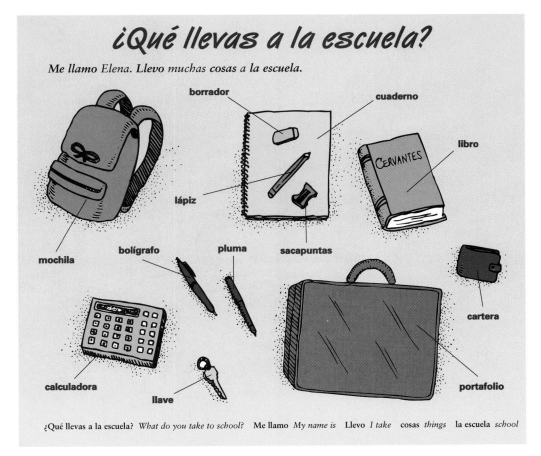

borrador
cuaderno
libro
lápiz
mochila
bolígrafo
pluma
sacapuntas
calculadora
llave
cartera
portafolio

¿Qué llevas a la escuela? *What do you take to school?* **Me llamo** *My name is* **Llevo** *I take* **cosas** *things* **la escuela** *school*

Capítulo 4 ¿De quién es? **77**

TEACH / MODEL

¿Qué llevas a la escuela?

PRESENTATION

 TRANSPARENCIES 21 AND 21A

Use actual objects for the most effective presentation of this vocabulary: **¿Qué es?** (pointing to or drawing a backpack) **Es una mochila. ¿Qué es?** (pointing to a pen) **¿Es una mochila también?** No, es un **bolígrafo.** Point to other objects, using this pattern. As you progress, go back to other groups to review and reinforce.

VOCABULARY EXPANSION

Introduce new words **papel, una hoja de papel, tijeras.** Point out that **billetera** is also used for wallet. **Un bolígrafo** is a ball-point pen. **Una pluma** is a fountain pen. **Borrador** is the generic term for eraser. Another common word for the eraser on a pen or pencil is **goma.**

Linguistic Comparisons 4.1

Etapa Support Materials

- Workbook: pp. 38-42
- TRB: Textbook Activity Masters: pp. 72, 73
- Textbook Cassettes/CDs: Cassette 1, Side A; CD 1, Track 25
- Tapescript: Textbook Cassettes/CDs p. 192
- Overhead Transparencies: 21, 21a, 22
- Middle School Activities: pp. 34, 35
- Lesson Plan Book: pp. 25-27

- Testing Program: Quiz pp. 39-41; Answer Key & Testing Cassettes Tapescript p. T17
- Testing Cassettes: Cassette Side B
- Computerized Testing Program: Windows™; Macintosh®
- Atajo Writing Assistant Software: Student Text p. 18

PRACTICE/APPLY

A. ¿Qué es?

ANSWERS

TRANSPARENCY 22

1. Es un libro
2. Es una mochila.
3. Es una calculadora.
4. Es un bolígrafo.
5. Es un cuaderno.
6. Es una cartera.
7. Es un borrador/una goma.
8. Es un sacapuntas. (*Point out that this is masculine singular despite its feminine plural ending.*)

B. No es...

SUGGESTION

Have students work in pairs; or do this activity as a class by using the **pregúntale** format.

ANSWERS
1. No es un bolígrafo. Es un libro.
2. ...Es una mochila.
3. ...Es una calculadora.
4. ...Es un bolígrafo.
5. ...Es un cuaderno.
6. ...Es una cartera.
7. ...Es un borrador/una goma.
8. ...Es un sacapuntas.

C. ¿Qué llevas tú a la escuela?

SUGGESTION

Have students write out sentences alone; then form pairs and have students correct each other's mistakes.

ANSWERS
1. Julia lleva una mochila a la escuela.
2. Jaime lleva un cuaderno...
3. Tú llevas unos bolígrafos...
4. Nosotros llevamos unos cuadernos...
5. Yo llevo un bolígrafo...
6. Él lleva una cartera...
7. Ella lleva una bolsa...
8. Ud. lleva una calculadora...

EXPANSION
Show students drawings, transparencies, or actual objects, and ask **¿Llevas un/una... a la escuela?**

▲ Visual-Spatial

¡Te toca a ti!

A. ¿Qué es? Identify the objects in the numbered drawings. Follow the model.

MODELO   *Es un lápiz.*

1.   2.   3.   4.

5.   6. 7. 8.

B. No es... Based on the numbered drawings in the previous exercise, correct the initial assumptions. Follow the model.

MODELO   ¿Es un libro?
No es un libro. Es un lápiz.

1. ¿Es un bolígrafo?   5. ¿Es un sacapuntas?
2. ¿Es una cartera?   6. ¿Es un borrador?
3. ¿Es un cuaderno?   7. ¿Es un portafolio?
4. ¿Es un lápiz?   8. ¿Es una llave?

C. ¿Qué llevas tú a la escuela? Indicate what each person takes to school according to the drawings. Follow the model.

MODELO   Juan
Juan lleva un libro a la escuela.

1. Julia   2. Jaime   3. tú   4. nosotros

MULTIPLE INTELLIGENCES

- Linguistic: All activities
- Logical-Mathematical: D, E, F
- Auditory-Musical: **Pronunciación**, D, **Aquí escuchamos**
- Visual-Spatial: **¿Qué llevas a la escuela?**, A, B, C, H
- Interpersonal: **Yo llevo...**
- Intrapersonal: **¿Qué llevas a la escuela?**

The Standards

- Interpersonal Communication 1.1: B, C, G, H, **Yo llevo**
- Interpretive Communication 1.2: F, I, **Aquí escuchamos ¿Qué llevas tú a la escuela?**
- Linguistic Comparisons 4.1: **Pronunciación, Estructura**

5. yo   6. él   7. ella   8. Ud.

PRONUNCIACIÓN   THE CONSONANT **p**

The sound of the consonant **p** is similar to the sound of *p* in English, but is pronounced without the puff of air that accompanies the English sound. Put your hand in front of your mouth and note the puff of air that is produced when you pronounce the English word *pan* and the absence of this puff of air when you say *speak*. The Spanish **p** is more like the *p* in the English word *speak*.

Práctica

D. Listen and repeat as your teacher models the following words.

1. papa
2. política
3. pájaro
4. pintura
5. problema
6. póster
7. pronto
8. pluma
9. lápiz
10. sacapuntas

ESTRUCTURA

The definite article

	Singular	Plural
Masculine	**el** libro	**los** libros
Feminine	**la** mochila	**las** mochilas

1. In Spanish, the definite article has four forms. The form used depends on whether the noun is masculine or feminine and singular or plural.

Capítulo 4 ¿De quién es?   **79**

TEACH/MODEL

Pronunciación

PRESENTATION

🔘 TEXTBOOK CASSETTE/CD CASSETTE 1, SIDE A; CD 1, TRACK 25

▭ TAPESCRIPT P. 192

Demonstrate that the puff of air that accompanies the sound of *p* in English can be seen by holding a piece of paper in front of your mouth as you pronounce English words that begin with *p*.

Then have students listen to the explanation for the consonant **p** on the Textbook Cassette/CD. The speaker will model the correct pronunciation of the words in **Práctica D**. Have students follow along in their texts and repeat after each word.

◢◣ Auditory-Musical

Estructura

PRESENTATION

Introduce definite articles by contrasting them with indefinite articles. Read several sentences where you stress the articles, and then have students repeat them. **Julia lleva** *un* **libro a** *la* **escuela. Allí está** *el* **libro de Julia.** Other objects: **calculadora, llaves, bolígrafos, cuaderno.**

You may want to point out that the definite article is omitted in direct address: **Buenos días, señor García; Hasta mañana, doctora Hernández.**

◢◣ Linguistic

☀ Spanish for Spanish Speakers

What Professionals Bring

Have Spanish speakers pick a professional and decide what items he (she) needs when traveling. For example, a student may pick an actress and write that she should travel with her script, costume, and makeup kit. Encourage students to look up words they do not know. Have them write their ideas down and exchange with another student to engage in peer-editing.

◯ Presentational Communication 1.3

PRACTICE/APPLY

E. ¿Un o el?

SUGGESTION

Have students do this activity with their books closed. Read the words with the indefinite articles and have students repeat them, substituting the corresponding definite articles.

VARIATION

Discuss with students some of the uses of the definite and indefinite articles. Elicit from them the difference between referring to a general person and a specific person.

 Activating Prior Knowledge
Drawing Inferences

 Linguistic Comparisons 4.1

ESTRUCTURA (continued)

2. One of the two main uses of the definite article is to designate nouns in a specific sense. In this situation, the English equivalent of **el, la, los,** and **las** is *the.*

Necesito **los** libros.

I need the books. (that is, the specific books already mentioned)

Aquí está **la** llave.

Here is the key. (that is, the specific key that someone is referring to)

3. The other main use of the definite article is to designate nouns in a general or collective sense. In this situation, English usually does not use an article.

El café es una bebida popular aquí.

Coffee is a popular drink here. (that is, coffee in general)

Me gusta **la** música.

I like music. (that is, music in general)

4. When talking about someone who has a title, always use the definite article in front of the title. However, when you talk directly to such a person, the definite article is not used with his (her) title.

El señor Herrera es ecuatoriano.

Mr. Herrera is Ecuadorian.

La señora Martínez lleva un libro a la escuela.

Mrs. Martínez takes a book to school.

Buenas tardes, **señorita Díaz.**

Good afternoon, Miss Díaz.

Aquí practicamos

E. ¿Un o el? Replace the indefinite article with the appropriate definite article (**el, la, los, las**). Follow the models.

MODELOS   un cuaderno   unos libros
el cuaderno   *los libros*

1. un café
2. una estudiante
3. un sándwich
4. una mochila
5. unas bebidas
6. unos médicos
7. un bolígrafo
8. una cartera

9. unos refrescos
10. un jugo
11. una profesora
12. unos estudiantes
13. una llave
14. una calculadora
15. un borrador
16. un sacapuntas

Vocabulary Expansion

Ask Spanish speakers if they know other words in Spanish for those in column B of Activity F. Then have students think of other items not mentioned that people in column A might need (i.e., **computadora, regla**).

 Linguistic Comparisons 4.1

F. ¿Qué necesita cada (each) persona? Based on the activities and people mentioned in Column A of the chart on your activity master, decide which items from Column B the people need. Follow the models to write your responses on your activity master. You may want to use some items from Column B more than once.

MODELOS   Yo quisiera leer.   Tina va a casa.
          Tú necesitas un libro.   *Ella necesita la llave.*

A	B
1. Ana estudia matemáticas.	bolígrafo(s)
2. Nosotros vamos a escribir.	calculadora(s)
3. Juan lleva muchos cuadernos a la escuela.	cuaderno
4. Miguel y María quisieran leer.	llave(s)
5. Tú vas a escribir (*write*) mucho con un lápiz.	libro(s)
6. Ustedes estudian mucho las matemáticas.	mochila
	sacapuntas

NOTA GRAMATICAL

Expressing possession with **de**

el libro de Ana	*Ana's book*
la calculadora de Juan	*Juan's calculator*
los cuadernos de Marta	*Marta's notebooks*
las llaves de Jorge	*Jorge's keys*

1. The following construction is often used in Spanish to express possession in the third person:

> *the definite article + noun + **de** + the name of the possessor*

2. To ask to whom a singular noun belongs, use **¿De quién es...?** Use **¿De quién son...?** to ask to whom a plural noun belongs.

¿De quién es la pluma?	*Whose pen is it?*
¿De quién son las plumas?	*Whose pens are they?*

Capítulo 4 ¿De quién es?   **81**

PRACTICE/APPLY

G. Es de...

ANSWERS

1. Es el cuaderno de Vicente.
2. Es la mochila de Marcos.
3. Es la calculadora de Bárbara.
4. Es la llave de Victoria.
5. Son los bolígrafos de María.
6. Son las llaves de Pedro.
7. Son los cuadernos de José.
8. Son los lápices de Juanita.

H. ¿De quién es... ?

SUGGESTION

 Students must remember to change the word order from the English way of forming possessive phrases: from *John's house* to *the house of John.*

 Sequencing

Linguistic Comparisons 4.1

ANSWERS

1. ¿De quién es la calculadora? Es de Enrique.
2. ¿De quién es el borrador? Es de Patricio.
3. ¿De quién es el sacapuntas? Es de Miguel.
4. ¿De quién es la cartera? Es de Anita.
5. ¿De quién es el bolígrafo? Es de Emilia.
6. ¿De quién son las llaves? Son de Mercedes.

Aquí escuchamos

 TEXTBOOK CASSETTE/CD CASSETTE 1, SIDE A; CD 1, TRACK 26

TAPESCRIPT P. 192

TRB: ACTIVITY MASTER, P. 73

Después de escuchar

ANSWERS

Todos los días: cuadernos, libros, mochilas; A veces: calculadora

---

G. Es de... After class one day, you and a friend notice that your classmates have left behind several of their belongings. You show these objects to your friend, who identifies the owners. With a singular noun, use **es**. With a plural noun, use **son**. Follow the models.

MODELOS   un libro (Beatriz)   unos libros (Juan)
              Es el libro de Beatriz.   *Son los libros de Juan.*

1. un cuaderno (Vicente)   5. unos bolígrafos (María)
2. una mochila (Marcos)   6. unas llaves (Pedro)
3. una calculadora (Bárbara)   7. unos cuadernos (José)
4. una llave (Victoria)   8. unos lápices (Juanita)

H. ¿De quién es...? You are trying to sort out who owns each of several items that have been left in the classroom. Ask a question and have a classmate answer according to the model.

MODELO   Tú: ¿De quién es el lápiz?   Carlos
             Compañera(o): Es de Carlos.

1. Enrique   2. Patricio   3. Miguel

4. Anita   5. Emilia   6. Mercedes

Aquí escuchamos

¿Qué llevas a la escuela? *Carmen describes her life as a high-school student.*

Antes de escuchar Think about items Carmen might take to school every day.

 A escuchar As you listen to the monologue, put a check mark on your activity master next to each of the following words when you hear it.

__bolígrafo	__cuaderno
__calculadora	__libro
__cartera	__mochila

Después de escuchar On your activity master, check the appropriate column to show how often Carmen takes each thing she mentions to school.

	Todos los días	A veces
bolígrafo		
calculadora		
cartera		
cuaderno		
libro		
mochila		
lápices		

¡ADELANTE!

 Yo llevo... Make a list of five items that you usually take to school with you. Then interview three classmates to find out what they have on their lists. Keep track of their answers so that you can report whose list is most like yours and whose list is most different.

 ¿Qué llevas tú a la escuela? Write a short paragraph telling what you take to school with you. Mention...

1. something that you sometimes take.
2. something that you take every day.
3. something that you like to take (**me gusta llevar**).
4. something that you do not like to take.

For at least one of the items you mention, offer an explanation; for example: **Siempre llevo el libro de español porque estudio el español todos los días.**

ETAPA SYNTHESIS

Yo llevo...
SUGGESTION
Call on a few students to say what they usually bring to class and have others report what their classmates said.

¿Qué llevas tú a la escuela?
FYI

 ATAJO WRITING ASSISTANT SOFTWARE

You might want to have students use this software program when doing this activity.

SUGGESTION
Write new vocabulary on cards and call on students to pick a card and draw the item on the board or on the overhead transparency. Have students guess what the item is.
Visual-Spatial

EXPANSION
Have students write more expansive statements, connecting clauses with **y**, **pero**, or **porque**. For example, **Llevo... a veces y llevo... todos los días. Llevo... porque....**

"SIMÓN DICE" GAME
For more hands-on and visual practice, have students put their school supplies in front of them, and then do a quick **"Simón dice toca el cuaderno, Simón dice levanta el lápiz"** activity.
 Bodily-Kinesthetic

Additional Practice and Recycling
FYI

WORKBOOK, PP. 38-42

For recycling and additional practice of the vocabulary, structures, and language functions presented throughout this **etapa**, you can assign the workbook activities as in-class work and/or homework. Answers to the activities are overprinted on each page of the Teacher's Edition of the Workbook.

¿Qué hay en tu cuarto?

PRESENTATION

🖵 TRANSPARENCIES 23, 23A, 24, 24A

Using the transparencies, introduce first the items in Marta's room: **Hay una cama, un escritorio y una silla. También hay un/una...** , etc. Then summarize: **Ella tiene una cama...** , etc. (**Tiene** should be treated only as a lexical item at this time.) Then move to Jorge's room. Begin by reviewing items already seen in Marta's room. Ask: **¿Hay una silla? ¿una cama? ¿unas plantas?** Eventually introduce items that are found only in his room.

VARIATION

If you prefer not to use the transparencies, bring in pictures of the various objects. Present the vocabulary (with books closed), then have students open their books and do Activities A and B.

WHAT CAN YOU REMEMBER? GAME

You can follow up on this presentation with an oral memory game that can take the place of Activities A and B. Ask (with the overlay removed): **¿Hay una cama en el cuarto de Marta? ¿un televisor? ¿una computadora? ¿Qué hay en el cuarto de Jorge? Y tú, ¿qué hay en tu cuarto?** etc.

VOCABULARY EXPANSION

Introduce **lámpara, osito de felpa** (in some countries **osito de peluche**), **espejo, pared, techo, piso (suelo), ventana, cortinas, ropero.** Tell students that **clóset** is now common in some countries. Another word for **póster** is **cartel.** A compact disc is a **disco compacto** or **CD.** It is played on a **reproductor de discos compactos.**

⊗ Linguistic Comparisons 4.1

SEGUNDA ETAPA

Preparación

- As you get ready to begin this **etapa,** think about what you have in your room at home.
- Make a list of at least eight items you have in your room.

¿Qué hay en tu cuarto?

*Marta Gómez y Jorge de Vargas son **una muchacha** y **un muchacho** que son estudiantes en una escuela en Quito, Ecuador.*

Me llamo Marta. **En mi cuarto hay...**

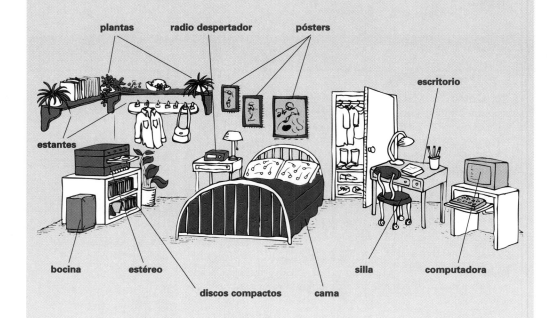

plantas   radio despertador   pósters   escritorio

estantes

bocina   estéreo   silla   computadora

discos compactos   cama

¿Qué hay en tu cuarto? What is there in your room? Una muchacha *a young woman* un muchacho *a young man*
En mi cuarto hay... *In my room there is/are . . .*

Etapa Support Materials

- Workbook: pp. 43-46
- TRB: Textbook Activity Masters: p. 74
- Textbook Cassettes/CDs: Cassette, Side A; CD 1, Track 27
- Tapescript: Textbook Cassettes/CDs p. 192
- Overhead Transparencies: 23, 23a, 24, 24a
- Middle School Activities: p. 36
- Lesson Plan Book pp. 19-20

- Testing Program: Quiz pp. 42, 43; Answer Key & Testing Cassettes Tapescript pp. T17, T18
- Testing Cassettes: Cassette Side B
- Computerized Testing Program: Windows™; Macintosh®
- Atajo Writing Assistant Software: Student Text p. 87

Me llamo Jorge. En mi cuarto hay...

cómoda · cámara · cintas · grabadora · televisor · estantes

cama · alfombra · silla · máquina de escribir · escritorio

¡Te toca a ti!

A. ¿Dónde hay...? (Where is/are there . . . ?) Based on the pictures, answer the following questions about Marta's and Jorge's rooms. Follow the models.

MODELOS

¿un televisor?
En el cuarto de Jorge hay un televisor.

¿una cama?
En el cuarto de Marta hay una cama y en el cuarto de Jorge hay una cama también.

1. ¿una computadora?
2. ¿una grabadora?
3. ¿un radio despertador?
4. ¿una cama?
5. ¿un estéreo?
6. ¿unos pósters?
7. ¿una máquina de escribir?

8. ¿una cámara?
9. ¿unas cintas?
10. ¿unos discos compactos?
11. ¿unas plantas?
12. ¿unos estantes?
13. ¿una silla?
14. ¿una alfombra?

B. ¿Y tú? Indicate what you have and do not have in your room at home. Follow the model.

MODELO

En mi cuarto, hay una cama y una cómoda, pero no hay un escritorio. También hay pósters en la pared (on the wall).

PRACTICE/APPLY

A. ¿Dónde hay... ?
ANSWERS
1. En el cuarto de Marta hay una computadora.
2. Jorge—grabadora
3. Marta—radio despertador
4. Marta—cama; Jorge—cama
5. Marta—estéreo
6. Marta—póster
7. Jorge—máquina de escribir
8. Jorge—cámara
9. Jorge—cintas
10. Marta—discos compactos
11. Marta—plantas
12. Marta—estantes
13. Marta—silla; Jorge—silla
14. Jorge—alfombra

B. ¿Y tú?
SUGGESTION

Expand into a writing activity, being sure to set a time limit if done in class. Have students write a paragraph comparing their rooms with those of their partners. They should draw from information gathered in interviews with their partners and recorded on a chart. Then have them check their partners' papers for errors in spelling or agreement of articles. You might also have volunteers read their paragraphs to the class.

Comparing and Contrasting

MULTIPLE INTELLIGENCES

- Linguistic: All activities
- Logical-Mathematical: E, F, G
- Visual-Spatial: **¿Qué hay en tu cuarto?**, A, D, G
- Auditory-Musical: **Pronunciación**, C, **Aquí escuchamos**
- Interpersonal: H, **¿Qué hay en tu cuarto?**

The Standards

- Interpersonal Communication 1.1:G, H, **Adelante** activities
- Interpretive Communication 1.2: A, H, **Aquí escuchamos**
- Presentational Communication 1.3: B, D, G, **¿Qué hay?**
- Linguistic Comparisons 4.1: **Pronunciación**

Pronunciación

PRESENTATION

 TEXTBOOK CASSETTE/CD CASSETTE 1, SIDE A; CD 1, TRACK 27

 TAPESCRIPT P. 192

Have students pronounce English words that begin with *t*, telling them to take notice of the position of the tip of the tongue. Then have them move the tip of the tongue from the gum ridge to the back of the upper front teeth and practice saying these Spanish syllables: **ta, te, ti, to, tu.**

Then have students listen to the explanation for the consonant **t** on the Textbook Cassette/CD. The speaker will model the correct pronunciation of the words in **Práctica C.** Have students follow along in their texts and repeat after each word.

Auditory-Musical

D. ¿Qué llevan a la escuela?

SUGGESTION

Review by doing a **pregúntale** exercise. **(María), pregúntale a... si lleva un/una... a la escuela.**

Palabras útiles

PRESENTATION

You may have presented these numbers in the **Etapa preliminar.** If that is the case, review them quickly. To present numbers for the first time, have students repeat number series in chorus: 0; 0, 1; 0, 1, 2; etc. Then have them count backwards and in twos, with books closed, introducing the notion of **pares** (even numbers) and **impares** (odd numbers). You could also have students practice saying zip codes.

Categorizing
Sequencing

Connections with Other Disciplines 3.1

PRONUNCIACIÓN THE CONSONANT t

The sound of **t** in Spanish is produced by placing the tip of the tongue behind the back of the upper front teeth, while *t* in English is pronounced by placing the tip of the tongue on the gum ridge behind the upper front teeth. Pronounce the English word *tea* and note where the tip of your tongue is. Now pronounce the Spanish word **ti** being careful to place the tip of the tongue on the back of the upper front teeth.

Práctica

C. Listen and repeat as your teacher models the following words.

1. tú	5. tipo	9. fútbol
2. tomo	6. tenis	10. cinta
3. tapas	7. tonto	
4. taza	8. política	

Repaso

D. ¿Qué llevan a la escuela? Look at the drawings that follow and tell what each person takes to school.

Martín   Julio

PALABRAS ÚTILES

Numbers from 0 to 20

cero	0	seis	6	doce	12	dieciocho	18
uno	1	siete	7	trece	13	diecinueve	19
dos	2	ocho	8	catorce	14	veinte	20
tres	3	nueve	9	quince	15		
cuatro	4	diez	10	dieciséis	16		
cinco	5	once	11	diecisiete	17		

 Spanish for Spanish Speakers

Diagramming a Room

Have Spanish speakers or more-prepared students draw diagrams of their rooms on the board, pointing out where items are. Then have Spanish speakers come up with additional items, using words not yet presented, and share them with the class.

Creating

Visual-Spatial

Aquí practicamos

E. **Cuenta (Count) mucho** Follow the directions in Spanish.

1. Cuenta del 0 al 10. Cuenta del 11 al 20.
2. Cuenta los números pares *(even):* 0, 2, 4, 6, 8, 10, 12, 14, 16, 18, 20.
3. Cuenta los números impares *(odd):* l, 3, 5, 7, 9, 11, 13, 15, 17, 19.

F. **Sumar y restar (Adding and subtracting)** Solve the following addition and subtraction problems, forming complete sentences with the solved problems. Follow the models.

MODELOS	$2 + 1 =$	$3 - 1 =$
	Dos más (plus)	*Tres menos* (minus)
	uno son tres.	*uno son dos.*

1. $2 + 5 =$	5. $4 - 1 =$	9. $7 + 13 =$	13. $3 + 5 =$
2. $6 - 3 =$	6. $0 + 4 =$	10. $18 - 2 =$	14. $1 + 2 =$
3. $6 + 10 =$	7. $5 + 4 =$	11. $8 - 3 =$	15. $9 - 4 =$
4. $17 - 2 =$	8. $19 - 6 =$	12. $12 + 5 =$	16. $19 - 8 =$

PALABRAS ÚTILES

Hay + noun

Hay lápices en el escritorio.	*There are pencils on the desk.*
Hay un libro en mi cuarto.	*There is a book in my room.*
Hay tres pósters en mi cuarto.	*There are three posters in my room.*

1. The Spanish word **hay** *(there is, there are)* may be followed by either a singular or a plural noun. **Hay** may also be followed by an indefinite article or a number.

2. When **hay** is used in the negative, the indefinite article is usually omitted.

No hay plantas en mi cuarto.	*There are no plants in my room.*

3. To ask how many people or things there are, use **¿Cuántos(as)... hay?**

¿Cuántos pósters hay en la pared?	*How many posters are there on the wall?*
¿Cuántas sillas hay aquí?	*How many chairs are there here?*

Capítulo 4 ¿De quién es?   **87**

PRACTICE/APPLY

E. **Cuenta mucho**
SUGGESTION
 Divide the class into two sections, having one section count the odd numbers, and the other count the even numbers.

Auditory-Musical

F. **Sumar y restar**
VARIATION
You do the calculations, making errors from time to time and having students correct you.

EXPANSION
Dictate some simple math problems to students with their books closed. Have students volunteer to read the problems and answers out loud.

TEACH/MODEL

Palabras útiles
PRESENTATION
Place some school supplies and classroom objects on a desk or table. Then ask: **¿Qué hay sobre (en) la mesa (el escritorio)? ¿Hay unos libros? ¿Hay un bolígrafo?** Have students point out other objects around the room.

You might also want to introduce **cuántos/cuántas** as a lexical item and ask questions such as, **¿Cuántas ventanas hay aquí?, ¿Cuántos pósters hay en la pared?** etc.

Point out that **hay** is never followed by a definite article, only by indefinite articles or numbers.

Linguistic
Visual-Spatial

☀ Spanish for Spanish Speakers

Adding pennies

Have Spanish speakers ask other classmates for pennies: **¿Tienes un centavo? ¿Me das un centavo, dos centavos, cinco... ? ¿Cuántos tienes?** Students can answer **sí** or **no**, answering with a number (e.g. **tengo tres**) if appropriate. Spanish speakers should circulate the classroom, asking for pennies before a set amount of time expires. Then have the class practice adding by combining collected pennies and stating out loud the equations.

Bodily-Kinesthetic
Logical-Mathematical

PRACTICE / APPLY

G. El cuarto de Marta

SUGGESTION

Have students use the drawing of Marta's room to create questions to ask a partner; their answers should be based on what's in the drawing. Example: **¿Hay una cama? Sí, hay una cama.**

ANSWERS

1. Hay unos pósters.
2. Hay una silla.
3. No hay cintas.
4. Hay una computadora.
5. No hay televisor.
6. Hay un estéreo.
7. Hay unos libros.
8. Hay unos lápices.
9. Hay unos bolígrafos.
10. Hay un escritorio.
11. Hay unas plantas.
12. No hay máquina de escribir.
13. No hay cuadernos.
14. No hay cámaras.
15. No hay cómoda.

H. Hay...

SUGGESTION

Have one member of a pair look at the drawing and ask questions. The other studies the picture, closes the book, then tries to remember the correct answers—without peeking. After five or six questions, have partners switch roles.

Aquí escuchamos

TEXTBOOK CASSETTE/CD CASSETTE 1, SIDE A; CD 1, TRACK 28

TAPESCRIPT P. 192

TRB: ACTIVITY MASTER, P. 74

Después de escuchar

ANSWERS

plantas, escritorio, cama, silla, grabadora, cintas, póster

Aquí practicamos

G. El cuarto de Marta Indicate whether each item is or is not found in the room pictured on page 84. Follow the models.

MODELOS　　una cama　　　　　　unas grabadoras
　　　　　　　Hay una cama.　　　*No hay grabadoras.*

1. unos pósters	6. un estéreo	11. unas plantas
2. una silla	7. unos libros	12. una cómoda
3. unas cintas	8. unos lápices	13. unos cuadernos
4. una computadora	9. unos bolígrafos	14. unas cámaras
5. un televisor	10. un escritorio	15. una máquina de escribir

H. Hay... Working with another student, take turns pointing out items in the room pictured below. Each of you should also point out one item that is not in the room. Each of you should mention five items. Follow the model.

MODELO　　*Hay una cama allí* (there).

☀ **Spanish for Spanish Speakers**

Vocabulary Expansion–Synonyms

Have Spanish speakers listen carefully to the **Aquí escuchamos** recording and write down five words they hear for which they know or want to find synonyms. Tell them not to limit themselves to just one or two parts of speech, but to choose nouns, verbs, adjectives, adverbs, prepositions, etc. Then give students copies of the dialogue from the Tapescript and have them work with a partner to combine their lists and create a transformed dialogue. Have Spanish speakers and other class volunteers roleplay the dialogue with the new words for the rest of the class.

 Creating

 Auditory-Musical Linguistic

Presentational Communication 1.3

Aquí escuchamos

¿Qué hay en tu cuarto? *Miguel mentions some items he has in his room.*

Antes de escuchar Think about what you have in your room at home. Then, think about the items Miguel might have in his room.

 A escuchar Listen twice to the monologue before checking off the mentioned items on your activity master.

Después de escuchar Check off on your activity master the items that Miguel has in his room.

cama	estéreo
cintas	grabadora
computadora	plantas
discos compactos	póster
escritorio	silla
estantes	

¡ADELANTE!

 ¿Qué hay? Find out from several of your classmates what they have and do not have in their rooms at home. Then tell them what you have and do not have in your own room. Follow the model.

MODELO		
	Tú:	*¿Qué hay en tu cuarto?*
	Compañero(a):	*En mi cuarto hay dos plantas, una cama...*

 Cosas importantes A foreign exchange student has just arrived at your school. A couple with no children has agreed to host the student. They have asked for help in furnishing their guest's room appropriately for a teen. With a partner, decide on the six most important items to include.

ETAPA SYNTHESIS

¿Qué hay?

SUGGESTION

 Have students report how many members of each group have the same items in their rooms. A group *reporter* should state the number of shared items in full sentences. Write the name of each item on the board. Example: **Hay plantas en los cuartos de tres alumnos, y hay escritorios en los cuartos de dos.** You write: **plantas, escritorios.** Then, enter the appropriate number of *tick* marks to represent the number of owners.

Categorizing
Comparing and Contrasting
Sequencing

VARIATION

 Discuss the highest and lowest frequency items while practicing the **hay** and **gustar** structures. Example: **¿De qué cosa hay más en nuestros cuartos? (Hay más escritorios; hay diecinueve escritorios.)** Encourage students to draw inferences about the *sample group* (their class). Ask **¿Por qué hay muchos escritorios? (Porque somos alumnos.)**

Drawing Inferences
Interpersonal

Cosas importantes

FYI

 ATAJO WRITING ASSISTANT SOFTWARE

You might want to have students use this software program when doing this activity.

Additional Practice and Recycling

FYI

WORKBOOK, PP. 43-46

For recycling and additional practice of the vocabulary, structures, and language functions presented throughout this **etapa**, you can assign the workbook activities as in-class work and/or homework.

En mi casa

PRESENTATION

TRANSPARENCIES 25 AND 25A

Using the transparency of houses and possessions, begin each vocabulary group by talking about yourself: **Yo vivo en una casa, ¿y tú? ¿Quién vive en un apartamento? En nuestra casa hay un estéreo y un televisor a colores. ¿Qué hay en tu casa?**

VARIATION

If you do not use the transparencies, describe the homes of two people. Use real examples and illustrate them with sketches on the board or by asking questions of Spanish-speaking students. Example: **Marta vive en una casa. En su casa hay un televisor a colores y... ,** etc.

VOCABULARY EXPANSION

Point out to students that **sillón** means *armchair*, or *easy chair*. Introduce **sofá, condominio.** Note that the technical word for *VCR* is **videocasete** or **videocasetera.** In Spain, the word **vídeo** is used for both the VCR and the tape that it plays.

Linguistic

Linguistic Comparison 4.1

TERCERA ETAPA

Preparación

- As you get ready to begin this **etapa,** think about where you and your friends and relatives live (house, apartment, condominium, etc.); what you have where you live; and how you get around town.

- Make a list with the headings *house, apartment, condominium* and/or *townhouse*; then list one to three acquaintances under each heading who live in that type of residence.

- Next to each name, list three interesting items that your friend or relative has at home.

- Name the different modes of transportation that each of you uses to get to school, go shopping, and to go to a friend's house.

En mi casa

Vivo en...

una casa

un apartamento

En mi casa *In my house*   Vivo en... *I live in...*

Etapa Support Materials

- Workbook: pp. 47-51
- TRB: Textbook Activity Masters: pp.75, 76
- Textbook Cassettes/CDs: Cassette 1, Side A; CD 1, Track 29
- Tapescript: Textbook Cassettes/CDs p. 193
- Overhead Transparencies: 25, 25a
- Middle School Activities: pp.37, 38
- Lesson Plan Book: pp. 23-24

- Testing Program: Quiz pp. 44, 45; Answer Key & Testing Cassettes Tapescript pp. T18, T19
- Testing Cassettes: Cassette Side B
- Computerized Testing Program: Windows™; Macintosh®
- Atajo Writing Assistant Software: Student Text p. 98

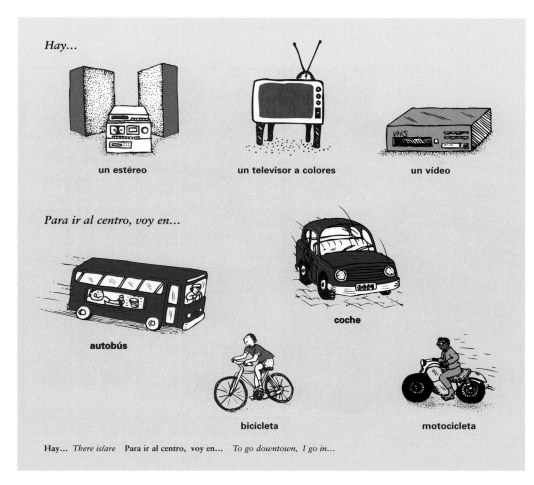

Hay...

un estéreo

un televisor a colores

un vídeo

Para ir al centro, voy en...

autobús

coche

bicicleta

motocicleta

Hay... *There is/are* Para ir al centro, voy en... *To go downtown, I go in...*

¡Te toca a ti!

A. Mi casa Answer the following questions about where you live.

1. ¿Vives tú *(Do you live)* en una casa o en un apartamento?
   Vivo…

2. ¿Hay un estéreo en tu casa? ¿Y un televisor? ¿Y una computadora?
   ¿Y un vídeo?
   Hay…

3. ¿Cómo vas *(How do you go)* al centro? ¿En coche? ¿En moto?
   ¿En bicicleta? ¿En autobús?
   Yo voy…

Capítulo 4 ¿De quién es?   **91**

VOCABULARY EXPANSION
Point out that **camioneta** means *van*. Introduce **autobús, camión** (*bus, truck* in Mexico).

PRACTICE / APPLY

A. Mi casa

SUGGESTION

Have students interview a partner to find out about the other's home. Then call on different *interviewers* to report their findings to the class.

POSSIBLE ANSWERS

1. Vivo en una casa.
2. Hay un televisor y un estéreo.
3. Yo voy al centro en bicicleta.

MULTIPLE INTELLIGENCES

- Linguistic: All activities
- Logical-Mathematical: E, F, G
- Visual-Spatial: **En mi casa**, B, G
- Auditory-Musical: **Pronunciación**, C, **Aquí escuchamos**
- Interpersonal: **Mi casa y tu casa**
- Intrapersonal: **Mi cuarto y mis actividades**

The Standards

- Interpersonal Communication 1.1: A, D, F, G, **Mi casa y tu casa**
- Interpretive Communication 1.2: A, B, E, F, **Aquí escuchamos**
- Presentational Communication 1.3: **Adelante** activities
- Linguistic Comparisons 4.1: **Pronunciación**

B. María, Antonio y Cristina

1. Vivo en <u>una casa</u>. Allí hay <u>unas plantas y un televisor</u>, pero no hay <u>estéreo</u>. Para ir al centro, voy en <u>coche</u>.

2. Yo vivo en un <u>apartamento</u>. Allí hay <u>un televisor, un vídeo y un estéreo</u>, pero no hay <u>una computadora</u>. Para ir al centro, voy en <u>motocicleta</u>.

3. Yo vivo en <u>una casa</u>. Allí hay <u>una computadora y una grabadora</u>, pero no hay <u>plantas</u>. Para ir al centro, voy en <u>bicicleta</u>.

STRIP STORIES GAME

Divide students into teams of two pairs. Have each pair work together to prepare a completion of one of the three strip stories.

Have pairs present variations of their strip stories to their team partners. (They may consult each other to confirm understanding.)

Visual-Spatial

B. María, Antonio y Cristina Using the drawings, complete each person's description of where he (she) lives.

1. Me llamo María González. Vivo en… Allí hay…, pero no hay… Para ir al centro, voy en…

2. Me llamo Antonio Martínez. Yo vivo en… Allí hay… y… Pero no hay… Para ir al centro, voy en…

3. Me llamo Cristina Sánchez. Yo vivo en… Allí hay…, pero no hay… Para ir al centro, voy en…

Focus on Culture

Transportation Worldwide

Use the transportation drawings as the basis for a discussion of typical ways of getting around. Begin by having students talk about how they travel back and forth across their cities or towns: How do you get to school? the mall? the movies? to friends' houses or special classes? How do family members get to work?, etc. Then give students some information about Spanish-speaking countries: Mopeds (**motobicicletas**) are a common alternative to cars (cheaper) or bicycles (faster) in some towns and cities in Spain. Mexico City has a large subway (**metro**) system; but people wanting to travel long distances from Mexico City usually take a bus or a plane, since not all roads are well equipped for cars.

Cultural Comparisons 4.2

PRONUNCIACIÓN The Sound of /k/

In Spanish the sound of /k/ can be spelled with a **c** before the vowels **a**, **o**, and **u**, as in **caso, cosa, culpa**, or before the consonants **l** and **r** as in **clase** and **cruz**. It can also be spelled with **qu** as in **Quito** and **queso;** in this combination, the **u** is always silent. A few Spanish words that have been borrowed from other languages are spelled with the letter **k**—for example, **koala, kimono,** and **kilómetro**. In all of these cases the sound of /k/ in Spanish is identical to the sound of /k/ in English.

Práctica

C. Listen and repeat as your teacher models the following words.

1. casa	6. que
2. cómoda	7. quien
3. cama	8. queso
4. computadora	9. pequeño
5. calculadora	10. kilómetro

Repaso

D. ¿Qué hay? Ask a classmate the following questions, and have him (her) answer them.

1. En tu cuarto, ¿hay libros? ¿Hay plantas? ¿Hay pósters en la pared?

2. ¿Hay un estéreo en tu casa? ¿Hay discos compactos? ¿Hay discos compactos de jazz? ¿Y de rock? ¿Y de música clásica?

3. ¿Hay un radio despertador en tu cuarto? ¿Hay un estéreo? ¿Hay cintas?

4. En tu casa, ¿hay una máquina de escribir? ¿Hay una computadora? ¿Hay una cámara?

Capítulo 4 ¿De quién es? **93**

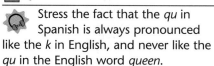

TEACH/MODEL

Pronunciación

PRESENTATION

TEXTBOOK CASSETTE/CD CASSETTE 1, SIDE A; CD 1, TRACK 29

TAPESCRIPT P. 193

Stress the fact that the *qu* in Spanish is always pronounced like the *k* in English, and never like the *qu* in the English word *queen*.

Then have students listen to the explanation of **k** on the Textbook Cassette/CD. The speaker will model the correct pronunciation of the words in the **Práctica**. Have students follow along in their texts and repeat after each word.

Auditory-Musical

PRACTICE/APPLY

D. ¿Qué hay?

SUGGESTION

Have students ask their partners the questions and then have volunteers report back to the class.

Interpersonal Communication 1.1

Focus on Culture

Linguistic Borrowing

Introduce the concept of linguistic borrowing. Explain that it is common for languages to borrow words from other languages. Give examples of words that English has borrowed from Spanish, such as *patio, rodeo, plaza, mosquito,* and *chocolate*. Then point out that any word spelled with a **k** in Spanish has been borrowed from another language.

Linguistic comparisons 4.1

Estructura

SUGGESTION

Collect some items from the students and place them on your desk or table. Ask: **¿Es tu libro? ¿Son tus lápices?**, etc. Have students respond using negative or affirmative statements: **Sí, es mi libro**, or **No, no es mi libro.** Then practice the plural forms. Walk around the room, stopping occasionally to take objects from various students. Then ask the neighbors of these students: **¿Son sus cuadernos?**, etc. Instruct them when to respond with the **nuestro** form. (It may be helpful to write this pattern on the board.)

Vuestro and its other forms have not been introduced. You may present them here if you wish.

Point out that the possessive adjective **tu** is written without the accent mark, unlike the subject pronoun **tú**.

FYI

Possessive adjectives are presented in two parts in order to establish the notion of double agreement (agreement with the modified noun as well as with the possessor) before the confusing his/her problem is introduced. Third-person possessive adjectives are presented in Chapter 9. You may wish to review gender and number before beginning the presentation of the possessive adjectives.

E. ¿Es mi libro?

EXPANSION

Have students work in groups to act out the above **Estructura** suggestion. They can use the nouns presented in this activity for ideas.

Bodily-Kinesthetic

ESTRUCTURA

Possessive adjectives: First and second persons

—¿Necesitas **tu** lápiz?	*Do you need your pencil?*
—Sí, necesito **mi** lápiz.	*Yes, I need my pencil.*
—¿Es **su** coche?	*Is this your car?*
—Sí, es **nuestro** coche.	*Yes, it is our car.*
—¿Escuchan **mis** cintas?	*Are they listening to my tapes?*
—Sí, escuchan **sus** cintas.	*Yes, they are listening to your (formal) tapes.*

Possessive Adjectives

	Singular		Plural	
yo	**mi**	*my*	**mis**	*my*
tú	**tu**	*your*	**tus**	*your*
usted	**su**	*your*	**sus**	*your*
nosotros(as)	**nuestro(a)**	*our*	**nuestros(as)**	*our*
vosotros(as)	**vuestro(a)**	*your*	**vuestros(as)**	*your*
ustedes	**su**	*your*	**sus**	*your*

1. Like articles and other adjectives, possessive adjectives agree in gender and number with the noun they modify. This means that they agree with what is possessed or owned.
2. Note that possessive adjectives are placed before the noun they modify.

Aquí practicamos

E. ¿Es mi libro? Replace the nouns in italics and make changes if necessary.

1. Es mi *libro*. (lápiz / apartamento / bolígrafo)
2. Es mi *casa*. (calculadora / cámara / máquina de escribir)
3. Son mis *discos compactos*. (llaves / amigos / plantas)
4. Allí está tu *casa*. (apartamento / cuaderno / cámara)
5. Quisiera escuchar tus *discos compactos*. (cintas / estéreo / grabadora)
6. Nosotros necesitamos nuestros *libros*. (cuadernos / calculadoras / computadora)
7. Es nuestro *coche*. (cuarto / mochila / calculadora)
8. ¿Son sus *libros*? (cintas / amigos / llaves)
9. Es nuestra *escuela*. (disco compacto / llave / televisor)
10. Llevamos nuestros *libros* a clase. (calculadoras / cuadernos / mochilas)

F. ¡Qué confusión! Everyone seems confused about what belongs to whom. First, someone you don't know tries to take your things, but you politely set him (her) straight. Remember to use **es** with a singular noun and **son** with a plural noun. Follow the models.

> **MODELO** Ah, mi lápiz.
> *Perdón. No es su lápiz. Es mi lápiz.*

1. Ah, mi cuaderno.
2. Ah, mi mochila.
3. Ah, mi calculadora.
4. Ah, mi borrador.

> **MODELO** Ah, mis libros.
> *Perdón. No son sus libros. Son mis libros.*

5. Ah, mis cintas.
6. Ah, mis llaves.
7. Ah, mis cuadernos.
8. Ah, mis discos compactos.

Now your neighbors are confused about what belongs to them and what belongs to your family.

> **MODELO** ¿Es nuestro coche?
> *No, no es su coche. Es nuestro coche.*

9. ¿Es nuestro televisor a colores?
10. ¿Es nuestra cámara?
11. ¿Es nuestro radio despertador?
12. ¿Es nuestra computadora?

> **MODELO** ¿Son nuestras plantas?
> *No, no son sus plantas. Son nuestras plantas.*

13. ¿Son nuestros discos compactos?
14. ¿Son nuestras bicicletas?
15. ¿Son nuestras llaves?
16. ¿Son nuestras cintas?

Finally, your friend thinks your things belong to him (her).

> **MODELO** Dame *(Give me)* mi llave.
> *Perdón. No es tu llave. Es mi llave.*

17. Dame mi cuaderno.
18. Dame mi cinta.
19. Dame mi borrador.
20. Dame mi mochila.

> **MODELO** Dame mis libros.
> *Perdón. No son tus libros. Son mis libros.*

21. Dame mis pósters.
22. Dame mis discos compactos.
23. Dame mis llaves.
24. Dame mis cuadernos.

Capítulo 4 ¿De quién es? **95**

? ¿Qué crees?

Spanish television often features **telenovelas**, both here in the United States and in other parts of the Spanish-speaking world. Telenovelas are:

a) TV plays
b) novels read on TV
c) soap operas
d) game shows

respuesta ☞

PRACTICE / APPLY

F. ¡Qué confusión!

ANSWERS

1. Perdón. No es su cuaderno. Es mi cuaderno.
2. ...No es su mochila. Es mi mochila.
3. ...No es su calculadora. Es mi calculadora.
4. ...No es su borrador. Es mi borrador.
5. ...No son sus cintas. Son mis cintas.
6. ...No son sus llaves. Son mis llaves.
7. ...No son sus cuadernos. Son mis cuadernos.
8. ...No son sus discos compactos. Son mis discos compactos
9. No, no es su televisor a colores. Es nuestro televisor a colores.
10. No, no es su cámara. Es nuestra cámara.
11. No, no es su radio despertador. Es nuestro radio despertador.
12. No, no es su computadora. Es nuestra computadora.
13. No, no son sus discos compactos. Son nuestros discos compactos.
14. No, no son sus bicicletas. Son nuestras bicicletas.
15. No, no son sus llaves. Son nuestras llaves.
16. No, no son sus cintas. Son nuestras cintas.
17. Perdón. No es tu cuaderno. Es mi cuaderno.
18. ...No es tu cinta. Es mi cinta.
19. ...No es tu borrador. Es mi borrador.
20. ...No es tu mochila. Es mi mochila.
21. ...No son tus pósters. Son mis pósters.
22. ...No son tus discos compactos. Son mis discos compactos.
23. ...No son tus llaves. Son mis llaves.
24. ...No son tus cuadernos. Son mis cuadernos.

☀ Spanish for Spanish Speakers

Commands

Have Spanish speakers give the correct pronunciation for **Dame** (used in 17-24). Tell the class to listen for the syllable stressed, and ask them to repeat **Dame** after the student giving the pronunciation.

🔊 Auditory-Musical

G. No, no es mi libro

ANSWERS

1. ¿Es tu calculadora? No, no es mi calculadora.
2. tus lápices/mis lápices
3. tus bolígrafos/mis bolígrafos
4. tu mochila/mi mochila
5. tu computadora/mi computadora
6. tu portafolio/mi portafolio
7. tu borrador/mi borrador
8. tu bicicleta/mi bicicleta
9. tu moto/mi moto
10. tu coche/mi coche
11. tus discos compactos/mis discos compactos
12. tus llaves/mis llaves
13. tu cuaderno/mi cuaderno
14. tus libros/mis libros
15. tu cartera/mi cartera

VARIATION

After denying ownership of an item, the student states that the questioner owns it. **No, no es mi libro, es tu libro.**

Individual Needs

More-prepared Students

Have the more prepared students redo the activity with their partners, this time using the **su/nuestro** format: **¿Es su cámara? No, no es nuestra cámara.**

Less-prepared Students

Less prepared students should write the names of several of the items first, and then do the activity orally.

G. No, no es mi libro Now *you're* confused! When you point out the following items and ask a classmate if they belong to him (her), your classmate responds negatively. Follow the models.

MODELOS

Tú: ¿Es tu cámara?
Compañera(o): No, no es mi cámara.

Tú: Son tus plantas?
Compañera(o): No, no son mis plantas.

c

1.
2.
3.
4.
5.

6.
7.
8.
9.
10.

11.
12.
13.
14.
15.

☀ Spanish for Spanish Speakers

What teens own

Ask Spanish speakers if they know whether it is common to have a car, a computer, a bike, or a motorcycle in their/their families' countries of origin. Have them discuss why they think these things are/are not common possessions among teens both here and in their countries of origin.

Cultural Comparisons 4.2

Aquí escuchamos

¿Dónde vives? *Carmen describes her home.*

Antes de escuchar Think about where Carmen might live, what she might have there, and how she might get around town.

 A escuchar Listen twice to the monologue and check off on your activity master the items that Carmen mentions.

__ apartamento	__ coche	__ motocicleta	__ televisor
__ bicicleta	__ estéreo	__ plantas	__ vídeo
__ casa	__ libros	__ pósters	

Después de escuchar On your activity master, write down some notes on what Carmen says about where she lives, what she has there, and how she gets around.

¡ADELANTE!

 Mi casa y tu casa Share information with a partner about your home and belongings.

1. Ask what he (she) has at home. (**¿Qué hay en tu casa?**)
2. Describe your own home. (**En mi casa hay…**)
3. While listening to your partner's description, point out something he (she) has that you also have at home. (**Hay un coche japonés en mi casa también.**)
4. Listen for something that there is at your partner's home but not at yours and comment on it. (**No hay moto en mi casa, pero hay tres bicicletas.**)

Finally, prepare a report together in which you identify…

1. a few items that are in both of your homes. (**En nuestras casas hay…**)
2. other items that are only in your home. (**En mi casa hay…, pero no hay… en su casa.**)
3. items that are only in his (her) home. (**En su casa hay…, pero no hay… en mi casa.**)

Capítulo 4 ¿De quién es? **97**

Aquí escuchamos

 TEXTBOOK CASSETTE/CD CASSETTE 1, SIDE A; CD 1, TRACK 30

 TAPESCRIPT P. 193

TRB: ACTIVITY MASTER, P. 75

Después de escuchar
ANSWERS
1. Vive en un apartamento.
2. Hay un estéreo, un televisor, unas plantas y muchos libros.
3. Va al centro en bicicleta.

ETAPA SYNTHESIS

Mi casa y tu casa
Have students ask their partners questions about the photograph on page 98. They could also compare their room to the one in the photo, saying what they have that the photo does not.

 Interpersonal Communication 1.1

Spanish for Spanish Speakers

Spoken Spanish

Ask Spanish speakers to listen to the Spanish used in the **Aquí escuchamos** recording and to compare it to the Spanish they use in their communities. Encourage student to focus, for example, on the consonant **s**: Does it sound similar to the *s* in English? Is it barely audible (as is often the case in Spanish spoken in the Caribbean)? Is it similar to the *th* sound in English? How does it contrast with their spoken Spanish? You might want to have the rest of the class participate in this activity.

☀ Comparing and Contrasting

◣◣ Auditory-Musical

⊛ Linguistic Comparisons 4.1

Mi cuarto y mis actividades

FYI

 ATAJO WRITING ASSISTANT SOFTWARE

You might want to have students use this software program when doing this activity.

SUGGESTION

 For extra practice, have students draw on the information in their strip stories to produce a written group story, including the similarities and differences among individual members of their group. Help students with additional vocabulary and phrases they may need.

Comparing and Contrasting
Creating

Presentational Communication 1.3

Additional Practice and Recycling

FYI

 WORKBOOK, PP. 47-51

For recycling and additional practice of the vocabulary, structures, and language functions presented throughout this **etapa**, you can assign the workbook activities as in-class work and/or homework. Answers to the activities are overprinted on each page of the Teacher's Edition of the Workbook.

Resources for Spanish-speaking Students

FYI

 WORKBOOK FOR SPANISH-SPEAKING STUDENTS: PP. 21-26

 ANSWER KEY TO SSS WORKBOOK PP. 7-9

Activities specially written to meet the needs of Spanish-speaking students are available in this workbook for the reinforcement and extension of the topics and language presented in this chapter.

 Mi cuarto y mis actividades Prepare your own personal picture strip story describing your own home, what you have in it, and how you travel when you go out, based on the models in activity B on page 92. In your writing, include things you have in your home or room and mention what you like to do with those things. You may wish to start out with: **En mi casa** (or **cuarto**) **hay….** Include in your description things you do not have at home (**En mi casa no hay…**). Follow the model.

MODELO *En mi cuarto hay un estéreo y muchos discos compactos Mis discos compactos son de música rock. Me gusta escuchar música cuando estudio. Hay un teléfono también en mi cuarto. Me gusta mucho hablar con mis amigos. También me gusta visitar a mis amigos. A veces voy a casa de mis amigos en bicicleta.*

En mi cuarto hay muchas muñecas (dolls).

 **EN LÍNEA**

Connect with the Spanish-speaking world! Access the *¡Ya verás! Gold* home page for Internet activities related to this chapter.

http://yaveras.heinle.com

98 *Segunda unidad* ¡Vamos a conocernos!

Additional Etapa Resources

Refer to the **Etapa** Support Materials list on the opening page of this **etapa** for detailed cross-references to these assessment options.

VOCABULARIO

Para charlar

Para expresar posesión
¿De quién es…?
¿De quién son…?
Es(Son) de…
mi(s)
tu(s)
su(s)
nuestro(s)
nuestra(s)

Para contar
cero
uno
dos
tres
cuatro
cinco
seis
siete
ocho
nueve
diez
once
doce
trece
catorce
quince
dieciséis
diecisiete
dieciocho
diecinueve
veinte

Temas y contextos

En la escuela
un(a) alumno(a)
un bolígrafo
un borrador
una calculadora
una cartera
un cuaderno
un lápiz
un libro
una llave
una mochila
una pluma
un portafolio
un sacapuntas

Los medios de transporte
un autobús
una bicicleta
un coche
una motocicleta

Las viviendas
un apartamento
una casa
un cuarto

En mi cuarto
una alfombra
una bocina
una cama
una cámara
una cinta
una cómoda
una computadora
un disco compacto
un escritorio
un estante
un estéreo
una grabadora
una máquina de
  escribir
una planta
un póster
un radio
  despertador
una silla
un televisor
  (a colores)
un vídeo

Vocabulario general

Verbos
llevar

Artículos
el
la
los
las

Otras palabras y expresiones
allí
cosa
¿Cuántos hay?
¿Dónde hay?
En mi cuarto hay…
éstos
más
Me llamo…
menos
muchacha
muchacho
Para ir al centro,
  voy en…
¿Qué hay en tu
  cuarto?
¿Qué llevas (tú) a la
  escuela?
telenovelas
Vivo en…

Capítulo 4 ¿De quién es? **99**

CHAPTER WRAP-UP

Vocabulario
VOCABULARY GAME
Play **el juego de las categorías** as a wrap-up activity. You name a category, for example, **la escuela, el cuarto**, or **los medios de transporte**. With books closed, students write as many items as they can remember for each category.

Categorizing

Improvised Conversation
SUGGESTION

	TEXTBOOK CASSETTE/CD CASSETTE 1, SIDE A; CD 1, TRACK 31
	TAPESCRIPT P. 193
	TRB: ACTIVITY MASTER, P. 76

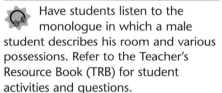 Have students listen to the monologue in which a male student describes his room and various possessions. Refer to the Teacher's Resource Book (TRB) for student activities and questions.

Listening Skills Development
FYI

	LAB MANUAL PP. 23-29
	LAB PROGRAM CASSETTE SIDE A, CD2, TRACKS 9-17
	TAPESCRIPT: LAB PROGRAM PP. 31-40

It is now appropriate to work through the lab manual activities and their accompanying recordings in class or in the language laboratory. These materials provide reinforcement of the pronunciation points, vocabulary, structures, and language functions presented throughout the **etapas** and continue the development of listening comprehension skills provided in the **Aquí escuchamos** sections and the Improvised Conversation.

Additional Chapter Resources

Refer to the Chapter Support Materials list on the opening page of this chapter for detailed cross-references to *¡Ya verás! Gold*'s student-centered technology components and various assessment options.

Spanish for Spanish Speakers

Keeping a Vocabulary Notebook
Remind Spanish-speaking students to add words and expressions from this vocabulary section to the problematic spelling combination categories and personal new vocabulary lists they started in their notebooks in Chapter 1. Reinforce that they should continue to do this each time a chapter in the textbook is completed.

PRACTICE/APPLY

"Caballo de acero"
Antes de leer
SUGGESTION
Have students review the photos to predict the content of the reading. Have them also discuss the format of this letter. How was it written? How was it sent? What are the benefits of this kind of correspondence? What are the drawbacks? Ask students if they correspond this way.

 Activating Prior Knowledge

VARIATION
Have students look for the nicknames used by the writer of this letter. What do these nicknames mean? Ask students if they use nicknames for their friends.

EXPANSION
Have students discuss the various uses of the bicycle, and why it is a such a popular mode of transportation in so many places around the world. Then have students talk about the attraction of cycling as a sport.

 Interpersonal

Guía para la lectura
VOCABULARY EXPANSION
Remind students that the other seasons of the year are **verano** (summer), **otoño** (fall), and **invierno** (winter).

Activating Prior Knowledge

"Caballo de acero"

Antes de leer

> **Reading Strategy**
> • Using photos, artwork and illustrations to predict content

1. What sports do you enjoy the most? The least?
2. What kind of format is the reading in?
3. Do you participate in cycling, either recreationally or competitively?

De: reinaroja@arols.com
Para: Pedro "El Pollo" Villar, Club de ciclismo "Caballo de acero"<pollovila@arols.com>
Fecha: 5 de febrero 19... 11:50AM
Tema: Carreras de bicicleta

¡Hola pollo!

¿Cómo estás? Y los padres, ¿qué tal? Yo tengo una fuerte gripe. Mi bicicleta está en el garaje y estoy aquí, en la cama, sin apetito. Solo tomo té con limón y pan tostado. Me gustan tus cartas, pero especialmente ahora.

Te envío pronto una copia de una revista que compro aquí todos los meses. Tiene un artículo muy interesante sobre el ciclismo. Gracias por la información que enviaste por correo electrónico sobre la "Vuelta a Colombia" de este año. Yo también pienso que esta es una competencia muy importante para el ciclismo latinoamericano. La "Vuelta a México" es muy importante también. Me parece que es bueno saber que si no ganas un campeonato de bicicleta en Colombia o en México, a lo mejor ganas en Ecuador, en Uruguay o en Argentina. ¡Hay tantas competencias para escoger! Los campeonatos de primavera están cerca y todos tenemos que entrenar mucho. Yo estoy muy nerviosa, pues tengo demasiado trabajo de la escuela y no hay mucho tiempo más para entrenar bien este año.

Bueno pollo, chao, te escribo pronto.

Un abrazo,

Isabel, "La Reina Roja"

Focus on Culture

El ciclismo

Cycling is growing in popularity in Latin America. Spain has always been strong in bicycle racing and hosts several races each year, including the Tour of Spain and the San Sebastian World Cup Road Race. A famous cycler is Spaniard Miguel Induráin, winner of the prestigious Tour de France race in 1992, 1993, and 1994 and the Tour de Italy in 1992 and 1993. Some major races in Latin America include: **Vuelta a Colombia** and **Vuelta a México**. Mountain bike riding is also growing in popularity in mountainous regions of Central and South America.

 Connections with Other Disciplines 3.1

Guía para la lectura

Here are some words and expressions to keep in mind as you read.

Caballo de acero	*name of a cycling club (literally, "iron horse")*
pollo	*chicken, used here as a nickname*
gripe	*common cold—also known by other names in Spanish: catarro, resfriado*
revista	*magazine*
correo electrónico	*e-mail*
competencia	*competition*
campeonato	*championship*
a lo mejor ganas	*maybe you'll win*
primavera	*spring (season)*
todos tenemos que entrenar	*everyone has to to train*

Después de leer

1. According to the context of the reading, what do you think the "Vuelta a Colombia" and the "Vuelta a México" are?

2. What is the author's opinion about these two events? And about participating in cycling events in Latin America in general?

3. Is cycling popular in the United States? Would you say that it is more popular in the United States than in other countries? Why?

4. Would you rather own a bicycle or a car? Why? What are the advantages of each?

Capítulo 4 ¿De quién es? **101**

Despues de leer
POSSIBLE ANSWERS
1. bicycle races
2. The **Vuelta a Colombia** and **Vuelta a México** are both important bicycle races in Latin America. There are other bicycle races in Ecuador, Uruguay and Argentina; She thinks it is a good thing that there are so many races in which to participate, because it gives cyclists more chances to win.
3. Answers will vary.
4. Answers will vary.

SUGGESTION
Have students compare and contrast owning a bicycle and owning a car. Have them evaluate which form of transportation is better suited for where they live. After students list the advantages and disadvantages of each, they can take a vote for the best mode of transportation.

Comparing and Contrasting
Determining Preferences
Evaluating

Focus on Culture

Cycling in the U.S.
Bicycling is the third largest participation sport in the United States with bike sales topping 100 million during the past six years. (Walking and swimming are the first two.) In addition, the number of Americans who have watched a cycling race also has exceeded the 100 million mark.

Connections to Other Disciplines 3.1

CAPÍTULO 5

OBJECTIVES

Functions
• Talking about preferences
• Obtaining information about other people

Context
• Various settings

Accuracy
• **Gustar (me gustan/te gustan)**
• Review of **ser + de** for possession
• **-Er** and **-ir** verbs

Pronunciation
• The consonant **d**

CHAPTER WARM-UP

Setting the Context

In preparation for their learning about how to express one's own preferences and how to find out more about other people, have students study this photo. Where are these two friends? What might they be talking about? Let students discuss their own tastes in music. Remind them that preferences are simply one's personal likes and dislikes—not matters of absolute right and wrong. As they study this chapter, encourage students to explore their own preferences and to find out more about other people without being judgmental.

Determining Preferences

Me gusta mucho...

—¿Te gusta la música?
—Claro. Me gusta mucho la música.

Objectives

● **talking about preferences**
● **getting information about other people**

102 *Segunda unidad* ¡Vamos a conocernos!

Chapter Support Materials

• Lab Manual: pp. 30-35
• Lab Program: Cassette Side B; CD 3, Tracks 1-9
• TRB: Textbook Activity Masters: pp. 77-80
• Textbook Cassettes/CDs: Cassette 1, Side A; CD 1, Track 38
• Tapescript: Lab Program pp. 41-50; Textbook Cassettes/CDs p. 195
• Middle School Activities: pp. 39-42
• Workbook for Spanish-speaking Students: pp. 27-32
• Answer Key to SSS Workbook: pp. 9-10
• Practice Software: Windows™; Macintosh®
• Testing Program: Chapter Test pp. 53-56; Answer Key & Testing Cassettes Tapescript p. T22; Oral Assessment p. T23
• Testing Cassettes: Cassette Side B
• Computerized Testing Program: Windows™; Macintosh®
• Video Program: Cassette 1, 40:09-53:48
• Video Guide: Videoscript pp. 22-24; Activities pp. 99-101
• **Mundos hispanos 1**
• Internet Activities: Student Text p. 119

PRIMERA ETAPA

Preparación

- As you get ready to begin this **etapa,** think about your likes and dislikes. On a sheet of paper, make headings for two lists: 1) *I like . . .* and 2) *I don't like . . . .*

- Write each of the following interests under the appropriate heading to express your personal tastes: music, animals, sports, nature, art, school subjects (science, history, foreign language, math).

Mis gustos

*Buenos días. Me llamo José. **Ésta** es Ana. Es mi **novia**, pero nuestros gustos son muy diferentes.*

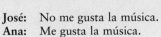

| José: | No me gusta la música. | José: | Me gustan los animales. |
| Ana: | Me gusta la música. | Ana: | No me gustan los animales. |

Mis gustos *My tastes*   **Ésta** *This*   **novia** *girlfriend*

Capítulo 5 Me gusta mucho...   **103**

TEACH/MODEL

Mis gustos
PRESENTATION

 TRANSPARENCIES 8

TEXTBOOK CASSETTE/CD CASSETTE 1, SIDE A; CD 1, TRACK 32

TAPESCRIPT PP. 193-194

You may introduce the new vocabulary by using transparencies and the Textbook Cassette/CD (with students' books closed). Prepare students for the listening comprehension by telling them that they are about to hear a conversation between a male student (José) and his girlfriend (Ana). They like each other a lot, but they have very different interests. After playing the Textbook Cassette/CD once or twice, ask questions such as, **¿A quién le gusta la música, a Ana o a José?** Tell students to answer with just the name.

Another option is to read different statements, such as, **Me gustan los animales**, and have students say who made the statement, Ana or José. If students are unable to answer, verify comprehension, then read the dialogue, having students repeat first as a whole class, then in groups, and then individually. Ask again those questions with which they had difficulty.

Point out that in most cases the adjective of nationality is also the word used for the languages.

Auditory-Musical

Interpretive Communication 1.2

Etapa Support Materials

- Workbook: pp. 52-57
- TRB: Textbook Activity Masters: pp. 77, 78
- Textbook Cassettes/CDs: Cassette 1, Side A; CD 1, Track 32
- Tapescript: Textbook Cassettes/CDs p. 192
- Overhead Transparencies: 26, 27
- Middle School Activities: p. 43
- Lesson Plan Book: pp. 26-27

- Testing Program: Quiz pp. 49-50; Answer Key & Testing Cassettes: Tapescript p. T21
- Testing Cassettes: Cassette Side B
- Computerized Testing Program: Windows™; Macintosh®
- Atajo Writing Assistant Software: Student Text p. 111

Mis gustos

VOCABULARY EXPANSION

Introduce **física, matemáticas (álgebra, trigonometría, cálculo, geometría), arte surrealista, arte moderno, pintura (cuadro), museo.**

Write the words on the board and then ask students simple questions with the new vocabulary, using either **gustar** or other **-ar** verbs that they have learned. **¿Qué ciencia estudias? ¿Te gusta el arte surrealista? ¿Visitas los museos mucho o poco?**

Interpersonal Communication 1.1

José: Me gustan los **deportes.**
Ana: No me gustan los deportes.

José: Me gusta la **naturaleza.**
Ana: No me gusta la naturaleza.

José: No me gusta el arte.
Ana: Me gusta el arte.

José: Me gustan las **lenguas.**
Ana: No me gustan las lenguas.

José: No me gustan las **ciencias…**
       no me gusta la **química.**
Ana: Me gustan las ciencias…
       me gusta la química.

José: No me gusta la biología.
Ana: Me gusta la biología.

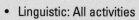

deportes *sports*   **naturaleza** *nature*   **lenguas** *languages*   **ciencias** *science*   **química** *chemistry*

104   *Segunda unidad* ¡Vamos a conocernos!

MULTIPLE INTELLIGENCES

- Linguistic: All activities
- Logical-Mathematical: C, E, G
- Visual-Spatial: **Mis gustos**, A, G, I, J
- Auditory-Musical: **Pronunciación**, F, **Aquí escuchamos**
- Interpersonal: H, **Los gustos de la clase**
- Intrapersonal: A, **Entrevista**

The Standards

- Interpersonal Communication 1.1: A, B, D, E, **Adelante** activities
- Interpretive Communication 1.2: C, H, I **Aquí escuchamos**
- Presentational Communication 1.3: H
- Connections with Distinctive Viewpoints 3.2: D
- Linguistic Comparisons 4.1: **Pronunciación, Nota gramatical**

¡Te toca a ti!

A. ¡(No) Me gusta! Indicate how you feel about each activity pictured. Follow the model.

> **MODELO** *Me gusta la música.* o:
> *No me gusta la música.*

1.
2.
3.
4.
5.
6.

B. ¿Y tú? Ask a classmate whether he (she) likes the activities pictured in the previous activity. Follow the model.

> **MODELO** Tú: *¿Te gusta la música?*
> Compañera(o): *No, no me gusta la música.*

ESTRUCTURA

The verb gustar

Me gusta el disco compacto.	*I like the compact disc.*
Te gusta la cinta.	*You like the tape.*
Me gusta estudiar.	*I like to study.*
Te gusta trabajar.	*You like to work.*
Me gustan los discos compactos.	*I like the compact discs.*
Te gustan las cintas.	*You like the tapes.*

1. **Gustar** is different from other Spanish verbs you know in that it does not use subject pronouns. As you learned in Chapter 1, to express *I like* and *you like*, you use the pronouns **me** and **te** in front of a form of the verb **gustar**.

2. Only two forms of **gustar** are used—the singular form **gusta** and the plural form **gustan**. Use **gusta** if what is liked is a singular noun or an infinitive. If what is liked is a plural noun, use **gustan**.

Capítulo 5 Me gusta mucho... **105**

PRACTICE/APPLY

C. Los gustos

SUGGESTION

 Reinforce the grammatical concepts and the idea of *agreement* in this activity by having students create a *word web*. First, have students complete the activity, adding other conjugated verbs and subject pronouns as appropriate.

Then, have students graph the elements in the columns. Direct them as follows: Put the subjects in a center circle; the plural verb(s) in a circle to the upper right of the first circle; the singular verb(s) in a circle to the lower right of the first circle. Then put the plural objects in a circle beside the plural verb(s). Put the singular objects in a circle beside the singular verb(s). Connect the correct elements with lines; label all the circles with the appropriate grammatical terms.

When students have completed this activity, call students to the board to re-graph what they have done there. Correct as necessary, emphasizing word order and the concept of agreement.

🔆 Analyzing

🔺 Visual-Spatial

VARIATION

Have pairs discuss and report their greatest shared interest and top mutual dislike. Take a tally on the board to determine the most and least popular class tastes. Label each column, **Nos gusta(n) más** and **Nos gusta(n) menos**. To follow up, ask: **¿A quién(es) le(s) gusta más... ? ¿Qué nos gusta menos?**

🔆 Comparing and Contrasting

Individual Needs

Less-prepared Students
Less-prepared students can find magazine ads and photos to create a personal poster on which they write their likes and dislikes and illustrate them in a creative way.

Aquí practicamos

C. Los gustos Create a sentence by combining an element from Column A, one from Column B, and one from Column C. Follow the model.

MODELO *Me gustan los licuados.*

A	B	C
me	gusta	el sándwich
te	gustan	los licuados
		los refrescos
		el póster
		el disco compacto
		los deportes
		la música clásica
		las ciencias
		las lenguas
		los animales

D. ¡Me gustan muchísimo los deportes! An exchange student from Peru will be living with your family for the next six months. You are getting to know each other and she (he) is asking you about your likes and dislikes. Be as specific as possible in your answers. Follow the model.

MODELO ¿Te gustan los deportes?
¡Sí, me gustan muchísimo los deportes! o:
No, no me gustan los deportes.

1. ¿Te gusta estudiar?
2. ¿Te gusta bailar?
3. ¿Te gusta la química?
4. ¿Te gustan las lenguas?
5. ¿Te gustan los animales?
6. ¿Te gusta la música?

☀ Spanish for Spanish Speakers

Interviewing

For Activity D, Spanish speakers and/or more-prepared students can interview each other as if they were looking for a compatible roommate for a study abroad program or for college. Have them list their likes and dislikes and then find others with similar interests.

 Categorizing
Determining Preferences

 Interpersonal

E. Me gustan los deportes, pero no me gusta la política You and your friends are talking about what you like and dislike. In each case, say that the person indicated by the pronoun likes the first activity or item but dislikes the second one. Follow the model.

> MODELO   me / deportes / política
> *Me gustan los deportes, pero no me gusta la política.*

1. me / naturaleza / animales
2. te / música / arte
3. me / lenguas / literatura
4. me / lenguas / ciencias
5. te / política / matemáticas
6. te / música / deportes

PRONUNCIACIÓN THE CONSONANT **d**

In Spanish, when **d** is the first letter of a word or comes after **l** or **n**, it is produced by placing the tip of the tongue behind the back of the upper front teeth. In English, *d* is pronounced by placing the tip of the tongue on the gum ridge behind the upper front teeth. Pronounce the English word *dee* and note where the tip of your tongue is. Now pronounce the Spanish word **di** being careful to place the tip of the tongue on the back of the upper front teeth.

Práctica

F. Listen and repeat as your teacher models the following words.

1. disco
2. de
3. domingo
4. dos
5. diez
6. grande
7. aprender
8. Donaldo
9. Aldo
10. donde

Repaso

G. ¿Cuántos hay? Tell how many objects are in each of the drawings below. Follow the model.

> MODELO   *Hay dos lápices.*

1.

2.

Capítulo 5 Me gusta mucho... **107**

PRACTICE/APPLY

G. ¿Cuántos hay?

SUGGESTION
Dictate the numbers to students with their books closed. Then have them read the numbers back to you in Spanish. Students could then do simple addition problems orally.

ANSWERS
1. tres bolígrafos
2. cinco plantas
3. una calculadora
4. cuatro sillas
5. tres cintas
6. siete lápices
7. once libros
8. ocho discos compactos

H. Nosotros llevamos...

FYI
This activity provides preparation for the **Charlemos un rato** activities at the end of Unit 2.

TEACH/MODEL

Estructura

PRESENTATION
Remind students that to express possession in Spanish they must change the word order of possessives in English. Instead of *John's keys* they must think *the keys of John*.

Linguistic Comparisons 4.1

PRACTICE/APPLY

I. El libro es de...

SUGGESTIONS
Have students do the activity orally with their partners or have them write out the statements and check their partners' work for mistakes.

ANSWERS
1. La calculadora es de Anita.
2. La computadora es de Elena.
3. La cámara es de Juan.
4. Los bolígrafos son de ella.
5. La bicicleta es de Tomás.
6. Los lápices son de Julián.
7. Las cintas son de él.
8. La mochila es de Carmen.
9. La radio es de Alicia y Susana.
10. Las llaves son de ellos.

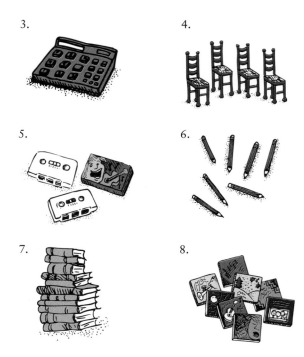

3.
4.
5.
6.
7.
8.

H. Nosotros llevamos... Make a list of five things you take to school every day. Compare your list with those of several other students in class. When you find that an item on your list is also on someone else's list, put a check mark beside it. Count the marks and report which items are most and least popular.

ESTRUCTURA

Ser + de for possession

El libro **es de Juan.**	*The book is Juan's.*
La calculadora **es de María.**	*The calculator is María's.*
Los lápices **son de él.**	*The pencils are his.*
Las mochilas **son de ellas.**	*The knapsacks are theirs* (female).

In Chapter 4, you learned two ways to express possession—the preposition **de** with nouns and possessors' names for the third person, and the possessive adjectives for first and second persons. You can also use the verb **ser** + **de** followed by the possessor's name or by a pronoun (**él, ella, ellos,** or **ellas**) to express possession in the third person.

Spanish for Spanish Speakers

School Items
Have Spanish speakers ask older members of their family or community what items they always took with them to school when they were younger in their native countries. Have students compare their findings with the answers given by students in Activity H.

Cultural Comparisons 4.2

Aquí practicamos

I. El libro es de... Look at the drawings and indicate to whom the items belong. Follow the models.

MODELOS   *El cuaderno es de José.*
Los libros son de Bárbara.

José   Bárbara

1. Anita   2. Elena   3. Juan   4. ella   5. Tomás

6. Julián   7. él   8. Carmen   9. Alicia y Susana   10. ellos

J. ¿De quién es? A classmate asks you to whom each of the following items belongs. Use **ser + de** to answer. Take turns asking and answering questions. Follow the models.

MODELOS   **Compañera(o):**   *¿De quién es la mochila?*
            Tú: *La mochila es de María.*

            Tú: *¿De quién son los cuadernos?*
    Compañera (o):   *Los cuadernos son de José.*

María   José

1. Juan   2. ella   3. Catarina   4. Alicia

5. Miguel   6. él   7. Anita   8. Lorenzo

Capítulo 5   Me gusta mucho...   **109**

J. ¿De quién es?

SUGGESTION

Do a singular and a plural example for the class first, before having them work in pairs. Stress **¿De quién es... ?** for singular items and **¿De quién son... ?** for plural.

ANSWERS

1. ¿De quién es la computadora? La computadora es de Juan.
2. ...son los discos compactos? Los discos compactos son de ella.
3. ...es el bolígrafo? El bolígrafo es de Catarina.
4. ...es la llave? La llave es de Alicia.
5. ...son los lápices? Los lápices son de Miguel.
6. ...son los libros? Los libros son de él.
7. ...son las plantas? Las plantas son de Anita.
8. ...son las cintas? Las cintas son de Lorenzo.

BUYER BEWARE GAME
Write the following twenty words/phrases on the board: **barco, coche, computadora, casas, videocaseteras, cintas, radios, plantas, discos compactos, televisor, gato, perros, motocicleta, pósters, libros, bicicleta, apartamentos, estéreo, radio despertador, grabadoras**

Then, divide the class into two teams. Have students study the words, then give students the set-up: (1) They have a lot of money. (2) They want to buy something listed on the board. (3) They have to find out who owns the item they want. Next, walk around the class whispering the names of items in *owners* ears; check off an item once you've assigned it.

Then, have students from each team take turns coming to the board, asking: **¿De quién es... ?, or ¿De quién son... ?** If a buyer gets the question correct, (**Es mi... ; Son mis...**) his (her) team gets one point. If the *owner* gets the answer correct, his (her) team gets one point. If they both speak correctly, they each get one point. Points should be tallied on the board. An object gets crossed out as soon as it's bought. The team that gets the most points wins.

 Interpersonal Communication 1.1

Linguistic

Aquí escuchamos

 TEXTBOOK CASSETTE/CD CASSETTE 1, SIDE A; CD 1, TRACK 34

 TAPESCRIPT P. 194

 TRB: ACTIVITY MASTER, P. 77

Después de escuchar
ANSWERS
She likes: **animales, biología, matemáticas**
She doesn't like: **arte, literatura**

Aquí escuchamos

Mis gustos *Carmen talks about her likes and dislikes.*

Antes de escuchar Think about how Carmen might say that she likes something, how she might say that she doesn't like some thing, and how the words **también, tampoco, y,** and **pero** are used.

 A escuchar As you listen, check the appropriate column on your activity master to show Carmen likes and what she doesn't like.

	She likes	She doesn't like
animales		
arte		
biología		
lenguas		
literatura		
matemáticas		
música		
química		

Después de escuchar On your activity master, answer the following question.

Which subject area do you think is Carmen's favorite: liberal arts, science, or technology?

✺ Spanish for Spanish Speakers

Vocabulary Expansion–Antonyms

Have Spanish speakers listen carefully to the **Aquí escuchamos** recording and write down five words they hear for which they know or want to find antonyms. Tell them not to limit themselves to just one or two parts of speech, but to choose nouns, verbs, adjectives, adverbs, prepositions, etc. Then give students copies of the dialogue from the Tapescript and have them work with a partner to combine their lists and create a transformed dialogue. Have Spanish speakers and other class volunteers roleplay the dialogue with the new words for the rest of the class.

Auditory-Musical Linguistic

Creating

Presentational Communication 1.3

¡ADELANTE!

 Los gustos de la clase Form pairs and prepare a profile of your partner's likes and dislikes using the chart on your activity master. Interview your partner and rate how much he (she) likes each activity or item with the numbers on the following scale. Write the appropriate number next to each item on your activity master. Be ready to report on your partner's favorite and least favorite activities and items.

no = 0   **poco** = 1   **bastante** *(okay,*
mucho = 3   **muchísimo** = 4   *pretty well)* = 2

MODELO		
Tú:	*¿Te gusta mucho la biología?*	
Compañera(o):	*No, me gusta la biología muy poco.*	
	(1 la biología) o:	
	No, pero me gusta la química	
	bastante. (2 la química)	

__ **la biología**	__ **la música clásica**	__ **los animales**
__ **la química**	__ **el jazz**	__ **los deportes**
__ **las ciencias**	__ **el arte moderno**	__ **la comida italiana**
__ **la historia**	__ **el arte clásico**	__ **la comida vietnamita**
__ **la literatura**	__ **los pósters**	__ **bailar**
__ **las lenguas**	__ **la política**	__ **viajar**
__ **la música rock**	__ **la naturaleza**	__ **cantar**

 Entrevista Using the list in the previous activity, along with other Spanish vocabulary you have learned, write a description of your likes and dislikes. Mention…

1. at least three things you like a lot
2. at least two that you don't like very much

Among them, mention…

3. something that you do well
4. something that you do every day
5. something else that you do occasionally

Use **también, tampoco, y,** and **pero** to connect your ideas. Compare your paragraph with that of a classmate. What are the similarities? What are the differences?

Capítulo 5 Me gusta mucho… **111**

Los gustos de la clase

SUGGESTION

 TRB: ACTIVITY MASTER, P. 78

Encourage your students to ask and answer their questions in complete sentences in Spanish. Tell them to say "**¿Cómo?**" or "**Repite, por favor**" if they don't understand a classmate's response.

Entrevista

FYI

 ATAJO WRITING ASSISTANT SOFTWARE

You might want to have students use this software program when doing this activity.

EXPANSION

 Develop a sample profile of the class from their interview responses:

Select one category of items from the list for your sample.

On the board, label your activity **Nuestros gustos** and then write the category title. Have students help you select all the items from the list that fit in that category.

Then have students tally their numbers for the items on the board.

Write those sums on the board and add them together to get a cumulative *profile* for the class.

 Categorizing

Additional Practice and Recycling

FYI

 WORKBOOK, PP. 52-57

For recycling and additional practice of the vocabulary, structures, and language functions presented throughout this **etapa**, you can assign the workbook activities as in-class work and/or homework.

TEACH/MODEL

¿Qué te gusta más?

PRESENTATION

 TRANSPARENCIES 8

 TEXTBOOK CASSETTE/CD CASSETTE 1, SIDE A; CD 1, TRACK 35

TAPESCRIPT P. 194

Point out the appropriate pictures on the transparencies as you play the Textbook Cassette/CD. Then have several students answer the questions. **¿Qué te gustan más, las películas de horror o las películas de aventura?**, etc. You might also want to use the opener as oral practice for students, reading the dialogue and having the class repeat after you. Then ask them questions based on the pictures.

▲▲ Auditory-Musical

FYI

Most new vocabulary words in this **etapa** are not glossed because they are cognates.

VOCABULARY EXPANSION

Introduce **pez de colores** (*goldfish*), **hámster** (pl. **hámsters**), **loro** (*parrot*), **perico/periquito** (*parakeet*), **natación, ciclismo, atletismo, lucha libre** (*wrestling*), **boxeo, los Juegos Olímpicos/las Olimpiadas**. Write the words on the board and continue discussing students' preferences: **¿Qué deportes practicas?/¿Qué deportes te gusta practicar? ¿Qué deportes miras en la televisión?**, etc.

 Interpersonal Communication 1.1

SEGUNDA ETAPA

Preparación

In this **etapa** you will continue to learn to talk about your likes and dislikes. Before you begin, think more specifically about the things you like and dislike. For example:

- Various sports
- Kinds of movies
- Types of art
- Types of animals
- Kinds of music
- Your school subjects

¿Qué te gusta más?

Un muchacho y una muchacha hablan de sus gustos.

Muchacho: Me gustan las **películas**.
Muchacha: ¿Qué te gusta más—las películas cómicas, las películas de horror, las películas de aventura o las películas de ciencia ficción?
Muchacho: Me gustan más las películas de horror.

¿Qué te gusta más? What do you like more? **películas** *movies*

112 *Segunda unidad* ¡Vamos a conocernos!

Etapa Support Materials

- Workbook: pp. 58-63
- TRB: Textbook Activity Masters: pp. 79, 80
- Textbook Cassettes/CDs: Cassette 1, Side A; CD 1, Track 32
- Tapescript: Textbook Cassettes/CDs pp. 194-195
- Overhead Transparencies: 28, 29
- Middle School Activities: pp. 44-46
- Lesson Plan Book: pp. 28-29

- Testing Program: Quiz pp. 51, 52; Answer Key & Testing Cassettes Tapescript pp. T21, T22
- Testing Cassettes: Cassette Side B
- Computerized Testing Program: Windows™; Macintosh®
- Atajo Writing Assistant Software: Student Text pp. 119; Workbook p. 63

Muchacho: Me gusta el arte.
Muchacha: ¿Qué te gusta más—la **pintura** o la **escultura?**
Muchacho: Me gusta más la escultura.

Muchacha: Me gustan los animales.
Muchacho: ¿Qué te gusta más—los **perros,** los **gatos** o los **pájaros?**
Muchacha: Me gustan más los pájaros.

Muchacha: Me gustan los deportes.
Muchacho: ¿Qué te gusta más—el **fútbol,** el fútbol americano, el básquetbol, el béisbol o el vólibol?
Muchacha: Me gusta más el béisbol.

Muchacho: Me gusta mucho la música.
Muchacha: ¿Qué te gusta más—la música rock, el jazz o la música clásica?
Muchacho: Me gusta más la música rock.

pintura *painting* **escultura** *sculpture* **perros** *dogs* **gatos** *cats* **pájaros** *birds* **fútbol** *soccer*

Capítulo 5 Me gusta mucho... **113**

SUGGESTION
At this time you might want to discuss sports in Spanish-speaking countries. Start by asking students what sports they associate with Spanish-speaking countries. Did they watch the 1992 Summer Olympic games in Barcelona? Can they remember which Spanish-speaking countries won medals? Point out the difference between American football and soccer. Soccer is the number one sport in Hispanic countries. Boxing and baseball are also very popular, especially in Mexico and the Caribbean countries. (Cuba won the Olympic gold medal for baseball in 1992.) Cubans also lead the world in boxing. (They won seven gold medals in boxing in Barcelona.)

Cultural Comparisons 4.2

VOCABULARY EXPANSION
Introduce students to some popular Latin music/rhythms, such as **flamenco, salsa, cumbia, merengue, mambo,** and **chachachá.**

Focus on Culture

Latin Musicians

Ask students if they are familiar with the types of music or rhythms listed in the vocabulary expansion. Do they know any singers from Latin American backgrounds? (Kid Frost, Mellow Man Ace, Gipsy Kings, Carlos Santana, Gloria Estefan, Rubén Blades, Linda Ronstadt, Tito Puente, Jon Secada, etc.) If you can, bring in some music by one or some of these performers or suggest that students bring in some tapes for a demonstration. If possible, make copies of the lyrics so that students can follow along.

Auditory-Musical

Cultural Comparisons 4.2

PRACTICE/APPLY

A. ¿Qué te gusta más?

SUGGESTIONS

 Have students work in pairs asking each other **¿Qué te gusta más,... ?** using the cues provided. Or have them write out sentences and edit their partners' work. You could also do this as a whole class activity using the **pregúntale** format.

Individual Needs

More-prepared Students
Ask more-prepared students additional preference questions to develop listening skills. Ask individual students randomly or use the **pregúntale** format. Since these questions are longer, students will have to listen carefully. You may have to repeat the questions.

🔊 Auditory-Musical

B. Me gusta más...

VARIATION

After students have completed Activities A and B, you may want to take a poll of the class' preferences. Record the results of the class poll on a graph. Have a student write each choice on the board. Enter *tick marks* by each item on the list as it is selected by a student response. Ask the summative question, **De todo esto, ¿qué nos gusta más?** Another variation would be to record the results on two different charts according to gender differences. Then ask the questions, **¿Qué les gusta más a las chicas? ¿y a los chicos?**

✏️ Comparing and Contrasting

¡Te toca a ti!

A. ¿Qué te gusta más?
Of the following items, indicate which you like more. Follow the model.

MODELO	el fútbol o el básquetbol
	Me gusta más el básquetbol.

1. el fútbol americano o el béisbol
2. los perros o los gatos
3. la pintura o la escultura
4. las películas de ciencia ficción o las películas cómicas
5. la música clásica o la música rock
6. la biología o la química
7. las lenguas o las matemáticas
8. la historia o el español

B. Me gusta más...
Ask two of your classmates to choose from the following sets of items. Follow the model.

MODELO	la música clásica, el jazz, la música rock
Tú:	*¿Te gusta más la música clásica, el jazz o la música rock?*
Compañero(a) 1:	*Me gusta más la música clásica.*
Tú:	*¿Y a ti?* (And you?)
Compañero(a) 2:	*Me gusta más la música rock.*

1. el fútbol, el fútbol americano, el básquetbol
2. la pintura, la escultura, la arquitectura
3. la música, el baile *(dancing)*, las películas
4. la música rock, el jazz, la música clásica
5. las hamburguesas, los sándwiches de jamón, las hamburguesas con queso
6. las películas de horror, las películas de aventura, las películas cómicas
7. el tenis, el golf, la natación *(swimming)*
8. la historia, las lenguas, las ciencias
9. el español, el francés, el inglés
10. la biología, la química, la física

PRONUNCIACIÓN THE CONSONANT **d**

The consonant **d** also has a sound that is similar to *th* in the English words *these, them, the, those,* etc. When you say these words note that the tip of the tongue touches the upper teeth. In Spanish, **d** is pronounced this way when it is between vowels or after any consonant except l or n or when it is the last letter in a word.

 MULTIPLE INTELLIGENCES

- Linguistic: All activities
- Logical-Mathematical: E, F
- Visual-Spatial: D, G, **Mi familia y yo**
- Auditory-Musical: **Pronunciación**, C, **Aquí escuchamos**
- Interpersonal: B, **Yo me llamo**
- Intrapersonal: **Yo me llamo**

 The Standards

- Interpersonal Communication 1.1: A, B, **Adelante** activities
- Interpretive Communication 1.2: D, E, F, G **Aquí escuchamos**
- Presentational Communication 1.3: **Mí familia y yo**
- Connections with Distinctive Viewpoints 3.2: H
- Linguistic Comparisons 4.1: **Pronunciación**

Práctica

C. Listen and repeat as your teacher models the following words.

1. todo
2. cada
3. madre
4. apellido
5. cuaderno

6. gordo
7. padre
8. universidad
9. verdad
10. usted

Repaso ♻

D. ¿De quién es? Identify each item. When a classmate asks you to whom each belongs, respond with the name of the person indicated under each picture. Follow the models.

MODELOS

Tú:	*Es un coche.*
Compañero(a):	*¿De quién es?*
Tú:	*El coche es de María.*
Tú:	*Son unos lápices.*
Compañero(a):	*¿De quién son?*
Tú:	*Los lápices son de Felipe.*

María

Felipe

1. Juan

2. Jaime

3. Rosa

4. Marta

5. Mario

6. Susana

7. Ana

8. José

Capítulo 5 Me gusta mucho... **115**

TEACH/MODEL

Pronunciación

PRESENTATION

💿 TEXTBOOK CASSETTE/CD CASSETTE 1, SIDE A; CD 1, TRACK 33

📖 TAPESCRIPT PP. 194-195

Review the sound of **d** and when it is used (after **l** or **n** or at the beginning of a word). Then tell students that everywhere else it is pronounced like the *th* in the English word *the*. Have students pronounce the English words *the*, *them*, *these*, and *those*, and notice the position of the tip of the tongue. Then have them pronounce the Spanish words **todo** and **nada**, and compare the sound of the **d** in these words to the *th* in the English words.

🔊 Read the words in **Práctica C**, having students repeat first as a whole class and then individually. Use the Textbook Cassette/CD for additional practice.

🎵 Auditory-Musical

D. ¿De quién es?

👥 **SUGGESTIONS** Model the activity before having students work in groups. You can also do this as a whole class, so you can see whether students understand how to use the structure.

PRACTICE/APPLY

ANSWERS

1. Es una casa. ¿De quién es? La casa es de Juan.
2. Es una computadora. ¿De quién es? La computadora es de Jaime.
3. Es una bicicleta. ¿De quién es? La bicicleta es de Rosa.
4. Son unas llaves. ¿De quién son? Las llaves son de Marta.
5. Es una videocasetera. ¿De quién es? La videocasetera es de Mario.
6. Es una cámara. ¿De quién es? La cámara es de Susana.
7. Es una moto. ¿De quién es? La moto es de Ana.
8. Son unos libros. ¿De quién son? Los libros son de José.

Estructura

PRESENTATION

Introduce **-er** verbs by making simple statements. Vocally stress the endings, using verbs that students know or that can easily be mimed: **Yo como en la cafetería. Tú comes en la cafetería también.** Then ask **tú** questions based on the previous statements: **¿Bebes refrescos todos los días? ¿Comes tú en la cafetería?**, etc.

Summarize using third-person forms: **Ella (Él) bebe refrescos todos los días. Él (Ella) come en la cafetería.** etc. Continue by making statements using the **nosotros** and the **Uds.** forms: **Nosotros comemos en la cafetería. Uds. comen en la cafetería. Nosotros bebemos agua todos los días.** etc. Then ask **Uds.** questions based on the statements you have just made: **¿Comen Uds. en la cafetería?**, etc.

🔺🔺 Auditory-Musical

VARIATION

Direct your questions to a small group, and have one student answer for the others: **Sí, comemos en la cafetería.**, etc. Then summarize: **Ellos (ellas), comen en la cafetería.**

When students understand the structure, establish the **nosotros** form for **-ir** verbs. Make statements with the verb **escribir: Nosotros escribimos en la clase de inglés.** (Mime writing.) Vocally stress the **-imos** endings of these verbs. Then make up a variety of other sentences with the **-er/-ir** verbs under item 3 on the student page, and have students repeat. Remind them that **Ud.** and **Uds.** take third-person endings. Then make statements in the singular form and have students change them to plural.

🔺🔺 Auditory-Musical
Bodily-Kinesthetic

ESTRUCTURA

The present tense of regular -er and -ir verbs

Yo **como** en la cafetería.	*I eat in the cafeteria.*
¿**Vives** tú aquí?	*Do you live here?*
Él **lee** siempre.	*He is always reading.*
Nosotros **comprendemos** inglés.	*We understand English.*
Uds. no **escriben** francés.	*You do not write French.*

Present Tense of Regular -er and -ir Verbs

Subject Pronoun	Verb Ending	Conjugated Verb Forms **correr** *(to run)* **vivir** *(to live)*	
yo	-o	corro	vivo
tú	-es	corres	vives
él ella Ud.	-e	corre	vive
nosotros(as)	-emos/-imos	corremos	vivimos
vosotros(as)	-éis/-ís	corréis	vivís
ellos ellas Uds.	-en	corren	viven

1. Note that, except for the **nosotros(as)** and **vosotros(as)** forms, the endings for **-er** and **-ir** verbs in the present tense are exactly the same. To conjugate any regular **-er** or **-ir** verb, drop the **-er** or **-ir** and replace it with the ending corresponding to its subject.

2. Here are some common **-er** and **-ir** verbs that you should learn.

aprender	*to learn*	comer	*to eat*
correr	*to run*	vender	*to sell*
compartir	*to share*	recibir	*to receive*
beber	*to drink*	comprender	*to understand*
leer	*to read*	vivir	*to live*
escribir	*to write*		

Vocabulary Expansion

For a challenge, have Spanish speakers come up with synonyms for the common **-er** and **-ir** verbs presented in the **Estructura: instruirse** for **aprender, huir** for **correr; dividir** for **compartir**, and so forth.

🔺🔺 Linguistic

Aquí practicamos

E. ¿Comprenden español? Create original sentences using words from each column.

A	B	C
Raúl	comer	en la cafetería
Teresa y Sara	vivir	en un apartamento
yo	comprender	español
nosotros	compartir	un cuarto
Uds.		
tú		

F. Durante el verano... (During the summer...)
Tell what you and five friends do and don't do during the summer. Write one sentence about each of your classmates, using the words in Columns A, B, and C. Use a different verb from Column B in each sentence. Follow the model.

MODELO   *John corre todos los días. o:*
John no corre todos los días.

A	B	C
(no)	comer	en la cafetería
	correr	todos los días
	leer	muchos libros
	beber	muchas cartas *(letters)*
	recibir	en Cuba
	vivir	leche cada mañana
	escribir	en un restaurante

PRACTICE/APPLY

E. ¿Comprenden español?
SUGGESTION

Have students exchange sentences with a partner and engage in peer-editing.

F. Durante el verano...

Individual Needs

Less-prepared Students
Alert less-prepared students to the fact that the verbs in Column B do not necessarily work with the phrases in the corresponding rows of column C.

Spanish for Spanish Speakers

Playing Teacher

Have Spanish-speaking students write sentences describing what their classmates are doing. Then, have them role-play their sentences for some other classmates to encourage these classmates to describe themselves. If students need help answering, encourage

Spanish speakers to help with words and accents.

Activating Prior Knowledge

Interpersonal
Intrapersonal

G. ¿Qué hacen?

ANSWERS

1. Miguel escribe una carta.
2. Rogelio y Lilia comparten (beben) un licuado.
3. Adela y Nívea corren.
4. Leo recibe una carta.
5. Nosotros leemos revistas.
6. Antonio come una hamburguesa.

VARIATION

 Have students ask their partners simple questions based on the pictures. For example: **¿Qué escribe Miguel?** Have them answer with a subject pronoun: **Él escribe una carta.** Or pretend that your drawing is unclear, and make a false statement about it. Have students correct you. (**"Miguel lee el menú." "No, Miguel escribe una carta."**)

 Visual-Spatial

 Interpersonal Communication 1.1

Aquí escuchamos

💿	TEXTBOOK CASSETTE/CD CASSETTE 1, SIDE A; CD 1, TRACK 35
📓	TAPESCRIPT P. 195
📕	TRB: ACTIVITY MASTER, P. 79

Después de escuchar

ANSWERS

Carmen likes: **películas de horror**; doesn't like: **películas de aventura.**

José likes: **fútbol americano, básquetbol**; doesn't like: **películas.**

G. ¿Qué hacen? (What are they doing?) Look at the drawings that follow and indicate what these people are doing.

1. Miguel

2. Rogelio y Lilia

3. Adela y Nívea

4. Leo

5. nosotros

6. Antonio

Aquí escuchamos

¿Qué te gusta más? *Carmen and José discuss their likes and dislikes.*

Antes de escuchar Think about how Carmen and José might say that they like or don't like something.

 **A escuchar** Listen twice to the conversation and pay attention to each person's preferences.

Después de escuchar Write down on the chart on your activity master what Carmen and José say they like and don't like.

	José	Carmen
animales		
básquetbol		
béisbol		
deportes		
fútbol americano		
música		

118 *Segunda unidad* ¡Vamos a conocernos!

	José	Carmen
películas		
de aventura		
de ciencia ficción		
de horror		
tenis		

¡ADELANTE!

 Yo me llamo...   Imagine this is your first day in an international school where the common language is Spanish.

1. Go up to another student and introduce yourself.
2. Say where you are from.
3. Ask his (her) name.
4. Ask the other student where he (she) is from.

Then share information about yourselves.

5. Indicate at least three things that you like.
6. Mention one thing that you do not like.

 Mi familia y yo   Write a short paragraph in which you describe where you and your family live and what you have in your home.

1. Mention where you are from if you do not live in your birthplace.
2. Say whether you live in a house or apartment.
3. Name at least three items in your home.
4. Mention the mode of transportation that each family member uses to go to work or to school. Follow the model.

MODELO   *Mi familia y yo somos de Nueva York, pero vivimos en Pennsylvania. Vivimos en una casa. En nuestra casa hay un estéreo, un televisor y una grabadora. No hay una computadora. Yo voy al centro en bicicleta, pero mis padres van al centro en coche.*

EN LÍNEA

Connect with the Spanish-speaking world!
Access the *¡Ya verás! Gold* home page for
Internet activities related to this chapter.

http://yaveras.heinle.com

Capítulo 5 Me gusta mucho...   **119**

Yo me llamo...

Individual Needs

More-prepared Students
More prepared students can extend
the conversation, asking and answering questions: **¿Qué necesito en
esta escuela? ¿Una mochila?
¿Cuántos cuadernos?**

Mi familia y yo

FYI

 ATAJO WRITING ASSISTANT SOFTWARE

You might want to have students use
this software program when doing this
activity.

Additional Practice and Recycling

FYI

 WORKBOOK PP. 58-63

For recycling and additional practice
of the vocabulary, structures, and
language functions presented throughout this **etapa**, you can assign the
workbook activities as in-class work
and/or homework. Answers to the
activities are overprinted on each page
of the Teacher's Edition of the
Workbook.

**Additional
Etapa
Resources**

Refer to the **Etapa**
Support Materials
list on the opening
page of this **etapa**
for detailed cross-
references to
these assessment
options.

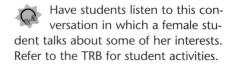

Vocabulario

VOCABULARY GAME

You may want to play **el juego de las categorías** as a wrap-up activity.

Improvised Conversation

SUGGESTION

 TEXTBOOK CASSETTE/CD CASSETTE 1, SIDE A; CD 1, TRACK 38

 TAPESCRIPT P. 195

 TRB: ACTIVITY MASTER, P. 80

 Have students listen to this conversation in which a female student talks about some of her interests. Refer to the TRB for student activities.

Listening Skills Development

FYI

 LAB CASSETTE SIDE B, CD 3, TRACKS 1-9

 TAPESCRIPT: LAB PROGRAM PP. 41-50

 LAB MANUAL PP. 30-35

It is now appropriate to work through the lab manual activities and their accompanying recordings in class or in the language laboratory. These materials provide reinforcement of the pronunciation points, vocabulary, structures, and language functions presented throughout the **etapas** and continue the development of listening comprehension skills provided in the **Aquí escuchamos** sections and the Improvised Conversation.

Resources for Spanish-speaking Students

FYI

 WORKBOOK FOR SPANISH-SPEAKING STUDENTS: PP. 27-32

 ANSWER KEY TO SSS WORKBOOK PP. 9-10

Activities specially written to meet the needs of Spanish-speaking students are available in this workbook for the reinforcement and extension of the topics and language presented in this chapter.

VOCABULARIO

Temas y contextos

Los animales
un gato
un pájaro
un perro

El arte
la escultura
la pintura

Las ciencias
la biología
la química

Los deportes
el básquetbol
el béisbol
el fútbol
el fútbol americano
el tenis
el vólibol

La música
el jazz
la música clásica
la música rock

Las películas
cómicas
de aventura
de ciencia ficción
de horror

Vocabulario general

Verbos
aprender
beber
compartir
comprender
correr
escribir
leer
recibir
vender
vivir

Otras palabras y expresiones
¡Claro!
Me gusta(n) más…
gustos
las lenguas
la naturaleza
una novia
la política
¿Qué te gusta más?

120 *Segunda unidad* ¡Vamos a conocernos!

 **Spanish for Spanish Speakers**

Keeping a Vocabulary Notebook

Remind Spanish-speaking students to add words and expressions from this vocabulary section to the problematic spelling combination categories and personal new vocabulary lists they started in their notebooks in Chapter 1. Reinforce that they should continue to do this each time a chapter in the textbook is completed.

Additional Chapter Resources

Refer to the Chapter Support Materials list on the opening page of this chapter for detailed cross-references to *¡Ya verás! Gold's* student-centered technology components and various assessment options.

ENCUENTROS CULTURALES

◆

La agenda de Mabel

Antes de leer

1. Look at the document below. Can you identify it? Do you use something similar?

2. Scan the document to find at least five cognates.

3. What extracurricular activities do you take part in during the week? Where do they take place?

4. What do you usually do on weekends? With whom do you spend time on weekends?

> ### Reading Strategies
> - Using illustrations to predict content
> - Scanning for specific information
> - Recognizing cognates

LUNES **20 de abril**	4:00	Clase de arte -Academia Sabrina. (Tengo una nueva profe.)
MARTES **21 de abril**	4:00	Clase de Badminton - Club El Frontón. A jugar con el "chistoso" de Max. Afortunadamente Loli y Jan aceptan su sentido de humor.
MIÉRCOLES **22 de abril**	4:30	Café Colón - Encontrarme con Sonia, Jochi y Gil antes de ir al cine para ver la nueva película de Disney. Me encantan nuestras sesiones de chismarreo.
JUEVES **23 de abril**	5:00	Café el Parisino - Encontrarme con la pandilla para 1) planear la fiesta, 2) decidir adónde ir para la excursión de clase. Si no presentamos opciones al profe Martínez mañana, no hay viaje; ¡Horror de horrores!
VIERNES **24 de abril**	9:00	¡Fiesta en casa de Jorge! ¡Toda la pandilla y otros amigos! También sus padres, claro. No son muy pesados pero se dejan ver.

SÁBADO **25 de abril**	9:00-2:00 p.m. Comprar el traje largo para la quinceañera de Sandra. 8:00-1:00 a.m. Quinceañera de Sandra en el Hotel El Conquistador. El guaperas de Nando es mi acompañante.	**DOMINGO** **26 de abril** 3:00-8:00 p.m. Discoteca Amazonas, Matiné Juvenil. ¡Bailar, bailar y bailar de todo y <u>sin padres</u>! Ánimos para el lunes...

Capítulo 5 Me gusta mucho **121**

PRACTICE/APPLY

La agenda de Mabel
Antes de leer
POSSIBLE ANSWERS
1. Answers will vary.
2. ballet, clase, humor, sesiones, decidir, excursión, opciones
3. Answers will vary.
4. Answers will vary.

EXPANSION
Students can be asked to make a list of their own extracurricular activities in the form of an agenda for the week ahead. This agenda should include the dates, the days of the week, the activity, and the location of each activity.

 Creating

Intrapersonal

> ### Focus on Culture
>
> ### La Quinceañera
> In most Spanish-speaking countries, it is still a popular tradition to have a special birthday party when a girl reaches age fifteen. This celebration is called **la quinceañera** and includes extended family members and many friends. Point out that a **quinceañera** is similar to the "sweet sixteen" birthday that marks the new phase of a teenager in the United States.
>
> Cultural Practices and Perspectives 2.1

> ### ☼ Spanish for Spanish Speakers
>
> ### Vocabulary Expansion
> Have Spanish Speakers give other words they would use instead of **chistoso, pandilla** or **guapera**. This is a good opportunity to discuss the richness of regional vocabulary in Spanish.
>
> Linguistic Comparisons 4.1

Después de leer

1. Ballet at Academia Sabrina, badminton at Club El Frontón
2. There is a new professor.
3. Max is funny.
4. They are not too smothering.
5. Hotel El Conquistador. Many friends and family will be there.
6. Answers will vary.
7. Answers will vary; Answers might include Sweet Sixteen parties, Barmitzvahs, and Batmitzvahs.

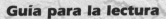

Guía para la lectura

1. Here are some words to keep in mind as you read.

chistoso	*joker*
encontrarme con	*to meet up with*
me encantan	*I love (literally, they enchant me)*
chismarreo	*gossip*
pandilla	*the gang, group of friends (coll.)*
no pesados pero se dejan ver	*not heavy (i.e. smothering), but they let themselves be seen*
traje largo	*ballgown, formal dress for a dance*
guaperas	*handsome*
Ánimos	*courage*

2. **La quinceañera,** or *fifteenth birthday party, is a very important "coming of age" celebration for young women in Latin America. It is considered the official entry into society, and usually includes a formal dance party and a lavish dinner.*

Después de leer

1. Where does Mabel take her art and her badminton classes?

2. Why might this week's art class be particularly interesting?

3. What personality trait is Max known for?

4. What does Mabel think of Jorge's parents?

5. Where is Sandra celebrating her fifteenth birthday? Who do you think will be there?

6. Did you find any of Mabel's activities or their locations surprising or unusual? If so, which ones and why?

7. Are **quinceañeras** held in your community? What similar celebrations do you know of in the United States?

CAPÍTULO 6

Ésta es mi familia

Ésta es mi familia: mi madre, mi hermano y mi hermana con su esposo.

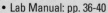
Objectives

- talking about one's family
- getting information about other people

Capítulo 6 Ésta es mi familia **123**

Chapter Support Materials

- Lab Manual: pp. 36-40
- Lab Program: Cassette Sides A&B; CD 3, Tracks 10-17
- TRB: Textbook Activity Masters: pp. 81-83
- Textbook Cassettes/CDs: Cassette 1, Side B; CD 1, Track 45
- Tapescript: Lab Program pp. 51-60; Textbook Cassettes/CDs p. 196
- Middle School Activities: pp. 47-49
- Workbook for Spanish-speaking Students: pp. 33-38
- Answer Key to SSS Workbook: pp. 11-12

- Practice Software: Windows™; Macintosh®
- Testing Program: Chapter Test pp. 62-64; Answer Key & Testing Cassettes Tapescript pp. T25, T26; Oral Assessment p. T26
- Testing Cassettes: Cassette Side B
- Computerized Testing Program: Windows™; Macintosh®
- Video Program: Cassette 1,
- Video Guide: Videoscript pp. 25-28; Activities pp. 103-104
- **Mundos hispanos 1**
- Internet Activities: Student Text p. 142

OBJECTIVES

Functions
- Talking about one's family
- Obtaining information about other people

Context
- Home

Accuracy
- Present tense of the verb **tener** (**tener que** + infinitive)
- Questions with **dónde, cuántos, cuántas, quién, qué**, and **por qué**
- **Ser +** descriptive adjectives

Pronunciation
- The consonant **b**

CHAPTER WARM-UP

Setting the Context

In preparation for their talking about families in this chapter, have students study the photo on this page. Ask them to compare Carmen Candelaria's family to their own. Is this a typical *nuclear family*? What do they observe about the decor of the house? about the way the family members are dressed? Do they notice anything that is different? anything similar?

 Analyzing

Cultural Comparisons 4.2

FYI
Throughout this chapter students will be studying the subject of family. Let students know that it's okay if they don't know a lot about their families or if they feel hesitant to share the attributes of their respective families; students can still do the activities using an imaginary family tree (or using any family they know of as a model, if they wish). Many families in the United States today are non-traditional; students should understand that their trees will probably differ from those shown in the book.

Yo vivo con...

PRESENTATION

 TRANSPARENCIES 8

 TEXTBOOK CASSETTE/CD CASSETTE 1, SIDE B; CD 1, TRACK 39

 TAPESCRIPT P. 195

With books closed, play the Textbook Cassette/CDs while students look at the transparency. After listening to the recording of Ernesto's monologue, you may want to replay it, stopping from time to time to ask students personal questions. Do not insist that they answer in complete sentences; comprehension should be the goal at this time.

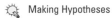 Auditory-Musical

VOCABULARY EXPANSION

Tell students the meanings of **bisabuelo/bisabuela** (great-grandfather/grandmother), and **tío abuelo/tía abuela** (great uncle/aunt). Ask students to look at the prefix **bis** and to guess what it might mean. Tell them that **bis**, when used as an adjective, means **duplicado**, or **repetido** (duplicated, repeated).

 Making Hypotheses

Linguistic

Linguistic Comparisons 4.1

PRIMERA ETAPA

Preparación

As you get ready to begin this **etapa,** think about the various members of your immediate family.

- Do you have a traditional family?
- Do you have stepparents?
- Do you have brothers and sisters?
- Do you have stepbrothers or stepsisters?

Yo vivo con...

Ésta es la familia de Ernesto.

madre   padre   hermano   hermana

abuelo   abuela

Buenos días. Me llamo Ernesto Torres. Ernesto es mi **nombre** y Torres es mi **apellido.** Hay siete personas en mi familia. **Tengo** un **padre,** una **madre,** un **hermano** y una **hermana.**

Mi padre se llama Alberto, y mi madre se llama Catalina. Mi hermano se llama Patricio, y mi hermana se llama Marta. Vivimos en una casa en la **Ciudad de México** con mi **abuelo** y mi **abuela.**

nombre *first name*   apellido *last name*   Tengo *I have*   padre *father*   madre *mother*   hermano *brother*
hermana *sister*   Mi padre se llama *My father's name is*   Ciudad de México *Mexico City*   abuelo *grandfather*
abuela *grandmother*

124   *Segunda unidad*   ¡Vamos a conocernos!

Etapa Support Materials

- Workbook: pp. 64-70
- TRB: Textbook Activity Masters: p. 81
- Textbook Cassettes/CDs: Cassette 1, Side B; CD 1, Track 39
- Tapescript: Textbook Cassettes/CDs p. 195
- Overhead Transparency: 30
- Middle School Activities: p. 50
- Lesson Plan Book: pp. 31-32

- Testing Program: Quiz pp. 57, 58; Answer Key & Testing Cassettes Tapescript p. T24
- Testing Cassettes: Cassette Side B
- Computerized Testing Program: Windows™; Macintosh®
- Atajo Writing Assistant Software: Student Text p. 131

¡Te toca a ti!

A. Tu familia

Complete these sentences with information about you and your family. Some additional words are listed for your use.

hermanastra *stepsister*
hermanastro *stepbrother*
madrastra *stepmother*
padrastro *stepfather*

1. Me llamo...
2. Mi nombre es...
3. Mi apellido es...
4. Hay... personas en mi familia.
5. Mi padre se llama...
6. Mi madre se llama...
7. Tengo... hermanos.
   (o: No tengo hermanos.)
8. Ellos se llaman...
9. Tengo... hermanas.
   (o: No tengo hermanas.)
10. Ellas se llaman...
11. Vivo con...

B. La familia de un(a) compañero(a)

Ask a classmate these following questions about himself (herself) and his (her) family.

1. ¿Cómo te llamas?
2. ¿Cuál *(What)* es tu nombre?
3. ¿Cuál es tu apellido?
4. ¿Cuántas personas hay en tu familia?
5. ¿Cómo se llama tu padre?
6. ¿Cómo se llama tu madre?
7. ¿Cuántos hermanos tienes?
8. ¿Cómo se llaman?
9. ¿Cuántas hermanas tienes?
10. ¿Cómo se llaman?
11. ¿Cuántos abuelos tienes?
12. ¿Cuántas abuelas tienes?

Comentarios CULTURALES

Los apellidos

Perhaps you have noticed that Spanish speakers often use more than one last name. This is because many use their mother's maiden name after their father's last name. For example, Mario González Cruz would use the last name of his father first (González), followed by his mother's last name (Cruz). Mario might also use the initial instead of the complete maiden name (Mario González C.). When addressing someone, you use the first of the two last names (Mario González). What would be your complete name according to this tradition?

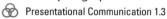
PRACTICE / APPLY

A. Tu familia

SUGGESTION

Have students write out the statements in paragraph form like the reading. Then have volunteers read their paragraphs to the class.

Presentational Communication 1.3

B. La familia de un(a) compañero(a)

SUGGESTION

You may want to do this first as a **pregúntale** exercise. Have students answer in complete sentences and point out mistakes if necessary. Students tend to say **Me llamo es...** and may be confused about how to form some of the other answers in this activity. You could also have students ask you the questions so they could hear your model.

Linguistic

Interpersonal Communication 1.3

ANSWERS

1. Me llamo...
2. Mi nombre es...
3. Mi apellido es...
4. Hay... personas en mi familia.
5. Mi padre se llama...
6. Mi madre se llama...
7. Tengo... hermanos. / Tengo un hermano. / No tengo hermanos.
8. Se llaman... y.../ Se llama...
9. Tengo... hermanas. / Tengo una hermana. / No tengo hermanas.
10. Se llaman... y... / Se llama...
11. Vivo con...

MULTIPLE INTELLIGENCES

- Linguistic: All activities
- Logical-Mathematical: A, H, I
- Visual-Spatial: D, G
- Auditory-Musical: **Pronunciación**, C, **Aquí escuchamos**
- Interpersonal: E, **Esta semana tengo que...**

The Standards

- Interpersonal Communication 1.1: A, B, E, G, **Adelante** activities
- Interpretive Communication 1.2: A, D, F, G, H, I, **Aquí escuchamos**
- Presentational Communication 1.3: **¿Qué tienes en tu casa?**
- Connections with Distinctive Viewpoints 3.2: **Comentarios culturales**

TEACH/MODEL

Pronunciación

PRESENTATION

 TEXTBOOK CASSETTE/CD CASSETTE 1,
SIDE B; CD 1, TRACK 40

TAPESCRIPT P. 195

Have students pronounce English words beginning with *b*, such as Bob, Bill, and Betty. Explain that this is also the sound for the Spanish consonant **v**. Then read the words in **Práctica C**, stressing the sound of the **v** pronounced as a *b* in numbers 4, 5, and 7.

You can also have students listen to the explanation for **b** on the Textbook Cassette/CD. The speaker will model the correct pronunciation of the words. Have students follow along in their texts and repeat after each word.

▲▲ Auditory-Musical

PRACTICE/APPLY

D. ¿Qué hacen?

SUGGESTION

Have students make statements to their partners, or tell them to write out the answers and have them edit their partners' work.

You could also have six students write the answers on the board while the rest write at their seats. Then have the whole class point out any errors.

Interpersonal Communication 1.1

POSSIBLE ANSWERS

1. Alicia y Carlos comen en un restaurante.
2. Ana lee un libro.
3. Alberto escribe una carta.
4. Marirrosa y Juan corren.
5. El Sr. García vende libros.
6. Sofía bebe leche.

---

a
z é
f
g ñ

PRONUNCIACIÓN THE SOUND OF /b/

In Spanish the sound of /b/ can be spelled with the letter **b** or **v** and is pronounced like the *b* in *Bill* when it is the first letter of a word or after **n** or **m**.

Práctica

C. Listen and repeat as your teacher models the following words.

1. bueno	6. hombre
2. bien	7. un video
3. bocadillo	8. un beso
4. vaso	9. también
5. vamos	10. hambre

Repaso ♻

D. ¿Qué hacen? Describe what the people in the drawings are doing.

1. Alicia y Carlos

2. Ana

3. Alberto

4. Marirrosa y Juan

5. el Sr. García

6. Sofía

126 *Segunda unidad* ¡Vamos a conocernos!

Focus on Culture

Last Names

You may want to discuss names a little more, since students may find them confusing. Write José Pérez Morales and Beatriz García Sánchez on the board. Explain to students that the first last name is called the **apellido paterno**. (Circle both of the apellidos paternos on the board.) The second last name is called the **apellido materno** and is the mother's maiden name. Ask students what would be the full name of José and Beatriz's first-born son, José, if this couple were to marry. If they can't answer, point to the circled name of the father (Pérez) and write it on the board, adding José before it. Then point to the circled name of the mother (García) and write it down after Pérez. Thus, José Pérez García would be their son's name.

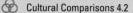 Cultural Comparisons 4.2

E. ¿Qué te gusta más? From the choices below, ask a class-mate what he (she) likes more.

1. el fútbol, el fútbol americano, el básquetbol
2. la música, el baile, las películas
3. la música rock, el jazz, la música clásica
4. las hamburguesas, los sándwiches de jamón, las hamburguesas con queso
5. las películas de horror, las películas de aventura, las películas cómicas
6. la historia, las lenguas, las ciencias

¿Qué crees?

When a woman marries she usually adds **de** plus her husband's last name to her own name. If María Pérez Clemente married José Román Caño, what would her name be?

a) María Clemente de Caño
b) María Pérez de Román
c) María Clemente de Román
d) María Pérez de Cañorespuesta

respuesta

ESTRUCTURA

The verb **tener**

Yo **tengo** dos hermanas.	*I have two sisters.*
¿**Tienes** tú un hermano?	*Do you have a brother?*
Él **tiene** un abuelo en Miami.	*He has a grandfather in Miami.*
Nosotros **tenemos** dos gatos.	*We have two cats.*
Ellos no **tienen** un perro.	*They don't have a dog.*

tener *(to have)*			
yo	**tengo**	nosotros(as)	**tenemos**
tú	**tienes**	vosotros(as)	**tenéis**
él ella Ud.	**tiene**	ellos ellas Uds.	**tienen**

In Spanish, the irregular verb **tener** can be used to talk about possessions.

Capítulo 6 ¡Ésta es mi familia! **127**

E. ¿Qué te gusta más?
SUGGESTION

Do as a **pregúntale** exercise with books closed to develop listening skills, or have students work in pairs.

Interpersonal

TEACH/MODEL

Estructura

PRESENTATION

Students have seen and used some forms of **tener** in the vocabulary activities, so it should be easy to present the verb inductively. Start out by making a statement about yourself, then ask a **tú** question based on your statement; finally summarize using the third-person singular form. Example: **Yo tengo dos hermanos. ¿Cuántos hermanos tienes tú? Ella (Él) tiene un hermano.**

Continue by making statements using the **nosotros** and the **Uds.** forms. **Nosotros tenemos muchos libros. Uds. tienen muchos libros también.** Then make other **nosotros** statements and ask **Uds.** questions based on those statements. Point to two or three students as you direct these questions and have one answer as a spokesperson for the others. **Nosotros tenemos muchos amigos. ¿Tienen Uds. muchos amigos?** Then summarize their answers using the third-person plural form: **Ellas (Ellos) tienen muchos amigos.**

Linguistic

Interpersonal Communication 1.1

Spanish for Spanish Speakers

Routine Activities

If Activity D is too easy, have Spanish speakers write sentences describing some of their routine activities. For example: Do they regularly play sports, go to the movies, talk on the phone, visit friends, etc. When finished, ask students to act out their paragraphs; have students guess what they are doing (in English or Spanish—depending on the vocabulary).

Bodily-Kinesthetic

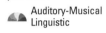

PRACTICE / APPLY

G. ¿Qué tienen Ana y Esteban?

SUGGESTION

Have students do this activity orally in pairs, or have them write out sentences and edit their partners' work.

Auditory-Musical
Linguistic

POSSIBLE ANSWERS

Answers will vary, but should reflect Ana and Esteban's possesions accurately: **Ana tiene una cámara, tres libros, un radio, un cuaderno, un lápiz y una mochila. Esteban tiene un portafolio, dos lápices, una cartera, una calculadora y un sacapuntas.**

VARIATION

Tell students they have 30 seconds to look at the drawings for Activity G and then they must close their books. When you say, "**Preparados, listos, ¡ya!**" they will have to write down as many items as they can remember in front of each person. Have volunteers read their answers; the one with the most items correct wins.

Linguistic

Aquí practicamos

F. **Tienen muchas cosas** Tell what your friends have and do not have, using words from Columns A, B, C, and D.

A	B	C	D
José	(no)	tener	dos hermanos
yo			una hermana
nosotros			un gato
Juan y Catarina			dos perros
tú			un pájaro
Uds.			

☞ b

G. **¿Qué tienen Ana y Esteban?** Look at the drawings below and tell what Ana and Esteban have and do not have. Follow the model.

> **MODELO** *Ana tiene una cámara, pero Esteban no tiene una cámara. o: Ellos tienen unos lápices.*

PALABRAS ÚTILES

Tener que + infinitive

Yo **tengo que** comer.	*I have to eat.*
Tú **tienes que** estudiar.	*You have to study.*
Él **tiene que** escribir la lección.	*He has to write the lesson.*

In Spanish, when you want to say that you have to do something, you do so by using the expression **tener que** followed by the infinitive form of the verb that expresses what must be done.

Aquí practicamos

H. ¿Qué tengo que hacer? Replace the words in italics and make the necessary changes.

1. Yo tengo que *comer*. (trabajar / estudiar / correr)
2. *Ellos* no tienen que estudiar. (Juan / Bárbara y Alicia / tú)
3. ¿Tienes *tú* que trabajar hoy *(today)?* (Julio y Santiago / Elena / Uds.)

I. Tenemos que... Tell what you and your friends have to do, using words from Columns A, B, and C.

A	B	C
yo	tener que	trabajar después de la escuela
nosotros(as)		estudiar para un examen
Jaime		hablar con un(a) amigo(a)
tú		comprar un disco compacto
Uds.		hacer un mandado *(errand)* para su padre (madre)

Capítulo 6 ¡Ésta es mi familia! **129**

Aquí escuchamos

	TEXTBOOK CASSETTE/CD CASSETTE 1, SIDE B; CD 1, TRACK 41
	TAPESCRIPT PP. 195-196
	TRB: ACTIVITY MASTER, P. 81

Después de escuchar

ANSWERS

familia: pequeña; padre: ingeniero; madre: periodista; un hermano; dos perros

Additional Practice and Recycling

FYI

| | WORKBOOK, PP. 64-70 |

For recycling and additional practice of the vocabulary, structures, and language functions presented throughout this **etapa**, you can assign the workbook activities as in-class work and/or homework.

Aquí escuchamos

Mi familia *Carmen is going to provide some basic information about her family.*

Antes de escuchar What information about her family do you expect Carmen to include in her monologue?

 A escuchar Listen twice to the monologue before circling on your activity master the words that describe Carmen's family.

Después de escuchar On your activity master, circle the choices that match what Carmen says about her family.

familia	padre	madre	hermanos	animales
grande	contador	enfermera	gatos	uno
pequeña	ingeniero	periodista	perros	dos
	mecánico	profesora		

Tengo que estudiar para un examen, mirar una película y jugar al fútbol con mis amigos. Y tú, ¿qué tienes que hacer?

 Spanish for Spanish Speakers

Vocabulary Expansion–Antonyms

Have Spanish speakers listen carefully to the **Aquí escuchamos** recording and write down five words they hear for which they know or want to find antonyms. Tell them not to limit themselves to just one or two parts of speech, but to choose nouns, verbs, adjectives, adverbs, prepositions, etc. Then give students copies of the dialogue from the Tapescript and have them work with a partner to combine their lists and create a transformed dialogue. Have Spanish speakers and other class volunteers role-play the dialogue with the new words for the rest of the class.

- Auditory-Musical Linguistic
- Creating
- Presentational Communication 1.3

¡ADELANTE!

Esta semana (This week) tengo que... Make a list of at least three things that you have to do this week. Then ask several classmates what they have to do this week. When someone mentions an activity that is not on your list, add it to a second list labeled **Mis compañeros** *(classmates)* **tienen que...**

¿Qué tienes en tu casa? Tengo... Write a paragraph about your family and their activities, interests, and belongings.

1. Begin by telling how many people are in your family.
2. State their relationship to you.
3. Tell something that each person does or likes.
4. Tell something that each person has or would like to have that relates to his (her) activities or interests.

Use **le gusta(n)** for *he (she) likes* and **les gusta(n)** for *they like.*

MODELO
Hay cuatro personas en mi familia: mi padre, mi madre, mi hermano y yo. Mi padre es contador y tiene una calculadora. Mi madre es abogada y escribe mucho. Ella tiene una computadora en su oficina, pero quisiera una computadora en casa también. Mi hermano tiene muchas cintas porque le gusta mucho la música. Me gusta la música también. Yo quisiera una grabadora.

Family Picnic

Capítulo 6 ¡Ésta es mi familia! **131**

Additional Etapa Resources

Refer to the **Etapa** Support Materials list on the opening page of this **etapa** for detailed cross-references to these assessment options.

 ETAPA SYNTHESIS

Esta semana tengo que...

SUGGESTION
 Have students draw a poll graph labeled **Esta semana tenemos que...** Make a list on the board of the different activities on the students' *to do* lists. Use tick marks to keep track of how many people have mentioned the same *to do* activity.

A follow-up discussion can include questions like **¿Quiénes tienen que... ?** with responses practicing the different forms of the verb.

 Logical-Mathematical

Individual Needs

More-prepared Students
More-prepared students can write a letter to a pen pal coming to visit for the first time, telling him (her) about activities and interests of family members.

Creating

¿Qué tienes en tu casa?

FYI
 ATAJO WRITING ASSISTANT SOFTWARE

You might want to have students use this software program when doing this activity.

SUGGESTION
Have students imagine that they must evacuate their houses immediately and can only take with them what they can carry. Write what each family member would probably take, and why.

Making Hypotheses
Prioritizing

 Interpersonal

Tengo una familia grande

PRESENTATION

 TRANSPARENCIES 31

 TEXTBOOK CASSETTE/CD CASSETTE 1, SIDE B; CD 1, TRACK 42

TAPESCRIPT P. 196

 To introduce and practice the new vocabulary you can use the transparency and have students listen to the Textbook Cassette/CD with their books closed. Or draw the family tree on the board and read the monologue, pointing to the different family members as they are introduced. Then read (or play the tape) again and ask simple questions to test comprehension.

Auditory-Musical
Visual-Spatial

VOCABULARY EXPANSION

Introduce additional extended family vocabulary, such as **cuñado/cuñada** (brother/sister-in-law), **abuelo paterno/materno, abuela paterna/materna** (paternal/maternal grandfather/grandmother).

SUGGESTION

Have students prepare a family tree identifying each family member on page 132 with the appropriate word in Spanish.

 Creating
 Visual-Spatial

SEGUNDA ETAPA

Preparación

- As you begin this **etapa,** think about your extended family.
- Do you have grandparents? Uncles? Aunts? Cousins?

Tengo una familia grande

La familia de Jaime es **grande** (large).

Juan   Elena   Rosa   Fernando   Jaime

Sergio

Guadalupe

María Catarina

Teresa

Diana

Yo me llamo Jaime y ésta es mi familia. Mi abuelo se llama Sergio y mi abuela se llama Guadalupe. Mi abuela es la **esposa** de mi abuelo. Mis abuelos tienen un **hijo** y una **hija.** La hija se llama Rosa y el hijo se llama Juan. Rosa es mi madre y **está casada con** mi padre. Él se llama Fernando. Mi hermana se llama Diana.

Juan, el hermano de mi madre, es mi **tío.** Él está casado con mi **tía.** Ella se llama Elena. Mi tío Juan y mi tía Elena tienen dos hijas que se llaman Teresa y María Catarina. Ellas son mis **primas. Cada domingo** nosotros vamos a la casa de mis abuelos.

esposa *wife* **hijo** *son* **hija** *daughter* **está casada con** *is married to* **tío** *uncle* **tía** *aunt* **primas** *(female) cousins* **Cada domingo** *Every Sunday*

132 *Segunda unidad* ¡Vamos a conocernos!

Etapa Support Materials

- Workbook: pp. 71-76
- TRB: Textbook Activity Masters: pp. 82, 83
- Textbook Cassettes/CDs: Cassette 1, Side B; CD 1, Track 42
- Tapescript: Textbook Cassettes/CDs p. 196
- Overhead Transparencies: 31, 32
- Middle School Activities: pp. 51-54
- Lesson Plan Book: pp. 33-34

- Testing Program: Quiz pp. 59-61; Answer Key & Testing Cassettes Tapescript pp. T24, T25
- Testing Cassettes: Cassette Side B
- Computerized Testing Program: Windows™; Macintosh®
- Atajo Writing Assistant Software: Student Text p. 142; Workbook p. 75

¡Te toca a ti!

A. ¿Quién es? (Who is it?)
Fill in the blanks to express the correct family relationships based on the information on page 132. Follow the model.

MODELO   María Catarina es *la hija* de Juan.

1. Rosa es _____ de Juan.
2. Fernando es _____ de Jaime.
3. Juan es _____ de Jaime.
4. Teresa es _____ de Juan.
5. Guadalupe es _____ de Rosa.
6. Sergio es _____ de Juan.
7. Sergio es _____ de Jaime.
8. Elena es _____ de Juan.
9. Guadalupe es _____ de María Catarina.
10. Fernando es _____ de Rosa.

B. Mi familia
Draw a family tree of your own family. Using your family tree as a reference, tell your partner the name of each member on your family tree and their relationship to you.

PRONUNCIACIÓN   THE SOUND OF /b/
When the letter **b** or **v** is between vowels or after any consonant except **n** or **m**, it is pronounced with the lips coming together but not allowing the lips to stop the passage of air.

Práctica

C. Listen and repeat as your teacher models the following words.

1. favor
2. acabar
3. ¡Qué bueno!
4. cubano
5. jueves
6. a veces
7. una botella
8. abogado
9. noviembre
10. el vaso

Capítulo 6 ¡Ésta es mi familia!   **133**

PRACTICE / APPLY

A. ¿Quién es?
ANSWERS

1. la hermana	6. el padre
2. el padre	7. el abuelo
3. el tío	8. la esposa
4. la hija	9. la abuela
5. la madre	10. el esposo

B. Mi familia
SUGGESTION

Have students identify family members as far back as they can. You may need to draw a model family tree on the board. If necessary, provide them with supplementary vocabulary. Then, have students work with partners to ask and answer questions about their family members. (using **gustar**, for example).

Intrapersonal

 Interpersonal Communication 1.1

TEACH / MODEL

Pronunciación
PRESENTATION

 TEXTBOOK CASSETTE/CD CASSETTE 1, SIDE B; CD 1, TRACK 40

TAPESCRIPT P. 196

Have students practice pronouncing the fricative **b**. Point out that it is similar to the **b** practiced on page 126 but there is not a complete stoppage of the air that passes between the lips. If students have problems producing this sound, tell them that it is better to pronounce it more closely to an English *b* than to an English *v*.

You can also have students listen to the explanation for **b** on the Textbook Cassette/CD. The speaker will model the correct pronunciation of the words in **Práctica C**. Have students follow along in their texts and repeat after each word.

Auditory-Musical

MULTIPLE INTELLIGENCES

- Linguistic: **Aquí escuchamos**
- Logical-Mathematical: A, E, J
- Visual-Spatial: B, **Una fiesta**
- Auditory-Musical: **Pronunciación, C, Aquí escuchamos**
- Interpersonal: C, G

The Standards

- Interpersonal Communication 1.1:B, D, F, G, **Una fiesta**
- Interpretive Communication 1.2: A, E, F, H, I, **Aquí escuchamos**
- Presentational Communication 1.3: **Adelante** activities
- Cultural Practices and Perspectives 2.1: **Comentarios culturales**, F
- Cultural Comparisons 4.2: **Comentarios culturales**

C. Quisiera... , pero tengo que...

SUGGESTION

To develop listening skills, have a few students read their lists and then call on different students to report what has just been said.

Auditory-Musical

Individual Needs

Less-prepared Students

For students not yet prepared to combine sentences with **pero** as in the model, first have them write five things under each of two columns labeled **Quisiera hacer** and **Tengo que hacer**.

Comentarios CULTURALES

La familia

When Hispanics talk about their families, they do not just mean their parents, brothers, and sisters as we often do in the United States. Many Hispanic families are very close and include many other relatives **(parientes)**, such as grandparents, uncles and aunts, cousins, godparents, and in-laws. Sometimes one set of grandparents will live in the same house with one of their children and their grandchildren. This is becoming less common, especially in modern cities, but families generally remain very close.

Repaso

C. Quisiera..., pero tengo que... Make a list of five things you would like to do but cannot because you have to do something else. Compare your list with a classmate's. Follow the model.

MODELO   *Quisiera mirar la TV, pero tengo que estudiar.*

134   *Segunda unidad* ¡Vamos a conocernos!

ESTRUCTURA

Information questions: dónde, cuántos, cuántas, quién, qué, por qué

You have already learned how to ask and answer *yes/no* questions. Frequently, however, you ask a question because you seek specific information. In Chapter 4 you learned to ask to whom something belongs, using **¿De quién es?** and **¿De quién son?** The following words are commonly used in Spanish when seeking information. Note that each of these words has an accent mark in its written form.

1. To find out *where* something is or someone is located, use **¿dónde?**

—**¿Dónde** vive tu hermano?	*Where does your brother live?*
—Él vive en Pittsburgh.	*He lives in Pittsburgh.*
—**¿Dónde** está mi libro?	*Where is my book?*
—Tu libro está en la mesa.	*Your book is on the table.*

2. To find out *how many* there are, use **¿cuántos?** if what you are asking about is masculine and **¿cuántas?** if what you are asking about is feminine.

—**¿Cuántos** hermanos tienes?	*How many brothers do you have?*
—Tengo dos.	*I have two.*
—**¿Cuántos** perros tienes?	*How many dogs do you have?*
—Tengo uno.	*I have one.*
—**¿Cuántas** hermanas tiene él?	*How many sisters does he have?*
—Él tiene seis.	*He has six.*
—**¿Cuántas** cintas tienes?	*How many tapes do you have?*
—Tengo una.	*I have one.*

3. To find out *who* does something, use **¿quién?**

—**¿Quién** come en la cafetería?	*Who eats at the cafeteria?*
—Bárbara come en la cafetería.	*Bárbara eats at the cafeteria.*
—**¿Quién** estudia en la biblioteca?	*Who studies at the library?*
—Roberto estudia en la biblioteca.	*Roberto studies at the library.*

4. To find out *what*, use **¿qué?**

—**¿Qué** buscan ellos?	*What are they looking for?*
—Ellos buscan la casa de Marta.	*They are looking for Marta's house.*
—**¿Qué** compran ellos?	*What are they buying?*
—Ellos compran una mochila.	*They are buying a knapsack.*

Capítulo 6 ¡Ésta es mi familia! **135**

Estructura (cont.)

Introduce **cuál** for recognition only. Say that **cuál**—meaning *what*—is used in some information questions, such as **¿Cuál es tu apellido?** or **¿Cuál es tu número de teléfono?**

Give answer-statements; students should form questions that would logically precede your answers. For example: Answer—**María estudia en la biblioteca.** Question—**¿Dónde estudia María?** If students find this difficult, have them write down your statements before changing them. Or send a few students to the board and dictate a sentence to each of them. Then have the whole class suggest how to change them to questions.

Linguistic

Interpretive Communication 1.2

ESTRUCTURA (continued)

5. To find out *why*, use **¿por qué?** The answers to such questions often includes **porque** *(because)*, which is one word and does not have an accent mark.

—**¿Por qué** estudias?   *Why are you studying?*
—**Porque** tengo un examen mañana.   *Because I have a test tomorrow.*

—**¿Por qué** comes pizza?   *Why do you eat pizza?*
—**Porque** me gusta.   *Because I like it.*

**Me llamo Lourdes. Ahora estoy en los Estados Unidos pero vivo en Bogotá, Colombia. Tengo dos hermanos y una hermana. Mis hermanos trabajan en Cartagena y mi hermana es estudiante de escuela secundaria (high school).
¿Cuántos hermanos tienes tú?
¿Qué hacen?**

136   *Segunda unidad* ¡Vamos a conocernos!

Aquí practicamos

E. ¿Cuándo estudia Josefina? Create original questions using words from each column.

A	B	C
dónde	trabajar	Josefina
qué	tener	tu padre
por qué	buscar	tú
quién	estudiar	Juan y Pablo
cuándo	comer	ellas
	correr	Uds.

F. Más detalles (More details) You are talking with some of the Spanish-speaking exchange students in your school. After a student makes a statement, ask a follow-up question that makes sense. Follow the model.

> **MODELO** Esteban: No vivo en Valencia.
> Tú: *¿Dónde vives?*

1. **Esteban:** Tengo hermanos, pero no tengo hermanas.
2. **Esteban:** Mis hermanos no viven con nosotros.
3. **Esteban:** Ellos no estudian ciencias.
4. **Bárbara:** Mi padre y mi madre trabajan.
5. **Bárbara:** Mi hermana estudia muchas horas todos los días.
6. **Bárbara:** Mi hermano tiene muchos discos compactos.
7. **Carlos:** No tengo el libro de química.
8. **Carlos:** Como en la cafetería.
9. **Carlos:** No vivo aquí.

Capítulo 6 ¡Ésta es mi familia! **137**

PRACTICE/APPLY

E. ¿Cuándo estudia Josefina?

EXPANSION

Have students work in pairs to answer questions they have formed from the words.

F. Más detalles

POSSIBLE ANSWERS

1. ¿Cuántos hermanos tienes?
2. ¿Dónde viven tus hermanos?
3. ¿Qué estudian?
4. ¿Dónde trabajan tus padres?
5. ¿Cuántas horas estudia tu hermana?
6. ¿Cuántos discos compactos tiene?
7. ¿Qué estudias?
8. ¿Qué comes?
9. ¿Dónde vives?

EXPANSION

Make statements about members of your family. Have students ask you follow-up questions. You might want to write **su/sus** on the board and point out that the **Ud.** form of the possessive is **su**.

Linguistic

G. ¿Dónde vives?

SUGGESTION

Since this is the first time that students will be doing an activity of this type, you may want to work through the items with the whole class before students work with partners. Pair students up with partners other than those with whom they worked in Activity B.

POSSIBLE ANSWERS

1. ¿Dónde viven tus abuelos?
2. ¿Cuántos hermanos tienes?
   ¿Cuántas hermanas tienes?
3. ¿Cuántos animales (perros, gatos, pájaros) tienes en tu casa?
4. ¿Qué estudias?

VARIATION

Put interrogatives on slips of paper in a hat. Have students draw a question word out of the hat, form a question with it, and call on someone to answer. The student who answers correctly can draw the next word out of the hat.

Interpretive Communication 1.1

G. ¿Dónde vives? Ask a classmate questions in order to get the information listed. Do not translate word for word. Instead, find a Spanish expression that will help you get the information. Your classmate will answer your questions. Follow the models.

MODELOS   where he (she) lives
           Tú: *¿Dónde vives?*
   Compañera(o):   *Vivo en Los Ángeles.*

          where his (her) father and mother work
           Tú: *¿Dónde trabajan tu padre y tu madre?*
   Compañera(o):   *Mi padre trabaja en First National Bank of Los Ángeles, y mi madre trabaja en City Hospital.*

1. where his (her) grandparents live
2. how many brothers and sisters he (she) has
3. how many pets (dogs, cats, birds) he (she) has
4. what he (she) is studying

ESTRUCTURA

Descriptive adjectives

Él es **alto.**	He is tall.
Ella es **alta.**	She is tall.
Juan y José son **altos.**	Juan and José are tall.
María y Carmen son **altas.**	María and Carmen are tall.

1. Remember that, in Spanish, adjectives agree in gender and number with the noun they modify. Masculine singular adjectives that end in **-o** have three other forms—feminine singular that ends in **-a**, masculine plural that ends in **-os**, and feminine plural that ends in **-as**. Here are some adjectives of this type used to describe people and things:

aburrido	*boring, bored*	**guapo**	*handsome*
alto	*tall*	**malo**	*bad*
antipático	*disagreeable*	**moreno**	*dark-haired, brunette*
bajo	*short*	**pelirrojo**	*red-haired*
bonito	*pretty*	**pequeño**	*small, little*
bueno	*good*	**rubio**	*blond*
delgado	*thin*	**serio**	*serious*
divertido	*fun, amusing*	**simpático**	*nice*
feo	*plain, ugly*	**tonto**	*stupid, foolish*
gordo	*fat*		

☀ Spanish for Spanish Speakers

Vocabulary Expansion

Encourage Spanish speakers to come up with cognates to describe people's personal traits. Have them use their vocabulary notebooks to keep lists of the adjectives. For example: (ending in **-e**—these have only one singular and one plural form) **elegante, eficiente, independiente, paciente, responsable, valiente**; (ending in **-a**—these have only one singular and one plural form) **egoísta, realista, idealista, optimista,** **pesimista, materialista**; (ending in **-o** or **a**) **extrovertido(a), introvertido(a), impulsivo(a), sincero(a), tímido(a), generoso(a), romántico(a)**; (ending in **-l**—these have only one singular and one plural form) **cruel, emocional, sentimental**. You might want to have all your students so this activity.

Categorizing

Linguistic Comparisons 4.1

ESTRUCTURA (continued)

pelirroja   moreno   rubia

2. Adjectives that end in -e have only two forms—one singular and one plural. Some common adjectives of this type are **inteligente** *(intelligent)*, **interesante** *(interesting)*, and **grande** *(big, large)*.

Alina y Bárbara son **inteligentes.**   *Alina and Bárbara are intelligent.*

Nuestra casa es **grande.**   *Our house is big.*

3. **¿Cómo es...?** and **¿Cómo son ...?** are used to ask what someone or something is like.

—**¿Cómo es** el libro?   *What is the book like?*
—Es aburrido.   *It is boring.*

El libro es muy interesante.

4. In Spanish, when adjectives are used with the nouns they modify, they usually follow the noun.

Me gustan **los restaurantes italianos.**   *I like Italian restaurants.*

Mi primo es **un estudiante serio.**   *My cousin is a serious student.*

El español es una **lengua interesante.**   *Spanish is an interesting language.*

Capítulo 6 ¡Ésta es mi familia!   **139**

Estructura

PRESENTATION
Since students have used **ser** with adjectives of nationality and adjectives that describe food, they know how to make adjectives agree. To reinforce adjective agreement, show pictures of famous people and describe them using the descriptive adjectives presented in this section (and other cognates if you choose to do so). Or describe yourself and different students in the class using all forms of the adjectives, so that students associate the adjective endings with the gender and number of the people being described. For example: **Teresa y Ana son rubias. También son bonitas y simpáticas. Karen es pelirroja.**

VARIATION
After writing these cognates (or having Spanish-speakers write them) on the board, say different adjectives and have students give their opposites, telling them to look at the lists on pages 138 and 139 or on the board to find the answer.

◣ Linguistic

TEACH/MODEL

H. ¿Cómo son?

PRESENTATION

To introduce **¿Cómo es... ?** or **¿Cómo son... ?** make statements about your family, and then ask students about theirs. Follow up your questions with some possible answers. For example: **Mi mamá es paciente y generosa. ¿Cómo es tu mamá? ¿Es generosa también?**

PRACTICE/APPLY

SUGGESTION

A possible way to present Activity H would be through the creation of a *word web*.

I. No, no es... , es...

Individual Needs

Less-prepared Students

Give less-prepared students more practice with adjectives by having them name famous people or characters and give an adjective that readily describes that person: (Michael Jordan—**alto**; Maya Angelou—**generosa**; Bugs Bunny—**divertido**, etc.).

▲▲ Interpersonal

POSSIBLE ANSWERS

1. ¿Es gordo Juan? No, no es gordo, es delgado.
2. ¿Es rubia Anita? No, ..., es morena.
3. ¿Es inteligente David? No, ..., es tonto.
4. ¿Es divertida Marina? No, ..., es aburrida.
5. ¿Es simpático Antonio? No, ..., es antipático.
6. ¿Son feos Miguel y Luis? No, ..., son guapos.
7. ¿Son bajas Éster y Marisa? No, ..., son altas.
8. ¿Son simpáticos ellos? No, ..., son antipáticos.
9. ¿Son aburridas ellas? No, ..., son divertidas.
10. ¿Son buenos los hijos? No, ..., son malos.

Aquí practicamos

H. ¿Cómo son? Describe the following people, using words from Columns A, B, and C. Follow the model.

MODELO *Él es alto.* o: *Él no es alto.*

A	B	C
él	(no)ser	alto
tú		inteligente
Elizabeth		bajo
Linda y Paula		rubio
Javier y Roberto		moreno
nosotros		pelirrojo
		aburrido
		tonto
		antipático
		bueno

I. No, no es..., es... A classmate asks you whether one of your friends has a certain quality. You respond by saying that your friend is the opposite. Follow the model.

MODELO alto / María
Compañera(o): *¿Es alta María?*
Tú: *No, no es alta, es baja.*

1. gordo / Juan
2. rubio / Anita
3. inteligente / David
4. divertido / Marina
5. simpático / Antonio
6. feo / Miguel y Luis
7. bajo / Éster y Marisa
8. simpático / ellos
9. aburrido / ellas
10. bueno / los hijos

☀ Spanish for Spanish Speakers

Adjective Practice

Have Spanish-speaking students describe in some detail a famous person or character and the rest of the class will guess who it is.

▲▲ Interpersonal

 Presentational Communication 1.3

J. ¿Cómo es? Use the adjectives in parentheses to tell something about the words in italics. Make any necessary changes to the adjective. Follow the model.

> **MODELO** (delicioso) Maribel come unas *patatas*.
> *Maribel come unas patatas deliciosas.*

1. (simpático) Leo y Jorge son dos *muchachos*.
2. (gordo) Mi amiga tiene un *perro*.
3. (divertido) Quisiera mirar una *película*.
4. (interesante) Clara lee un *libro*.
5. (pelirrojo) Tu primo tiene una *novia*.

Aquí escuchamos

La familia de Isabel
Isabel, a friend of Carmen's, is going to give some information about her family.

Antes de escuchar Given what you have learned in this **etapa,** what information about Isabel's family do you think she will include in her description?

 A escuchar Listen twice to the monologue before choosing on your activity master the items that match Isabel's description of her family.

Después de escuchar On your activity master, circle the items that match what Isabel says about her family.

familia	padre	madre	animales	hermanos
grande	contador	enfermera	gatos	uno
pequeña	ingeniero	periodista	perros	dos
	mecánico	profesora		

Capítulo 6 ¡Ésta es mi familia! **141**

Aquí escuchamos

  TEXTBOOK CASSETTE/CD CASSETTE 1, SIDE B; CD 1, TRACK 44

TAPESCRIPT P. 196

TRB: ACTIVITY MASTER, P. 82

Después de escuchar
ANSWERS
familia: grande; padre: contador; madre: profesora; dos hermanos; un perro; un pájaro

 Spanish for Spanish Speakers

Summarizing
Have Spanish speakers listen to the **Aquí escuchamos** recording and summarize the dialogue. Encourage students to write down any difficult vocabulary or structures, and work with a partner to better understand how these are used in this recording. Review summaries with Spanish speakers to determine problematic structures and vocabulary.

Creating
Synthesizing

ETAPA SYNTHESIS

Una fiesta

SUGGESTION

 TRANSPARENCY 32

 Have students write out the descriptions and then have them edit their partners' papers.

Tu familia

FYI

 ATAJO WRITING ASSISTANT SOFTWARE

You might want to have students use this software program when doing this activity.

Individual Needs

More-prepared Students
More-prepared students can write two different descriptions of themselves—one from their own point of view (**Yo soy...**), and another as if a family member were doing the describing (**Mi hijo Andrew es...**).

Additional Practice and Recycling

FYI

 WORKBOOK, PP. 71-76

For recycling and additional practice of the vocabulary, structures, and language functions presented through-out this **etapa**, you can assign the workbook activities as in-class work and/or homework.

Improvised Conversation

SUGGESTION

 TEXTBOOK CASSETTE/CD CASSETTE 1, SIDE B; CD 1, TRACK 45

 TAPESCRIPT P. 196

 TRB: ACTIVITY MASTER, P. 76

Have students listen to this conversation in which two students talk about their families. Refer to the TRB for student activities.

¡ADELANTE!

 Una fiesta Describe the people pictured in the following image.

 Tu familia Choose three members of your extended family. Write a description of each one, including at least three adjectives for each.

EN LÍNEA

Connect with the Spanish-speaking world! Access the **¡Ya verás!** *Gold* home page for Internet activities related to this chapter.

http://yaveras.heinle.com

Spanish for Spanish Speakers

Tu familia

Spanish-speaking students can interview a Spanish-speaking relative and write about him(her). Perhaps he(she) could record the interview and play it for the class.

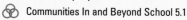 Communities In and Beyond School 5.1

Additional Etapa Resources

Refer to the **Etapa** Support Materials list on the opening page of this **etapa** for detailed cross-references to these assessment options.

VOCABULARIO

VOCABULARIO

Para charlar

Para preguntar

¿Cómo es(son)?
¿Cuántos(as)?
¿Dónde?
¿Qué?
¿Por qué?
¿Quién?

Temas y contextos

La familia

una abuela
un abuelo
una esposa
un esposo
una hermana
un hermano
una hija
un hijo
una madre
un padre
un pariente
una prima
un primo
una tía
un tío

Vocabulario general

Sustantivos

un apellido
una ciudad
un nombre
unas personas

Adjetivos

aburrido(a)
alto(a)
antipático(a)
bajo(a)
bonito(a)
bueno(a)
delgado(a)
divertido(a)
feo(a)
gordo(a)
grande
guapo(a)
inteligente
interesante
malo(a)
moreno(a)
pelirrojo(a)
pequeño(a)
rubio(a)
serio(a)
simpático(a)
tonto(a)

Verbos

tener

Otras expresiones

cada domingo
Está casado(a) con…
Se llama(n)…
tener que

Capítulo 6 ¡Ésta es mi familia!   **143**

CHAPTER WRAP-UP

Vocabulario

ROUND TABLE GAME

Divide the class into several teams and give one person on each team a piece of paper. Announce a category, such as **La familia**. The first person quickly writes down a word that fits the category, then passes the sheet of paper to the next student who writes down another word, and so on. Change categories to cover the vocabulary to be reviewed.

When finished, check each team's sheet. The team with the most words written correctly wins.

WHAT'S THE OPPOSITE? GAME

You might want to play a game of opposites to practice the adjectives. Read a list of adjectives, including the cognates from the vocabulary expansion, and have students write down the opposites.

Listening Skills Development

FYI

	LAB MANUAL PP. 36-40
	CASSETTE SIDE A&B; CD 3, TRACKS 10-17
	TAPESCRIPT: LAB PROGRAM PP. 51-60

It is now appropriate to work through the lab manual activities and their accompanying recordings in class or in the language laboratory.

Resources for Spanish-speaking Students

FYI

	WORKBOOK FOR SPANISH-SPEAKING STUDENTS: PP. 33-38
	ANSWER KEY TO SSS WORKBOOK PP. 11-12

Activities specially written to meet the needs of Spanish-speaking students are available in this workbook for the reinforcement and extension of the topics and language presented in this chapter.

Additional Chapter Resources

Refer to the Chapter Support Materials list on the opening page of this chapter for detailed cross-references to *¡Ya verás! Gold's* student-centered technology components and various assessment options.

 Spanish for Spanish Speakers

Keeping a Vocabulary Notebook

Remind Spanish-speaking students to add words and expressions from this vocabulary section to the problematic spelling combination categories and personal new vocabulary lists they started in their notebooks in Chapter 1. Reinforce that they should continue to do this each time a chapter in the textbook is completed.

ENCUENTROS
CULTURALES
◆

PRACTICE/APPLY

Un árbol ecuatoriano

SUGGESTION

Review the vocabulary for family members and the custom of using both maternal and paternal last names. You may want to write your own family tree on the board, identifying both maternal and paternal last names.

Visual-Spatial

Antes de leer

POSSIBLE ANSWERS

1. a family tree
2. Answers will vary.
3. Answers will vary.
4. Upon marriage, a woman can take her husband's last name instead of her own maiden name; he and/or she can hyphenate the two last names, or she can keep her maiden name, even in marriage.

Un árbol ecuatoriano

Reading Strategies

- Using illustrations to predict content
- Activating background knowledge

Antes de leer

1. Look at the illustration. What kind of diagram is this?

2. Do you know where your grandparents and great-grandparents came from?

3. How many last names do you use? Do you use a hyphenated family name? Do you know people who do? Explain the changes that a person's last name sometimes undergoes when he or she gets married.

Queridos papás:

¿Cómo están? Escribo esta nota porque quiero mostrarles el árbol genealógico que preparo para la clase de historia. Como se presentan los apellidos es bien diferente aquí, en los Estados Unidos. Mamá, ¿sabes que en los Estados Unidos mucha gente no usa el apellido materno? Es como un secreto. También, ¡cómo se sorprende a veces la gente de que mis parientes vengan de tantas partes del mundo! Quizás es que la gente no se acuerda de que en América Latina muchas personas también vinieron de otras partes del mundo, igual que por acá. Bueno, chau, me voy a hacer los deberes. Les escribo pronto.

Un beso,

Carlos

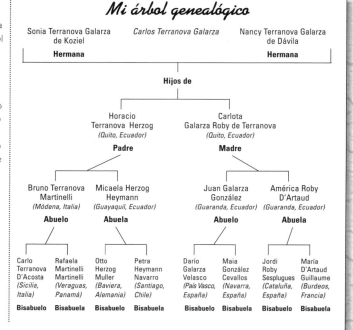

Mi árbol genealógico

Guía para la lectura

1. Here are some words and expressions to keep in mind as you read.

quiero mostrarles	*I want to show you*
sabes	*do you know*
vengan	*might possibly come*
Quizás	*perhaps*
no se acuerda	*do not remember (reflex.)*
vinieron	*came*
los deberes	*homework (used in Ecuador)*

2. In Spanish-speaking countries, **de** is sometimes used after a woman's maiden name to separate it from her husband's last name.

Después de leer

1. Why do you think Carlos says that "el apellido materno en los Estados Unidos es como un secreto"? Are you known by both your mother's maiden name and your father's last name? What is the usefulness of using the last name of both one's parents?

2. Why does it bother Carlos that people in the United States are surprised that his ancestors came from all over the world?

3. A diagram depicting the growth of a family through several generations is often called "a family tree." Why do you think this term is used? Why do you think family trees might be useful? Have you or other family members ever prepared a family tree?

Guía para la lectura
VOCABULARY EXPANSION

In addition to **deberes**, other words for "homework" are **tarea** and **trabajo de casa**.

 Linguistic Comparisons 4.1

Después de leer
POSSIBLE ANSWERS

1. Not many people use their mother's last name with their father's last name.
2. Because many North Americans do not realize that Latin America attracted immigrants as did the United States and Canada.
3. Answers will vary.

¡Sigamos adelante! Resource

FYI

 LESSON PLAN BOOK P. 36

You might find it helpful to refer to the Lesson Plan Book before you and your students begin the end-of-unit materials.

 **PRACTICE / APPLY**

A. Vamos a conocernos

SUGGESTION

Pair students together who have not yet worked together on an interview-type activity.

Interpersonal Communication 1.1
Cultural Practices and Perspectives 2.1

B. Un diálogo de contrarios

SUGGESTION

Have students present their dialogues to the class after they have practiced and rehearsed them.

Interpersonal Communication 1.1
Cultural Practices and Perspectives 2.1

INSIDE/OUTSIDE CIRCLE GAME

Start playing a recording of popular Spanish music. Set up equal numbers of chairs in two concentric circles, with the inside circle facing out and the outside circle facing in. Tell students to sit down when you stop the music. Once students are seated, announce a question, which the students on the inside circle are to ask the students they are facing on the outside circle. (Questions should reflect chapter content.) Students on the outside circle answer, and then ask the student on the inside circle the same question.

After both students have asked and answered the question, ask the students to stand, start the music, and have the students proceed around their circles until the music stops again. Repeat the exercise until all students have asked and answered all the questions. To ensure individual accountability, call on students randomly to answer the questions.

Auditory-Musical
Interpersonal

Conversemos un rato

A. Vamos a conocernos Role-play the following situation with a classmate.

1. Imagine that you are at a party feeling lonely and bored. You strike up a conversation with an interesting person sitting next to you. Work with a partner to prepare a dialogue based on the suggestions below.

   a. Greet each other using any of the **saludos y respuestas** you learned in the first chapter. Find out your classmate's first and last names.

   b. Find out where your classmate lives.

   c. Ask your partner to describe his or her family members (*parientes*). Ask how many brothers and sisters your partner has, and whether he or she has a small or large family.

   d. Find out the names of your friend's grandparents (*abuelos*).

   e. Ask if there are dogs or cats at home. Find out their names.

   f. Ask your partner to describe his or her parents and what do they do for a living.

B. Un diálogo de contrarios After reviewing pp. 103-104 and 112-113 in your textbook, prepare a dialogue with a classmate, based on the following scenario.

1. Imagine your family is hosting an exchange student from Bolivia. Discuss likes and dislikes with the exchange student.

   a. Greet each other using your full names and shake hands.

   b. Offer your new friend some snacks. Your friend should decline politely.

   c. For each of the categories below, express differing opinions.

   The type of movies you like

   The sports you watch

   Your favorite subjects in school

   What type of pet you like

   d. Dinner is ready and finally you find there's something you agree on; you both love to eat!

146   *Segunda unidad*   ¡Vamos a conocernos!

MULTIPLE INTELLIGENCES
- Auditory-Musical
- Bodily-Kinesthetic
- Interpersonal

The Standards
- Presentational Communication 1.3

Taller de escritores

Writing a paragraph

For practice, write a paragraph in Spanish to a pen pal or email-pal, describing your room at home or another room you like.

> Mi cuarto es pequeño pero bonito. Tiene una ventana grande donde uno ve la próxima casa. Tiene mucha luz. Contiene muchas cosas para su tamaño: mi estéreo, mi ropa, mi computadora. Hay una cama, un escritorio, un estante con mis libros...

Writing Strategy
• List writing

A. Reflexión Choose a room to describe, then list as many details about it as you can think of. Narrow your list to a few main points.

B. Primer borrador Write a first draft of the paragraph.

C. Revisión con un(a) compañero(a) Exchange paragraphs with a classmate. Read each other's work and comment on it, based on these questions: What aspect of the description is the most interesting? What part of the room can you most easily visualize? Is the paragraph appropriate for its audience? Does the paragraph reflect the task assigned? What aspect of the paragraph would you like to have clarified or made more complete?

D. Versión final Revise your first draft at home, based on the feedback you received. Check grammar, spelling, punctuation, and accent marks. Bring your final draft to class.

E. Carpeta Your teacher may choose to place your work in your portfolio, display it on a bulletin board, or use it to evaluate your progress.

147

MULTIPLE INTELLIGENCES

• Linguistic
• Visual-Spatial

The Standards

• Interpretive Communication 1.2
• Presentational Communication 1.3

Taller de escritores Resource

FYI

 ATAJO WRITING ASSISTANT SOFTWARE

You might want to have students use this software program when doing their writing assignment. The following language references in **Atajo** will be helpful in their work.

Phrases: Describing objects; Expressing location; Writing a letter (informal)

Vocabulary: House: Bedroom, furniture, kitchen, living room

Grammar: Possessive Adjectives: **mi(s)**, **tu(s)**; Verbs: Use of **estar**, Use of **tener**

A. Reflexión
SUGGESTION
Remind students to refer to the **Estructura** and **Nota gramatical** sections, as well as to the **Vocabulario** list at the end of each chapter.

B. Primer borrador
SUGGESTION
Tell students to keep in mind why they are writing and for whom.

C. Revisión con un(a) compañero(a)
SUGGESTION
Model a peer review by showing sample descriptions on a transparency and answering the revision questions in class.

D. Versión final
SUGGESTION
Tell students they do not have to incorporate all the suggestions given by their classmates, but rather use the ideas that they feel would improve the message.

E. Carpeta
Point out that as students add samples of their written work to their **carpeta** they will be able to see the progress in their writing in Spanish.

A. ¿Con quién vives?

SUGGESTION

 Have students look over the list of people and point out the words they do not know. Then give them simple hints so that they can make educated guesses: **Su cuñado es el esposo de su hermana**.

Activating Prior Knowledge
Making Hypotheses

Tipos de familias

SUGGESTION

You may want to ask some of the following questions to help guide students through the reading:

1. **¿Cuáles tipos de familias tienen dos padres?**
2. **¿Cuáles grupos no tienen dos padres?**
3. **¿Cuántos padres hay en una familia monoparental?**
4. **¿Qué tipo de famlia quisieras tener en veinte años?**

FYI

Many families in the United States today are nontraditional, so be supportive of the students in their expression of their individual lives. Let students know that the book portrays a variety of families, and affirm that families are unique and many possibilities exist.

Linguistic
Logical-Mathematical

Conexión con la sociología

La familia en nuestra sociedad

Para empezar La familia es la base de nuestra **sociedad** humana. Algunas familias son grandes y otras son pequeñas. Nuestra sociedad es interesante y diversa porque todos tenemos familias diferentes.

A. ¿Con quién vives? Look over the following list of people.

1. Write down relatives you live with.
2. Write down how many of each you have in your family.

madre	tía	hijo
padre	primo	hija
hermano	prima	**sobrino**
hermana	padrastro	**sobrina**
abuelo	madrastra	**cuñado**
abuela	hermanastra	**cuñada**
tío	hermanastro	otros: _____

3. Tengo _____ personas en mi familia.

Tipos de familias

La familia nuclear: es ahora el tipo de familia más común en el mundo. En esta familia, hay dos esposos que viven con sus hijos o **hijastros**. Otros **parientes** llegan de visita pero no viven con ellos.

La familia extendida: Cuando otros parientes viven con dos esposos y sus hijos, es una familia extendida. En muchas familias extendidas, los abuelos, y a veces los primos, tíos y **parientes políticos** viven en la misma casa. En Latinoamérica todavía hay muchas familias extendidas.

La familia monoparental: En una familia monoparental, **sólo** hay una madre o un padre que vive con sus hijos o hijastros. No hay dos padres. A veces la madre o el padre está divorciado(a). A veces la madre o el padre es **viudo(a)**.

sociedad *society* sobrino(a) *nephew (niece)* cuñado(a) *brother-in-law (sister-in-law)*
hijastros *stepchildren* parientes *relatives* parientes políticos *relatives by marriage* sólo *only*
viudo(a) *widower (widow)*

  The Standards

- Linguistic
- Logical-Mathematical

B. ¿Qué tipo de familia es?

Now complete the chart below using your knowledge from the reading to identify the kinds of families that the following people have. The first one is done for you.

persona	vive con	tipo de familia
Carmen	su madre y padre, sus hermanos y hermanas	*nuclear*
Luis	sus abuelos, padres y hermanos	
Elena	su esposo y su hijo	
Carlos	su hijo	
Mónica	su hijo y sus dos hijas	
Yo	¿?	¿?

C. ¿Verdadero o falso?

Answer **verdadero** or **falso** based on the information in the chart below.

1. En esta gráfica, hay información sobre personas solteras (*single*).
2. La gráfica tiene información sobre las familias extendidas.
3. El 12% de las personas viven con su madre, pero no con su padre.
4. El 15% de las personas viven en familias monoparentales.
5. La sección azul (*blue*) representa las familias nucleares.

FAMILIAS EN LOS ESTADOS UNIDOS

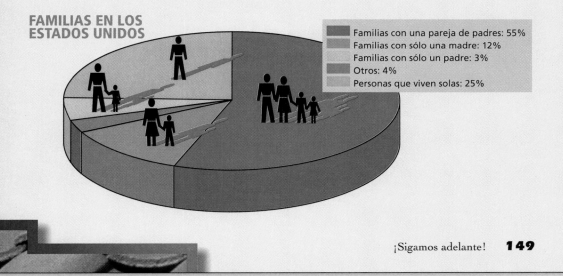

Familias con una pareja de padres: 55%
Familias con sólo una madre: 12%
Familias con sólo un padre: 3%
Otros: 4%
Personas que viven solas: 25%

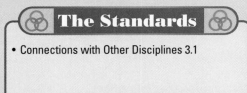

The Standards

• Connections with Other Disciplines 3.1

B. ¿Qué tipo de familia es?

ANSWERS

Carmen: una familia nuclear
Luis: una familia extendida
Elena: una familia nuclear
Carlos: una familia monoparental
Mónica: una familia monoparental

C. ¿Verdadero o falso?

ANSWERS

1. verdadero
2. falso
3. verdadero
4. verdadero
5. verdadero

EXPANSION

Put the following sentences on an overhead transparency or on the board and ask students to decide which kind of family each describes. Mark *N* for **una familia nuclear**, *E* for **una familia extendida** or *MP* for **una familila monoparental**.

El padre y la madre no viven en la misma casa. (MP)
Los abuelos viven con los padres y sus hijos. (E)
Los hijos viven con su madre y su padrasto. (N)
Los tíos y tías viven con los padres y sus hijos. (E)
Los esposos viven con los padres de la esposa. (E)

TEACH/MODEL

Ecuador

PRESENTATION

Tell students that Ecuador is the smallest of the Andean countries. It is know for its spectacular volcanic and jungle landscapes, Indian markets, and a rich colonial history. The Galápagos Islands, part of Ecuador, are considered one of the world's natural history treasures.

Connections with Other Disciplines 3.1

Vistas
de los países hispanos

Ecuador

Capital: Quito

Ciudades principales: Guayaquil, Cuenca, Ambato

Población: 10.500.000

Idiomas: español, quechua

Área territorial: 270.670 km²

Clima: la costa mantiene una temperatura de 23° a 25° C; en la región de la sierra de 20° a 26° C

mantiene *maintains*   sierra *mountains*

150   *Segunda unidad* ¡Vamos a conocernos!

MULTIPLE INTELLIGENCES

- Visual-Spatial

The Standards

- Connections with Distinctive Viewpoints 3.2

Focus on Culture

Quechua

Quechua, the language of the Indians of Inca descent, is spoken by over 8 million people in South America. Some English words borrowed from Quechua include: **condor, guano, llama, puma, quinoa,** and **vicuña.**

Linguistic Comparisons 4.1

Chile

Capital: Santiago

Ciudades principales: Concepción, Valparaíso, Viña del Mar,

Población: 13.200.000

Idiomas: español

Área territorial: 756.626 km²

Clima: seco en el norte, templado en la region central, frio y húmedo en el sur

seco *dry*   templado *temperate, moderate* húmedo *humid*

EXPLORA

Find out more about Ecuador and Chile! Access the **Nuestros vecinos** page on the **¡Ya verás!** *Gold* web site for a list of URLs.

http://yaveras.heinle.com/vecinos.htm

¡Sigamos adelante! **151**

Chile

PRESENTATION

Tell students that Chile has flourishing cosmopolitan cities, spectacular Pacific coastlines, and beautiful Andean mountains. The country is known for its many opportunities for adventure sports. There are skiing and hiking in the mountains and national parks and plenty of water sports along the Pacific coast. Easter Island, off the coast of Chile, is a very remote inhabited island and is home to about 2000 people of Polynesian descent and hundreds of huge stone statues called **moais**.

Connections with Other Disciplines 3.1

MULTIPLE INTELLIGENCES

- Visual-Spatial

The Standards

- Connections with Distinctive Viewpoints 3.2

Honduras

PRESENTATION

Honduras is still one of the least developed and least industrial countries in Central America. The slow pace and natural beauty make it a nice place to visit. Most Hondurans speak Spanish but Creole English and Indian dialects are also spoken. One of the sites to visit is the **Ruinas de Copan**, an ancient Maya ruin.

 Connections with Other Disciplines 3.1

FYI

When Honduras became independent from Spain in 1821, it united with El Salvador, Costa Rica, Guatemala, and Nicaragua to form the Central American Federation until 1839. The present version of the Honduran flag is almost identical to the one used by the federation. The two blue bands around one white band represent the geographic position of Honduras between the Pacific Ocean and the Caribbean Sea. The five blue stars, introduced in 1866, reflect the hope that the five Central American countries may once again form an association.

 Connections with Distinctive Viewpoints 3.2

Honduras

Capital: Tegucigalpa

Ciudades principales: San Pedro Sula, Choluteca

Población: 5.800.000

Idiomas: español, dialectos indígenas

Área territorial: 112,492 km²

Clima: tropical en la costa, templado en el interior

indígenas *indigenous, native*

EXPLORA

Find out more about Honduras! Access the **Nuestros vecinos** page on the *¡Ya verás! Gold* web site for a list of URLs.

http://yaveras.heinle.com/vecinos.htm

152 *Segunda unidad ¡Vamos a conocernos!*

MULTIPLE INTELLIGENCES

- Visual-Spatial

The Standards

- Connections with Distinctive Viewpoints 3.2

Focus on Culture

Cloud Forests

Honduras has the most **bosques nublosos** or cloud forests in Central America. Some national parks in Honduras are: **Parque nacional de Cerro Azul** and **Pico Bonito**. The Mosquito Coast, on the northern coast of Honduras is another natural treasure.

 Connections with Distinctive Viewpoints 3.2 Linguistic Comparisons 4.1

En la comunidad

¡Programa tu carrera!

"My name is Adam Weiss. The summer of my junior year in high school, I took three years of high school Spanish and one big bag and went to Madrid on a cultural exchange. A month later, I brought home a passion for languages and a lifelong friendship with a Spanish family. It was exciting to actually use a foreign language!

A background in Spanish and computer science turned out to be a requirement for my first job. Now I work as an international software engineer at a company that creates voice recognition software. If you want to talk to your computer in Spanish or in other European languages and have it do your typing for you, you'll use our software. Although my primary responsibility is programming, I've also traveled to Mexico and South America for trade shows to show off our products. I also collect voice and accent samples for our programs so they can recognize varying ways to pronounce the same words. My career has been a lot more interesting because I've learned Spanish!"

¡Ahora te toca a ti!

Adam's cultural exchange led to "a passion for languages and a lifelong friendship with a Spanish family." Why do you think he enjoyed the exchange program so much?

Do you think that spending time in Spain improved his Spanish? Why?

If you have visited a Spanish-speaking country or participated in an exchange program, you may want to prepare a short presentation in Spanish about your experiences. If you wish, bring photographs to class to help you describe the country as well as the people you met there.

If you haven't participated in an exchange program or traveled to a Spanish-speaking country, you might like to interview someone who has. Be prepared to share with your classmates what you find out.

You might also want to imagine that you're going on a cultural exchange program to a Spanish-speaking country. At the library, research places you would like to visit and choose a destination. Be prepared to discuss with your classmates why you want to visit that particular country.

 ¡Sigamos adelante! **153**

PRACTICE/APPLY

¡Ahora te toca a ti!

SUGGESTION

This might be a good opportunity to discuss students' own language learning goals and previous experiences with Spanish.

Cultural Practices and Perspectives 2.1
Connections with Distinct Viewpoints 3.2

SUGGESTION

Have students research exchange programs in Ecuador, Chile, or Honduras—the countries highlighted in the **Vistas de los países hispánicos** section of this unit. Then they can present what they found to the class. If any students have participated in an exchange program, to a Spanish-speaking country or elsewhere, have them give a short presentation to the class.

Presentational Communication 1.3

MULTIPLE INTELLIGENCES

- Linguistic
- Interpersonal
- Intrapersonal

The Standards

- Communities In and Beyond School 5.1

UNIDAD 3

Setting the Context

Unit 3 features José Rivas, a young man from Spain. The basic theme of the unit is getting around towns and cities. Chapter 7 offers a generic introduction to a town or city. Chapter 8 focuses on how to give directions for getting around in a city. Chapter 9 discusses many of the celebrations in the Hispanic world.

UNIDAD 3

¿Dónde y a qué hora?

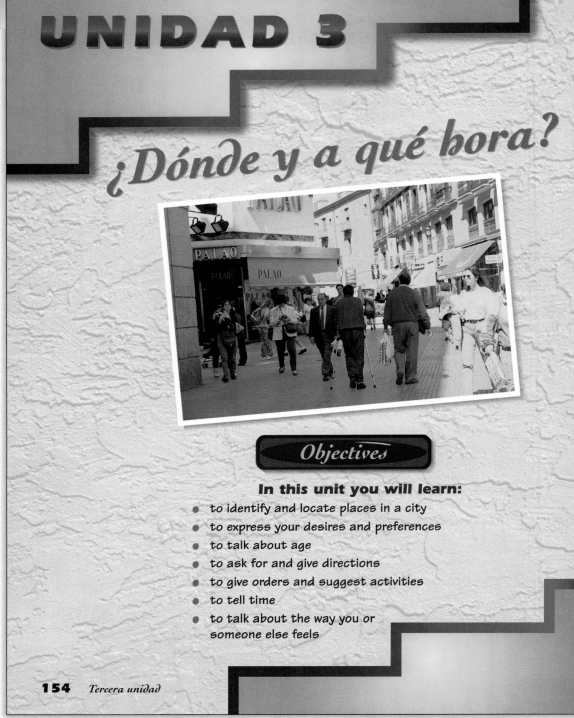

Objectives

In this unit you will learn:

- to identify and locate places in a city
- to express your desires and preferences
- to talk about age
- to ask for and give directions
- to give orders and suggest activities
- to tell time
- to talk about the way you or someone else feels

154 *Tercera unidad*

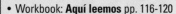

Unit Support Materials

- Workbook: **Aquí leemos** pp. 116-120
- Lab Manual: **Ya llegamos** pp. 64-66
- Lab Program: Cassette Side B; CD 10, Tracks 8-10
- Tapescript: Lab Program pp. 96, 97
- TRB: Unit Grammar Review Masters: pp. 24-30; Answer Key pp. 53-55
- Lesson Plan Book: **¡Sigamos adelante!** p. 54
- Workbook for Spanish-speaking Students: pp. 59, 60
- Answer Key to SSS Workbook: pp. 13-14
- Testing Program: Unit Test pp. 102-108; Answer Key & Testing Cassettes Tapescript pp. T43, T44;

- Oral Assessment p. T44; Portfolio Assessment pp. Pxi-Pxii
- Testing Cassettes: Cassette Side A
- Computerized Testing Program: Windows™; Macintosh®
- Atajo Writing Assistant Software: Student Text p. 223
- Video Program: Cassette 1, 1:22:04-1:25:35
- Video Guide: Videoscript pp. 30-34; Activities pp. 107-108
- Internet Explorations: Student Text p. 226

¿Qué ves?

- Where are the people in the photo at left?
- What kind of store do you think is in the photo at left?
- What public buildings do you see in the photos on this page?

 ¿Adónde vamos?
Primera etapa: Los edificios públicos
Segunda etapa: ¿Quieres ir al cine?
Tercera etapa: Las tiendas

 ¿Dónde está... ?
Primera etapa: ¿Está lejos de aquí?
Segunda etapa: ¿Cómo llego a... ?

 ¡La fiesta del pueblo!
Primera etapa: ¿A qué hora son los bailes folklóricos?
Segunda etapa: ¿Cómo están Uds.?

155

UNIT WARM-UP

Planning Strategy

 WORKBOOK, P. 81

If you do not assign the Planning Strategy (Workbook, p. 81) for homework, or if students have difficulty coming up with English expressions, you might try asking several students to role play each of the situations in English: you can ask someone to find out from a stranger the location of the town library; you can have another student find out from a friend if there is a drugstore nearby; etc. After each response, point out the expressions used and then ask the class to suggest other possibilities.

Presentational Communication 1.3

Focus on Culture

José Rivas

Have students study the photo of José Rivas on page 156. Ask them to compare and contrast the way he dresses to the way people his age in the United States dress.

Cultural Comparisons 4.2

CAPÍTULO 7

OBJECTIVES

Function
- Identifying public buildings and places

Context
- City or town

Accuracy
- Present tense of the verb **ir**
- The contraction **al**
- Expressions of frequency
- Present tense of **querer** and **preferir**
- Numbers from 20 to 100
- Expressions with **tener**

Pronunciation
- The consonants **g** and **j**

CHAPTER WARM-UP

Setting the Context

In preparation for their learning about identifying public buildings and places, show students a map of a typical—classically structured—Latin American city. (You can refer them to p. 166 of the text or p. 94 of the Workbook.) Ask them to compare the layout of the town or city where they live to that of the Latin American town or city. What differences do they notice? How might they explain these differences?

 Comparing and Contrasting Hypothesizing

 Visual-Spatial

 Cultural Comparisons 4.2

CAPÍTULO 7

¿Adónde vamos?

José Rivas va a la farmacia.

Objectives

- identifying places in a city
- identifying public buildings

Chapter Support Materials

- Lab Manual: pp. 43-51
- Lab Program: Cassette Side A; CD 4, Tracks 1-10
- TRB: Textbook Activity Masters: pp. 84-88
- Textbook Cassettes/CDs: Cassette 1, Side B; CD 2, Track 8
- Tapescript: Lab Program pp. 65-77; Textbook Cassettes/CDs pp. 30-34
- Middle School Activities: pp. 55-58
- Workbook for Spanish-speaking Students: pp. 41-46
- Answer Key to SSS Workbook: pp. 13-14
- Practice Software: Windows™; Macintosh®

- Testing Program: Chapter Test pp. 79-81; Answer Key & Testing Cassettes Tapescript pp. T31, T32; Oral Assessment pp. T32, T33
- Testing Cassettes: Cassette Side A
- Computerized Testing Program: Windows™; Macintosh®
- Video Program: Cassette 1, 57:20-1:06:12
- Video Guide: Videoscript pp. 30-34 Activities pp. 107-108

- **Mundos hispanos 1**
- Internet Activities: Student Text p. 180

PRIMERA ETAPA

- What are some buildings that can be found in most cities or towns?
- What does the word **plaza** make you think of?
- Where are most of the public buildings located in your city or town?
- Which public buildings are within walking distance from where you live?

Los edificios públicos

*En nuestra ciudad hay muchos **edificios públicos*** (public buildings).

un aeropuerto
una estación de trenes
un banco
un hospital
una biblioteca *a library*
una iglesia *a church*
una catedral
un mercado *a market*
un colegio *a school*
una oficina de correos *a post office*
una escuela secundaria *a high school*
una plaza *a town, city square*
una estación de autobuses *a bus station*
una universidad
una estación de policía

Capítulo 7 ¿Adónde vamos? **157**

TEACH/MODEL

Los edificios públicos

PRESENTATION

 TRANSPARENCY 33

With students' books closed, show the class the transparency. Introduce all the vocabulary, using the following pattern: **un hospital/¿Qué es?/(Es un hospital.)/Sí, es un hospital.** Then continue by making mistakes and having students correct you: **Es una iglesia. (No, no es una iglesia, es un hospital.)** If the class performs well with the transparency, move directly to Activity B.

 Visual-Spatial

Interpretive Communication 1.2

VARIATION

Write the names of the places (grouped by category: transportation, schools, public buildings) on the board. Many of the words are recognizable as cognates. Have students ask you about the others: **¿Qué es una iglesia?**, etc.

 Activating Prior Knowledge Categorizing

Linguistic Comparisons 4.1

Etapa Support Materials

- Workbook: pp. 82-85
- TRB: Textbook Activity Masters: p. 84
- Textbook Cassettes/CDs: Cassette 1, Side B; CD 2, Track 1
- Tapescript: Textbook Cassettes/CDs p. 197
- Overhead Transparency: 33
- Middle School Activities: pp. 59, 60
- Lesson Plan Book: pp. 55-56

- Testing Program: Quiz pp. 72, 73; Answer Key & Testing Cassettes Tapescript p. T29
- Testing Cassettes: Cassette Side A
- Computerized Testing Program: Windows™; Macintosh®
- Atajo Writing Assistant Software: Student Text p. 163; Workbook p. 84

PRACTICE / APPLY

Comentarios culturales

SUGGESTION

Have students describe the town or city where they live. Ask them to focus on the location of the government buildings, police station, churches, post office, and other major buildings. Then read about the **plaza** and ask students to compare and contrast their town or city with those described in **La ciudad típica**.

 Comparing and Contrasting

Cultural Comparisons 4.2

A. ¿Qué es?

SUGGESTION

This activity could be written or done orally in pairs.

ANSWERS

1. Es una estación de autobuses.
2. Es el centro.
3. Es una estación de policía.
4. Es un mercado.
5. Es un aeropuerto.
6. Es una estación de trenes.
7. Es un hospital.
8. Es una oficina de correos.
9. Es una iglesia.

Comentarios CULTURALES

La ciudad típica

Many cities in the Spanish-speaking world are built based on the same pattern. There is usually a **plaza** in the middle of town with several important buildings facing it: the cathedral or main church at one end; the main government building and a police station at the other; and shops, banks, hotels, and cafés on the two sides in between. Families and young people gather at the central plaza on weekends and summer evenings to take a walk, see their friends, and have a drink or a meal. Walking around a city and its plaza is considered one of life's pleasures by many different people in Spanish-speaking societies. The streets are full of life, movement, and music.

¡Te toca a ti!

A. ¿Qué es? Identify each building or place in the drawings that follow. Follow the model.

MODELO	*Es una catedral.*

1.　　　　　　　　2.

3.　　　　　　4.　　　　　　5.

MULTIPLE INTELLIGENCES

- Linguistic: All activities
- Logical-Mathematical: B, E, F
- Visual-Spatial: A,
- Auditory-Musical: **Pronunciación**, D, **Aquí escuchamos**
- Interpersonal: C

The Standards

- Interpersonal Communication 1.1: C, G, H, J, **Adelante** activities
- Interpretive Communication 1.2: B, C, K, A, E, F, I, **Aquí escuchamos**
- Presentational Communication 1.3: **Más números**
- Cultural Practices and Perspectives 2.1: **Comentarios culturales**
- Linguistic Comparisons 4.1: **Pronunciación**
- Cultural Comparisons 4.2: **Comentarios culturales**

6.   7.   8.   9.

B. ¿Dónde está...? (Where is . . . ?)
You have just arrived in town and are looking at a map. Using the appropriate form of the definite article (**el, la**), ask where each building or place is located. Follow the model.

> **MODELO**   oficina de correos
> *¿Dónde está la oficina de correos?*

1. estación de trenes	8. biblioteca
2. aeropuerto	9. catedral
3. iglesia	10. oficina de correos
4. estación de autobuses	11. estación de policía
5. universidad	12. hospital
6. plaza	13. mercado
7. escuela secundaria	14. colegio

C. ¡Aquí está! (Here it is!)
Now that you are familiar with the map of the town, a tourist asks you where certain buildings and places are. A classmate will play the role of the tourist. Using the expression **Aquí está,** indicate the various locations on the map. Follow the model.

> **MODELO**   la plaza
> **Turista:**   *¿Dónde está la plaza?*
> **Tú:**   *¿La plaza? Aquí está.*

1. la catedral	7. el aeropuerto
2. la oficina de correos	8. la estación de policía
3. la universidad	9. la iglesia
4. la biblioteca	10. el hospital
5. la estación de trenes	11. la estación de autobuses
6. la escuela secundaria	12. el colegio

Capítulo 7 ¿Adónde vamos?   **159**

Focus on Culture

Spanish Towns and Cities

Most Spanish towns and cities date back to the Middle Ages-when the major city planning concern was protection. Often towns grew around a **castillo** or a church, with houses crowded together behind defensive walls. (Try to bring in pictures of Ávila or other walled cities.) As a result, the streets were narrow and winding and did not follow any predetermined pattern. The basic street pattern of Spanish cities has changed very little since the fifteenth century: many of the walls have come down and towns have expanded, but plazas with a church in the middle are still central to Spanish towns and cities.

   Connections with Other Disciplines 3.1

Pronunciación

PRESENTATION

 TEXTBOOK CASSETTE/CD CASSETTE 1, SIDE B; CD 2, TRACK 1

 TAPESCRIPT P. 197

Have students listen to the explanation for the consonant **g** on the Textbook Cassette/CD. The speaker will model the correct pronunciation of the words in **Práctica D**. Have students follow along in their texts and repeat after each word.

🎵 Auditory-Musical

Estructura

PRESENTATION

To present the verb **ir** inductively, you can combine the presentation of the verb with that of the adverbs frequently used with the idea of going (see the **Palabras útiles** on pp. 161-162).

Write these new adverbs and the adverbs of frequency learned in Chapter 1 on the board (**nunca, rara vez, a veces/de vez en cuando, a menudo, todos los días/siempre**). Illustrate their meanings with verbs that students already know (**estudiar, cantar, hablar español**, etc.)

Then choose a well-known city and start by telling about yourself: **Yo voy a Chicago rara vez, pero voy a Nueva York a menudo.** Then ask a student: **¿Tú vas a Chicago a menudo?** Summarize using third-person forms. **Él(Ella) nunca va a Chicago.** Continue until you have used all of the forms, stressing the conjugated forms of **ir** each time with voice inflection. (Make statements using the **nosotros** form, then ask **Uds.** questions, and summarize the answers in the third-person plural.) End the presentation by writing the forms of ir on the board.

VARIATION

Have students repeat the conjugation while you write the subject pronouns on the board: **yo/tú/él, ella, Ud./ nosotros(as), vosotros(as), Uds./ellos, ellas.** Repeat with the negative. Then add the verb forms to the pronouns.

PRONUNCIACIÓN THE CONSONANT **g**

In Spanish, **g** is pronounced like the *g* in the English word *goal* when it is before the vowels **a, o,** and **u,** as in **gato, gota,** and **gusta** or before the consonants **l** and **r** as in **globo** or **grupo.** It has this sound before **ue** and **ui** as in **guerra** and **guitarra,** in which cases the **u** is silent. The letter **g** is also pronounced this way when it is the first letter of a word or follows the consonant **n.**

Práctica

D. Listen and repeat as your teacher models the following words.

1. gato	4. ganas	7. Gustavo	9. un gato
2. grupo	5. gracias	8. tengo	10. un globo
3. gordo	6. globo		

ESTRUCTURA

The verb **ir** and the contraction **al**

¿Adónde **van** Uds.?	*Where are you going?*
Yo **voy** a Nueva York.	*I am going to New York.*
Alicia **va** a la plaza.	*Alicia is going to the (town) square.*
Vamos al mercado.	*We are going to the market.*

ir *(to go)*			
yo	**voy**	nosotros(as)	**vamos**
tú	**vas**	vosotros(as)	**vais**
él		ellos	
ella	**va**	ellas	**van**
Ud.		Uds.	

1. The verb **ir** is irregular, so you need to memorize its forms.
2. When the preposition **a** is followed by the definite article **el,** they contract to form one word, **al.**

☀ Spanish for Spanish Speakers

Cities of Origin

Have Spanish speakers conduct interviews with a former resident of a Spanish-speaking country. Students can prepare by writing questions that ask the following: (1) where that person's former home was, (2) how she(he) traveled around town, (3) where everyday destinations were located, i.e. market, movie theater, favorite restaurants, school, work, or best friend's house, and (4) where important city attractions were, etc. Interviews should take place as homework; answers should be written down. When interviews have been completed, have students do simple class presentations, using the board, maps, or photos to facilitate communication.

🌐 Connections with Distinctive Viewpoints 3.2
Communities In and Beyond School 5.1

Aquí practicamos

E. ¿Adónde vas? Pick an activity from the first column, and then choose the place associated with it from the second column. Form a sentence, following the model.

> **MODELO** Me gusta viajar. el aeropuerto
> *Me gusta viajar; por eso* (because of that) *voy al aeropuerto.*

A	B
1. Tienes que ver al médico.	la biblioteca
2. Necesitamos más libros.	el banco
3. Quisieran comprar fruta.	el museo
4. Me gusta caminar (*walking*).	la oficina de correos
5. Usted necesita dinero.	la estación de policía
6. Ellos tienen que aprender.	el hospital
7. Me gusta el arte moderno.	la iglesia
8. Tengo que mandar una carta.	la escuela
9. Quiero hablar con un policía.	el mercado
10. Desean escuchar música religiosa.	el aeropuerto
	el parque

F. En la estación de trenes You are at the railroad station with a group of friends who are all leaving to visit different Spanish cities. Each time you ask a friend if someone is going to a certain city, he (she) tells you that you are wrong. Ask and answer questions with a partner, following the model.

> **MODELO** Raquel / Salamanca / Cádiz
> **Tú:** *¿Va Raquel a Salamanca?*
> **Amigo(a):** *No, Raquel no va a Salamanca. Ella va a Cádiz.*

1. Teresita / León / Burgos
2. Carlos / Valencia / Granada
3. Antonio / Málaga / Córdoba
4. Carmencita / Sevilla / Toledo
5. Miguel / Pamplona / Ávila
6. Mari / Barcelona / Valencia
7. Juan / Córdoba / Segovia

Capítulo 7 ¿Adónde vamos? **161**

PRACTICE/APPLY

E. ¿Adónde vas?
SUGGESTION
Since it may not be immediately apparent to students, point out that the subject for the second verb (**ir**)—shown in the model—may be logically deduced from that of the first verb.

Drawing Inferences

F. En la estación de trenes
ANSWERS
All answers follow the model. Students simply substitute the name of the person and places in each of their questions and answers.
1. ¿Va Teresita a León? No, Teresita no va a León. Ella va a Burgos, etc.
2. ¿Va Carlos a Valencia? No, Carlos no va a Valencia. Él va a Granada.
3. ¿Va Antonio a Málaga? No, Antonio no va a Málaga. Él va a Córdoba.
4. ¿Va Carmencita a Sevilla? No, Carmencita no va a Sevilla. Ella va a Toledo.
5. ¿Va Miguel a Pamplona? No, Miguel no va a Pamplona. Él va a Ávila.
6. ¿Va Mari a Barcelona? No, Mari no va a Barcelona. Ella va a Valencia.
7. ¿Va Juan a Córdova? No, Juan no va a Córdoba. Él va a Segovia.

Focus on Culture

Some Spanish Cities

Point out a few facts about some of the cities mentioned in Activity F; bring in pictures if you can. Suggestions: (2) Valencia (Spain's third largest city, probably best known for the millions of orange trees that surround it); (2) Granada (site of the Alhambra-a magnificent palace built by the Arabs); (5) Pamplona (**Fiesta de San Fermín** [in July] and the running of the bulls, location of Hemingway's novel *The Sun Also Rises*); (6) Barcelona (Spain's second largest city and site of the 1992 Summer Olympics, probably best known for **las Ramblas, el Museo de Picasso**, and the buildings by the architect Antonio Gaudí).

Connections with Other Disciplines 3.1

Palabras útiles

PRESENTATION

If you have not introduced these adverbs along with **ir**, put on the board a continuum running from **nunca** to **siempre** (see the notes for p.160). Use expressions such as **ir a la biblioteca**, and **ir al centro**, to practice the adverbs and expressions.

FYI

The use of **nunca** after the verb will be presented later. For now, students should use it only before the verb.

PRACTICE/APPLY

G. Una encuesta

POSSIBLE ANSWERS

1. Sí todos los domingos.
2. Múy rara vez.
3. Sí todos los días
4, Nó, nunca.
5. Sí, siempre.
6. No, nunca.

H. Los resultados

EXPANSION

Divide the class into teams of four to conduct **una encuesta.**

Then, explain that each question in Activities G and H will be answered by a different student, who will then ask each of his (her) team members the same question. For example, the first student might say, **Voy a menudo a la iglesia. Tomás, ¿vas tú a la iglesia a menudo?**

Next, each team should designate a "recorder" to keep track of everyone's answers. Tell the recorder to summarize the responses for his(her) teammates for **Los resultados**.

Finally, call on one member of each team (not the recorder) to report the team's results to the class in complete sentences.

Drawing Inferences
Synthesizing

PALABRAS ÚTILES

Expressing frequency

Following are some more phrases used in Spanish to say how often you do something.

rara vez rarely	**a menudo** frequently, often
nunca never	**de vez en cuando** from time to time

Nunca usually precedes the verb. The other adverbs may be placed at the beginning or end of a sentence.

Nunca vamos a la estación de policía.	We *never* go to the police station.
Rara vez voy al hospital.	I *rarely* go to the hospital.
Andrés va a la biblioteca **a menudo.**	Andrés goes to the library *often*.

Aquí practicamos

G. Una encuesta (A survey) Ask three other students the following questions and write down their answers. They do not need to answer with complete sentences. Your classmates should use a variety of expressions of frequency in the answers, including **siempre, todos los días, a veces,** and those learned in Chapter 1. Follow the model.

> MODELO
> Tú: ¿Vas al aeropuerto a menudo?
> Compañero(a): *Muy rara vez.* o: *Sí, a menudo.* o: *No, nunca.*

1. ¿Vas a la iglesia a menudo?
2. ¿Vas a la catedral a menudo?
3. ¿Vas a la plaza a menudo?
4. ¿Vas al mercado a menudo?
5. ¿Vas a la biblioteca a menudo?
6. ¿Vas al hospital a menudo?

H. Los resultados *Using complete sentences, report your findings from Activity G to your classmates. Follow the model.*

> MODELO
> *Josh nunca va a la biblioteca. Linda va a la biblioteca de vez en cuando y Denise va a menudo.*

162 *Tercera unidad* ¿Dónde y a qué hora?

Aquí escuchamos

El autobús *An announcement describes the route that a city bus takes on a typical day and the stops it makes.*

Antes de escuchar To prepare for the announcement you will hear, review the vocabulary you have learned for buildings and places.

 A escuchar Listen to the announcement twice before marking the order of the stops on your activity master.

Después de escuchar Based on what you just heard, write numbers next to the stops mentioned to indicate their order along the route.

__ el aeropuerto	__ la estación de auto-buses	__ el mercado
__ la biblioteca		__ la oficina de correos
__ la catedral	__ la estación de policía	__ la plaza
__ la escuela secundaria	__ el hospital	__ la universidad

¡ADELANTE!

 En la calle (On the street) You run into a classmate on the street. 1) Greet each other. 2) Then ask where he (she) is going, 3) what he (she) is going to do there, and 4) whether he (she) goes there often. Follow the model.

MODELO

Estudiante 1:	¡Hola! ¿Qué tal?
Estudiante 2:	Muy bien, ¿y tú?
Estudiante 1:	Bien, gracias. ¿Adónde vas?
Estudiante 2:	Voy a la biblioteca.
Estudiante 1:	¿Qué vas a hacer?
Estudiante 2:	Voy a estudiar.
Estudiante 1:	¿Vas a menudo a la biblioteca?
Estudiante 2:	Sí, todos los días. o: No, voy de vez en cuando.

 ¿Cuándo? Write a list of sentences using each of the following expressions to indicate how frequently you go to different public buildings in your town or city.

a menudo   nunca   siempre

a veces   rara vez   todos los días

de vez en cuando

Capítulo 7 ¿Adónde vamos? **163**

Aquí escuchamos

 TEXTBOOK CASSETTE/CD CASSETTE 1, SIDE B; CD 2, TRACK 2

 TAPESCRIPT P. 197

 TRB: ACTIVITY MASTER, P. 84

Después de escuchar

ANSWERS
1. aeropuerto, 2. universidad, 3. centro, 4. catedral, 5. la oficina de correos, 5. la escuela secundaria, 6. hospital, 7. mercado, 8. estación de autobuses

ETAPA SYNTHESIS

En la calle

Individual Needs

Less-prepared Students
Make a list on the board of possible greetings, expressions of frequency, and different destinations so that there is extra reinforcement of these items as students improvise their dialogues and then perform them for the class or for their group.

¿Cuándo?

FYI

 ATAJO WRITING ASSISTANT SOFTWARE

You might want to have students use this software program when doing this activity.

Additional Practice and Recycling

FYI

 WORKBOOK, PP. 82-85

For recycling and additional practice of the vocabulary, structures, and language functions presented throughout this **etapa**, you can assign the workbook activities as in-class work and/or homework. Answers to the activities are overprinted on each page of the Teacher's Edition of the Workbook.

Additional Etapa Resources

Refer to the **Etapa** Support Materials list on the opening page of this **etapa** for detailed cross-references to these assessment options.

SEGUNDA ETAPA

TEACH/MODEL

¿Quieres ir al cine?

PRESENTATION

 TRANSPARENCIES 34

 TEXTBOOK CASSETTE/CD CASSETTE 1, SIDE B; CD 1, TRACK 3

TAPESCRIPT P. 197

Describe the town where your school is located. Begin by using words from the previous **etapa: En esta ciudad hay un colegio, pero no hay una universidad...** . Move from the public buildings to the entertainment topic by using cognates: **En esta ciudad hay lugares interesantes y divertidos. ¿Te gusta bailar? ¿Vas a las discotecas? ¿Te gusta ver películas en el cine? Hay... cines en nuestra ciudad**, etc.

 Have students repeat the new vocabulary items after each sentence or two. Work in non-cognate expressions, mentioning also what the town does not have. After introducing the vocabulary, play the Textbook Cassette/CD to present the dialogue. Or, you may want to read it to the students, having them listen carefully, trying to understand as much as possible.

Auditory-Musical

Linguistic Comparisons 4.1

Preparación

- Besides the places you learned about in the previous **etapa**, what other public buildings or public places can you think of that are meant for leisure-time activities, recreation, or entertainment?

- What is your favorite place for recreation in your city or town?

- What do you wish your town had for recreation that it currently does not have?

¿Quieres ir al cine?

Una conversación telefónica:

Isabel:	¡Hola! ¿Celia?
Celia:	Sí. ¿Quién habla?
Isabel:	Habla Isabel.
Celia:	Hola, Isabel. ¿Qué tal?
Isabel:	Muy bien. Delia y yo vamos al cine esta **tarde. ¿Quieres venir** con nosotras?
Celia:	Mm..., **lo siento,** pero no es posible porque voy al museo con Marcos, y esta noche vamos a la discoteca.
Isabel:	Bueno, **en otra oportunidad.**
Celia:	Gracias, Isabel. Hasta luego.
Isabel:	De nada. Adiós.

Otros lugares *(places)* **en la ciudad:**

un cine *a movie theater*	un parque	**un estadio** *a stadium*
un museo *a museum*	una discoteca	un teatro
un club	**una piscina** *a swimming pool*	

tarde *afternoon*   **Quieres venir** *Do you want to come*   lo siento *I'm sorry*   esta noche *tonight*
en otra oportunidad *some other time*

164   *Tercera unidad* ¿Dónde y a qué hora?

Etapa Support Materials

- Workbook: pp. 86-90
- TRB: Textbook Activity Masters: p. 85
- Textbook Cassettes/CDs: Cassette 1, Side B; CD 2, Track 3
- Tapescript: Textbook Cassettes/CDs pp. 197-198
- Overhead Transparencies: 34-36
- Middle School Activities: p. 61
- Lesson Plan Book: pp. 51-52

- Testing Program: Quiz pp. 74-76; Answer Key & Testing Cassettes Tapescript pp. T29, T30
- Testing Cassettes: Cassette Side A
- Computerized Testing Program: Windows™; Macintosh®
- Atajo Writing Assistant Software: Student Text p. 172; Workbook p. 87

Comentarios CULTURALES

El teléfono

 here are different ways of answering the phone in Spanish, depending on the country. **Bueno** is used in Mexico, **hola** and **aló** are used in several South and Central American countries, and **diga** or **dígame** is used in Spain.

¡Te toca a ti!

A. ¿Qué lugares son? Identify each building or place that follows.

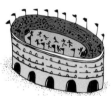

1.   2.   3.

4.   5.   6.

B. ¿Hay un(a)... en el barrio (neighborhood)? Ask a passerby if the places listed are in the neighborhood. The passerby will answer affirmatively and tell you the street where each can be found. Act this out with a partner, alternating roles.

> **MODELO**   restaurante / en la calle (street) San Martín
>   **Tú:**   *Perdón, señor (señorita). ¿Hay un restaurante en el barrio?*
>   **Compañero(a):**   *Sí, hay un restaurante en la calle San Martín.*

Capítulo 7 ¿Adónde vamos?   **165**

PRACTICE/APPLY

A. ¿Qué lugares son?
SUGGESTION

   TRANSPARENCY 35

Use the transparency and ask simple questions using cognates: **¿Dónde practicamos la natación? ¿Dónde podemos mirar obras de Shakespear o de Tenessee Williams?**, etc.

   Activating Prior Knowledge

ANSWERS
1. Es un estadio.
2. Es un teatro
3. Es un parque
4. Es una piscina
5. Es un cine
6. Es un museo

B. ¿Hay un(a)... en el barrio?
ANSWERS

Following the model, students substitute the cues given and add the articles to these words:

1. un parque
2. una discoteca
3. un teatro
4. un museo
5. un cine
6. una piscina
7. una oficina de correos

C. ¿Qué hay en Nerja?

SUGGESTION

 TRANSPARENCY 36

Have students look at the transparency when doing this activity.

Individual Needs

Less-prepared Students

After less-prepared students have made their lists, have them relate the information orally to each other as a double check. Write a model on the board for them to follow: **En Nerja hay un/una _____ pero no hay un/una_____.**

More-prepared Students

Have more-prepared students explain in Spanish why their additional buildings are most needed and why others aren't. (You may need to supply additional vocabulary.) Suggest that they try to also use expressions of frecuency in their work. For example, **Nerja necesita un hospital porque a menudo hay accidentes. Nerja no necesita una librería porque las personas van a la biblioteca frecuentemente.**

 Analyzing

---

1. parque / en la calle Libertad
2. discoteca / en la calle Tucumán
3. teatro / en la avenida 9 de Julio
4. museo / en la calle Cervantes
5. cine / en la avenida Lavalle
6. piscina / en la calle Bolívar
7. oficina de correos / en la calle Independencia

C. ¿Qué hay en Nerja? Following are examples of public buildings that are found in many cities and towns. Using the map of Nerja and its legend, make two lists, indicating what there is and what there is not in this small beach town. Use the headings **Hay...** and **No hay...** Then, with a partner, decide on the three additional public buildings that you think the town most needs to add.

estación de trenes · museo · parque · restaurante · hospital · oficina de correos · cine · estadio

hotel · discoteca · aeropuerto · café · biblioteca · iglesia · plaza

166 *Tercera unidad* ¿Dónde y a qué hora?

Focus on Culture

About Nerja

Nerja is a beach town on the Costa del Sol, 45 km east of Málaga. It is visited by many tourists in the summer months and boasts the **Balcón de Europa**, a palm-fringed promenade built on the top of a cliff that juts out onto the Mediterranean Sea.

 Interpersonal Communication 1.1

PRONUNCIACIÓN THE CONSONANT **g**

When the letter **g** (in the same combinations you studied in the previous **etapa**) follows a vowel or any consonant except **n,** it is pronounced like the *g* in the English word *sugar* when it is said very quickly.

Práctica

D. Listen and repeat as your teacher models the following words.

1. lago
2. amigo
3. llego
4. nos gusta
5. conmigo

6. Ortega
7. regular
8. lugar
9. hasta luego
10. jugar

Repaso ☯

E. ¿Adónde van? Félix and his family are visiting Medellín, Colombia, for the day. Because they all want to go to different places, they decide to split up. Based on the drawings, give Félix's explanation of where each person is headed. Follow the model.

MODELO   mi tío
Mi tío va a la catedral.

1. mis padres

2. mi prima y yo

3. mi tía

Capítulo 7 ¿Adónde vamos? **167**

SEGUNDA ETAPA

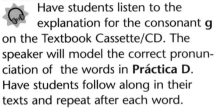

TEACH/MODEL

Pronunciación
PRESENTATION

TEXTBOOK CASSETTE/CD CASSETTE 1, SIDE B; CD 1, TRACK 4

TAPESCRIPT PP. 197-198

Have students listen to the explanation for the consonant **g** on the Textbook Cassette/CD. The speaker will model the correct pronunciation of the words in **Práctica D.** Have students follow along in their texts and repeat after each word.

▲▲ Auditory-Musical

PRACTICE/APPLY

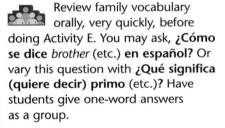

E. ¿Adónde van?
SUGGESTION

Review family vocabulary orally, very quickly, before doing Activity E. You may ask, **¿Cómo se dice** *brother* (etc.) **en español?** Or vary this question with **¿Qué significa (quiere decir) primo** (etc.)**?** Have students give one-word answers as a group.

ANSWERS
1. Mis padres van al parque.
2. Mi prima y yo vamos a la estación de trenes.
3. Mi tía va a la oficina de correos.
4. Mi hermana va a la iglesia.
5. Mi hermano va al centro.
6. Mis primas van a la piscina.

Focus on Culture

About Córdoba

Córdoba's history is marked by two different Golden Ages: the Romans made it the largest city on the Iberian peninsula; then, in the Middle Ages, it became one of the cultural centers of Europe under Muslim rule, well-known for its science and art. After the Reconquest, it was the custom for the Catholic Spaniards to destroy mosques and build churches on the ruins. Fortunately, in Córdoba they spared one of the world's largest and most beautiful mosques (begun in the year 785) and built a cathedral inside it called the **Mezquita-Catedral** (Mosque-cathedral).

⊛ Connections with Other Disciplines 3.1

4. mi hermana 5. mi hermano 6. mis primas

TEACH/MODEL

F. ¿Adónde quisiera ir... ?

SUGGESTION

Before doing Activity F, review the idea of conjugated verb + infinitive, using **quisiera** as your example on the board.

VARIATION

As alternatives to **quisiera**, you may wish to also include verbs such as **desear, necesitar**, and **acabar de** in this activity after listing them on the board. This also will serve as an introduction to the verbs **querer** and **preferir**, presented in the **Estructura** on page 169.

PRACTICE/APPLY

ANSWERS

1. ¿Adónde quisiera ir Elsa? Elsa quisiera ir a la piscina.
2. ...Isabel? ...al parque.
3. ...Roberto? ...a la discoteca.
4. ...Mónica? ...a la disco
5. ...Manuel? ...al museo.
6. ...Pilar? ...al teatro.
7. ...Luis? ...al estadio.
8. ...Lidia? ...al café.

F. **¿Adónde quisiera ir...?** You are talking to a friend about where other friends want to go this weekend. Ask him (her) about each of the following people and he (she) will answer using the places suggested. Follow the model.

> **MODELO**   Miguel / el club
>
> **Tú:** *¿Adónde quisiera ir Miguel?*
> **Amigo(a):** *Miguel quisiera ir al club.*

1. Elsa / la piscina
2. Isabel / el parque
3. Roberto / la discoteca
4. Mónica / el cine
5. Manuel / el museo
6. Pilar / el teatro
7. Luis / el estadio
8. Lidia / el café

ESTRUCTURA

The verbs **querer** and **preferir**

querer (to want, to love)			
yo	**quiero**	nosotros(as)	**queremos**
tú	**quieres**	vosotros(as)	**queréis**
él		ellos	
ella	**quiere**	ellas	**quieren**
Ud.		Uds.	

preferir (ie) (to prefer)			
yo	**prefiero**	nosotros(as)	**preferimos**
tú	**prefieres**	vosotros(as)	**preferís**
él		ellos	
ella	**prefiere**	ellas	**prefieren**
Ud.		Uds.	

1. The verb **querer** is used to express desire. It is more commonly used than the verb **desear** *(to wish, to want)*.

2. In Spanish, some verbs are called stem-changing verbs because they have irregular stems (infinitives minus the -ar, -er, or -ir ending) that change when the verbs are conjugated. **Querer** and **preferir** are examples of verbs in which the final vowel in the stems changes from **e** to **ie** in all forms except **nosotros(as)** and **vosotros(as)**. The Spanish-English and English-Spanish glossaries at the end of your textbook, as well as many dictionaries, list stem-changing verbs with their vowel change in parentheses, as done here in the charts for **querer (ie)** and **preferir (ie).**

3. **Querer** and **preferir** may be followed by a noun or an infinitive. To make these constructions negative, place **no** before the conjugated forms of **querer** and **preferir**.

Tú quieres un taco.	*You want a taco.*
Rosa quiere comer algo también.	*Rosa wants to eat something too.*
Javier no quiere comer.	*Javier doesn't want to eat.*
Ellos prefieren el tren.	*They prefer the train.*
Yo no prefiero el tren.	*I don't prefer the train.*
Yo prefiero viajar en autobús.	*I prefer to travel by bus.*

Capítulo 7 ¿Adónde vamos? **169**

TEACH/MODEL

Estructura

PRESENTATION

To introduce the verbs **querer** and **preferir** inductively, start out by making simple statements in the **yo** form and follow them up by asking **tú** questions based on the information given in the statements. Summarize the responses in the third person: **Yo quiero ir al cine pero tengo que estudiar./¿Quieres tú ir al cine?/Ella (Él) quiere ir al cine.**

Continue by making statements in the **nosotros** form, asking **Uds.** questions based on the statements, and then summarize students' responses in the third person.

Proceed in the same manner to introduce **preferir.** Continue practicing by having students ask each other questions using the **pregúntale** format. Then proceed to the activities on the following page.

◣◣ Linguistic

☀ Spanish for Spanish Speakers

Family Connections

Ask Spanish speakers to write three things they want this year. If students are uncertain writers, let them use the present tense of **querer** for this activity. Advanced students can use whatever forms they think natural. As a variation, have students ask the same question to a family member.

 Intrapersonal

⊕ Communities In and Beyond School 5.1

PRACTICE / APPLY

G. Preferencias
EXPANSION
Have students add two or three new words/phrases for each column and practice using them in sentences.

✎ Creating

H. ¿Adónde quieres ir?
ANSWERS
1. ¿Quieres ir a la biblioteca? No, quiero ir a la piscina
2. ...al club? ...al teatro.
3. ...al museo? ...a la oficina de correos.
4. ...a la plaza? ...al parque.
5. ...a la estación de trenes? ...a la estación de autobuses.
6. ...a la escuela secundaria? ...al mercado.

I. ¿Qué quieres hacer?
POSSIBLE ANSWERS
1. ¿Quieres comer en un café? Sí quiero comer en un café./No, prefiero comer en casa.
2. ¿Quieres ir a la piscina? Sí, .../No, prefiero ir a la playa.
3. ¿Quieres bailar en un a disciteca? Sí, .../No, prefiero bailar sola.
4. ¿Quieres visitar un museo? Sí, .../No, prefiero ir al cine.
5. ¿Quieres estudiar toda la mañana? Sí, .../No, prefiero jugar al fútbol.
6. ¿Quieres correr por el parque? Sí, .../No, prefiero pasear.
7. ¿Quieres escuchar música? Sí, .../No, prefiero dormir.
8. ¿Quieres tomar algo? Sí, .../No, prefiero no tomar nada.

Aquí practicamos

G. Preferencias Create original sentences using words from each column to indicate what the following people want or prefer to do.

A	B	C
Mario	querer	ir a la discoteca
ellos	preferir	un coche
yo	ir al parque	
nosotros	leer este libro	
tú	viajar en tren	
Uds.		

H. ¿Adónde quieres ir? You and a friend are visiting a town in Mexico. Each of you wants to see something different. Find out what she (he) wants to see by asking specific questions. Follow the model.

MODELO   la plaza / la iglesia
        Tú: ¿Quieres ir a la plaza?
    Amiga(o):   No, quiero ir a la iglesia.

1. la biblioteca / la piscina
2. el club / el teatro
3. el museo / la oficina de correos
4. la plaza / el parque
5. la estación de trenes / la estación de autobuses
6. la escuela secundaria / el mercado

I. ¿Qué quieres hacer? You and your friend are making plans for the afternoon. Your friend makes a suggestion. Tell him (her) if you agree with the suggestion. If you don't agree, express your own preference. Follow the model.

MODELO   ir al teatro
    Amigo(a):   ¿Quieres ir al teatro?
        Tú: Sí, quiero ir al teatro. o: Mm... no, prefiero ir al cine.

1. comer en un café   5. estudiar toda la mañana
2. ir a la piscina   6. correr por el parque
3. bailar en la discoteca   7. escuchar música
4. visitar un museo   8. tomar algo

J. Decisiones

J. Decisiones You and a friend need to decide what you want to do after school. In pairs, decide what you want to do, alternating roles in asking and answering questions. Then give your answer to the class. Follow the model.

> **MODELO** ¿ir en bicicleta o caminar?
>
> **Tú:** ¿Quieres ir en bicicleta o caminar?
> **Amigo(a):** Yo prefiero caminar.
> **Tú:** Nosotros preferimos caminar.

1. ¿jugar *(to play)* al tenis o al vólibol?
2. ¿ir a mi casa o al café?
3. ¿visitar a nuestros amigos o estudiar?
4. ¿ir a la plaza o al parque?
5. ¿comer o tomar un refresco?

Aquí escuchamos

En el centro *Gloria and Marilú have a conversation on their way downtown to run some errands.*

Antes de escuchar Based on the information you have learned in this chapter, answer the following questions.

1. What are some of the places where Gloria and Marilú might go to on a trip downtown?
2. How do you say in Spanish that you have to do something?

 A escuchar Listen twice to the conversation between Gloria and Marilú, paying attention to the places where they plan to go.

Después de escuchar On your activity master, list as many of the places that Gloria and Marilú mention as you can.

Capítulo 7 ¿Adónde vamos? **171**

J. Decisiones

ANSWERS
Answers will follow the model.

Aquí escuchamos

 TEXTBOOK CASSETTE/CD CASSETTE 1, SIDE B; CD 2, TRACK 5

 TAPESCRIPT PP. 197-198

 TRB: ACTIVITY MASTER, P. 85

Antes de escuchar

ANSWERS
1. la plaza, el musea, el parque, la biblioteca, etc.
2. Tengo que...

Después de escuchar

ANSWERS
el nuevo restaurante mexicano, la librería, el hospital, el banco, el correo, el parque, el mercado

---

☀ Spanish for Spanish Speakers

Spoken Spanish

Ask Spanish speakers to listen to the Spanish used in the **Aquí escuchamos** recording and to compare it to the Spanish they use in their communities. Encourage students to focus, for example, on the consonant **s**: Does it sound similar to the **s** in English? Is it barely audible (as is often the case in Spanish spoken in the Caribbean)? Is it similar to the *th* sound in English? How does it contrast with their spoken Spanish? You might want to have the rest of the class participate in this activity.

🔍 Comparing and Contrasting
🎵 Auditory-Musical
⊛ Linguistic Comparisons 4.1

ETAPA SYNTHESIS

En la calle

SUGGESTIONS

 Give the same destination to three or four students and ask them to find as many people as possible to go with them. Before beginning the activity, model two conversations involving you and a student: in one, the two of you have the same destination; in the other, you have different destinations.

 Bodily-Kinesthetic

Individual Needs

More-prepared Students
First have more-prepared students do this activity as a dialogue for the less-prepared students.

Less-prepared Students
Have the less-prepared students do their own pair work orally, then have them write their partner's answers.

Una invitación

FYI

 ATAJO WRITING ASSISTANT SOFTWARE

You might want to have students use this software program when doing this activity.

Additional Practice and Recycling

FYI

📖 WORKBOOK, PP. 86-90

For recycling and additional practice of the vocabulary, structures, and language functions presented throughout this **etapa**, you can assign the workbook activities as in-class work and/or homework. Answers to the activities are overprinted on each page of the Teacher's Edition of the Workbook.

¡ADELANTE!

 En la calle While heading for a place of your choice in town, you bump into a friend.

1. Greet your friend.
2. Find out how he (she) is.
3. Ask where he (she) is going.
4. He (she) will ask you where you are going.
5. If you are going to the same place, suggest that you go there together. (**¡Vamos juntos/juntas!**)
6. If not, say good-bye and continue on your way.

 Una invitación Write a note to a Spanish-speaking friend.

1. Invite him (her) to go to the movies with you.
2. Say what movie you want to see.
3. Ask if he (she) prefers to see a different one.
4. Mention where you can meet downtown.
5. Ask if he (she) wants to eat dinner before the movie.
6. Close by asking him (her) to call you on the phone with an answer.

Additional Etapa Resources

Refer to the **Etapa** Support Materials list on the opening page of this **etapa** for detailed cross-references to these assessment options.

TERCERA ETAPA

Preparación

- What is the difference between a department store and a mall?

- How would you describe a specialty shop?

- Make a list of five different kinds of specialty shops that you can think of.

- On your list, mark the shops where you like to go. Be prepared to discuss whether you prefer them to a department store or a large discount center and why.

Las tiendas

*En nuestra ciudad hay muchas **tiendas** (stores).*

una carnicería *a butcher shop*
una farmacia *a drugstore*
una florería *a flower shop*

una librería *a book store*
una panadería *a bakery*

Capítulo 7 ¿Adónde vamos? **173**

TEACH/MODEL

Las tiendas

PRESENTATION
The suggestions in the previous two **etapas** can be used for presenting this vocabulary. You might also try to find one or two large photos of Spanish street scenes that illustrate the shops introduced here.

VOCABULARY EXPANSION
Introduce **salchichonería**, which is similar to a deli (they sell sausages, cold meats, and cheeses of all kinds). Have students guess what they think **pastelerías** and **zapaterías** are.

 Linguistic Comparisons 4.1

Etapa Support Materials

- Workbook: pp. 91-96
- TRB: Textbook Activity Masters: pp. 86-88
- Textbook Cassettes/CDs: Cassette 1, Side B; CD 2, Tracks 6-7
- Tapescript: Textbook Cassettes/CDs p. 198
- Overhead Transparency: 37
- Middle School Activities: pp. 62, 63
- Lesson Plan Book: pp. 41-42

- Testing Program: Quiz pp. 77, 78; Answer Key & Testing Cassettes Tapescript pp. T30, T31
- Testing Cassettes: Cassette Side A
- Computerized Testing Program: Windows™; Macintosh®
- Atajo Writing Assistant Software: Student Text p. 180

Unit 3, Chapter 7 **T173**

Comentarios culturales

VOCABULARY EXPANSION

Point out that the bread sold in the **panadería** is usually baked fresh at least twice daily. It is crusty on the outside and soft on the inside and is usually sold in several sizes. Fancy pastries are sold at **pastelerías**.

 Cultural Products and Perspectives 2.2

PRACTICE/APPLY

A. ¿Qué es?

SUGGESTION

 TRANSPARENCY 37

You may want to use the suggestions given for Activity A on page 165.

ANSWERS
1. Es un mercado.
2. Es una florería
3. Es un banco
4. Es una librería
5. Es una panadería
6. Es una carnicería

Comentarios CULTURALES

Las tiendas

In many parts of the Spanish-speaking world, small stores are more common than large supermarkets. Each one of these stores sells only one type of article or food. The name of the shop is taken from the products sold; for example, **pan** (bread) is sold at the **panadería; flores** (flowers) are sold at the **florería.**

¡Te toca a ti!

A. ¿Qué es? Identify each of the following buildings or places.

1.

2.

3.

4.

5.

6.

MULTIPLE INTELLIGENCES
- Linguistic: All activities
- Logical-Mathematical: B, C, E
- Visual-Spatial: A
- Auditory-Musical: **Pronunciación**, D, **Aquí escuchamos**
- Interpersonal: **Adelante** activities

The Standards
- Interpersonal Communication 1.1: B, C, F, H, I, J, **En la calle**
- Interpretive Communication 1.2: E, F, G, I, J, **Aquí escuchamos**
- Presentational Communication 1.3: **Una invitación**
- Cultural Practices and Perspectives 2.1: **Comentarios culturales**
- Linguistic Comparisons 4.1: **Pronunciación**

B. Cerca de aquí (Near here)
You ask a passerby whether certain stores and places are nearby. A classmate will play the role of the passerby. He (she) will answer affirmatively and indicate the street where you can find each building. Follow the model.

> **MODELO** banco / en la calle Alcalá
> **Tú:** *Perdón, señorita (señor). ¿Hay un banco cerca de aquí?*
> **Compañero(a):** *Sí, hay un banco en la calle Alcalá.*

1. farmacia / en la avenida Libertad
2. hotel / en la calle Perú
3. librería / en la calle Mayor
4. banco / en la calle San Marco
5. panadería / en la avenida Independencia
6. florería / en la avenida Colón

C. ¿Adónde vamos primero (first)?
Whenever you run errands with your friend, you like to know where you are headed first. However, each time you suggest a place, your friend has another idea. Follow the model.

> **MODELO** banco / librería
> **Tú:** *¿Adónde vamos primero? ¿Al banco?*
> **Amigo(a):** *No, primero vamos a la librería. Luego (Then) vamos al banco.*

1. carnicería / mercado
2. librería / florería
3. museo / banco
4. farmacia / panadería
5. hotel / oficina de correos
6. biblioteca / colegio

PRONUNCIACIÓN THE SOUND OF SPANISH j
The Spanish **jota** is similar to the sound of the *h* in the English word *hot*. This sound is spelled with **.g** when it is followed by the vowels **e** or **i**. The consonant *j* (**j**) ia always pronounced in this way.

Práctica

D. Listen and repeat as your teacher models the following words.

1. Juan
2. trabajo
3. julio
4. jueves
5. jugar
6. tarjeta
7. geografía
8. biología
9. general
10. Jorge

Capítulo 7 ¿Adónde vamos? **175**

Spanish for Spanish Speakers

Shopping Abroad
Ask Spanish speakers to question friends or relatives who have lived in Spanish-speaking countries: (1) Are there things they could buy there that they can't buy here? (2) How do shops differ in Spanish-speaking countries from those in America? (3) What items are specific to certain Spanish-speaking countries?

Cultural Products and Perspectives 2.2
Cultural Comparisons 4.2

B. Cerca de aquí
ANSWERS
Following the model, students substitute the cues provided and add definite articles to these words:
1. ...una farmacia
2. ...un hotel
3. ...una librería
4. ...un banco
5. ...una panadería
6. ...una florería

C. ¿Adónde vamos primero?
SUGGESTION
 Write the model sentences on the board, then have students close their books. Prepare ahead small pieces of paper or cards with photocopied icons of the different places. Hand one out to each student, and do a chain **pregúntale** activity with the whole class.

Interpersonal Communication 1.1

ANSWERS
Following the model, students supply the preposition **a** with the correct definite article along with the other cues provided.
1. ...a la carnicería/...al mercado
2. ...a la librería/...a la florería
3. ...al museo/...al banco
4. ...a la farmacia/...a la panadería
5. ...al hotel/...a la oficina de correos
6. ...a la biblioteca/...al colegio

Pronunciación
PRESENTATION
 TEXTBOOK CASSETTE/CD CASSETTE 1, SIDE B; CD 2, TRACK 6

 TAPESCRIPT P. 198

Have students listen to the explanation for the consonant **j** on the Textbook Cassette/CD. The speaker will model the correct pronunciation of the words in **Práctica D**. Have students follow along in their texts and repeat after each word.

Auditory-Musical

E. Los padres de tus amigos

ANSWERS
Following the model, students supply the preposition with the correct definite article.
1. ...en la estación de trenes/...al cine
2. ...en la universidad/...al parque
3. ...en la oficina de correos/...al museo
4. ...en el restaurante/...al mercado
5. ...en la biblioteca/...a la librería

TEACH/MODEL

Palabras útiles

PRESENTATION
Have students count from 1 to 20. Continue by saying slowly, **veintiuno, veintidós, veintitrés,** and point to a student to continue, **veinticuatro,** so on up to 29. Then say slowly **treinta, treinta y uno, treinta y dos, treinta y tres,** and point to a student to continue. Proceed in this manner up to 100. Then count to 100 by fives and then by tens, having the class repeat.

Write **veintiún, veintiuna** and **treinta y un, treinta y una** on the board. Explain how they are used before masculine and feminine nouns. Mention that the other numbers are invariable and do not agree with nouns. You may also want to point out the accents written on the last stressed vowel in the numbers **veintidós, veintitrés,** and **veintiséis.**

Logical-Mathematical

Repaso

E. Los padres de tus amigos Your parents are curious about your friends. Tell them where your friends' parents work and where they often go when they're not working. Follow the model.

MODELO   el padre de Cristina (hospital / biblioteca)
El padre de Cristina trabaja en el hospital. Va a la biblioteca a menudo.

1. el padre de Roberto (estación de trenes / cine)
2. la madre de Isabel (universidad / parque)
3. el padre de Vicente (oficina de correos / museo)
4. la madre de Marilú (restaurante / mercado)
5. el padre de Josefina (biblioteca / librería)

Comentarios CULTURALES

Las direcciones y los teléfonos

Usually when an address (**una dirección**) is given in Spanish, the name of the street is followed by the number. Also, when the numbers of addresses go over a hundred, they are usually grouped in sets of two. Thus, the number in **Avenida Bolívar, número 1827** would be said as **dieciocho, veintisiete.** Phone numbers (**los números de teléfono**) are also usually grouped in sets of two. For example, the number 925–6534 would be read as **nueve, veinticinco, sesenta y cinco, treinta y cuatro.**

PALABRAS ÚTILES

Numbers from 20 to 100

20 veinte	24 veinticuatro	28 veintiocho	32 treinta y dos	70 setenta
21 veintiuno	25 veinticinco	29 veintinueve	40 cuarenta	80 ochenta
22 veintidós	26 veintiséis	30 treinta	50 cincuenta	90 noventa
23 veintitrés	27 veintisiete	31 treinta y uno	60 sesenta	100 cien

176   *Tercera unidad* ¿Dónde y a qué hora?

Aquí practicamos

F. Cuenta tú

1. Cuenta *(Count)* del 0 al 30, y luego del 30 al 0.
2. Cuenta del 20 al 100 de cinco en cinco.
3. Cuenta los números pares *(even)* del 0 al 100.
4. Cuenta los números impares *(odd)* del 1 al 99.
5. Cuenta de diez en diez del 0 al 100.

G. ¿Cuántos hay en la ciudad?
While working for the tourist bureau during the summer, you have to research the number of hotels, movie theaters, etc., that the city has. Interview the city's leading statistician in order to collect this information. Work in pairs and take turns playing the role of the statistician. Remember to use **¿Cuántos?** or **¿Cuántas?** according to the noun that follows. Follow the models.

MODELOS	hoteles / 15
Tú:	*¿Cuántos hoteles hay?*
Compañero(a):	*Hay quince hoteles.*
	piscinas / 17
Compañero(a):	*¿Cuántas piscinas hay?*
Tú:	*Hay diecisiete.*

1. librerías / 11
2. panaderías / 18
3. clubes / 13
4. mercados / 26
5. farmacias / 16
6. carnicerías / 27
7. teatros / 14
8. cines / 12
9. florerías / 20
10. cafés / 22

H. ¡Diga!
You want to make several telephone calls from a small town where you need to talk to the operator to get connected. Tell him (her) the number that you want. Follow the model.

MODELO	730–89–70
	Siete, treinta, ochenta y nueve, setenta, por favor.

1. 825–5978
2. 654–6783
3. 222–5160
4. 382–6791
5. 943–5690
6. 537–4087
7. 795–4670
8. 497–5530

Capítulo 7 ¿Adónde vamos? **177**

? ¿Qué crees?
You are traveling in Uruguay and the schedule says that your bus leaves at 22:00 hrs. When will it go?

a) It's a misprint; you don't know when the bus leaves.
b) at 2 o'clock
c) at 10:00 p.m.

respuesta ☞

PRACTICE/APPLY

G. ¿Cuántos... hay en la ciudad?
ANSWERS

1. ¿Cuántas librerías hay?/Hay once librerías.
2. ...panaderías.../...dieciocho panaderías.
3. ¿Cuántos clubes hay?/...trece clubes.
4. ...mercados.../...veintiséis mercados.
5. ¿Cuántas farmacias hay? / ...dieciséis farmacias.
6. ...carnicerías.../...veintisiete carnicerías.
7. ¿Cuántos teatros hay?/...catorce teatros.
8. ...cines.../...doce cines.
9. ...¿Cuántas florerías hay?/...veinte florerías.
10. ¿Cuántos cafés hay?/...veintidos cafés

H. ¡Diga!
ANSWERS

1. Ocho, veinticinco, cincuenta y nueve, setenta y ocho, por favor.
2. Seis, cincuenta y cuatro, sesenta y siete, ochenta y tres...
3. Dos, veintidos, cincuenta y uno, sesenta...
4. Tres, ochenta y dos, sesenta y siete, noventa y uno...
5. Nueve, cuarenta y tres, cincuenta y seis, noventa...
6. Cinco, treinta y siete, cuarenta, ochenta y siete...
7. Siete, noventa y cinco, cuarenta y seis, setenta...
8. Cuatro, noventa y siete, cincuenta y cinco, treinta...

EXPANSION

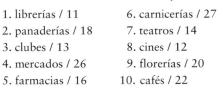
Have students practice their own phone numbers by asking several of their classmates, **¿Cuál es tu número de teléfono?** For seven-digit numbers, have them say a single number first and then the rest of the numbers in pairs. For example: 7-61-09-38 (**siete, sesenta y uno, cero nueve, treinta y ocho**).

Interpretive Communication 1.2

Palabras útiles

PRESENTATION

Bring in some photos of people of various ages (including children and elderly people) and indicate the age of each, by saying, **Este niño tiene ocho años.** etc. Then ask some students how old they are.

▲▲ Visual-Spatial

To introduce the expressions **tener hambre** and **tener sed**, use gestures to indicate hunger and thirst while making statements. Then ask students follow-up questions. For example: **Quiero comer ahora porque tengo hambre. ¿Tienes hambre tú? También quiero tomar un refresco porque tengo sed. ¿Quieres tomar algo? ¿Tienes sed?**, etc.

▲▲ Bodily-Kinesthetic

PRACTICE/APPLY

I. ¿Cuántos años tienes?

ANSWERS

1. Carmelita tiene diecisiete años.
2. ...sesenta y cuatro...
3. ...veinte...
4. ...doce...
5. ...ochenta y dos...
6. ...cincuenta y cinco...

Individual Needs

Less-prepared Students
Review family vocabulary. Have students write-out a list of questions such as: **¿Cuántos años tienes tú? ¿Cuántos años tiene tu mamá/papá/hermano/hermana/primo?**, etc. Remind students to chart or take notes of other students' answers so that they can report back to the class.

J. ¿Tienen hambre?

SUGGESTION

Call out on students to report back all of the information they found out: **Joe quiere comer un taco, pero Mary y John tienen sed y quieren tomar agua**, etc.

PALABRAS ÚTILES

Expressions with tener

1. To ask someone's age in Spanish, use **tener.**

—¿Cuántos años tienes?   *How old are you?*
—Tengo catorce años   *I am fourteen years old.*

—¿Cuántos años tiene tu hermana?   *How old is your sister?*
—Tiene cuatro.   *She's four.*

2. Other expressions with **tener** are **tener hambre** *(to be hungry)* and **tener sed** *(to be thirsty).*

—Tengo hambre. ¿Y tú?   *I'm hungry. And you?*
—No, yo no tengo hambre, pero sí tengo mucha sed.   *No, I'm not hungry, but I am very thirsty.*

☞ C

Aquí practicamos

I. **¿Cuántos años tienes?** You want to find out how old the people you know are. Working with a classmate, take turns asking and telling how old the following people are. Use the verb **tener** and the word **años.** Follow the model.

> **MODELO**
> Tú: ¿Cuántos años tiene Felipe? (13)
> Compañero(a): *Felipe tiene trece años.*

1. ¿Cuántos años tiene Carmelita? (17)
2. Y el señor Ramos, ¿cuántos años tiene? (64)
3. ¿Cuántos años tiene Ana María? (20)
4. ¿Cuántos años tiene Roberto? (12)
5. ¿Cuántos años tiene don Alberto? (82)
6. Y doña Ester, ¿cuántos años tiene ella? (55)

J. **¿Tienen hambre?** You are hosting a picnic and you want to know if your guests are hungry or thirsty and what they would like to have. Ask five classmates what they want. Follow the model.

> **MODELO**
> Tú: *¿Tienes hambre? ¿Tienes sed?*
> Compañero(a) 1: *Sí, tengo mucha hambre. No tengo sed.*
> Tú: *¿Qué quieres comer?*
> Compañero(a) 1: *Un taco, por favor.*

Aquí escuchamos

Números *Several people give their names, addresses, and telephone numbers.*

Antes de escuchar Review the numbers 1–100 in Spanish before listening to the information that follows.

 A escuchar Each person on the recording will give a phone number, name, and address. Listen to each person repeat himself (herself), paying particular attention to the telephone numbers and the cities mentioned. On your activity master, write down as many of the phone numbers as you can.

Después de escuchar On your activity master, put a check mark next to the cities that were mentioned in the information you just heard. Next to the cities that you mark, write down the nationality of a person from that city.

__Bogotá, Colombia

__Buenos Aires, Argentina

__Caracas, Venezuela

__Ciudad de México, México

__Lima, Perú

__Madrid, España

__San Juan, Puerto Rico

__Santiago, Chile

23-0662	VARGAS CANTO NESTOR MANUEL		CALLE 30 N° 334
	CALLE 100 N° 120 CP 97240	21-5451	VARGAS MENDEZ JC
26-5072	VARGAS CASTILLO MANUEL AUGUSTO		CALLE 65 N° 570
	CALLE 55 N° 417 CP 97160	24-4442	VARGAS MIRIAM SC
26-5852	VARGAS CASTRO GRACIA IRMA		CALLE 8 N° 128-
	CALLE 75 N° 561-D ZP 97	21-2513	VARGAS MONZON E
24-6827	VARGAS CECILIA CAMPOS DE		
	CALLE 51 N° 287 CP 97119	26-1624	VARGAS NIDIA AVI
23-5894	VARGAS CELIA AGUILAR DE		CALLE 57 A N°
	CALLE 23 N° 222	21-0965	VARGAS NIDIA CRI
24-8169	VARGAS CERVERA ALBERTO		VARGAS OLGA EST
	CALLE 26 N° 299-A CP 97148	26-3349	CALLE 29-A N°
24-9655	VARGAS CERVERA AMADO-CALLE 30 N° 501 M	21-8303	VARGAS PACHECO
24-1519	CALLE 54 N° 521 B 1	21-6829	VARGAS PATRON
	CALLE 65 N° 429 ZP 97	24-2920	VARGAS PERAZA
23-4418	VARGAS CERVERA JORGE-CALLE 49 N° 558-C	23-6529	CALLE 11 PTE
	CALLE 9 N° 226	25-1682	VARGAS PERAZA
25-6829	VARGAS CETINA ELSA-CALLE 7 A N° 281	27-0748	CALLE 95 N° 5
	VARGAS CETINA RAUL M PROF		VARGAS PERERA
24-6358	CALLE 63 B N° 224	21-5753	CALLE 88 N°
	VARGAS CHACON ADELA-CALLE 48 N° 517	23-8658	VARGAS PINZON
25-6206	VARGAS CLARA ELENA DIAZ DE		VARGAS QUIJAN
21-2058	CALLE 25 N° 496 B	27-1435	CALLE 61 N°
	VARGAS CORREA ANDRES DR		VARGAS QUINTA
27-3503	CALLE 109 N° 349 CP 97270	24-1253	CALLE 83 N°
	VARGAS CORREA JORGE BERNARDO DR		VARGAS QUINTA
24-0449	CALLE 25 N° 212 CP 97140	26-0366	CALLE 46 N°
	VARGAS CRUZ RAYMUNDO		VARGAS RAMIRE
27-7773	CALLE 39 N° 325 CP 97119	24-3449	CALLE 18 N° 1
	VARGAS DE LA PEÑA FERNANDO DR		CALLE 64 N° 5
23-9413	CALLE 36 N° 428	27-8225	VARGAS RAMIRE
	COLON 203-A	25-5899	CALLE 15 N° 1
21-4050	VARGAS DIAZ RAYMUNDO		VARGAS RAMOS
	CALLE 21 N° 12 CP 97070	25-8927	VARGAS RIVERO
24-2776	VARGAS DOMITILA DIAZ DE		VARGAS ROSA EL
	CALLE 40 N° 440 A	27-6069	CALLE 44 N° 5
	...AS DURAN HUMBERTO		VARGAS ROSA PA
	...203 ZP 97	...-1277	

Capítulo 7 ¿Adónde vamos? **179**

Después de escuchar

ANSWERS

Cuidad de México; mexicano
Lima, Perú; peruana
Madrid, España; español
Buenos Aires, Argentina; argentina
Santiago, Chile; chileno

 Spanish for Spanish Speakers

Summarizing

Have Spanish speakers listen to the **Aquí escuchamos** recording and summarize the dialogue. Encourage students to write down any difficult vocabulary or structures, and work with a partner to better understand how these are used in this recording. Review summaries with Spanish speakers to determine problematic structures and vocabulary.

Creating
Synthesizing

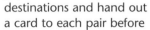

ETAPA SYNTHESIS

En la oficina de correos

VARIATION

Prepare cards or small pieces of paper with different destinations and hand out a card to each pair before they begin work. Try pairing up a less-prepared student with a more-prepared one so that the stronger student can help the weaker one. Remind all students that conversations go two ways, so if someone asks you about your brothers or sisters, you might want to ask them about theirs or else ask another family-related question.

Más números

FYI

 ATAJO WRITING ASSISTANT SOFTWARE

You might want to have students use this software program when doing this activity.

SUGGESION

 TRB: ACTIVITY MASTER, P. 87

Have students do the project outside of class with another classmate. Then ask students to take the information they have recorded about their classmate and exchange it with another student in class. Each student will then read all the *vital statistics*, minus the student's name, and see if the class can guess who the student is.

 Activating prior knowledge

 Interpretive communications 1.2

Additional Practice and Recycling

FYI

 WORKBOOK, PP. 91-96

For recycling and additional practice of the vocabulary, structures, and language functions presented throughout this **etapa**, you can assign the workbook activities as in-class work and/or home-work. Answers to the activities are over-printed on each page of the Teacher's Edition of the Workbook.

¡ADELANTE!

 En la oficina de correos While standing in line at the post office, you strike up a conversation with the person standing next to you.

1. Greet him or her.
2. Find out how many brothers and sisters he (she) has.
3. Ask what their ages are.
4. When you leave, find out where your new friend is going.
5. Tell him (her) where you are going.
6. Ask if you can walk together (**¡Vamos juntos/juntas!**).
7. If not, say good-bye.

 Más números You want to find out the "vital statistics" of some of your classmates. On the chart in your activity master, record the appropriate information (name, age, address, and phone number) for yourself and three of your classmates. Write out the numbers in Spanish and be prepared to tell them to your classmates when asked. Follow the model.

MODELO

Nombre de mi amigo(a)	Su edad	Su dirección	Su teléfono
Carlos	16 (dieciséis) años	Calle Central 2586 (veinticinco, ochenta y seis)	845-3370 (ocho, cuarenta y cinco, treinta y tres, setenta)

 **EN LÍNEA**

Connect with the Spanish-speaking world! Access the *¡Ya verás! Gold* home page for Internet activities related to this chapter.

http://yaveras.heinle.com

180 *Tercera unidad* ¿Dónde y a qué hora?

Additional Etapa Resources

Refer to the **Etapa** Support Materials list on the opening page of this **etapa** for detailed cross-references to these assessment options.

VOCABULARIO

Para charlar	Temas y contextos		Vocabulario general

Para contestar el teléfono

¡Bueno!
¡Diga! / ¡Dígame!
¡Hola!

Para preguntar la edad

¿Cuántos años tienes?

Para contar

veinte
veintiuno
veintidós
veintitrés
veinticuatro
veinticinco
veintiséis
veintisiete
veintiocho
veintinueve
treinta
treinta y uno
treinta y dos
cuarenta
cincuenta
sesenta
setenta
ochenta
noventa
cien

Los edificios y los lugares públicos

un aeropuerto
un banco
una biblioteca
una catedral
un cine
un club
un colegio
una discoteca
una escuela
  secundaria
una estación de
  autobuses
una estación de
  policía
una estación de
  trenes
un estadio
un hospital
un hotel
una iglesia
un museo
una oficina de
  correos
un parque
una piscina
una plaza
un teatro
una universidad

Las tiendas

una carnicería
una farmacia
una florería
una librería
un mercado
una panadería

Verbos

ir
querer (ie)
preferir (ie)

Expressions of frequency

a menudo
de vez en cuando
rara vez
nunca

Otras palabras y expresiones

¿Adónde vamos?
al
cerca de aquí
una dirección
en otra oportunidad
esta noche
llamar a
Lo siento.
primero
¿Quieres venir?
la tarde
tener hambre
tener sed

Capítulo 7 ¿Adónde vamos? **181**

CHAPTER WRAP-UP

Vocabulario

SUGGESTION

Have students bring in maps of distant towns. Have a questioner ask what is in the town and where it is—without peeking at the mapholder's map. Then—with the mapholder's help—the questioner should try to sketch the mapholder's map on a separate piece of paper.

 Visual-Spatial.

Improvised Conversation

SUGGESTION

 TEXTBOOK CASSETTE/CD CASSETTE 1, SIDE B; CD 2, TRACK 8

 TAPESCRIPT PP. 198-199

 TRB: ACTIVITY MASTER, P. 88

Have students listen to this conversation in which a male student calls a female student to ask her for a date. The segment draws upon vocabulary and structures from all three **etapas**.

Listening Skills Development

FYI

LAB MANUAL PP. 43-51

LAB CASSETTE SIDE A; CD 4, TRACKS 1-10

 TAPESCRIPT: LAB PROGRAM PP. 65-77

It is now appropriate to work through the lab manual activities and their accompanying recordings in class or in the language laboratory.

Resources for Spanish-speaking Students

FYI

WORKBOOK FOR SPANISH-SPEAKING STUDENTS: PP. 41-46

 ANSWER KEY TO SSS WORKBOOK PP. 13-14

Activities specifically written to reinforce language and extend topics for Spanish speakers are available for each chapter in this workbook.

Additional Chapter Resources

Refer to the Chapter Support Materials list on the opening page of this chapter for detailed cross-references to *¡Ya verás! Gold*'s student-centered technology components and various assessment options.

Spanish for Spanish Speakers

Keeping a Vocabulary Notebook

Remind Spanish speakers to add words and expressions from the **Vocabulario** to the problematic spelling combination categories and personal new vocabulary lists in their notebooks. Encourage them to do this each time a chapter is completed.

PRACTICE/APPLY

La Pequeña Habana
Antes de leer
POSSIBLE ANSWERS
1. Miami, Orlando, Tampa, New York City, San Antonio, Dallas, Houston, El Paso, Phoenix, Los Angeles, San Diego, Chicago, among others.
2. Answers will vary.
3. Miami

SUGGESTION
Try to find copies of *El Nuevo Herald*, Miami's leading Spanish language newspaper, and look for articles or advertisements about places and events in **La Pequeña Habana**. Or have students review the Spanish newspaper and try to find activities or events that might interest them.

▲ Visual-Spatial

ENCUENTROS CULTURALES
◆

La Pequeña Habana

Reading Strategies
• Activating background knowledge
• Scanning for specific information

Antes de leer

1. In which cities in the United States are there large numbers of Spanish-speaking people?

2. Have you visited some of these cities? If so, what do you remember about them?

3. Briefly scan the reading. What part of the United States is this reading about?

La Pequeña Habana es un barrio de la ciudad de Miami. Aquí se reúnen muchos de los cubanos que llegaron de Cuba porque no quisieron vivir bajo el sistema político impuesto en la isla por Fidel Castro en 1959. Hoy en día, este sector de la ciudad es un centro social importante, no sólo para los cubanos sino también para numerosas personas de otros países de habla hispana. Para ellos, la Pequeña Habana es como un segundo hogar.

En la Pequeña Habana, la gente se reúne en los cafetines del barrio para charlar y jugar al dominó.

Para los norteamericanos y los turistas extranjeros que la visitan, el área es uno de los sectores más atractivos del sur de la Florida. Los vistantes disfrutan enormemente de la cultura cubana: de su comida, sus fiestas y su artesanía. En todas partes de la Pequeña Habana—en los cafetines, en las calles, en el sonido de los dominós, la música y las radios—el corazón cubano y la imagen de Cuba siguen vivos.

Focus on Culture

La Pequeña Habana

La Pequeña Habana not only attracts Cuban-Americans, but also Spanish-speakers of other Central and South American countries. The main street in **La Pequeña Habana** is called **Calle Ocho**. Other Florida cities with a large Spanish-speaking population include Orlando and Tampa-St. Petersburg. Both have thriving Cuban-American communities.

⊗ Connections with Distinctive Viewpoints 3.2

Guía para la lectura

Here are some words and expressions to keep in mind as you read.

se reúnen	*get together*
cafetines	*small coffee shops*
impuesto	*imposed*
hogar	*home*
disfrutan	*enjoy*
corazón	*heart*
siguen vivos	*live on*

Después de leer

1. Where is la Pequeña Habana located?

2. **La Habana** is the capital of Cuba. Why is this area of Miami called **La Pequeña Habana**?

3. Do you know of any other American cities, towns, or neighborhoods that maintain especially strong links with the culture of another country? In what ways do these communities express their ties to other cultures?

Capítulo 7 ¿Adónde vamos? **183**

Después de leer

POSSIBLE ANSWERS

1. Miami

2. It is an important social center for many Cubans who came over from Cuba, as well as other Spanish-speaking Americans.

3. Possible Answers: Mexican-Americans in Southwestern cities, Chinese and other Asian groups in Chinatown (San Francisco or New York), Irish Americans in Boston or New York, Italian Americans in Little Italy in New York or the North End of Boston, among others.

CAPÍTULO 8

CAPÍTULO 8

OBJECTIVES

Functions
- Asking for and giving directions
- Getting people to do something

Context
- Cities and towns

Accuracy
- The preposition **de**
- The contraction **del**
- Present tense of **estar**
- Commands with **Ud.** and **Uds.**
- Irregular command forms

Pronunciation
- The sound of **/s/**

CHAPTER WARM-UP

Setting the Context

In preparation for their learning about asking for and giving directions, have students discuss important cultural sites that might be found in a city or town. Focus, for example, on museums and ask the following: What museums have they visited and in what cities? What North American museums have they heard about? Ask why they think museums are important. Are they familiar with any famous museums in Spain or Latin America? Do they think they could describe these museums and explain to another student how to get there?

Connections with Other Disciplines 3.1
Cultural Comparisons 4.2

¿Dónde está...?

—¿Dónde está el museo de arte?
—Está al final de la Avenida Libertad.

Objectives

- asking for directions
- giving directions
- telling people to do something

Chapter Support Materials

- Lab Manual: pp. 52-57
- Lab Program: Cassette Side B; CD 4, Tracks 11-19
- TRB: Textbook Activity Masters: pp. 89-91
- Textbook Cassettes/CDs: Cassette 1, Side B; CD 2, Track 14
- Tapescript: Lab Program pp. 78-86; Textbook Cassettes/CDs p. 200
- Middle School Activities: pp. 64-66
- Workbook for Spanish-speaking Students: pp. 47-52
- Answer Key to SSS Workbook: pp. 15-16
- Practice Software: Windows™; Macintosh®

- Testing Program: Chapter Test pp. 88-90; Answer Key & Testing Cassettes Tapescript pp. T36, T37; Oral Assessment p. T37
- Testing Cassettes: Cassette Side A
- Computerized Testing Program: Windows™; Macintosh®
- Video Program: Cassette 1, 1:05:54-1:13:00
- Video Guide: Videoscript pp. 35-37; Activities: pp. 109-110

- **Mundos hispanos 1**
- Internet Activities: Student Text p. 199

PRIMERA ETAPA

Preparación

- How would you find your way around a city if you had never been there before?
- When you ask for directions, what do you usually want to find out?
- When someone asks you how to get to a particular place in town, what information do you give?

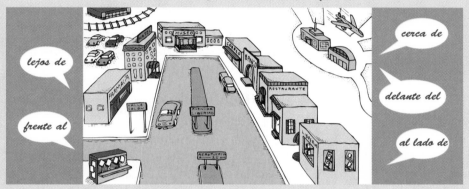

¿Está lejos de aquí?

lejos de — *frente al* — *cerca de* — *delante del* — *al lado de*

¿Dónde están (where are) *los edificios públicos de la ciudad?*

¿Dónde **está** el aeropuerto?	Está **lejos de** la ciudad.
¿Dónde está la estación de trenes?	Está **cerca del** hotel.
¿Dónde está la oficina de correos?	Está **frente al** hotel
¿Dónde está la farmacia?	Está **al lado del** hotel.
¿Dónde está el museo?	Está **al final de** la avenida Libertad.
¿Dónde está el **quiosco de periódicos?**	Está **en la esquina** de la calle Colón y la avenida Libertad.
¿Dónde está el coche de Mario?	Está en un **estacionamiento detrás del** hotel.
¿Dónde está el coche de Teresa?	Está en la avenida **delante del** banco.
¿Dónde está el banco?	Está **entre** el restaurante y la oficina de correos.

está is (located) **lejos de** *far from* **cerca de** *near* **frente a** *across from, facing* **al lado de** *next to* **al final de** *at the end of* **quiosco de periódicos** *newspaper kiosk* **en la esquina de** *at the corner of* **estacionamiento** *parking lot* **detrás de** *behind* **delante de** *in front of* **entre** *between*

Capítulo 8 ¿Dónde está…? **185**

TEACH/MODEL

¿Está lejos de aquí?

PRESENTATION

TRANSPARENCY 38

Introduce the new vocabulary and prepositions of place by using the transparency. Have students keep their books closed as they look at the transparency and listen to you say the expressions. After each pair or group of expressions, have students repeat.

🎵 Auditory-Musical

VARIATION

Read the expressions while students look at the picture in their books. Have them repeat after each pair or group of expressions.

🎵 Auditory-Musical

Etapa Support Materials

- Workbook: pp. 97-102
- TRB: Textbook Activity Masters: p. 89
- Textbook Cassettes/CDs: Cassette 1, Side B; CD 2, Track 9
- Tapescript: Textbook Cassettes/CDs p.199
- Overhead Transparency: 38
- Middle School Activities: pp. 67-69
- Lesson Plan Book: pp. 44-45
- Testing Program: Quiz pp. 82-85; Answer Key & Testing Cassettes Tapescript p. T34
- Testing Cassettes: Cassette Side A
- Computerized Testing Program: Windows™; Macintosh®
- Atajo Writing Assistant Software: Student Text p. 192

PRACTICE / APPLY

A. Mi ciudad

VARIATION

Situate your school in relationship to places around it. For example: **La escuela está en la esquina de la calle... y la avenida....** Ask students: **¿Qué hay delante de la escuela?**

▲▲ Visual-Spatial

B. No, te equivocas...

ANSWERS

1. No, te equivocas, está frente a la iglesia.
2. ...cerca del museo.
3. ...al lado de la librería.
4. ...en la esquina de la avenida Libertad y la calle Colón.
5. ...al final de la avenida Libertad.
6. ...delante del banco.
7. ...entre la librería y el restaurante.

¡Te toca a ti!

A. Mi ciudad When a tourist asks you about the town pictured on page 185, you answer using the suggested expressions. Follow the model.

> **MODELO** Turista: ¿Dónde está la estación de trenes? (cerca del hotel)
>
> Tú: *Está cerca del hotel.*

1. ¿Dónde está el hotel? (al lado de la farmacia)
2. ¿Dónde está el banco? (frente a la iglesia)
3. ¿Dónde está el aeropuerto? (lejos de la ciudad)
4. ¿Dónde está la oficina de correos? (cerca del restaurante)
5. ¿Dónde está la farmacia? (en la esquina de la calle Colón y la avenida Libertad)
6. ¿Dónde está la estación de trenes? (al lado del museo)
7. ¿Dónde está el restaurante? (entre la florería y el banco)

B. No, te equivocas (you're wrong)... A young man (woman) asks you for information about the town pictured on page 185. He (she) is not quite right about the locations. You politely tell the person he (she) is wrong and point out the correct information. Follow the model.

> **MODELO** Muchacho(a): El aeropuerto está cerca de la ciudad, ¿no? (lejos de)
>
> Tú: *No, te equivocas; está lejos de la ciudad.*

1. El restaurante está al lado de la iglesia, ¿verdad? (frente a)
2. La estación de trenes está lejos del museo, ¿no? (cerca de)
3. La florería está frente a la librería, ¿verdad? (al lado de)
4. El quiosco de periódicos está al final de la avenida Libertad, ¿verdad? (en la esquina de la avenida Libertad y la calle Colón)
5. El museo está al lado del banco, ¿no? (al final de la avenida Libertad)
6. El coche de Teresa está detrás de la iglesia, ¿verdad? (delante del banco)
7. La florería está frente a la librería y el restaurante, ¿no? (entre)

186 *Tercera unidad* ¿Dónde y a qué hora?

Focus on Culture

Museums

Madrid alone has more than 30 museums, including the new Museo Nacional Centro de Arte Reina Sofía, which houses the most famous of Picasso's paintings, the Guernica. Ask students to find out the history of the Guernica; have students research the painting at the library or on the Internet and bring in pictures.

◉ Connections with other Disciplines 3.1

MULTIPLE INTELLIGENCES

- Linguistic: All activities
- Logical-Mathematical: A, B, F, G
- Visual-Spatial: C, H, **Para ir a mi escuela**
- Auditory-Musical: **Pronunciación**, D, **Aquí escuchamos**
- Interpersonal: E, **Intercambio**

C. En la cola (In line)
While waiting to get into the movies, you point out some of your friends to your brother. Tell him where each person is located in the line. Use the drawing that follows to give your answers. Follow the model.

MODELO Estela / detrás
¿Estela? Ella está detrás de Alejandro.

1. Amanda / delante
2. Pablo / detrás
3. Marcos / entre
4. Antonio / detrás
5. Alejandro / delante
6. Estela / entre

Antonio   Amanda   Marcos   Pablo   Estela   Alejandro

PRONUNCIACIÓN THE SOUND OF /s/

The sound of Spanish /s/ is spelled with the consonants s or z. Usually, these are pronounced in the same way as s in the English word *say*. Note that z is never pronounced as the z in the English words *zoo*, *zebra*, and *zero*.

Práctica

D. Listen and repeat as your teacher models the following words.

1. siempre
2. salsa
3. sábado
4. zapato
5. plaza
6. señor
7. semana
8. López
9. arroz
10. lápiz

Capítulo 8 ¿Dónde está…? **187**

PRACTICE/APPLY

E. ¿Vas a... a menudo?

SUGGESTION

Before doing Activity E, quickly review expressions of frequency by asking "¿cómo se dice?" or "¿qué significa?" questions. Alternatively, you could ask **¿Cuál es una palabra/expresión similar a frecuentemente? (a menudo);** or work with opposites, **¿Cuál es lo contrario de nunca? (siempre).**

🔺 Linguistic

ANSWERS

Students will follow the model using **nunca** or **todos los días**, depending on their own experiences.

F. ¿Qué cuarto tienes?

SUGGESTION

Before doing Activity F, quickly review numbers from 1 to 100 orally. Divide the class into groups. Have one group count by 10s to 100, the other by 5s, then by 3s, then by 4s.

🔺 Logical-Mathematical

ANSWERS

1. ¿Qué cuarto tiene Claudia? Claudia tiene el cuarto número sesenta y ocho.
2. Bill tiene... veinte.
3. Betty y Rosa tienen... quince.
4. Paul tiene... treinta y seis.
5. Martha y Ann tienen... setenta y dos.
6. Antonio tiene... ochenta y nueve.
7. Sue y Clara tienen... cuarenta y siete.
8. John y Tom tienen... once.

Repaso ♻

E. ¿Vas a... a menudo? Find out how often your partner goes to the places listed. Take turns interviewing each other. Keep track of his (her) answers and make a list of places ranging from most to least frequently visited. When you have completed your lists, compare them to see which places you go to with the same frequency. Follow the model.

MODELO la panadería

Tú: *¿Vas a la panadería a menudo?*

Compañera(o): *No, nunca voy a la panadería.* o: *Voy a la panadería todos los días.*

1. la farmacia
2. el banco
3. la librería
4. la panadería
5. la florería
6. la piscina
7. la oficina de correos
8. la carnicería

F. ¿Qué cuarto tienes? Your class has just arrived at a hotel in Panama City where you are going to spend a week. You want to find out your friends' room numbers. Ask a partner where each person is staying. Follow the model.

MODELO Anita / 23

Tú: *¿Qué cuarto tiene Anita?*

Compañero(a): *Anita tiene el cuarto número veintitrés.*

1. Claudia / 68
2. Bill / 20
3. Betty y Rosa / 15
4. Paul / 36
5. Martha y Ann / 72
6. Antonio / 89
7. Sue y Clara / 47
8. John y Tom / 11

188 *Tercera unidad* ¿Dónde y a qué hora?

Focus on Culture

Zócalo

The center of Mexico City today, called the Zócalo, was also the center of the ancient Aztec city the Gran Tenochtitlán. The Spaniards destroyed the Aztecs' palaces and pyramids and over the ruins built the National Cathedral, a palace for the **conquistador** Hernán Cortés, and many other splendid buildings of Spanish sixteenth century architecture. Today Cortés' palace is called the Palacio Nacional. It is the official seat of the presidency and houses paintings by the great Mexican muralist Diego Rivera. In the early 1980s, archeologists began to explore the area under the palace and cathedral and discovered rich Aztec treasures and ceremonial buildings.

🌐 Connections with Other Disciplines 3.1

NOTA GRAMATICAL

The preposition de and the definite article el

Es el portafolio **del** profesor. *It's the teacher's briefcase.*

El coche de Teresa está al lado **del** hotel. *Teresa's car is next to the hotel.*

1. When the preposition **de** is followed by the definite article **el**, they contract to form one word, **del.**

2. Many of the phrases used to indicate location that have been presented in this **etapa** include **de.** When they are followed by the definite article **el,** the same rule for contraction applies.

al final **del** estacionamiento	cerca **del** aeropuerto	detrás **del** museo
al lado **del** banco	delante **del** quiosco	lejos **del** estadio

Aquí practicamos

G. ¿Dónde está? Replace the words in italics with the words in parentheses and make the necessary changes.

1. El banco está *cerca de* la estación. (al lado de / detrás de / lejos de)
2. Nosotros vivimos *al lado del* restaurante. (detrás de / delante de / frente a)
3. ¿Hay una farmacia frente a *la iglesia?* (museo / estadio / cine / casa)
4. Hay un café lejos de *la panadería.* (carnicería / hotel / oficina de correos / florería)
5. —¿De quién es el coche nuevo?
   —Es *de la señorita Galdós.* (profesor / Sr. Álvarez / Sra. Ruiz / muchacho)

H. Direcciones Using the drawing on page 185, answer these questions that different people ask about the city. Be as precise as possible. Follow the model.

> **MODELO**
> Señora: Perdón. ¿Dónde está el quiosco de periódicos, por favor?
> Tú: *¿El quiosco? Está en la esquina de la calle Colón y la avenida Libertad, cerca de la farmacia.*

1. Perdón, ¿el restaurante, por favor?
2. Perdón, ¿Dónde está el hotel, por favor?
3. Perdón, ¿el museo, por favor?
4. Por favor, ¿la farmacia?
5. ¿Dónde está la oficina de correos, por favor?
6. ¿Hay una librería cerca de aquí?

Capítulo 8 ¿Dónde está...? **189**

TEACH/MODEL

Nota gramatical

PRESENTATION

 TRANSPARENCY 38

You can combine the presentation of contractions with **de** and contractions of prepositions of place by using the transparency for the buildings or by having them look at the drawing on page 185. Begin by using two places that have the article **la** and are near each other. Then find two places that use the article **el** that are near each other. For each place, ask: **¿Qué está cerca de... ?** or **¿Dónde está... ?** (Point to a place that is near or next door or across the street.) Once you have established the patterns for **de la** and **del,** you can then mix genders.

▲▲ Visual-Spatial

PRACTICE/APPLY

G. ¿Dónde está?

ANSWERS
1. al lado de/detrás de/lejos de
2. detrás del/delante del/frente al
3. al museo/al estadio/al cine/a la casa
4. de la carnicería/del hotel/de la oficina de correos/de la florería
5. del profesor/del señor Álvarez/de la señora Ruiz/del muchacho

H. Direcciones

ANSWERS
Answers may vary slightly.
1. Está al lado del banco.
2. ...frente a la oficina de correos.
3. ...al final de la avenida Libertad.
4. ...al lado del hotel, en la esquina de la calle Colón.
5. ...al lado del banco y frente al hotel.
6. ...frente al quiosco de periódicos.

Estructura

PRESENTATION

To introduce the verb **estar** inductively, follow the suggestions given for presenting other verbs on page T169. Make statements in the **yo** form using prepositions of location: **Estoy en la escuela.**, etc. Continue by asking a **tú** question and summarize the answer in the third person. Proceed with the plural forms. Point out the written accents on the second- and third-person forms.

▲ Linguistic

PRACTICE/APPLY

I. ¿Cómo y dónde?

EXPANSION

Have students create new sentences replacing the words in columns A and C with words of their choice.

✎ Creating

ESTRUCTURA

The verb estar

Yo **estoy** en el hotel Trinidad.   *I am at the Hotel Trinidad.*

Ana y Raúl **están** en el coche.   *Ana and Raúl are in the car.*

estar (to be)			
yo	**estoy**	nosotros(as)	**estamos**
tú	**estás**	vosotros(as)	**estáis**
él / ella / Ud.	**está**	ellos / ellas / Uds.	**están**

1. The **yo** form of the verb **estar** is irregular, and all second and third person forms have a written accent on the **a** of the verb endings.

2. Spanish has two verbs that mean *to be:* **estar** and **ser.** Each verb has its own specific uses. In Chapter 1, you learned to use **estar** to ask and talk about health as in ¿**Cómo estás?** **Estar** is also used to express the location of people and things.

Aquí practicamos

I. ¿Cómo y dónde? Taking information from each column, use different forms of the verb **estar** to create complete sentences. Follow the model.

MODELO   Mario / Madrid
      Mario está en Madrid.

A	B	C
Graciela y Ana		en Buenos Aires
el (la) profesor(a)		en el banco
mi amigo(a)		cerca de la iglesia
la biblioteca	estar	con José
tú		mal
los abogados		en la calle Alameda
nosotros		cerca de la iglesia
la panadería		bastante bien
yo		al lado del hotel
Esteban		

J. ¿Dónde están?

When you get home, your sister is the only person there. Ask her where everybody is. Follow the model.

MODELO   la abuela / mercado
          Tú: *¿Dónde está la abuela?*
  Tu hermana: *Está en el mercado.*

1. tía Ana / piscina
2. papá y mamá / banco
3. Lourdes / café de la esquina

4. Ángel / cine
5. las primas / estadio
6. mi perro / tu cuarto

¿Dónde estamos?

Aquí escuchamos

No está lejos   *A woman asks a man for the location of a building.*

Antes de escuchar   Review the phrases used to indicate place (page 185). Then, answer the following questions.

1. What is the opposite of **lejos de**?
2. What verb is used in Spanish to indicate location of people, animals, places, or things?

 A escuchar   Listen twice to the conversation and write down the four public places that are mentioned.

J. ¿Dónde están?
ANSWERS
1. ¿Dónde está la tía Ana? Está en la piscina.
2. ¿Dónde están papá y mamá? Están en el banco.
3. ¿Dónde está Lourdes? Está en el café de la esquina.
4. ¿Dónde está Ángel? Está en el cine.
5. ¿Dónde están las primas? Están en el estadio.
6. ¿Dónde está mi perro? Está en tu cuarto.

Aquí escuchamos

 TEXTBOOK CASSETTE/CD CASSETTE 1, SIDE B; CD 2, TRACK 10

 TAPESCRIPT P. 199

TRB: ACTIVITY MASTER, P. 89

Antes de escuchar
ANSWERS
1. cerca de
2. estar

A escuchar
ANSWERS
la biblioteca, el banco, la oficina de correos, la biblioteca en la universidad

Después de escuchar
ANSWERS
1. F, She wants to go to the library.
2. T
3. T
4. F, The university is far away.
5. T

 Spanish for Spanish Speakers

Summarizing
Have Spanish speakers listen to the **Aquí escuchamos** recording and summarize the dialogue. Encourage students to write down any difficult vocabulary or structures, and work with a partner to better understand how these are used in this recording. Review summaries with Spanish speakers to determine problematic structures and vocabulary.

Creating
Synthesizing

ETAPA SYNTHESIS

Intercambio

Individual Needs

More-prepared Students
Have more-prepared students approach the activity as a conversation; emphasize that often after a person answers a question, he (she) asks a related question in return—even something as simple as **¿y tú?**.

Por favor, ¿dónde está... ?

VARIATION
Have some students describe the location of a place using the expression **Este lugar está...** . Let others try to identify the place.

 Creating

Para ir a mi escuela

FYI
ATAJO ATAJO WRITING ASSISTANT SOFTWARE

You might want to have students use this software program when doing this activity.

Individual Needs

More-prepared Students
Supply more-prepared students with additional vocabulary from the next **etapa** (p. 193) in order to give more complex directions.

Additional Practice and Recycling

FYI
WORKBOOK, PP. 97-102

For recycling and additional practice of the vocabulary, structures, and language functions presented throughout this **etapa**, you can assign the workbook activities as in-class work and/or homework.

Después de escuchar Based on the conversation you just heard, decide whether the following statements are true or false. If a statement is false, provide the correct information in English.

1. The woman wants to go to the bank.
2. The man indicates that the place the woman is looking for is nearby.
3. The woman finds out that the bank and the post office are on the same street.
4. The man says there is a university right in the downtown area of the city.
5. The woman discovers that there are two libraries she can visit.

¡ADELANTE!

 Intercambio Ask a classmate the following questions.

1. ¿Vas al aeropuerto de vez en cuando? ¿Está cerca de la ciudad? ¿Cerca de tu casa?
2. ¿Vas al cine a menudo? ¿Hay un cine cerca de tu casa? ¿Qué hay al lado del cine?
3. ¿Hay una panadería cerca de tu casa? ¿Qué hay frente a la panadería?
4. ¿Qué hay entre tu casa y la escuela? ¿Casas? ¿Edificios de apartamentos? ¿Una biblioteca? ¿Tiendas?
5. ¿Qué hay delante de la escuela? ¿Y detrás de la escuela?

 Por favor, ¿dónde está...? You are walking down the street in your town when a Spanish-speaking person stops you and asks where a certain place (movie theater, bank, train station, drugstore, etc.) is located. You indicate the street or avenue and then try to describe the area (such as what the building is near to, next to, across from, behind, between).

 Para ir a mi escuela Write out in Spanish directions for some out-of-town guests from Honduras. Tell them how to get from your school to the downtown area of your city or town, where you will meet them at a restaurant for lunch. Refer to specific buildings as well as streets in your description.

Additional Etapa Resources

Refer to the **Etapa** Support Materials list on the opening page of this **etapa** for detailed cross-references to these assessment options.

SEGUNDA ETAPA

Preparación

- What do you say when you stop somebody on the street to ask for directions?
- What sorts of things do you say when you give someone directions?
- Is it easy for you to understand directions? Why or why not?
- What helps you to remember directions?

¿Cómo llego a... ?

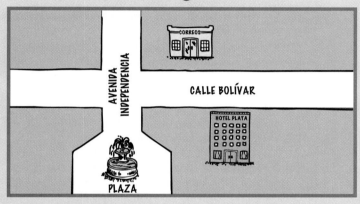

*Una señora quiere ir a la oficina de correos, pero necesita **ayuda** (help).*

Señora: Perdón, señor. ¿Hay una oficina de correos cerca de aquí?
Señor: Sí, señora. En la calle Bolívar.
Señora: **¿Cómo llego a** la calle Bolívar, por favor?
Señor: Mm..., **cruce** la plaza y **tome** la avenida Independencia, **siga derecho por** Independencia **hasta** llegar a la calle Bolívar. **Doble a la derecha.** La oficina de correos está **a la izquierda,** frente al Hotel Plata.
Señora: Muchas gracias.
Señor: De nada.

¿Cómo llego a...? *How do I get to...?*   cruce *cross*   tome *take*   siga derecho por *go, continue straight along*
hasta *until*   Doble a la derecha. *Turn right.*   a la izquierda *on the left*

Capítulo 8 ¿Dónde está...? **193**

Etapa Support Materials

- Workbook: pp. 103-106
- TRB: Textbook Activity Masters: pp. 90, 91
- Textbook Cassettes/CDs: Cassette 1, Side B; CD 2, Track 11
- Tapescript: Textbook Cassettes/CDs p.199
- Overhead Transparencies: 39, 40, 41
- Middle School Activities: pp. 70, 71
- Lesson Plan Book: pp. 46-47
- Testing Program: Quiz pp. 86, 87; Answer Key & Testing Cassettes Tapescript pp. T35
- Testing Cassettes: Cassette Side A
- Computerized Testing Program: Windows™; Macintosh®
- Atajo Writing Assistant Software: Student Text p. 199; Workbook p. 106

TEACH/MODEL

¿Cómo llego a... ?
PRESENTATION

 TRANSPARENCY 39

 TEXTBOOK CASSETTE/CD CASSETTE 1, SIDE B; CD 2, TRACK 11

 TAPESCRIPT P. 199

Begin by having students listen to the recording of the dialogue on the Textbook Cassette/CD. Ask: **¿Qué busca la señora?** Then replay the dialogue while students look at the transparency. **¿Qué cruza la señora para ir a la oficina de correos? Ella sigue derecho por qué calle? ¿Adónde dobla al llegar a la calle Bolívar, a la derecha o a la izquierda? ¿Dónde está la oficina de correos?** The goal is to make clear the meanings of the new expressions. Use gestures whenever necessary and accept phrases as answers. You may wish to let different pairs of students read the dialogue after initially listening to you, or the recording on the Textbook Cassette/CD.

Auditory-Musical
Bodily-Kinesthetic

PRACTICE / APPLY

A. Cómo llegar

SUGGESTION

Answers will follow the model by replacing the words in italics.

B. Perdon, señorita. ¿Cómo llego a... ?

SUGGESTION

 TRANSPARENCY 40

 Do the first destination with the class (or have one of your more-prepared students do it), using the transparency of the city map. Then have students work in pairs. Finally, verify their work by using the transparency and having various students go over the directions they came up with while working in pairs.

Visual-Spatial

Presentational Communication 1.3

VARIATION

With students looking at the map in their book, describe an itinerary students are to follow with their fingers on the page. When you arrive at your final destination, ask someone to indicate where you are. Once you have done this receptive activity a few times, divide the students into pairs and have them do the activity. This is a good listening comprehension activity.

Auditory-Musical
Visual-Spatial

Comentarios CULTURALES

El español en el mundo

Spanish is the fourth most widely spoken language in the world after Chinese, Hindi, and English. It is spoken by more than 400 million people in Spain, the Americas, and in other areas of the world that were once Spanish possessions. Today, after English, Spanish is by far the most widely spoken and studied language in the United States.

¡Te toca a ti!

A. Cómo llegar Give the following directions by replacing the words in italics.

1. Cruce *la calle.* (la plaza / la avenida / el parque)
2. Siga derecho hasta *la avenida de las Américas.* (la plaza San Martín / la calle Corrientes / la catedral)
3. Doble a la derecha *en la esquina.* (al llegar al río [river] / en la calle Córdoba / al llegar a la avenida Libertad)
4. Doble a la izquierda en *la avenida 9 de Julio.* (la calle Santa Fe / la calle Florida / la calle Esmeralda)

B. Perdón, señorita. ¿Cómo llego a...? Work with a partner and take turns playing the role of the police officer at **la Puerta del Sol** (circled in red on the following map). Explain how to get to the places that follow. Follow the model.

MODELO la estación de metro Antón Martín
Señor(ita): *Perdón, señor (señorita). ¿Cómo llego a la estación de metro Antón Martín?*
Policía: *Tome la calle Carretas hasta llegar a la Plaza Benavente. Tome la calle Atocha a la izquierda de la plaza. Siga derecho. La estación de metro Antón Martín está a la izquierda.*

1. la Plaza Mayor
2. la Capilla del Obispo
3. la Plaza de la Villa
4. el Teatro Real
5. la Telefónica en la Gran Vía

194 *Tercera unidad* ¿Dónde y a qué hora?

 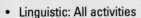

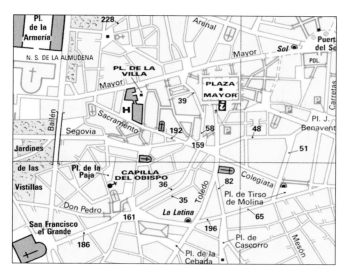

 ¿Qué crees?

In which Latin American city were many archaeological findings discovered while building a subway system? One of the stations is decorated by an excavated pyramid.

a) Buenos Aires, Argentina
b) Mexico City, Mexico
c) Caracas, Venezuela

respuesta

PRONUNCIACIÓN THE SOUND OF /s/

The sound of /s/ can also be spelled with the consonant **c** when it is before the vowels **e** and **i** as in **cena** and **cine**.

Práctica

C. Listen and repeat as your teacher models the following words.

1. cena	5. a veces	9. cien
2. centro	6. cine	10. gracias
3. cerca	7. cinta	
4. dulce	8. cita	

Repaso

D. ¿Por favor...? Some tourists stop you in the Zócalo to ask where certain places are located. Work in a group. Using the map that follows, tell the tourist as precisely as possible the location of each of the places that they are looking for. Follow the model.

> **MODELO** Escuela Normal Preparatoria
> **Turista:** *¿La Escuela Normal Preparatoria, por favor?*
> **Tú:** *La Escuela Normal Preparatoria está frente al Templo Mayor.*

Capítulo 8 ¿Dónde está…? **195**

TEACH/MODEL

Pronunciación

PRESENTATION

 TEXTBOOK CASSETTE/CD CASSETTE 1, SIDE B; CD 2, TRACK 12

 TAPESCRIPT P. 199

Point out that in some regions of Spain, the **c** before an **i** or an **e** is pronounced like the *th* in the English word *think*, just like the Spanish **z**.

Linguistic Comparisons 4.1

Have students listen to the explanation for the sound of **s** on the Textbook Cassette/CD. The speaker will model the correct pronunciation of the words in **Practica C**. Students can repeat after the speakers as they follow along in their text

Auditory-Musical

PRACTICE/APPLY

D. ¿Por favor... ?

SUGGESTION

TRANSPARENCY 41

Quickly review prepositions of place before doing Activity D. Ask students to supply the words while you write them on the board.

Individual Needs

Less-prepared Students
A review of prepositions before Activity D should be especially useful for less-prepared students; it also serves as a introduction to the activity for all students.

More-prepared Students
Encourage more-prepared students to expand their answers by explaining how to get from one locale to another—according to the map on page 196—by using other direction-giving vocabulary.

Focus on Culture

The Languages of Spain

Ask students if they know the names of any official languages (other than Spanish) spoken in Spain. Point out that Catalán is spoken in the region of Cataluña, and that it is similar to both French and Spanish. At the Barcelona Olympic games, the scores and other announcements were given in Catalán, Spanish, English, and French. Then mention that Gallego is spoken in Galicia. The Basque language (Vascuence or Euskera) is not related to any other European language and is the oldest language spoken in Spain.

Connections with Distinctive Viewpoints 3.2
Linguistic Comparisons 4.1

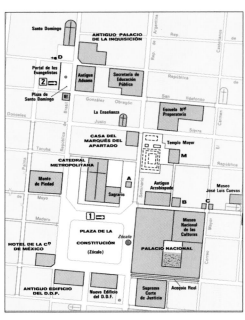

1. Casa del Marqués del Apartado
2. Monte de Piedad
3. Suprema Corte de Justicia
4. Hotel de la Ciudad de México
5. Antiguo Arzobispado
6. Nuevo Edificio del D.D.F.

Estructura

PRESENTATION

Introduce the commands inductively by doing a whole class activity. Use commands such as **levántense/siéntense**, then move on to verbs such as **mirar (por la ventana, a la profesora), hablar, bailar, cantar, correr, escribir (en la pizarra)**, doing both positive and negative forms, as well as singular and plural (one student or whole class). Allow students to use gestures for verbs such as **cantar, correr**, and **comer**.

Auditory-Musical
Bodily-Kinesthetic
Linguistic

☞ **b**

ESTRUCTURA

The imperative with **Ud.** and **Uds.**: Regular second-person commands

Tome la avenida Atocha.	*Take Atocha Avenue.*
¡**Escuchen** bien!	*Listen well!*
¡No **doble** por esa calle!	*Don't turn onto that street!*

Regular Second-person Commands

	Singular	Plural
-ar verbs	Cante.	Canten
-er verbs	Coma.	Coman
-ir verbs	Escriba.	Escriban

1. Command forms of a verb are used to tell someone to do something, as when giving orders, directions, or suggestions.

2. To form the **Ud.** commands, drop the -o from the **yo** form of the present tense and add -**e** for regular -**ar** verbs and -**a** for regular -**er** and -**ir** verbs. To form the **Uds.** commands, do the same, but add -**en** for regular -**ar** verbs and -**an** for regular -**er** and -**ir** verbs.

196   *Tercera unidad* ¿Dónde y a qué hora?

ESTRUCTURA (continued)

hablar			
yo **hablo**	**habl-**	**hable** (Ud.)	**hablen** (Uds.)
beber			
yo **bebo**	**beb-**	**beba** (Ud.)	**beban** (Uds.)
escribir			
yo **escribo**	**escrib-**	**escriba** (Ud.)	**escriban** (Uds.)
tener			
yo **tengo**	**teng-**	**tenga** (Ud.)	**tengan** (Uds.)

3. Commands are made negative by placing **no** in front of the verb forms: ¡No baile! ¡No canten!

Aquí practicamos

E. Hablen español Use the **Ud.** and **Uds.** command forms of the following verbs. Follow the model.

> **MODELO** doblar a la derecha
> *Doble a la derecha.*
> *Doblen a la derecha.*

1. estudiar
2. no beber mucho
3. aprender español
4. tener paciencia
5. no comer mucho
6. leer todos los días

F. A mi profesor(a) Use the **Ud.** command to tell your teacher to do the following. Follow the model.

> **MODELO** no bailar en clase
> *No baile en clase.*

1. tener paciencia
2. no trabajar mucho
3. escribir las instrucciones
4. leer en la biblioteca
5. viajar mucho
6. no hablar tan despacio *(so slowly)*

G. ¡Vamos! Using the suggested verbs, tell two of your classmates to do something. Use the suggested verbs. Follow the models.

bailar	correr	escuchar	trabajar
cantar	escribir	mirar	usar

> **MODELOS** *Luisa y Marta, ¡canten bien!*
> *Antonio y Marta, ¡bailen mucho!*

Capítulo 8 ¿Dónde está…? **197**

PRACTICE/APPLY

E. Hablen español
ANSWERS
1. Estudie/Estudien.
2. No beba/Beban mucho.
3. Aprenda/Aprendan español.
4. Tenga/Tengan paciencia.
5. No coma/Coman mucho.
6. Lea/Lean todos los días.

F. A mi profesor(a)
ANSWERS
1. Tenga paciencia.
2. No trabaje mucho.
3. Escriba las instrucciones.
4. Lea en la biblioteca.
5. Viaje mucho.
6. No hable tan despacio.

Individual Needs

Less-prepared Students
 Have less-prepared students work in pairs to write out the commands.

More-prepared Students
Have more-prepared students improvise additional commands to put you on the spot. You may wish to put a list of verbs on the board for them to use.
 Creating

G. ¡Vamos!
ANSWERS
Answer may vary, but should include the following verb forms:
bailen/canten/corran/escriban/escuchen/miren/trabajen/usen

Nota gramatical

PRESENTATION

Gesture to several students to come forward telling them, **Vayan a la pizarra**. Tell each one to write a verb that involves a spelling change for the command form. For example, **Juan, escribe "llegar"**. Then have the student write the **yo** form of the verb. Ask the class to give the command ending and have the student at the board erase the **o** from the **yo** form and write the command ending.

Remind them that **g** before an **i** or an **e** is pronounced like the English **h** in *heal*. A **u** is needed to make it sound like the **g** in *game*. In **cruce** a spelling change is necessary because the **z** usually changes to a **c** before an **i** or an **e** in Spanish.

H. Lleguen temprano

ANSWERS

1. Sea bueno./Sean buenos.
2. Vaya/Vayan a bailar.
3. No sea antipático./No sean antipáticos.
4. Vaya/Vayan a clase.
5. Practique/Practiquen el piano.
6. No llegue/No lleguen tarde.
7. No cruce/No crucen la calle.
8. Busque/Busquen las llaves.

Aquí escuchamos

 TEXTBOOK CASSETTE/CD CASSETTE 1, SIDE B; CD 2, TRACK 13

 TAPESCRIPT P. 200

 TRB: ACTIVITY MASTER, P. 90

Antes de escuchar

ANSWERS

1. **doble a la izquierda**
2. **derecho** means straight and derecha means **right**.

A escuchar

ANSWERS

calle Bolívar, calle San Vicente

ESTRUCTURA

The imperative with **Ud.** and **Uds.**: Irregular second-person commands			
-car verbs	c → qu	Practi**que**. (Ud.)	Practi**quen**. (Uds.)
-gar verbs	g → gu	Lle**gue**. (Ud.)	Lle**guen**. (Uds.)
-zar verbs	z → c	Cru**ce**. (Ud.)	Cru**cen**. (Uds.)

1. Note the spelling changes that verbs ending in **-car**, **-gar**, and **-zar** have in the **Ud.** and **Uds.** commands. Another **-car** verb you should learn is **buscar** *(to look for)*.

2. The verbs **ir** and **ser** have irregular command forms: **Vaya** (Ud.) and **vayan** (Uds.) for **ir**; **sea** (Ud.) and **sean** (Uds.) for **ser**.

Aquí practicamos

H. Lleguen temprano Use the **Ud.** and the **Uds.** command forms of these verbs. Follow the model.

> **MODELO**   ir de vacaciones
> *Vaya de vacaciones.*
> *Vayan de vacaciones.*

1. ser bueno
2. ir a bailar
3. no ser antipático
4. ir a clase
5. practicar el piano
6. no llegar tarde *(late)*
7. cruzar la calle
8. buscar las llaves

Aquí escuchamos

Está cerca de aquí   *A man is looking for the Museo Nacional.*

Antes de escuchar   Review the command forms that you just learned about (pages 196-198). Then, answer the following questions.

1. How do you tell someone to turn to the left in Spanish?
2. What is the difference between **derecho** and **derecha?**

Vocabulary Expansion–Synonyms

Have Spanish speakers listen carefully to the **Aquí escuchamos** recording and write down five words they hear for which they know or want to find synonyms. Tell them not to limit themselves to just one or two parts of speech, but to choose nouns, verbs, adjectives, adverbs, prepositions, etc. Then give students copies of the dialogue from the Tapescript and have them work with a partner to combine their lists and create a transformed dialogue. Have Spanish speakers and other class volunteers role-play the dialogue with the new words for the rest of the class.

 Creating

 Auditory-Musical Linguistic

 Presentational Communication 1.3

A escuchar Listen twice to the conversation, and pay special attention to the name of the street the man is looking for. Write the name of the street on your activity master, as well as any other street names you hear.

Después de escuchar On your activity master, put a check mark next to the phrases that you heard in the conversation.

__ ahí está	__ ¿Dónde está?	__ frente al banco
__ doble a la derecha	__ está cerca	__ siga cinco cuadras
__ doble a la izquierda	__ está lejos	__ siga tres cuadras

¡ADELANTE!

 Vamos a la escuela Explain to one of your classmates how you get from where you live to your school.

1. Give specific directions, including street names and turns.
2. Name at least three buildings that you pass on the way.
3. Include in your explanation the verbs **ir, cruzar,** and **doblar.**

 Para ir a la Plaza Mayor You and a Peruvian pen pal have just arrived in Madrid. While having lunch at **la Puerta del Sol,** you look at a map similar to the one on page 195 and find the red circle marking where you are. You are headed to **la Plaza Mayor** and your friend is meeting his (her) family in front of **el Teatro Real.** Discuss the best way to get to your destinations. Together, write down specific directions in Spanish from your current location to each destination.

EN LÍNEA

Connect with the Spanish-speaking world! Access the *¡Ya verás! Gold* home page for Internet activities related to this chapter.

http://yaveras.heinle.com

Additional Etapa Resources

Refer to the **Etapa** Support Materials list on the opening page of this **etapa** for detailed cross-references to these assessment options.

Después de escuchar
ANSWERS
¿Dónde está?/ está cerca/ doble a la izquierda/ahí está

ETAPA SYNTHESIS

Vamos a la escuela

Individual Needs

Less-prepared Students
Help less-prepared students brainstorm and organize a list of expressions to use when giving directions.

More-prepared Students
For more-prepared students, have one partner explain how to get from home to school and the other explain how to get from the school back to the first partner's house.

Para ir a la Plaza Mayor
FYI

 ATAJO WRITING ASSISTANT SOFTWARE

You might want to have students use this software program when doing this activity.

Individual Needs

Less-prepared Students
Have less-prepared students trace their route with their finger first. Then have them return to Sol and retrace, stopping to write down the street names and the directions as they go along.

 Visual-Spatial

Additional Practice and Recycling
FYI

 WORKBOOK, PP. 103-106

For recycling and additional practice of the vocabulary, structures, and language functions presented throughout this **etapa**, you can assign the workbook activities as in-class work and/or homework.

VOCABULARIO

Para charlar

Para dar (to give) direcciones

Cruce la calle.
Doble a la derecha.
Doble a la izquierda.
Está a la derecha.
Está a la izquierda.
Está al final de…
Está al lado de…
Está cerca de…
Está delante de…
Está detrás de…
Está en la esquina de…
Está entre…
Está frente a…
Está lejos de…
Tome la calle, la avenida…
Siga derecho por… hasta…

Para pedir (to ask for) direcciones

¿Cómo llego a…?
¿Dónde está…?
¿Está cerca de aquí?
¿Está lejos de aquí?

Vocabulario general

Sustantivos

un estacionamiento
un quiosco de periódicos

Verbos

buscar
cruzar
doblar
estar
llegar

Otras palabras y expresiones

ayuda
del
Sea Ud…
Sean Uds…
Vaya Ud…
Vayan Uds…

200 *Tercera unidad* ¿Dónde y a qué hora?

El centro colonial de Quito

Antes de leer

1. According to the title, what will this reading be about?

2. Are you familiar with any historic sites or tourist attractions in your city or town?

3. In what kind of document might you find this text?

Reading Strategies
• Examining format for content clues
• Activating background knowledge

Si vas a Quito, Ecuador, visita el viejo centro colonial. Coge un taxi o un autobús hasta la Plaza de la Independencia. Al lado oeste de la Plaza está el Palacio de Gobierno original. Hoy es en parte un museo. Al lado sur está La Compañía; la catedral original y una joya artística. Al lado norte, en la esquina, hay un hotel con un buen café. En la misma vecindad hay una serie de tiendas y restaurantes. Al lado este, hay más tiendas y restaurantes.

Cerca de la Plaza vas a encontrar muchos museos, iglesias llenas de arte y calles angostas de piedra. Allí hay arquitectura con más de 500 años. Esta área ha sido restaurada. Visita el viejo centro quiteño y camina por uno de los Monumentos de la Humanidad. Las Naciones Unidas designan así al viejo centro colonial de Quito.

Capítulo 8 ¿Dónde está...? **201**

Focus on Culture

El centro colonial de Quito

Quito, Ecuador, is one of the most beautiful cities in South America. It is located in a valley, surrounded by mountains and snow-capped volcanoes. It is only 22 kilometers from the equator, so it always has spring-like weather. The old colonial center has many white-washed houses, red-tiled roofs, colonial churches, and pretty parks.

🌐 Connections with Other Disciplines 3.1

Guía para la lectura

VOCABULARY EXPANSION

The word **quiteño** refers to something from Quito. **El viejo centro quiteño** means *the old Quito center.*

Linguistic Comparisons 4.1

Después de leer

ANSWERS

Answers will vary.

Guía para la lectura

Here are some words and expressions to keep in mind as you read.

coge	*take*
joya	*jewel*
vecindad	*vicinity*
angostas	*narrow*
de piedra	*stone, cobbled*
restaurada	*restored*

Después de leer

1. If you visited Quito, which aspects of the city would interest you most—the old colonial section described here, or the Avenida Amazonas, a modern area with nightlife and shopping?

2. Do you prefer modern architecture or older architecure? Why?

3. Choose an historical site or tourist attraction in your town or city. With a classmate, take turns explaining why she or he might want to visit your chosen site, and give him or her directions for getting there.

202 *Tercera unidad* ¿Dónde y a qué hora?

CAPÍTULO 9

¡La fiesta del pueblo!

¡Bienvenidos a la fiesta del pueblo!

Objectives

- talking about leisure-time activities
- making plans
- telling and asking for the time

Capítulo 9 ¡La fiesta del pueblo! **203**

OBJECTIVES

Functions
- Talking about leisure-time activities
- Making plans
- Telling and asking for the time

Context
- Festivals

Accuracy
- Telling time
- Present tense of **venir**
- **Estar** + adjectives of condition
- Possessive adjectives (third person)

Pronunciation
- The consonants **m**, **n**, and **ñ**

CHAPTER WARM-UP

Setting the Context

In preparation for their learning to discuss leisure time activities, have students look at the photograph on page 203 and describe what they see. Ask them to figure out what kind of **fiesta** is depicted and have them translate the caption. Then engage in a discussion about the kinds of celebrations or festivals they participate in throughout the year, and ask them to describe the dancing, food, and activities that typically accompany these events.

Visual-Spatial

Chapter Support Materials

- Lab Manual: pp. 58-63
- Lab Program: Cassette Side A, B; CD 5, Tracks 1-9
- TRB: Textbook Activity Masters: pp. 92-94
- Textbook Cassettes/CDs: Cassette 1, Side B; CD 2, Track 23
- Tapescript: Lab Program pp. 87-95; Textbook Cassettes/CDs p. 202
- Middle School Activities: pp. 72-76
- Workbook for Spanish-speaking Students: pp. 53-58
- Answer Key to SSS Workbook: pp. 49-50
- Practice Software: Windows™; Macintosh®

- Testing Program: Chapter Test pp. 98-101; Answer Key & Testing Cassettes Tapescript pp. T40, T41; Oral Assessment p. T41
- Testing Cassettes: Cassette Side A
- Computerized Testing Program: Windows™; Macintosh®
- Video Program: Cassette 1, 1:13:08-1:21:56
- Video Guide: Videoscript pp. 38-41; Activities pp. 111-112
- **Mundos hispanos 1**
- Internet Activities: Student Text p. 218

PRIMERA ETAPA

TEACH/MODEL

¿A qué hora son los bailes folklóricos?

PRESENTATION

TRANSPARENCY 42

Present the information inductively in Spanish, allowing the students to answer in phrases. First, either read or have a student read the introduction. Then begin by stating, **Nuestro día de la independencia es el 4 de julio.** (perhaps writing the date on the board). **¿Cuándo es el día de la independencia en Guatemala?** Reinforce by restating after student attempts: **Sí, el quince de septiembre.**

Direct students to look at the schedule of events: **Miren las actividades.** Gesturing to your watch, ask, **¿A qué hora es la misa?** Reinforce comprehension by saying with emphasis, **Sí, a las diez y media** (perhaps writing this on the board). **¿A qué hora es la feria? ...Sí, a las doce.**

Interpretive Communication 1.2

EXPANSION

Ask students about other times, having them convert the 24-hour clock to the 12-hour one. Ask other questions, such as **¿Dónde ocurre el baile folklórico? ¿Qué actividad te gusta?**, etc. Then, ask students in English for places or occasions when a twenty-four hour clock could be useful and why (in situations where any possible confusion between A.M. and P.M. must be prevented, e.g. airline travel, the military, or ocean navigation).

Logical-Mathematical

Preparación

- What are some of the holidays that are important to the people who live in your town or city? What kinds of events or activities does your town or city hold to celebrate national holidays, such as the Fourth of July?

- Have you ever celebrated a special holiday in another country? Where did this happen and what was it like?

- Do you think it is a good idea for people to get together to celebrate a holiday? Why or why not?

¿A qué hora son los bailes folklóricos?

En Guatemala la gente se prepara para (people are getting ready for) *la fiesta del Día de la Independencia.*

Octavio García vive en Guatemala. Como en **la mayoría** de las ciudades y **pueblos hispanos**, la Ciudad de Guatemala tiene una **gran fiesta una vez al año**. En Guatemala celebran el Día de la Independencia el 15 de septiembre. Octavio mira el póster que **anuncia** los programas **para** el festival.

Día de la Independencia
Ciudad de Guatemala

10:30	**Misa** de **Acción de Gracias** en la Catedral
12:00	**Feria** de la comida
13:30	Bailes folklóricos en la Plaza Mayor
14:45	**Concurso de poesía—Premio al mejor poema**
16:30	**Desfile** de las escuelas
19:00	Banquete en el Club Independencia
21:00	**Fuegos artificiales** en el Parque Nacional
22:00	Baile popular (Parque Nacional)

la mayoría de *most* pueblos *towns* hispanos *Hispanic* gran fiesta *large party, festival* una vez al año *once a year* anuncia *announces* para *for* Misa *Mass* Acción de Gracias *Thanksgiving* Concurso de poesía *Poetry contest* Premio *Prize* el mejor *the best* poema *poem* Desfile *Parade* Fuegos artificiales *Fireworks*

204 *Tercera unidad* ¿Dónde y a qué hora?

Etapa Support Materials

- Workbook: pp. 107-111
- TRB: Textbook Activity Masters: p. 92
- Textbook Cassettes/CDs: Cassette 1, Side B; CD 2, Track 15
- Tapescript: Textbook Cassettes/CDs p. 200
- Overhead Transparencies: 42, 43
- Middle School Activities: pp. 77, 78
- Lesson Plan Book: pp. 49-50

- Testing Program: Quiz pp. 91-93; Answer Key & Testing Cassettes Tapescript p. T38
- Testing Cassettes: Cassette Side A
- Computerized Testing Program: Windows™; Macintosh®
- Atajo Writing Assistant Software: Student Text p. 211

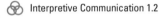

Comentarios CULTURALES

La fiesta del pueblo

Many towns in the Hispanic world have at least one big celebration each year. There are religious festivals in honor of the patron saints of the towns, celebrations for the coming of spring and harvest, grape-pressing festivals, and more. The whole town participates in these celebrations. The festivals often begin with a religious ceremony and prayers said in the local churches. In the evening there are parties with dancing, eating, and sometimes fireworks.

¡Te toca a ti!

A. El Día de la Independencia Elena is planning her activities for the day of the festival. Complete the following paragraph according to the information found on the poster on page 204.

Primero voy a la catedral para escuchar la Misa de _____ __ _____. Luego voy a comer en la casa de Adela. Después de comer, Adela y yo vamos a ver los bailes _____ en la _____ Mayor. Adela va a leer su poema en el _____ de _____. No vamos a ver el _____ de las escuelas porque va a ser muy largo. Tampoco vamos a ir al _____ en el _____ Independencia, porque es muy caro (*expensive*). Por la noche, vamos a ver los _____ _____ en el Parque Nacional, y luego vamos al _____ popular. Va a ser (*It's going to be*) un día divertido.

B. ¿Qué quisieran hacer durante la fiesta? Look at the schedule on page 204 and list the three events that you would most like to attend. Then, ask several classmates what they would like to do at the **fiesta.** Find out whose itineraries are most similar to yours. Follow the model.

> **MODELO** Tú: ¿Qué quisieras hacer tú, Jaime?
> Jaime: Yo quisiera ver el desfile.

Capítulo 9 ¡La fiesta del pueblo! **205**

A. El Día de la Independencia
ANSWERS
Acción de Gracias/folklóricos/Plaza/ concurso/poesía/desfile/banquete/ Club/fuegos artificiales/baile

B. ¿Qué quisieran hacer durante la fiesta?
SUGGESTION
Very quickly before doing Activity B, review the forms of the present tense of the verb **querer** and re-emphasize its use with an infinitive.

Linguistic

Individual Needs

Less-prepared Students
Have less-prepared students make a chart to mark their own responses and those of classmates, and then use the chart to report back to the class.

Comparing and Contrasting

More-prepared Students
Have more-prepared students use this activity for conversation by asking follow-up questions such as, **¿Por qué quisieras ver el desfile?, ¿Dónde ocurre?, ¿A qué hora es?**

VARIATION
Ask students to look at the festival schedule and decide what they would like to see. Then ask them to tell the class. You might want to have your Spanish-speaking students say why they want to do each activity mentioned.

Interpersonal Communication 1.1

 MULTIPLE INTELLIGENCES

- Linguistic: All activities
- Logical-Mathematical: A, E, F, I
- Visual-Spatial: D
- Auditory-Musical: **Pronunciación**, C, **Aquí escuchamos**
- Interpersonal: B, J

 The Standards

- Interpersonal Communication 1.1: B, D, J, **Adelante** activites
- Interpretive Communication 1.2: A, E, F, G, H, I
- Presentational Communication 1.3: **Adelante** activities
- Cultural Practices and Perspectives 2.1: **¿A qué hora son los bailes folklóricos?**
- Cultural Products and Perspectives 2.2: **Comentarios culturales**
- Connections with Distinctive Viewpoints 3.2: **Estructura**
- Linguistic Comparisons 4.1: **Pronunciación**

Pronunciación

PRESENTATION

TEXTBOOK CASSETTE/CD CASSETTE 1, SIDE B; CD 2, TRACK 15

TAPESCRIPT P. 200

Have students listen to the explanation for the consonants **m** and **n** on the Textbook Cassette/CD. The speaker will model the correct pronunciation of the words in **Práctica C.** Have students follow along in their texts and repeat after each word.

Auditory-Musical

PRACTICE/APPLY

D. ¿Dónde hay un (una)...?

SUGGESTION

TRANSPARENCY 43

Use transparency to help students better see the streets and destinations. If necessary, have students repeat the names of the streets and sites after you, and before they begin working with their partners.

Auditory-Musical
Visual-Spatial

PRONUNCIACIÓN THE CONSONANTS **m** AND **n**

When the consonants **m** and **n** are the first letters of a word or syllable, they are pronounced exactly like *m* and *n* in English.

Práctica

C. Listen and repeat as your teacher models the following words.

1. mamá
2. mal
3. más
4. merienda
5. mermelada
6. tener
7. una
8. nada
9. noche
10. bueno

Repaso

D. ¿Dónde hay un (una)...? You are a tourist in Lima and want to find out where various places are, so you ask the clerk at the Hotel Bolívar. Among the places you can ask directions for are **el estadio, el Museo de Arte, la oficina de correos, la catedral,** etc. Enact the conversation with a partner, following the model.

MODELO

Tú: *¿Dónde está la Plaza Grau, por favor?*
Compañero(a): *Está en la esquina del Paseo de la República y la avenida Grau.*

206 *Tercera unidad* ¿Dónde y a qué hora?

Focus on Culture

Festivals

Many cities and towns in Spain, Latin America, and the United States organize annual festivals celebrating some aspect of the area's culture. Have students list some celebrations they are familiar with and some festivities for these celebrations in their communities. Ask them to compare the activities on their lists with those in Spanish-speaking countries, that they learned about in the **etapa** opener and the **Comentarios culturales** reading on page 205. Finally, ask if students find any festivities in these readings that they would not expect to see practiced in their own community.

Comparing and Contrasting

Cultural Comparisons 4.2

ESTRUCTURA

Telling time

¿Qué hora es?   *What time is it?*

Es la una.

Son las dos.

Son las dos y diez.

Son las dos
y cuarto.

Son las dos
y media.

Son las tres
menos veinte.

Son las tres
menos cuarto.

Es medianoche
(*midnight*).

Es mediodía
(*noon*).

1. To distinguish between A.M. and P.M., use the expressions **de la mañana** (*in the morning*), **de la tarde** (*in the afternoon*), or **de la noche** (*in the evening*).
2. Notice that in Spanish **es la** is used for one o'clock and **son las** is used for all other hours.

Capítulo 9 ¡La fiesta del pueblo!   **207**

TEACH/MODEL

Estructura

PRESENTATION

Use a model clock (or draw one on the board). Begin by having students repeat the hours from one to midday (contrast with midnight). Then have them repeat the time every five minutes.

As a way to reinforce what they have learned and to give students practice you can begin and end each class by asking someone what time it is. Or, you can have several students become responsible for giving the time whenever anyone needs to know it for a few weeks (to know when a dance begins, when a football game starts, etc.).

◢◣ Logical-Mathematical

VOCABULARY EXPANSION

In order to say *on the dot* or *sharp* when telling time, Spanish speakers use the expression **en punto**. Therefore, *It is two o'clock sharp* becomes **Son las dos en punto**.

⊗ Linguistic Comparisons 4.1

Focus on Culture

The Incas

Have students locate Lima, Peru on the map of South America in the front of the book. Ask what they know about the ancient Incan empire. What was its capital? (Cuzco) Bring in a picture of Machu Picchu; explain that no one knew it existed until the twentieth century. Mention some achievements of the Incas: they had the most intricate and advanced agricultural system of their time using irrigation canals; they built terraces in mountainsides to grow crops; they invented a freeze-dried potato which could be stored for up to six years. Over 26,000,000 descendants of the Incas still speak the languages of their empire: **Quechua** and **Aymará**.

Cultural Practices and Perspectives 2.1
Connections with Other Disciplines 3.1
Cultural Comparisons 4.2

PRACTICE/APPLY

F. La hora

SUGGESTION

After students have practiced for a while and are comfortable, have students work as a class to give the time as quickly as possible. Call on students in rapid succession until they have given every five interval. Then repeat the activity, giving the times between 8:00 and 9:00, 10:00 and 11:00, etc.

ANSWERS

1. Son las ocho y veinte de la mañana.
2. Es la una (en punto) de la tarde.
3. Es la una y media de la mañana.
4. Son las tres y diez de la tarde.
5. Son las once menos cinco de la mañana.
6. Son las doce menos cuarto de la noche.
7. Son las cuatro y cuarto de la tarde.
8. Son las seis menos veinticinco de la mañana.
9. Son las ocho menos cuarto de la mañana.
10. Son las diez y veinticinco de la noche.

TEACH/MODEL

Palabras útiles

PRESENTATION

Write additional times on the board. Then prepare to ask your students questions about time. Begin by talking to the students about their Spanish class. **Nuestra clase de español comienza a las... y continúa hasta las... . La clase dura desde las... hasta las... . Entonces, hablamos español entre las... y las... .** Then ask them to verify the information: **¿A qué hora comienza nuestra clase de español? ¿Hasta qué hora continúa? ¿Cuándo es que hablamos español? (Desde las... hasta...** or **Entre las... y las...)** Then switch topics. For example, talk about when they eat lunch or dinner, when they arrive at school or get home, etc. Have students refer to the schedule of events on page 204 and ask them similar questions.

Aquí practicamos

E. La hora Give the time for every five minutes between 9:00 and 10:00.

F. ¿Qué hora es? Find out the time from a classmate. He (She) should indicate whether it is morning (**de la mañana**), afternoon (**de la tarde**), or evening (**de la noche**). Take turns telling the time. Follow the model.

> **MODELO**   2:20 A.M.
> **Tú:** *¿Qué hora es?*
> **Compañera(o):** *Son las dos y veinte de la mañana.*

1. 8:20 A.M.
2. 1:00 P.M.
3. 1:30 A.M.
4. 3:10 P.M.
5. 10:55 A.M.
6. 11:45 P.M.
7. 4:15 P.M.
8. 5:35 A.M.
9. 7:45 A.M.
10. 10:25 P.M.

PALABRAS ÚTILES

Questions about time

1. To ask someone what time something happens, use **¿A qué hora...?** The response to this question requires the preposition **a.**

   —**¿A qué hora** comes?   *¿At what time do you eat?*
   —**A las 6:15.**   *At 6:15.*

2. To ask someone when something occurs, use **¿cuándo?** To indicate that something happens between two times, use either **entre las... y las...** or **desde las... hasta las...** .

   —**¿Cuándo** corres?   *When do you run?*
   —**Entre las 5:00 y las 6:00.** *Between 5:00 and 6:00.*

   —**¿Cuándo** trabaja tu madre?   *When does your mother work?*
   —**Desde las 9:00 hasta las 5:00.** *From 9:00 to 5:00.*

Aquí practicamos

G. ¿A qué hora? Your friend asks you at what time you do each of the following activities. Tell him (her) between what times you do them. Follow the model.

> **MODELO**   mirar la TV
> **Amigo(a):** *¿A qué hora miras la TV?*
> **Tú:** *Miro la TV entre las 7:00 y las 9:00 de la noche.*

208 *Tercera unidad* ¿Dónde y a qué hora?

Focus on Culture

Jornada continua

In some parts of the Spanish-speaking world, students begin school early in the morning and go through to one or two P.M. without a break for lunch and then they go home for the day. This schedule is known as **Jornada continua.** Ask students to discuss this schedule and compare it to their own. Would they like to be on this schedule? Why or why not?

Cultural Comparisons 4.2

1. preparar la tarea *(to prepare homework)* de español
2. usar el laboratorio de lenguas
3. comer
4. practicar el tenis
5. trabajar
6. leer

ESTRUCTURA

The verb venir

¿A qué hora **viene** Mónica?	*What time is Mónica coming?*
Nosotros **venimos** a las tres.	*We are coming at three.*

venir *(to come)*			
yo	**vengo**	nosotros(as)	**venimos**
tú	**vienes**	vosotros(as)	**venís**
él		ellos	
ella	**viene**	ellas	**vienen**
Ud.		Uds.	

The irregular verb **venir** follows a pattern similar to the verb **tener,** with variations in the **nosotros** and **vosotros** forms.

Aquí practicamos

H. ¿Quién viene? Create original sentences using words from each column.

A	B	C
Laura	venir	a la fiesta
Cristina y yo		de Acapulco
Uds.		a mi casa
tus amigos		del supermercado
la profesora		
tú		

PRACTICE / APPLY

G. ¿A qué hora?

SUGGESTION

Do first as a whole class, using the **pregúntale** format to practice listening comprehension. Call on more-prepared students first to establish the pattern. Then have the students do it again in pairs, teaming up more-prepared students with less-prepared ones.

Interpersonal Communication

EXPANSION

Expand and personalize Activity G. Begin by brainstorming with the class, reviewing vocabulary for day-to-day activities. Then have students list activities that they normally do or participate in during the week. With each activity, have them tell what time of the day they usually do these activities. When the lists are completed, the results can be examined on a *tick mark* graph on the blackboard to determine: which activities appear on the most lists, which ones come earlier or later in the day, and which ones might be limited to certain seasons.

Visual-Spatial

Logical-Mathematical

TEACH / MODEL

Estructura

PRESENTATION

Begin by making statements using the present tense of **venir** in the **yo** form. Continue by asking questions in the **tú** form and then summarize the answers in the third-person plural. Proceed in the same way for the plural forms. (See the presentation for the **-er** and **-ir** verbs in Chapter 5.) Then write the conjugation on the board and proceed with the activities.

PRACTICE / APPLY

H. ¿Quién viene?

SUGGESTION

Let students create additional sentences by adding more places (with prepositions) to Column C.

I. ¿Quién viene al baile con nosotros?

ANSWERS

1. Elena y su hermano no vienen al baile.
2. Elvira no viene...
3. Tú vienes...
4. Mis abuelos vienen...
5. David y Juliana vienen...
6. Uds. no vienen...

Individual Needs

More-prepared Students
Have more-prepared students make a list of personalized questions.

Less-prepared Students
Help less-prepared students answer short questions to reinforce verb forms and listening comprehension, **¿Vienes tú?/¿Viene María?** Then ask longer, more meaningful questions and have these students make up their own questions.

J. ¿Quieres venir a mi fiesta esta noche?

Individual Needs

Less-prepared Students
Have less-prepared students circulate with a chart (**sí/no/porque**), and check off or make notes.

Aquí escuchamos

 TEXTBOOK CASSETTE/CD CASSETTE 1, SIDE B; CD 2, TRACKS 16-19

 TAPESCRIPT PP. 200-201

 TRB: ACTIVITY MASTER, P. 92

Después de escuchar

ANSWERS

1. a las diez de la mañana
2. hasta las once y media
3. Es la una.
4. Son las diez de la mañana
5. a las siete y media
6. a las nueve
7. a las dos y media de la tarde
8. a las cuatro y media

I. **¿Quién viene al baile con nosotros?** You and your boyfriend (girlfriend) are going to the dance for **el Día de la Independencia.** You talk about who else is coming with you. Follow the model.

> **MODELO** Ana / sí
> *Ana viene al baile.*

1. Elena y su hermano / no
2. Elvira / no
3. tú / sí
4. mis abuelos / sí
5. David y Juliana / sí
6. Uds / no

J. **¿Quieres venir a mi fiesta esta noche?** You are giving a party tonight and you are inviting people in your class. Ask five people whether they want to come. If they cannot come, they give you an excuse. Follow the model.

> **MODELO** Tú: *Rob, ¿quieres venir a mi fiesta esta noche?*
> Rob: *Sí, ¡cómo no! o: No, lo siento, pero tengo que estudiar.*

Aquí escuchamos

La hora *Some people are talking about time: class times, time zones, plans for an evening's activity, and bus schedules.*

Antes de escuchar Review the different ways of telling time (pages 207 and 208).

 A escuchar Listen twice to the conversations and pay special attention to the times given. On your activity master, write down as many of the times as you can.

Después de escuchar On your activity master, answer the following questions, based on what you heard.

Conversación 1	Conversación 2	Conversación 3	Conversación 4
1. ¿Cuándo empieza *(begins)* la clase de inglés?	3. ¿Qué hora es en Nueva York cuando son las 7:00 en Madrid?	5. ¿A qué hora van a ir a un restaurante el muchacho y la muchacha?	7. ¿A qué hora va el autobús a Santa Fe?
2. ¿Hasta qué hora es la clase?	4. ¿Qué hora es en Los Ángeles cuando son las 7:00 en Madrid?	6. ¿A qué hora es la película que van a ver?	8. ¿A qué hora llega el autobús a Santa Fe?

210 *Tercera unidad* ¿Dónde y a qué hora?

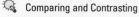 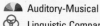 **Spanish for Spanish Speakers**

Spoken Spanish

Ask Spanish speakers to listen to the Spanish used in the **Aquí escuchamos** recording and to compare it to the Spanish they use in their communities. Encourage student to focus, for example, on the consonant s: Does it sound similar to the *s* in English? Is it barely audible (as is often the case in Spanish spoken in the Caribbean)? Is it similar to the *th* sound in English? How does it contrast with their spoken Spanish? You might want to have the rest of the class participate in this activity.

- Comparing and Contrasting
- Auditory-Musical
- Linguistic Comparisons 4.1

¡ADELANTE!

 En la fiesta del pueblo Imagine that your class is in Guatemala for the annual **Día de la Independencia**. Consult the poster on page 204.

1. Decide on three events that you would like to attend.
2. Working with two classmates, reach an agreement on one event on each person's list that you will attend together.
3. Finally, create a schedule, indicating at what time each event begins and how long you will be at the **fiesta**. Be prepared to report on your choices and your schedule.

 Un programa Work with a classmate and prepare a poster in Spanish announcing a celebration in your town or city for the Fourth of July, or for some other holiday of your choice. Write down the events for an entire day and evening as well as the times they will take place. If you wish, you can use the program on page 204 as a model.

Capítulo 9 ¡La fiesta del pueblo! **211**

ETAPA SYNTHESIS

En la fiesta del pueblo
SUGGESTION

 Follow up with a discussion of the group decisions. Elicit these from the group reporters, keeping track of the activities mentioned, how many different groups plan to attend them, and how long each group plans to spend at the **fiesta**. (Given a model, students can respond to the question, **¿Cuántas horas van a pasar en la fiesta?** by converting times expressed in such terms as **desde las diez hasta las dos** into total hours.) Have students determine which events are most popular and the average length of time to be spent at the celebration.

Categorizing
Determining Preferences

Logical-Mathematical

Un programa
FYI

 ATAJO WRITING ASSISTANT SOFTWARE

You might want to have students use this software program when doing this activity.

Additional Practice and Recycling
FYI

 WORKBOOK, PP. 107-111

For recycling and additional practice of the vocabulary, structures, and language functions presented throughout this **etapa**, you can assign the workbook activities as in-class work and/or homework. Answers to the activities are overprinted on each page of the Teacher's Edition of the Workbook.

Additional Etapa Resources

Refer to the **Etapa** Support Materials list on the opening page of this **etapa** for detailed cross-references to these assessment options.

TEACH/MODEL

¿Cómo están Uds.?

PRESENTATION

 TRANSPARENCY 44

 TEXTBOOK CASSETTE/CD CASSETTE 1, SIDE B; CD 2, TRACK 20

TAPESCRIPT P. 201

Discuss with students what details have to be settled when making plans, for example, where to go, when and where to meet. Then have them listen to the dialogue on the Textbook Cassette/CD and answer the following questions:

1. ¿Qué quiere hacer Julia?
2. ¿Adónde van Consuelo y Miguel?
3. ¿Dónde se van a encontrar con Julia?

SEGUNDA ETAPA

> **Preparación**
>
> • What kinds of special events does your town or city plan for special holidays?
>
> • If you could help plan events for a public holiday celebration, what suggestions would you make?

¿Cómo están Uds.?

Hay muchas actividades para ver (to see) *durante la fiesta del pueblo.*

Ana:	**Entonces,** ¿adónde vamos **ahora**? ¿Hay más actividades?
Julia:	**Por supuesto,** pero estoy muy **cansada.** Quisiera **descansar** por una hora.
Miguel:	Pues, yo estoy muy bien. Estoy **listo** para continuar la fiesta.
Consuelo:	Ahora es el concurso de poesía. Yo quiero ver quién gana el premio.
Julia:	Bueno, vayan Uds.
Ana:	Muy bien. ¿Dónde **nos encontramos**?
Miguel:	Delante del cine Odeón en la avenida Los Andes.
Julia:	**De acuerdo.** ¡Hasta luego!

Entonces *Then*   ahora *now*   Por supuesto *Of course*   cansada *tired*   descansar *rest*   listo *ready*
nos encontramos *we meet*   De acuerdo. *O.K., Agreed.*

212   *Tercera unidad* ¿Dónde y a qué hora?

Etapa Support Materials

• Workbook: pp. 112-115
• TRB: Textbook Activity Masters: pp. 93, 94
• Textbook Cassettes/CDs: p. 201

• Tapescript: Textbook Cassettes/CDs p. 201
• Overhead Transparency: 44
• Middle School Activities: pp. 79-81
• Lesson Plan Book: pp. 51-52

• Testing Program: Quiz pp. 94-97; Answer Key & Testing Cassettes Tapescript p. T39
• Testing Cassettes: Cassette Side A
• Computerized Testing Program: Windows™; Macintosh®
• Atajo Writing Assistant Software: Student Text p. 218

¡Te toca a ti!

A. De acuerdo

You and a classmate are planning to attend the **fiesta del pueblo** in Guatemala City. Ask your classmate what he (she) wants to do at the festival. When your classmate suggests an activity, indicate your agreement or disagreement by saying **De acuerdo. ¡Buena idea!** or **No, prefiero....** Agree on three of the activities listed. Follow the model.

> **MODELO**   ir a ver el desfile
>
> **Tú:**   *Entonces, ¿adónde vamos?*
> **Compañero(a):**   *Vamos a ver el desfile.*
> **Tú:**   *De acuerdo. ¡Buena idea!*

1. ir a la feria de las comidas regionales`
2. ir a mirar los fuegos artificiales
3. ir a ver los bailes folklóricos
4. ir al banquete
5. ir al baile popular

B. ¿A qué hora nos encontramos? ¿Y dónde?

You and your classmate have decided where you want to go. Now you need to arrange a time and place to meet. Follow the model.

> **MODELO**   10:00 / delante del cine Odeón
>
> **Compañero(a):**   *¿A qué hora nos encontramos?*
> **Tú:**   *A las 10:00.*
> **Compañero(a):**   *¿Dónde?*
> **Tú:**   *Delante del cine Odeón.*
> **Compañero(a):**   *De acuerdo, a las 10:00, delante del cine Odeón.*

1. 11:00 / delante de la catedral
2. 3:00 / delante del Club San Martín
3. 4:00 / en la avenida Los Andes, esquina de la calle Corrientes
4. 9:00 / en el Parque Nacional

❓ ¿Qué crees?

One of the shows that is common in town festivals in Spain is the **Toros de Fuego** *(Bulls of Fire)*. Do you think they are:

a) bullfights
b) bulls set on fire
c) people dressed as bulls carrying fireworks on their backs

respuesta

PRONUNCIACIÓN   THE CONSONANT ñ

The consonant ñ is pronounced like the *ni* in the English word *onions.*

Práctica

C. Listen and repeat as your teacher models the following words.

1. año
2. mañana
3. señorita
4. baño
5. señor
6. español

Capítulo 9 ¡La fiesta del pueblo!   **213**

PRACTICE/APPLY

A. De acuerdo
ANSWERS

1. Entonces, ¿adónde vamos? Vamos a la feria de las comidas regionales. De acuerdo. ¡Buena idea!
2. Entonces, ¿adónde vamos? Vamos a mirar los fuegos artificiales. No, prefiero ir al concurso de poesía.

Answers 3 through 5 will follow the same model.

B. A qué hora nos encontramos? ¿Y dónde?
ANSWERS

1. ¿A qué hora nos encontramos? A las 11:00. ¿Dónde? Delante de la catedral. De acuerdo, a las 11:00, delante de la catedral.

Answers 2 through 5 will follow the same model.

TEACH/MODEL

Pronunciación
PRESENTATION

💿 TEXTBOOK CASSETTE/CD CASSETTE 1, SIDE B; CD 2, TRACK 21

📼 TAPESCRIPT P. 201

🔆 Have students listen to the explanation for the consonant ñ on the Textbook Cassette/CD. The speaker will model the correct pronunciation of the words in **Práctica C.** Have students follow along in their texts and repeat after each word.

🔊 Auditory-Musical

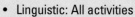

- Linguistic: All activities
- Logical-Mathematical: A, B, H
- Visual-Spatial: F
- Auditory-Musical: **Pronunciación**, C, **Aquí escuchamos**
- Interpersonal: F, G
- Intrapersonal: E

- Interpersonal Communication 1.1: A, B, G, **¿Cómo estás?**
- Interpretive Communication 1.2: A, G, D, E, F, H, **Aquí escuchamos**
- Presentational Communication 1.3: G, **Una encuesta**
- Connections with Distinctive Viewpoints 3.2: A
- Linguistic Comparisons 4.1: **Pronunciación, Nota gramatical**

PRACTICE / APPLY

D. ¿Qué hora es?

ANSWERS

1. Son las siete y veinticinco.
2. Son las doce menos ocho.
3. Son las diez y cuarto.
4. Son las tres y media.
5. Son las ocho y diez.
6. Son las dos menos cuarto.
7. Son las cinco menos veinte.
8. Son las doce y cinco.
9. Son las nueve y dieciséis.

TEACH / MODEL

Estructura

PRESENTATION

Introduce students to **estar** + adjectives of condition; bring in pictures from magazines that show different physical states or emotional conditions. Make statements about the pictures and ask students follow-up questions about themselves. For example: **Estos jugadores de básquetbol están cansados. ¿Estás tú cansado ahora?**, etc. Point out that **estar** is only used with adjectives that describe physical or mental states and emotional conditions (or feelings). Remind students that adjectives ending in **-e**, like **triste**, have the same feminine and masculine form. They only change in the plural.

Visual-Spatial

VOCABULARY EXPANSION

Introduce students to the adjectives **desilusionado, sorprendido, preocupado, nervioso, decepcionado, celoso.** Have them guess what they might mean.

Linguistic Comparisons 4.1

D. ¿Qué hora es? A friend asks what time it is. Answer according to the cues, following the model.

MODELO   2:30
Amigo(a):   ¿Qué hora es?
Tú: Son las dos y media.

1. 7:25	4. 3:30	7. 4:40
2. 11:52	5. 8:10	8. 12:05
3. 10:15	6. 1:45	9. 9:16

ESTRUCTURA

Estar + adjectives of condition

Yo estoy muy cansada.   *I am very tired.*

Yo estoy listo para   *I am ready to continue with the*
   continuar la lección.   *lesson.*

1. **Estar** is used with adjectives that describe physical or emotional conditions.

aburrido	*bored*	enojado	*angry*
cansado	*tired*	listo	*ready*
contento	*happy*	tarde	*late*
enfermo	*sick*	triste	*sad*

2. Like all adjectives, these agree in gender and number with the person they describe.

Ella está **cansada.**   Ellas están **cansadas.**

Él está **cansado.**   Ellos están **cansados.**

☞ C

Aquí practicamos

E. ¿Qué hacen? (What are they doing?) Complete the following sentences with an adjective from the above **Estructura**. Tell how you and the people mentioned feel when they do each activity. Follow the model.

MODELO   Voy al cine cuando...
          Voy al cine cuando estoy aburrido(a).

1. Voy al hospital cuando...
2. Tomamos una siesta cuando...
3. Ustedes necesitan correr cuando...
4. Mis amigos comen cuando...

214   *Tercera unidad* ¿Dónde y a qué hora?

Focus on Culture

Latin American Heroes

Most Latin American countries celebrate their independence from Spain. Ask if students know any of the leaders in the 19th century movements for independence from Spain. Mention that Simón Bolívar is known as the **Libertador** of South America. He is to South America what George Washington is to the United States. You may also want to mention Miguel Hidalgo (who led the movement for independence in Mexico) and Bernardo O'Higgins (Chile's hero), among others.

Cultural Practices and Perspectives 2.1
Connections with Other Disciplines 3.1
Cultural Comparisons 4.2

5. Mi hermana va de compras cuando...

6. Escuchamos música cuando...

7. Llamo a mi mejor amigo(a) cuando...

8. Raquel y Pablo no hablan cuando...

9. Tomas el examen cuando...

10. Voy al centro cuando...

F. ¿Estás bien? Look at the pictures and describe how these people feel today.

1. Marisol

2. Graciela

3. Santiago

4. Diego y Fernando

5. Julia

6. Benjamín y Laura

G. ¿Cómo están Uds.? Ask five of your classmates how they are feeling today. Then report to the class. Follow the model.

MODELO

Tú: *¿Cómo estás?*

Compañero(a) 1: *Estoy muy contento(a).*

PRACTICE / APPLY

E. ¿Qué hacen?

POSSIBLE ANSWERS

1. Voy al hospital cuando estoy enfermo(a).

2. Tomamos una siesta cuando estamos cansados(as).

3. Ustedes necesitan correr cuando llegan tarde.

4. Mis amigos comen cuando están listos.

5. Mi hermana va de compras cuando está aburrida.

6. Escuchamos música cuando estamos contentos(as).

7. Llamo a mi mejor amigo(a) cuando estoy aburrido(a).

8. Raquel y Pablo no hablan cuando están enojados.

9. Tomas el examen cuando estás listo.

10. Voy al centro cuando estoy contento(a).

F. ¿Estás bien?

POSSIBLE ANSWERS

1. Marisol está cansada.

2. Graciela está enferma.

3. Santiago está contento.

4. Diego y Fernando están tristes.

5. Julia está aburrida.

6. Benjamín y Laura están enojados.

EXPANSION

Write the adjectives from the Vocabulary Expansion on page T214 on the board. Practice listening comprehension by asking personal questions. For example: **¿Cómo estás cuando no tienes clases? ¿Aburrido?** Start out with simple questions and work up to more complicated ones such as, **Si tú llegas a casa a la 1:00 de la mañana, ¿cómo reacciona tu mamá?**

◢◣ Bodily-Kinesthetic

Estructura

PRESENTATION

Students are now familiar with the basic notion of possessive adjectives, so the transition to the third person should be fairly easy. Begin discussing third-person possessive adjectives by asking: **¿De quién es el libro?** Students respond: **El libro es de (Juan).** You say: **Sí, es su libro.** After a few more similar examples, put together objects belonging to two students and ask: **¿De quiénes son los... ?** Students respond: **Los... son de Pedro y Miguel. You say: Sí, son sus...,** etc.

Work your way through various objects, alternating singular and plural things to underline the fact that the *possessive adjectives agree with the objects,* not the possessor(s). To make sure that they understand how to use these possessives, ask questions in English such as: "How do you say *their house* or *his cars* in Spanish?" If they answer incorrectly, write a few examples on the board and point out again how these adjectives agree.

Visual-Spatial

Linguistic Comparisons 4.1

ESTRUCTURA

Possessive adjectives: Third person

—¿Es la bicicleta de Vicente? *Is it Vicente's bike?*
—Sí, es **su** bicicleta. *Yes, it's his bike.*

Possessive Adjectives

		Singular		Plural
él, ella	**su**	his, her, its	**sus**	his, her, its
ellos, ellas	**su**	their	**sus**	their

1. Like other possessive adjectives, **su** and **sus** agree in gender and number with the noun they modify.

2. **Su** and **sus** have several English equivalents: **your** (formal; singular and plural), **his, her, its,** and **their.** To clarify who the possessor is, the phrases **de él (ella), de Ud., de Uds.,** and **de ellos (ellas)** can be used instead of **su** and **sus.**

—Es **su** coche? *Is it her car?*
—Sí, es **el coche de ella.** *Yes, it's her car.*

Aquí practicamos

H. Sí, es su... Answer the questions affirmatively, following the model.

MODELO   ¿Es el cuaderno de Pedro?
Sí, es su cuaderno.

1. ¿Es el libro de Ana María?   2. ¿Son las llaves de Antonio?   3. ¿Son las amigas de Raquel y Susana?

4. ¿Es el perro de Pilar?

5. ¿Es el gato de Mariano y Adela?

6. ¿Son las hijas de Marcos y Carmen?

7. ¿Es la hermana de Raúl?

8. ¿Es la casa de Benito?

Aquí escuchamos

¿Cómo están? *A man asks five people how they are. They answer and say why they feel this way.*

Antes de escuchar Review the adjectives of condition or mood (page 214). Then, answer the following questions.

1. What verb is used in Spanish with the adjectives listed to describe how a person feels?

2. What ending does the adjective usually have if referring to a male? to a female?

 A escuchar Listen twice to the conversation. On your activity master, write next to each name mentioned the adjective that the person uses to describe how she (he) feels.

	Adjective
Alejandra	
Beatriz	
Patricia	
Mónica	
Raimundo	
Ramón	
Raquel	
Roberto	

Capítulo 9 ¡La fiesta del pueblo! **217**

PRACTICE/APPLY

H. Sí, es su...
ANSWERS
1. Sí, es su libro.
2. Sí, son sus llaves.
3. Sí, son sus amigas.
4. Sí, es su perro.
5. Sí, es su gato.
6. Sí, son sus hijas.
7. Sí, es su hermana.
8. Sí, es su casa.

EXPANSION
Continue the activity by asking questions using various objects that belong to students.

▲ Linguistic
Visual-Spatial

Aquí escuchamos

💿	TEXTBOOK CASSETTE/CD CASSETTE 1, SIDE B; CD 2, TRACK 22
📼	TAPESCRIPT PP. 201-202
📕	TRB: ACTIVITY MASTER, P. 93

Antes de escuchar
ANSWERS
1. estar
2. **o** referring to a male
   a referring to a female

Después de escuchar
ANSWERS
1. She feels sick because it is cold, she doesn't sleep well, and she doesn't eat well.
2. Ramón is happy because his father is going to buy him a car.
3. She is worried because she has two exams tomorrow and she has a lot of work to do.
4. He wants a raise and he's mad.
5. Alejandra is sad because there are no more tickets available for the concert.

☀ **Spanish for Spanish Speakers**

Vocabulary Expansion–Antonyms

Have Spanish speakers listen carefully to the **Aquí escuchamos** recording and write down five words they hear for which they know or want to find antonyms. Tell them not to limit themselves to just one or two parts of speech, but to choose nouns, verbs, adjectives, adverbs, prepositions, etc. Then give students copies of the dialogue from the Tapescript and have them work with a partner to combine their lists and

create a transformed dialogue. Have Spanish speakers and other class volunteers role-play the dialogue with the new words for the rest of the class.

✏ Creating

▲ Auditory-Musical
Linguistic

⊕ Presentational Communication 1.3

ETAPA SYNTHESIS

¿Cómo estás?

Individual Needs

Pair up a less-prepared and a more-prepared student to work together on this oral activity.

Una encuesta

FYI

 ATAJO WRITING ASSISTANT SOFTWARE

You might want to have students use this software program when doing this activity.

Additional Practice and Recycling

FYI

WORKBOOK, PP. 112-115

For recycling and additional practice of the vocabulary, structures, and language functions presented throughout this **etapa**, you can assign the workbook activities as in-class work and/or homework. Answers to the activities are overprinted on each page of the Teacher's Edition of the Workbook.

Después de escuchar On your activity master, answer the following questions in English, based on what you heard. Use the notes that you took while listening.

1. How does Raquel feel and why does she feel this way?
2. Which person is happy and what is the reason?
3. What does Patricia say about the mood she is in?
4. What does Raimundo want and how is he?
5. What about Alejandra? How does she feel?

¡ADELANTE!

 ¿Cómo estás? Tell a partner how you feel when you carry out the following activities. Then he (she) tells you about his (her) feelings. Follow the model.

MODELO
Cuando voy a un concierto...
Cuando voy a un concierto, estoy contento(a).

1. Cuando corro...
2. Cuando voy a clase...
3. Cuando escucho música...
4. Cuando estudio...
5. Cuando hablo con mis amigos...
6. Cuando recibo una F...

 Una encuesta Take a poll of four classmates.

1. Write down a sentence or two about how each of your classmates feels today.
2. Include the reason each person gives for feeling that way.
3. Then, organize a chart based on your findings, grouping the names of your classmates by the feeling they expressed. Be prepared to report back to the class.

EN LÍNEA

Connect with the Spanish-speaking world! Access the *¡Ya verás! Gold* home page for Internet activities related to this chapter.

http://yaveras.heinle.com

Additional Etapa Resources

Refer to the **Etapa** Support Materials list on the opening page of this **etapa** for detailed cross-references to these assessment options.

VOCABULARIO

Para charlar

Para pedir la hora
¿Qué hora es?
¿A qué hora?
¿Cuándo?

Para dar la hora
a la medianoche
a las cinco de la
  mañana
a las nueve de la noche
a la una de la tarde
al mediodía
desde la(s)… hasta
  la(s)…
entre la(s)… y la(s)…
Es la una y media.
Son las dos y cuarto.
Son las tres menos
  veinte.

Temas y contextos

La fiesta del pueblo
un baile popular
unos bailes folklóricos
un concurso de poesía
un desfile
el Día de la Independencia
una feria
unos fuegos artificiales
una gran fiesta
la misa de Acción de
  Gracias
un premio

Vocabulario general

Verbos
anunciar
celebrar
descansar
estar
preparar
venir

Adjetivos
aburrido(a)
cansado(a)
contento(a)
enfermo(a)
enojado(a)
hispano(a)
listo(a)
tarde
triste

Otras expresiones
ahora
¡Buena idea!
De acuerdo.
¿Dónde nos encontramos?
entonces
la mayoría de
el mejor
por supuesto
su
sus
la tarea
todo(a)
una vez al año

Capítulo 9 ¡La fiesta del pueblo! **219**

CHAPTER WRAP-UP

Vocabulario
SUGGESTION
Plan activities for a traditional celebration from the Spanish-speaking world, such as **el 5 de mayo** from Mexico. If students have a celebration they wish to know more about, have them do research and then plan activities for it.

Improvised Conversation
SUGGESTION

 TEXTBOOK CASSETTE/CD CASSETTE 1, SIDE B; CD 2, TRACK 23

 TAPESCRIPT P. 202

 TRB: ACTIVITY MASTER, P. 94

 Have students listen to the conversation in which three people make plans to meet at the town fair.

Listening Skills Development
FYI

 LAB MANUAL PP. 58-63

 LAB CASSETTE SIDE A, B; CD 5, TRACKS 1-9

 TAPESCRIPT: LAB PROGRAM, 87-95

It is now appropriate to work through the lab manual activities and their accompanying recordings in class or in the language laboratory.

Resources for Spanish-speaking Students
FYI

 WORKBOOK FOR SPANISH-SPEAKING STUDENTS: PP. 53-58

 ANSWER KEY TO SSS WORKBOOK PP. 49-50

Activities specially written to meet the needs of Spanish-speaking students are available in these workbooks for the reinforcement and extension of the topics and language in this chapter.

Additional Chapter Resources

Refer to the Chapter Support Materials list on the opening page of this chapter for detailed cross-references to *¡Ya verás! Gold*'s student-centered technology components and various assessment options.

Spanish for Spanish Speakers

Keeping a Vocabulary Notebook
Remind Spanish-speaking students to add words and expressions from this vocabulary section to the problematic spelling combination categories and personal new vocabulary lists in their notebooks.

PRACTICE / APPLY

Los muchos colores del júbilo: las fiestas en el mundo hispano

SUGGESTION

Have students discuss any local festivals or celebrations they attend. What kinds of events are there? What kinds of attractions are there? Who attends these celebrations? Who participates in these celebrations? Do visitors come from other countries?

Antes de leer

POSSIBLE ANSWERS

1. The word **júbilo** means jubilation or joy, festival, celebration, parade.
2. Students may have heard of **Día de los Muertos** (Day of the Dead, celebrated November 1) from Mexico or Guatemala. Some students may also know Carnaval which takes place in many Catholic countries before the start of Lent.
3. Answers will vary.

Los muchos colores del júbilo

Reading Strategies

- Using the title and the photos to predict content
- Scanning for specific information
- Activating background knowledge

Antes de leer

1. Look at the title. Can you guess the meaning of the word *júbilo*? Look at the photos, what do you think the reading will be about?

2. Scan the reading and take note of the different festivals mentioned. Are you familiar with any of them?

3. What festivals are held in your area? What is the purpose of these festivals?

Públicas o privadas, religiosas o seculares, las fiestas de un pueblo dicen mucho sobre su historia y temperamento. Tanto España como los países en Latinoamérica celebran muchísimas fiestas y carnavales, que simbolizan tanto la gran imaginación de sus ciudadanos como la complicada historia de sus tradiciones.

Entre las más hermosas festividades hispanas están las celebraciones del Día de los Muertos. En Guatemala, en la provincia de Santiago de Sadatepeques, el pueblo eleva gigantescas cometas para recordar a sus muertos. Estas "mensajeras" suben al cielo llevando en sus colas mensajes a los muertos de la familia. En México, es tradicional preparar golosinas que se ofrecen al espíritu del muerto para complacerlo durante esta celebración.

Varios países latinos celebran el carnaval en febrero; otra celebración llena de colorido, música y diversión. La gente—niños, adolescentes y adultos—se disfrazan. Participan en desfiles y concursos de disfraces. También hay muchas fiestas de disfraces en casas privadas y en clubes.

220 *Tercera unidad* ¿Dónde y a qué hora?

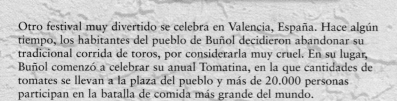

Otro festival muy divertido se celebra en Valencia, España. Hace algún tiempo, los habitantes del pueblo de Buñol decidieron abandonar su tradicional corrida de toros, por considerarla muy cruel. En su lugar, Buñol comenzó a celebrar su anual Tomatina, en la que cantidades de tomates se llevan a la plaza del pueblo y más de 20.000 personas participan en la batalla de comida más grande del mundo.

Guía para la lectura

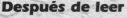

recuerda	*remembers*
eleva	*flies*
cometas	*kites*
colas	*tails*
mensajeras	*messengers*
golosinas	*sweets, candy*
complacerlo	*to please (him/her)*
llena de colorido	*full of color, colorful*
diversión	*fun*
se disfrazan	*dress in costumes, disguises*
disfraces	*costumes, disguises*
concursos	*competitions*
corrida de toros	*bullfight*

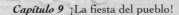

Después de leer

1. Did you know anything about these festivals? Did you have any previous opinions about them? Have your opinions changed? If so, how?

2. Think about holidays or festivals celebrated in the United States. Make lists of differences and similarities between the festivals mentioned in the reading and those you're familiar with.

3. How did Buñol's *tomatina* begin? Would you enjoy participating in the *tomatina*? Why or why not?

Después de leer
POSSIBLE ANSWERS
1. Answers will vary.
2. Students can discuss such U.S. holidays as Halloween, Fourth of July, and Mardi Gras in New Orleans and compare them to the festivals in the reading.
3. Buñuel's Tomatina is a huge food fight using tomatoes. The townspeople decided to replace bull fights with tomato fights.

¡Sigamos adelante! Resource

FYI

 LESSON PLAN BOOK: P. 54

You might find it helpful to refer to the Lesson Plan Book before you and your students begin the end-of-unit materials.

PRACTICE / APPLY

A. Un día en la vida de...

SUGGESTION

 To prepare for this role-play, have each student write down his (her) daily schedule, including the time and place where each activity occurs. Suggest that students include a map to go with the directions to their partners' houses.

Individual Needs

Less-prepared Students

You may want to review how to give directions to a place using the formal commands presented in Chapter 8. (See pages 196-198.) Students can make a list of verbs, vocabulary expressions, and street names to get them started. Remind them to use the verbs **ir**, **cruzar**, and **doblar**.

B. El festival

SUGGESTION

You can review the present tense forms of the verb **querer** and its use with an infinitive to indicate the events and activities students want to do.

EXPANSION

Have students plan a series of events for celebrating some local festival or special day in their lives. In small groups students can plan an itinerary listing the events, their locations, and the time of day that each occurs. You can have students create a poster to announce their special celebration.

Creating
Sequencing
Synthesizing

Conversemos un rato

A. Un día en la vida de... Role-play the following situations with another classmate.

1. You and your partner have decided to switch lives for an afternoon. You will take over your partner's classes, afternoon activities, and you will eat dinner at your partner's home. Your partner will take over your day. Give each other the information needed to complete your routine.

a. Tell your partner the rest of your class schedule. Don't forget to tell him/her where and when the classes are.

b. Give your partner your after-school routine and explain where and when each activity occurs.

c. Give your partner the directions to your house so he/she can eat dinner there tonight. Be sure to tell him/her what time to be there.

d. Give your partner any other information you think he/she might need.

2. Now switch partners with another pair of classmates and tell your new partner about a day in your first partner's life. Which daily routine do you prefer; your day or your partner's day?

B. El festival You and two of your classmates are in Guatemala for the annual festival. Using the poster on page 204, plan your activities for the day.

1. Decide on at least two different activities to do together.

2. Choose one activity that each of you will do alone.

3. Make plans to meet later in the day. Set a time and a place where you will meet.

222 *Tercera unidad* ¿Dónde y a qué hora?

Focus on Culture

Fiestas patronales

Most cities and towns in the Spanish-speaking world have annual festivals that may celebrate a religious holiday like a patron saint's day, a local event like the arrival of the harvest season, or independence day, a political event. Have students think of any local celebrations in their hometown that might compare to **Día de la Independencia** in Guatemala.

 Cultural Comparisons 4.2

MULTIPLE INTELLIGENCES

- Auditory-Musical
- Bodily-Kinesthetic
- Interpersonal

 The Standards

- Presentational Communication 1.3

Taller de escritores

Writing a persuasive description

Create a short description of your city or town aimed at Spanish speakers who might be considering vacationing or working there.

Writing Strategy
- Group brainstorming using clusters

¡Bienvenidos a mi pueblo!

Cuando estás en mi pueblo estás en casa. Las personas son simpáticas. Es pequeño pero tiene de todo: en el centro, por ejemplo, hay una oficina de correos, dos bancos, restaurantes, librerías, y la estación de policía. También hay hoteles, dos hospitales, bibliotecas y supermercados. Tiene un aeropuerto, una estación de trenes y de autobuses. Mi pueblo está cerca de la playa.

A. Reflexión In a small group as assigned by your teacher, brainstorm the topic; that is, think about all the points you would like to include and share them with your group. Then, working in the same group, form clusters by relating the topics to the major points you wish to cover.

B. Primer borrador Write a first draft of the description.

C. Revisión con un(a) compañero(a) Exchange descriptions with a classmate. Read each other's work and comment on it, based on these questions. What aspect of the description is the most interesting? What aspect of the town/city can you most easily visualize? Is the writing appropriate for its audience? Does the writing reflect the task assigned? What aspect of the writing would you like to have clarified or made more complete?

D. Versión final Revise your first draft at home, based on the feedback you received. Check grammar, spelling, punctuation, and accent marks. Bring your final draft to class.

E. Carpeta Your teacher may choose to place your work in your portfolio, display it on a bulletin board, or use it to evaluate your progress.

223

MULTIPLE INTELLIGENCES
- Interpersonal
- Linguistic
- Visual-Spatial

 The Standards
- Interpretive Communication 1.2
- Presentational Communication 1.3

☀ **Spanish for Spanish Speakers**

Summarizing
Have students go through each of the activities that accompany the readings in this program. Then they can summarize the readings in Spanish for extra writing practice. They might also create a list of new vocabulary they find in the readings to include in their Vocabulary notebook.

Taller de escritores Resource

FYI

 ATAJO WRITING ASSISTANT SOFTWARE

You might want to have students use this software program when writing the first draft and final version of their writing assignment. Tell them that the following language references in **Atajo** are directly related to and will be helpful to their work.

Phrases: Describing objects; Describing places; Expressing location
Vocabulary: City; Direction & distance; Means of transportation
Grammar: Prepositions: **a**; Verbs: Use of **estar**, Use of **haber**

A. Reflexión
SUGGESTION
It might be helpful for students to draw a rough map of their town and use it as a point of departure for their description. You can use the map of the students' town to compare to the map of a typical Hispanic town on page 166 of the textbook.

 Visual-Spatial
Cultural Comparisons 4.2

B. Primer borrador
SUGGESTION
Remind students that the adjectives and nouns must agree in gender and number.

C. Revisión con un(a) compañero(a)
SUGGESTION
Model a peer review with the whole class by showing a sample description on a transparency and answering the six revision questions together. Remind students to start their feedback with something positive and to include some constructive suggestions to improve the description.

Para empezar
SUGGESTION
Ask students if they have ever taken a trip to a place located in a different time zone. Where? Also ask them if they have friends or family who live in a different time zone. It might be helpful to have a globe in the classroom to further illustrate the concept of time zones.

▲▲ Visual-Spatial

Conexión con la geografía

Los husos horarios

Para empezar Nuestro planeta tiene veinticuatro husos horarios (zonas de tiempo) porque hay veinticuatro horas en el día. Mientras el planeta **da vueltas**, las horas del día pasan de un huso horario a otro. Por ejemplo, en el **dibujo** siguiente, la hora "mediodía" pasa de Nueva York a Chicago, y luego de Chicago a Denver. Cuando es mediodía en Denver, es la una en Chicago y son las dos en Nueva York.

El mapa tiene todos los husos horarios del mundo. Siempre es la misma hora en las ciudades que están en el mismo huso horario. Con este mapa, es posible contar la diferencia de horas entre dos ciudades que están muy lejos.

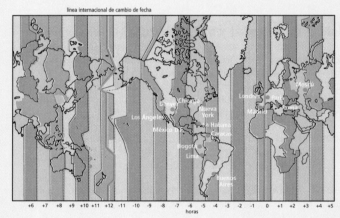

Países que tienen diferencias de media hora con los husos horarios al lado, o que no participan en el sistema de husos horarios.

da vueltas *rotates*   dibujo *drawing*

224   *Tercera unidad* ¿Dónde y a qué hora?

MULTIPLE   INTELLIGENCES

• Linguistic
• Logical-Mathematical
• Visual-Spatial

A. Cuando es la una...

Answer the following questions based on the drawings and the reading passage.

1. Cuando es la una en Nueva York, ¿qué hora es en Denver?
2. Cuando es la una en Nueva York, ¿qué hora es en Los Ángeles?
3. Cuando es mediodía en Denver, ¿dónde es la una?
4. Cuando es mediodía en Denver, ¿dónde son las once?

B. Los horarios de las ciudades

1. ¿Cuáles ciudades latinoamericanas están en el mismo huso horario que Nueva York?
2. ¿Hay otras ciudades europeas que están en el mismo huso horario que Madrid? ¿Cómo se llaman?
3. ¿En qué huso horario está tu ciudad?
4. ¿Cuántos husos horarios hay entre Nueva York y Madrid? ¿entre Nueva York y Los Ángeles? ¿entre Los Ángeles y Madrid? ¿entre Londres y Madrid?

C. ¿A qué hora...?

Work with a partner and find out at what time he or she performs the following daily activities. Make a list of the activities and the time your partner does each activity. Use your knowledge of time zones to imagine what people in other parts of the world do at that hour.

MODELO comer el desayuno

> Estudiante 1: ¿A qué hora comes el desayuno?
> Estudiante 2: Desayuno a las siete de la mañana.
> Estudiante 1: Cuando tú desayunas, la gente en París...

1. estudiar
2. ir a la escuela
3. llegar a casa
4. estar cansado(a)
5. descansar en la cama
6. mirar la televisión
7. comer en la cafetería
8. pasar el tiempo con amigos

¡Sigamos adelante! **225**

A. Cuando es la una...

ANSWERS
1. 11:00
2. 10:00
3. Chicago
4. Los Angeles

EXPANSION

Use the map to discuss other Spanish-speaking cities and their time zones, such as México D.F., Bogotá, Lima, Caracas. Then have students guess about other cities not listed on this map, for example, San Juan, Puerto Rico; Sevilla, España; Santo Domingo, La República Dominicana; San José, Costa Rica; and others. Students can use the maps in their textbook as a reference.

 Logical-Mathematical
Visual-Spatial

B. Los horarios de las ciudades

ANSWERS
1. Bogotá, Lima, Havana
2. Londrés
3. Answers will vary.
4. 5, 3, 8, 0

C. ¿A qué hora?

EXPANSION

 Students can reverse the task in this activity and find out what time it is here when people in another part of the world may be doing some of their daily activities. Have students use their knowledge of time zones and daily activities to speculate about different countries. You may want to limit this activity to one or two locations. Follow the model.

Student 1	Student 2
Cuando la gente de Londres...	Aquí
come el desayuno	Son las...
toma la siesta	Son las...
come la comida	Son las...
come la cena	Son las...
Se acuesta	Son las...

TEACH/MODEL

Costa Rica

PRESENTATION

Costa Rica has many natural attractions, fascinating wildlife, and enlightened policies for conservation. Many scientists and conservation-minded tourists visit Costa Rica every year, making it a leader in "ecotourism" (tourism that tries to leave minimal impact on wildlife and natural preserves). National parks cover almost 12% of the country, and forest preserves and Indian reservations increase the protected land to 27% of the country. Tourism now surpasses bananas as the main source of foreign exchange, drawing more than 800,00 foreign visitors each year, and providing jobs to thousands.

EXPANSION

Costa Rica became independent from Spain in 1821 and united with Nicaragua, El Salvador, Guatemala, and Honduras to form the Central American Federation until 1839. The blue and white stripes were taken from the flag of that federation and represent the geographic position of Costa Rica between the Pacific Ocean and Caribbean Sea. The red was added in 1848 to commemorate the revolutionary activity in France that year.

Connections with Other Disciplines 3.1

FYI

Did you know that Costa Ricans call themselves **ticos**?

Vistas
de los países hispanos

Costa Rica

Capital: San José

Ciudades principales: Alajuela, Cartago, Heredia

Población: 2.800.000

Idiomas: español

Área territorial: 50.700 km^2

Clima: cálido y húmedo, temperatura media anual de 25º a 27º

Moneda: colón

cálido *warm*

EXPLORA

Find out more about Costa Rica! Access the **Nuestros vecinos** page on the *¡Ya verás! Gold* web site for a list of URLs.

http://yaveras.heinle.com/vecinos.htm

226 *Tercera unidad* ¿Dónde y a qué hora?

MULTIPLE  INTELLIGENCES

- Visual-Spatial

The Standards

- Connections with Distinctive Viewpoints 3.2

En la comunidad

Paul Kearney: **En caso de una emergencia**

"After being burned in a fire as a child, you would think the last career I would choose would be that of firefighter. However, later in life I knew that's what I wanted to be because I wanted to help people who were in trouble.

My desire to help people suits my profession: I know a lot about fires, a lot about rescue procedures, and a lot about how to talk to both English- and Spanish-speaking people during emergencies. My Spanish isn't polished, but it's still very useful when I need to know things like: Who's in the building? Are there any pets to rescue? How did the fire start? What else is flammable in the building? And, even, what's on the other side of a particular window or door, in case there's a danger I'm unaware of."

¡Ahora te toca a ti!

With a partner, find out who the "emergency specialists" are in your city or town. Research who is in charge and how to reach them. Find the phone number for the fire department, the police department, a local hospital, or other emergency specialists in your community. Give the phone numbers in Spanish and give simple directions for how a Spanish-speaking person might contact each emergency specialist in the case of an emergency.

¡Sigamos adelante! **227**

UNIDAD 4

Setting the Context

Unit 4 features Elena González, a young high school student from Madrid. The basic task of this unit is getting around a city. Chapter 10 centers on making plans for typical city activities (shopping, errands, meeting people). Chapter 11 deals with the Madrid **metro** system. Chapter 12 focuses on cars and taxis.

UNIDAD 4

Vamos al centro

Objectives

In this unit you will learn:

- to make plans for various activities in town
- to talk about the future
- to use the Madrid subway
- to give directions for using the Madrid subway

228 *Cuarta unidad*

Unit Support Materials

- Workbook: **Aquí leemos** pp. 158-160
- Lab Manual: **Ya llegamos** pp. 82-84
- Lab Program: Cassette Side B; CD 10, Tracks 11-14
- Tapescript: Lab Program pp. 124-126
- TRB: Unit Grammar Review Masters: pp. 31-37; Answer Key pp. 55-57
- Lesson Plan Book: **¡Sigamos adelante!** p. 72
- Workbook for Spanish-speaking Students: pp. 79, 80
- Testing Program: Unit Test pp. 140-144; Answer Key & Testing Cassettes Tapescript pp. T57, T58; Oral Assessment pp. T59; Portfolio Assessment pp. Pxiii-Pxv
- Testing Cassettes: Cassette Side B
- Computerized Testing Program: Windows™; Macintosh®
- Atajo Writing Assistant Software: Student Text pp. 292, 293; Workbook p. 159
- Video Program: Cassette 2, 21:02-24:49
- Video Guide: Videoscript p. 52; Activities pp. 121-122
- Internet Explorations: Student Text p. 296

UNIT WARM-UP

Planning Strategy

 WORKBOOK, P. 121

If you do not assign the Planning Strategy for homework, do it in class by having students role play inviting a friend to go somewhere. Then have them invite a friend's parents to do something, using appropriate forms of address. Discuss modes of transportation in small towns and cities. Note the kinds of information you need in order to use each form of transportation.

Presentational Communication 1.3

¿Qué ves?

- Who are these people in the photographs?
- Where are they going? How?
- Where do you think they are?

 ¿Quieres ir al centro?
10
Primera etapa: ¿Para qué?
Segunda etapa: ¿Cuándo vamos?
Tercera etapa: ¿Cómo prefieres ir, en coche o a pie?

 Vamos a tomar el metro
11
Primera etapa: ¿En qué dirección?
Segunda etapa: En la taquilla

 ¿Cómo vamos?
12
Primera etapa: ¡Vamos a tomar un taxi!
Segunda etapa: En la agencia de viajes

229

Spanish for Spanish Speakers

Examining the Photos

Have Spanish speakers mention, in Spanish, what they see. Ask them to tell what the people in the various photos are doing. Write new vocabulary on the board to help them with the spelling.

Visual-Spatial

CAPÍTULO 10

OBJECTIVES

Functions
- Making plans to go downtown
- Identifying what to do in town
- Talking about when and how to go downtown

Context
- Cities and towns

Accuracy
- The immediate future: **Ir a +** infinitive
- **Tener ganas de +** infinitive
- The days of the week
- Present tense of **hacer** and **poder**

Pronunciation
- The consonant **h**

CHAPTER WARM-UP

Setting the Context

In preparation for their learning about planning excursions and activities to do downtown, tell students to walk around the room, greeting other students. Have them find a person they do not know well and work with her (him). Then tell them that one of the pair should say what she (he) is going to do after school. The other student will first confirm her (his) understanding by paraphrasing what the partner said, and then tell the partner what she (he) is going to do. Ask some of the students to report on what other students do after school. Ask students if they often go downtown with their friends. What do they do there?

▲▲ Bodily-Kinesthetic

⊛ Interpretive Communication 1.2

¿Quieres ir al centro?

—¿Quieres ir al centro conmigo?
—Sí, tengo que comprar algo.

Objectives

- making plans to go downtown
- identifying what to do in town
- talking about when and how to go downtown

230 *Cuarta unidad* Vamos al centro

Chapter Support Materials

- Lab Manual: pp. 67-72
- Lab Program: Cassette Side A; CD 5, Tracks 10-18
- TRB: Textbook Activity Masters: p. 95
- Textbook Cassettes/CDs: Cassette 1, Side B; CD 2, Track 31
- Tapescript: Lab Program pp. 99-107; Textbook Cassettes/CDs p. 204
- Middle School Activities: pp. 82-85
- Workbook for Spanish-speaking Students: pp. 61-66
- Answer Key to SSS Workbook: pp. 19-20
- Practice Software: Windows™; Macintosh®

- Testing Program: Chapter Test pp. 117-121; Answer Key & Testing Cassettes Tapescript p. T49; Oral Assessment p. T50
- Testing Cassettes: Cassette Side B
- Computerized Testing Program: Windows™; Macintosh®
- Video Program: Cassette 1, 00:00-8:24
- Video Guide: Videoscript pp. 43-46 Activities pp. 115-116
- **Mundos hispanos 1**
- Internet Activities: Student Text p. 253

PRIMERA ETAPA

Preparación

- What do you do when you go downtown?
- Why do you go there?
- How do you invite someone to go with you?

¿Para qué?

Estas personas tienen planes en el centro.

Miguel: Voy al centro para ver a mis amigos.
Sandra: Ah, tienes una **cita** con tus amigos.

Andrés: Voy al centro para **ir de compras.**
Adela: Ah, quieres comprar algo.

Cristina: Voy al centro para ir al cine.
Javier: Ah, **tienes ganas de** ver una película.

Natalia: Voy al centro para **hacer un
          mandado** para mi madre.
Pedro: Ah, **debes** hacer un mandado.

¿Para qué? *For what reason?*   **cita** *date*   **ir de compras** *to go shopping*   **tienes ganas de** *you feel like*
hacer un mandado *do an errand*   **debes** *you must*

Capítulo 10 ¿Quieres ir al centro? **231**

TEACH/MODEL

¿Para qué?

PRESENTATION

 TRANSPARENCIES 46 AND 47

 TEXTBOOK CASSETTE/CD CASSETTE 1,
SIDE B; CD 2, TRACK 24

 TAPESCRIPT P. 202

Have students look at the drawings on the transparency while
they listen to the short conversations
on the Textbook Cassette/CD. After
each conversation ask questions, moving from comprehension of the
dialogue (**¿Adónde va para ver a sus
amigos?**) to personalized variations
(**¿Adónde vas tú para ver a tus amigos?**)

Auditory-Musical
Visual-Spatial

FYI

This **etapa** shows that an idea can
be expressed in more than one way.
Students need not learn to produce
all of the expressions. They should
understand both forms and be able
to use one of the expressions for each
activity. It is important for all students
to realize that there is always more
than one way to express an idea.

Individual Needs

Less-prepared Students
Have less-prepared students
concentrate on one of the
expressions, incorporate it well,
and then learn the others.

More-prepared Students
Encourage more-prepared students
to learn each expression actively and
to interchange them.

Etapa Support Materials

- Workbook: pp. 122-126
- Textbook Cassettes/CDs: Cassette 1, Side B;
  CD 2, Track 24
- Tapescript: Textbook Cassettes/CDs pp. 202
- Overhead Transparencies: 46, 47
- Middle School Activities: p. 86
- Lesson Plan Book: pp. 55-56

- Testing Program: Quiz pp. 109-111; Answer Key &
  Testing Cassettes Tapescript p. T26
- Testing Cassettes: Cassette Side B
- Computerized Testing Program: Windows™;
  Macintosh®
- Atajo Writing Assistant Software: Student
  Text p. 240; Workbook pp. 122-126

VOCABULARY EXPANSION
Additional questions to use while presenting and practicing this new vocabulary include: **¿Vas al centro a veces para ir de compras? ¿Con quién? ¿Adónde vas? ¿Qué compras? ¿Te gusta el cine? ¿Tienes ganas de ver una película esta noche? ¿Haces mandados para tu madre? ¿Vas a la oficina de correos? ¿Y al supermercado? ¿Te gusta dar paseos? ¿Dónde? ¿Qué vas a hacer después de la escuela hoy? ¿Tienes ganas de ir al centro para ver las tiendas?**

Remember that the idea during the presentation of this **etapa** is to familiarize students with the meanings and basic structures of these expressions, not to get them to produce complete sentences.

🔺 Linguistic

Daniel:	¿Para qué vas al centro?
Noemí:	Voy al centro para **dar un paseo.**

Una situación

Elena:	¿Francisco, quieres ir al centro conmigo?
Francisco:	¿Para qué?
Elena:	Para hacer un mandado para mi padre. Tengo que ir a la farmacia.
Francisco:	Mm, bueno, quiero comprar un disco compacto. ¡Vamos!
Elena:	De acuerdo. ¡Vamos!

dar un paseo *take a walk*

¡Te toca a ti!

A. **¿Para qué va al centro?** Your teacher wants to know why the following students are going downtown. On the basis of the following drawings, explain why. Follow the model.

> **MODELO**   ¿Para qué va María al centro?
> *Ella va al centro para ver a una amiga.*

232   *Cuarta unidad* Vamos al centro

☀ Spanish for Spanish Speakers

Places and Reasons to go Downtown
Ask Spanish speakers for variations to the places and reasons young people might go downtown. They may know how to pronounce these variations, but not how to write them. Help them with the spelling of these variations by writing them on the board or overhead. Have them focus on the more difficult spelling combinations such as the **c** in **cita** and **cine**, the **h** and **c** in **hacer** and the **s** in **paseo**.

MULTIPLE INTELLIGENCES

- Linguistic: All activities
- Logical-Mathematical: D, G
- Visual-Spatial: A, B, H
- Auditory-Musical: **Pronunciación**, C, **Aquí escuchamos**
- Interpersonal: **¿Quieres ir al centro conmigo?**
- Intrapersonal: **Este fin de semana tengo ganas de...**

1. ¿Para qué va Vicente al centro?

2. ¿Para qué va Anita al centro?

3. ¿Para qué va José al centro?

4. ¿Para qué va Laura al centro?

5. ¿Para qué van Patricio y Julia al centro?

6. ¿Para qué van Mario y Luis al centro?

Capítulo 10 ¿Quieres ir al centro? **233**

B. ¿Quieres ir al centro conmigo?

SUGGESTION

 Call on pairs of students to perform one of the situations for the class.

ANSWERS
The answers to this activity require no grammatical changes. Students replace **a la oficina de correos** with these cues, following the model:
1. a la biblioteca
2. a la librería
3. a la panadería
4. al banco
5. a la farmacia

TEACH/MODEL

Pronunciación

TEXTBOOK CASSETTE/CD CASSETTE 1, SIDE B; CD 2, TRACK 25

TAPESCRIPT PP. 202-203

Have students listen to the explanation for **h** on the Textbook Cassette/CD. The speaker will model the correct pronunciation of the words in **Práctica C**. Have students follow along in their texts and repeat after each word.

Auditory-Musical

B. ¿Quieres ir al centro conmigo? You are going downtown and invite a friend to go along. When you explain the reason for going, your friend decides to accompany you. Use the following drawings to explain your reasons for going. Follow the model.

MODELO		
	Tú:	¿Quieres ir al centro conmigo?
	Amigo(a):	¿Para qué?
	Tú:	Tengo que ir a la oficina de correos.
	Amigo(a):	Bueno. Vamos.

1.   2.

3.   4.   5.

PRONUNCIACIÓN THE CONSONANT **h**

In Spanish, unlike English, the letter **h** is always silent.

Práctica

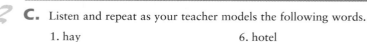

C. Listen and repeat as your teacher models the following words.

1. hay	6. hotel
2. hospital	7. hablar
3. hola	8. hispano
4. hoy	9. ahora
5. hace	10. hora

En el centro de Madrid, España

ESTRUCTURA

The immediate future: Ir a + infinitive

Voy a comer.	*I am going to eat.*
Vamos a estudiar.	*We are going to study.*
Vas a dar un paseo.	*You are going to take a walk.*
¿Qué van a hacer esta tarde?	*What are they going to do this afternoon?*

1. One way to express a future action, especially one that will occur in the near future, is to use a present tense form of **ir** + **a** + infinitive. This structure is equivalent to the English *to be going to* + verb.

2. To make a sentence or question that uses **ir a** + infinitive negative, place **no** before the conjugated form of **ir**.

No voy a comer en el centro.	*I'm not going to eat downtown.*
Ellos **no van a estudiar**.	*They're not going to study.*

Capítulo 10 ¿Quieres ir al centro? **235**

Estructura
PRESENTATION
Since students are already familiar with the conjugation of **ir** and its meaning, begin using the future in a conversational question-and-answer format.

Start by asking what they are going to do tonight and then, before they answer, say what you and others are going to do: **¿Qué van a hacer Uds. esta noche? Yo voy a comer con mis hijos y voy a ver la televisión un poco. Después voy a preparar las lecciones para mañana y voy a leer un libro divertido.**

Then ask them questions, occasionally summarizing their answers and adding comments. After several students have answered correctly, write **ir a +** infinitive on the board and explain that this is an idiomatic expression similar to the English expression *going to +* verb.

 Interpersonal Communication 1.1
Linguistic Comparisons 4.1

 Spanish for Spanish Speakers

The verb ir

Most Spanish speakers will know how to conjugate the verb **ir** and how to use it to form this tense, but they may not know that it is called the immediate future tense. Ask students if they know another way to talk about future activities or events and have them think about when they use the immediate future in conversation (as opposed to the future tense). While it is not necessary to introduce the future structure to Spanish speakers at this time, tell them that as they continue their studies, they will learn how to write this tense as well.

☼ Activating Prior Knowledge

◢◣ Linguistic

PRACTICE/APPLY

D. ¿Qué van a hacer?

SUGGESTION

Have students carry out this activity with a "word web." On a separate piece of paper, students should draw a web, and then connect elements from the columns in ways that form grammatically correct sentences, writing in the correct forms of the verb **ir**.

Logical-Mathematical

E. ¿Qué vas a hacer el sábado por la tarde?

SUGGESTION

Point out to students that they should use the correct form of the verb **ir** and that they do not need to repeat the names of the subjects in their answers, because the verb form will make the subject clear.

ANSWERS

1. Voy a estudiar en la biblioteca.
2. Va a ver a una amiga en el centro.
3. Van a dar un paseo.
4. Van a ir de compras.
5. Voy a comprar un disco compacto.

F. ¿Qué vas a hacer este fin de semana?

Individual Needs

More-prepared Students

Have more-prepared students ask two or three classmates about their plans and then report back, including their own plans, too: **John va a escribir una carta, Mary va a comprar un libro y yo voy a estudiar español.**

EXPANSION

After students have done the activity in the singular, have them redo it, using **Uds./nosotros** forms. Have less-prepared students write the questions on the board. Have one student ask a group of others for their plans. Designate one student to answer for the whole group.

Aquí practicamos

D. ¿Qué van a hacer? Use words from each column to form sentences expressing future plans.

A	B	C
yo	ir a	dar un paseo
Susana		comer en un restaurante
Marcos		estudiar en la biblioteca
nosotros		comprar un disco compacto
Juan y su novia		mirar un programa de televisión
Uds.		
tú		
Ud.		

E. ¿Qué vas a hacer el sábado por la tarde (Saturday afternoon)? You are trying to find out what your friends are going to do Saturday afternoon. Ask your classmates these questions, and they will use the expressions in parentheses to answer. Follow the model.

> **MODELO** Tú: Marcos, ¿qué vas a hacer el sábado por la tarde? (comer en un restaurante)
> Compañero(a): *Voy a comer en un restaurante.*

1. Carlos, ¿qué vas a hacer el sábado por la tarde? (estudiar en la biblioteca)
2. ¿Y qué va a hacer Juan? (ver a una amiga en el centro)
3. ¿Y Fernando y su amigo? (dar un paseo)
4. ¿Y Bárbara y Julián? (ir de compras)
5. Marcos, ¿qué vas a hacer? (comprar un disco compacto)

F. ¿Qué vas a hacer este fin de semana (this weekend)? Answer the following questions about your weekend plans.

1. ¿Vas a estudiar español?
2. ¿Vas a leer un libro? ¿Qué libro?
3. ¿Vas a comprar algo?
4. ¿Vas a mirar un programa de televisión? ¿Qué programa?
5. ¿Vas a bailar en una fiesta?
6. ¿Vas a hablar por teléfono con un(a) amigo(a)? ¿Con qué amigo(a)?

236 *Cuarta unidad* Vamos al centro

 Spanish for Spanish Speakers

Personalizing

To pose a challenge in Activity D, have Spanish speakers come up with a column chart of their own that includes the names of people they know and the places they go in order to reflect the real world in their daily lives. Help them with the spelling of their ideas.

Categorizing
Creating

PALABRAS ÚTILES

Tener ganas de + infinitive

Tengo ganas de estudiar.	*I feel like studying.*
Tienes ganas de comer una hamburguesa con queso.	*You feel like eating a cheeseburger.*
Tenemos ganas de bailar.	*We feel like dancing.*
Tienen ganas de escuchar la radio.	*They feel like listening to the radio.*

In Spanish, when you want to say you feel like doing something, use the expression **tener ganas de** + infinitive. Simply conjugate **tener** and use the infinitive form of the verb that expresses what you feel like doing.

G. Tienen ganas de... Create original sentences, using words from each column.

A	B	C
Esteban	tener ganas de	comer en un restaurante
yo		estudiar
nosotros		bailar
tú		mirar la televisión
Marta y Julia		ir a un museo
Uds.		dar un paseo
		ir al centro

H. ¿Qué tiene ganas de hacer...? Tell what the people in the following drawings feel like doing. Follow the model.

> **MODELO**   ¿Qué tienen ganas de hacer Isabel y Juan?
> *Isabel y Juan tienen ganas de bailar.*

¿Qué tienen ganas de hacer Isabel y Juan?

Capítulo 10 ¿Quieres ir al centro?   **237**

TEACH/MODEL

Palabras útiles
PRESENTATION
Start out by asking **tú** questions using **querer** and then make follow-up questions and statements using the new expression. For example: **¿Tú quieres estudiar esta noche? Ah, ¿no? ¿No tienes ganas de estudiar? ¿Qué quieres hacer? ¿Ver televisión? Ah, ¿sí? ¿Tienes ganas de ver televisión? Yo también tengo ganas de ver televisión.** Then write **tener ganas de** + infinitive on the board and explain that it is a common idiomatic expression. Ask a few more questions, preferably in the **Uds.** form.

PRACTICE/APPLY

G. Tienen ganas de...
SUGGESTION
For students who learn better with visual cues and manual manipulation, you may wish to have them write each of the items in the columns as well as the conjugated forms of **tener ganas de** on separate index cards. They can combine the cards in different ways to come up with their sentences.

Linguistic
Visual-Spatial

Focus on Culture

Cataluña

The region of Cataluña was an independent nation with its own language and parliamentary system long before the formation of the Spanish state. It was historically one of the main commercial powers of the Mediterranean and by the year 1850 had become the world's fourth manufacturing power. Starting with the marriage of Fernando de Aragón to Isabel de Castilla in 1469, Cataluña has had to fight suppression from the Spanish government. Since the end of the Franco regime in 1975, Cataluña has undergone a cultural resurgence. Some of the region's world-famous artists are painters Pablo Picasso, Joan Miró, and Salvador Dalí; musician Pablo Casals; and the sculptor and architect Antonio Gaudí.

Connections with Other Disciplines 3.1

H. ¿Qué tiene ganas de hacer...?

ANSWERS

1. Irma tiene ganas de dar un paseo.
2. Julián y Javier tienen ganas de ir al museo.
3. Eva tiene ganas de comer.
4. Mis amigos tienen ganas de hacer la tarea.
5. Esteban tiene ganas de escuchar la radio.
6. Bárbara y Carolina tienen ganas de mirar la televisión.

TEACH/MODEL

I. Tengo ganas de... pero debo...

SUGGESTIONS

Before beginning the activity, review the idea of verb + infinitive by listing on the board alternatives introduced in Chapter 7 to **tener ganas de**, such as **querer** or **preferir**. Do the same for **deber** with expressions such as **tener que** and **necesitar**. This refresher will also be useful later in this chapter, when the verb **poder** is presented.

PRACTICE/APPLY

Individual Needs

Less-prepared Students
Have less-prepared students concentrate on using the verb **deber** until they grasp the concept well.

More-prepared Students
Encourage more-prepared students to vary their answers with as many alternative expressions as possible.

EXPANSION

Ask personalized questions to continue the activity. Remember to ask some in the **Uds.** form. You might also want to ask a few questions using the **pregúntale** format.

Interpersonal Communication 1.1

1. ¿Qué tiene ganas de hacer Irma?

2. ¿Qué tienen ganas de hacer Julián y Javier?

3. ¿Qué tiene ganas de hacer Eva?

4. ¿Qué tienen ganas de hacer tus amigos?

5. ¿Qué tiene ganas de hacer Esteban?

6. ¿Qué tienen ganas de hacer Bárbara y Carolina?

I. Tengo ganas de... pero debo... A friend invites you to do something. You say that you want to but cannot because you ought to do something else. Give him (her) a good excuse. Follow the model.

MODELO   ir al centro
Amigo(a):   *¿Tienes ganas de ir al centro conmigo?*
Tú: *Sí, pero debo estudiar español.*

1. comprar un disco compacto
2. ver una película
3. caminar al centro
4. ir a la librería
5. comer en un restaurante
6. dar un paseo

238   *Cuarta unidad* Vamos al centro

Aquí escuchamos

¿Quieres ir al centro?
Elena invites Francisco to go downtown with her.

 Antes de escuchar Think about how you would invite someone to go downtown with you in Spanish.

A escuchar Listen twice to the conversation between Elena and Francisco before answering the questions about it that follow.

Después de escuchar Answer the following questions based on what you heard.

1. Why is Elena going downtown?
2. Where is she going?
3. Why does Francisco want to go downtown?
4. What else does Elena invite Francisco to do?
5. What phrase does Francisco use to agree to accompany Elena?

—¿Quieres ir al cine conmigo?
—Sí, pero no hay un cine por aquí.
—¿Entonces quieres ir al centro?
—¡Vamos!

Capítulo 10 ¿Quieres ir al centro? **239**

Aquí escuchamos

 TEXTBOOK CASSETTE/CD CASSETTE 1, SIDE B; CD 2, TRACK 26

 TAPESCRIPT REFERENCE P. 203

Después de escuchar
ANSWERS
1. to do an errand for her father
2. to the bank
3. to buy a CD
4. to see a movie
5. ¡De acuerdo! ¡Vamos!

Spanish for Spanish Speakers

Summarizing

Have Spanish speakers listen to the **Aquí escuchamos** recording and summarize the dialogue. Encourage students to write down any difficult vocabulary or structures, and work with a partner to better understand how these are used in this recording. Review summaries with Spanish speakers to determine problematic structures and vocabulary.

Creating
Synthesizing

ETAPA SYNTHESIS

¿Quieres ir al centro conmigo?

SUGGESTION

Point out that **no puedo** means *I can't* and that later in the chapter (page 250) they will learn the verb formally.

Este fin de semana tengo ganas de...

FYI

 ATAJO WRITING ASSISTANT SOFTWARE

You might want to have students use this software program when doing this activity.

SUGGESTION

Encourage students to elaborate on their sentences by telling for whom as well as with whom they plan to do things and by giving reasons for some of their tasks. For example: **Tengo ganas de ir al centro con mi padre. Tenemos que comprar un radio para mamá, porque es su cumpleaños.**

VOCABULARY EXPANSION

Since the days of the week are presented later in this chapter, you may want to do some premapping by introducing **el sábado** and **el domingo** as expansion vocabulary. Have students tell what they plan to do each day, and review time in this activity by having students use expressions such as **el sábado por la noche** and **el domingo a la una.**

Additional Practice and Recycling

FYI

 WORKBOOK, PP. 122-126

For recycling and additional practice of the vocabulary, structures, and language functions presented throughout this **etapa**, you can assign the workbook activities as in-class work and/or homework.

¡ADELANTE!

 ¿Quieres ir al centro conmigo? Make a list of things you want or need to do in town. Then interview several classmates to find someone who would like to go downtown for some of the same reasons. When you find someone who wants to join you, try to arrange a time that will be convenient for both of you. Use **no puedo** to say *I can't.* Follow the model.

MODELO

Tú:	*¡Hola, Catalina! ¿Qué vas a hacer en el centro?*
Catalina:	*Debo ir a la farmacia. Y tengo ganas de ir de compras.*
Tú:	*Yo quiero ir de compras también. ¿Quieres ir conmigo?*
Catalina:	*Sí, cómo no. ¿A qué hora?*
Tú:	*¿A las once?*
Catalina:	*No, no puedo a las once, porque tengo una cita con mi abuela a mediodía. Nosotras vamos a comer juntas.*
Catalina:	*Entonces, vamos al centro a las tres.*
Tú:	*De acuerdo.*

 Este fin de semana tengo ganas de... Write a note to a friend in which you tell what you feel like doing this weekend. Mention four different activities. For each one, write when, where, or with whom you want to do these things. Name a fifth activity that you are not going to do because of a previous commitment.

240 *Cuarta unidad* Vamos al centro

SEGUNDA ETAPA

Preparación

- In this **etapa** you will be talking about various activities that you do on certain days and at specific times of the day. What are some ways of dividing a day into different parts?

- Do you know the names of the days of the week in Spanish?

- How do you ask someone what he (she) is going to do on a specific day or during a specific part of a day?

¿Cuándo vamos?

Voy a hacer muchas cosas hoy y mañana.

Hoy

1. **Esta mañana,** yo voy a la escuela.

3. **Esta tarde,** yo voy a estudiar.

Mañana

2. **Mañana por la mañana,** voy a dormir tarde.

4. **Mañana por la tarde,** voy a ir de compras.

hoy *today*   **mañana** *tomorrow*   **viernes** *Friday*   **Esta mañana** *This morning*   **sábado** *Saturday*   **Mañana por la mañana** *Tomorrow morning*   **Esta tarde** *This afternoon*   **Mañana por la tarde** *Tomorrow afternoon*

Capítulo 10 ¿Quieres ir al centro?   **241**

TEACH/MODEL

¿Cuándo vamos?

PRESENTATION

	TRANSPARENCY 48
	TEXTBOOK CASSETTE/CD CASSETTE 1, SIDE B; CD 2, TRACK 27
	TAPESCRIPT P. 203

Begin by writing today's date on the board. Have the class repeat: **Hoy es el...** . Then write tomorrow's date and have students say: **Mañana es el...** . Under today's date, write *9:30 a.m.* and have students repeat **esta mañana**. Continue with an afternoon and an evening time. Then have students look at the transparency while you read the captions, having them repeat. Finally have them listen to the Textbook Cassette/CD recording of the conversation. Then ask comprehension questions such as, **¿Adónde van? ¿Cuándo? ¿Esta mañana?** etc.

For additional practice, have students look at the pictures in the book while you read the captions, having them repeat. Then read the dialogue and follow up with comprehension questions. Finally, ask personalized questions: **¿Vas a estudiar esta noche? ¿Vas a escribir una carta esta tarde? ¿Cuándo vas a escribir?**

Auditory-Musical

Interpretive Communication 1.2

Etapa Support Materials

- Workbook: pp. 127-131
- Textbook Cassettes/CDs: Cassette 1, Side B; CD 2, Track 27
- Tapescript: Textbook Cassettes/CDs p. 203
- Overhead Transparency: 48
- Middle School Activities: pp. 87, 88
- Lesson Plan Book: pp. 57-58

- Testing Program: Quiz pp. 112, 113; Answer Key & Testing Cassettes Tapescript p. T47
- Testing Cassettes: Cassette Side B
- Computerized Testing Program: Windows™; Macintosh®
- Atajo Writing Assistant Software: Student Text p. 247; Workbook pp. 127-131

Hoy

Mañana

5. Esta noche, yo voy a mirar la televisión en casa.

6. Mañana por la noche, voy a ver a mis amigos en el cine.

Una situación

Liliana: ¿Quieres ir al centro **conmigo?** Tengo que ir a la oficina de correos.

Guillermo: Sí, yo también. Tengo que hacer un mandado para mi padre. ¿Cuándo quieres ir? ¿Esta mañana?

Liliana: No, es imposible. **No puedo ir** esta mañana. Tengo que estudiar hasta las 12:00. ¿Esta tarde? **¿Está bien?**

Guillermo: Sí, está bien. Vamos al centro esta tarde.

Esta noche *Tonight*   **Mañana por la noche** *Tomorrow night*   **conmigo** *with me*   **No puedo ir** *I can't go*
¿Está bien? *Is that O.K.?*

¡Te toca a ti!

A. ¿Cuándo vas al centro? Based on the drawings that follow, indicate when the following activities take place. Pretend that today's date is the fifth of March. Follow the model.

la mañana   la tarde   la noche

MODELO   ¿Cuándo va Anita al centro?
Ella va al centro esta noche.

el 5 de marzo

el 5 de marzo

el 6 de marzo

el 5 de marzo

1. ¿Cuándo van a ir al cine tus padres?

2. ¿Cuándo va Enrique al centro?

3. ¿Cuándo va a estudiar tu hermana?

242   *Cuarta unidad* Vamos al centro

PRACTICE/APPLY

A. ¿Cuándo vas al centro?

SUGGESTION

Direct students to form pairs and sit or stand back-to-back. Distribute the questions from Activity A to one student and drawings indicating dates and times of day to the other. Tell the student with the questions to begin with the first cue by asking **¿Cuándo van a ir al cine tus padres?** The partner answers, using an appropriate date and time of day chosen from the drawings. After three questions, tell students to switch roles. The second student asks a question, and the first student answers with a different time of day than the one used by the second student. Direct the pairs to continue until finished.

 Auditory-Musical

ANSWERS

1. Ellos van al cine esta noche.
2. Él va al centro mañana por la tarde.
3. Ella va a estudiar esta mañana.
4. Él va a comprar el disco compacto mañana por la mañana.
5. Voy a ver a mis amigos mañana por la noche.
6. Mis hermanos van a hacer el mandado esta tarde.

VARIATION

Ask pairs of students to make up personalized questions about times and activities of other students in the class. Have the pairs ask and answer their personalized questions in front of the class.

 Creating

 Interpersonal

 Interpretive Communication 1.2

MULTIPLE INTELLIGENCES

- Linguistic: All activities
- Logical-Mathematical: B, D, E, F, G, H
- Visual-Spatial: A
- Auditory-Musical: **Aquí escuchamos**
- Interpersonal: C
- Intrapersonal: **Este fin de semana**

The Standards

- Interpersonal Communication 1.1: C, G, J, **¿Qué haces los fines de semana?**
- Interpretive Communication 1.2: A, B, C, D, E, F, H, **Aquí escuchamos**
- Presentational Communication 1.3: **Adelante** activities

el 6 de marzo

el 6 de marzo

el 5 de marzo

4. ¿Cuándo va a comprar Julián el disco compacto?

5. ¿Cuándo vas a ver a tus amigos?

6. ¿Cuándo van a hacer el mandado tus hermanos?

B. ¿Cuándo quieres ir? Make plans with a friend. Using the information provided, imitate each of the model conversations.

> **MODELO**　　ir al cine, esta noche / sí
> 　　　　　　　Tú:　　　¿Quieres ir al cine conmigo?
> 　　　　Amiga(o):　　Sí. ¿Cuándo quieres ir?
> 　　　　　　　Tú:　　　Esta noche. ¿Está bien?
> 　　　　Amiga(o):　　Sí, por supuesto. Vamos al cine esta noche.

1. ir al centro, esta noche / sí

2. ir a la biblioteca, mañana por la tarde / sí

3. ir a la piscina, mañana por la tarde / sí

> **MODELO**　　ir al centro, esta tarde / no (trabajar) / mañana
> 　　　　　　　por la tarde / sí
> 　　　　Amiga(o):　　¿Quieres ir al centro conmigo?
> 　　　　　　　Tú:　　　Sí, ¿cuándo quieres ir?
> 　　　　Amiga(o):　　Esta tarde. ¿Está bien?
> 　　　　　　　Tú:　　　No, es imposible. Tengo que trabajar.
> 　　　　　　　　　　　¿Mañana por la tarde?
> 　　　　Amiga(o):　　Claro que sí. Vamos al centro mañana por la
> 　　　　　　　　　　　tarde.

4. ir al museo, esta tarde / no (hacer un mandado) / mañana por la tarde / sí

5. dar un paseo, esta mañana / no (dormir) / esta tarde / sí

6. ir al cine, esta noche / no (estudiar) / mañana por la noche / sí

Repaso

C. Preguntas Your partner will play the role of an exchange student who has just arrived at your school. He (she) wants to get to know you. Answer his (her) questions, paying close attention to whether each question is general and therefore requires the present tense, or whether it deals with a specific future time and thus calls for **ir a** + infinitive.

1. ¿Estudias mucho? ¿Vas a estudiar esta noche?

2. Usualmente, ¿qué haces por la noche? ¿Qué vas a hacer esta noche?

Capítulo 10 ¿Quieres ir al centro? **243**

Estructura

PRESENTATION

First, have students repeat the days of the week after you. Then write on the board today's date and the dates for the next six days. Ask: **¿Qué día es hoy? Ah, hoy es (lunes, el 9 de...). Y el 10 de..., ¿es (miércoles)? Ah, bien, es (martes).** etc. Continue by writing the days of the week on the board, beginning with **lunes.** Then write **el** before the days and make a statement with each one. Explain that when you use an article before the days of the week, it means *on*. Then make more statements with follow-up questions using both **el** and **los** before the days mentioned.

VOCABULARY EXPANSION

Write **fin de semana** on the board and explain its meaning in Spanish using the days of the week. For example: **Me gusta mucho el fin de semana. Los viernes por la noche, voy a comer en un restaurante y voy al cine. Los sábados voy de compras y leo un buen libro. También trabajo en la casa. Los domingos... ¿Te gusta también el fin de semana? ¿Qué te gusta hacer?**

D. Hoy es...

ANSWERS

1. ¿Es jueves hoy? No, hoy no es jueves. Hoy es viernes.
2. ¿Es sábado hoy? ...sábado. Es domingo.
3. ¿Es miércoles hoy? ...miércoles. Es jueves.
4. ¿Es domingo hoy? ...domingo. Es lunes.
5. ¿Es viernes hoy? ...viernes. Es sábado.
6. ¿Es martes hoy? ...martes. Es miércoles.

---

3. ¿Vas frecuentemente al centro? ¿Qué haces en el centro? ¿Vas al centro mañana?
4. ¿Estudias español? ¿ruso? ¿chino? ¿francés? ¿Vas a estudiar otra lengua?
5. ¿Te gusta dar un paseo? ¿Vas a dar un paseo esta noche?

ESTRUCTURA

The days of the week

El jueves yo voy al cine.	*On Thursday I'm going to the movies.*
El domingo vamos a dar un paseo.	*On Sunday we're going to take a walk.*
Los domingos vamos a la iglesia.	*On Sundays we go to church.*
Los sábados no vamos a la escuela.	*On Saturdays we don't go to school.*

1. In Spanish the days of the week (**los días de la semana**) are as follows:

lunes	*Monday*	**jueves**	*Thursday*	**sábado**	*Saturday*
martes	*Tuesday*	**viernes**	*Friday*	**domingo**	*Sunday*
miércoles	*Wednesday*				

2. Spanish speakers consider the week to begin on Monday and end on Sunday. The names of the days are masculine and are not capitalized.

3. To express the idea of *on a certain day* or *days*, use the definite article **el** or **los** with the day of the week. When you are simply telling what day it is, however, the article is omitted.

—¿Qué día es hoy?	*What day is it today?*
—Es miércoles.	*It is Wednesday.*

Aquí practicamos

D. Hoy es... Form questions using the day indicated. Then, answer each question negatively using the next day in your response. Follow the model.

> **MODELO** lunes
> ¿Es lunes hoy?
> *No, hoy no es lunes. Hoy es martes.*

1. jueves	3. miércoles	5. viernes
2. sábado	4. domingo	6. martes

Spanish for Spanish Speakers

The consonants j and v

Have Spanish speakers focus on the **j** and **v** of **jueves** and the **v** of **viernes**. Then have them come up with other words in Spanish that use **j** and **v**. Provide examples such as **verano, julio, vaca,** and **jugar** to get students started.

Auditory-Musical

E. Ellos llegan el jueves

Some students from Bolivia are going to visit your school. They come from different cities and will arrive on different dates. Using the following calendar, indicate on what day of the week each student will arrive. Follow the model.

MODELO   Miguel va a llegar el 18.
Ah, él llega el jueves.

1. Enrique va a llegar el 15.
2. Mario y Jaime van a llegar el 17.
3. María y Anita van a llegar el 20.
4. Francisco va a llegar el 21.
5. Roberto va a llegar el 16.
6. Todos los demás *(All the rest)* van a llegar el 19.

Enero

L	M	M	J	V	S	D
15	16	17	18	19	20	21

ESTRUCTURA

The verb hacer

1. In the present tense, the **yo** form of the verb **hacer** (**hago**) is irregular, but all other forms are conjugated in the same way as regular -er verbs.

hacer *(to do, to make)*			
yo	**hago**	nosotros(as)	**hacemos**
tú	**haces**	vosotros(as)	**hacéis**
él ella Ud.	**hace**	ellos ellas Uds.	**hacen**

2. When asked a question that includes **hacer** or one of its forms, you normally answer with the verb that expresses what it is you do.

—¿Qué **haces** los lunes?   *What do you do on Mondays?*
—**Voy** a la escuela.   *I go to school.*

—¿Qué **vas a hacer** el viernes?   *What are you going to do on Friday?*

—**Voy a estudiar.**   *I'm going to study.*

Capítulo 10 ¿Quieres ir al centro?   **245**

E. Ellos llegan el jueves

ANSWERS

1. Ah, él llega el lunes.
2. Ah, ellos llegan el miércoles.
3. Ah, ellas llegan el sábado.
4. Ah, él llega el domingo.
5. Ah, él llega el martes.
6. Ah, ellos llegan el viernes.

TEACH/MODEL

Estructura

PRESENTATION

Begin by asking, in English, what several students are going to do later in the week. Point out that while a form of the verb *to do* is part of the question, it is not part of the answer. The response contains a form of the verb that expresses what they will do, but not the verb *to do* itself. Then present the verb in a manner similar to other verbs that you have presented, making statements and then asking follow-up questions, etc. **Yo hago ejercicio a menudo. ¿Tú haces ejercicio también?** Continue by writing the verb on the board, and have students point out its similarities and differences from other verbs that they have studied.

 Linguistic

Linguistic Comparisons 4.1

PRACTICE/APPLY

F. ¿Qué hacen?

ANSWERS

1. hace Anita, haces tú, hacen Uds., hacen Susana y Enrique, hago yo, hace Ud.

2. vas a hacer tú, van a hacer Uds., va a hacer Alberto, voy a hacer yo, van a hacer Linda y Mario, vamos a hacer nosotros

G. ¿Qué hace Juan...?

ANSWERS

1. Martín mira la televisión.
2. Lucía come en un restaurante.
3. Elisa y Jaime van al cine.
4. Marina va de compras.
5. Mario y Susana dan un paseo.

H. ¿Qué va a hacer Timoteo...?

ANSWERS

1. José va a escuchar discos compactos esta noche.
2. Ernestina va a estudiar el viernes.
3. Antonio y Catarina van a ir al museo mañana.
4. Pepita va a ver a una amiga en el centro el martes.
5. Teodoro y Alicia van a hacer un mandado el sábado.

Aquí practicamos

F. **¿Qué hacen?** Replace the words in italics with each of the words in parentheses, making all necessary changes.

1. ¿Qué hace *Juan* los sábados? (Anita / tú / Uds. / Susana y Enrique / yo / Ud.)

2. ¿Qué van a hacer *ellos* el domingo por la tarde? (tú / Uds. / Alberto / yo / Linda y Mario / nosotros)

G. **¿Qué hace Juan...?** Your sister asks you what your friends usually do on a certain day of the week. Respond with the activities in parentheses. Follow the model.

> **MODELO** Tu hermana: ¿Qué hace Martín los lunes por la noche? (estudiar)
> Tú: *Martín estudia.*

1. ¿Qué hace Martín los martes por la noche? (mirar la televisión)
2. ¿Qué hace Lucía los viernes? (comer en un restaurante)
3. ¿Qué hacen Elisa y Jaime los sábados por la noche? (ir al cine)
4. ¿Qué hace Marina los jueves en el centro? (ir de compras)
5. ¿Qué hacen Mario y Susana los domingos? (dar un paseo)

H. **¿Qué va a hacer Timoteo... ?** Your teacher asks you what your friends are going to do on a certain day. Respond with the activities in parentheses. Follow the model.

> **MODELO** Tu profesora: ¿Qué va a hacer Timoteo esta noche? (leer)
> Tú: *Timoteo va a leer esta noche.*

1. ¿Qué va a hacer José esta noche? (escuchar discos compactos)
2. ¿Qué va a hacer Ernestina el viernes? (estudiar)
3. ¿Qué van a hacer Antonio y Catarina mañana? (ir al museo)
4. ¿Qué va a hacer Pepita en el centro el martes? (ver a una amiga)
5. ¿Qué van a hacer Teodoro y Alicia el sábado? (hacer un mandado)

Aquí escuchamos

¿Cuándo vamos? *Elena and Francisco discuss their plans to go downtown.*

Antes de escuchar Think about how Elena might invite Francisco to do something, how he might agree or disagree, and how they could settle on a time of day.

A escuchar Listen twice to the conversation before answering the questions about it that follow.

Después de escuchar Answer the following questions, based on what you heard.

1. What does Elena have to do downtown?
2. Why does Francisco have to go downtown?
3. Why can't Francisco go in the morning?
4. When do they decide to go?

¡ADELANTE!

 ¿Qué haces los fines de semana? Ask several of your classmates what they do on the weekends. Keep track of your findings and be ready to report back to the class. Ask as many classmates as you can in the time allotted.

 Este fin de semana Write a note to a friend, explaining what you are going to do this weekend. Include at least five activities. Ask your friend what he (she) is going to do.

Este fin de semana, voy a la feria con Jorge.

Capítulo 10 ¿Quieres ir al centro? **247**

Aquí escuchamos

 TEXTBOOK CASSETTE/CD CASSETTE 1, SIDE B; CD 2, TRACK 28

 TAPESCRIPT P. 203

Después de escuchar
ANSWERS
1. to go to the post office
2. to do an errand for his mother
3. he has to study
4. in the afternoon

ETAPA SYNTHESIS

¿Qué haces los fines de semana?
SUGGESTION
Before having students report to the class, ask students to guess the most popular weekend activity and to write it (in Spanish) on a piece of paper. After students report to the class, find out which student(s) guessed correctly.

 Making Hypotheses

Este fin de semana
FYI

 ATAJO WRITING ASSISTANT SOFTWARE

You might want to have students use this software program when doing this activity.

SUGGESTION

 After students write their notes, have them exchange papers and edit each other's work. You may want to pair up a less-prepared student with a more-prepared one for this activity.

Additional Practice and Recycling
FYI

 WORKBOOK, PP. 127-131

For recycling and additional practice of the vocabulary, structures, and language functions presented throughout this **etapa**, you can assign the workbook activities as in-class work and/or homework.

TERCERA ETAPA

 TEACH/MODEL

¿Cómo prefieres ir, en coche o a pie?

PRESENTATION

	TRANSPARENCY 49
	TEXTBOOK CASSETTE/CD CASSETTE 1, SIDE B; CD 2, TRACK 29
	TAPESCRIPT PP. 203-204

Have students repeat the expressions being introduced while looking at the transparency. Then make statements that are not true based on the drawings, and have students correct them. For example: **¿El Sr. Valdés va en coche? No, va en metro.** Then have students listen to the short conversation on the Textbook Cassette/CD. Ask comprehension questions such as **¿Adónde quiere ir Andrés? ¿Cómo van a ir allí?** Then replay the recording and have students repeat the dialogue.

VARIATION

Have students repeat the expressions as they look at the pictures in the book. Then tell them about how a Colombian family gets around. For example, tell them about los García: **Los Sres. García trabajan. El Sr. García va a su oficina en metro. La Sra. García va en autobús. Sus hijos van a la escuela. Su hija va en bicicleta. Su hijo va a pie.** Act out or draw on the board the various means of transportation. Then proceed as above with the recorded dialogue, or read it to the class yourself.

Auditory-Musical
Bodily-Kinesthetic
Visual-Spatial

Preparación

- How do you get around town? Buy car? By bus? By bike?
- How do you ask someone if he (she) can do something?
- How do you politely say you can't do something?

¿Cómo prefieres ir, en coche o a pie?

*Hay muchas **maneras** (ways) de ir al centro.*

El Sr. Valdés va en metro.

La Sra. Candelaria va en en coche.

La Sra. López va en autobús.

El Sr. Cano va en taxi.

Pedro va en bicicleta.

Fernando va a pie *(on foot)*.

248 *Cuarta unidad* Vamos al centro

Etapa Support Materials

- Workbook: pp. 132-136
- TRB: Textbook Activity Masters: p. 95
- Textbook Cassettes/CDs: Cassette 1, Side B; CD 2, Track 29
- Tapescript: Textbook Cassettes/CDs pp. 203-204
- Overhead Transparency: 49
- Middle School Activities: pp. 89, 90
- Lesson Plan Book: pp. 59-60

- Testing Program: Quiz pp. 114-116; Answer Key & Testing Cassettes Tapescript p. T48
- Testing Cassettes: Cassette Side B
- Computerized Testing Program: Windows™; Macintosh®
- Atajo Writing Assistant Software: Student Text p. 253; Workbook pp. 132-136

Una situación

Andrés:	¿Quieres ir al Museo del Prado hoy?
Gabriela:	Sí. Me gustan las pinturas de Velázquez. ¿Vamos a pie?
Andrés:	No. Está muy lejos. Vamos en metro.
Gabriela:	Bien, de acuerdo. Vamos a **tomar** *(take)* el metro.

Museo del Prado: *Located in Madrid, the Prado is considered one of the most important art museums in the word. It contains over 6,000 works by Spanish artists such as Velázquez, Goya, and El Greco, as well as masterpieces by other artists such as Bosch, Rubens, and Raphael.*

¡Te toca a ti!

A. ¿Cómo van? Based on the drawings that follow, tell how each person gets downtown. Follow the model.

MODELO
Jorge va...
Jorge va en bicicleta.

1. Francisco va...   2. La Sra. Fernández va...   3. Carlos va...   4. Marta va...

5. El Sr. González va...   6. Santiago y su hermana van...   7. El Sr. López va...

Capítulo 10 ¿Quieres ir al centro?   **249**

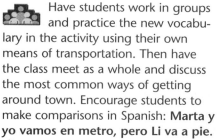

B. ¿Tú quieres ir...?

FYI

When possible, this book introduces functional expressions in activities rather than in isolated lists, in order to provide immediate practice, for example, **claro que sí** (*of course*), **de acuerdo** (*agreed*). Encourage students to try several ways of agreeing to a suggestion. By learning to use these functional expressions in different contexts, they will be taking an important step in becoming truly communicative in the language, even though the "quantity" of Spanish they know may still be quite limited.

SUGGESTION

Have students do the activity first in pairs, then correct the activity with the whole class, eliciting alternative versions and expressions. You may also want students to write their own original cues on cards and distribute them, writing some appropriate expression on the board for their use in sentences.

C. Intercambio

SUGGESTIONS

Have students work in pairs and then ask follow-up questions to give them the opportunity to report back. You might also want to do it as a **pregúntale** activity with books closed to practice listening comprehension.

Auditory-Musical

B. ¿Tú quieres ir...? You invite a friend to go somewhere with you. He (she) responds affirmatively, saying **Claro que sí.** Your friend then suggests a way of going there, but you have a different idea. Follow the model.

> **MODELO** museo / metro / a pie
> **Tú:** *¿Quieres ir al museo?*
> **Amigo(a):** *Claro que sí. ¿Vamos en metro?*
> **Tú:** *No. ¡Vamos a pie!*
> **Amigo(a):** *De acuerdo. Vamos a pie.*

1. cine / a pie / autobús
2. centro / autobús / coche
3. biblioteca / taxi / metro
4. parque / coche / a pie
5. restaurante / metro / autobús
6. farmacia / autobús / metro /
7. estadio / bicicleta / a pie
8. mercado / a pie / coche

Repaso ♻

C. Intercambio Ask the following questions of a classmate, who will answer them.

1. ¿Qué tienes ganas de hacer el sábado próximo *(next)*?
2. ¿Qué haces los domingos por la mañana?
3. ¿Qué haces los lunes por la mañana? ¿Por la tarde?
4. ¿Cuándo estudias? ¿Cómo vas a la escuela? ¿Cuándo vas al centro? ¿Para qué? ¿Cuándo vas al cine?

250 *Cuarta unidad* Vamos al centro

Focus on Culture

Museo del Prado

The Museo del Prado is one of Madrid's greatest attractions. It houses the world's greatest collection of Spanish paintings and hundreds of foreign masterpieces. It was meant to serve as a museum of natural history, but its construction was interrupted by the Napoleonic wars and it wasn't finished until decades later. It was then opened up as an art museum and filled with treasures collected by Spain's Hapsburg and Bourbon kings, other patrons of the arts, and Spanish monasteries and convents. Some of its most famous paintings include *Las Meninas* by Velázquez, *Nobleman with a Hand on His Chest* by El Greco, *the Majas* and *Executions of the Rioters* by Goya, and *Holy Family with a Little Bird* by Murillo.

Connections with Other Disciplines 3.1

ESTRUCTURA

The present tense of the verb poder

poder (ue) *(to be able)*			
yo	puede	nosotros(as)	**podemos**
tú	puedes	vosotros(as)	**podéis**
él ella Ud.	puede	ellos ellas Uds.	pueden

1. The verb **poder** is a stem-changing verb in which the vowel in the stem (**pod-**) changes from **o** to **ue** in all forms except **nosotros(as)** and **vosotros(as)**. The verb **contar** *(to count, to tell a story)* follows this same pattern: **yo cuento,** but **nosotras contamos.**

2. **Poder** is followed directly by an infinitive. To make this construction negative, place **no** before the conjugated form of the verb **poder.**

—¿**Puede hablar** francés Marcos?   *Can Marcos speak French?*

—No, **no puede hablar** francés.   *No, he cannot speak French.*

Aquí practicamos

D. Podemos... Tell what the following people can do, using words from each column.

A	B	C
Linda yo tú Gregorio y Verónica Uds. nosotros	poder	ir al centro ir a un restaurante ir al concierto ir al museo ir al cine

---

TEACH/MODEL

Estructura

PRESENTATION
Begin by making **yo** statements with the verb **poder** and then ask follow-up questions based on the statements. For example, **Yo quiero ir al cine hoy, pero no puedo. Tengo que preparar las lecciones para mañana. ¿Puedes tú ir al cine hoy?** Proceed in a manner similar to the way in which you have presented other verbs (pages 127 and 160). Have students identify the pattern of the stem change. Point out that there is no stem change in the **nosotros** form.

Activating Prior Knowledge

PRACTICE/APPLY

D. Podemos...

SUGGESTION
You may want to use a word web or separate index cards to have students visually match up the elements from the different columns.

Visual-Spatial

☀ Spanish for Spanish Speakers

Linguistic Variations
Ask Spanish speakers for variations of modes of transportation that are listed here. It is common for people in Mexico to call a bus a **camión**, while in Puerto Rico, Cuba, and the Dominican Republic the word **guagua** is used. They might also have heard **carro** and **auto** for **coche**.

Linguistic Comparisons 4.1

E. Hoy no puedo...

ANSWERS

1. ¿Puedes ir al centro ahora? No, ahora no puedo, pero puedo ir el viernes por la tarde.
2. ¿Puedes ir a un restaurante esta noche? No, esta noche no puedo, pero puedo ir mañana por la noche.
3. ¿Puedes ir al museo esta tarde? No, esta tarde no puedo, pero puedo ir el domingo por la tarde.
4. ¿Puedes ir al concierto esta semana? No, esta semana no puedo, pero puedo ir la semana próxima.
5. ¿Puedes ir de compras esta mañana? No, esta mañana no puedo, pero puedo ir el sábado por la mañana.

F. No, no puedo

ANSWERS

Answer will follow the model, substituting the cues.

E. Hoy no puedo... A classmate invites you to do something. You cannot do it at the time he (she) suggests, but you suggest another time when you can. Follow the model.

> **MODELO** ir al cine, hoy / sábado por la noche
> **Compañero(a):** *¿Puedes ir al cine hoy?*
> **Tú:** *No, hoy no puedo, pero puedo ir el sábado por la noche.*

1. ir al centro, ahora / viernes por la tarde
2. ir a un restaurante, esta noche / mañana por la noche
3. ir al museo, esta tarde / domingo por la tarde
4. ir al concierto, esta semana / la semana próxima
5. ir de compras, esta mañana / sábado por la mañana

F. No, no puedo You suggest an activity to a friend. He (she) is interested, but cannot do it on the day you have proposed and gives you a reason why not. You then suggest a different day, which is fine with your friend. Follow the model.

> **MODELO** dar un paseo, mañana / trabajar / sábado
> **Tú:** *¿Puedes dar un paseo mañana?*
> **Amigo(a):** *No, no puedo. Tengo que trabajar.*
> **Tú:** *¿El sábado? ¿Está bien?*
> **Amigo(a):** *Sí. Vamos a dar un paseo el sábado.*

1. ir al centro, esta noche / ir al cine con mis padres / mañana por la noche
2. hacer un mandado, el sábado / trabajar / domingo
3. ir al museo, esta tarde / estudiar / sábado
4. ir a tomar un café, el sábado / ir de compras con mi madre / domingo
5. ir al cine, mañana / hacer un mandado / viernes
6. ir a la biblioteca, hoy / ver a un amigo / martes

252 *Cuarta unidad* Vamos al centro

☀ **Spanish for Spanish Speakers**

Dialect Variations

Most students will know the verb **poder**, but they may not know how to spell the forms. One possible variation might occur in the **nosotros** form where some students, by analogy with the other forms, might say "**puedemos.**" Tell students that while they may use "**puedemos**" in their speech community, "**podemos**" is the standard, widely accepted form used in formal Spanish.

⊕ Linguistic Comparisons 4.1

Aquí escuchamos

¿Puedes ir conmigo? *Elena invites Francisco to accompany her to a building downtown.*

Antes de escuchar Think about how you invite someone in Spanish to accompany you to do something. Try to predict how Elena might invite Francisco to do something, how he could agree or disagree, and how they could settle on a means of transportation.

 A escuchar Listen twice to the conversation before answering the questions about it that follow.

Después de escuchar Answer the following questions, based on what you heard.

1. Where does Elena invite Francisco to go?
2. When does she want to go?
3. When does Francisco suggest they go?
4. How do they decide to go?
5. What phrase does Elena use to agree when Francisco suggests a new time?

¡ADELANTE!

 ¿Puedes ir conmigo? Ask a classmate if she (he) can do something with you. When you get an affirmative response, arrange a day, a time, and a place to meet. Then agree on a means of transportation.

 El sábado... Write a short note to a classmate.

1. Ask if he (she) can accompany you to do something on Saturday.
2. Mention where you want to go.
3. Tell him (her) what you plan to do when you get there.
4. Mention how you expect to get there.
5. Be sure to suggest a time of day.

EN LÍNEA

Connect with the Spanish-speaking world!
Access the **¡Ya verás!** *Gold* home page for
Internet activities related to this chapter.

http://yaveras.heinle.com

Capítulo 10 ¿Quieres ir al centro? **253**

Aquí escuchamos

 TEXTBOOK CASSETTE/CD CASSETTE 1, SIDE B; CD 2, TRACK 30

 TAPESCRIPT P. 204

Después de escuchar

ANSWERS

1. to the Museo del Prado
2. in the afternoon
3. the next morning
4. by train
5. Sí, ¡cómo no!

ETAPA SYNTHESIS

¿Puedes ir conmigo?

SUGGESTION

Review the days of the week, then ask questions such as, **¿Qué día es hoy? ¿Qué días vamos a la escuela?**

El sábado...

FYI

 ATAJO WRITING ASSISTANT SOFTWARE

You might want to have students use this software program when doing this activity.

Additional Practice and Recycling

FYI

 WORKBOOK, PP. 132-136

For recycling and additional practice of the vocabulary, structures, and language functions presented throughout this **etapa**, you can assign the workbook activities as in-class work and/or homework.

Resources for Spanish-speaking Students

FYI

 WORKBOOK FOR SPANISH-SPEAKING STUDENTS: PP. 61-66

 ANSWER KEY TO SSS WORKBOOK PP. 19-20

Activities specially written to meet the needs of Spanish-speaking students are available in this workbook for the reinforcement and extension of the topics and language presented in this chapter.

Additional Etapa Resources

Refer to the **Etapa** Support Materials list on the opening page of this **etapa** for detailed cross-references to these assessment options.

Vocabulario

SUGGESTION

 Have students write to a classmate asking if they can do something together. Have all students exchange notes with each other. Instruct them to write an answer saying they can't go at the suggested day or time, but offering an alternative. Students can exchange notes one more time, this time writing to agree to the alternative. Remind all students to use communicative phrases such as **claro que sí** in their responses.

Improvised Conversation

SUGGESTION

	TEXTBOOK CASSETTE/CD CASSETTE 1, SIDE B; CD 2, TRACK 31
	TAPESCRIPT P. 204
	TRB: ACTIVITY MASTER, P. 95

Have students listen to this conversation between two people who are making plans to do something together. Ask them to try to identify what each person wants to do. You may wish to write **parada del autobús** on the board and have students guess at the possible meaning of **parada**. Beginning with this unit, you may want to have students discuss recorded segments in Spanish.

 Interpretive Communication 1.2

Listening Skills Development

FYI

	LAB MANUAL PP. 67-72
	LAB PROGRAM CASSETTE SIDE A CD 5, TRACKS 10-18
	TAPESCRIPT: LAB PROGRAM PP. 99-107

It is now appropriate to work through the lab manual activities and their accompanying recordings in class or in the language laboratory.

VOCABULARIO

Para charlar

Para hablar de los planes

¿Está bien?
ir + a + *infinitive*
poder + *infinitive*
tener ganas + de + *infinitive*

Para decir adónde vas

Voy a dar un paseo.
Voy a hacer un mandado.
Voy a ir de compras.
Voy a ver a un amigo.

Para decir cuándo

Vamos esta mañana.
…esta tarde.
…hoy.
…mañana.
…mañana por la mañana.
…mañana por la tarde.
…mañana por la noche.

Para decir sí o no

¡Claro que sí!
Es imposible.
No, no puedo.
No puedo ir.
Sí, puedo.
Sí, tengo ganas de…

Para ir al centro

Voy en autobús.
…a pie.
…en bicicleta.
…en coche.
…en metro.
…en taxi.

Para preguntar qué día es

¿Qué día es hoy?

Temas y contextos

Los días de la semana

el lunes
el martes
el miércoles
el jueves
el viernes
el sábado
el domingo
el fin de semana

Vocabulario general

Verbos

deber
hacer
poder
tomar

Otras palabras y expresiones

una cita
conmigo
¿Para qué?
próximo(a)
usualmente

Spanish for Spanish Speakers

Keeping a Vocabulary Notebook

Remind Spanish-speaking students to add words and expressions from this vocabulary section to the problematic spelling combination categories and personal new vocabulary lists they started in their notebooks in Chapter 1. Reinforce that they should continue to do this each time a chapter in the textbook is completed.

Additional Chapter Resources

Refer to the Chapter Support Materials list on the opening page of this chapter for detailed cross-references to *¡Ya verás! Gold*'s student-centered technology components and various assessment options.

ENCUENTROS CULTURALES

Estrellas de la música latina

Antes de leer

1. Look at the photos to see if you recognize these people. What do they do?

2. Do you know the names of any other Spanish-speakers within this profession? Where are they from?

Si se va a una tienda de discos en una de las grandes ciudades de los Estados Unidos o de Europa, es posible encontrar una gran variedad de música latina. Dos de los ritmos musicales más populares en Latinoamérica son la salsa y el merengue. A pesar de que la salsa se originó en Puerto Rico y el merengue en la República Dominicana, hoy en día esta música se baila en toda Latinoamérica y en muchas de las ciudades de los Estados Unidos y el mundo.

> **Reading Strategies**
> - Using photos to predict content
> - Activating background knowledge

Ruben Blades

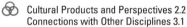

Rubén Blades, abogado panameño graduado de la universidad de Harvard, trae una dimensión social y panamericana a la salsa. Escribe muchas de sus propias canciones y cuenta historias mejor que nadie. Canciones como "Decisiones" y "Buscando América" reflejan la vida y la realidad latinoamericana.

Celia Cruz

Celia Cruz, "la reina de la salsa", es cubana y tiene una voz potente, con toda la gracia y el color de los trópicos. Embajadora de la música del Caribe, viaja constantemente por el mundo, actuando en compañía de Tito Puente, otro salsero legendario. Muchas personas que van a los conciertos de Celia Cruz se ponen a bailar porque es imposible resistir el ritmo de su música.

Estrellas de la música latina

SUGGESTION

Bring in some examples of salsa or merengue to play for the class. It would be helpful to find tapes of Celia Cruz, Tito Puente, Rubén Blades or Juan Luis Guerra (his band was called **cuatro-cuarenta**), those featured in this reading. If you have the lyrics to some of the songs, let the students listen once for music appreciation, then have them listen again and follow the words.

🎵 Auditory-Musical

🔵 Cultural Products and Perspectives 2.2
Connections with Other Disciplines 3.1

Antes de leer

POSSIBLE ANSWERS

1. They are musicians.
2. Other Spanish-speaking musicians include: Julio Iglesias, José Feliciano, Jose Luís Rodriguez. Some Hispanic-Americans musician that students might be familiar with include: Gloria Estefan, Jon Secada, and Selena.

Después de leer

POSSIBLE ANSWERS

1. Rubén Blades's music appeals to a variety of Latin American countries by dealing with more global themes.
2. Juan Luis Guerra.
3. Students may name Julio Iglesias, José Feliciano, Jose Luís Rodríguez, Gloria Estefan, Jon Secada, Linda Ronstadt, and Selena.
4. Answers will vary.

Juan Luis Guerra

Juan Luis Guerra, de la República Dominicana, canta sobre los problemas sociales y económicos de su gente mientras los invita a desahogarse de la mejor manera que saben: bailando. Con canciones como "Ojalá que llueva café" y "Burbujas de amor", este cantante dinámico le da al merengue una nueva popularidad.

Guía para la lectura

1. Here are some words and expressions to keep in mind as you read.

voz	*voice*
Embajadora	*Ambassador (female)*
se ponen a	*begin to*
propias	*own*
mientras	*while*
desahogarse	*unburden themselves*
Burbujas	*Bubbles*

2. **"Ojalá que llueva café"** ("Oh how I wish it would rain coffee") In this song Guerra describes a landscape so abundant with food that it rains coffee, the plains sprout sweet potatoes and strawberries, and there are hills of wheat and rice. Here everyone is happy and the children sing. Although Guerra is dealing with a serious subject, the catchy rhythm and playful lyrics have made the song extremely popular.

Después de leer

1. According to the reading, which singer has given salsa a more Pan-American flavor? What does this mean? Do you think it's good for this artist's music to have a Pan-American dimension? Why or why not?

2. According to the reading, which singer's music calls to people to release their frustrations by dancing? How might dancing help people express themselves? Do you think dancing is a good way to express emotions? Why or why not?

3. The music of these three Hispanic musicians is popular in the United States and in other countries around the world. What other Hispanic musicians are you familiar with? What kinds of music do they create?

4. Are you a musician? If so, what kinds of music do you play? Do you believe your music helps you to express yourself? If so, how?

256 *Cuarta unidad* Vamos al centro

☀ Spanish for Spanish Speakers

Favorite Music

Have the Spanish Speakers in the class discuss any music or favorite groups they may have. Ask them to bring in any favorite music they may have to share with the class. Ask them to discuss the music they hear in their speech community, from younger people to the older generations.

 Cultural Products and Perspectives 2.2
Cultural Comparisons 4.2

CAPÍTULO 11

Vamos a tomar el metro

—¿Tomamos un autobús?
—No, vamos a tomar el metro.

Objectives

- talking about taking the Madrid subway
- buying subway tickets
- making and accepting invitations

Capítulo 11 Vamos a tomar el metro **257**

OBJECTIVES

Functions
- Taking the subway and taxis
- Making and accepting invitations

Context
- Subway stations

Accuracy
- Adverbs used for expressing present and future time
- Talking about the future with **pensar**

Pronunciation
- The consonant **ch**

CHAPTER WARM-UP

Setting the Context

In preparation for their learning about taking public transportation, put students who have not worked together into teams of three and have them assign numbers within the group. Give each team a map of their hometown. Tell students to explain in round robin fashion (taking turns clockwise) how to get to three local landmarks from school. Ask Student 1 of each team to explain to the class how to get to one of the landmarks. Have Student 2 ask questions about the directions. Then have Student 3 rephrase the directions, answering the questions.

Visual-Spatial

Chapter Support Materials

- Lab Manual: pp. 73-76
- Lab Program: Cassette Side B; CD 6, Tracks 1-9
- TRB: Textbook Activity Masters: p. 96
- Textbook Cassettes/CDs: Cassette 2, Side A; CD, Track 37
- Tapescript: Lab Program pp. 108-115; Textbook Cassettes/CDs p. 206
- Middle School Activities: pp. 91-94
- Workbook for Spanish-speaking Students: pp. 62-72
- Answer Key to SSS Workbook: pp. 20-21
- Practice Software: Windows™; Macintosh®

- Testing Program: Chapter Test pp. 127-130; Answer Key & Testing Cassettes Tapescript pp. T52, T53; Oral Assessment p. T53
- Testing Cassettes: Cassette Side B
- Computerized Testing Program: Windows™; Macintosh®
- Video Program: Cassette 2, 8:31-13:38
- Video Guide: Videoscript pp. 47-48; Activities pp. 117-118
- **Mundos hispanos 1**
- Internet Activities: Student Text p. 296

PRIMERA ETAPA

TEACH/MODEL

¿En qué dirección?

PRESENTATION

TRANSPARENCY 50

TEXTBOOK CASSETTE/CD CASSETTE 1, SIDE A; CD 2, TRACK 32

TAPESCRIPT P. 204

Because of the large amount of cultural information involved in doing the **metro** activities, you may wish to have students follow along in the text while they listen to the Textbook Cassette/CD. You can then ask them if there are things they do not understand. Use the transparency of the metro map to point out the basic information given in the **Comentario cultural** on page 260 (**líneas, estaciones,** etc.) as well as to trace the girls' route.

🔺🔺 Auditory-Musical

SUGGESTION

Have students study the photo on page 257. Point out that the girls are looking at a **mapa del metro** like the one on page 259. Ask students if they have ever traveled in a subway system, either in the United States or in a foreign country. Mention that the subways in the Spanish-speaking world are excellent but very busy, especially during rush hours, as in the United States.

Cultural Comparisons 4.2

Preparación

- Have you ever ridden a subway?

- What cities in the U.S. have subways? Have you heard of the "L" in Chicago; the "T" in Boston; "BART" in San Francisco; "MARTA" in Atlanta; or the Metro in Washington, DC?

¿En qué dirección?

¿Cómo van a llegar Elena y Clara al Museo del Prado?

Elena y su prima Clara van a tomar el metro al Museo del Prado. Están cerca de la Plaza de España, donde hay una estación de metro. Las dos **jóvenes** miran el **plano** del metro en la **entrada** de la estación.

Estás aquí

Elena: Bueno. Estamos aquí, en la Plaza de España.
Clara: ¿Dónde está el Museo del Prado?
Elena: Está cerca de la Estación Atocha. Allí.
Clara: Entonces, ¿qué hacemos?
Elena: Es fácil. Tomamos la dirección de Legazpi.
Clara: ¿Es necesario **cambiar** de trenes?
Elena: Sí. Cambiamos en Sol, dirección de Portazgo.
Clara: Y debemos **bajar** en Atocha, ¿verdad?
Elena: Exacto, allí en Atocha bajamos.

jóvenes *young people* **plano** *map* **entrada** *entrance* **cambiar** *to change* **bajar** *to get off*

¡Te toca a ti!

A. Cambiamos en... Bajamos en... A friend asks you questions about where to change lines and where to get off the subway in order to get to his (her) destination. Based on the cues, answer his (her) questions. The place to change lines is listed first and the destination is second. Follow the model.

MODELO Sol / la Plaza de España
    Amigo(a): *¿Es necesario cambiar de trenes?*
    Tú: *Sí, tienes que cambiar en Sol.*

258 *Cuarta unidad* Vamos al centro

Etapa Support Materials

- Workbook: pp. 137-142
- Textbook Cassettes/CDs: Cassette 2, Side A; CD 2, Track 32
- Tapescript: Textbook Cassettes/CDs p. 204
- Overhead Transparencies: 50, 51
- Middle School Activities: pp. 95, 96
- Lesson Plan Book: pp. 62-63

- Testing Program: Quiz pp. 122-124; Answer Key & Testing Cassettes Tapescript pp. T51
- Testing Cassettes: Cassette Side B
- Computerized Testing Program: Windows™; Macintosh®
- Atajo Writing Assistant Software: Student Text p. 265

Amigo(a): ¿Dónde bajo del tren?
Tú: Debes bajar en la Plaza de España.

1. Pacífico / Manuel Becerra
2. Callao / Lavapiés
3. Bilbao / Goya
4. Ópera / Cuatro Caminos
5. Ventas / Banco de España
6. Goya / Sol

B. ¡Vamos a tomar el metro!
Use the metro map that follows to explain how to use the subway. The metro line number (shown in parentheses after the name of each station mentioned) will help you locate the stations. Follow the model.

MODELO   Juan / la Plaza de España (3, 10) → Ventas (2)
Juan, para ir a Ventas desde la Plaza de España, es necesario tomar la dirección Legazpi. Tienes que cambiar de tren en Callao, dirección de Canillejas, y debes bajar en Ventas.

1. Marcos / Argüelles (4) → Rubén Darío (5)
2. Pilar / Nueva Numancia (1) → Embajadores (3)
3. Felipe / Delicias (3) → Atocha (1)
4. Nilda / Manuel Becerra (6) → Plaza de Castilla (1)

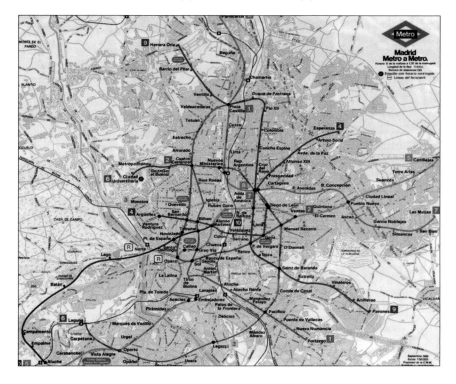

Capítulo 11 Vamos a tomar el metro **259**

PRACTICE / APPLY

A. Cambiamos en... Bajamos en...
ANSWERS
1. ¿Es necesario cambiar de trenes? Sí, tienes que cambiar en Pacífico. ¿Dónde bajo del tren? Debes bajar en Manuel Becerra.

Questions 2 through 6 will follow the same pattern.

B. ¡Vamos a tomar el metro!
SUGGESTIONS

TRANSPARENCY 50

Demonstrate the model using the transparency or by holding up your book while students follow along with their fingers. Then have them work in pairs. If students first read the **Comentarios culturales** on page 260, the activity will be easier to understand.

POSSIBLE ANSWERS
1. Marcos, es necesario tomar la dirección de Esperanza. Tienes que cambiar de tren en A. Martínez, dirección de Canillejas, y debes bajarte en Rubén Darío.
2. Pilar ... la dirección de la Plaza de Castilla, ... cambiar de tren en Sol, ... dirección de Legazpi, ... bajarte en Embajadores.
3. Felipe ... la dirección de Moncloa, ... cambiar de tren en Sol, ... dirección de Portazgo, ... bajarte en Atocha.
4. Nilda ... la dirección de la Ciudad Universitaria, ... cambiar de tren en Nuevos Ministerios, ... dirección de Fuencarral, ... bajarte en la Plaza de Castilla.

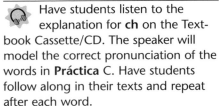

TEACH/MODEL

Pronunciación

 TEXTBOOK CASSETTE/CD CASSETTE 1, SIDE A; CD 2, TRACK 33

 TAPESCRIPT P. 205

Have students listen to the explanation for **ch** on the Text-book Cassette/CD. The speaker will model the correct pronunciation of the words in **Práctica** C. Have students follow along in their texts and repeat after each word.

Auditory-Musical

D. Como de costumbre

SUGGESTION

Quickly review the forms of the verb **ir**, days of the week and modes of transportation before doing this activity. Use the **¿Cómo se dice?** and **¿Qué quiere decir?** question format.

EXPANSION

Review the other forms of **ir** by asking personalized questions in both the **tú** and the **Uds.** forms. For example: **¿Adónde vas mañana por la mañana? ¿El domingo por la mañana? ¿Cómo vas? ¿Adónde van tú y tus amigos(as) los sábados por la noche?** etc.

PRONUNCIACIÓN THE CONSONANT **ch**

The sound of **ch** in Spanish is like the *ch* in the English word *church*.

Práctica

C. Listen and repeat as your teacher models the following words.

1. chocolate	6. ocho
2. Chile	7. leche
3. mucho	8. noche
4. muchacho	9. ochenta
5. coche	10. mochila

Comentarios CULTURALES

El metro

The **metro** is one of the most popular means of transportation in Madrid. The rate for each trip on the subway is fixed. Booklets of tickets are available, and buying tickets by the booklet is cheaper than buying individual tickets. To get around on the **metro** you must first find the **línea** on which you want to travel. Then look for the direction you want to go on that line and find the name of the last station. Follow the signs for that station.

Repaso

D. Como de costumbre (As usual) Some members of your family follow a regular routine. On a certain day of the week, they always do the same thing. Describe where they go and how they get there, based on the following drawings. Follow the model.

MODELO tu madre
Los lunes mi madre va al centro.
Usualmente ella va a pie.

LUNES

The Standards

- Interpersonal Communication 1.1: A, **Adelante** activities
- Interpretive Communication 1.2: A, B, D, E, F, G, **Aquí escuchamos**
- Cultural Products and Perspectives 2.2: **Comentarios culturales**
- Connections with Other Disciplines 3.1: B
- Linguistic Comparisons 4.1: **Pronunciación**

Focus on Culture

The ch and the ll

Tell students that **ch** is no longer part of the Spanish alphabet. It was decided by the **Real Academia Española de la Lengua** in 1993 to eliminate both the **ch** and the **ll** as letters. Words that start with **ch** and **ll** will now be put under the **c** and **l** categories.

Linguistic Comparisons 4.1

1. tu abuelo

2. tu primo

3. tu hermana

4. tu tío y tu tía

5. tus primas

6. tus padres

ESTRUCTURA

Adverbs for the present and the future

Mi mamá trabaja **hoy.**	*My mother is working today.*
Mañana ella no va a trabajar.	*Tomorrow she's not going to work.*
¿Dónde están **ahora?**	*Where are they now?*

1. You have already learned several adverbs that express present or future time.

hoy	mañana
esta mañana	mañana por la mañana
esta tarde	mañana por la tarde
esta noche	mañana por la noche

2. Here are some additional expressions you should learn.

ahora *now*	la semana próxima *next week*
esta semana *this week*	el mes próximo *next month*
este mes *this month*	el año próximo *next year*
este año *this year*	

Capítulo 11 Vamos a tomar el metro **261**

PRACTICE/APPLY

ANSWERS
1. Los sábados mi abuelo va al café. Usualmente él va a pie.
2. Los sábados mi primo va al museo. ...él va en taxi.
3. Los martes mi hermana va a la escuela. ...ella va en autobús.
4. Los viernes mis tíos van al banco. ...ellos van en coche.
5. Los jueves mis primas van al cine. ...ellas toman el metro.
6. Los domingos mis padres van a la iglesia. ...ellos van a pie.

TEACH/MODEL

Estructura
PRESENTATION
On the board write today's date, dates for this week and next, the present year, and next year. Review and introduce the adverbs by using the dates. Begin with the present and move to the future. Continue by talking about your own plans for next week and next year. Then have students answer questions about their plans, gradually familiarizing them with the notion of **próximo(a).** For example: **¿Qué van a hacer Uds. la semana próxima? ¿Y en las próximas vacaciones?**

☼ Spanish for Spanish Speakers

Directions
Ask students for variations to the vocabulary and/or expressions introduced in this **etapa.** A common variation might be the use of the verb **quedar** for **estar** when asking where some building is. For example, **¿Dónde queda el Museo del Prado?**

◉ Linguistic Comparisons 4.1

E. ¿Cuándo van?

SUGGESTION

You could have students create a "word web." On a separate piece of paper, students would draw a web, and then connect elements from the columns in ways that form grammatically correct sentences. They would have to write in the correct forms of the verb in column B. Word web formats will vary from activity to activity.

▲▲ Visual-Spatial

F. Esta noche no

ANSWERS

1. El miércoles por la noche no... . Vamos al centro el miércoles por la tarde.
2. ...Voy a hacer un mandado el sábado por la mañana.
3. ...Va a comer en un restaurante la semana próxima.
4. ...Va a estudiar español el año próximo.
5. ...Vamos al cine el viernes por la noche.
6. ...Va a llevar el coche el domingo por la tarde.
7. ...Van a llegar el jueves próximo.
8. ...Voy a estudiar esta noche.

ESTRUCTURA (continued)

3. The expressions **por la mañana, por la tarde, por la noche,** and **próximo(a)** can be combined with the days of the week: **el lunes por la mañana, el sábado por la tarde, el domingo por la noche, el lunes próximo,** etc. Time expressions are usually placed at the very beginning or end of a sentence.

El domingo por la noche *On Sunday night, I am*
  voy a mirar la televisión. *going to watch television.*

Aquí practicamos

E. ¿Cuándo van? Create original sentences using words from each column.

A	B	C	D
Yo	ir	al cine	hoy
Roberto		a Madrid	esta tarde
Nosotros		al museo	el viernes por la noche
mi hermana		al banco	el domingo por la mañana
Uds.		a la iglesia	la semana próxima
Tú		a la escuela	el jueves por la noche
			ahora

F. Esta noche no... Your mother asks you about people's activities, but she has them confused. Correct her statements, using the information given. Follow the model.

MODELO ¿Van al cine tú y Luis esta noche? (mañana por la noche)
Esta noche no podemos ir al cine. Vamos al cine mañana por la noche.

1. ¿Van tú y Felipe al centro el miércoles por la noche? (miércoles por la tarde)
2. ¿Vas a hacer un mandado mañana por la mañana? (el sábado por la mañana)
3. ¿Va a comer Mario en un restaurante esta semana? (la semana próxima)
4. ¿Va a estudiar español tu hermano este año? (el año próximo)
5. ¿Van al cine tú y Yolanda esta noche? (el viernes por la noche)
6. ¿Va a usar el coche tu hermana esta tarde? (el domingo por la tarde)
7. ¿Van a llegar tus abuelos hoy? (el jueves próximo)
8. ¿Vas a estudiar ahora? (esta noche)

262 *Cuarta unidad* Vamos al centro

G. El horario (schedule) de los González Answer the questions about what the González family did during the month of February. Choose the appropriate time expressions, assuming that today is the morning of February 15. Follow the models.

FEBRERO

lunes	martes	miércoles	jueves	viernes	sábado	domingo
1	2	3	4	5 *restaurante*	6	7 *iglesia*
8	9	10	11	12 *restaurante*	13	14 *iglesia*
15 *Sr y Sra teatro en el centro (noche)*	16 *Sr. jugar al tenis*	17 *Sr. trabajo (noche)*	18 *Sra. museo*	19 *Sra trabajo (mañana) restaurante*	20 *Sra curso de francés (tarde)*	21 *iglesia*
22 *catedral*	23 *los Martínez*	24	25	26 *restaurante*	27	28 *iglesia*

MODELO ¿Cuándo va a visitar el museo la Sra. González?
El jueves.

1. ¿Qué noche va a trabajar el Sr. González?
2. ¿Cuándo van a visitar los González la catedral?
3. ¿Cuándo van a comer en un restaurante?
4. ¿Cuándo van a llegar los Martínez?
5. ¿Cuándo va a jugar al tenis el Sr. González?
6. ¿Qué mañana va a trabajar la Sra. González?

MODELO ¿Qué va a hacer el Sr. González el miércoles por la noche?
Él va a trabajar.

7. ¿Qué van a hacer los González esta noche?
8. ¿Qué van a hacer el Sr. y la Sra. González el domingo?
9. ¿Qué va a hacer la Sra. González el sábado por la tarde?
10. ¿Qué van a hacer los González el viernes próximo?

Capítulo 11 Vamos a tomar el metro **263**

G. El horario de los González

 TRANSPARENCY 51

ANSWERS
1. El miércoles.
2. El lunes próximo.
3. Este viernes y el viernes próximo.
4. El martes próximo.
5. Mañana.
6. El viernes.
7. Van al teatro.
8. Van a la iglesia.
9. Va al curso de francés.
10. Van al restaurante.

EXPANSION
Have students practice giving the date of some of the activities of the González family.

Individual Needs

Less-prepared Students
Have less-prepared students write three questions in the **Ud.** form to ask you about next week, using new expressions.

More-prepared Students
Have more-prepared students improvise questions to you using the **Ud.** forms.

Aquí escuchamos

 TEXTBOOK CASSETTE/CD CASSETTE 2, SIDE A; CD 2, TRACK 34

 TAPESCRIPT P. 205

Antes de escuchar

POSSIBLE ANSWERS

They might want to go downtown in order to shop, to see a movie, to sightsee, to go to a museum, or to see a play. They could go by subway or by bus.

Después de escuchar

ANSWERS

1. to buy a CD
2. to see a movie
3. by bus
4. Ventas
5. Ópera

ETAPA SYNTHESIS

¿Qué dirección tomamos?

SUGGESTION

Model this activity first for less-prepared students.

VARIATION

Pose an alternate problem: You are at a **pensión** near the Legazpi Station (3) and want to go to the bullfights near the Ventas Station (2). For a controlled version of this situation, write these guidelines on the board: 1) Tell the desk clerk that you want to take the subway. 2) Ask if the American Express office near the Banco de España Station is near or far from the hotel. 3) Find out what direction to take. 4) Ask if you have to change trains. 5) Summarize what you have heard.

 Interpretive Communication 1.2

EXPANSION

Change the location of the hotel and/or the destination. Prepare cards with several different destinations for your more-prepared students to role-play.

Presentational Communication 1.3

Aquí escuchamos

¿Tomamos el metro? *Elena and Francisco are making plans to go downtown.*

Antes de escuchar Based on what you've learned in this **etapa,** what do you expect Elena and Francisco might say about why they have to go downtown and about how they will get there?

A escuchar Listen twice to the conversation between Elena and Francisco. Pay special attention to what they plan to do and how they plan to get there.

Después de escuchar Answer the following questions based on what you heard.

1. Why does Elena want to go downtown?
2. What does Francisco want to do?
3. How does Francisco suggest they go?
4. Where will they get on the subway?
5. Where do they change trains?

264 *Cuarta unidad* Vamos al centro

¡ADELANTE!

 ¿Qué dirección tomamos? You and your family are staying in Madrid at a hotel near the Plaza de Castilla (line 1). You need to go to the American Express office near Banco de España (line 2). You have just arrived in Madrid and do not understand the subway system yet, so you ask the desk clerk for help. Have a classmate play the role of the desk clerk. After he (she) explains how to get there, you repeat the instructions to make sure you have understood. Use the metro map on page 259.

 Muchas cosas que hacer A foreign exchange student from Caracas will arrive at your school next week. You and two partners want to introduce the student to some of your favorite places and activities. You will have a week of vacation left before classes, so you can plan your schedule over several days.

1. Begin by brainstorming on places to go (favorite restaurants, museums, parks) and things to do (concerts, movies, parties, sports).
2. Narrow your list down so that you have time to do it all during your vacation.
3. Then write out a schedule, beginning when your guest arrives (**llega**). Decide on which days and at what time of day you will do each item on your list (**el sábado próximo por la tarde, el martes entre el mediodía y las tres**, etc.).

 Mis actividades este mes Make a calendar for the current month and indicate what you will be doing on various days of the month. Use the calendar in activity G on page 263 as an example.

DICIEMBRE

lunes	martes	miércoles	jueves	viernes	sábado	domingo
1	2	3	4	5	6	7
8	9	10	11	12	13	14
15	16	17	18	19	20	21
22	23	24	25	26	27	28

Capítulo 11 Vamos a tomar el metro **265**

Muchas cosas que hacer

FYI

 ATAJO WRITING ASSISTANT SOFTWARE

You might want to have students use this software program when doing this activity.

VARIATION

Ask the different groups what they have on their itineraries. Write the places and activities on the board. Then have the class decide which three items are most important.

Categorizing
Prioritizing

EXPANSION

You may want to have a follow-up discussion about the cultural relevance of the students' choices of sites and activities to share with a foreign visitor. Have them come up with categories such as *typically American, unique to our city, ways to meet people.* Help them see that fun activities, e.g., local theme parks, have cultural significance, especially for foreign visitors.

Categorizing

 Cultural Comparisons 4.2

Mis actividades este mes

SUGGESTION

Brainstorm with students to help them come up with a variety of activities that are not on the calendar on page 263.

Additional Practice and Recycling

FYI

 WORKBOOK, PP. 137-142

For recycling and additional practice of the vocabulary, structures, and language functions presented throughout this **etapa**, you can assign the workbook activities as in-class work and/or homework.

Additional Etapa Resources

Refer to the **Etapa** Support Materials list on the opening page of this **etapa** for detailed cross-references to these assessment options.

TEACH/MODEL

En la taquilla

PRESENTATION

 TRANSPARENCY 52

 TEXTBOOK CASSETTE/CD CASSETTE 2, SIDE A; CD 2, TRACK 35

TAPESCRIPT P. 205

 Begin by having students look at the tickets on page 268 and by going over the information in the **Comentarios culturales** on that page. Ask your students if they are familiar with any subway systems in the United States that have automated ticket sales, like the metro in Washington, D.C. Then play the recording on the Textbook Cassette/CD. Ask simple comprehension questions, such as **¿Van a comprar un billete sencillo? ¿Por qué no? ¿Cuánto cuesta un billete de diez viajes?** etc. Then read the dialogue again with students' books open and have students repeat after you.

🎵 Auditory-Musical

⊛ Interpretive Communication 1.2

SEGUNDA ETAPA

Preparación

- What does it cost to ride public transportation in your town or city?
- Do you pay with currency or can you use tokens?
- Can you use a pass?
- What do you do if you do not have exact change?

En la taquilla

Elena y Clara entran en la estación del metro y van a la **taquilla** *(ticket booth).*

Elena: ¿Vas a comprar un **billete sencillo**?

Clara: No, voy a comprar un **billete de diez viajes**. Es más **barato**. Un billete sencillo **cuesta** 125 pesetas y un billete de diez viajes cuesta 625. ¿Y tú, vas a comprar un billete?

Elena: No, yo tengo una **tarjeta de abon transportes**. Con esta tarjeta puedo tomar el metro o el autobús **sin** límite por **un mes entero**.

Clara: ¡Qué bien! Por favor, señorita, un billete de diez viajes.

La empleada: Seiscientas veinticinco pesetas, señorita.

billete sencillo *single ticket* **billete de diez viajes** *ten-ride ticket* **barato** *cheap* **cuesta** *costs*
tarjeta de abono transportes *commuter pass* **sin** *without* **un mes entero** *a whole month*

266 *Cuarta unidad* Vamos al centro

Etapa Support Materials

- Workbook: pp. 143-146
- TRB: Textbook Activity Masters: p. 96
- Textbook Cassettes/CDs: Cassette 2, Side A; CD 2, Track 35
- Tapescript: Textbook Cassettes/CDs p. 205
- Overhead Transparency: 52
- Middle School Activities: pp. 97, 98
- Lesson Plan Book: pp. 64-65

- Testing Program: Quiz pp. 125, 126; Answer Key & Testing Cassettes Tapescript p. T52
- Testing Cassettes: Cassette Side B
- Computerized Testing Program: Windows™; Macintosh®
- Atajo Writing Assistant Software: Student Text p. 271

¡Te toca a ti!

A. En la taquilla
At the ticket booth, ask for the indicated metro tickets. Follow the model.

MODELO
1 ticket
Un billete sencillo, por favor.

1. 2 tickets
2. 1 book of ten tickets
3. 2 books of ten tickets
4. 1 ticket that allows you to travel for a month

B. En el metro
Explain to the people described in the following activity how to take the subway to get where they need to go. Specify the kind of ticket they need to buy. Consult the **metro** map on page 259. **Metro** line numbers are given in parentheses. Follow the model.

MODELO
Your friend Andrea is with you near Menéndez Pelayo (1). She wants to go to Estrecho (1).
Tú vas a la estación Menéndez Pelayo. Compras un billete sencillo, tomas la dirección de Plaza de Castilla y bajas en Estrecho.

1. Gina, your Italian friend, is in Madrid for a couple of days. Her hotel is near Cuatro Caminos (2). She wants to go see a church that is near Atocha (1).
2. Mr. and Mrs. Dumond, French friends of your family, are spending three weeks in Madrid. Their hotel is near the Cruz del Rayo station (9) and they want to go to the bullfights. The Madrid Plaza de Toros *(bullring)* is near the Ventas station (2).
3. Near the Delicias station (3), you meet a disoriented tourist who wants to get to the American Express office near the Banco de España station (2).

—Un billete sencillo, por favor.

PRACTICE/APPLY

A. En la taquilla
ANSWERS
1. Dos billetes sencillos, por favor.
2. Un billete de diez viajes, por favor.
3. Dos billetes de diez viajes, por favor.
4. Una tarjeta de abono de transportes mensual, por favor.

B. En el metro

Individual Needs

Less-prepared Students
Brainstorm a list of expressions, such as **debes tomar/debes cambiar/en dirección**, with less-prepared students before they begin. You may wish to write the expressions on the board for continued reference.

More-prepared Students
Have more-prepared students role-play this activity. The roles will vary, but always have two students giving different directions to the same destination.

MULTIPLE INTELLIGENCES

- Linguistic: All activities
- Logical-Mathematical: A, B, D
- Auditory-Musical: **Aquí escuchamos**
- Visual-Spatial: B, **Por favor...**
- Interpersonal: **¿Qué piensas hacer la semana próxima?**

The Standards

- Interpersonal Communication 1.1: B, **Por favor...**
- Interpretive Communication 1.2: A, D, E, **Aquí escuchamos**
- Presentational Communication 1.3: **¿Qué piensas hacer la semana próxima?**
- Cultural Practices and Perspectives 2.1: **En la taquilla**
- Cultural Products and Perspectives 2.2: **Comentarios culturales**

C. ¿Qué haces?

SUGGESTION

Before doing this activity, quickly review days of the week using the **¿Cómo se dice? ¿Qué quiere decir?** format. Also review the verb **ir**.

VARIATION

Ask the students personalized questions based on the information from the activity. In order to emphasize the habitual vs. future time, ask things like, **¿Qué haces los sábados por la tarde?** vs. **¿Qué vas a hacer el sábado próximo?**, perhaps writing the two questions on the board. Once you establish a pattern, you could continue this as a **pregúntale** activity. This can also serve as an introduction to the next **Estructura**.

EXPANSION

With students' books closed, do a **pregúntale** activity to develop listening skills and practice the new vocabulary. For example: **Juan, pregúntale a José cuándo dan su programa favorito en la televisión**, etc.

Interpretive Communication 1.2

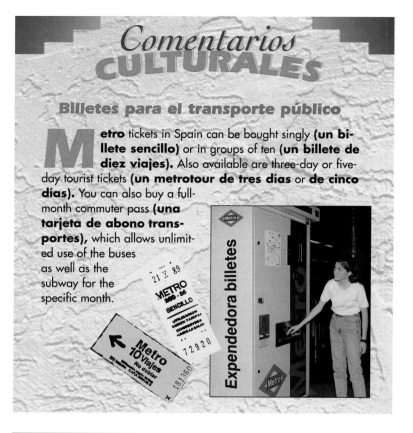

Comentarios CULTURALES

Billetes para el transporte público

Metro tickets in Spain can be bought singly (**un billete sencillo**) or in groups of ten (**un billete de diez viajes**). Also available are three-day or five-day tourist tickets (**un metrotour de tres días** or **de cinco días**). You can also buy a full-month commuter pass (**una tarjeta de abono transportes**), which allows unlimited use of the buses as well as the subway for the specific month.

Repaso

C. ¿Qué haces? Using the adverbs of time that you learned on page 261, tell your classmates about your usual activities (**los sábados, los lunes por la mañana**, etc.) and then about your upcoming plans (**el sábado próximo, el lunes próximo**, etc.). Follow the model.

> **MODELO** los lunes / el lunes próximo
> *Usualmente, los lunes voy a la escuela.*
> *Pero el lunes próximo voy a visitar a mis abuelos.*

1. los sábados por la tarde / el sábado próximo
2. los viernes por la noche / el viernes próximo
3. los domingos por la mañana / el domingo próximo
4. los lunes por la mañana / el lunes próximo
5. los jueves por la tarde / el jueves próximo
6. los sábados / el sábado próximo por la noche

268 *Cuarta unidad* Vamos al centro

Focus on Culture

Subway Stations

Have students study the photo on page 267. Ask them to compare this station to one in the United States, if they are familiar with subway stations. What else do they notice? You may want to bring in pictures of subway stations in the United States to facilitate comparisons.

Comparing and Contrasting

Cultural Comparisons 4.2

Spanish for Spanish Speakers

Vocabulary Variations

A common variation for **billete** is **boleto**. Although Spanish speakers may know how to pronounce these variations, many may have never seen how they are written. Help them with the spelling of these variations by writing them on the board or overhead. Point out to them the spelling of **billete** with an **ll** and **sencillo** with an **ll** and **c**.

Linguistic Comparisons 4.1

ESTRUCTURA

The verb pensar and pensar + infinitive

pensar (ie) *(tothink, to plan)*			
yo	pienso	nosotros(as)	pensamos
tú	piensas	vosotros(as)	pensáis
él ella Ud.	piensa	ellos ellas Uds.	piensan

1. Like **querer** and **preferir**, **pensar** is a stem-changing, **e** to **ie** verb.

2. When **pensar** is followed by an infinitive, it means *to plan (to do something)*. This construction is useful for talking or writing about your future plans.

—¿Qué **piensas hacer** mañana?   *What do you plan to do tomorrow?*
—**Pienso ir** al centro.   *I plan to go downtown.*

—¿Qué **piensa hacer** Juan esta noche?   *What does Juan plan to do tonight?*
—**Piensa estudiar** en la biblioteca.   *He plans to study at the library.*

Aquí practicamos

D. ¿Qué piensan hacer? Using words from each column, create sentences that express future plans.

A	B	C	D
Julia Enrique y yo tú yo Uds.	pensar	ir al cine comer en un restaurante hacer un mandado estudiar dar un paseo	mañana por la tarde el sábado por la noche el viernes por la tarde mañana

？¿Qué crees?

What city does not have a subway system?

a) Barcelona, Spain
b) Buenos Aires, Argentina
c) Bogotá, Colombia
d) Mexico City, Mexico

respuesta ☞

Capítulo 11 Vamos a tomar el metro   **269**

TEACH/MODEL

Estructura

PRESENTATION

First stress the structure: conjugated form of **pensar** + the infinitive. Then say what you plan to do later this week and follow up by asking students about their plans. For example: **Juan, ¿qué piensas hacer el viernes por la noche? María, ¿qué piensan hacer tú y tus amigas este fin de semana?** etc.

PRACTICE/APPLY

D. ¿Qué piensan hacer?

SUGGESTION

These column activities are meant to provide controlled practice. A possible way to present these would be with a "word web". Ask students to write in the forms of the verb in the middle column.

◢◣ Logical-Mathematical

Focus on Culture

Bus Passes

Ask students what might be the advantages of having a full month bus pass. Point out that there are 90 bus routes in Madrid and they all provide excellent and efficient service.

🔍 Evaluating

E. Piensan hacer otra cosa

ANSWERS

1. No, él piensa ver a un amigo en el centro.
2. No, ellos piensan comer en un restaurante.
3. No, ella piensa ir a la biblioteca.
4. No, ellos piensan dar un paseo.
5. No, ellos piensan mirar la televisión en casa.
6. No, ella piensa ir de compras con su madre.

Aquí escuchamos

 TEXTBOOK CASSETTE/CD CASSETTE 2, SIDE A; CD 2, TRACK 36

 TAPESCRIPT P. 205

Antes de escuchar

POSSIBLE ANSWERS

¿Piensas ir a... ?
¿Qué piensas hacer?
dar un paseo
estudiar
hacer un mandado
comer en un restaurante
ir al cine

Después de escuchar

ANSWERS

1. to go to a concert
2. to study
3. to go downtown, eat at a restaurant, and buy books
4. to go to the movies with a friend
5. to go to the **Restaurante Caracol**

Interpretive Communication 1.2

E. Piensan hacer otra cosa (something else)

Your father asks if you plan to go to the movies with your friends. Explain to him that your friends all seem to have other plans. Follow the model.

> **MODELO**   Susana / ir a un concierto
> **Tu padre:**   *¿Piensas ir al cine con Susana?*
> **Tú:**   *No, ella piensa ir a un concierto.*

1. Esteban / ver a un amigo en el centro
2. tus hermanos / comer en un restaurante
3. Linda / ir a la biblioteca
4. tus primos / dar un paseo
5. José y Catarina / mirar la televisión en casa
6. Anita / ir de compras con su madre

Aquí escuchamos

¿Qué piensan hacer?   *Elena and Francisco are talking about their plans for the weekend.*

Antes de escuchar   Based on what you have learned in this **etapa,** what words and expressions do you expect Elena and Francisco to use to ask each other about their plans and to say what they might do?

 A escuchar   Listen twice to the conversation between Francisco and Elena. Pay particular attention to what they say they will do each day.

Después de escuchar
Answer the following questions based on what you heard.

1. What does Elena plan to do on Friday?
2. What does Francisco plan to do on Friday?
3. What does Elena plan to do on Saturday?
4. What does Francisco plan to do on Saturday?
5. What will they do on Saturday night?

☞ c

Hoy pensamos ir al cine.

270   *Cuarta unidad* Vamos al centro

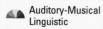 **Spanish for Spanish Speakers**

Vocabulary Expansion–Synonyms

Have Spanish speakers listen carefully to the **Aquí escuchamos** recording and write down five words they hear for which they know or want to find synonyms. Tell them not to limit themselves to just one or two parts of speech, but to choose nouns, verbs, adjectives, adverbs, prepositions, etc. Then give students copies of the dialogue from the Tapescript and have them work with a partner to combine their lists and create a transformed dialogue. Have Spanish speakers and other class volunteers role-play the dialogue with the new words for the rest of the class.

Auditory-Musical Linguistic

Creating

Presentational Communication 1.3

¡ADELANTE!

 Por favor... You have now become an expert on the Madrid metro. While you are waiting at the Plaza de Colón station (4) for a bus to take you to the airport for your trip home, a group of Japanese tourists, just arriving in Madrid, ask you for help in getting to their hotel near the Puerta del Sol station (1). Give them directions, referring to the map on page 259. Have one of your classmates play the role of the group leader for the tourists.

 ¿Qué piensas hacer la semana próxima? Write a note to a friend indicating at least one thing you plan to do each day next week. Specify when you will do each thing by using **por la mañana, por la tarde,** and **por la noche.** Add a sentence in which you say that you *want* to do one of the activities and that you *have* to do another one.

EN LÍNEA

Connect with the Spanish-speaking world!
Access the *¡Ya verás! Gold* home page for
Internet activities related to this chapter.

http://yaveras.heinle.com

Capítulo 11 Vamos a tomar el metro **271**

Additional Etapa Resources

Refer to the **Etapa** Support Materials list on the opening page of this **etapa** for detailed cross-references to these assessment options.

ETAPA SYNTHESIS

Por favor...

EXPANSION

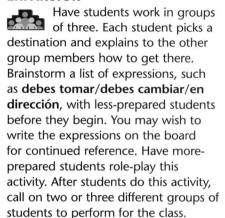 Have students work in groups of three. Each student picks a destination and explains to the other group members how to get there. Brainstorm a list of expressions, such as **debes tomar/debes cambiar/en dirección**, with less-prepared students before they begin. You may wish to write the expressions on the board for continued reference. Have more-prepared students role-play this activity. After students do this activity, call on two or three different groups of students to perform for the class.

Interpersonal Communication 1.1
Presentational Communication 1.3

¿Qué piensas hacer la semana próxima?

FYI

ATAJO ATAJO WRITING ASSISTANT SOFTWARE

You might want to have students use this software program when doing this activity.

SUGGESTION

Brainstorm with the class a list of verbs in two columns, one for expressing wants (**querer, pensar, ir, preferir**), and the other for obligations (**necesitar, tener que, deber**). Keep the lists on the board for less-prepared students to refer to as they write, and encourage more-prepared students to vary their expressions.

 Categorizing

Additional Practice and Recycling

FYI

WORKBOOK, PP. 143-146

For recycling and additional practice of the vocabulary, structures, and language functions presented throughout this **etapa**, you can assign the workbook activities as in-class work and/or homework.

CHAPTER WRAP-UP

Listening Skills Development

FYI

 LAB MANUAL, PP. 73-76

 LAB CASSETTE SIDE B; CD 6, TRACKS 1-9

 TAPESCRIPT: LAB PROGRAM 108-115

It is now appropriate to work through the lab manual activities and their accompanying recordings in class or in the language laboratory.

Improvised Conversation

SUGGESTION

 TEXTBOOK CASSETTE/CD CASSETTE 2, SIDE A; CD 2, TRACK 37

 TAPESCRIPT P. 206

 TRB: ACTIVITY MASTER, P. 96

Have students listen to this conversation in which two people are using a map of the Madrid **metro** to get to the Puerta del Sol. Tell them to try to identify some of the names of the Madrid **metro** stations that are mentioned. You may want to have them look at page 259 of their books to aid their comprehension, or provide photocopies of the map and have students trace the route they hear.

 Auditory-Musical
Visual-Spatial

 Interpretive Communication 1.2

Resources for Spanish-speaking Students

FYI

 WORKBOOK FOR SPANISH-SPEAKING STUDENTS: PP. 67-72

 ANSWER KEY TO SSS WORKBOOK PP. 20-21

Activities specially written to meet the needs of Spanish-speaking students are available in this workbook for the reinforcement and extension of the topics and language presented in this chapter.

VOCABULARIO

Para charlar

Para tomar el metro

Bajamos en Plaza de España.
bajar
Cambiamos en Sol.
cambiar
¿En qué dirección?

Para hablar del futuro

pensar + *infinitive*
esta semana
este mes
este año
la semana entera
el mes entero
el año entero
la semana próxima
el mes próximo
el año próximo
el domingo por la noche

Temas y contextos

El metro

un billete sencillo
un billete de diez viajes
una entrada
una estación de metro
una línea
un metrotour de tres días
un metrotour de cinco días
un plano del metro
una taquilla
una tarjeta de abono transportes

Vocabulario general

Otras palabras y expresiones

barato
cuesta
un horario
jóvenes
jugar (al tenis)
sin

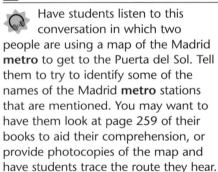

Additional Chapter Resources

Refer to the Chapter Support Materials list on the opening page of this chapter for detailed cross-references to *¡Ya verás! Gold's* student-centered technology components and various assessment options.

Spanish for Spanish Speakers

Keeping a Vocabulary Notebook

Remind Spanish-speaking students to add words and expressions from this vocabulary section to the problematic spelling combination categories and personal new vocabulary lists they started in their notebooks in Chapter 1. Reinforce that they should continue to do this each time a chapter in the textbook is completed.

ENCUENTROS CULTURALES

◆

Viaje por Latinoamérica

Antes de leer

Viaje por Latino-américa
SUGGESTION
You may want to review vocabulary for transportation: **el autobús (la guagua), la bicicleta, el coche (el auto, el carro), la motocicleta, el metro, el taxi, el avión, el tren, el barco.**
 Linguistic Comparisons 4.1

1. Skim the first paragraph. What is this reading going to be about?

2. What means of transportation are available where you live?

3. Do you know of any places where people get around differently? What forms of transportation are used there?

Reading Strategies
• Skimming for the gist
• Activating background knowledge

Antes de leer
POSSIBLE ANSWERS
1. Transportation in Latin America
2. Answers will vary.
3. Answers will vary.

El transporte en América Latina varía de país en país. Hay aviones, trenes, metros, autobuses, taxis, y coches particulares y otras formas de transporte modernas en todos los países. También hay formas de transporte más interesantes para los aventureros. Todo depende de la geografía o la cultura del país y dónde quieres ir.

Colombia fue el primer país en Sudamérica en tener una línea aérea. Se estableció como ACADTA en 1919 y ahora se llama Avianca. Las líneas aéreas colombianas tienen aviones enormes y avionetas pequeñas que vuelan entre las ciudades de Sudamérica y por el resto del mundo. Dentro de Colombia, otras formas de transporte incluyen las chivas— antiguos autobuses de madera usados en áreas rurales— y los colectivos, entre un autobús y un taxi de tamaño.

También hay muchos trenes y metros. Ciudades como Caracas y la Ciudad de México disfrutan de unos sistemas de trenes subterráneos rápidos y baratos. El metro de la Ciudad de México es uno de los sistemas más extensos del mundo. Al contraste, Paraguay tiene trenes anticuados de vapor, a base de leña. No son caros y ofrecen la oportunidad de viajar tranquilamente.

Si prefieres viajar en barco, hay muchos cruceros de lujo que viajan entre las ciudades latinoaméricanas y las islas del Caribe. También hay partes de la costa nicaragüense del Caribe y en el Lago de Nicaragua que sólo tienen acceso por barco. En Panamá los barcos son el medio principal de transporte en varias zonas.

Algunos sitios son bellos pero pocos accesibles. Venezuela, por ejemplo, tiene unos 40 parques nacionales que ofrecen una gran variedad de excursiones. Hay caminos bien marcados y caminos en la jungla que requieren un guía y machete. Para viajar al Salto Aponguao, una de las cataratas más espectaculares, tienes que salir de la carretera, viajar 40 kilómetros por caminos pequeños al pueblo indio de Iboribó, pagarle a un residente para que te lleve por canoa por el Río Aponguao, y caminar media hora hasta llegar a la catarata. Pero vale la pena porque se puede ver una catarata bellísima y nadar en las piscinas naturales debajo.

Capítulo 11 Vamos a tomar el metro **273**

Después de leer

ANSWERS

Answers will vary.

SUGGESTION.

In this series of questions, students are asked to state preferences, give opinions, and speculate about the future. Remind them to use the **ir + a** + infinitive structure to discuss the future.

 Determining Preferences

Guía para la lectura

Here are some words and expressions to keep in mind as you read.

línea aérea	*airline*
vuelan	*fly*
avionetas	*small, 2-engine planes*
madera	*wood*
tamaño	*size*
disfrutan	*enjoy*
vapor	*steam*
leña	*firewood*
barco	*ship, boat*
cruceros de lujo	*luxury cruise ships*
caminos	*paths*
cataratas	*waterfalls*
carretera	*highway*
para que te lleve	*to take you*

Después de leer

1. The reading mentioned various types of transportation in Latin America. Which types of transportation did you find particularly interesting? Explain your choices.

2. Do you enjoy challenges in getting places, or do you prefer to use quick and easy forms of transportation? Why?

3. Technology is gradually changing the face of transportation around the world. Do you think the more colorful forms of transportation in Latin America, such as wooden buses, canoes and steam-powered trains, will survive through the 21st century? Why or why not?

4. In your opinion, what kinds of transportation will be available around the world in 20 years? In 50 years?

274 *Cuarta unidad* Vamos al centro

CAPÍTULO 12

¿Cómo vamos?

—¿Cómo vamos? ¿A pie o en el coche de tu padre?
—Vamos en autobús.

Objetivos

- taking a taxi
- expressing wishes and desires

OBJECTIVES

Functions
- Taking a taxi
- Expressing wishes and desires

Context
- Cities and towns

Accuracy
- Numbers from 100 to 1,000,000
- Discussing plans with **esperar** and **querer** + infinitive

Pronunciation
- The consonant **ll**

CHAPTER WARM-UP

Setting the Context

In preparation for learning more about taking public transportation, have students look at the photo on this page. Do they ever go places with their friends by bus? Point out that there are several sizes and kinds of buses used in Spanish-speaking countries, and that depending on the country or region in which you are traveling, the bus you are taking might be called an **autobus**, **bus**, **microbus**, **buseta**, or **guagua**, just to name a few.

Visual-Spatial

Linguistic Comparisons 4.1

Chapter Support Materials

- Lab Manual: pp. 77-81
- Lab Program: Cassette Side A, B; CD 6, Tracks 10-16
- TRB: Textbook Activity Masters: pp. 97
- Textbook Cassettes/CDs: Cassette 2, Side A; CD 2, Track 43
- Tapescript: Lab Program pp. 116-123; Textbook Cassettes/CDs pp. 207-208
- Middle School Activities: pp. 99-102
- Workbook for Spanish-speaking Students: pp. 73-78
- Answer Key to SSS Workbook: pp. 22-23
- Practice Software: Windows™; Macintosh®

- Testing Program: Chapter Test pp. 135-139; Answer Key & Testing Cassettes Tapescript pp. T55, T56; Oral Assessment p. T53
- Testing Cassettes: Cassette Side B
- Computerized Testing Program: Windows™; Macintosh®
- Video Program: Cassette 2, 13:48-20:53
- Video Guide: Videoscript pp. 49-52; Activities pp. 119-120
- **Mundos hispanos 1**
- Internet Activities: Student Text p. 287

TEACH/MODEL

¡Vamos a tomar un taxi!

PRESENTATION

TEXTBOOK CASSETTE/CD CASSETTE 2, SIDE A; CD 2, TRACK 38

TAPESCRIPT P. 206

Begin by doing a mini-planning strategy about taking a taxi. Have students generate the address, how long the trip will take, and how much it will cost. Then have students listen to the recording on the Textbook Cassette/CD. Ask: **¿Adónde van Linda y Julia? ¿Cuál es la dirección del Restaurante Julián Rojo? ¿Cuánto tarda en llegar? ¿Cuesta mucho el taxi?**

Since this conversation is fairly challenging, you will probably want to replay it with students looking at the book. You can then ask again any questions that may have caused difficulty.

Auditory-Musical

Interpretive Communication 1.2

PRIMERA ETAPA

Preparación

- Have you ever taken a taxi?
- What information must you give to the taxi driver?
- What information can you expect him or her to give you?
- What do you know about payment?
- Are you expected to give a tip?

¡Vamos a tomar un taxi!

Linda y Julia van a una **agencia de viajes** *(travel agency)* **pero antes** *(before), van a* **almorzar** *(eat lunch) en un restaurante que está cerca de la agencia. Piensan tomar un taxi.*

Linda:	¡Taxi! ¡Taxi!
El chófer:	¿Señoritas? ¿Adónde van? *Ellas* **suben** *(get in) al taxi.*
Linda:	Queremos ir al Restaurante Julián Rojo, avenida Ventura de la Vega 5, por favor. **¿Cuánto tarda** para llegar?
El chófer:	Diez minutos... quince **como máximo.**

Ellas llegan al restaurante. Julia baja del taxi y Linda va a **pagar.**

Linda:	¿Cuánto es, señor?
El chófer:	**Trescientas ochenta** pesetas, señorita.
Linda:	Aquí tiene **quinientas** pesetas, señor.
El chófer:	Aquí tiene Ud. el **cambio, ciento veinte** pesetas. *Linda le* **da** *70 pesetas al chófer como* **propina.**
Linda:	Y **esto es para Ud.,** señor.
El chófer:	Muchas gracias, señorita. Hasta luego.

Cuánto tarda *How long does it take* **como máximo** *at most* **pagar** *to pay* **trescientas ochenta** *Three hundred eighty* **quinientas** *five hundred* **cambio** *change* **ciento veinte** *one hundred twenty* **da** *gives* **propina** *tip* **esto es para Ud.** *this is for you*

Etapa Support Materials

- Workbook: pp. 147-152
- Textbook Cassettes/CDs: Cassette 2, Side A; CD 2, Track 38
- Tapescript: Textbook Cassettes/CDs p. 206
- Middle School Activities: pp. 105-107
- Lesson Plan Book: pp. 67-68

- Testing Program: Quiz pp. 131, 132; Answer Key & Testing Cassettes Tapescript p. T54
- Testing Cassettes: Cassette Side B
- Computerized Testing Program: Windows™; Macintosh®
- Atajo Writing Assistant Software: Student Text p. 282

¡Te toca a ti!

A. ¿Adónde van?
A taxi driver asks you where you and a friend are going. Have a classmate play the driver. Tell him (her) the name of the place and the address. Follow the model.

> **MODELO** Restaurante Capri / calle Barco 27
> **Compañera(o):** ¿Adónde van?
> **Tú:** Queremos ir al Restaurante Capri, Calle Barco 27.

1. Hotel Praga / calle Antonio López 65
2. Restaurante Trafalgar / calle Trafalgar 35
3. Hotel Don Diego / calle Velázquez 45
4. Café Elche / calle Vilá-Vilá 71
5. Hotel Ramón de la Cruz / calle Don Ramón de la Cruz 91

B. ¿Cuánto tarda para llegar?
As you make plans with a friend, you discuss how long it will take to get to your destination. The answer will depend on the means of transportation you choose. Remember that in Spanish the preposition **en** is used in the expressions **en coche, en autobús, en metro, en taxi,** and **en bicicleta,** but **a** is used in **a pie.** Follow the model.

> **MODELO** al parque / en autobús (10 minutos) / a pie (30 o 35 minutos)
> **Tú:** ¿Cuánto tardas para ir al parque?
> **Amigo(a):** Para ir al parque en autobús, tardo diez minutos.
> **Tú:** ¿Y para llegar a pie?
> **Amigo(a):** ¿A pie? Tardo treinta o (or) treinta y cinco minutos.

1. a la biblioteca / a pie (25 minutos) / en bicicleta (10 minutos)
2. a la catedral / en metro (20 minutos) / en autobús (25 o 30 minutos)
3. al aeropuerto / en taxi (45 minutos) / en metro (30 o 35 minutos)
4. a la estación de trenes / en coche (20 minutos) / en metro (10 minutos)
5. al centro / a pie (35 minutos) / en autobús (15 minutos)

PRACTICE / APPLY

A. ¿Adónde van?
SUGGESTION
Ask students personalized questions about places in their town or city. For example: **¿Cuánto tardas para ir a tu casa de la escuela?** etc.

ANSWERS
1. Queremos ir al Hotél Praga, calle Antonio López 65.
2. …al Restaurante Trafalgar, calle Trafalgar 35.
3. …al Hotel Don Diego, calle Velázquez 45.
4. …al Café Elche, calle Vilá-Vilá 71.
5. …al Hotel Ramón de la Cruz, calle Don Ramón de la Cruz 91.

B. ¿Cuánto tarda para llegar?
EXPANSION
Have pairs of students of equal abilities make up questions to ask the class, using the new expressions. Instruct them to write both singular and plural versions, such as **¿Cuánto tardas para ir a tu casa desde la escuela?** and **¿Cuánto tardan Uds. para ir al centro desde la casa?** Call on a variety of students to ask and answer the questions.

☀ Linguistic
✇ Interpretive Communication 1.2

ANSWERS
Answers will follow the model.

MULTIPLE INTELLIGENCES

- Linguistic: All activities
- Logical-Mathematical: A, B, **Palábras útiles**, F
- Auditory-Musical: **Pronunciación**, C, **Aquí escuchamos**
- Interpersonal: D, **Tenemos que tomar un taxi**

☀ **Spanish for Spanish Speakers**

Vocabulary Variations
Ask Spanish speakers if they are familiar with the situation presented in **¡Vamos a tomar un taxi!** If they bring up any variations, help them with the spelling of the variations they provide. Point out that the word **chófer** is also pronounced **chofer**. Both pronunciations are acceptable.

✇ Linuistic Comparisons 4.1

Pronunciación

SUGGESTION

 TEXTBOOK CASSETTE/CD CASSETTE 2, SIDE A; CD 2, TRACK 39

 TAPESCRIPT P. 206

Have students listen to the explanation for the consonant **ll** on the Textbook Cassette/CD. The speaker will model the correct pronunciation for the words in **Práctica C**. Have students repeat the words as they follow along in their texts.

Auditory- Musical

D. Pensamos hacer...

SUGGESTION

Brainstorm with students to help them come up with a list of activities that can be done with classmates.
Examples: **ir de compras, hacer mandados, mirar un vídeo, ir al cine, visitar el museo, jugar al básquetbol, ir a la biblioteca, dar un paseo, comer en el café, ir a un concierto, estudiar español**.

To elicit expressions with pensamos, poll the different groups to find out what they plan to do and when they plan to get together.

Interpersonal Communication 1.1

VARIATION

Do a three-step interview. Direct the students to form teams of four and number off. Explain that Student 1 will state the task (**Pregúntales a los otros si...**), Student 2 will ask the question (**¿Piensas ir de compras?...**), Student 3 will answer the question, and Student 4 will summarize the answers. Tell the students to rotate roles. When students have finished, you may want to ask one question of every student in the class, and then ask a volunteer to try to remember and summarize the answers.

Presentational Communication 1.3

PRONUNCIACIÓN THE CONSONANT **ll**

You will recall when you learned the alphabet in **Capítulo 1** that the letters **ll** represent a sound in Spanish that is similar to the y in the English word *yes*.

Práctica

C. Listen as your teacher models the following words.

1. llamar	4. tortilla	7. ella	9. maravilla
2. calle	5. ellos	8. Sevilla	10. pollo
3. milla	6. llegar		

Repaso

D. Pensamos hacer... Think of four different things that you plan to do during the coming week and write them down. Then ask several classmates about their plans. When you find someone who plans to do something that is on your list, try to arrange a day and time that you can do it together. Follow the model.

MODELO

Estudiante 1: *¡Hola! ¿Qué piensas hacer esta semana?*

Estudiante 2: *Pienso ver una película el sábado próximo por la tarde.*

Estudiante 1: *Bueno, yo quiero ir al cine también. Vamos juntos.*

Estudiante 2: *Buena idea. ¿A qué hora quieres ir?*

Estudiante 1: *¿A la una?*

Estudiante 2: *De acuerdo. o: No puedo a la una porque tengo que hacer mandados con mi madre. ¿Puedes ir a las cuatro?*

Spanish for Spanish Speakers

Spelling with ll

The spelling of words with **ll** can pose a problem for Spanish speakers, who may use those words with a **y**. Have them focus on the spelling of the words listed here. Tell them that **ll** is no longer listed as a separate letter in the Spanish alphabet. The **Real Academia Español de la Lengua** decided in 1993 to eliminate both the **ch** and **ll** as separate letters.

 Connections with Distinctive Viewpoints 3.2

The Standards

- Interpersonal Communication 1.1: D, F, **Adelante** activities
- Interpretive Communication 1.2: A, B, E, F, **Aquí escuchamos**
- Presentational Communication 1.3: **¿Cuál es la distancia entre Washington D.C. y ...?**
- Connections with Distinctive Viewpoints 3.2: **Comentarios culturales**, G
- Linguistic Comparisons 4.1: **Pronunciación**

Comentarios CULTURALES

La Puerta del Sol en Madrid

La Puerta del Sol is one of the most lively and popular **plazas** in Madrid. Several **metro** lines intersect there, and it is the location of **kilómetro 0,** the point from which official distances from Madrid to other cities in Spain and Portugal are measured. Below are the official distances from the capital to some major Spanish and Portuguese cities. Note that distances in Spain, as well as in most Spanish-speaking countries, are measured in kilometers **(kilómetros),** the metric equivalent of about 5/8 of a mile **(milla).**

Segovia	99 km	Granada	423 km
Salamanca	209 km	Málaga	532 km
Burgos	237 km	Porto	561 km
Valencia	351 km	Barcelona	617 km
Córdoba	389 km	Cádiz	624 km
Pamplona	401 km	Lisboa	632 km

⁇ ¿Qué crees?

The distance between Madrid, Spain, and Paris, France is approximately equal to the distance between:

a) Detroit, MI and Atlanta, GA

b) Boston, MA and Washington DC

c) Chicago, IL and New Orleans, LA

d) Albuquerque, NM and Oklahoma, OK.

respuesta

PALABRAS ÚTILES

Numbers from 100 to 1,000,000

100	cien	1.000	mil
101	ciento uno	2.000	dos mil
102	ciento dos	4.576	cuatro mil quinientos setenta y seis
200	doscientos(as)	25.489	veinticinco mil cuatrocientos ochenta y nueve
300	trescientos(as)	1.000.000	un millón
400	cuatrocientos(as)	2.000.000	dos millones
500	quinientos(as)		
600	seiscientos(as)		
700	setecientos(as)		
800	ochocientos(as)		
900	novecientos(as)		

Capítulo 12 ¿Cómo vamos? **279**

TEACH/MODEL

Palabras útiles

PRESENTATION

Begin by having students count from one to ten and then by tens to 100. Then count slowly from 101 to 110 and then by tens to 200, and so on up to 1,000. Continue by writing a few three-digit numbers on the board; say them out loud and have students repeat. Go through the points listed on page 280. Then write some dates on the board, show how they are formed, and have the class repeat them.

PRACTICE/APPLY

EXPANSION

 Write **nací** and **nació** on the board and have students write out in Spanish the year in which they were born: **Nací en mil novecientos... .** Then have them do the same for one of their parents or siblings using **mi papá (mamá, hermano, hermana, etc.) nació en... .**

⊛ Interpersonal Communication 1.1

E. Los números

ANSWERS

1. doscientos setenta y ocho, quinientos cuarenta y seis, ciento cincuenta y seis, cuatrocientos ochenta, seiscientos diez, ochocientos diecisiete, setecientos veintinueve

2. mil ochocientos, cinco mil quinientos setenta y cinco, siete mil novecientos dos, tres mil setecientos veintiuno, seis mil ciento treinta y cuatro

3. once mil doscientos noventa y siete, cuarenta y nueve mil setecientos noventa y cinco, sesenta y siete mil setecientos cincuenta y dos, ochenta y siete mil novecientos setenta y dos, noventa y ocho mil trescientos ochenta y seis

4. doscientos veinticinco mil cuatrocientos ochenta y nueve, trescientos sesenta y nueve mil setecientos sesenta y cinco, quinientos sesenta y nueve mil cuatrocientos treinta y dos, setecientos ochenta y nueve mil quinientos veintiocho, ochocientos cincuenta y dos mil doscientos ochenta y nueve

5. un millión quinientos mil, dos milones ochocientos mil, cincuenta y seis millones doscientos cincuenta mil, setenta y seis mil cuatrocientos cincuenta mil

EXPANSION

Divide the class into two teams and then dictate some basic math problems. Teams win a point for coming up with the correct answer first. Write the plus, minus, multiplication, and division symbols on the board and write out their Spanish equivalents to use in the math problems: **más, menos, por, dividido por.**

🔺 Logical-Mathematical

PALABRAS ÚTILES (conTiNUED)

1. The word **cien** is used before a noun: **cien discos compactos.**

2. **Ciento** is used with numbers from 101 to 199. There is no **y** following the word **ciento:** 120 = **ciento veinte.**

3. **Cientos** changes to **cientas** before a feminine noun: **doscientos hombres, doscientas mujeres.**

4. Spanish uses a period where English uses a comma: **3.400** = 3,400 (three thousand four hundred).

5. **Millón/millones** is followed by **de** when it accompanies a noun: **un millón de dólares, tres millones de habitantes.**

☞ **a**

Aquí practicamos

E. Los números Read the following numbers out loud.

1. 278	2. 1.800	3. 11.297	4. 225.489	5. 1.500.000
546	5.575	35.578	369.765	2.800.000
156	7.902	49.795	569.432	56.250.000
480	3.721	67.752	789.528	76.450.000
610	6.134	87.972	852.289	
817		98.386		
729				

F. ¿Cuál es la distancia entre Madrid y...? Take turns with a partner asking and answering questions about the distance between Madrid and each of the following cities. Consult the chart that follows to find the information you will need for your answers. Take notes and together create a list of the cities in the order of their distance from Madrid. Start your list with the city that is closest. Follow the model.

MODELO　　Segovia / Lisboa

Estudiante 1: *¿Cuál es la distancia entre Madrid y Segovia?*
Estudiante 2: *Noventa y nueve kilómetros.*
Estudiante 1: *¿Está más lejos que Lisboa?*
Estudiante 2: *No, Lisboa está a seiscientos treinta y dos kilómetros de Madrid.*

1. Valencia / Lisboa　　3. Pamplona / Barcelona
2. Granada / Porto　　4. Burgos / Málaga

280 *Cuarta unidad* Vamos al centro

Focus on Culture

Currencies

Introduce the names of currencies used in other countries, including **pesos** in Mexico, Colombia, Chile, Argentina, and Bolivia, **colones** in Costa Rica and El Salvador, **sucres** in Ecuador, **bolívares** in Venezuela, and U.S. dollars (**dólares**) in Puerto Rico. Point out that even if countries call their currencies by the same name, currencies are usually different and have different values in each country.

🔻 Cultural Comparisons 4.2

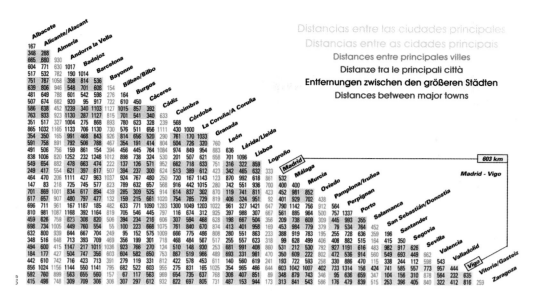

Distancias entre las ciudades principales
Distancias entre as cidades principais
Distances entre principales villes
Distanze tra le principali città
Entfernungen zwischen den größeren Städten
Distances between major towns

603 km

Madrid - Vigo

Aquí escuchamos

¡Taxi, taxi! *Elena and Francisco are going to take a taxi to a museum in the city.*

Antes de escuchar Based on what you've learned in this **etapa**, what do you expect Elena and Francisco 1) to ask the taxi driver, 2) to tell the taxi driver, and 3) to be told by the taxi driver?

 A escuchar Listen twice to the conversation and pay special attention to the numbers mentioned.

Después de escuchar Answer the following questions based on what you heard.

1. Where do Elena and Francisco want to go?
2. What is the name of the street?
3. What is the street number?
4. How long will it take to get there?
5. How much did the taxi ride cost?

Capítulo 12 ¿Cómo vamos? **281**

F. ¿Cuál es la distancia entre Madrid y...?
ANSWERS
1. trescientos kilómetros, seiscientos treinta y dos kilómetros
2. cuatrocientos veintitrés kilómetros, quinientos sesenta y un kilómetros
3. cuatrocientos y un kilómetros, novecientos sesenta y tres kilómetros
4. doscientos treinta y siete kilómetros, cuatrocientos kilómetros

Aquí escuchamos

 TEXTBOOK CASSETTE/CD CASSETTE 2, SIDE A; CD 2, TRACK 40

 TAPESCRIPT PP. 206-207

Antes de escuchar
ANSWERS
1. ¿Cuánto tarda para llegar a... ?
2. Queremos ir a...
3. They might be told how long it will take to get to their destination and how much it will cost.

Después de escuchar
ANSWERS
1. to the Museo Reina Sofía
2. calle Santa Isabel
3. 52
4. about 15 minutes
5. 730 **pesetas** plus 70 **pesetas** as tip

  Spanish for Spanish Speakers

Vocabulary Expansion–Synonyms

Have Spanish speakers listen carefully to the **Aquí escuchamos** recording and write down five words they hear for which they know or want to find synonyms. Tell them not to limit themselves to just one or two parts of speech, but to choose nouns, verbs, adjectives, adverbs, prepositions, etc. Then give students copies of the dialogue from the Tapescript and have them work with a partner to combine their lists and create a transformed dialogue. Have Spanish speakers and other class volunteers role-play the dialogue with the new words for the rest of the class.

Creating

Auditory-Musical Linguistic

Presentational Communication 1.3

ETAPA SYNTHESIS

Tenemos que tomar un taxi

SUGGESTION

 Create activity cards by writing the destination on one side of the card (Plaza Mayor) and the time (15 minutes) and price (**1.200 pesetas**) on the other. Model the dialogue and write the steps to be represented. For each step, ask the class to suggest appropriate expressions. Then divide the class into pairs and have each pair choose a card. Students playing the American tourist look at side 1 of the card for the address. Their partner then looks at side 2 for time and price.

¿Cuál es la distancia entre Washington, DC, y...?

FYI

ATAJO ATAJO WRITING ASSISTANT SOFTWARE

You might want to have students use this software program when doing this activity.

SUGGESTION

Bring a map or almanac in which students can research the distances of American cities from Washington.

EXPANSION

Have students include further information about the cities they chose to write about: New Orleans (French/Cajun/Creole culture and cuisine, jazz, Mardi Gras), Miami (Cuban culture/arts, beaches), San Antonio (history, missions, Mexican culture/ arts/architecture).

Additional Practice and Recycling

FYI

 WORKBOOK, PP. 147-152

For recycling and additional practice of the vocabulary, structures, and language functions presented throughout this **etapa**, you can assign the workbook activities as in-class work and/or homework.

¡ADELANTE!

 Tenemos que tomar un taxi. You are in Madrid with your parents, who don't speak Spanish. They want to go from their hotel (the Euro Building) to the Plaza Mayor. They ask you to go with them in a taxi. A classmate will play the role of the taxi driver.

1. Hail the taxi.
2. Tell the driver where you want to go.
3. Ask if your destination is nearby.
4. Ask how long the trip will take.
5. On arriving at your destination, ask how much the ride costs.
6. Give the driver a tip.

 ¿Cuál es la distancia entre Washington, DC, y...? In Washington, DC, there is also a point from which distances are measured. It is on the Ellipse, between the White House and the Washington Monument. A friend from Spain writes to you and is curious about distances between Washington, DC, and some other major cities, including where you live. Choose two cities in addition to your own and find out what the distances are. Write a letter giving your friend the information.

Additional Etapa Resources

Refer to the **Etapa** Support Materials list on the opening page of this **etapa** for detailed cross-references to these assessment options.

SEGUNDA ETAPA

Preparación

- Have you ever been to a travel agency?
- When would you go to one?
- Where would you want to go on a trip?

En la agencia de viajes

Linda y Julia visitan la
agencia de viajes.

Agente:	¿En qué puedo servirles?
Linda:	Queremos planear un **viaje.**
Agente:	¿Adónde piensan ir?
Linda:	**Esperamos** viajar a París. ¿Cuánto cuesta viajar a París **en avión?**
Agente:	Muchísimo. Un **viaje de ida y vuelta** cuesta 31.000 pesetas.
Julia:	¿Y **en tren?**
Agente:	En tren es más barato. Un billete de ida y vuelta **sólo** cuesta 15.000 pesetas.
Linda:	**Es mucho. Sólo tengo** 10.000 pesetas y mi amiga tiene 9.000.
Agente:	Entonces, por 7.000 pesetas pueden ir a Barcelona o a Málaga.
Julia:	¡Mm, Málaga tiene unas **playas hermosas!**
Linda:	¡Buena idea! Pero primero tenemos que discutir los planes con nuestros padres.
Agente:	Muy bien. **Aquí estoy para servirles.**
Linda:	Muchísimas gracias.
Julia:	Hasta luego.

¿En qué puedo servirles? *How may I help you?* **viaje** *trip* **Esperamos** *We hope* **en avión** *by plane*
viaje de ida y vuelta *round trip* **en tren** *by train* **sólo** *only* **Es mucho.** *That's a lot.* **Sólo tengo** *I only have*
playas hermosas *gorgeous beaches* **Aquí estoy para servirles.** *I'm here to help you.*

Capítulo 12 ¿Cómo vamos? **283**

TEACH/MODEL

En la agencia de viajes

PRESENTATION

	TRANSPARENCY 53
	TEXTBOOK CASSETTE/CD CASSETTE 2, SIDE A; CD 2, TRACK 41
	TAPESCRIPT P. 207

Play the Textbook Cassette/CD or read the dialogue for students (with books closed) and follow up by asking simple comprehension questions. Then play the Textbook Cassette/CD (or read) again and have students follow along in their books. Ask more comprehension questions and then have students read the dialogue in groups of three, alternating the roles.

▲▲ Auditory-Musical

Presentational Communication 1.3

EXPANSION
Find out the current **peseta**/dollar exchange rate and have students calculate the dollar amounts of the costs discussed.

▲▲ Logical-Mathematical

Etapa Support Materials

- Workbook: pp. 153-157
- TRB: Textbook Activity Masters: p. 97
- Textbook Cassettes/CDs: Cassette 2, Side A; CD 2, Track 41
- Tapescript: Textbook Cassettes/CDs p. 207
- Overhead Transparency: 53
- Middle School Activities: pp. 103, 104
- Lesson Plan Book: pp. 69-70

- Testing Program: Quiz pp. 133, 134; Answer Key & Testing Cassettes Tapescript pp. T54, T55
- Testing Cassettes: Cassette Side B
- Computerized Testing Program: Windows™; Macintosh®
- Atajo Writing Assistant Software: Student Text p. 287

PRACTICE/APPLY

A. ¿Adónde esperas viajar?

SUGGESTION

Have students ask their partners the question **¿Adónde esperas viajar?** and then answer, following the model. Then have students form groups and alternate asking similar questions in the **Uds.** form.

Interpersonal Communication 1.1

B. ¿Adónde quiere viajar?

ANSWERS

1. Los Sres. Cano quieren viajar a México.
2. Raúl quiere viajar a París.
3. Bárbara quiere viajar a Quito.
4. Los estudiantes quieren viajar a Madrid.
5. Tú quieres viajar a Buenos Aires.
6. Yo quiero viajar a Caracas.

C. Una encuesta

SUGGESTION

After students have circulated around the room asking questions of their fellow students, ask follow-up questions to give them the opportunity to report back.

EXPANSION

With the help of students, you might create a summative graph on the board to determine the most popular points of interest for travel for the class. Label your graph "**Queremos viajar a… .**"

Visual-Spatial

Connections with Other Disciplines 3.1

¡Te toca a ti!

A. ¿Adónde esperas viajar? Tell where you hope to travel, using the cities listed. Follow the model.

> **MODELO** San Juan
> *Espero viajar a San Juan.*

1. San José
2. Lisboa
3. París
4. Nueva York
5. Quito
6. San Antonio
7. Seattle
8. Buenos Aires
9. Miami
10. Bogotá

B. ¿Adónde quiere viajar? Tell where each of the people in the drawings below want to travel based on what it says on their luggage.

1. Sr. y Sra. Cano

2. Raúl

3. Bárbara

4. los estudiantes

5. tú

6. yo

C. Una encuesta Ask as many classmates as possible where they hope to travel.

MULTIPLE INTELLIGENCES

- Linguistic: All activities
- Logical-Mathematical: E, F
- Visual-Spatial: B
- Auditory-Musical: **Aquí escuchamos**
- Interpersonal: G, **¿Qué planes tienes para el verano próximo?**

The Standards

- Interpersonal Communication 1.1: C, G, **Adelante** activities
- Interpretive Communication 1.2: A, D, E, I, **Aquí escuchamos**
- Presentational Communication 1.3: **La semana próxima…**
- Cultural Products and Perspectives 2.2: **En la agencia de viajes**

Repaso ☉

D. ¿Cuánto es? You and a friend are going over how much money you have paid for certain things. Each time you say a price, your friend asks for confirmation so you repeat more clearly. Follow the model.

MODELO	320
Tú:	*Trescientos veinte.*
Amiga(o):	*¿Cuánto?*
Tú:	*Trescientas veinte pesetas.*

1. 430
2. 350
3. 1.250
4. 790
5. 940
6. 7.500
7. 860
8. 670
9. 30.750
10. 570
11. 760
12. 2.400.000

ESTRUCTURA

Esperar + infinitive and a summary of expressions for discussing plans

Espero comprar un coche nuevo el año próximo.
I hope to buy a new car next year.

Esperamos ir al cine el viernes próximo.
We hope to go to the movies next Friday.

1. **Esperar** *(to hope)* is a regular -ar verb. Like the other constructions you have learned for expressing future plans (**querer, pensar, ir a**), it is followed by an infinitive.

2. Note how the meanings of the four constructions you have learned for expressing future actions progress from uncertain to certain.

Quiero comprar un coche nuevo.   *I want to buy a new car.*

Espero comprar un coche nuevo.   *I hope to buy a new car.*

Pienso comprar un coche nuevo.   *I plan to buy a new car.*

Voy a comprar un coche nuevo.   *I am going to buy a new car.*

Aquí practicamos

E. En el futuro Using words from each column of the following table, form sentences to discuss future plans.

Capítulo 12 ¿Cómo vamos? **285**

D. ¿Cuánto es?
SUGGESTION

Before doing this activity, review numbers. Have students count from 100 to 1000 by hundreds and then by 50s. Have them count from 1000 to 10,000 by thousands; from 10,000 to 100,000 by ten thousands, etc. Write on the board and recite one or two large numbers together, such as 2,436,789.

🔊 Auditory-Musical

ANSWERS

1. cuatrocientas treinta pesetas
2. trescientas cincuenta...
3. mil doscientas cincuenta...
4. setecientas noventa...
5. novecientas cuarenta...
6. siete mil quinientas...
7. ochocientas sesenta...
8. seiscientas setenta...
9. treinta mil setecientas cincuenta...
10. quinientas setenta...
11. setecientas sesenta...
12. dos millones cuatrocientas mil...

TEACH/MODEL

Estructura
PRESENTATION

Since students have already been using these expressions, a quick review is all that is necessary before practicing them. Begin by having students discuss in English the differences between I want to go, I hope to go, I plan to go, and I'm going to go. Then introduce **quiero ir, espero ir, pienso ir, and voy a ir**. Continue by having students form sentences with one of the four expressions to give their personal reactions to the following activities: **comprar un coche nuevo, ir al cine, hacer mi tarea**, etc.

🔵 Linguistic Comparisons 4.1

Focus on Culture

RENFE

The Spanish rail system is called **RENFE**, which stands for **Red Nacional de los Ferrocarriles Españoles**. Point out that long distance trains (especially the **Talgo**) are fast and punctual. The bullet trains built for Expo '92 that run between Sevilla and Madrid travel up to 180 m.p.h. Local trains (especially the **Exprés**) are slow but offer the opportunity to see a lot of the country. There is not much difference between first and second class accommodations on Spanish trains. People between the ages of 12 and 26 are eligible for a **Tarjeta Joven**, with which they receive a 30-50% dicount on train travel if they travel on the **Días Azules** (off-peak days when **RENFE** discounts tickets).

🌐 Connections with Distinctive Viewpoints 3.2

E. En el futuro

SUGGESTION

These column activities are meant to provide controlled practice. A possible way to present these would be through the creation of a "word web." Word web formats will vary in each activity.

 Visual-Spatial

F. Algún día

EXPANSION

Have students write questions to ask each other emphasizing what they want or hope to do versus what they are going to do. For example: **¿Esperas comer en un restaurante hoy? ¿Vas a comer en un restaurante hoy?** Call on different pairs of students to ask and answer these questions.

G. Intercambio

SUGGESTION

Review the meaning of **tener ganas de** + infinitive and **tener que** + infinitive before doing the activity.

EXPANSION

Continue asking similar questions with students' books closed to develop listening comprehension skills. Include some **Uds.** questions to give students more practice answering in the **nosotros** form.

 Interpretive Communication 1.2

Aquí escuchamos

TEXTBOOK CASSETTE/CD CASSETTE 2, SIDE A; CD 2, TRACK 42

TAPESCRIPT P. 207

Antes de escuchar

POSSIBLE ANSWERS

The agent might tell them about the most affordable transportation to get to their destination and things to see and do when they get to their destination.

T286 Unit 4, Chapter 12

A	B	C	D
yo Uds. nosotros Esteban Linda y su amiga tú	(no)	esperar pensar ir a querer	viajar a Argentina algún día visitar a un(a) amigo(a) en Boston el mes próximo cenar con un(a) amigo(a) el sábado por la noche vivir en Colombia el año próximo

F. Algún día Indicate how each person in parentheses feels about doing the following activities. Use the verbs **esperar, pensar, querer,** and **ir a.** Follow the model.

> **MODELO**　ir a Panamá (tu padre / tus amigos / tú)
> *Mi padre no quiere ir a Panamá.*
> *Mis amigos esperan ir a Panamá algún día.*
> *Yo pienso ir a Panamá el año próximo.*

1. ir a Lima (tu madre / tus hermanos [hermanas, amigos] / tú)
2. ser presidente (tú y tus amigos / tu padre / tu hermana [amigo])
3. tener un Rolls Royce (tu padre / tus amigos / tú)
4. vivir en Alaska (tu madre / tu hermana [hermano, amigo] / tú)

G. Intercambio Ask the following questions of a classmate, who will answer them.

1. ¿Qué piensas hacer esta noche?
2. ¿Qué vas a hacer el sábado por la tarde?
3. ¿Qué tienes ganas de hacer el sábado?
4. ¿Qué quieres hacer el domingo?
5. ¿Qué piensas hacer el año próximo?
6. ¿Qué esperas hacer algún día?

Aquí escuchamos

Vamos de viaje *Elena and Francisco are going to a travel agent to talk about plans for a trip.*

> **Antes de escuchar** Based on what you've learned in this **etapa,** what information do you expect Elena and Francisco to find out from the travel agent?

> **A escuchar** Listen twice to the conversation before answering the questions about it that follow.

Después de escuchar Answer the following questions based on what you heard.

1. Where do Elena and Francisco want to go at the beginning of the conversation?
2. What is the price if they go by train?
3. What is the price if they fly?
4. Where do they decide to go?
5. How will they get there?

¡ADELANTE!

 ¿Qué planes tienes para el verano próximo?
You and a partner are making plans to spend part of next summer together.

1. Agree to take a trip to at least three major destinations. (**Pensamos viajar a...**)
2. Determine at least one good reason to go to each place that you plan to visit. (**Quiero... Deseo ver... Me gusta ir de compras.**)
3. Decide on how long you will stay at each place. (**Pensamos estar allí cinco días.**)
4. Determine a means of transportation to use while at each destination. (**en taxi, en autobús, a pie**)
5. Decide how to get there and back. (**en avión, en tren**)
6. Estimate how much the transportation and lodging portions of your trip will cost. (**Un viaje de ida y vuelta cuesta...**)

 La semana próxima Write a note to a friend indicating your plans for each day of next week. Use each of the expressions for making plans that you've learned in this **etapa**.

 **EN LÍNEA**

Connect with the Spanish-speaking world!
Access the **¡Ya verás!** *Gold* home page for Internet activities related to this chapter.

http://yaveras.heinle.com

Capítulo 12 ¿Cómo vamos? **287**

☀ Spanish for Spanish Speakers

Important Dates

You may wish to have some of the Spanish speakers in your class research and choose two or three important dates in their or their relatives' country of origin and make a short presentation for the class telling why each date is important. You may want to ask them to write their dates on the board before their presentation and have the class repeat each date.

 Presentational Communication 1.3

Después de escuchar
ANSWERS
1. to Alicante or Málaga
2. 30.000 ptas.
3. 42.000 ptas.
4. to Cádiz
5. by train

ETAPA SYNTHESIS

La semana próxima
FYI

 ATAJO WRITING ASSISTANT SOFTWARE

You might want to have students use this software program when doing this activity.

Individual Needs

Less-prepared Students
Review days of the week with less-prepared students as well as expressions for the future.

Additional Practice and Recycling
FYI

WORKBOOK, PP. 153-157

For recycling and additional practice of the vocabulary, structures, and language functions presented throughout this **etapa**, you can assign the workbook activities as in-class work and/or homework.

Resources for Spanish-speaking Students
FYI

WORKBOOK FOR SPANISH-SPEAKING STUDENTS: PP. 73-78

 ANSWER KEY TO SSS WORKBOOK PP. 22-23

Activities specially written to meet the needs of Spanish-speaking students are available in this workbook for the reinforcement and extension of the topics and language presented in this chapter.

Vocabulario

SUGGESTION

Have students complete a transportation questionnaire, reviewing the vocabulary of this chapter and of Chapter 10. Ask a series of questions, such as, **¿Tiene tu familia un coche? ¿Qué marca de coche tiene? ¿Quién conduce el coche? ¿Cómo vienes a la escuela? ¿Cuánto tardas para ir de tu casa a la escuela?** etc. After everyone has written the answers, you can then do a summary survey of the class by dividing the class into teams and assigning a question or questions to each team.

Improvised Conversation

SUGGESTION

 TEXTBOOK CASSETTE/CD CASSETTE 2, SIDE A; CD 2, TRACK 43

 TAPESCRIPT PP. 207-208

TRB: ACTIVITY MASTER, P. 97

 Have students listen to this conversation in which two students are making travel plans. You may want to refer students back to the Focus on Culture box about **RENFE** on page 285 so that they can better understand the references to the **Tarjeta Joven** and the **Días Azules**. Refer to the TRB for the corresponding activity master.

 Auditory-Musical

Listening Skills Development

FYI

 LAB MANUAL PP. 77-81

 LAB CASSETTE SIDE A, B; CD 6, TRACKS 10-16

 TAPESCRIPT: LAB PROGRAM PP. 116-123

It is now appropriate to work through the lab manual activities and their accompanying recordings in class or in the language laboratory.

VOCABULARIO

Para charlar

Para ir al centro

¿Cuánto tarda en
 llegar a…?
Tarda diez minutos,
 como máximo.
Esto es para Ud., señor
 (señora, señorita).

Para viajar

Aquí estoy para servirles.
¿En qué puedo servirles?
Queremos planear un viaje.
¿Cuánto cuesta un viaje
 de ida y vuelta en avión?
Es mucho. Sólo tengo
 2.500 pesetas.

Los planes

esperar + *infinitive*

Para contar

cien
ciento
ciento veinte
doscientos(as)
trescientos(as)
cuatrocientos(as)
quinientos(as)
seiscientos(as)
setecientos(as)
ochocientos(as)
novecientos(as)
mil
un millón

Temas y contextos

Los viajes

una agencia de viajes
billete de ida y vuelta
en avión
en taxi
en tren
kilómetro
milla
propina

Vocabulario general

Sustantivos

el cambio
la playa

Verbos

almorzar
discutir
pagar

Adjetivos

famoso(a)
hermoso(a)
nuevo(a)

Otras palabras y expresiones

algún día
antes
o
si
sólo

Spanish for Spanish Speakers

Keeping a Vocabulary Notebook

Remind Spanish-speaking students to add words and expressions from this vocabulary section to the problematic spelling combination categories and personal new vocabulary lists they started in their notebooks in Chapter 1. Reinforce that they should continue to do this each time a chapter in the textbook is completed.

Additional Chapter Resources

Refer to the Chapter Support Materials list on the opening page of this chapter for detailed cross-references to *¡Ya verás! Gold*'s student-centered technology components and various assessment options.

ENCUENTROS CULTURALES

◆

Explora el "Agua Grande"

Antes de leer

1. The title indicates that the reading is about a scenic attraction that some call *Agua Grande*. Why might a place be called *Agua Grande*?

2. What kinds of brochures would you expect to pick up at the information center in a national park? What information would such brochures usually contain?

3. Briefly scan the brochures about the Parque Nacional de Iguazú. Where are the Iguazú falls located?

Reading Strategies

- Using the title to predict content
- Activating background knowledge
- Scanning for specific information

Parque Nacional del Iguazú

Horas: 7:30 A.M.–12:00 A.M. lunes a domingo
Estación de primeros auxilios, Cuartos de baño, Cafetería

Datos importantes:

- Las cataratas del Iguazú (que significa "Agua grande" en el idioma guaraní) están localizadas en la frontera entre Brasil y Argentina, y son las cataratas más espectaculares de Sudamérica.
- El sistema de cataratas tiene forma de herradura y tiene aproximadamente dos y media millas de ancho.
- Numerosas islas dividen las aguas en 275 cascadas, con un altitud de entre 200 y 269 pies.

Algunos puntos de interés:

- Puerto Peligro e Isla de San Martín
- Catarata principal: Garganta del diablo
- Cataratas mayores: Arrechea, San Martín, Tres mosqueteros
- Recorridos por la selva: camino Yacaretea y camino Macuco

Iguazú desde un helicóptero

Capítulo 12 ¿Cómo vamos? **289**

Explora el "Agua Grande"

Antes de leer

POSSIBLE ANSWERS

1. Big Waters. It might be a large body of water.
2. Brochures that describe local attractions, the local wildlife, and instructions on how to get there, and what to do there.
3. Between Brazil and Argentina.

SUGGESTION

You can ask students the following questions to activate their prior knowledge about visiting natural sites.

Have you visited any interesting or exciting natural sites in the United States or elsewhere? Which is the most surprising site you have visited? Which of the following activities would you like to do: camping, whitewater rafting, flying in a helicopter, horseback riding or mountain biking? Where did you do them? Did you have any unusual experiences?

Activating Prior Knowledge
Determining Preferences

Después de leer

1. Transportation includes: helicopter, all-terrain vehicles, canoe, mountain bike, horse, airplane or boat. Answers will vary.

2. **a.** false, they have a horseshoe shape
   b. true, including helicopter, all-terrain vehicles, canoe, mountain bike, horse, boat
   c. false, it means *Big Water*.
   d. true
   e. false, they have tourist guides at a cost of 460,000 (**pesos argentinos**) per person
   f. true

3. Answer will vary.

Guía para la lectura

Here are some words and expressions to keep in mind as you read.

Recorrido	*tour*
Estación de primeros auxilios	*First aid station*
herradura	*horseshoe*
selva	*jungle*
estadía	*stay, sojourn*
nocturnos	*nighttime*

Agencia turística Del Salto:
Iguazú

Guía de excursiones: Costos y medios de transporte (pesos argentinos)

Excursión para acampar . . . . Duración: 3 días
Costo: 87,00 por día.

Recorrido de las cataratas . . . . Duración: 3 horas
Costo: 4,00 por persona.

Excursión en helicóptero . . . . Duración: 7 minutos
Costo: 52,00 por persona.

Safari fotográfico (con guía) . . . . . . Duración: 2 horas
Costo: 25,00 por grupo.

Paseos nocturnos por las cataratas.
Costo: 38,00 por persona.

Excursiones Yusumí: . . . . Duración: 3 días
● Boleto de avión incluido
● Estadía en el Hotel Nacional (cuartos para dos personas)
● Guía turístico especializado
   Costo: 460,00 por persona.

Aventuras en la selva:
● Recorrido en jeep, caballo, bote o canoa . . . . *Costo:* 5,00-25,00 por persona.
● Alquiler de bicicletas de montaña
   Costo: 10,00 por día.
● Alquiler de canoas
   Costo: 10,00 por 30 minutos.

Despúes de leer

1. Mention at least 3 different means of transportation you can use at the park. Which ones would you use to explore the park? Explain your choices.

2. Indicate whether the following statements are true or false. Please correct the false statements.

   a. The falls have a rectangular shape.

   b. There are few means of transportation available to explore the Falls.

   c. Iguazú means *Fast Water*.

   d. You can rent a mountain bike at the falls.

   e. You need to get your own guide if you participate in one of the *Excursiones Yusumí*.

   f. You can see the waterfalls during the nighttime.

3. Would you enjoy visiting this park? Why or why not? What other scenic areas would you like to visit? Why?

290 *Cuarta unidad* Vamos al centro

Conversemos un rato

A. Explorando Quito Role-play the following situations.

1. You have just met a young traveler in Quito, Ecuador and the two of you decide to travel together for a few days. First you must get acquainted with each other. Some places to go to in Quito include many cathedrals and churches, museums (the Museo Aqueológico and Casa de la Cultura), El Jido park, the Colonial City, and shopping in outdoor markets or La Avenida Amazonas.

   a. Greet your new friend and invite him/her to join you for a drink at a café.

   b. Tell each other where you are from and what types of activities you like to do.

   c. Discuss three things you each would like to do in Quito, Ecuador.

   d. Then decide on one thing to do together and make plans to get together.

2. You and your new friend are making plans to spend Saturday in downtown Quito.

   a. Decide when and where you will meet.

   b. Agree on four places to visit or activities to do together.

   c. Decide on the best means of transportation to get downtown and back home.

   d. Finally describe your itinerary to two other classmates and invite them to go with you. Make any necessary changes to your plans to convince them to accompany you.

291

¡Sigamos adelante! Resource

FYI

 LESSON PLAN BOOK: P. 72

You might find it helpful to refer to the Lesson Plan Book before you and your students begin the end-of-unit materials.

 PRACTICE / APPLY

A. Explorando Quito

SUGGESTION

 It may be helpful to have a map of Quito or other tourist information on Quito in order for students to do this activity.

Visual-Spatial

VARIATION

If you don't have enough information on Quito, you can change the location to Mexico City, San Juan, or any other city that students may be familiar with.

Taller de escritores Resource

FYI

 ATAJO WRITING ASSISTANT SOFTWARE

You might want to have students use this software program when writing the first draft and final version of their writing assignment. Tell them that the following language references in **Atajo** are directly related to and will be helpful to their work.

Phrases: Expressing location; Expressing distance; Planning a vacation; Writing a letter (informal)
Vocabulary: Beach; Camping; City; Countries; Direction & distance; Time; Traveling
Grammar: Prepositions: **a**; Verbs: Future with **Ir**

Taller de escritores

Writing a letter

In this unit you will write a letter describing a place you'd like to visit. A sample letter follows.

Writing Strategy
• Individual brainstorming using clusters

---

21 de septiembre de 19__

Querida Estela,

¡Estoy muy contenta! Mis padres me van a llevar a México. Vamos a pasar la semana de vacaciones en Manzanillo en el Hotel Las Hadas. Mi padre va hoy a la agencia de viajes para comprar los **boletos de avión**. Pensamos salir de aquí el 26 de diciembre y volver el 2 de enero. ¡Qué bueno, ¿verdad?!

Dicen mis padres que vamos a pasar un día en Colima donde hay un museo arqueológico muy interesante. Interesante para ellos. No me interesa mucho. Yo tengo ganas de pasar todo el tiempo en la playa. Mi madre dice que puedo comprar un **traje de baño** nuevo antes de ir. Voy a ir de compras mañana. ¡No puedo esperar!

Te escribo con más detalles.

Miles de besos y abrazos de

Carolina

Querida *Dear*   boletos de avión *airline tickets*   traje de baño *bathing suit*
Miles de besos y abrazos de *lots of hugs and kisses from*

MULTIPLE INTELLIGENCES

• Linguistic
• Visual-Spatial
• Interpersonal

The Standards

• Interpretive Communication 1.2
• Presentational Communication 1.3

A. Reflexión First think of a place you would like to go, then write down as many ideas about that place as possible. Create two major ideas and relate other minor points to each of them. Each cluster then forms the basis for a paragraph.

B. Primer borrador Write the first draft of your letter to your pen pal. To organize your thoughts, use the clusters you created.

C. Revisión con un(a) compañero(a) Exchange letters with a classmate. Read each other's work and comment on it, based on these questions.

1. What aspect of the letter do you like the best?
2. In which activities mentioned would you like to participate?
3. Is the letter appropriate for its audience?
4. Does the letter reflect the task assigned?
5. What aspect of the letter would you like to have clarified or made more complete?

D. Versión final At home revise your first draft, incorporating changes based on the feedback from your classmate. Revise content and check your grammar, spelling, punctuation, and accent marks. Bring your final draft to class.

E. Carpeta After you turn in your letter, your teacher may choose to place it in your portfolio, display it on a bulletin board, or use it to evaluate your progress.

☀ Spanish for Spanish Speakers

Immediate Future

Most students will know how to conjugate and use the verb **ir** but they might not know that it is called the *immediate future*.

¡SIGAMOS ADELANTE!

A. Reflexión
SUGGESTION

With the whole class brainstorm a list of words and ideas about travel and vacationing. Then have them create a list of the locations they would like to visit and the activities they would do there.

Remind students that they can use **ir + a + infinitive** to express the immediate future. This structure can be very useful when discussing future plans. They can refer back to page 235 for some examples.

B. Primer borrador
SUGGESTION

Remind students to keep in mind for whom they are writing, about what they are writing, and why they are writing. A personal letter to a friend will have a familiar tone.

C. Revisión con un(a) compañero(a)
SUGGESTION

You may want to model a peer review with the whole class by showing a sample letter on a transparency and answering the six revision questions together. Remind students to start their feedback with something positive and to include some constructive suggestions to improve the writing in the letter.

D. Versión final
SUGGESTION

Students should be aware that they do not have to incorporate all the suggestions given by their classmates, but rather take the ideas or corrections that they feel would improve the content and expression of the message.

EXPANSION

As a follow up activity, have students exchange letters and write a short response to the letter. It should include a reaction to the travel plans and any questions the student may have about the trip.

Para empezar

SUGGESTION

To start discussion on libraries, ask students the following questions: **¿Para qué vas a la biblioteca? ¿Cómo encuentras la información que necesitas? ¿Sabes cómo se organizan los libros en una biblioteca? ¿Usas una computadora en la biblioteca?**

 Interpersonal Communication 1.1

Conexión con la biblioteconomía

Para empezar Most libraries now use computers to store information regarding book location. In fact, many libraries now offer access to books located in other libraries. Nevertheless, most libraries still need to use one of two systems of classification to organize their collection by subject; the Dewey Decimal system or the Library of Congress (LC) system. Do you know which system your school library uses? Which system does your local public library use?

Below is an abridged version of the LC subject headings in Spanish. Single letters indicate the major subject headings and the double letters indicate subcategories within each subject.

Clasificación de la Biblioteca del Congreso

A **Obras generales**
   AE Enciclopedias generales
   AG Diccionarios

B **Filosofía-religión**
   B   Filosofía general
   BF Psicología
   BL Religiones, mitología

D **Historia y topografía (excepto continentes de América)**
   DP España y Portugal

E y F **Historia (los continentes de América)**

G **Geografía y antropología**
   G   Mapas, átlases
   GR Folklore
   GV Recreación y tiempo libre

J **Ciencia política**
   JK Historia constitucional (Estados Unidos)
   JV Colonias y colonización

M **Música**

N **Bellas artes y artes visuales**
   NA Arquitectura
   NC Dibujo, diseño
   ND Pintura

P **Lenguaje y literatura**
   PQ Literatura romance
   PR Literatura inglesa
   PS Literatura de los Estados Unidos

Q **Ciencias puras**
   QA Matemáticas
   QB Astronomía
   QC Física
   QD Química
   QE Geología
   QK Botánica

S **Agricultura**

T **Tecnología**

MULTIPLE INTELLIGENCES

• Logical-Mathematical

 **The Standards**

• Connections with Other Disciplines 3.1

A. ¿Verdadero o falso?

A classmate has written down call numbers and topics to help you find some books. Decide which of the following are correct (*verdadero*) or incorrect (*falso*), based on the chart above. Then correct the topics and letters that are wrong.

MODELO	Tema	Cifra de clasificación
Ludwig von Beethoven	música	M
1. El Greco	mapas, atlases	G
2. William Shakespeare	literatura inglesa	PR
3. Sigmund Freud	Agricultura	S
4. Stephen Hawkings	Física	QC
5. Albert Einstein	Historia y topografía	D
6. Mikhail Barysnikov	Bellas artes y artes visuales	N

B. En la biblioteca

You are a student library assistant at a school in Bogotá. Today library patrons have been forgetting to write down the first letters of the call numbers. Supply the missing portions of the call numbers for the titles below.

MODELO	Enciclopedia universal ilustrada	AE 61.E56 1994
1.	Como agua para chocolate	__6323.A5A6 1989
2.	El estilo de Frank Lloyd Wright	__813.G7Z8 1993
3.	Mitología griega y romana	__725.S62 1998
4.	Música y músicos en Panamá	__L106.M6T3 1991
5.	Plantas de Costa Rica	__217.P57 1985
6.	Planetas y satélites	__501.S3 1997
7.	Historia de Paraguay	__66.H5572 1995
8.	Atlas geográfico de la República Argentina	__1755.A77 1992

C. Pair up with a classmate.

Each of you is to write down three topics that interest you, and give them to your partner. Your partner will write the Library of Congress letters which correspond to each topic.

MODELO   Uso de las bicicletas de montaña en los Estados Unidos
GV

A. ¿Verdadero o falso?
ANSWERS
1. falso
2. verdadero
3. falso, (Freud: Psicología, BF)
4. verdadero
5. verdadero
6. falso (Colón: Colonias y colonización, JV)

B. En la biblioteca
ANSWERS
1. PQ (novel written by Mexican author, Laura Esquivel)
2. NA (American architect, known for modern style)
3. BL
4. M
5. QK
6. QB
7. E y F
8. G

EXPANSION
You may want to read the titles aloud to the students before they do the activity. Some additional titles are: **El ingenioso hidalgo Don Quijote de la Mancha, El artista Goya en Andalucia, Historia de España, La Iglesia Católica en Latinoamérica, Los árboles de los Andes.**

C. Pair up with a classmate
EXPANSION
After each partner has learned the LC letters of the three topics that interest them, have them go to the library and find the call numbers of 3–4 references. If the school library doesn't use the Library of Congress system, a local university or public library might.

Communities In and Beyond School 5.1

TEACH/MODEL

Mexico

PRESENTATION

Tell students that Mexico is the most populous Spanish-speaking country in the world, and that Mexico City is the world's largest city with more than 20 million people.

This city was once an island in Lake Texcoco, and was connected to the shore by causeways. The lake was filled in by the Spanish conquistadors to create extra real estate. However, today the swampy soil is causing some buildings in the capital to sink.

 Connections with Distinctive Viewpoints 3.2

EXPANSION

An Aztec legend said that the Aztec capital should be built where an eagle was seen devouring a snake (two strong images with religious significance). Supposedly Aztec priests saw such a scene on a rock in the middle of Lake Texcoco and so they established their capital city there. It was known then as Tenochtitlán and now is the site of Mexico City. This scene is depicted on the Mexican flag and on Mexican coins.

Connections with Other Disciplines 3.1

Vistas
de los países hispanos

México

Capital: Ciudad de México

Ciudades principales: Guadalajara, Monterrey, Puebla, León, Ciudad Juárez

Población: 86.200.000

Idiomas: español

Área territorial: 1.972.547 km^2

Clima: tiene una zona tropical y otra árida; mantiene una variedad climática muy grande.

Moneda: peso

árida *arid*

EXPLORA

Find out more about México! Access the **Nuestros vecinos** page on the *¡Ya verás! Gold* web site for a list of URLs.

http://yaveras.heinle.com/vecinos.htm

296 *Cuarta unidad* Vamos al centro

MULTIPLE INTELLIGENCES

• Visual-Spatial

 **The Standards**

• Connections with Distinctive Viewpoints 3.2

En la comunidad

Caryl Feinstein—preparada para el siglo XX

"My father jokes that his daughter works in transportation just as he did. The difference between us, he says, is that he sat still so others could travel, whereas I've always traveled so others didn't have to. My father was an air traffic controller; I'm a regional director for an international company that sells telecommunication equipment and I travel throughout Latin America. When my company wanted to send customer representatives to Central America, where we were selling ever-greater quantities of equipment, I decided I would be that person. I started taking classes in business administration, and set out to refresh my high school Spanish. I took an intensive, day-long class every Saturday, plus I listened to Spanish language-learning tapes in the car as I commuted to work. At the end of two years, my company sent me to Bogotá!

Now, as the Latin American regional director, I manage eight employees in Bogotá as well as offices in Venezuela, Chile, Argentina, and Costa Rica. I'm the youngest such manager I know, and I spend all day speaking Spanish—to negotiate, to talk to employees and clients, or when I travel."

¡Ahora te toca a ti!

Make your information travel, so you don't have to! Look through classified ads in Spanish to see if there is a job overseas that might interest you. You can use a computer with Internet access, or go to a local library and look at foreign or Spanish edition newspapers (e.g. The Miami Herald). Use the computer or the newspaper to locate the classified *(los clasificados)* section of a Spanish language newspaper. Use a dictionary as necessary to find your dream job. Then write out in Spanish the corresponding information for the list below.

Job Title:

Company:

Newspaper/Source:

Date:

Responsibilities:

Experience needed:

Salary:

TEACH/MODEL

En la comunidad

SUGGESTION

If you know of any adults in the community that may do business in Latin America consider inviting them in to talk about there cross-cultural experiences while doing business in a new country.

Cultural Practices and Perspectives 2.1

¡Ahora te toca a ti!

SUGGESTION

If you can't find Spanish language newspapers, have students bring in classified ads from an English language newspaper to use as a model and create their own job listing in Spanish for their dream job.

Cultural Practices and Perspectives 2.1
Connections with Other Disciplines 3.1

VARIATION

You can also have students research large American corporations that might do business in Latin America. Have students create their dream job in a U.S. company that wants to expand into the Latin American country of their choice.

Connections with Other Disciplines 3.1

MULTIPLE INTELLIGENCES

- Linguistic
- Visual-Spatial

The Standards

- Communities In and Beyond School 5.1

UNIDAD 5

Setting the Context

Unit 5 does not feature any one student. Instead, it deals with a variety of sports and pastimes around the Spanish-speaking world. Chapter 13 centers on pastimes and extra-curricular activities. Chapter 14 deals with sports that students participate in, and Chapter 15 focuses on two international professional sports that include many Spanish-speaking stars: baseball and tennis.

SUGGESTION

Ask students about their favorite sports and pastimes. Do they like to participate in the same sports they watch regularly? Let them know that many of the same sports that are popular in the United States are also popular in the Spanish-speaking world. People in both cultures like to play baseball, tennis, and basketball and to go cycling. The most popular spectator sport in the United States is football, whereas soccer is the spectator and participatory favorite in Spanish-speaking countries.

Cultural Comparisons 4.2

UNIDAD 5

Tu tiempo libre

Objectives

In this unit you will learn:

- to understand short readings about various aspects of the Spanish-speaking world
- to find out information about various activities in the Spanish-speaking world
- to talk about past, present, and future activities and events

298 *Quinta unidad*

Unit Support Materials

- Workbook: **Aquí leemos** pp. 201-204
- Lab Manual: **Ya llegamos** pp. 105-106
- Lab Program: Cassette Side B; CD 10, Tracks 15-17
- Tapescript: Lab Program pp. 154-155
- TRB: Unit Grammar Review Masters: pp. 38-42; Answer Key pp. 57-58
- Lesson Plan Book: **¡Sigamos adelante!** p. 90
- Workbook for Spanish-speaking Students: pp. 99,100
- Testing Program: Unit Test pp. 179-183; Answer Key & Testing Cassettes Tapescript pp. T70-T71; Oral

Assessment pp. T71-T72; Portfolio Assessment pp. Pxvi-Pxvii
- Testing Cassettes: Cassette Side A
- Computerized Testing Program: Windows™; Macintosh®
- Atajo Writing Assistant Software: Student Text pp. 370-371; Workbook, p. 203
- Video Program: Cassette 2, 55:55-58:48
- Video Guide: Videoscript p. 66; Activities pp. 135-136
- Internet Explorations: Student Text p. 374

¿Qué ves?

- Where are the people in the photographs?
- What are they doing?
- What do you see in the photos that is similar to what you would do in the United States?
- What do you see that is different?

UNIT WARM-UP

Planning Strategy

WORKBOOK, P. 161

If you do not assign the Planning Strategy for homework (Workbook, p. 161) you may want to go over the items in class before beginning Chapter 13.

Los pasatiempos

CAPÍTULO 13

Primera etapa: ¿Qué te gusta hacer?
Segunda etapa: ¿Adónde fuiste?
Tercera etapa: Una semana típica

Actividades deportivas

CAPÍTULO 14

Primera etapa: Los deportes
Segunda etapa: Deportes de verano

Dos deportes populares

CAPÍTULO 15

Primera etapa: El béisbol
Segunda etapa: El tenis

299

CAPÍTULO 13

OBJECTIVES

Functions
- Talking about past events and activities
- Situating activities in the past

Context
- Leisure-time activities

Accuracy
- Preterite of regular **-ar**, **-er**, **-ir** verbs
- Preterite of the irregular verbs **hacer**, **ir**, **andar**, **estar**, and **tener**
- Adverbs, prepositions and other expressions used to designate the past

CHAPTER WARM-UP

Setting the Context

In preparation for their learning about sports and pastimes in Spanish-speaking countries, have students look at the photograph on this page and share what they know about the sport of tennis. There are many professional tennis players from Spanish-speaking countries, as well as those of Hispanic/Latino descent who are from the United States. Ask students if they can name any Hispanic tennis players, and if they know where the players are from. Possibilities include: Gabriela Sabatini from Argentina, Arantxa Sánchez Vicario from Spain, Mary Joe Fernández from the United States, Conchita Martínez from Spain, and Jaime Yzaga from Peru.

 Activating Prior Knowledge

Los pasatiempos

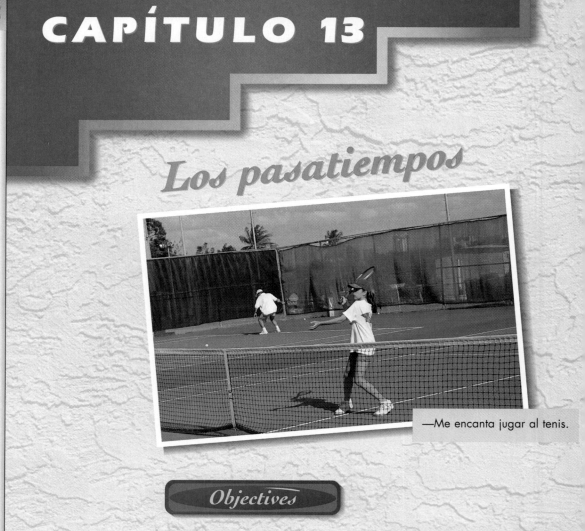

—Me encanta jugar al tenis.

Objectives

- talking about events and activities that took place in the past
- situating activities in the past

300 *Quinta unidad* Tu tiempo libre

Chapter Support Materials

- Lab Manual: pp. 85-91
- Lab Program: Cassette Side A; CD 7, Track 1-10
- TRB: Textbook Activity Masters: pp. 98-105
- Textbook Cassettes/CDs: Cassette 2, Side A; CD 3, Track 6
- Tapescript: Lab Program pp. 127-138; Textbook Cassettes/CDs p. 209
- Middle School Activities: pp. 108-111
- Workbook for Spanish-speaking Students: pp. 81-86
- Answer Key to SSS Workbook: pp. 23-25
- Practice Software: Windows™ Macintosh®

- Testing Program: Chapter Test pp. 135-139; Answer Key & Testing Cassettes Tapescript pp. T61, T62; Oral Assessment p. T62
- Testing Cassettes: Cassette Side A
- Computerized Testing Program: Windows™; Macintosh®
- Video Program: Cassette 2, 24:53-32:44
- Video Guide: Videoscript pp. 53-55; Activities pp. 123-125
- **Mundos hispanos 1**
- Internet Activities: Student Text p. 324

PRIMERA ETAPA

Preparación

- What do you like to do in your free time? Make a list of your favorite activities.
- What don't you like to do? Make a list of these activities.

¿Qué te gusta hacer?

A estas personas les gusta hacer cosas diferentes.

Me gusta ir de compras.

Me gusta leer.

Me gusta hablar por teléfono.

Me gusta escuchar música.

Me gusta alquilar vídeos.

Nos gusta montar en bicicleta.

Capítulo 13 Los pasatiempos **301**

TEACH/MODEL

¿Qué te gusta hacer?
PRESENTATION
After students answer the questions in the **Preparación** activity, have students discuss in class some of the things they wrote in their lists. What do most students like to do? What don't students like to do? Write students' answers on the board. Allow extra space after writing an item on the board.

PRACTICE/APPLY

TRANSLATION GAME
Call on students to read the captions under **¿Qué te gusta hacer?**, then read them as a class in unison. When you have finished, have students close their books and put them on the floor. Then, divide the class into two teams; have team members take turns coming to the board to write Spanish translations of the items listed there (see above Presentation). Provide translations for those items not covered in the activity, or have students provide them from the dictionary. The team with the most correct answers wins.

Linguistic

Etapa Support Materials

- Workbook: pp. 162-167
- TRB: Textbook Activity Masters: pp. 98-101
- Textbook Cassettes/CDs: Cassette 2, Side A; CD 3, Track 1
- Tapescript: Textbook Cassettes/CDs p. 208
- Middle School Activities: pp. 112-113
- Lesson Plan Book: pp. 91-92

- Testing Program: Quiz pp.145, 146; Answer Key & Testing Cassettes Tapescript p. T60
- Testing Cassettes: Cassette Side A
- Computerized Testing Program: Windows™; Macintosh®
- **Atajo** Writing Assistant Software: Student Text, p. 309

A. Me gusta...

SUGGESTION

Before proceeding to Activity A, explain to students that the captions in the activity may be translated two ways: **Me gusta ir de compras** = I like to go shopping; I like shopping. **Me gusta leer** = I like reading; I like to read.

Individual Needs

Less-prepared Students

Allow students a minute or two to look at the drawings and recall vocabulary. Or brainstorm vocabulary items with students before having them begin their work.

More-prepared Students

Have them create additional pictograms of activities for their partners to identify and use with **gustar**.

▲ Visual-Spatial

Me gusta escribir cartas.

Nos gusta ir al cine.

Me gusta nadar.

Me gusta hacer ejercicio.

Nos gusta correr.

Nos gusta bailar.

¡Te toca a ti!

A. Me gusta... Imagine you are the person in the drawings that follow. Respond accordingly when one of your classmates asks you what you like to do. Follow the model.

MODELO ¿Qué te gusta hacer?
Me gusta nadar.

1.

2.

3.

4.

MULTIPLE INTELLIGENCES

- Linguistic: All activities
- Logical-Mathematical: B, C, D, F, H
- Visual-Spatial: G
- Auditory-Musical: **Aquí escuchamos**
- Interpersonal: A, E, **¿Qué hiciste tú durante el fin de semana?**, **La semana pasada**

5.
6.
7.
8.

B. ¿Qué te gusta hacer? Survey your classmates to find out what they like to do and what they don't like to do in their free time. Following the model, interview six classmates in Spanish. They can use the suggested activities or come up with their own. As you interview people, write down their likes and dislikes in the appropriate column on the chart on your activity master.

aprender	charlar	hacer ejercicio
bailar	comer	ir de compras
caminar	correr	mirar
cantar	descansar	trabajar

MODELO

Tú: *¿Qué te gusta hacer en tu tiempo libre?*
Compañero(a): *Me gusta estudiar, pero no me gusta escribir cartas.*

Nos gusta hacer estas actividades	No nos gusta hacer estas actividades
estudiar	*escribir cartas*

When you finish your survey, work in Spanish with a partner to study the results. 1) Compare your lists. Did you both get similar responses? 2) Count the number of times each activity occurs in the "like-to-do" column and how many times each occurs in the "don't-like-to-do" column. 3) Based on your tallies, what are the three most popular leisure activities among your classmates? What are the three least popular? 4) Did any activities come up in both columns?

Capítulo 13 Los pasatiempos **303**

B. ¿Qué te gusta hacer?

SUGGESTION

TRB: ACTIVITY MASTER, P. 98

Help students work efficiently. Remind them that they will need to write down the activities only once if they use tick marks to keep count of how often each activity is mentioned. Most students will be familiar with the concept of surveys and polling. But, you may want to take advantage of this activity to help them better understand the process as they work through it. Emphasize the different stages before students begin:
(1) collecting information, i.e., data;
(2) reviewing and analyzing data;
(3) reporting conclusions.

Connections with Other Disciplines 3.1

VARIATION

Have students analyze the polling process. When students have finished, poll the whole class for activities (1) liked/disliked by all and for activities (2) appearing in both columns. For these items, you may wish the class to discuss/explore possible reasons for the differences in likes and dislikes. For example, is there an item that only males or females like, or only sports-oriented students like? etc. Review the three stages of polling/surveying again before concluding this activity.

Comparing and Contrasting Analyzing

TEACH/MODEL

Estructura

PRESENTATION

In a monologue, contrast what you (and your family or friends) habitually do with what you did yesterday or last week. For example: **Usualmente, preparo la cena, miro la televisión y hablo con mis amigos.**, etc. Then write **ayer** on the board along with the day of the week and the date. Redo the monologue in the preterite tense. Then quickly show on the board how the preterite is formed and point out the accent marks. Explain that the stress is on the endings rather than on the stem as it is in the present tense. Contrast **yo hablo** with **él habló**. Have students point out which form is the same as the present tense (**nosotros** form).

Analyzing
Comparing and Contrasting

ESTRUCTURA

Preterite tense of -ar verbs

Yo **hablé** con Juan ayer.

I talked with Juan yesterday.

Él **bailó** mucho anoche.

He danced a lot last night.

Preterite of **-ar** Verbs		
Subject Pronoun	Verb Ending	Conjugated Form of the Verb **cantar**
yo	**-é**	**canté**
tú	**-aste**	**cantaste**
él ella Ud.	**-ó**	**cantó**
nosotros(as)	**-amos**	**cantamos**
vosotros(as)	**-asteis**	**cantasteis**
ellos ellas Uds.	**-aron**	**cantaron**

1. In Spanish, the preterite is a verb tense used to talk about actions that happened in the past. To conjugate **-ar** verbs in the preterite, drop the **-ar** to find the stem (**cant-** for **cantar**) and add the verb ending that corresponds to the subject. Note that there is a written accent on the endings of the **yo** and the **él, ella, Ud.** forms.

2. You already know several **-ar** verbs such as **alquilar** and **preparar**. Here are some new verbs you should learn:

andar	*to walk*
cenar	*to eat dinner*
cocinar	*to cook*
contestar	*to answer*
desayunar	*to eat breakfast*
invitar	*to invite*
pasar	*to pass, to occur, to spend (time)*
preguntar	*to ask*
terminar	*to finish*
usar	*to use*

304 *Quinta unidad* Tu tiempo libre

Aquí practicamos

C. Anoche (Last night) Di *(say)* lo que *(what)* tú y tus amigos hicieron *(did)* anoche. Sigue *(Follow)* el modelo.

> **MODELO** *Yo compré un disco compacto nuevo.*
> *Roberto no compró un disco compacto nuevo.*

A	B	C	D
yo	(no)	comprar	un programa de televisión
tú		mirar	para un examen
Roberto		estudiar	por teléfono
nosotros		hablar	un disco compacto nuevo
Uds.		escuchar	música rock
Elena y Juan			

D. Por supuesto... Your parents went out to dinner and returned late at night. They ask what you did while they were out. As they ask you questions, answer in the affirmative. Follow the model.

> **MODELO** *¿Terminaste tu tarea?*
> *Sí, por supuesto, terminé mi tarea.*

1. ¿Hablaste por teléfono con tu amigo?
2. ¿Cenaste aquí?
3. ¿Estudiaste para el examen de español?
4. ¿Miraste un programa de televisión?
5. ¿Tomaste algo *(something)*?

E. El sábado pasado (Last Saturday) Pregúntales *(Ask)* a tus compañeros(as) lo que hicieron el sábado pasado. Usa preguntas *(questions)* de tipo **sí/no** con las actividades que siguen *(that follow)*. Sigue el modelo.

> **MODELO** **Tú:** *¿Estudiaste el sábado pasado?*
> **Compañero(a):** *No, no estudié el sábado pasado.* o:
> *Sí, estudié para mi examen*
> *de matemáticas.*

alquilar un vídeo	escuchar tu estéreo
caminar al centro	hablar por teléfono
cenar con un(a) amigo(a)	mirar televisión
comprar un disco compacto	pasar tiempo con tu familia
desayunar en un restaurante	visitar a un(a) amigo(a)

Capítulo 13 Los pasatiempos **305**

PRACTICE/APPLY

C. Anoche
SUGGESTION
This column activity is meant to provide controlled practice. A possible way to present it is through the creation of a "word web".

Logical-Mathematical
Visual-Spatial

E. El sábado pasado

Individual Needs

More-prepared Students
Have students construct follow-up questions using interrogative words. For example: **¿Qué programa miraste en la televisión? ¿Quién caminó al centro? ¿A qué hora cenaste con una amiga?** Then have them construct yes/no questions using the **Uds.** form, for example: **¿Miraron Uds. la televisión?** Next, go on to information questions using **Uds.** as the subject, i.e., **¿Qué miraron Uds. en la televisión?**

Less-prepared Students
As extra reinforcement of forms, have students formulate their answers and write out the appropriate verb forms for the first half of the list, before starting the activity orally. Have them follow a similar procedure with the question forms.

ANSWERS
¿Alquilaste... ? ...alquilé... .
¿Caminaste... ? ...caminé... .
¿Cenaste... ? ...cené... .
¿Compraste... ? ...compré... .
¿Desayunaste... ? ...desayuné... .
¿Escuchaste... ? ...escuché…
¿Hablaste... ? ...hablé... .
¿Miraste... ? ... miré... .
¿Pasaste... ? ...pasé...
¿Visitaste... ? ...visité... .

Nota gramatical

PRESENTATION

Introduce **hacer** by contrasting an action in the present and the past. For example: **Yo hago ejercicio todos los sábados. Yo hice ejercicio el sábado pasado.** (Gesture with your hands to indicate the past.) **También hice ejercicio ayer. ¿Hiciste tú ejercicio ayer?** Then summarize in the third person. **Él (Ella) (no) hizo ejercicio ayer.** Continue in the same manner with the plural forms. Then write the conjugation on the board and have students point out how it differs from the preterite of **-ar** verbs they have learned (no written accent marks, **i** instead of **a** predominates, etc.) Be sure to point out the spelling change in the third-person singular (**c** to **z**) if students do not notice it.

🔺🔺 Linguistic

FYI

Hacer is introduced here before students have seen **-er** and **-ir** verbs in the preterite, so students can learn to ask meaningful questions at an early stage (**¿Qué hiciste anoche?, ¿Qué hizo María ayer?**), while continuing to answer with the many **-ar** verbs they know.

NOTA GRAMATICAL

The preterite of the verb hacer

—¿Qué **hizo** Tomás ayer?
—Tomás habló con el profesor.

What did Tomás do yesterday?
Tomás talked to the teacher.

—¿Qué **hicieron** ellos anoche?
—Ellos estudiaron mucho.

What did they do last night?
They studied a lot.

—¿Qué **hiciste** tú anoche?
—No **hice** nada.
—**Hice** mi tarea de español.

What did you do last night?
I didn't do anything.
I did my Spanish homework.

hacer *(to do, to make)*			
yo	hice	nosotros(as)	hicimos
tú	hiciste	vosotros(as)	hicisteis
él ella Ud.	hizo	ellos ellas Uds.	hicieron

1. The verb **hacer** is used in the preterite to talk about what was done in the past.

2. When you are asked a question about the past with the verb **hacer**, you often respond with a different verb that expresses what was done.

3. Here are some common expressions with **hacer**.

hacer un viaje	to take a trip
hacer la cama	to make the bed
hacer las maletas	to pack
hacer ejercicio	to exercise
hacer un mandado	to run an errand

Ellos **hicieron un viaje** a Bogotá, Colombia el año pasado.

They took a trip to Bogotá, Colombia last year.

Ernestito **hizo la cama** ayer.

Ernestito made the bed yesterday.

¿**Hiciste las maletas** para tu viaje a Honduras?

Did you pack for your trip to Honduras?

306 *Quinta unidad* Tu tiempo libre

Do, Make, and Hacer

Direct pairs to use Spanish-English dictionaries and thesauruses to explore the concepts of *do, make,* and **hacer**. Then have students write brief essays addressing the following points: (1) How does English generally distinguish between the two? Give examples. (Note: Generally *do,* meaning to accomplish, implies utility; whereas *make,* meaning to cause to exist, implies creativity— but there are many exceptions.) (2) How does **hacer** express the dual concept of *do/make*? Give examples. (3) What part of speech encompasses the concept of *do/does* when asking questions in Spanish? Give examples.

Interpretive Communication 1.2
Linguistic Comparisons 4.1

Aquí practicamos

F. Lo que hice Sustituye las palabras en cursiva *(italics)* con las palabras que están entre paréntesis y haz *(make)* los cambios *(changes)* necesarios.

1. *Yo* no hice nada anoche. (nosotros / ella / ellos / tú / Ud. / Elena y yo)
2. ¿Qué hizo *Ud.* ayer? (tú / él / yo / Uds. / ellos / nosotras)
3. *Julio* hizo las maletas ayer. (yo / tú / María / nosotros / ellas)

G. ¿Qué hicieron anoche? Un(a) compañero(a) quiere saber lo que tú y tus amigos hicieron anoche. Tu compañero(a) te hace las preguntas. Responde según *(according to)* el modelo y los dibujos *(drawings)*.

Roberto

MODELO
Compañero(a): *¿Qué hizo Roberto anoche?*
Tú: *Roberto habló con María.*

1. José

2. Marta y Ana

3. Melisa

4. Luis y Elena

5. Esteban

6. Sara

Capítulo 13 Los pasatiempos **307**

PRACTICE/APPLY

F. Lo que hice
ANSWERS
1. nosotros no hicimos, ella no hizo, ellos no hicieron, tú no hiciste, Ud. no hizo
2. hiciste tú, hizo él, hice yo, hicieron Uds., hicieron ellos
3. yo hice, tú hiciste, María hizo, nosotros hicimos, ellas hicieron

G. ¿Qué hicieron anoche?
POSSIBLE ANSWERS
Note: Descriptive verbs may vary.
1. hizo / cenó
2. hicieron / escucharon
3. hizo / estudió
4. hicieron / miraron
5. hizo / alquiló
6. hizo / habló

EXPANSION
Have students create additional pictographs for their partners to identify and use in their answers. Draw pictographs of someone doing exercises/making their bed/doing their homework in one column; in another have students draw pictographs of someone walking/talking on the phone/watching TV, etc. Ask **¿Qué hizo Juan (María, etc.) anoche?** for each pictograph and have the whole class say what happened in each one. Point out and contrast very strongly those cases where **hacer** is used in the answers. Remind students again of the **c** to **z** spelling change in **hizo**.
Visual-Spatial

Individual Needs

More-prepared Students
Have students ask and answer about their real-life activities from last night.

H. ¿Qué hiciste en casa de tu prima?

ANSWERS

Students substitute the cues, using the forms of these verbs:

1. visitaste / visité
2. estudiaste / estudié
3. hablaste / hablé
4. tomaste / tomé
5. escuchaste / escuché

EXPANSION

Have students create three additional items for each half of the activity.

Aquí escuchamos

TEXTBOOK CASSETTE/CD CASSETTE 2, SIDE A; CD 3, TRACK 1

TAPESCRIPT P. 208

TRB: ACTIVITY MASTER, P. 99

Antes de escuchar

POSSIBLE ANSWERS

Shopping, reading, talking on the phone, listening to music, renting videos, riding bikes, writing letters, going to the movies, swimming, exercising, running, dancing

Después de escuchar

ANSWERS

Juan: likes swimming and exercising, doesn't like listening to music

Eva: likes riding a bicycle, doesn't like talking on the phone

Esteban: likes renting videocassettes, doesn't like going to the movies

Elena: likes shopping, doesn't like exercising

H. ¿Qué hiciste en casa de tu prima? Your parents were out of town, so you spent the day yesterday at your cousin Anita's house. Today, a friend wants to know how you spent the day. Work with a partner and follow the model.

MODELO hablar con María, Linda
Amiga(o): *¿Hablaste con María?*
Tú: *No hablé con María, pero hablé con Linda.*

1. visitar a Julián, Alicia
2. estudiar con Teresa, Julia
3. hablar con los padres de Miguel, su hermana
4. tomar café, jugo de naranja
5. escuchar la radio, una cinta de Janet Jackson

Aquí escuchamos

¿Qué te gusta hacer? *Various students talk about what they like and don't like to do in their free time.*

Antes de escuchar What activities do you think the students might mention? On your activity master, make a list based on the leisure-time activities you have learned to discuss in Spanish.

 A escuchar Listen twice to what the students say and pay attention to what they like and do not like to do.

Después de escuchar On the chart in your activity master, indicate what each person likes to do and doesn't like to do by checking off the appropriate column.

	Sí	No
Juan		
Eva		
Esteban		
Elena		

Spanish for Spanish Speakers

Spoken Spanish

Ask Spanish speakers to listen to the Spanish used in the **Aquí escuchamos** recording and to compare it to the Spanish they use in their communities. Encourage students to focus, for example, on the consonant **s**: Does it sound similar to the *s* in English? Is it barely audible (as is often the case in Spanish spoken in the Caribbean)? Is it similar to the *th* sound in

English? How does it contrast with their spoken Spanish? You might want to have the rest of the class participate in this activity.

⚙ Comparing and Contrasting

◣▲ Auditory-Musical

⊕ Linguistic Comparisons 4.1

¡ADELANTE!

 ¿Qué hiciste tú durante el fin de semana?
It's Monday morning, and you and your friend are telling each other what you did and did not do over the weekend. Working in pairs, interview your partner to find out how he (she) spent last weekend. Record your partner's responses on your activity master. When you are asking questions, use expressions like **¿Qué hiciste el viernes pasado por la tarde?** When you are answering questions, choose from the suggestions provided, using the preterite. Possible activities are **trabajar mucho, mirar la televisión, bailar mucho, hablar por teléfono, estudiar,** etc.

viernes por la noche	
sábado por la mañana	
sábado por la noche	
domingo por la tarde	
domingo por la noche	

La semana pasada Make a list of five things you did last week.

1. For each activity on your list, tell on which day and at what time of day you did it.
2. When you have completed your list, work with a partner to fill out the chart on your activity master.
3. For the activities that you both did, find out if you had a similar schedule (**¿Cuándo estudiaste para el examen de inglés?**).

Mis actividades	Las actividades de nosotros(as) dos	Las actividades de mi compañero(a)

 ETAPA SYNTHESIS

¿Qué hiciste tú durante el fin de semana?

SUGGESTION

 TRB: ACTIVITY MASTER, P. 100

Have students add at least one time not included on the chart and at least 1-2 activities not listed in their text.

La semana pasada

FYI

 ATAJO WRITING ASSISTANT SOFTWARE

You might want to have students use this software program when doing this activity.

EXPANSION

 TRB: ACTIVITY MASTER, P. 101

Have students use information from their charts to write a short paragraph comparing and contrasting their week with their partner's. You may wish to have them read and edit each other's work.

Comparing and Contrasting

Additional Practice and Recycling

FYI

 WORKBOOK, PP. 162-167

For recycling and additional practice of the vocabulary, structures, and language functions presented throughout this **etapa**, you can assign the workbook activities as in-class work and/or homework. Answers to the activities are overprinted on each page of the Teacher's Edition of the Workbook.

TEACH/MODEL

¿Adónde fuiste?

PRESENTATION

 TEXTBOOK CASSETTE/CD

TAPESCRIPT

Using the questions from **Preparación**, have students discuss their free time. Then ask them what they think students from the Spanish-speaking world do in their free time. Do they think their activities will be the same or different, and in what ways?

After this brief discussion, have students listen to the conversation between Cristina and Carmen on the Textbook Cassette/CD. Encourage them to listen for the overall meaning of the dialogue. Then have them look at the drawings on page 311 as they listen to the dialogue a second time to help them have a firmer grasp of the new structures and vocabulary.

Auditory-Musical
Visual-Spatial

SEGUNDA ETAPA

> **Preparación**
>
> - Where do you go in your free time?
> - What are some of the events you attend?

¿Adónde fuiste?

Un muchacho y una muchacha hablan de lo que hicieron anoche.

Olga: ¿Adónde fuiste anoche?
Daniel: A un **partido** de fútbol. ¿Y tú?
Olga: Fui a un concierto.

It's Monday morning and before class begins, Carmen and her friend, Cristina, are talking about where they and some of their friends went last Saturday afternoon.

Carmen: Hola, Cristina, ¿cómo estás?
Cristina: Bien, y tú, ¿qué tal?
Carmen: Muy, muy bien. ¿Qué hiciste el sábado pasado? **¿Fuiste** al cine?
Cristina: No, no. No **fui** al cine. Roberto y yo **fuimos** al concierto. ¿Y tú?
Carmen: Yo fui a la biblioteca.
Cristina: ¿Fuiste con tu novio?
Carmen: No, él **fue** al gimnasio.
Cristina: Y tu hermano, ¿qué hizo? ¿Fue al gimnasio, también?
Carmen: No, mi hermano y su novia **fueron** al partido de fútbol.

partido *game, match*   **fuiste** *you went*   **fui** *I went*   **fuimos** *we went*   **fue** *he, she went*   **fueron** *they went*

310   *Quinta unidad* Tu tiempo libre

Etapa Support Materials

- Workbook, pp. 168-171
- TRB: Textbook Activity Masters: pp. 102, 103
- Textbook Cassettes/CDs: Cassette 2, Side A; CD 3, Track 2
- Tapescript: Textbook Cassettes/CDs p. 208
- Middle School Activities: pp. 114-116
- Overhead Transparency: 54
- Lesson Plan Book: pp. 73-74

- Testing Program: Quiz pp. 147-149; Answer Key & Testing Cassettes Tapescript p. T60
- Testing Cassettes: Cassette Side A
- Computerized Testing Program: Windows™; Macintosh®
- **Atajo** Writing Assistant Software: Student Text, p. 317; Workbook, p. 171

T310 Unit 5, Chapter 13

a la biblioteca

a casa de un(a) amigo(a)

al centro

al cine

de compras

a una fiesta

al gimnasio

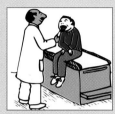

al médico

a un museo

al parque

al parque zoológico

a la playa

a un restaurante

a la piscina

Capítulo 13 Los pasatiempos **311**

EXPANSION

As a follow-up to the dialogue and to present new expressions from the captions on page 311 in the student text, ask *yes/no* questions about the girls' activities: **¿Cristina fue al médico? ¿Carmen fue de compras? ¿Cristina fue a la biblioteca? ¿No? ¿Quién fue a la biblioteca?**

 Interpretive Communication 1.2

MULTIPLE INTELLIGENCES

- Linguistic: All activities
- Logical-Mathematical: A, B, D
- Visual-Spatial: G
- Auditory-Musical: **Aquí escuchamos**
- Interpersonal: C, F, **¿Adónde fuiste y qué hiciste el verano pasado?**
- Intrapersonal: **La semana pasada**

Estructura

PRESENTATION

Begin by making statements in the present tense. Then change them to the past tense and ask follow-up questions. For example: **Yo siempre voy al cine los sábados. Yo fui al cine el sábado pasado.** (Gesture to show the past.) **¿Tú fuiste al cine también, Juan?** Summarize his answer in the third person. Continue with the plural forms. Then write the conjugations on the board and have students point out what they notice is different from the other verbs they have studied in the preterite (no accents, etc.).

Bodily-Kinetic
Visual-Spatial

PRACTICE / APPLY

A. ¿Adónde fue... ?

ANSWERS

Students substitute the cues, using these verbs and articles:
1. fue / fue al
2. fue / fue al
3. fuiste / fui a la
4. fueron / fueron al
5. fueron / fueron al
6. fue / fue al
7. fueron / fueron al
8. fue / fue al

EXPANSION

Ask different students where they went last night or last weekend. Add third-person follow-up questions occasionally to see if students have been listening. Try to practice all forms of the verbs.

Auditory-Musical

Interpretive Communication 1.1

ESTRUCTURA

The preterite of the verb ir

Yo **fui** al cine anoche.	*I went to the movies last night.*
Ellos **fueron** a un concierto el sábado pasado.	*They went to a concert last Saturday.*
Nosotros **fuimos** al centro ayer.	*We went downtown yesterday.*
—¿**Fuiste** tú a la fiesta de Julia el viernes pasado?	*Did you go to Julia's party last Friday?*
—No, no **fui** a la fiesta.	*No, I didn't go to the party.*

ir *(to go)*			
yo	**fui**	nosotros(as)	**fuimos**
tú	**fuiste**	vosotros(as)	**fuisteis**
él ella Ud.	**fue**	ellos ellas Uds.	**fueron**

¡Te toca a ti!

A. ¿Adónde fue...? Un(a) compañero(a) pregunta adónde fueron todos *(everyone)* ayer *(yesterday)* por la tarde. Sigue el modelo.

> **MODELO**   David / cine
> **Compañera(o):** *¿Adónde fue David?*
> **Tú:** *Fue al cine.*

1. Carmen / concierto
2. tu hermana / museo
3. tú / biblioteca
4. Jorge y Hernando / banco
5. Victoria y Claudia / restaurante
6. la profesora / médico
7. tus padres / centro
8. Mario / parque zoológico

312   *Quinta unidad* Tu tiempo libre

  The Standards

- Interpersonal Communication 1.1: A, B, E, F, G, **¿Adónde fuiste y qué hiciste el verano pasado?**
- Interpretive Communication 1.2: C, D, **Aquí escuchamos**
- Presentational Communication 1.3: **La semana pasada**

B. ¿Adónde fuiste? Ahora pregúntale a un compañero(a) adónde fue ayer. Sigue el modelo.

> **MODELO** biblioteca /cine
> **Tú:** *¿Adónde fuiste ayer? ¿A la biblioteca?*
> **Compañero(a):** *No, fui al cine.*

1. a la playa / a la piscina
2. a un restaurante / a casa de un(a) amigo(a)
3. al parque / al gimnasio
4. al partido de básquetbol / al concierto
5. a la biblioteca / de compras
6. a la piscina / a una fiesta

C. ¿Adónde fuiste anoche? Ask eight of your classmates where they went last night. Record their responses on the chart on your activity master, showing who went where. Be prepared to report your findings to the class.

	Nombre	Nombre	Nombre	Nombre
a un restaurante	Luis	Carla		
al parque				
al cine	David			
a una fiesta				
a casa de un(a) amigo(a)				
a un partido de básquetbol				
al trabajo				
...				
...				

Capítulo 13 Los pasatiempos **313**

B. ¿Adónde fuiste?

ANSWERS
Answers will follow the model, substituting the cues.

C. ¿Adónde fuiste anoche?

SUGGESTION

 TRB: ACTIVITY MASTER, P. 102

 Brainstorm with the class to create a list on the board of some additional places they could include on their activity masters of places people went last night.

FYI

 When the ellipses (...) appear as additional lines in a chart, it is intended that the students come up with and add in other personalized options that are appropriate for their discussion.

EXPANSION
Poll students informally to find out what activities were the most/least popular, how many students had the same activities, etc. You may also want to have students write up their information as a short report. If so, have them read and edit each other's work before they turn it in.

Comparing and Contrasting

Interpretive Communication 1.2

D. No, no me gusta... , prefiero...

SUGGESTION

Before doing Activity D, review the verb **gustar** with students. Remind them that usually only third-person singular and plural forms are used, i.e., **gusta/gustan**. Do a short oral substitution drill. Or write on the board or a transparency items such as **Me gusta(n) la canción/las canciones, el libro/los libros, la casa/las casas**, etc.

Then do a similar one using infinitives (**-r** forms), reminding students to use the singular in these cases. For example: **Me gusta bailar/estudiar/ mirar la televisión/hacer la tarea/ cenar en un restaurante**, etc.

Estructura

PRESENTATION

After you have introduced the verbs using a monologue, write the forms on the board and have students point out how they are the same or different from the other preterite verbs they have studied. (You might want to write the conjugation of an **-ar** verb and the verb **hacer** on the board so they can compare them.) Ask them which form is the same in both the present and the preterite tenses (**nosotros** form of **-ir** verbs).

Activating Prior Knowledge
Comparing and Contrasting

Repaso ⟳

D. No, no me gusta..., prefiero... You are discussing what you like and do not like to do. When your partner asks you if you like to do something, you respond negatively and indicate what you prefer to do instead. Follow the model.

MODELO estudiar

Compañera(o): *¿Te gusta estudiar?*

Tú: *No, no me gusta estudiar. Prefiero ir al cine.*

1. estudiar
2. leer
3. hacer ejercicio
4. ir al cine
5. caminar por el parque
6. mirar la televisión
7. correr
8. alquilar vídeos
9. ir de compras

ESTRUCTURA

Preterite tense of -er and -ir verbs

Yo **comí** en un restaurante anoche.	*I ate in a restaurant last night.*
Nosotros **escribimos** una carta ayer.	*We wrote a letter yesterday*
Susana **no comprendió** la lección.	*Susana did not understand the lesson.*
¿**Recibieron** Uds. una invitación a la fiesta?	*Did you receive an invitation to the party?*
Ella **salió** de casa temprano ayer.	*She left home early yesterday.*

comer (to eat), vivir (to live)							
yo	-í	comí	viví	nosotros(as)	-imos	comimos	vivimos
tú	-iste	comiste	viviste	vosotros(as)	-isteis	comisteis	vivisteis
él ella Ud.	-ió	comió	vivió	ellos ellas Uds.	-ieron	comieron	vivieron

1. Note that the preterite endings for **-er** and **-ir** verbs are identical, and that the **yo** and the **él, ella, Ud.** forms have a written accent.

2. You already know several **-er** and **-ir** verbs such as **correr** and **discutir.** Here are some new verbs you should learn:

perder	*to lose*	**asistir a**	*to attend*
vender	*to sell*	**salir con**	*to go out with*
volver	*to return*	**salir de**	*to leave*
repetir	*to repeat*	**servir**	*to serve*

314 *Quinta unidad* Tu tiempo libre

Focus on Culture

Media

Ask students if they have or can acquire television advertisements/magazines in Spanish. Ask them to bring them in and then talk about them as a class. Are they advertising the same shows/movies as English-language print media? Compare and contrast visuals, marketing techniques, and content with print media in English.

Cultural Products and Perspectives 2.2
Cultural Comparisons 4.2

Aquí practicamos

E. Ayer después de la escuela Di lo que tú y tus amigos hicieron ayer después de la escuela. Usa las palabras *(words)* de cada *(each)* columna.

A	B	C	D
yo	(no)	comer	pizza
Miguel		escribir	dos cartas
tú		recibir	un(a) amigo(a)
Pedro y yo		salir con	un partido
Linda y Fernando		asistir a	un libro
Ud.		correr	dos millas
		perder	los ejercicios del libro

F. El fin de semana Compare notes with your partner about what you did over the weekend. Use the following expressions to begin your questions, alternating turns. Find at least one activity that you both did. Follow the model.

MODELO   comer en un restaurante

    Tú: *¿Comiste en un restaurante?*
Compañero(a): *Sí, comí en un restaurante.* o: *No, no comí en un restaurante.*

1. aprender información interesante
2. asistir a un concierto
3. perder la cartera
4. escribir una carta a tu amigo(a)
5. discutir un problema
6. recibir un regalo *(gift)*
7. correr un poco
8. comer en un restaurante
9. salir con un(a) amigo(a)
10. volver a casa tarde con un(a) amigo(a)

Capítulo 13 Los pasatiempos   **315**

PRACTICE / APPLY

E. Ayer después de la escuela

EXPANSION
Have students insert other verbs listed in the **Estructura** under 2 (student text page 314) in column C and new words and phrases in column D to create more sentences.

Creating

F. El fin de semana

ANSWERS
1. aprendiste / aprendí
2. asististe / asistí
3. perdiste / perdí
4. escribiste / escribí
5. discutiste / discutí
6. recibiste / recibí
7. corriste / corrí
8. comiste / comí
9. saliste / salí
10. volviste / volví

EXPANSION
Continue to ask questions with interrogative words to practice listening comprehension. Ask follow-up questions in the third person to practice all of the forms. Start out with **tú** questions and then practice **Uds.** questions. For example: **¿Qué hiciste anoche, Juan? (Yo estudié.) ¿Qué hizo Juan? ¿Miró la televisión?**, etc.

¿Qué hicieron tú y tus amigos/amigas el sábado pasado? (Asistimos a un partido de básquetbol.) ¿Qué hicieron ellos? ¿Estudiaron para un examen?, etc.

Auditory-Musical

Interpretive Communication

G. Una tarde típica

POSSIBLE ANSWERS

 TRANSPARENCY 54

1. Tomamos el autobús.
2. Estudiamos español.
3. Caminamos a su casa.
4. Escuchamos música y ella bailó.
5. Salimos de su casa.
6. Compramos un libro.
7. Comimos en un restaurante mexicano.
8. Miramos la televisión.
9. Escribimos una carta.
10. Bebimos un refresco en un café.

EXPANSION

Now that students have additional verbs at their disposal, you can redo the **¡Adelante!** activities from the first **etapa** in this chapter. Have students use **-er** and **-ir** verbs along with **hacer** and **ir**. This time, they can give more details about their activities. It is often a good idea to brainstorm some possible verbs and expressions before beginning a free-writing activity. This also provides an opportunity to introduce expressions for things that students are curious to know how to express.

Interpersonal Communication 1.1

G. Una tarde típica Using the drawings and verbs that follow as guides, explain to your parents how you and your boyfriend (girlfriend) spent the afternoon. Follow the model.

MODELO salir
Salimos de la escuela.

1. tomar

2. estudiar

3. caminar

4. escuchar

5. salir

6. comprar

7. comer

8. mirar

9. escribir

10. beber

316 *Quinta unidad* Tu tiempo libre

Aquí escuchamos

¿Qué hiciste anoche? *Olga and Esteban talk about what they did last night.*

Antes de escuchar Based on what you have been studying in this **etapa,** what do you think Olga and Esteban might say they did?

 A escuchar Listen twice to the conversation and pay special attention to the activities mentioned by each speaker.

Después de escuchar On your activity master, check off what each person did last night, based on what you heard.

	Olga	Esteban
caminar		
correr		
cenar con amigos		
escribir cartas		
estudiar		
hablar por teléfono		
leer		
mirar televisión		

¡ADELANTE!

 ¿Adónde fuiste y qué hiciste el verano pasado? Talk to five of your classmates. 1) Find out one place they went and one activity that they did last summer. 2) Make a list of their responses. 3) Select the most interesting place and the most interesting activity and report them to the class.

 La semana pasada Your pen pal in Argentina has reminded you that it is your turn to write. Write a note telling what you did and where you went last week. Indicate at least five things that you did and include at least two places that you went.

Capítulo 13 Los pasatiempos **317**

Aquí escuchamos

 TEXTBOOK CASSETTE/CD CASSETTE 2, SIDE A; CD 3, TRACK 3

 TAPESCRIPT PP. 208-209

TRB: ACTIVITY MASTER, P. 103

Después de escuchar
ANSWERS
Olga: leer, escribir cartas
Esteban: hablar por teléfono, mirar televisión

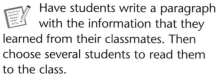
ETAPA SYNTHESIS

¿Adónde fuiste y qué hiciste el verano pasado?
VARIATION

 Have students write a paragraph with the information that they learned from their classmates. Then choose several students to read them to the class.

 Presentational Communication 1.3

La semana pasada
FYI

ATAJO WRITING ASSISTANT SOFTWARE

You might want to have students use this software program when doing this activity.

Individual Needs

More-prepared Students
Allow them to write responses to their partners' letters, telling about their own invented activities and including questions about the activities mentioned in the original letters.

Additional Practice and Recycling
FYI

WORKBOOK, PP. 168-171

For recycling and additional practice of the vocabulary, structures, and language functions presented throughout this **etapa,** you can assign the workbook activities as in-class work and/or homework.

Additional Etapa Resources

Refer to the **Etapa** Support Materials list on the opening page of this **etapa** for detailed cross-references to these assessment options.

TEACH/MODEL

Una semana típica

PRESENTATION

 TEXTBOOK CASSETTE/CD CASSETTE 2, SIDE A; CD 3, TRACK 4

TAPESCRIPT P. 209

Tell students they are about to hear about one person's schedule for the week. Have them close their books and listen to the recording on the Textbook Cassette/CD. Then have the students open their books and listen again before continuing on to Activities A and B.

🔵 Auditory-musical

SUGGESTION

Go back over the days of the week orally, and then write them on the board. Do a brief substitution review orally. For example: **Si hoy es lunes, ¿qué día es mañana? Si hoy es _____, ¿qué día es mañana?**

Then do the same with **pasado mañana**. Shift to **ayer** and **anteayer**: **Si hoy es lunes, ¿qué día fue ayer?**, etc.

🔵 Logical-Mathematical

Preparación

As you begin this **etapa**, think about what your routine was last week.

- Did you go to school every day?
- Did you participate in any extracurricular activities?
- Did you study?
- Did you go out? Where?

Una semana típica

Elisabeth habla de lo que hizo la semana pasada.

El lunes, miércoles y viernes asistí a mi clase de ejercicio aeróbico. El martes y jueves fui a la piscina y nadé por una hora. El jueves por la noche estudié para un examen por dos horas. El viernes después de mi clase de ejercicio aeróbico, cené con mi novio Jay. Comimos pizza en un restaurante italiano. Después fuimos a un partido de fútbol del **equipo** de nuestra escuela. Nuestro equipo perdió.

equipo *team*

El sábado a la una fui de compras con mi amiga Amy. Por la noche, alquilé un vídeo. Invité a mis amigos a mi casa y miramos el vídeo. El domingo fui al centro con mi amigo Billy. Compré dos discos compactos nuevos. Volví a casa a las 5:30 y cené con mis padres.

318 *Quinta unidad* Tu tiempo libre

Etapa Support Materials

- Workbook, pp. 172-177
- TRB: Textbook Activity Masters: pp. 104, 105
- Textbook Cassettes/CDs: Cassette 2, Side A; CD 3, Track 4
- Tapescript: Textbook Cassettes/CDs p. 209
- Middle School Activities: p. 117
- Lesson Plan Book: pp. 77-78

- Testing Program: Quiz pp.150-152 Answer Key & Testing Cassettes/CDs Tapescript p. T61
- Testing Cassettes: Cassette Side A
- Computerized Testing Program: Windows™; Macintosh®
- **Atajo** Writing Assistant Software: Student Text, pp. 324; Workbook, p. 177

¡Te toca a ti!

A. ¿Qué hizo Elisabeth? Con un(a) compañero(a) di lo que hizo Elisabeth cada día de la semana pasada. Empieza *(Begin)* con el lunes pasado: ¿Qué hizo Elisabeth el lunes pasado?

1. lunes
2. martes
3. jueves
4. viernes
5. domingo

B. ¿Qué hizo Marta la semana pasada? Di lo que hizo Marta la semana pasada. Basa *(Base)* tus respuestas *(answers)* en los dibujos. Sigue el modelo.

| MODELO | sábado
El sábado pasado
Marta alquiló un vídeo. |

1. viernes

2. miércoles

3. sábado

4. domingo

5. lunes

6. jueves

7. martes

8. domingo

Capítulo 13 Los pasatiempos **319**

A. ¿Qué hizo Elisabeth?

POSSIBLE ANSWERS

1. Asistió a su clase de ejercicio aeróbico.
2. Fue a la piscina y nadó por una hora.
3. Estudió para un examen por dos horas.
4. Cenó con su novio Jay.
5. Fue al centro con su amigo Billy.

B. ¿Qué hizo Marta la semana pasada?

POSSIBLE ANSWERS

1. El viernes pasado cenó con su novio.
2. El miércoles pasado estudió.
3. El sábado pasado miró la televisión.
4. El domingo pasado alquiló un vídeo.
5. El lunes pasado caminó en el parque.
6. El jueves pasado montó en bicicleta.
7. El martes pasado escuchó música.
8. El domingo pasado habló con sus padres.

MULTIPLE INTELLIGENCES

- Linguistic: All activities
- Logical-Mathematical: E, F
- Visual-Spatial: B, C
- Auditory-Musical: **Aquí escuchamos**
- Interpersonal: A, G, **Intercambio**
- Intrapersonal: **El fin de semana pasado**

The Standards

- Interpersonal Communication 1.1: A, B, E, F, **Intercambio**
- Interpretive Communication 1.2: C, F, **Aquí escuchamos**
- Presentational Communication 1.3: D, G, **El fin de semana pasado**

C. ¿Qué hicieron?

POSSIBLE ANSWERS

1. Marisol salió con su hermano el lunes por la mañana.
2. Marrirosa y Juanita fueron a un concierto de rock el viernes por la noche.
3. Juan fue al cine el miércoles por la tarde.

EXPANSION

Use interrogative words to ask personalized questions based on the pictures. (You may want to use the **pregúntale** format.) Be sure to ask follow-up questions in the third person, to see if students are listening carefully.

▲▲ Visual-Spatial

TEACH/MODEL

Estructura

PRESENTATION

Write on the board today's date plus dates for last week, this year, and last year. Work backwards from **hoy** through **ayer, la semana pasada, el mes pasado** to **el año pasado**. Then introduce the notion of duration (**por**). As you introduce these lexical items, it would be useful to introduce the interrogative phrase **¿Por cuánto tiempo?** For example: **¿Por cuánto tiempo estudiaste anoche? Por cuánto tiempo corriste esta mañana?**, etc.

☼ Categorizing

Repaso ♻

C. ¿Qué hicieron? Basándote en los dibujos, di lo que hicieron las personas y cuándo lo hicieron. Sigue el modelo.

MODELO   Martín y Catarina / el domingo por la tarde
Martín y Catarina corrieron el domingo por la tarde.

1. Marisol y su hermano / el lunes por la mañana
2. Marirrosa y Juanita / el viernes por la noche
3. Juan / el miércoles por la tarde

ESTRUCTURA

Adverbs, prepositions, and other expressions used to designate the past

La semana pasada compré un disco compacto	*Last week I bought a CD.*
El viernes pasado comimos en un restaurante.	*Last Friday we ate at a restaurant.*

1. Here are some expressions used to talk about an action or a condition in the past.

ayer	*yesterday*	anteayer	*the day before yesterday*
ayer por la mañana	*yesterday morning*	la semana pasada	*last week*
ayer por la tarde	*yesterday afternoon*	el fin de semana pasado	*last weekend*
anoche	*last night*	el mes pasado	*last month*
el jueves (sábado, etc.) pasado	*last Thursday (Saturday, etc.)*	el año pasado	*last year*

2. The preposition **por** will enable you to express how long you did something.

Estudié **por** dos horas.	*I studied for two hours.*
Corrió **por** veinte minutos.	*She ran for twenty minutes.*

320   *Quinta unidad* Tu tiempo libre

☀ Spanish for Spanish Speakers

Creating Comics

Tell Spanish speakers to bring newspaper comics to class; have them find "funnies" that illustrate action. Then, have students cut their strips out of the paper, cut out and discard all captions, and paste the-now captionless-comics onto blank paper. Direct them to create dialogues to match the drawings, using the preterite of common verbs as much as possible. They can either write in or paste on their new dialogues. If students are comfortable, distribute the books in class, and have students study them for an informal reading activity.

☼ Creating

🌐 Presentational Communication 1.3

Aquí practicamos

D. ¿Qué hicieron recientemente (recently)?
Di lo que tú y tus amigos hicieron recientemente. Usa palabras de cada columna.

A	B	C	D
nosotros	(no)	cenar en un restaurante	la semana pasada
tú		correr dos millas	ayer por la tarde
Margarita y Alicia		no asistir a clase	el viernes pasado
Julián		alquilar un vídeo	anteayer
yo		hacer ejercicio	ayer por la mañana
Marta y yo		caminar por el parque	el miércoles pasado

E. ¿Cuándo?
Usa las expresiones que están entre paréntesis para decir cuándo hiciste las actividades que siguen. Sigue el modelo.

> **MODELO** ¿Cuándo hablaste con María? (ayer por la mañana)
> *Hablé con María ayer por la mañana.*

1. ¿Cuándo estudiaste francés? (el año pasado)
2. ¿Cuándo corriste? (ayer por la tarde)
3. ¿Cuándo hablaste con tu novia(o)? (el viernes pasado)
4. ¿Cuándo compraste tu bicicleta? (el mes pasado)
5. ¿Cuándo recibiste la carta de Julia? (el jueves pasado)
6. ¿Cuándo comiste pizza? (el domingo pasado)

PRACTICE / APPLY

D. ¿Qué hicieron recientemente?

SUGGESTION
A possible way to present this activity is through the creation of a "word web". Word webs divide linguistic elements into different categories, allowing students to analyze each element visually as well as analytically. First, have students write in the correct answers in all appropriate columns. Next, have students draw a web horizontally, on a separate piece of paper, sketching circles large enough to let students write in the grammatical elements in each category. Then, have students label each circle (subject, verb, etc.). Finally, have them connect elements from the circles in ways that form grammatically correct sentences.

Categorizing

Logical-Mathematical
Visual-Spatial

E. ¿Cuándo?

ANSWERS
Students substitute the cues using the following verbs:

1. Estudié...   4. Compré...
2. Corrí...   5. Recibí...
3. Hablé...   6. Comí...

EXPANSION

Continue to ask personalized questions using **cuándo.** Ask some **Uds.** questions also. (**¿Cuándo fueron tú y un amigo/una amiga al cine?**)

Interpretive Communications 1.2

Estructura

PRESENTATION

Introduce **andar**, **estar**, and **tener** in the preterite with a series of self-explanatory statements, miming, if necessary, to clarify your speech. Follow the introductory patterns of other, similar presentations. Point out to students that learning irregular verbs in patterns is easier than learning each one individually.

 Categorizing

Bodily-Kinesthetic

PRACTICE/APPLY

F. ¿Qué hicieron?

ANSWERS

1. tú tuviste, Ud. tuvo, Ana y su novio tuvieron, yo tuve, nosotros tuvimos
2. Uds. no estuvieron, Diego no estuvo, yo no estuve, tú no estuviste, nosotras no estuvimos
3. anduvo Ud., anduvieron Santiago y Enrique, anduvo Alicia, anduviste tú

ESTRUCTURA

Preterite of the verbs **andar, estar,** and **tener**

Yo **estuve** en casa de Pablo anteayer.   *I was at Paul's house the day before yesterday.*

—¿**Anduviste** tú por el parque ayer?   *Did you walk in the park yesterday?*
—Sí, yo **anduve** con mi amiga Paula.   *Yes, I walked with my friend Paula.*

Nosotros no **tuvimos** que estudiar anoche. *We did not have to study last night.*

The verbs **andar, estar,** and **tener** are irregular in the preterite, but they are conjugated similarly.

Pronoun	**andar** *(to walk)*	**estar** *(to be)*	**tener** *(to have)*
yo	anduve	estuve	tuve
tú	anduviste	estuviste	tuviste
él ella Ud.	anduvo	estuvo	tuvo
nosotros(as)	anduvimos	estuvimos	tuvimos
vosotros(as)	anduvisteis	estuvisteis	tuvisteis
ellos ellas Uds.	anduvieron	estuvieron	tuvieron

Aquí practicamos

F. **¿Qué hicieron?** Sustituye las palabras en cursiva con las palabras que están entre paréntesis y haz los cambios necesarios.

1. *Catarina* tuvo que estudiar mucho anoche. (tú / Ud. / Ana y su novio / yo / nosotros)

2. *Juan y Roberto* no estuvieron en la fiesta de Sofía. (Uds. / Diego / yo / tú / nosotras)

3. ¿Anduvieron *Uds.* a la escuela ayer? (Ud. / Santiago y Enrique / Alicia / tú)

322   *Quinta unidad* Tu tiempo libre

 Spanish for Spanish Speakers

Vocabulary Expansion

Ask Spanish speakers if they know the spelling for the following irregular verbs in the preterite: **tener, poder, saber,** and **poner**. Have them practice using and writing verbs in the preterite.

Linguistic

G. La semana pasada Ask several classmates the following questions. Have them 1) name three places where they were last week, 2) indicate three places they walked to, and 3) tell three things they had to do. Follow the model.

MODELO	¿Dónde estuviste la semana pasada?
	Estuve en la piscina el viernes por la tarde.
	Estuve en el parque el domingo por la mañana.
	Estuve en casa el martes por la noche.

1. ¿Dónde estuviste la semana pasada?
2. ¿Adónde anduviste la semana pasada?
3. ¿Qué tuviste que hacer la semana pasada?

Aquí escuchamos

¿Qué hiciste este fin de semana? *Olga and Juan talk about what they did over the weekend.*

Antes de escuchar Think about what you did last weekend. Based on what you've learned in this **etapa,** what are some of the things you think that Olga and Juan might mention doing over the weekend?

 a escuchar Listen twice to the conversation between Olga and Juan before checking off on your activity master the activities that each of them did.

Capítulo 13 Los pasatiempos **323**

G. La semana pasada
EXPANSION

 Have students report back on their classmates' activities. Were there any activities in common? Was there anyone who did something completely different? Have students ask the teacher similar questions using the **Ud.** form.

 Comparing and Contrasting

 Presentational Communication 1.3

Aquí escuchamos

	TEXTBOOK CASSETTE/CD CASSETTE 2, SIDE A; CD 3, TRACK 5
	TAPESCRIPT P. 209
	TRB: ACTIVITY MASTER, P. 104

Antes de escuchar
POSSIBLE ANSWERS
studying, buying, something, eating in a restaurant, talking on the phone, going to a game, watching television, listening to music

Después de escuchar
ANSWERS
Olga: fue a un concierto, fue a una fiesta, fue al gimnasio, fue al cine, descansó
Juan: fue a cenar en un restaurante, fue a la biblioteca, fue de compras, estudió, descansó

Spanish for Spanish Speakers

Vocabulary Expansion–Synonyms

Have Spanish speakers listen carefully to the **Aquí escuchamos** recording and write down five words they hear for which they know or want to find synonyms. Tell them not to limit themselves to just one or two parts of speech, but to choose nouns, verbs, adjectives, adverbs, prepositions, etc. Then give students copies of the dialogue from the Tapescript and have them work with a partner to combine their lists and create a transformed dialogue. Have Spanish speakers and other class volunteers role-play the dialogue with the new words for the rest of the class.

 Creating

 Auditory-Musical Linguistic

Presentational Communication 1.3

ETAPA SYNTHESIS

Intercambio

SUGGESTION

Have students create a question-naire for this ahead of time. It should include different days of the week (**el lunes**, etc.), different amounts of time (**¿Por cuánto tiempo?**), and different periods during the day (**por la mañana**, etc.)

 Categorizing

El fin de semana pasado

FYI

 ATAJO WRITING ASSISTANT SOFTWARE

You might want to have students use this software program when doing this activity.

Individual Needs

Less-prepared Students
Brainstorm with students a possible list of activities, then have them recall the correct verb format before beginning.

More-prepared Students
Remind them that a letter is a two-way street and that they need to show interest in their correspondent by asking about his or her activities, as well as describing their own.

Additional Practice and Recycling

FYI

WORKBOOK, PP. 172-177

For recycling and additional practice of the vocabulary, structures, and language functions presented throughout this **etapa**, you can assign the workbook activities as in-class work and/or homework. Answers to the activities are overprinted on each page of the Teacher's Edition of the Workbook.

Después de escuchar On the chart on your activity master, check off each person's activities based on what you heard.

	Olga	Juan
fue al parque		
fue a la piscina		
fue a la biblioteca		
fue a cenar en un restaurante		
fue a un concierto		
fue a una fiesta		
fue al gimnasio		
fue de compras		
fue al cine		
estudió		
descansó		

¡ADELANTE!

 Intercambio Work with a partner and discuss what you did last week and for how long. Possible activities include: **estudiar, comprar, hablar con amigos, comer, asistir a un concierto, andar, tener que hacer algo,** etc.

 El fin de semana pasado Make a list of six things that you did last weekend. Write a postcard to a friend in Costa Rica, telling her (him) what you did.

EN LÍNEA

Connect with the Spanish-speaking world! Access the *¡Ya verás! Gold* home page for Internet activities related to this chapter.

http://yaveras.heinle.com

Additional Etapa Resources

Refer to the **Etapa** Support Materials list on the opening page of this **etapa** for detailed cross-references to these assessment options.

VOCABULARIO

Para charlar

Para hablar de una acción en el pasado

anoche
anteayer
el año pasado
ayer
ayer por la mañana
ayer por la tarde
el fin de semana
  pasado
el jueves (sábado,
  etc.) pasado
la semana pasada
el mes pasado
por una hora (un
  día, tres años, cua-
  tro meses, quince
  minutos, etc.)

Para hablar de las actividades

alquilar un vídeo
desayunar en un
  restaurante
montar en bicicleta
nadar

Lugares adónde vamos

el concierto
el gimnasio
el parque zoológico

Vocabulario general

Verbos

andar
asistir a
caminar
cenar
cocinar
comprar
contestar
invitar
pasar
perder
pregunatar
repetir
salir con
salir de
servir
terminar
usar
visitar
vender
volver

Otras palabras y expresiones

un equipo
hacer la cama
hacer ejercicio
hacer las maletas
hacer un viaje
nada
no hacer nada
un partido

Capítulo 13 Los pasatiempos **325**

CHAPTER WRAP-UP

Vocabulario

ADD-ON CHAIN GAME
One student begins by stating what he (she) did last evening. Each successive student repeats the previous statement(s) and adds a new statement. For example: **Juan cenó en un restaurante, María miró la tele y yo escuché un disco compacto.** Coach stuck students with non-verbal signals.

 Bodily-Kinesthetic
Linguistic

Listening Skills Development

FYI

 LAB MANUAL, PP. 85-91

 LAB CASSETTE SIDE A; CD 7, TRACKS 1-10

TAPESCRIPT: LAB PROGRAM, PP. 127-138

It is now appropriate to work through the lab manual activities and their accompanying recordings in class or in the language laboratory.

Improvised Conversation

SUGGESTION

 TEXTBOOK CASSETTE/CD CASSETTE 2, SIDE A; CD 3, TRACK 6

 TAPESCRIPT P. 209

 TRB: ACTIVITY MASTER, P. 105

Have students listen to this conversation in which two teenagers meet for the first time at a party. Refer to the TRB for student activities.

Resources for Spanish-speaking Students

FYI

 WORKBOOK FOR SPANISH-SPEAKING STUDENTS: PP. 81-86

 ANSWER KEY TO SSS WORKBOOK PP. 23-25

Activities specially written to meet the needs of Spanish-speaking students are available in these workbooks for the reinforcement and extension of the topics and language presented in this chapter.

Additional Chapter Resources

Refer to the Chapter Support Materials list on the opening page of this chapter for detailed cross-references to *¡Ya verás! Gold*'s student-centered technology components and various assessment options.

Spanish for Spanish Speakers

Keeping a Vocabulary Notebook

Remind Spanish-speaking students to add words and expressions from this vocabulary section to the problematic spelling combination categories and personal new vocabulary lists in their notebooks.

Tu tiempo libre
Antes de leer

ANSWERS

1. The reading is about what people like to do in their free time.
2. Answers based on photo
3. Answers may vary. Possible answers may be: **ir al cine, jugar con mis amigos, visitar a mis abuelos**.

SUGGESTION

Have students read the three sketches of leisure time activities and make a list of the activities mentioned. Then have them devise categories by which to classify the different recreations. Possible classifications might include: Physical activities, Social events, Cultural enrichment, Activities that can be done alone, Outdoor activities, Indoor activities, etc.

 Categorizing

ENCUENTROS CULTURALES

Tu tiempo libre

Antes de leer

Reading Strategies
• Activating background knowledge
• Using photos to predict content

1. Read the title of the reading. What do you think the reading will be about?

2. Look at the photos. Describe the people you see in Spanish. What do you think they might do during their free time?

3. What do you like to do during your free time? Try to name at least three activities in Spanish that you enjoy.

"Me llamo Nora Nieves y vivo en Puerto Rico. Soy estudiante en el colegio y no tengo mucho tiempo libre. Cuando no estoy en clase, me gusta salir con mis amigas. Vamos de compras al centro comercial. También tomo una clase de escultura. El arte me fascina.

En mi clase de escultura

Hola, me llamo Marta Barrios y soy de San Antonio, Texas. Me gustan los fines de semana porque no tengo que levantarme temprano. Por ejemplo, este sábado me levanté a las diez de la mañana y fui a correr. Por la tarde fui a la casa de una amiga y escuchamos música. El domingo mi familia y yo visitamos a mis abuelos y fui de pesca con mi abuelo. Por la noche miré la televisión antes de acostarme."

¡Mi abuelo con un pescado grandísimo!

"Soy Andrés. Vivo en Buenos Aires, capital de la Argentina. Durante los fines de semana tengo mucho tiempo libre y a veces mis amigos y yo vamos al parque a jugar al fútbol o a montar en bicicleta. Por la tarde nos reunimos para ir al cine o a alguna fiesta en casa de unos amigos."

En bicicleta con mis amigos

Guía para la lectura

Here are some words and expressions to keep in mind as you read.

centro comercial	*shopping mall*
jugar al fútbol	*to play soccer*
nos reunimos	*we get together*
levantarme temprano	*get up early*
fui de pesca	*I went fishing*
antes de acostarme	*before going to bed*

Después de leer

1. Based on the information given by Nora, Andrés and Marta, determine which of them is involved in the following activities during his or her free time.

   a. montar en bicicleta   e. jugar básquetbol

   b. ir de pesca   f. mirar le televisión

   c. escuchar música   g. ir al cine

   d. hacer escultura   h. estar con los(as) amigos(as)

2. Based on the activities they mention, with which of the teens do you have the most in common?

3. Who would you prefer to spend your free time with, your friends or your family? Explain your answer.

4. Do you think young people today have too much free time or too little free time? How would you change your weekly schedule?

Capítulo 13 Los pasatiempos **327**

Después de leer

ANSWERS

1. a. Andrés,
   b. Marta,
   c. Marta,
   d. Nora,
   e. nobody,
   f. Nora,
   g. Andrés,
   h. Nora y Marta
2. Answers will vary.
3. Answers will vary.
4. Answers will vary.

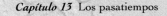
Focus on Culture

Evaluating Leisure Activities

Hold a discussion to explore the value of various types of leisure activities. What health benefits are derived from different pastimes? social benefits? emotional benefits? intellectual stimulation? Are some activities simply a waste of time? Or is it necessary in a fast-paced society to be able to unwind by doing little or nothing? How have attitudes toward leisure time changed as our culture has moved from an agricultural to an industrialized society? How do other cultures view the use of leisure time?

⬥ Evaluating

⬥ Cultural Practices and Perspectives 2.1
Cultural Comparisons 4.2

CAPÍTULO 14

OBJECTIVES

Functions
- Situating activities in the past

Contexts
- Sports
- Leisure-time activities

Accuracy
- **Hace** and **hace que**
- Preterite of verbs ending in **-gar** and **-car**
- Expressions used to talk about a series of actions

CHAPTER WARM-UP

Setting the Context

In preparation for their discussion on sports and leisure time activities, let students know that in addition to Latin America, Spain is one of several European countries where basketball has become very popular. It is played in gyms and on playgrounds across the country. The presence of the United States "Dream Team" caused particular excitement in Spain during the Olympics in Barcelona. The Spanish national team also did better than ever during the Barcelona Olympics. Many basketball players from the United States go to Spain to play professionally, and the professional basketball leagues there are pulling increasingly larger audiences.

Ask students why they think basketball has also become popular in Latin America. If time permits, introduce information on basketball phenomenon Rebecca Lobo, which can be found in the **Encuentro cultural** of Chapter 14, Level 2.

Cultural Practices and Perspectives 2.1
Connections with Other Disciplines 3.1

Actividades deportivas

El baloncesto es un deporte muy popular en América Latina. Es muy divertido para todos.

Objetives

- talking about and situating activities and events in the past
- talking about sports and leisure time activities

328   *Quinta unidad* Tu tiempo libre

Chapter Support Materials

- Lab Manual: pp. 92-98
- Lab Program: Cassette Side B; CD 7, Tracks 11-19
- TRB: Textbook Activity Masters: pp. 106-108
- Textbook Cassettes/CDs: Cassette 2, Side A; CD 3, Track 10
- Tapescript: Lab Program pp. 139-145; Textbook Cassettes/CDs pp. 210-211
- Middle School Activities: pp. 118, 119
- Workbook for Spanish-speaking Students: pp. 87-92
- Answer Key to SSS Workbook: pp. 25-27

- Practice Software: Windows™; Macintosh®

- Testing Program: Chapter Test pp. 163-167; Answer Key & Testing Cassettes Tapescript pp. T64, T65; Oral Assessment p. T65
- Testing Cassettes: Cassette Side A
- Computerized Testing Program: Windows™; Macintosh®
- Video Program: Cassette 2, 32:50-41:05
- Video Guide: Videoscript pp. 56-59; Activities pp. 127-129
- **Mundos hispanos 1**
- Internet Activities: Student Text p. 346

PRIMERA ETAPA

Preparación

As you begin this **etapa**, think about the sports you play.

- Do you play sports just for fun? For exercise?
- Are you on a sports team?

Los deportes

Esteban y Alberto hablan de los deportes que practican.

Esteban:	¡Hola! ¿Adónde vas?
Alberto:	Voy a jugar al fútbol.
Esteban:	¿Estás en algún **equipo**?
Alberto:	Sí, estoy en el equipo de nuestra escuela.
Esteban:	¿Vas a practicar?
Alberto:	Sí, tengo que practicar los lunes, martes, miércoles y jueves.
Esteban:	¿Cuándo son los partidos?
Alberto:	Los partidos son los viernes por la noche. Y tú, ¿estás en algún equipo?
Esteban:	No. Me gusta mucho jugar al baloncesto, pero no estoy en un equipo. Sólo juego para hacer ejercicio.

hacer ejercicios aeróbicos **jugar al baloncesto** **jugar al béisbol**

equipo *team*

Capítulo 14 Actividades deportivas **329**

TEACH/MODEL

Los deportes

PRESENTATION

 TEXTBOOK CASSETTE/CD CASSETTE 2, SIDE A; CD 3, TRACK 7

 TAPESCRIPT P. 210

With books closed, have students listen to the dialogue on the Textbook Cassette/CD. Tell them to listen for the cognates, and write them down as they hear them. Then have students open their books and listen to the dialogue again.

Auditory-Musical

PRACTICE/APPLY

SUGGESTION

To practice vocabulary, put up pictures of various sports around the room. Have students identify the sports offered at their school and nearby colleges and perhaps who plays on local teams. You can have students do a human graph of the most popular sports by asking them to line up in front of their favorite sport, then count the number of people in each line. Students might then enjoy graphing the results on paper.

Bodily-Kinesthetic
Visual-Spatial

Etapa Support Materials

- Workbook, pp. 178-182
- Textbook Cassettes/CDs: Cassette 2, Side A; CD 3, Track 7
- Tapescript: Textbook Cassettes/CDs p. 210
- Middle School Activities: pp. 120, 121
- Lesson Plan Book: pp. 80-81

- Testing Program: Quiz pp. 159, 160; Answer Key & Testing Cassettes Tapescript p. T63
- Testing Cassettes: Cassette Side A
- Computerized Testing Program: Windows™; Macintosh®
- Atajo Writing Assistant Software: Student Text, p. 337

EXPANSION

Tell students that the first game of basketball took place in 1891 in the United States. However, there already existed a similar sport that was played by pre-Columbian civilizations of Mexico, a sport known as **tlactli** in the language of the Mayans.

Connections with Distinctive Viewpoints 3.2

jugar al fútbol   jugar al fútbol americano   jugar al golf

jugar al hockey   jugar al hockey sobre hierba   jugar al tenis

jugar al vólibol   levantar pesas   montar en bicicleta

330   *Quinta unidad*   Tu tiempo libre

MULTIPLE INTELLIGENCES

- Linguistic: All activities
- Logical-Mathematical: A, D, E, F, H
- Visual-Spatial: G
- Auditory-Musical: **Aquí escuchamos**
- Interpersonal: B, C, I, J, K, **¿Qué pasó?**
- Intrapersonal: **Querido...**

patinar

patinar sobre hielo

¡Te toca a ti!

A. ¿Qué deporte prefieres? Pregúntale a un(a) compañero(a) qué deportes prefiere. Sigue el modelo.

> **MODELO**
> montar en bicicleta / jugar al vólibol
> **Tú:** ¿Te gusta montar en bicicleta?
> **Compañero(a):** No, no me gusta montar en bicicleta; prefiero jugar al vólibol.

1. correr / levantar pesas
2. patinar sobre hielo / jugar al vólibol
3. jugar al golf / jugar al tenis
4. nadar / hacer ejercicio aeróbico
5. jugar al baloncesto / jugar al béisbol
6. jugar al fútbol americano / jugar al fútbol
7. jugar al hockey / esquiar
8. montar en bicicleta / patinar

B. ¿Qué deporte te gusta más? 1) Choosing from the sports you have learned to say in Spanish, list your three favorites. 2) When you have your list, circulate among your classmates, looking for people who share your interests. 3) When you find someone with whom you have an activity in common, try to arrange a time that you can practice it together.

> **MODELO**
> **Tú:** ¿Qué deporte te gusta, Juana?
> **Juana:** Me gusta jugar al vólibol.
> **Tú:** ¿No te gusta nadar?
> **Juana:** Sí, me gusta mucho nadar. ¿Y a ti?
> **Tú:** ¡Claro que sí! ¿Quieres ir a la piscina con mi hermana y yo?
> **Juana:** ¿Cuándo van Uds.?
> **Tú:** El sábado próximo por la tarde.
> **Juana:** ¡Qué buena idea! o: No, no puedo ir el sábado. ¿Pueden Uds. ir el domingo?
> **Tú:** Sí, cómo no.

Capítulo 14 Actividades deportivas **331**

C. ¡Preguntas y más preguntas!

SUGGESTION

If students need a review of regular and irregular verbs in the preterite tense, provide the categories on the board: regular -**ar**, -**er**, and -**ir** verbs on one side, irregulars on the other. Students should brainstorm infinitives for each category and request a "pet verb" from the list to conjugate orally in the preterite.

EXPANSION

Ask **Uds.** questions (with books closed) of the whole class. Start with **¿Cuántos de ustedes... ?** and ask for a show of hands. Call on a student to answer for his (her) group in the **nosotros** form.

TEACH/MODEL

Estructura

PRESENTATION

Begin by making statements such as: **Aprendí a conducir un coche hace...años.** (Make a gesture indicating the past.) **Hice un viaje a México hace cinco años.** (Use gestures.) Then write the two *formulas* given in the **Estructura** on the board. Explain that Spanish has no equivalent for the English word *ago*. To express this concept in Spanish, they must use one of the two structures presented here.

Have students generate sentences in English in which they would use the word *ago*. (e.g., I lived in Indiana five years ago; I went to Disneyland three months ago.) Write some of these sentences on the board and have students substitute different lengths of time, subjects, and verbs in Spanish. Have students generate sentences in English in which they would use the word *for* + length of time. (e.g., I studied for two hours.) Write some of them on the board and substitute various lengths of time, subjects, and verbs in Spanish.

Analyzing

Linguistic Comparisons 4.1

C. ¡Preguntas y más preguntas! Quieres saber lo que hizo tu amigo(a) el fin de semana pasado. Hazle las preguntas que siguen a un(a) compañero(a).

1. ¿Qué hiciste el viernes pasado?
2. ¿Estuviste en la escuela el sábado pasado?
3. ¿Miraste un programa de televisión el sábado por la noche?
4. ¿Hablaste por teléfono con alguien? ¿Con quién? ¿Cuándo?
5. ¿Tuviste que hacer algo el domingo pasado?
6. ¿Anduviste al centro con tus amigos?
7. ¿Tuviste que estudiar el domingo?
8. ¿Comiste en un restaurante? ¿Cuándo?

ESTRUCTURA

Hace and **hace que** for expressing how long ago something occurred

—**¿Cuánto hace que** Raúl **compró** el disco compacto?

—**Hace dos semanas que** Raúl **compró** el disco compacto.

—Raúl **compró** el disco compacto **hace dos semanas.**

How long ago did Raúl buy the CD?

Two weeks ago, Raúl bought the CD.

Raúl bought the CD two weeks ago.

1. To express how long ago something happened, Spanish uses the following two constructions:

> **Hace** + *length of time* + **que** + *verb in the preterite*
>
> *Verb in the preterite* + **hace** + *length of time*

2. To ask how long ago something occurred, Spanish uses the following construction:

> **¿Cuánto** + **hace** + **que** + *verb in the preterite ?*

Spanish for Spanish Speakers

Expansion

For Activity C, have Spanish speakers and more-prepared students change questions 2-8 to open-ended questions, and then answer them. Then have them prepare an interview of a famous sports figure, writing a series of questions about his (her) past.

Creating

Aquí practicamos

D. ¿Cuánto hace? Sustituye las palabras en cursiva con las palabras que están entre paréntesis y haz los cambios necesarios.

1. Hace *2 días* que Juan habló con su novia. (5 horas / 4 meses / 6 días / 1 mes / 3 semanas)

2. Marirrosa vendió su bicicleta hace *3 meses*. (8 días / 1 año / 6 semanas / 2 horas / 3 meses)

E. Hablé con ella hace... Un(a) amigo(a) quiere saber *(wants to know)* cuánto tiempo hace que hiciste algo *(how long ago you did something)*. Habla con un(a) compañero(a) y sigue el modelo.

> **MODELO**   hablar con ella / 2 horas
> Compañera(o):   ¿Cuánto hace que hablaste con ella?
> Tú: Hablé con ella hace 2 horas.

1. vivir en Indiana / 10 años
2. estudiar francés / 2 años
2. comprar la bicicleta / 3 meses
4. recibir la carta de Ana / 5 días
5. comer en un restaurante / 2 semanas
6. ir al cine / 3 semanas

F. Hace... Now ask your partner the questions she (he) asked you in Exercise E. She (he) will answer, using the alternate construction below. Follow the model.

> **MODELO**   hablar con ella / 2 horas
> Tú: ¿Cuánto hace que hablaste con ella?
> Compañera(o):   Hace 2 horas que hablé con ella.

Capítulo 14 Actividades deportivas   **333**

D. ¿Cuánto hace?

EXPANSION

Have students supply other time frames and complete the sentences using them. For example, **Hace dos segundos que Juan habló con su novia.**

E. Hablé con ella hace...

ANSWERS

Students substitute the cues following the models, using these verb forms:
1. viviste / viví
2. estudiaste / estudié
3. compraste / compré
4. recibiste / recibí
5. comiste / comí
6. fuiste / fui

Individual Needs

More-prepared Students
Help students do additional practice by asking oral questions similar to those in Activities E and F.

Less-prepared Students
Help students review length-of-time expressions by listing common events or everyday activities (e.g. math class, lunch, bus ride to school) and about how long they take. They could also list favorite/most interesting things they have done in their lives, and how long ago they did them.

Intrapersonal

F. Hace...

EXPANSION

Ask **Uds.** questions (with books closed) similar to those in the activity. For example: **¿Cuánto hace que comieron Uds.?**, etc.

Spanish for Spanish Speakers

Sports and Games in Other Countries

Have individuals or pairs interview an adult from a Spanish-speaking country about games/sports he (she) played as a child. Students can tape-record the conversation or write a report—illustrated, if possible, with photos of the country or interviewee—for class presentation. Questions should include: (1) What games/sports did you play as a child? (2) Whom did you play with?

(3) Where did you play? (4) Did boys and girls play together? (5) If unknown or unusual, can you explain the rules of the game/sport? (6) What's your favorite game/sport now? (7) Do you think any games/sports played in the United States are strange?

Cultural Practices and Perspectives 2.1
Communities In and Beyond School 5.1

G. ¿Cuánto hace que...?

SUGGESTION

Encourage students to expand their descriptions of how long ago they did the (pictured) activities, perhaps telling where, with whom, and what it was like.

POSSIBLE ANSWERS

All of the questions will begin with **¿Cuánto hace que... ?**

1. ...comiste pizza? / Comí pizza hace...
2. ...fuiste al cine? / Fui al cine hace...
3. ...fuiste a la oficina de correos? / Fui a la oficina de correos...
4. ...corriste? / Corrí hace...
5. ...visitaste a tus abuelos? / Visité a mis abuelos hace...
6. ...compraste una mochila? / Compré una mochila hace...
7. ...miraste la televisión? / Miré la televisión hace...
8. ...alquilaste un vídeo? Alquilé un vídeo hace...

G. ¿Cuánto hace que...? Basándote en los dibujos, hazle preguntas a un(a) compañero(a). Empieza cada pregunta con la expresión **¿Cuánto hace que...?**

1.

2.

3.

4.

5.

6.

7.

8.

Focus on Culture

Tlactli

Have students do research on the pre-Columbian sport of **tlactli**. Tell them that a good place to find information, in addition to the local library, is the Internet.

Connections with Other Disciplines 3.1

ESTRUCTURA

The preterite of verbs ending in -gar

—A qué hora **llegaste** a la escuela ayer? *What time did you arrive at school yesterday?*
—**Llegué** a las ocho de la mañana. *I arrived at eight o'clock in the morning.*

—¿**Jugaron al** tenis tú y Julián el domingo pasado? *Did you and Julián play tennis last Sunday?*
—Yo **jugué,** pero Julián no **jugó.** *I played, but Julián did not play.*

—¿Cuánto **pagaste** tú por la bicicleta? *How much did you pay for the bicycle?*
—Yo **pagué** 150 dolares. *I paid 150 dollars.*

The Preterite of Verbs Ending in -gar

llegar (to arrive)			
yo	**llegué**	nosotros(as)	**llegamos**
tú	**llegaste**	vosotros(as)	**llegasteis**
él ella Ud.	**llegó**	ellos ellas Uds.	**llegaron**

1. In the **yo** form of verbs ending in **-gar,** the **g** of the stem (**lleg-** for **llegar**) changes to **gu** before the ending **-é.** The other forms of the verb are conjugated exactly like those you learned in Chapter 13 for **-ar** verbs in the preterite.

2. You already saw the verb **jugar,** which means *to play (a game or sport),* in Chapter 11. **Pagar** *(to pay)* is another verb ending in **-gar** that follows this pattern in the preterite.

Aquí practicamos

H. Pagamos, jugamos, llegamos Sustituye las palabras en cursiva con las palabras que están entre paréntesis y haz los cambios necesarios.

1. El año pasado, *nosotros* pagamos 150 dólares por la bicicleta. (Marisol / yo / Ud. / Ángela y su mamá / él)

2. *Julián* no jugó al tenis ayer por la tarde. (nosotros / Uds. / yo / tú / Mario y David)

3. ¿Llegaste *tú* tarde *(late)* a la clase ayer? (Juan / yo / Bárbara y yo / Linda y Clara / Ud.)

Capítulo 14 Actividades deportivas **335**

TEACH/MODEL

Estructura

PRESENTATION
Begin by asking **tú** questions with **llegar,** since students will automatically answer correctly in the **yo** form of the preterite. Then write **llegué** on the board and ask students why the **g** of verbs ending in -**gar** must change to **gu** before **e** or **i.** You might want to review other **Pronunciación** sections where the sounds of **g** are discussed.

 Analyzing
Auditory-Musical

PRACTICE/APPLY

H. Pagamos, jugamos, llegamos

ANSWERS
1. Marisol pagó, yo pagué, Ud. pagó, Ángela y su mamá pagaron, él pagó
2. nosotros no jugamos, Uds. no jugaron, yo no jugué, tú no jugaste, Mario y David no jugaron
3. llegó Juan, llegué yo, llegamos Bárbara y yo, llegaron Linda y Clara, llegó Ud.

I. ¿Cuánto pagaste por...?

SUGGESTION

 You can also have students say when and where they bought the item.

J. ¿Cuándo llegaste a...?

VARIATION

 This oral activity could also be transformed into a short writing activity. To adapt it, have students describe a trip they have taken—where and when they went, when they arrived, and what they did there.

K. ¿A qué deporte jugaste y cuándo?

EXPANSION

To practice other verb tenses, have students talk about the sport another classmate or other classmates played recently and when: **Hace dos semanas que él (ella) jugó al tenis; Hace tres días que ellos jugaron al tenis.**

Aquí escuchamos

TEXTBOOK CASSETTE/CD CASSETTE 2, SIDE A; CD 3, TRACK 8

TAPESCRIPT P. 210

Después de escuchar

ANSWERS

1. the school basketball team
2. She practiced for 3 hours.
3. on Friday
4. to her aerobics class
5. She was late two days ago.

I. ¿Cuánto pagaste por...? Ask several classmates how much they paid for something they bought recently. Suggestions include: **una mochila, un disco compacto, una pizza,** etc.

J. ¿Cuándo llegaste a...? Ask several classmates when they arrived at some place they went to recently. Suggestions include: **el partido, la escuela, a casa,** etc.

K. ¿A qué deporte jugaste y cuándo? Ask several classmates what sport they played recently and when.

Aquí escuchamos

Los deportes *Sonia and Mari run into each other after school and they talk briefly.*

Antes de escuchar Think about the sports activities that you and/or your classmates participate in after school. Then answer the following questions.

1. What do you think Sonia and Mari might talk about?
2. Where do you think they might be going after school?

 A escuchar Listen twice to the conversation before answering the questions about it that follow.

Después de escuchar Answer the following questions based on what you heard.

1. What team is Sonia on?
2. Why is she tired?
3. When is the big game?
4. Where is Mari going?
5. Is she going there early or late?

 Spanish for Spanish Speakers

Vocabulary Expansion–Antonyms

Have Spanish speakers listen carefully to the **Aquí escuchamos** recording and write down five words they hear for which they know or want to find antonyms. Tell them not to limit themselves to just one or two parts of speech, but to choose nouns, verbs, adjectives, adverbs, prepositions, etc. Then give students copies of the dialogue from the Tapescript and have them work with a partner to combine their lists and create a transformed dialogue. Have Spanish speakers and other class volunteers role-play the dialogue with the new words for the rest of the class.

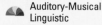 Creating

 Auditory-Musical Linguistic

Presentational Communication 1.3

¡ADELANTE!

 ¿Qué pasó? Work in pairs within groups of four. Ask your partner when the last time was he (she) went to a store (**tienda**), what he (she) bought, and how much he (she) paid for it. Ask your teacher to provide words you don't know, or use the dictionary. As a group, compile your responses. Your teacher will then record all the groups' responses on the board to determine the most popular purchases and their price ranges.

 Querido... A friend from Argentina wants to know what sorts of sports are popular in the United States and which ones you like. Write a note to him (her).

1. Name some popular sports.
2. Tell which ones you prefer.
3. Mention whether you like to attend the games, watch them on television, or participate.
4. In a second paragraph, tell whether you are on a team, if you participate in competitions (**competiciones**), or if you prefer to do sports for exercise.
5. Tell some details about a sport that you play, when you last participated in it, and where.

Capítulo 14 Actividades deportivas **337**

ETAPA SYNTHESIS

¿Qué pasó?

SUGGESTIONS

 Have groups create and fill out grids to organize their information easily. Then, write labels on the board, categorizing types of purchases, e.g., **diversión**, **cursos**, **ropa**, **regalos**, and any other category students suggest. Next, poll each group to find out the number of times any given category is included on their grids. (**¿Qué categorías tiene su grupo? ¿Y cuántas personas compraron algo para cada categoría?**) Keep count on the board using tick marks. When everyone has been polled, have students rank the categories in order of frequency (from least to most).

 Categorizing

Logical-Mathematical

Querido...

FYI

ATAJO WRITING ASSISTANT SOFTWARE

You might want to have students use this software program when doing this activity.

EXPANSION

Students could also provide the friend from Argentina with written copy and photos that describe, magazine-style, the popular sports in their state.

Creating

Additional Practice and Recycling

FYI

WORKBOOK, PP. 178-182

For recycling and additional practice of the vocabulary, structures, and language functions presented throughout this **etapa**, you can assign the workbook activities as in-class work and/or homework.

Deportes de verano

PRESENTATION

As in the **Primera Etapa,** have students look at various pictures of summer sports they participate in. Then have them focus on the sports and activities depicted in the drawings on pages 338 and 339, and hold a discussion on the popularity of these sports in the students' communities and towns. Model the correct pronunciation of the captions using your own preferences and ask students questions about each sport or activity: **Durante el verano, camino en la playa todos los días. Yolanda, ¿te gusta caminar en la playa tambien?,** etc. This will be good preparation for Activity A.

Auditory-Musical
Visual-Spatial

SEGUNDA ETAPA

Preparación

As you begin this **etapa**, think about sports or activities you like to do in the summer.

- Are you close to the beach?
- Do you go to a pool?
- Do you go camping?
- Do you go fishing?

Deportes de verano

*Durante el **verano** (summer), puedes practicar muchos deportes divertidos.*

practicar el esquí acuático

practicar el surfing

tomar el sol

practicar el windsurf

practicar la vela

ir de camping

338 *Quinta unidad* Tu tiempo libre

Etapa Support Materials

- Workbook, pp. 183-188
- TRB: Textbook Activity Masters: pp. 106-108
- Textbook Cassettes/CDs: Cassette 2, Side A; CD 3, Track 9
- Tapescript: Textbook Cassettes/CDs p. 210
- Middle School Activities: pp. 122-124
- Overhead Transparency: 55
- Lesson Plan Book: pp. 82-83

- Testing Program: Quiz pp. 161, 162; Answer Key & Testing Cassettes Tapescript pp. T63, T64
- Testing Cassettes: Cassette Side A
- Computerized Testing Program: Windows™; Macintosh®
- Atajo Writing Assistant Software: Student Text, p. 346

la natación / nadar practicar el alpinismo la pesca / ir de pesca

practicar el ciclismo el buceo / bucear caminar en la playa

¡Te toca a ti!

A. ¿Qué actividad prefieres? Pregúntale a un(a) compañero(a) qué actividades de verano prefiere. Sigue el modelo.

> **MODELO** el ciclismo / el alpinismo
> **Tú:** *¿Te gusta practicar el ciclismo?*
> **Compañera(o):** *No, no me gusta practicar el ciclismo. Prefiero practicar el alpinismo.*

1. ir de pesca / nadar
2. la vela / el windsurf
3. el esquí acuático / el buceo
4. el alpinismo / ir de camping
5. el ciclismo / tomar el sol
6. el surfing / caminar en la playa

Capítulo 14 Actividades deportivas **339**

A. ¿Qué actividad prefieres?

ANSWERS

1. ¿Te gusta ir de pesca?
   No, no me gusta ir de pesca.
   Prefiero nadar.
2. ¿Te gusta practicar la vela?
   No, no me gusta practicar la vela.
   Prefiero practicar el windsurf.
3. ¿Te gusta practicar el esquí acuático?
   No, no me gusta practicar el esquí acuático. Prefiero el buceo (bucear).
4. ¿Te gusta practicar el alpinismo?
   No, no me gusta practicar el alpinismo. Prefiero ir de camping.
5. ¿Te gusta practicar el ciclismo?
   No, no me gusta practicar el ciclismo. Prefiero tomar el sol.
6. ¿Te gusta practicar el surfing?
   No, no me gusta practicar el surfing. Prefiero caminar en la playa.

SUGGESTION

For more speaking practice, have students explain to their partners why they prefer the second sport.

Determining Preferences

MULTIPLE INTELLIGENCES

- Linguistic: All activities
- Logical-Mathematical: A, C, G, H, J
- Visual-Spatial: B, D
- Auditory-Musical: **Estructura**, **Aquí escuchamos**, I
- Interpersonal: C, G, **El verano pasado**
- Intrapersonal: E, **Durante las vacaciones**

The Standards

- Interpersonal Communication 1.1: A, B, C, D, F, H, **El verano pasado**
- Interpretive Communication 1.2: G, I, J, **Aquí escuchamos**
- Presentational Communication 1.3: E, **Durante las vacaciones**

PRACTICE / APPLY

B. ¿Qué hacen?

ANSWERS

1. Isabel practica el buceo.
2. Juan practica el alpinismo.
3. Mario y Julia caminan en la playa.
4. Elena practica el surfing.
5. Pedro practica la pesca/va a pescar.
6. Esteban y Roberto practican el ciclismo.
7. Tomás y Laura van de camping.
8. Elena practica la natación.

VARIATION

Use chapter vocabulary to describe the drawings to students; have 1-3 students at a time sketch one of the pictures-without peeking. Then, collect all pictures and pin one on the back of each student. Have students circulate, asking **sí/no** questions about the drawing. When they can correctly describe the picture to you, they can remove it, put it on the board, and write a description of it.

◭◭ Visual-Spatial

B. ¿Qué hacen? Basándote en los dibujos, di lo que hace cada persona. Sigue el modelo

MODELO   Julián
Julián practica el esquí acuático.

1. Isabel

2. Juan

3. Mario y Julia

4. Elena

5. Pedro

6. Esteban y Roberto

7. Tomás y Laura

8. Regina

340   *Quinta unidad* Tu tiempo libre

Focus on Culture

Actividades

Have students look at the drawings for Activity B and tell them to think about the Spanish-speaking countries they have read about. Ask students to cite a region/country where they think an activity is likely to be popular. Start them off with a sentence such as **Es muy popular ir a la playa en San Juan, Puerto Rico.**

☼ Activating Prior Knowledge

✪ Connections with Distinctive Viewpoints 3.2

C. ¿Qué actividad de verano te gusta?

Compare your opinions about summer sports and activities with those of your partner. 1) On your activity master, indicate your opinion of each activity in the left column, using the numbers on the following scale to indicate how much you like each one. 2) Then, interview your partner, writing the appropriate number to indicate his (her) preferences in the right column. 3) Go over your results as explained below.

no = 0, poco = 1, bastante = 2, mucho = 3, muchísimo = 4

No tengo experiencia con esta actividad = X

MODELO

Tú:	¿Te gusta practicar el surfing?
Compañero(a):	No, no me gusta practicar el surfing, pero me gusta mucho caminar en la playa.

Yo	Actividad	Mi amigo(a)
3	practicar el surfing	0
2	tomar el sol	3
	caminar en la playa	
	practicar el esquí acuático	
	ir de pesca	
4	nadar	3
	practicar la vela	
	ir de camping	
	practicar el ciclismo	
x	practicar el windsurf	x
	bucear	
	jugar al golf	
	jugar al tenis	

Go over the results with your partner. Name the activities about which your attitudes are the same and those about which your opinions are the most different.

MODELO

A los (las) dos nos gusta tomar el sol y nadar.
No nos gusta ir de pesca.
Tenemos opiniones diferentes sobre (about) practicar el surfing.
No tenemos experiencia con el windsurf.

Capítulo 14 Actividades deportivas **341**

C. ¿Qué actividad de verano te gusta?

 TRB: ACTIVITY MASTER, P. 106

SUGGESTION

 Have students play the role of travel agents, taking their information from Activity C and writing up a summer vacation itinerary for their partners. Have them refer to Chapter 13 vocabulary for more ideas.

VARIATION

 Ask students to do a three-paragraph team writing project. They should name their shared preferences in the first paragraph, the activities neither of them likes in the second, and point out their differences in the third.

 Comparing and Contrasting

EXPANSION

 Have pairs tally their points for the sports grid, reporting their totals to student statisticians who add up all totals for any one sport. The statisticians should report the results while you write them on the board. Practice the targeted vocabulary and structures while reading them, i.e.: **¿Qué deporte(s) le gusta(n) más a la clase? ¿Cuál(es) le gusta(n) menos? ¿Con qué actividad(es) no tenemos mucha experiencia?** Then lead students to draw inferences: **¿Por qué no? (No tenemos playa; no estamos cerca del mar.)**

 Analyzing
Drawing Inferences

Logical-Mathematical

PRACTICE/APPLY

D. ¿Qué hizo Esteban ayer?

SUGGESTION

 TRANSPARENCY 55

To check spelling and review the alphabet, have students spell the verbs they use in items 1-6.

POSSIBLE ANSWERS

1. Anduvo por el parque.
2. Llegó a las 2:00 de la tarde.
3. Jugó al fútbol.
4. Compró un refresco.
5. Pagó por el refresco.
6. Volvió a casa a las 5:30.

E. ¿Qué hiciste tú ayer?

ANSWERS

1. anduve   4. compré
2. llegué   5. pagué
3. jugué   6. volví

Individual Needs

More and Less-prepared Students

After Activity E, students could prepare and present "A Day in the Life of..." as if on television. Students could interview each other about the most interesting/unbelievable/unforgettable day of their lives. More-prepared students could use a wider range of activities, while less-prepared students could limit their descriptions to a day of sports/leisure activities.

Interpersonal

F. ¿Cuánto hace que... ?

SUGGESTION

Students can test their memories in this activity by saying what they remember about each specific activity. This is also an opportunity to discuss observation and memory and perhaps introduce some memory games.

Linguistic

Repaso

D. ¿Qué hizo Esteban ayer? Basándote en los dibujos, di lo que Esteban hizo ayer.

1. andar

2. llegar

3. jugar

4. comprar

5. pagar

6. volver

E. ¿Qué hiciste tú ayer? Ahora imagina que eres Esteban. Di lo que hiciste ayer usando los dibujos de la Actividad D.

F. ¿Cuánto hace que...? Ask several classmates when they last did a specific activity. For example, ask when they played tennis, when they ate at a restaurant, walked in the park, etc. Take notes on their responses and be prepared to report back to the class.

ESTRUCTURA

The preterite of verbs ending in -car

—¿Quién **buscó** el libro?   *Who looked for the book?*
—Yo **busqué** el libro.   *I looked for the book.*

—**Tocó** Julián la guitarra en la fiesta anoche?   *Did Julián play the guitar at the party last night?*
—No, yo **toqué** la guitarra anoche.   *No, I played the guitar last night.*

The Preterite of Verbs Ending in -car

buscar *(to look for)*			
yo	**busqué**	nosotros(as)	**buscamos**
tú	**buscaste**	vosotros(as)	**buscasteis**
él ella Ud.	**buscó**	ellos ellas Uds.	**buscaron**

1. In the **yo** form of verbs ending in -car, the **c** of the stem (**busc-** for **buscar**) changes to **qu** before the ending -é. The other forms of the verb are conjugated exactly like those you learned in Chapter 13 for -ar verbs in the preterite.

2. You already know the verbs **practicar** and **tocar**. The verb **sacar**, which means *to take out, to remove,* or *to obtain (a grade),* is another verb ending in -car that follows this pattern in the preterite.

Aquí practicamos

G. Todos buscan Sustituye las palabras en cursiva con las palabras que están entre paréntesis y haz los cambios necesarios.

1. *Elena* buscó la casa de Raúl. (tú / Ud. / Lilia y su novio / yo / Uds.)
2. *Olga* no tocó el piano anoche. (Uds. / Diego / yo / tú / nosotras)
3. ¿Practicaron *Uds.* ayer por la tarde? (nosotros / Santiago y Enrique / tú / yo / ella)

H. ¿Qué deporte practicaste el verano pasado?
Un(a) compañero(a) quiere saber qué deportes practicaste el verano pasado. Responde según el modelo.

Capítulo 14 Actividades deportivas   **343**

TEACH/MODEL

Estructura

PRESENTATION
Start out by asking **tú** questions in the preterite with **practicar**. After a few questions, write the **yo** form of the verb on the board and ask students why the **c** of verbs ending in -car must change to **qu** before **e** and **i**. You might want to review the **Pronunciación** sections where **que** and **qui** are discussed and where **ce** and **ci** are discussed. Point out that **tocar** also means *to touch* or *to knock*.

Auditory-Musical

VOCABULARY EXPANSION
For more practice with the verb **tocar**, introduce students to the following instruments: **trompeta, violín, órgano, flauta, clarinete, guitarra, piano, tambores.**

PRACTICE/APPLY

G. Todos buscan
ANSWERS
1. tú buscaste, Ud. buscó, Lilia y su novio buscaron, yo busqué, Uds. buscaron
2. Uds. no tocaron, Diego no tocó, yo no toqué, tú no tocaste, nosotras no tocamos
3. practicamos nosotros, practicaron Santiago y Enrique, practicaste tú, practiqué yo, practicó ella

SUGGESTION
This activity lends itself to the use of a small, soft ball. Toss it to a student as you say the new subject. The student substitutes the correct verb and tosses the ball back.

Bodily-Kinesthetic

H. ¿Qué deporte practicaste el verano pasado?
SUGGESTION
Tell students that if they have not participated in any of these sports, they can say that the sport interests them and tell why. This is an opportunity to review **Me interesa** and **Me fascina**.

Palabras útiles

PRESENTATION

The purpose of introducing these lexical items (**primero, entonces, por fin,** etc.) is to lead students to string sentences together and produce extended discourse, i.e., to begin to talk in paragraphs. These time indicators will be expanded throughout Unit 5.

You may wish to begin this presentation by enumerating things you did yesterday. Have students imitate your model before they go on to the activities. Also, have students generate English-language examples in order to clarify the concept of time transpositions.

PRACTICE/APPLY

I. ¿Qué hizo Felipe?

ANSWERS

1.—¿Practicaste el buceo el verano pasado?
—No, practiqué...(answers will vary).
2.—¿Practicaste el surfing...?
—No, practiqué....
3.—¿Practicaste el esquí acuática
—No, practiqué....
4.—¿Practicaste la vela...?
—No, practiqué....
5.—¿Practicaste el alpinismo...?
—No, practiqué....
6.—¿Practicaste el ciclismo...?
—No, practiqué....

SUGGESTION

You might want to practice this as a listening/memory activity, with students listening to the sequence and then attempting to retell what was done.

Auditory-Musical

MODELO	el windsurf	
	Compañera(o):	¿*Practicaste el windsurf el verano pasado?*
	Tú:	*No, no practiqué el windsurf, practiqué el buceo.*

1. el buceo
2. el surfing
3. el esquí acuático
4. la vela
5. el alpinismo
6. el ciclismo

PALABRAS ÚTILES

Expressions used to talk about a series of actions

Primero, yo estudié en la biblioteca. **Entonces,** caminé al parque y visité a un amigo. **Por fin,** volví a casa.

1. When talking about a series of actions in the past, you will find the following expressions useful.

primero	*first*
entonces, luego	*then*
por fin, finalmente	*finally*

2. These expressions are also useful when talking about future actions.

Primero, voy a estudiar en la biblioteca. **Entonces,** voy a caminar al parque y voy a visitar a un amigo. **Por fin,** voy a volver a casa.

3. You can also use them to talk about daily routines.

Todos los días después de la escuela, llego a casa a las 4:00. **Primero,** como un sándwich y bebo un vaso de leche. **Entonces,** saco la basura. **Por fin,** estudio por unas horas.

Aquí practicamos

I. ¿Qué hizo Felipe? Use the expressions in parentheses to tell what Felipe did in the past and in what order. Follow the model.

MODELO Felipe tomó el autobús al centro. (el domingo pasado)
El domingo pasado, Felipe tomó el autobús al centro.

1. Comió en un restaurante. (primero)
2. Compró un disco compacto. (entonces)
3. Visitó a una amiga en el parque. (luego)
4. Volvió a su casa a las 5:00 de la tarde. (finalmente)

344 *Quinta unidad* Tu tiempo libre

Spanish for Spanish Speakers

Summaries

Put Spanish speakers in pairs or small groups or team them with classmates so less-prepared students work with fluent or more-prepared students. Then, have each team write Spanish sentences summarizing the plot of a famous book or movie. Emphasize the use of time expressions (from **Palabras útiles**) to clarify the sequence of events. When all have finished, have teams present/role-play the summaries, and see who can guess the title.

Presentational Communication 1.3

Now tell what Felipe did last Saturday.

> **MODELO**   Felipe fue a la playa. (el sábado pasado)
> *El sábado pasado, Felipe fue a la playa.*

5. Practicó el windsurf. (primero)
6. Nadó en el mar. (entonces)
7. Tomó el sol. (luego)
8. Caminó a casa. (finalmente)

Now tell what Felipe is going to do at some point in the future.

9. Felipe va a viajar a Ecuador. (el mes próximo)
10. Va a ir a Quito. (primero)
11. Va a visitar la ciudad de Guayaquil. (entonces)
12. Va a volver el 5 de junio. (por fin)

J. **Primero... entonces... finalmente...**   Describe the order of each set of three activities. Choose logical verbs to go with the words provided. Follow the model.

> **MODELO**   nosotros / piscina / en casa / programa de televisión
> *Primero, nosotros fuimos a la piscina. Entonces, estudiamos en casa. Finalmente, miramos un programa de televisión.*

1. ellos / escuela / sándwich / televisión
2. yo / biblioteca / centro / disco compacto
3. nosotros / casa / jugo de naranja / estéreo
4. ella / café y pan tostado / autobús / un amigo
5. él / sándwich de jamón y queso / metro / centro
6. ellas / parque / refresco / casa

Capítulo 14 Actividades deportivas   **345**

J. Primero... entonces... finalmente...

POSSIBLE ANSWERS
Students substitute the cues and add the expressions following the model, using the verbs and other words in these forms:

1. fueron a la, comieron un, miraron la
2. fui a la, fui al, compré un
3. estuvimos en, tomamos (bebimos) un, escuchamos el
4. desayunó, tomó el, visitó a
5. comió un, tomó el, fue al
6. fueron/anduvieron al, tomaron un, volvieron a

Individual Needs

Less-prepared Students
These students might benefit from writing this challenging activity. You can check their work, and then have them try the activity orally.

More-prepared Students
These students might like to write additional, original dehydrated sentences for their partners to try.

PRACTICE/APPLY

Aquí escuchamos

| TEXTBOOK CASSETTE/CD CASSETTE 2, SIDE A; CD 3, TRACK 9 |
| TAPESCRIPT P. 210 |
| TRB: ACTIVITY MASTER, P. 107 |

Después de escuchar

ANSWERS

nadar, bucear, practicar el windsurf, cenar

ETAPA SYNTHESIS

El verano pasado

SUGGESTION

Encourage students to organize this activity using a calendar, and to select the most interesting or unusual events of the summer.

Sequencing

Durante las vacaciones...

FYI

ATAJO WRITING ASSISTANT SOFTWARE

You might want to have students use this software program when doing this activity.

SUGGESTION

Remind students that they can use information from the preceding activity to organize their letter. You can also have them include questions for the pen pal about his or her school and vacation schedule, and what the "winter" months of June, July, and August are like in Chile.

Additional Practice and Recycling

FYI

WORKBOOK, PP. 183-188

For recycling and additional practice of the vocabulary, structures, and language functions presented throughout this **etapa**, you can assign the workbook activities as in-class work and/or homework.

Aquí escuchamos

¡Qué bien lo pasaste! *Roberto tells Felipe about his weekend at the beach.*

Antes de escuchar Have you been to the beach before? Based on what you have learned in this **etapa**, what activities do you think Felipe might have done there?

A escuchar Listen twice to the conversation between Roberto and Felipe. Pay attention to the order of Roberto's activities and indicate the order on your activity master.

Después de escuchar On your activity master, write numbers next to the activities Roberto mentions to indicate the order in which he did them.

__bucear	__nadar
__caminar en la playa	__practicar el windsurf
__cenar	__tomar el sol

¡ADELANTE!

El verano pasado Both you and your partner were very busy last summer, participating in many summer sports and activities. To report your activities to each other, organize them in the order in which you did them. Use time expressions to list them in order. Include at least five activities each. Find at least one activity in which you both participated.

Durante las vacaciones... You've just come back to school from summer vacation and want to tell your pen pal in Chile what you did during the summer. Write your friend a note and indicate what you did, including at least five activities that you were involved in. Use time expressions to tell the order in which you did your summer activities.

EN LÍNEA

Connect with the Spanish-speaking world! Access the **¡Ya verás!** *Gold* home page for Internet activities related to this chapter.

http://yaveras.heinle.com

Additional Etapa Resources

Refer to the **Etapa** Support Materials list on the opening page of this **etapa** for detailed cross-references to these assessment options.

VOCABULARIO

Para charlar

Para hablar de una serie de acciones

primero
entonces
luego
finalmente
por fin

Para hablar del tiempo

un minuto
una hora
un día
una semana
un mes
un año

Temas y contextos

Deportes

hacer ejercicio aeróbico
jugar…
　al baloncesto
　al golf
　al hockey
　al hockey sobre hierba
levantar pesas
patinar
patinar sobre hielo

Deportes de verano

el buceo / bucear
caminar en la playa
ir de camping
la natación / nadar
la pesca / ir de pesca
practicar…
　el alpinismo
　el ciclismo
　el esquí acuático
　el surfing
　la vela
　el windsurf
tomar el sol

Vocabulario general

Verbos

sacar

Sustantivos

una guitarra

Otras expresiones

¿Cuánto hace que + *verb in the preterite?*
Hace + *length of time* + que + *subject* + *verb in the preterite.*
Subject + *verb in the preterite* + hace + *length of time.*

Capítulo 14 Actividades deportivas **347**

CHAPTER WRAP-UP

Vocabulario

SUGGESTION

 Have students divide into groups and use the maps in the front matter to plan a trip to Latin America. Ask them to decide where they will go, what they will visit, and how they will get there. Encourage them to use **primero, entonces, luego, por fin, finalmente**.

Listening Skills Development

FYI

 LAB MANUAL, PP.92-98

 LAB CASSETTE SIDE B; CD 7, TRACKS 11-19

TAPESCRIPT: LAB PROGRAM PP. 139-145

It is now appropriate to work through the lab manual activities and their accompanying recordings in class or in the language laboratory.

Improvised Conversation

SUGGESTION

 TRB: ACTIVITY MASTER, P. 108

 TEXTBOOK CASSETTE/CD CASSETTE 2, SIDE A; CD 3, TRACK 10

 TAPESCRIPT PP. 210-211

Have students listen to this conversation between a teenager, Julia, and her mother, Ángela. Refer to the TRB for student activities.

Resources for Spanish-speaking Students

FYI

 WORKBOOK FOR SPANISH-SPEAKING STUDENTS: PP. 87-92

 ANSWER KEY TO SSS WORKBOOK PP. 25-27

Activities specially written to meet the needs of Spanish-speaking students are available in these workbooks for the reinforcement of the topics and language presented in this chapter.

Additional Chapter Resources

Refer to the Chapter Support Materials list on the opening page of this chapter for detailed cross-references to *¡Ya verás!*'s student-centered technology components and various assessment options.

☀ Spanish for Spanish Speakers

Keeping a Vocabulary Notebook

Remind Spanish-speaking students to add words and expressions from this vocabulary section to the problematic spelling combination categories and personal new vocabulary lists they started in their notebooks in Chapter 1. Reinforce that they should continue to do this each time a chapter in the textbook is completed

Una página de "surfing" latinoamericano
Antes de leer

ANSWERS

1. It is a page from the Internet. **Página** is the word that refers to the format.
2. Costa Rica, El Salvador, Uraguay, Australia, Hawaii
3. Answers will vary
4. Answers will vary. Possible answer could be in tourist beach communities of Australia, Hawaii, Uruguay, etc...

SUGGESTION

Invite students to research the sport of surfing. What is some of the terminology used in surfing? What equipment is needed? What Latin American countries have international surfing competitions? What are the dangers of surfing?

ENCUENTROS CULTURALES
◆

Una página de "surfing" latinoamericano

Reading Strategies
- Previewing
- Activating background knowledge
- Scanning for specific information

Antes de leer

1. Can you identify the format of this reading? What word in the title refers to this kind of format?

2. Scan the whole text. Find the names of at least four different countries that are mentioned in relation to surfing activities.

3. What do you know about surfing?

4. Where does surfing usually take place?

Netsite: http:// www.the grid.net/fleming/sites.html/

El Salvador: "punto" desconocido

Muchos saben que las playas de Costa Rica son un excelente lugar para "surfear," pero pocos saben que en El Salvador también hay estupendos lugares para practicar este deporte. Hay varios lugares muy buenos para "surfear" a lo largo de la costa, pero el mejor oleaje lo ofrece La Libertad, una popular área turística al sur de San Salvador. Allí vas a encontrar un estupendo rompeolas cerca del muelle, además de muchos restaurantes y hoteles. Recomendamos también que visites Los Cobanos, en el sur, que tiene un estupendo oleaje y un hotel muy económico.

Otros dos puntos para visitar son Costa del Sol y El Cuco

¡Atención! Recuerda viajar durante la temporada de lluvias, que es entre junio y noviembre, si quieres disfrutar del mejor oleaje.

Médanos + tablas = felicidad

Como todo amante del "surfeo" sabe, los brasileños de la ciudad de Florianópolis inventaron, en 1986, el deporte del "sandboarding", o deslizamiento en tablas sobre arena. Este deporte ha alcanzado gran popularidad en el mundo. Los médanos de Valizas en Uruguay son los más grandes de Sudámerica y alcanzan los 30 metros de altura. ¡Diversión—y algunos moretones—garantizados!
Presiona aquí si quieres ver fotos de los mejores médanos del Uruguay.

348 *Quinta unidad* Tu tiempo libre

Muncoarena: "Surfea" en el Uruguay   ¡¡¡Disfruta tu estadía!!!

Netsite: http://www.greenarrow.com/ssurf.html

Todo el mundo ha oído hablar de Australia y Hawaii, pero pocos saben que el Uruguay ofrece algunos de los mejores puntos para "surfear" en el mundo. Aquí, algunas sugerencias para un viaje de "surfeo" uruguayo: Punta del Este/José Ignacio/Santa Teresa

Algunas recomendaciones para tu viaje de "surfing" a Punta del Este:

a. El aereopuerto principal se llama Aereopuerto Internacional Carrasco. Punta del Este está situada a 100 millas del aereopuerto. Para llegar, puedes tomar el bus o alquilar un automóvil.

b. Si necesitas comprar equipo para "surfear," visita la playa de La Olla, donde está la tienda de equipo de "surfing" más grande de Sur América, la tienda "Valle del Sol" de artículos deportivos.

c. En muchas áreas hay disponible alquiler de bicicletas y motoras.

d. Por último: ¡asegúrate de viajar durante la temporada de invierno—de octubre a diciembre—cuando el océano es más agresivo!

Guía para la lectura

1. Here are some words and expressions to keep in mind as you read.

"punto"	*spot, point—here it refers to a good surfing location*
oleaje	*surf, breaking waves*
muelle	*pier*
temporada de lluvias	*rainy season*
Médanos	*Sand dunes*
tablas	*boards (for surfing or sandboarding)*
deslizamiento	*sliding*
arena	*sand*
moretones	*bruises*
motoras	*motorboats*

2. Notice the different versions of the borrowed English word *surfing*: "surfear," "surfing," "surfeo."

Después de leer

1. This reading mentions two varieties of surfing. What are they? How are the two types of surfing similar, and how are they different?

2. If you wanted to go surfing, which of the sites mentioned in the reading would you visit? Explain your response.

3. Browsing the World Wide Web is commonly known as "surfing". Can you explain why?

Después de leer

ANSWERS

1. Surfing and sandboarding. A board is needed for both sports, but the first one slides on the water and the second one on sand.
2. Answers may vary
3. Answers may vary. A possible answer could be that browsing through the Web is like navigating through different sites.

EXPANSION

Have students compare surfing to two land sports: skateboarding and snowboarding. What are the similarities? the differences? Consider things like equipment, climate, source of power for movement, skills involved, tricks, etc. If students have participated in any of these sports requiring **tablas**, let them share with the class their observations. What does it feel like? Is it hard to learn? What tricks can be done?

Analyzing
Comparing and Contrasting

CAPÍTULO 15

CHAPTER WARM-UP

Setting the Context

In preparation for talking about sports played in Spanish-speaking countries, ask students to hypothesize what sports are popular in the Spanish-speaking world and why. Are those the same sports played here? Have students write their answers. Have them skim the chapter to get a better picture of the sports that are popular in Spanish-speaking countries.

Discuss cultural similarities and differences. Did students expect that baseball and tennis were popular? Why isn't soccer—so popular elsewhere in the Spanish-speaking world—popular here? Is this changing? Do students know that the United States hosted the World Cup Soccer Championship in 1994?

 Making Hypotheses

 Cultural Comparisons 4.2

Dos deportes populares

Es muy divertido mirar el tenis, pero es aún mejor practicarlo.

Objectives

- talking about actions in the past, present, and future
- talking about sports

Chapter Support Materials

- Lab Manual: pp. 99-104
- Lab Program: Cassette Side A, B; CD 8, Tracks 1-7
- TRB: Textbook Activity Masters: pp. 109, 110
- Textbook Cassettes/CDs: Cassette 2, Side A; CD 3, Track 13
- Tapescript: Lab Program pp.146-153 ; Textbook Cassettes/CDs p. 212
- Middle School Activities: pp. 125-127
- Workbook for Spanish-speaking Students: pp. 93-98
- Answer Key to SSS Workbook: pp. 27-29
- Practice Software: Windows™; Macintosh®

- Testing Program: Chapter Test pp. T174-T178; Answer Key & Testing Cassettes Tapescript pp. T68, T69; Oral Assessment p. T69
- Testing Cassettes: Cassette Side A
- Computerized Testing Program: Windows™; Macintosh®
- Video Program: Cassette 2, 41:16-55:47
- Video Guide: Videoscript pp. 60-65; Activities pp. 131-133
- **Mundos hispanos 1**
- Internet Activities: Student Text p. 365

PRIMERA ETAPA

- Think about the importance given to sports in the United States. When you think about sports in Latin America, what do you think of? This **etapa** begins with a short reading about a sport that is very popular in several Latin American countries.

El béisbol

El béisbol es un deporte muy popular en el Caribe.

Raúl Mondesi

Juan González

Roberto Alomar

Capítulo 15 Dos deportes populares **351**

El béisbol

PRESENTATION
Have students try to guess the countries where baseball is popular. List them on the board. Also ask students for the names of Latin American ball players and list them on the board. Leave them on the board to see if any of the countries or names appear in the reading.

FYI
Students may already know that soccer is very popular in the Spanish-speaking world, both as a spectator and a participatory sport. They may not be quite as aware of the popularity of baseball in Spanish-speaking countries. Let them know that the Caribbean countries, Mexico, and Central America all have thriving baseball leagues. Many of the best players in the North American leagues come from these countries.

Cultural Comparisons 4.2

SUGGESTION
After they read, ask students to think about what they already know about the game of baseball—how it's played, what makes a good player, when and where it's played here, for example. Instruct them to use this knowledge as they try to decipher Activities A (vocabulary) and B (comprehension).

Activating Prior Knowledge

Etapa Support Materials

- Workbook: pp. 189-193
- TRB: Textbook Activity Masters: p. 109
- Textbook Cassettes/CDs: Cassette 2, Side A; CD 3, Track 11
- Tapescript: Textbook Cassettes/CDs p. 211
- Middle School Activities: pp. 128-131
- Overhead Transparency: 56
- Lesson Plan Book: pp. 85-86
- Testing Program: Quiz pp.168-170; Answer Key & Testing Cassettes Tapescript p. T66
- Testing Cassettes: Cassette Side A
- Computerized Testing Program: Windows™; Macintosh®
- Atajo Writing Assistant Software: Student Text, p. 357

PRACTICE/APPLY

A. Estudio de Palabras

ANSWERS

1. leagues
2. qualities
3. reflexes
4. throw
5. hit

B. Comprensión

ANSWERS

1. Cuba and Dominican Republic
2. No
3. Japan, Taiwan and South Korea
4. physical strength, speed, quick reflexes
5. Because they are of Hispanic origin

VOCABULARY EXPANSION

Refer back to the list of Hispanic ball players on the board. Which ones did not appear in the reading? Of those that did, what position does each one play and on which major league team? You may wish to tell students that since baseball originated in the United States, most of its vocabulary in Spanish is borrowed from English, with a few modifications in spelling and pronunciation. Have students generate a vocabulary list and then do equivalents in Spanish. For example, a *home run* becomes a **jonrón**; a *bat*, **bate**; *first, second, third base*, **primera**, **segunda**, **tercera base**; a *pitcher* is either **lanzador** or **pícher**.

Linguistic Comparisons 4.1

Andrés Galarraga

El béisbol es el deporte nacional de los Estados Unidos. También es muy popular en varios países del mundo hispano, principalmente Cuba y la República Dominicana. En Canadá no es tan popular, pero hay dos equipos en las **ligas** mayores—un equipo en Montreal y otro en Toronto. El deporte también es muy popular en México, Puerto Rico, las naciones de Centroamérica, Venezuela y Colombia. También se juega en el Japón, Taiwan y en Corea del Sur.

Hay muchos beisbolistas de origen hispano que juegan en las ligas mayores. Por ejemplo, Juan González de los Texas Rangers, Andrés Galarraga de los Colorado Rockies, Raúl Mondesi de los Los Angeles Dodgers y Sandy Alomar de los Toronto Blue Jays. Hay ciertas **cualidades** que todos estos beisbolistas tienen en común: fuerza física, rapidez, **reflejos** rápidos. **Lanzar** la pelota y **golpearla** con el bate son actividades que requieren mucha práctica y preparación. ¿Te gusta el béisbol? ¿Cuál es tu equipo favorito?

¡Te toca a ti!

A. Estudio de palabras ¿Qué crees que significan las siguientes palabras que están en negrita en la lectura? *(What do you think the following words in boldface in the reading mean?)*

1. ligas
2. cualidades
3. reflejos
4. lanzar
5. golpear

B. Comprensión Responde a las siguientes preguntas sobre la lectura *(about the reading)*.

1. In what Latin American countries is baseball popular?
2. Is it popular in Canada?
3. Where else, besides the Americas, is baseball played?
4. What are some of the characteristics of good baseball players?
5. Why are the players mentioned in the reading significant?

352 *Quinta unidad* Tu tiempo libre

MULTIPLE INTELLIGENCES

- Linguistic: All activities
- Logical-Mathematical: A
- Visual-Spatial: C, F
- Auditory-Musical: **Aquí escuchamos**
- Interpersonal: **En este momento**
- Intrapersonal: D, E, **¿Qué está(n) haciendo?**

Repaso ♻

C. ¿Qué hizo Alicia ayer? Basándote en los dibujos que siguen, di lo que hizo Alicia por la tarde.

1. salir de

2. practicar

3. llegar

4. primero / sacar

5. entonces / practicar

6. luego / cenar

7. finalmente / mirar

D. ¿Qué hiciste tú ayer? Ahora imagina que tú eres la persona que está en los dibujos. Di lo que hiciste ayer.

ESTRUCTURA

The present progressive

—¿Qué **están haciendo** Uds. ahora mismo?

What are you doing right now?

—**Estamos estudiando.**

We are studying.

Mi madre **está escribiendo** una carta.

My mother is writing a letter.

1. In Spanish, the present progressive is formed with the present tense form of the verb **estar** plus the **-ndo** form of another verb. The **-ndo** form of the verb is known as the present participle. In English, the present progressive consists of the present tense form of the verb *to be* plus the present participle (the *-ing* form) of another verb *(Charlie is playing tennis. We are resting.).*

The Standards

- Interpersonal Communication 1.1: F, **En este momento**
- Interpretive Communication 1.2: C, **Aquí escuchamos**
- Presentational Communication 1.3: D, E,
- Cultural Practices and Perspectives 2.1: B
- Linguistic Comparisons 4.1: A, B, **Estructura**

C. ¿Qué hizo Alicia ayer?

ANSWERS

1. Alicia salió de la escuela.
2. Practicó deporte (el fútbol).
3. Llegó a su casa.
4. Primero sacó unos discos compactos.
5. Entonces practicó el piano.
6. Luego cenó.
7. Finalmente miró la televisión.

SUGGESTION

Have students re-do Activity C with different subjects, such as **los niños, nosotros, Juan y María, la profesora.**

D. ¿Qué hiciste tú ayer?

ANSWERS

Answers will follow model of Activity C, except for the verb form:

1. salí
2. practiqué
3. llegué
4. saqué
5. practiqué
6. cené
7. miré

SUGGESTION

As students do Activity D, suggest sample verbs, e.g., **llegar, practicar, sacar,** etc. Have them repeat **yo practiqué, yo saqué,** and **yo llegué** to reinforce the sound pattern. Remind students of the spelling changes between **practicó** and **practiqué, sacó** and **saqué, llegó** and **llegué.** Emphasize that this pattern is true for any verb ending in **-gar** or **-car** (**pagar, jugar, tocar, buscar,** etc.) and provide examples.

Auditory-Musical

TEACH/MODEL

Estructura

PRESENTATION

Make statements to introduce the present progressive. For example: **Estoy hablando en este momento. Estoy presentando el presente progresivo de los verbos. Uds. están escuchando. Uds. están aprendiendo una estructura nueva.**

Estructura (cont.)

Emphasize that the use of this tense means that an action is occurring right now. Have students create full sentences, using the present participle of other regular verbs: (**cantar, cenar, descansar, esperar, esquiar, mirar, tomar, trabajar, viajar, aprender, beber, vender, abrir, asistir, subir, vivir**). Make statements, using en **este momento, ahora mismo,** and **ahora.** Then ask questions such as: **¿Qué estás haciendo en este momento? ¿Qué están haciendo tus compañeros de la clase de español ahora mismo? ¿Qué está haciendo tu mamá/papá/ hermano/hermana ahora?,** etc.

 Linguistic Comparisons 4.1

 PRACTICE / APPLY

E. Ahora mismo

SUGGESTION

A possible way to present this activity is through the creation of a "word web." Word webs divide linguistic elements into different categories, allowing students to analyze each element visually as well as analytically. First, have students write in the correct answers in all appropriate columns. Next, have students draw a web horizontally, on a separate piece of paper, sketching circles large enough to let students write in the grammatical elements in each category. Then, have students label each circle (subject, verb, etc.). Finally, have them connect elements from the circles in ways that form grammatically correct sentences.

Categorizing

Visual-Spatial
Logical-Mathematical

ESTRUCTURA (continued)

2. To form the present participle of -ar verbs, drop the -ar and add -ando. For -er and -ir verbs, drop the -er or the -ir and add -iendo. Note that the present participles of **leer** *(to read)* and **dormir** *(to sleep)* are irregular.

nadar	nad-	nad**ando**
correr	corr-	corr**iendo**
salir	sal-	sal**iendo**
dormir	durm- (irregular)	durm**iendo**
leer	ley- (irregular)	ley**endo**

3. In Spanish, the use of the present progressive is limited solely to expressing an action that is in progress at that very moment. In English, the -ing form of the verb can be used to express several different verb tenses. In Spanish, however, separate tenses are required: the present progressive, the present tense, and **ir a** + infinitive.

Juan **busca** las llaves.	*Juan is looking for the keys.*
Ellas **vienen** a la una.	*They are coming at one o'clock.*
Voy a dar un paseo.	*I am going to take a walk.*

Aquí practicamos

E. Ahora mismo Di lo que tú y tus amigos están haciendo ahora mismo *(are doing right now)*. Usa palabras de cada columna.

A	B	C	D
ahora mismo	yo	estar	estudiar
	[nombre de un(a) amigo(a)] y yo		comer
	[nombre de un(a) amigo(a)]		escribir
	tú		dormir
	[un(a) amigo(a)] y [otro(a) amigo(a)]		leer

F. **¿Qué están haciendo en este momento?** Di lo que están haciendo en este momento las personas de los dibujos.

1. Jaime

2. Julia

3. Marirrosa y Juan

4. Alberto

5. Carmen y Cristina

6. Juanito

Aquí escuchamos

¿Vienes a la fiesta? *Marta calls Luis to tell him that she can't come to a party that Luis is hosting.*

Antes de escuchar How do you think Marta might ask Luis about what her friends are doing? How might he describe what everyone is doing?

A escuchar Listen twice to the phone conversation between Marta and Luis. Pay special attention to the activities that Luis says each person is doing.

Capítulo 15 Dos deportes populares **355**

F. ¿Qué estan haciendo en este momento?
POSSIBLE ANSWERS
1. Jaime está comprando algo.
2. Julia está corriendo.
3. Marirrosa y Juan están mirando la televisión.
4. Alberto está comiendo un bocadillo.
5. Carmen y Cristina están caminando por el parque.
6. Juanito está tomando/bebiendo leche.

Aquí escuchamos
SUGGESTION

 TEXTBOOK CASSETTE/CD CASSETTE 1, SIDE A; CD 3, TRACK 11

 TAPESCRIPT P. 211

 TRB: ACTIVITY MASTER, P. 109

 Have students write the information on their activity master as they listen to the Textbook Cassette/CD. Divide the recording into sections, stop after each, and ask for students to indicate who is doing what. Be sure to correct with the whole class afterwards.

Auditory-Musical

Antes de escuchar
POSSIBLE ANSWERS
Marta: ¿Qué está haciendo mis amigos?
Luis: Ellos están bailando (hablando, comiendo, etc.)

Después de escuchar
ANSWERS
Marta: está trabajando
Marcos y Carmen: están bailando
Felipe: está comiendo
Sara: está tocando la guitarra y cantando
María: está preparando comida

ETAPA SYNTHESIS

En este momento

SUGGESTION

For students who need more vocabulary practice, or just for a change of pace, create a master list on the board ahead of time, writing verbs that students might use in this activity. Then have pairs do a charade of one of the actions. Have the rest of the class guess which action is being performed.

Bodily-Kinesthetic

¿Qué está(n) haciendo?

FYI

ATAJO ATAJO WRITING ASSISTANT SOFTWARE

You might want to have students use this software program when doing this activity.

SUGGESTION

TRANSPARENCY 56

Have students recall different expressions to express "now" before they begin (**en este momento, ahora mismo, ahora**). Encourage them to vary their time expressions in their discussion.

Individual Needs

Less-prepared Students

Have students number each of the activities. Then point to each different activity and have them name the activity (verb) and write it down. When they have been quizzed on all activities, have students write sentences.

More-prepared Students

Brainstorm a list of adverbial expressions such as **debajo del árbol, cerca de la piscina, en el sol, en la sombra, en el suelo** to round out their sentences. When doing the second part, pair up a more-prepared student with a less-prepared one to write the composition. Have student pairs read and edit each other's work.

Después de escuchar On your activity master, indicate who is doing what by writing the name of the person next to the appropriate activity on the list.

_____ está bailando.	_____ está mirando el televisor.
_____ está cantando.	_____ está preparando.
_____ está comiendo.	_____ está tocanda la guitarra.
_____ está leyendo.	_____ está trabajando.

¡ADELANTE!

En este momento Think about various people in your life whose daily schedules are familiar to you. Make a list of four people who have different schedules, such as parents, brothers, sisters, boy/girl friends, best friends. Discuss with a partner what the people you each know are doing right now.

¿Qué está(n) haciendo? Look at the drawing that follows of people enjoying a weekend afternoon in the park. 1) Write at least six sentences telling what they are doing. Identify a different activity in each of your sentences. 2) Then, working with a partner, create a combined list of activities from which the two of you can write a brief composition describing how the people in the park are spending their afternoon. 3) Give your composition an introductory sentence and a closing sentence that briefly summarizes the point of the composition. Take care to organize the sentences between the beginning and end so that you guide your readers smoothly from one activity to the next.

356 *Quinta unidad* Tu tiempo libre

MODELO

(first sentence) *Hoy es domingo y hay muchas personas en el parque. Ellos están haciendo muchas cosas. Por ejemplo, hay una mujer que...*
(last sentence) *Siempre hay mucho para hacer en el parque durante el fin de semana.*

Capítulo 15 Dos deportes populares **357**

PRACTICE/APPLY

VARIATION

Encourage flexibility in paraphrasing. Have students notice the different descriptive interpretations possible for many of the actions in the drawing. For example, they may say of the woman using the telephone: **está hablando** or **está llamando (a un amigo)**; of the woman at the refreshment stand: **está comprando** or **está pagando**; of the seated couple with the dancers: **están escuchando** or **están mirando**; of the person under the tree with a book: **está leyendo, está estudiando**, or even **está pensando**; of the people with the guitar player: **están escuchando** or **están cantando**; of the person napping: **está durmiendo** or **está descansando**.

Point out that it may be appropriate to use two such options together for a more interesting sentence, and one that might help them achieve cohesion (flow) in their compositions. Have them create a list of "linking" expressions they know that might accomplish this. Some ideas are: **Mientras que**... (While...); **También**,... ; **En otro lugar**,... ; **Cerca del árbol**,... ; **Al quiosco de refrescos**... ; **A la cabina telefónica**,... ; **No muy lejos**,... .

Encourage students to include a summative paragraph in their composition mentioning activities they personally enjoy doing in the park.

 Creating

Additional Practice and Recycling

FYI

WORKBOOK, PP. 189-193

For recycling and additional practice of the vocabulary, structures, and language functions presented throughout this **etapa**, you can assign the workbook activities as in-class work and/or homework.

TEACH/MODEL

El tenis

PRESENTATION

Point out to students that the three women in the etapa opener photos are all roughly the same age. Does that suggest that tennis is dominated by people of a certain age? Note again that the pictures are all of women. Does that suggest that tennis is dominated by women? Who plays tennis? Is the sport more popular in some countries than in others? What kind of skills do you need to play tennis professionally? Is the sport accessible to all?

Have students discuss these topics before doing the reading to see how they analyze these issues. Then, after doing the reading and Activities A and B, return to these questions, and see how the reading has added to their discussion: Does the reading address these questions? Do students agree with some of the answers it gives?

Activating Prior Knowledge
Analyzing
Drawing Inferences

FYI

As an extension of the discussion of who plays tennis, refer to the Focus on Culture: *Surnames in the Spanish-speaking World,* found later in this **etapa**.

SEGUNDA ETAPA

Preparación

- Have you ever played tennis?
- Have you ever watched a match on television?
- Who are some of the great players that you know about?
- What are some of the major tournaments that are played around the world?

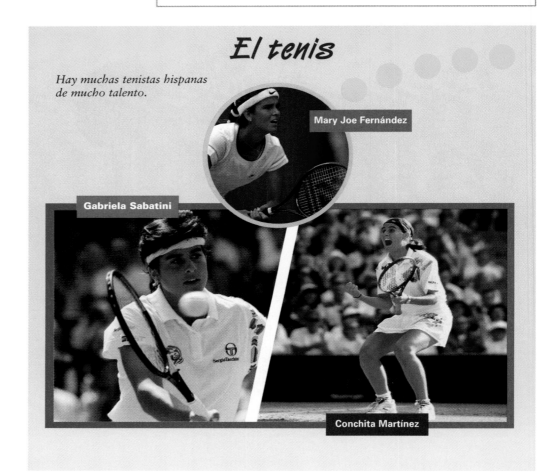

El tenis

Hay muchas tenistas hispanas de mucho talento.

Mary Joe Fernández

Gabriela Sabatini

Conchita Martínez

358 *Quinta unidad* Tu tiempo libre

Etapa Support Materials

- Workbook: pp. 194-200
- TRB: Textbook Activity Masters: p. 110
- Textbook Cassettes/CDs: Cassette 2, Side A; CD 3, Track 2
- Tapescript: Textbook Cassettes/CDs pp. 211-212
- Middle School Activities: p. 132
- Overhead Transparency: 57
- Lesson Plan Book: pp. 87-88

- Testing Program: Quiz pp.171-173; Answer Key & Testing Cassettes Tapescript pp. T66, T67
- Testing Cassettes: Cassette Side A
- Computerized Testing Program: Windows™; Macintosh®
- Atajo Writing Assistant Software: Student Text, p. 365, Workbook, p.199

El tenis requiere **agilidad** y control del cuerpo, pero no gran fuerza. Por eso es un deporte que pueden jugar personas de **diversas** edades y condiciones físicas. Al nivel profesional, se necesita una combinación de **habilidad,** buena técnica y una excelente condición física.

Entre las mejores tenistas femeninas del mundo, hay un grupo de hispanas: Gabriela Sabatini de Argentina, Mary Joe Fernández de los Estados Unidos, Arantxa Sánchez Vicario y Conchita Martínez de España. Todas juegan en los grandes **torneos** que se juegan en Inglaterra, en Francia y en los Estados Unidos. En 1994, Conchita ganó el prestigioso torneo en Wimbledon y Arantxa ganó el U.S. Open y el French Open. Arantxa es tan popular en España que tiene que vivir en Andorra, un pequeño país entre Francia y España, para **evitar** a los **admiradores** y periodistas. ¿Te gusta el tenis? ¿Te gusta jugarlo o mirarlo? ¿Quién es tu tenista favorito?

Arantxa Sánchez Vicario

¡Te toca a ti!

A. Estudio de palabras ¿Qué crees que significan las siguientes palabras que están en negrita en la lectura?

1. agilidad
2. diversas
3. habilidad
4. torneos
5. evitar
6. admiradores

B. Comprensión Responde a las siguientes preguntas sobre la lectura.

1. What characteristics are required of a tennis player?
2. Where are the tennis players featured in the reading from?
3. What did Martínez do in 1994?
4. What did Sánchez Vicario do in 1994?
5. Why does Sánchez Vicario live in Andorra?

Capítulo 15 Dos deportes populares **359**

PRACTICE / APPLY

A. Estudio de palabras
ANSWERS

1. agility
2. different
3. ability
4. avoid
5. tournaments
6. fans

As a lead-in to this activity, remind students to focus on cognates by having them skim the text and make a list of cognates. Have them tell the meaning of each word. Then brainstorm about how this information can help them understand the reading.

SUGGESTION

Use this opportunity to discuss cognates and word families. After students have guessed and explained the meaning of each word, have them identify other words in the same family in English, and look them up in Spanish (agility, agile; diverse, diversity, etc.).

 Linguistic Comparisons 4.1

B. Comprensión
ANSWERS

1. agilidad y control del cuerpo
2. Argentina, Estados Unidos, España
3. ganó el torneo de Wimbledon
4. ganó el U.S. Open y el French Open
5. para evitar a los admiradores y periodistas

EXPANSION

After students have answered the questions in this activity, have them go back to the earlier discussion begun prior to doing the reading: Does the reading confirm or disagree with their previous assumptions? What issues doesn't the reading address?

Analyzing

MULTIPLE INTELLIGENCES

- Linguistic: all, B
- Logical-Mathematical: A, D, G
- Visual-Spatial: C, F
- Auditory-Musical: **Aquí escuchamos**
- Interpersonal: E, **Intercambio**
- Intrapersonal: **Los fines de semana**

  The Standards

- Interpersonal Communication 1.1: C, D, E, G, **Intercambio, Los fines de semana**
- Interpretive Communication 1.2: F, **Aquí escuchamos**
- Cultural Practices and Perspectives 2.1: B
- Linguistic Comparisons 4.1: A, **Estructura**

C. En este momento...

SUGGESTION

Ask for as many variations or paraphrases of each drawing as students can think of in order to expand vocabulary usage.

For example, the first one could be **llamando a un amigo/hablando con un amigo/hablando por teléfono**. The activity can be done quickly as oral work or may be written out individually or in pairs.

Linguistic
Visual-Spatial

POSSIBLE ANSWERS

1. Roberto está hablando por teléfono.
2. Esteban y Carmen están estudiando.
3. Marirrosa y su amigo están comiendo pizza.
4. Carlos está haciendo la maleta.
5. Cristina está leyendo.
6. José y Patricio están jugando al tenis.
7. Mi papá está haciendo la cama.

Repaso

C. En este momento... Di lo que está haciendo en este momento cada persona de los dibujos que siguen.

1. Roberto

2. Esteban y Carmen

3. Marirrosa y su amigo

4. Carlos

5. Cristina

6. José y Patricio

7. mi papá

360   *Quinta unidad* Tu tiempo libre

Focus on Culture

Surnames

Point out that Sabatini is an Italian name and that in the late 19th century, there was a large wave of Italian immigration to Argentina, very similar to that in the United States. (Because of the Italian influence in Argentina, pizza is a common as well as popular dish there.) In the case of Mary Joe Fernández, point out the long Hispanic presence in what is now the United States and the large Hispanic population (around 20 million) in the United States. You may also wish to contrast the first names of the two Spanish players, and point out that Arantxa is a Basque, not a Spanish name. Use a map of Spain and point out the Basque region as well as Andorra.

Cultural Comparisons 4.2

ESTRUCTURA

Past, present, and future time: A review

Pasado: Ayer **hablé** por teléfono con mi abuelo.
Presente: Hoy **hablo** con mis amigos en la escuela.
Progresivo: Ahora mismo **estoy hablando** con mi amigo.
Futuro: Más tarde **voy a hablar** con mi profesor.

Pasado: Esta tarde el estudiante **comió** en la cafetería.
Presente: **Come** en el Café Hermoso los viernes por la tarde.
Progresivo: **Está comiendo** en casa ahora mismo.
Futuro: **Tiene ganas de comer** en un restaurante mañana.

Pasado: La semana pasada **salimos** con nuestros primos.
Presente: Cada mes, **salimos** con nuestra madre.
Progresivo: En este momento **estamos saliendo** con toda la familia.
Futuro: La semana próxima **esperamos salir** con nuestros amigos.

In Units 1–5, you learned how to express past, present, and future events using various verb tenses and constructions, as well as several expressions that situate events in the past, present, and future. Reviewing these materials will help you keep your communication skills sharp.

1. Past time: preterite tense

—¿Qué **hiciste** anoche? *What did you do last night?*
—**Cené** en un restaurante y **fui** al cine. *I ate dinner in a restaurant and went to the movies.*

2. Present time for routine activities: present tense

—¿Qué **haces** tú después de la escuela todos los días? *What do you do after school every day?*
—**Visito** a mis amigas. *I visit my girlfriends.*

3. Present time for actions occurring at that very moment: present progressive

—¿Qué **estás haciendo** ahora? *What are you doing now?*
—**Estoy buscando** mis libros. *I am looking for my books.*

4. Future time: **esperar** + infinitive, **ir a** + infinitive, **pensar** + infinitive, **querer** + infinitive, **quisiera** + infinitive, **tener ganas de** + infinitive

—¿Qué **van a hacer** Uds. durante las vacaciones? *What are you going to do during vacation?*
—Yo **voy a visitar** a amigos en Nueva York. *I am going to visit friends in New York.*
—Yo **quiero ir** a Nuevo México. *I want to go to New Mexico.*
—Y yo **quisiera viajar** a Colombia. *And I would like to travel to Colombia.*
—Pablo **espera volver** a la Argentina. *Pablo hopes to return to Argentina.*
—La profesora **piensa viajar** a Bolivia. *The teacher plans to travel to Bolivia.*
—Mis padres **tienen ganas de ir** a la playa. *My parents feel like going to the beach.*

Capítulo 15 Dos deportes populares **361**

Estructura

FYI
Note that there is no new material presented in this **Estructura**. It is designed to review and contrast the four time frames (preterite, present, present progressive, future) that students have already learned.

SUGGESTION
Make statements and then ask students simple questions that contrast the four tenses. For example: **Siempre hablo español en la clase. Ahora mismo estoy hablando español. Ayer hablé español y mañana voy a hablar español también. ¿Qué haces todos los días? ¿Qué estás haciendo ahora? ¿Qué hiciste ayer? ¿Qué vas a hacer mañana?**, etc.

🔅 Activating Prior Knowledge

☀ Spanish for Spanish Speakers

Then, Now, and Later

Have Spanish speakers write 15 sentences in their notebooks: five should describe what they did (or imagined they did) five years ago; five should describe what they are doing right now; and five should describe what they are going to do in five years. Students can describe silly, funny, or adventurous activities.

⊛ Presentational Communication 1.3

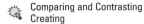
PRACTICE/APPLY

D. Hoy, ayer y mañana

SUGGESTION

A possible way to present it is through the creation of a *word web*.

⚫ Logical-Mathematical
Visual-Spatial

⚙ Categorizing

VARIATION

Have pairs create a small composition together, comparing and contrasting their habits based on the information they record on charts.

⚙ Comparing and Contrasting
Creating

E. Quisiera saber...

SUGGESTION

If you want to have students provide more information in their answers than simply **sí** or **no**, have them practice doing so as a class before putting them in groups. You might want students to suggest additional, more open-ended questions for this activity.

ANSWERS

Answers will vary, but the verbs will be in the following forms:
1. estoy, estuve, voy a estar
2. hago, hice, voy a hacer
3. desayuno, desayuné, voy a desayunar
4. miro, miré, voy a mirar
5. hablo, hablé, voy a hablar

EXPANSION

Ask follow-up questions in the third person, giving students the opportunity to report back some of the information they found out when questioning their partners.

Aquí practicamos

D. Hoy, ayer y mañana Di lo que tú y tus amigos están haciendo, hacen, hicieron y van a hacer.

A	B	C
ayer	yo	hablar por teléfono con sus amigos
ahora mismo	tú y ?	mirar un programa de televisión
todos los días	? y yo	estudiar para un examen
anoche	? y ?	comer en un restaurante
el fin de semana próximo	?	salir con sus amigos

E. Quisiera saber... Hazle las siguientes preguntas a un(a) compañero(a).

1. ¿Estás en la escuela todos los días? ¿Estuviste en la escuela el sábado pasado? ¿Vas a estar en la escuela el verano próximo?

2. ¿Haces un viaje todos los veranos? ¿Hiciste un viaje el año pasado? ¿Vas a hacer un viaje el año próximo?

3. ¿Desayunas todos los días? ¿Desayunaste ayer por la mañana? ¿Vas a desayunar mañana por la mañana?

4. ¿Miras algún programa de televisión los viernes? ¿Miraste un programa de televisión el domingo por la noche? ¿Vas a mirar un programa de televisión mañana por la noche?

5. ¿Hablas por teléfono con alguien cada noche? ¿Hablaste por teléfono con alguien anoche? ¿Vas a hablar por teléfono con alguien esta noche?

F. De costumbre... For each of the drawings that follow, explain what the people do normally (**de costumbre**), what they did in the past, and what they will do in the future. Begin each explanation with **De costumbre...**, continue it with **Pero...**, and finish it with **Y....** Follow the model.

MODELO ¿Qué hace José Luis durante las vacaciones de verano?
De costumbre él escucha música. Pero el año pasado estuvo en la playa. Y el año próximo piensa viajar a México.

de costumbre   el año pasado   el año próximo

1. ¿Qué hace Vera durante el fin de semana?

   de costumbre   el fin de semana pasado   el fin de semana próximo

2. ¿A qué hora llega Marcos a la escuela?

   de costumbre   anteayer   el viernes próximo

3. ¿Qué comen Sabrina y Carolina cuando van al centro?

   de costumbre   el sábado pasado   el sábado próximo

4. ¿Qué hace Óscar los viernes?

   de costumbre   el viernes pasado   el viernes próximo

F. De costumbre...

VARIATION

 TRANSPARENCY 57

You can personalize this activity by having students give information about themselves, their families, or their friends using the same kinds of questions as provided in Activity E.

Individual Needs

Less-prepared Students
Have students use the questions from Activity F and/or generate more examples—only in the **yo** form—by saying or writing what they usually do during the week or on weekends. They can then tell what they did differently at some time in the past, and then what they will do in the future.

POSSIBLE ANSWERS
Students substitute the cues and add the following information
1. ...mira la televisión./ ...fue al museo./ ...piensa ir a una fiesta.
2. ...llega a las ocho menos cuarto./ ...llegó a las ocho y media./ ...va a llegar a las siete y cuarto.
3. ...comen sándwiches./ ...comieron ensalada./ ...van a comer pizza.
4. ...va al cine./ ...estudió./ ...va a ir a un restaurante con su novia.

Spanish for Spanish Speakers

Expansion
For Activity F, have Spanish speakers write their own questions, interview another student, and write up a short biography of that person. Suggest a few questions to get students started: **¿Que haces durante las vacaciones? ¿Qué comes cuando estás en la escuela?**

Interpersonal Communication 1.1

G. Una entrevista

POSSIBLE ANSWERS
Students substitute the cues, using the following forms of the verbs:
1. No, voy a ir...
2. No, pienso viajar...
3. No, fui...
4. Sí, voy a visitar...
5. No, fui...
6. No, viajé a...

EXPANSION

To proceed from this controlled interview to a more creative one, have students who have done some traveling abroad or in this country volunteer to bring in souvenirs and be interviewed by classmates, who will organize the question-and-answer format themselves. Students often enjoy watching these activities on videotape.

Visual-Spatial

Cultural Products and Perspectives 2.2

Aquí escuchamos

SUGGESTION

 TEXTBOOK CASSETTE/CD CASSETTE 2, SIDE A; CD 3, TRACK 12

 TAPESCRIPT PP. 211-212

If you choose to practice this activity as a telephone conversation, it is an opportunity to stress the importance of good listening skills. Have students sit back-to-back and practice inviting each other somewhere, turning each other down, and making alternate plans.

Antes de escuchar

POSSIBLE ANSWERS
Isabel: ¿Quieres ir al centro conmigo?
Pedro: No puedo. **or** Sí, sí puedo.

Después de escuchar

ANSWERS
1. to buy a new CD
2. immediately
3. he will be working at 1 p.m.
4. tomorrow morning

G. Una entrevista
You are being interviewed by a reporter from your school newspaper about your many travels. Answer the questions using the cues given in parentheses. Follow the models.

MODELOS
¿Esperas viajar a España este año? (no, el año próximo)
No, voy a viajar a España el año próximo.
¿Piensas ir a México? (no, el año pasado)
No, fui a México el año pasado.

1. ¿Piensas ir de vacaciones mañana? (no, hoy)
2. ¿Viajaste a Costa Rica el verano pasado? (no, el mes próximo)
3. ¿Esperas viajar a Bogotá? (no, el año pasado)
4. ¿Quisieras visitar la Ciudad de Guatemala? (sí, el año próximo)
5. ¿Piensas ir a Santa Fe este año? (no, el año pasado)
6. ¿Quieres viajar a Europa el año próximo? (no, el verano pasado)

Aquí escuchamos

¿Para qué vas al centro? *Isabel invites Pedro to go downtown.*

Antes de escuchar How do you think Isabel might invite Pedro to go downtown? How might Pedro say he can or can't accompany her?

 A escuchar Listen twice to the conversation between Isabel and Pedro before answering the questions about it that follow.

Después de escuchar Answer the following questions based on what you heard.

1. Why does Isabel want to go downtown?
2. When does Isabel want to go?
3. Why can't Pedro go tomorrow afternoon?
4. When do they decide to go?

¡ADELANTE!

 Intercambio Using the verbs indicated, ask a partner questions to obtain the listed information. When asking questions about the future, be sure to use some of the following expressions: **pensar, esperar, ir a, quisiera, querer, tener ganas de.** Find one activity that you have in common and one in which you differ.

1. **estudiar:** Find out where your friend usually studies; whether he (she) studied there last night; whether he (she) is planning to study there tonight.

2. **ir al cine:** Find out if your friend goes to the movies a lot; if he (she) went to the movies last week; whether he (she) is going to the movies soon.

3. **viajar:** Find out if your friend travels a lot; if he (she) traveled last year, and if so, where he (she) went; whether he (she) hopes to travel next year, and if so, where he (she) intends to go.

4. **ir / tomar / andar:** Find out how your friend usually gets to school; if he (she) got to school the same way this morning; whether he (she) will get to school the same way next year.

 Los fines de semana You have just received a note from a friend in El Salvador in which she asks about how students your age in the United States spend their weekends. Write a note to her in which you tell three things that you do in a typical weekend, three things that you did last weekend, and three activities that you plan to do next weekend.

EN LÍNEA

Connect with the Spanish-speaking world! Access the *¡Ya verás! Gold* home page for Internet activities related to this chapter.

http://yaveras.heinle.com

Capítulo 15 Dos deportes populares **365**

Additional Etapa Resources

Refer to the **Etapa** Support Materials list on the opening page of this **etapa** for detailed cross-references to these assessment options.

CHAPTER WRAP-UP

Listening Skills Development

FYI

LAB MANUAL PP. 99-104

LAB CASSETTE SIDE A, B; CD 8, TRACKS 1-7

TAPESCRIPT: LAB PROGRAM PP.146-153

It is now appropriate to work through the lab manual activities and their accompanying recordings in class or in the language laboratory.

Improvised Conversation

SUGGESTION

TRB: ACTIVITY MASTER, P. 110

TEXTBOOK CASSETTE/CD CASSETTE 2, SIDE A; CD 3, TRACK 13

TAPESCRIPT P. 212

Have students listen to this conversation in which Nico and his father, Crístobal discuss sports. Refer to the TRB for student questions.

Resources for Spanish-speaking Students

FYI

WORKBOOK FOR SPANISH-SPEAKING STUDENTS: PP. 87-92

ANSWER KEY TO SSS WORKBOOK PP. 27-29

Activities specially written to meet the needs of Spanish-speaking students are available in these workbooks for extension and reinforcement.

VOCABULARIO

Para charlar

Para hablar de acciones en el futuro

esperar + *infinitive*
ir a + *infinitive*
pensar + *infinitive*
querer + *infinitive*
quisiera + *infinitive*
tener ganas de + *infinitive*

Para hablar de acciones que están pasando ahora

ahora
ahora mismo
en este momento
estar + *verb in present participle*

Vocabulario general

Otras palabras y expresiones

de costumbre
dormir
durante las vacaciones

366 *Quinta unidad* Tu tiempo libre

Spanish for Spanish Speakers

Keeping a Vocabulary Notebook

Remind Spanish-speaking students to add words and expressions from this vocabulary section to the problematic spelling combination categories and personal new vocabulary lists in their notebooks.

Additional Chapter Resources

Refer to the Chapter Support Materials list on the opening page of this chapter for detailed cross-references to ¡*Ya verás! Gold*'s student-centered technology components and various assessment options.

ENCUENTROS CULTURALES

Un héroe de Puerto Rico

Antes de leer

1. Look at the pictures that accompany the reading. What sport does this person play?

2. Look at the title. Where is this athlete from? Do you think he is held in great esteem in his country? Why?

3. Scan the second paragraph of the reading. Find two cognates or familiar terms related to baseball playing, then find the names of two baseball teams from the United States.

Reading Strategies
- Using title and context to predict meaning
- Scanning for specific knowledge
- Cognate recognition

Muchos jugadores en la historia del béisbol son famosos no sólo por sus logros atléticos, sino por su interés en ayudar a sus comunidades. Babe Ruth enseñó a batear a muchos niños y Cal Ripken, Jr. hoy en día promueve los programas de educación para adultos. Roberto Clemente, formidable atleta puertorriqueño, ha sido tal vez el único jugador que ha dado su vida por ayudar a otros.

Roberto Clemente nació en Carolina, Puerto Rico, en 1934. A los 20 años firmó su primer contrato para jugar al béisbol profesional con los Dodgers de Brooklyn. Un año más tarde, en 1955, firmó un contrato para jugar con los Piratas de Pittsburgh. Allí tuvo una brillante carrera y muchos todavía consideran a Clemente como uno de los mejores jugadores de la historia del béisbol. En octubre de 1971, los Piratas ganaron la Serie Mundial y Clemente fue el factor principal de ese triunfo. Clemente, nombrado el jugador más valioso (MVP) de esa serie, bateó en 1972 su hit número 3,000—algo que muy pocos jugadores logran.

Ese año, después de terminar la temporada de béisbol, Clemente volvió a Puerto Rico para pasar el invierno. A finales de diciembre, hubo un terremoto catastrófico en Nicaragua, que dejó a muchas personas sin casa y sin comida. Clemente, cuando oyó que se estaban robando las provisiones y medicinas de las víctimas del terremoto, decidió ir en persona a hacer la entrega.

El 31 de diciembre de 1972, un sobrecargado DC-7 despegó del Aeropuerto de Isla Verde hacia Nicaragua. Roberto Clemente era uno de los pasajeros. Minutos después, el avión explotó en el aire y desapareció para siempre en el fondo del océano. El verano después de su muerte, Clemente fue elegido para formar parte del Pabellón de la Fama en Cooperstown, Nueva York. Hoy lo recordamos con un monumento colocado frente al estadio de Pittsburgh y con un premio que celebra los logros de los jugadores de béisbol tanto en el estadio como en la comunidad.

Capítulo 15 Dos deportes populares **367**

Un héroe de Puerto Rico

Antes de leer

ANSWERS

1. Baseball
2. He is from Puerto Rico. He is a National hero.
3. cognates: **contrato**—contract **profesional**—professional teams: Brooklyn Dodgers Pittsburgh Pirates

EXPANSION

There are a number of topics from this reading that students could explore in more depth. Let them choose something that interests them and study it further. Possible topics include: Roberto Clemente's childhood in Puerto Rico, the earthquake that devastated Nicaragua, the Baseball Hall of Fame, Hispanic baseball greats.

Después de leer

ANSWERS

1. Answers may vary. Possible answer could be that he is the only one who has given his life in order to help others.
2. **a.** he signed a contract
   b. he was appointed the "most valuable player"
   c. they won the World Series
   d. he went personally to make the delivery
3. Answers may vary.

Guía para la lectura

logros	*achievements, feats*
batear	*to hit (baseball)*
promueve	*promotes*
programas de educación	*literacy programs*
ha dado su vida	*has given his life*
firmó	*he signed*
Serie Mundial	*World Series*
terremoto	*earthquake*
se estaban robando	*(supplies) were being stolen*
hacer la entrega	*make the delivery*
sobrecargado	*overloaded*
despegó	*took off*
explotó	*exploded*
premio	*award*

Después de leer

1. Explain in your own words the meaning of the last sentence of the first paragraph. What makes Roberto Clemente special?

2. Some vocabulary words in the reading have not been defined for you. Try to glean meaning from context and from the recognition of cognates.

   What is the meaning of these phrases in italics?

   a. firmó *un contrato*

   b. nombrado el *jugador más valioso*

   c. *ganaron* la serie mundial

   d. decidió ir *en persona* a hacer la entrega

3. Who are the public figures you admire? What is it about them that you find admirable? Do you think it's important to have "heroes?" Why or why not?

Focus on Culture

Puerto Rico

Many people think of Puerto Rico as a foreign country, but it actually has the unique status of a commonwealth in association with the United States. The inhabitants of the island have all the rights and responsibilities of United States citizens except the right to vote in national elections and the obligation to pay federal taxes. Have students research Puerto Rico to find out more about its people, geography, government, economy, etc. One theme they might want to explore is how much the Puerto Ricans have absorbed the dominant culture and how much they have retained their distinctive identity.

Cultural Practices and Perspectives 2.1
Cultural Comparisons 4.2

Conversemos un rato

A. La semana pasada In groups of three or four students, role-play the following discussion about what you each did last week. Try to decide who had the busiest week.

1. Each member of the group will take turns describing his or her past week by listing the events or activities in the order they occurred. Be sure to use a variety of verbs in the past and use appropriate time indicators.

2. The other members of the group will ask for clarification.

3. Reach an agreement about who had the busiest week in the group.

B. ¡Vivan las vacaciones! Imagine that your Spanish class has just won an all-expense-paid trip to the Spanish-speaking countries of your choice. There will be a competition to decide the itinerary for the class trip. The team with the winning itinerary will get to travel in first class.

1. In teams of three or four students, role-play the following discussion in order to plan an itinerary for the big trip.

   a. Each member of the team must suggest a country to visit. Decide on two.

   b. Each member must suggest an interesting activity to do and organize them into an itinerary.

   c. As a team, decide on the kind of transportation you will use and how you will travel from place to place.

2. Then, meet with another team to compare itineraries.

   a. Each team will describe their itinerary to the other team.

   b. Both teams will then combine their itineraries to create one travel plan, taking the most interesting ideas from each team.

   c. Finally, present your travel plan to the entire class and try to persuade them to adopt your itinerary. Remember, the winning team gets to travel in first class!

¡Sigamos adelante! **369**

¡Sigamos adelante! Resource

FYI

LESSON PLAN BOOK: P. 90

You might find it helpful to refer to the Lesson Plan Book before you and your students begin the end-of-unit materials.

PRACTICE/APPLY

A. La semana pasada

SUGGESTIONS

Review past tense verbs with students before beginning this activity. You might also want to go over common activities and list them on the board or transparency.

Linguistic
Visual-Spatial

B. ¡Vivan las vacaciones!

SUGGESTION

If students have access to the internet, they can find information about interesting activities for the countries they have chosen. Often, offices of tourism have home pages replete with information and photos on cultures, climate, places of interest, and social/cultural activities.

 Connections with Distinctive Viewpoints 3.2

Spanish for Spanish Speakers

Transportation

If students have traveled in a Spanish-speaking country, have them tell the rest of the class what they know about the transportation systems in those countries. Ask them if they are similar to or different from the transportation available in communities of the same size and population in the United States.

Connections with Distinctive Viewpoints 3.2
Cultural Comparisons 4.2

The Standards

• Interpersonal Communication 1.1

Taller de escritores Resource

FYI

 ATAJO WRITING ASSISTANT SOFTWARE

You might want to have students use this software program when writing the first draft and final version of their writing assignment. Tell them that the following language references in **Atajo** are directly related to and will be helpful to their work.

Phrases: Sequencing events; Talking about past events; Writing a news item
Vocabulary: Beach; Camping; City; Direction & distance; Leisure; Sports; Traveling
Grammar: Demonstrative Adjectives: **este, ese, aquel**; Relatives: **que**; Verbs: Preterite

Taller de escritores

Writing a report

You will practice your writing in Spanish by writing a two- or three-paragraph report on a trip you took or an exciting leisure-time experience you have had. Your audience will be the readers of the Spanish Club Newsletter.

Writing Strategy
• Making an outline

Un viaje a la playa

El mes pasado fuí de vacaciones con mis padres a Manzanillo, en la costa de México. Pasamos una semana en el Hotel Las Hadas. Hicimos el viaje en avión y salimos el 26 de diciembre y volvimos el 2 de enero. Tuvimos un viaje muy divertido.

Manzanillo tiene un clima muy bueno en el invierno. Pasamos mucho tiempo en la playa del hotel donde nadamos mucho. También nos acostamos cerca de la piscina grande del hotel. Un día fuimos a otra playa donde practicamos el esquí acuático y el buceo deportivo. Tomamos el sol todos los días, menos un día cuando no hizo sol.

Un día fuimos a Colima, la capital del estado. Allí vimos un museo de arqueología muy grande. También fuimos a comer a muchos restaurantes buenos. Nos sirvieron comidas muy variadas. Hicimos muchas cosas durante los siete días. Para unas vacaciones magníficas les recomiendo Manzanillo.

370 *Quinta unidad* Tu tiempo libre

MULTIPLE INTELLIGENCES

• Linguistic

PRACTICE/APPLY

A. Reflexión
SUGGESTIONS

Pair heterogeneous students together when writing outlines. Encourage peer editing and cooperative learning. As a class, have students discuss how they selected their main points and subpoints and elicit tips for understanding how to find these points.

B. Primer Borrador
SUGGESTION

After finishing their rough draft, have students circle or underline any vocabulary or structures that are causing them difficulty. As a class, have students discuss their markings and come up with a list of common problem areas to resolve together.

Analyzing

C. Revisión con un(a) compañero(a)
SUGGESTION

Model a peer review with the whole class by showing a sample letter on a transparency and answering the six revision questions together.

D. Versión final
SUGGESTIONS

Tell students that they do not have to incorporate all of the suggestions given by their classmate, but rather take their ideas or corrections that they feel will improve the content of the report.

A. Reflexión After choosing the trip you will describe, select the main point of each paragraph and write an outline. Add subheadings to each major heading to increase the detail.

B. Primer borrador Write a first draft of your description. Remember you are writing for a student newsletter.

C. Revisión con un(a) compañero(a) Exchange papers with a classmate. Read each other's work and comment on it, based on the questions below.

1. What do you like best about your classmate's first draft?
2. What part do you find the clearest?
3. What part do you find the most interesting?
4. Does the first draft keep the audience in mind?
5. Does the writing reflect the task assigned?
6. Does the first draft raise questions that, if answered, you think would make the writing clearer, more interesting, or more complete?

D. Versión final At home, revise your first draft, incorporating changes based on the feedback from your classmate. Revise content and check your grammar, spelling, punctuation and accent marks. Bring your final draft to class.

E. Carpeta After you turn in your report, your teacher may choose to place it in your portfolio, display it on a bulletin board, or use it to evaluate your progress.

¡Sigamos adelante! **371**

 The Standards

• Interpretive Communication 1.2

Para empezar

SUGGESTION

Have students discuss their favorite kinds of aerobic exercise. Then ask them to guess which forms of exercise burn the most calories and why.

Analyzing
Determining Preferences
Making Hypotheses

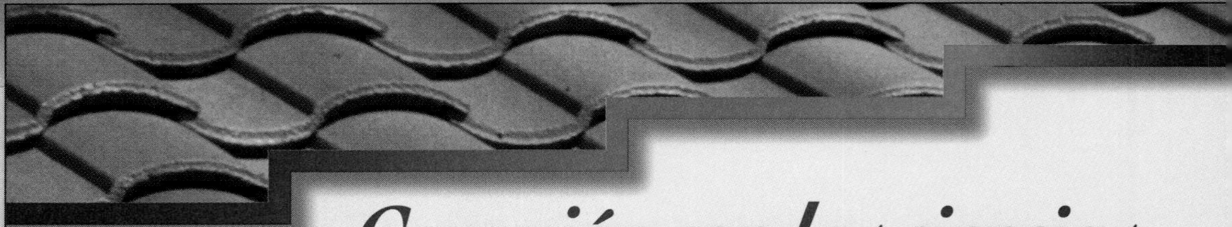

Conexión con las ciencias

Para empezar The following passage discusses aerobic exercises and the amount of energy we use (how many calories we burn) when we do certain activities.

El término aeróbico significa "vivir en la presencia del oxígeno". Los ejercicios aeróbicos, la natación, el ciclismo y el correr, por ejemplo, estimulan el corazón y los pulmones con el objetivo de aumentar la cantidad de oxígeno que el cuerpo pueda utilizar dentro de un período de tiempo. Los ejercicios aeróbicos también son ideales para quemar calorías y bajar de peso, ya que el coeficiente de utilización de energía (CUE) de estas actividades es muy alto. Esto quiere decir que utilizamos mucha energía cuando las practicamos.

Cuanto más tiempo se pasa haciendo ejercicios aeróbicos, más energía se utiliza. Las personas de mayor peso suelen utilizar más energía que las de menor peso haciendo la misma actividad.

La primera columna del siguiente esquema nos da el CUE de varias actividades, algunas aeróbicas y otras no. Se multiplica el CUE por el peso de una persona—en kilogramos—para determinar el número de calorías que se queman haciendo una actividad. ¿Cuánto pesas tú en kilogramos? La fórmula para convertir las libras en kilogramos no es muy complicada.

Fórmula:	libras X 0,45 =	kilogramos	
Ana pesa 100 lbs	X 0,45 =	Ana pesa 45 kilogramos	
Pedro pesa 150 lbs	X 0,45 =	Pedro pesa 68 kilogramos	

Ya mencionamos que las personas de mayor peso queman más calorías que las de menor peso haciendo la misma actividad. ¿Quién utiliza más energía haciendo las actividades de la lista, Pedro o Ana?

corazón *heart*   pulmones *lungs*   cuerpo *body*   bajar de peso *lose weight*   el coeficiente de utilización de energía *energy use coefficient*   esquema *chart*   libras *pounds*

MULTIPLE   INTELLIGENCES

- Linguistic
- Logical-Mathematical

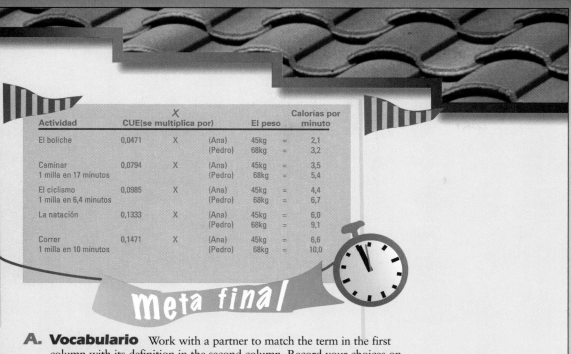

A. Vocabulario

ANSWERS

1. E
2. A
3. B
4. F
5. G
6. D
7. C

B. Taller

ANSWERS

1. 105 calorias
2. 54 minutos
3. 156 minutos
4. 74 minutos
5. Pedro

Actividad	CUE(se multiplica por)	X		El peso		Calorías por minuto
El boliche	0,0471	X	(Ana)	45kg	=	2,1
			(Pedro)	68kg	=	3,2
Caminar 1 milla en 17 minutos	0,0794	X	(Ana)	45kg	=	3,5
			(Pedro)	68kg	=	5,4
El ciclismo 1 milla en 6,4 minutos	0,0985	X	(Ana)	45kg	=	4,4
			(Pedro)	68kg	=	6,7
La natación	0,1333	X	(Ana)	45kg	=	6,0
			(Pedro)	68kg	=	9,1
Correr 1 milla en 10 minutos	0,1471	X	(Ana)	45kg	=	6,6
			(Pedro)	68kg	=	10,0

A. Vocabulario Work with a partner to match the term in the first column with its definition in the second column. Record your choices on a separate sheet of paper. Prepare for class discussion!

_____1. el kilogramo   A. unidad de energía
_____2. la caloría   B. la actividad de montar en bicicleta
_____3. el ciclismo   C. la actividad de nadar
_____4. aeróbico   D. gas que respiramos
_____5. los pulmones   E. unidad de peso del sistema métrico
_____6. el oxígeno   F. en la presencia del oxígeno
_____7. la natación   G. dos órganos que usamos para respirar

B. Taller Refer to the chart to answer the following questions.

1. Ana caminó por 30 minutos ayer por la tarde (velocidad = 1 milla en 17 minutos). ¿Cuántas calorías quemó ella?

2. Pedro comió una pizza que contenía unas 500 calorías el viernes por la noche. ¿Cuántos minutos tiene que nadar para quemar esas calorías?

3. Cuántos minutos tiene que jugar al boliche para quemar las 500 calorías?

4. Cuántos minutos tiene que montar en bicicleta para quemar las mismas 500 calorías?

5. Una persona misteriosa corrió en el parque por 45 minutos. Sabemos que la persona quemó 450 calorías. ¿Quién fue al parque, Pedro o Ana?

 The Standards

- Interpretive Communication 1.2
- Connections with Other Disciplines 3.1

TEACH/MODEL

California

SUGGESTIONS

Ask students to look at a detailed map of California and find the Spanish names of regions and towns. Have them point out towns and give the translation in English. If they chose Los Angeles, for example, ask them if they have ever heard this city referred to as "The city of Angels."

Have students choose an area of interest (agriculture, immigration, entertainment industry) and do a research project based on its relevance and relationship on some region of California. You might have students work in small groups and have each group present their information to the class.

 Presentational Communication 1.3
Connections with other Disciplines 3.1

Florida

SUGGESTIONS

Tell students that Florida has the largest Cuban American population in the United States and discuss with students why this is true. Then have students look in newspapers or on the internet to find articles on Florida and report what they find to the class. You might want to have students work on specific topics and report back as a group.

Connections with Distinctive Viewpoints 3.2

Vistas de los hispanos en los Estados Unidos

California

Capital: Sacramento

Ciudades principales: Los Angeles, San Francisco, San Diego, San José

Población: 29.839.225

Idiomas: inglés y español

Área territorial: 411.047 km²

Clima: muy variado, temperatura se mantiene de 32° C para bajo

Florida

Capital: Tallahassee

Ciudades principales: Miami, Jacksonville, Tampa, St. Petersburg, Orlando

Población: 12.937.926

Idiomas: inglés y español

Área territorial: 151.939 km²

Clima: tropical, húmedo

EXPLORA

Find out more about California and Florida! Access the **Nuestros vecinos** page on the *¡Ya verás! Gold* web site for a list of URLs.

http://yaveras.heinle.com/vecinos.htm

 374 *Quinta unidad* Tu tiempro libre

MULTIPLE INTELLIGENCES

• Visual-Spatial

The Standards

• Connections with Distinctive Viewpoints 3.2

En la comunidad

¡Se buscan estrellas de béisbol!

"My name is Anita Lopez-Jenkins. My father is a quiet man who was born in Detroit. He always wanted a child he could play baseball with. My mother is a gregarious Dominican-American who always wanted a child she could speak Spanish with. My father dreamed I'd be a famous female ball player. My mother thought I'd make a great Spanish teacher.

Fortunately, I've always liked Spanish and I've always liked sports. In high school, I took Spanish all four years and played hockey, track, and girl's basketball. In college, I double-majored in Spanish and physical education, while I continued playing basketball, plus took up tennis and swimming. Once I graduated, however, I wasn't sure how I could combine sports and Spanish. I thought about teaching, social work with kids, or working at a luxury resort as an activities director, but nothing seemed quite right for me. Then I saw an article in a sports magazine about sports recruiters, and a light went on. I wrote to the managers of major and minor league baseball teams all over the country. I described my background and my knowledge of sports and Spanish. On my third interview, I got a job! Nowadays, I spend most of the year traveling to Puerto Rico, the Dominican Republic, and other Spanish-speaking countries where baseball is an important sport. I help evaluate talent during professional try-outs and interview potential players in Spanish. It's a lot of fun; I love my job!"

¡Ahora te toca a ti!

Choose a well-known, Spanish-speaking actor, singer, writer, or athlete to research. Use the resources at your local library to locate an interview, a review, or an article with information on your subject. Consider your subject's hobbies, country of origin, occupation and contribution to his or her field. Then write a short paragraph in Spanish (at least five sentences), describing the person you have chosen. List your source(s). You may wish to share your research with the class.

MULTIPLE INTELLIGENCES

- Linguistic
- Interpersonal

 The Standards

- Connections with Other Disciplines 3.1
- Connections with Distinctive Viewpoints 3.2
- Communities In and Beyond School 5.1

En la comunidad
SUGGESTION

Tell students that combining language skills with other areas of interest can not only be interesting and rewarding, but it often gives that person a real advantage in the world of work. Ask students to come up with other professions that sometimes require or benefit from having employees that know a second language. Examples might include: teaching, publishing, medicine, law enforcement, computer technology, manufacturing, banking, sports-related fields, and social work.

¡Ahora te toca a ti!
FYI

More information on athletes and popular sports in Spanish-speaking countries can be found in Unit 5 of Level 2.

Setting the Context

The young Mexican woman featured in Unit 6 is Alicia Sánchez. The focus of this Unit is on shopping. In Chapter 16, we read about people going to specialty stores—a record shop, a stationery store, and a sporting goods store. In Chapter 17, we read about people shopping for food at an open-air market, as well as a supermarket. Finally, in Chapter 18, we read about people visiting a clothing boutique and a shoe store.

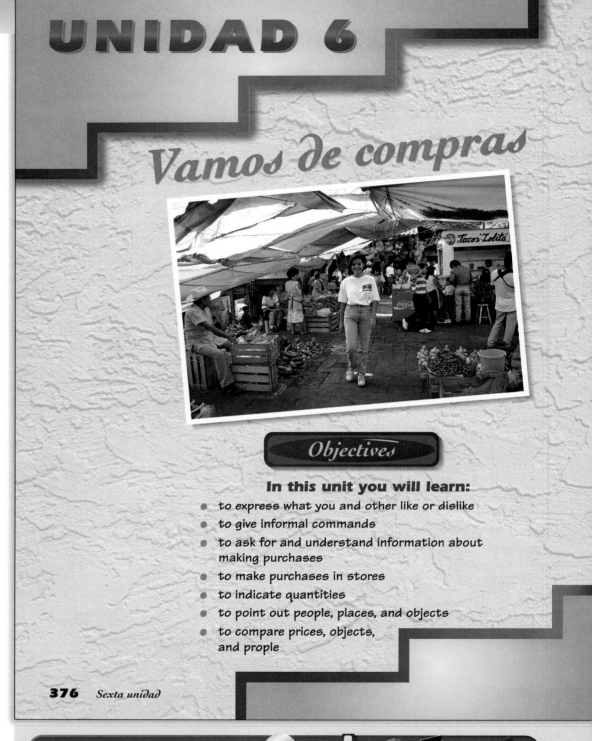

UNIDAD 6

Vamos de compras

Objectives

In this unit you will learn:

- to express what you and other like or dislike
- to give informal commands
- to ask for and understand information about making purchases
- to make purchases in stores
- to indicate quantities
- to point out people, places, and objects
- to compare prices, objects, and prople

376 *Sexta unidad*

Unit Support Materials

- Workbook: **Aquí leemos** pp. 247-252
- Lab Manual: **Ya llegamos** pp. 124-125
- Lab Program: Cassette Side B; CD 10, Tracks 18-20
- Tapescript: Lab Program pp.183-186
- TRB: Unit Grammar Review Masters: pp. 43-49; Answer Key pp. 58-59
- Lesson Plan Book: **¡Sigamos adelante!** p. 108
- Workbook for Spanish-Speaking Students pp. 119-120
- Testing Program: Unit Test pp.218-226; Chapter Test pp. 218-226; Chapter Test pp. 214-217; Answer Key

  & Testing Cassettes/Tapescript pp. T84, T85; Oral Assessment p. T86; Portfolio Assessment pp. Pxviii-Pxx
- Testing Cassettes: Cassette Side B
- Computerized Testing Program: Windows™; Macintosh®
- **Atajo** Writing Assistant Software: Student Text p. 439; Workbook p. 250, 252
- Video Program: Cassette 2, 1:28:44-1:32:38
- Video Guide: Videoscript p. 82; Activities pp. 149-150
- Internet Explorations: Student Text pp. 442-444

¿Qué ves?

- What is the girl in these photographs doing?
- Where is she?
- Why is she there?

Vamos al centro comercial
Primera etapa: En la tienda de música
Segunda etapa: En la papelería
Tercera etapa: La tienda de deportes

¿Cuánto cuesta...?
Primera etapa: Día de feria
Segunda etapa: En el supermercado

¿Qué quieres comprar?
Primera etapa: Tienda "La Alta Moda"
Segunda etapa: Zapateria "El Tacón"

377

UNIT WARM-UP
Planning Strategy

 WORKBOOK, P. 205

If you do not assign the Planning Strategy for homework (Workbook, p. 205), you may want to go over the questions in class before beginning Chapter 16.

CAPÍTULO 16

OBJECTIVES

Functions
- Making purchases and choices
- Expressing quantity
- Asking for prices

Contexts
- Various shops (music, stationary, sporting goods)

Accuracy
- The verb **gustar** (presented with all indirect object pronouns)
- Affirmative and negative familiar commands

Pronunciation
- The consonants **r** and **rr**

CHAPTER WARM-UP

Setting the Context

In preparation for their learning about making purchases in different kinds of stores, ask students to study the photo on this page. Where are Alicia and her friend? Explain that modern shopping malls can be found in all the capital cities as well as other larger cities in Latin America. Ask students if they usually shop in a traditional "downtown" or go to a mall when they want to get someone a birthday gift. Have students discuss the pros and cons of each and tell which they think their Latin American counterparts would prefer.

 Comparing and Contrasting

 Interpersonal Communication 1.1

FYI

The Chapter Warm-Up discussion is a prelude to more *shopping talk* in the Presentation of **En la tienda de música** on the next page. These can be used at the end of the chapter as expansion activities.

Vamos al centro comercial

—Quiero comprar un disco compacto nuevo.
—Yo también. ¡Vamos!

Objectives

- making purchases and choices
- expressing quantity
- asking for prices

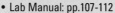

378 *Sexta unidad* Vamos de compras

Chapter Support Materials

- Lab Manual: pp.107-112
- Lab Program: Cassette Side A; CD 8, Tracks 8-15
- TRB: Textbook Activity Masters: pp. 111-113
- Textbook Cassettes/CDs: Cassette 2, Side B; CD 3, Track 22
- Tapescript: Lab Program pp. 157-167; Textbook Cassettes /CDs pp. 214-215
- Middle School Activities: pp. 133-136
- Workbook for Spanish-Speaking Students: pp.101-106
- Answer Key to SSS Workbook: pp. 29-30

- Practice Software: Windows™; Macintosh®
- Testing Program: Chapter Test pp. 191-194; Answer Key & Testing Cassettes Tapescript pp. T75, T76; Oral Assessment p. T76
- Testing Cassettes: Cassette Side B
- Computerized Testing Program: Windows™; Macintosh®
- Video Program: Cassette 2, 58:51-1:12:40
- Video Guide: Videoscript pp. 67-73; Activities pp. 137-139
- **Mundos hispanos 1**
- Internet Activities: Student Text p. 394

PRIMERA ETAPA

Preparación

- Do you like to go shopping? Why, or why not?
- Where do you usually go to buy the things you need?
- What kinds of questions do you normally need to ask when you are shopping?
- Do you do your grocery shopping at the same place where you buy such items as records, clothes, shoes, and sporting goods?

En la tienda de música

Beatriz y Mónica van de compras.

Anoche Beatriz y Mónica **fueron** a un concierto de rock en el Parque Luna. **A ellas les encantó** escuchar a su grupo favorito, Juan Luis Guerra y los 440. Hoy Mónica quiere comprar uno de sus discos compactos. **Por eso,** van a la tienda de música "La Nueva Onda". Beatriz quiere comprar un disco compacto de Jon Secada, pero es muy **caro.**

> **Beatriz:** ¡**Qué pena!** No tengo **suficiente dinero** para comprar el disco compacto.
> **Mónica:** Mira, yo encontré la cinta de Juan Luis Guerra y los 440 que me gusta y es muy barata.
> **Beatriz:** A ver. ¿Dónde están las cintas?
> **Mónica:** Allí, al lado de los vídeos.
> **Beatriz:** ¡Super! Aquí está la cinta que me gusta a mí.

fueron *went*   **A ellas les encantó** *They loved*   **Por eso** *That is why*   **caro** *expensive*   **¡Qué pena!** *What a shame*
suficiente *enough*   **dinero** *money*   **A ver.** *Let's see.*

¡Te toca a ti!

A. Para mi cumpleaños... Make up a "wish list" for your next birthday by completing the following sentences.

1. Yo quiero…
2. Quisiera…
3. Necesito…
4. Por favor, compra…
5. ¿Tienes suficiente dinero para comprar…?

Capítulo 16 Vamos al centro comercial **379**

Etapa Support Materials

- Workbook: pp. 206-210
- Textbook Cassettes/CDs: Cassette 2, Side B; CD 3, Track 14
- Tapescript: Textbook Cassettes/CDs p. 212
- Middle School Activities: pp. 137, 138
- Lesson Plan Book: pp. 91-92
- Testing Program: Quiz pp. 184-186; Answer Key & Testing Cassettes/CDs Tapescript p. T73
- Testing Cassettes/CDs: Cassette Side B
- Computerized Testing Program: Windows™; Macintosh®
- Atajo Writing Assistant Software: Student Text p. 383, Workbook p. 210

TEACH/MODEL

En la tienda de música

SUGGESTION

Introduce this topic by asking general questions about shopping: Do you like to go shopping? Why, or why not? Where do you usually go to buy the things you need? Do you shop out of necessity or for fun and browsing? Do you generally prefer the bigger stores where you can buy groceries as well as records, clothes, and sporting goods all at once, or do you prefer smaller specialty stores? Why? What are the favorite shopping places locally? Where do you spend the majority of your money? On what? Do you think you are treated well when you go out shopping with friends? Do you think the customer is always right? What kinds of questions do we normally ask in a shopping situation?

🔎 Analyzing

PRESENTATION

 TEXTBOOK CASSETTE/CD CASSETTE 2, SIDE B; CD 3, TRACK 14

 TAPESCRIPT P. 212

You can begin by playing the dialogue from the Textbook Cassettes/CDs (with books closed). You may want to play it twice before having students answer general comprehension questions. For example: **¿Dónde están las dos amigas? ¿Adónde fueron anoche? ¿Qué quieren comprar?** etc. Then have students open their books and read the dialogue. Follow up by asking personalized questions

🔊 Auditory-Musical

PRACTICE/APPLY

A. Para mi cumpleaños

SUGGESTION

Have students compare answers after completing this activity. What wishes are the most unique? What are the most common wishes?

🔎 Comparing and Contrasting

B. Los regalos

SUGGESTION

In talking about birthdays and gift-giving, students might enjoy doing a birthday lineup. Tell them that when you give the signal, they are to attempt to find everyone whose birthday falls in the same month as theirs. Then, instruct them to line up in chronological order of birth and tell the dates of their birthdays from January to December.

 Sequencing

 Bodily-Kinetic

VARIATION

 You may wish to have students review the verb **gustar** and some of its uses in various expressions as listed in the **Estructura** below before doing Activity B. Then, after students have completed the activity, encourage the whole class to compile a master list of alternative gift ideas for those people who don't like music or whose musical tastes are unknown, e.g., co-workers, grandparents, neighbors, etc. Help students with vocabulary as necessary.

TEACH/MODEL

Pronunciación

SUGGESTION

TEXTBOOK CASSETTE/CD CASSETTE 2, SIDE B; CD 3, TRACK 15

TAPESCRIPT P. 212

Pronounce the list of practice words clearly and slowly for students; have them repeat after you. For additional practice, call on random students, or have students call on one another.

Have students listen to the explanation for the consonant **r** on the Textbook Cassette/CD. The speaker will model the correct pronunciation of the words in **Práctica C** as students follow along in their texts.

 Auditory-Musical

B. Los regalos You are at "La Nueva Onda," buying presents for your family and friends. 1) Decide which tapes or CDs you will get for whom. 2) Develop a list of at least four people and gifts as you make your decisions. When you have made your choices, 3) discuss them with a partner. As you go through your list, 4) make a comment explaining each choice. Follow the model.

MODELO	**Tú:**	*Pienso comprar este disco compacto para mi prima. [X] es su cantante favorito. Y esta cinta es para papá. Escucha siempre la música de [X].*
	Compañero(a):	*Buena idea. Yo voy a comprar esta cinta para mi hermano. Le gusta mucho el jazz latino. Quisiera comprar el disco compacto pero es muy caro.*

PRONUNCIACIÓN   THE CONSONANT r

A single **r** within a word is pronounced like the *dd* in the English words *daddy* and *ladder*, that is, with a single tap of the tip of the tongue against the gum ridge behind the upper front teeth.

Práctica

C. Escucha a tu maestro(a) cuando lee las siguientes palabras y repítelas después para practicar la pronunciación.

1. cámara	5. pintura	9. parque
2. pájaro	6. estéreo	10. serio
3. farmacia	7. libro	
4. cuatro	8. hermano	

ESTRUCTURA

The verbs gustar and encantar

Le gusta tocar la guitarra.	*You (formal) like to play the guitar.*
Les gusta el concierto.	*You (plural) like the concert. They like the concert.*
No nos gustan las películas de horror.	*We don't like horror movies.*

1. To express what someone else likes or dislikes, Spanish uses the pronouns **le** (singular) and **les** (plural). The pronoun **nos** is used for **nosotros(as)**. Remember to use **gusta** if what is liked is a singular noun or an infinitive and to use **gustan** if what is liked is a plural noun.

MULTIPLE INTELLIGENCES

- Linguistic: All activities
- Logical-Mathematical: F
- Auditory-Musical: **Pronunciación, C, Aquí escuchamos**
- Interpersonal: B, E, G, **¿Qué te gusta hacer los fines de semana?**
- Intrapersonal: A, E, **Un diálogo de contrarios**

2. The verb **encantar** *(to like very much, to really like, to love)* follows the same pattern as the verb **gustar**.

Nos encanta el helado.   *We love ice cream.*

3. To clarify or emphasize who likes or dislikes something, use the preposition **a** plus the pronoun(s) or noun(s) that identify the person(s).

A mí me encantan los deportes.   *I really like sports.*

A ti no te gusta ir de camping.   *You don't like to go camping.*

A Ud. le gusta el jazz.   *You* (formal) *like jazz.*

A mi hermana le encanta la música latina.   *My sister loves Latin music.*

A Lucy y a mí nos gusta bailar.   *Lucy and I like to dance.*

A Uds. les encantan los vídeos.   *You* (plural) *love the videos.*

A Ana y Javier no les gusta la cinta.   *Ana and Javier don't like the tape.*

Aquí practicamos

D. Los gustos   Ask two classmates what items or activities they like most. After they answer, indicate the ones that both of them like. If they do not like the same things, indicate what each of your classmates likes. Follow the model.

MODELO

Tú:	*¿Les gusta más la radio o la grabadora?*
Estudiante 1:	*Me gusta más la grabadora.*
Estudiante 2:	*Me gusta más la grabadora.* o: *Me gusta la radio.*
Tú:	*Ah, a los dos les gusta la grabadora.* o: *Ah, a él (ella) le gusta la grabadora y a ella (él) le gusta la radio.*

1. los discos compactos o las cintas
2. el concierto o la película
3. ir de compras o hablar por teléfono
4. la computadora o la máquina de escribir
5. el jazz o la música clásica
6. las fotografías o los vídeos
7. la televisión o el cine
8. la radio o la grabadora
9. bailar o mirar la televisión

Capítulo 16 Vamos al centro comercial   **381**

  The Standards

- Interpersonal Communication 1.1: B, D, G, **Adelante** activities
- Interpretive Communication 1.2: A, D, E, F, **Aquí escuchamos**
- Presentational Communication 1.3: G, **¿Qué te gusta hacer los fines de semana?**, **Un diálogo de contrarios**
- Linguistic Comparisons 4.1: **Pronunciación**

Estructura

PRESENTATION

Illustrate how to report what someone else likes or dislikes by asking students questions about what they like or don't like (e.g, **¿Qué animal/clase/comida te gusta? ¿Les gustan las vacaciones?**). After students reply, repeat to the class what you have been told. Use mime to emphasize that so-and-so told you this information. Emphasize the correct verb-noun agreement in student sentences by writing them on the board and underlining the singular-singular or plural-plural agreement. (e.g. **Le gustan los gatos, Nos gustan las vacaciones. Le gusta la pizza.**) Then specifically address other students and explain—emphatically—what previous students have said (e.g., **A Michael le gusta la pizza; A nosotros nos gustan las vacaciones**). Use a number of examples of this construction with **gustar** and **encantar** until students are able to offer their own correct examples.

PRACTICE / APPLY

D. Los gustos

ANSWERS

While personalized responses will vary, grammatical forms will be as follows:

1. ...gustan más los discos compactos; ...gustan más las cintas
2. ...gusta más el concierto; ...gusta más la película
3. ...gusta más ir de compras; ...gusta más hablar por teléfono
4. ...gusta más la computadora; ...gusta más la máquina de escribir
5. ...gusta más el jazz; ...gusta más la música clásica
6. ...gustan más las fotografías; ...gustan más los vídeos
7. ...gusta más la televisión; ...gusta más el cine
8. ...gusta más la radio; ...gusta más la grabadora
9. ...gusta más bailar; ...gusta más mirar la televisión

E. ¿Qué les gusta hacer?

SUGGESTION

 Have students write out the answers on the board and then have the class point out any errors.

F. El concierto de rock

ANSWERS

1. A Benito y a mí nos encantó...
2. A Laura no le gustó...
3. A mi prima no le gustó...
4. A mí me encantó...
5. A ellos no les gustó...
6. A Ud. le encantó...
7. A nosotros nos encantó...
8. A Uds. les encantó...
9. A ella no le gustó...
10. A Eduardo y a mí nos encantó...

G. ¿Qué le encanta a tu compañero(a)?

VARIATION

Write the following categories on the board: **Comida, Lugares, Música, Cosas para hacer.** As students report on what their classmates like to do, write each classmate's name under the appropriate heading(s).

 Categorizing

Aquí escuchamos

 TEXTBOOK CASSETTE/CD

 TAPESCRIPT

📕 TRB: ACTIVITY MASTER, P. 111

Antes de escuchar

POSSIBLE ANSWERS

discos compactos, cintas, jazz, música clásica, artistas

Después de escuchar

ANSWERS

1. Isabel
2. la música latina; la música clásica
3. los CDs son muy caros
4. Isabel
5. Los Lobos
6. a la tienda de música

E. ¿Qué les gusta hacer? Do you know your friends and family well? What is the one thing they most like to do? Tell what each person listed likes to do. Follow the model.

> **MODELO**   mi hermana
> *A mi hermana le gusta estudiar.*

1. mi mejor amigo(a)
2. mi madre
3. mis abuelos
4. mis compañeros de clase
5. mis primos
6. mi padre
7. mi hermano(a)
8. mis profesores

F. El concierto de rock Tell who liked the concert a lot and who did not like it. Follow the models.

> **MODELOS**   a mi hermano / sí
> *A mi hermano le encantó el concierto.*
>
> a mis padres / no
> *A mis padres no les gustó el concierto.*

1. a Benito y a mí / sí
2. a Laura / no
3. a mi prima / no
4. a mí / sí
5. a ellos / no
6. a Ud. / sí
7. a nosotros / sí
8. a Uds. / sí
9. a ella / no
10. a Eduardo y a mí / sí

G. ¿Qué le encanta a tu compañero(a)? Find out from a classmate the things that he (she) likes and loves to do and eat, the places that he (she) likes to go, and the music or group (**grupo**) that he (she) likes to listen to. Then report that information to the class. Work with a partner and follow the model.

> **MODELO**   Tú: ¿Qué te gusta hacer?
> Compañera(o): *A mí me gusta... y me encanta...*
> Tú: *A Anita le gusta... y le encanta...*

382 *Sexta unidad* Vamos de compras

Aquí escuchamos

Me gusta la música... *Isabel and Miguel give information about their likes and dislikes.*

Antes de escuchar Based on what you've learned in this **etapa**, what are some of the likes and dislikes you expect Isabel and Miguel to talk about?

 A escuchar On your activity master, make a list of some of the things that Isabel likes and another of the things that Miguel likes.

Después de escuchar Responde a las siguientes preguntas sobre la conversación entre Isabel y Miguel.

1. ¿A quién le gustan muchos tipos de música?
2. ¿Qué música le gusta más a Isabel? ¿Y a Miguel?
3. ¿Por qué le gustan más a Miguel las cintas que los discos compactos?
4. ¿A quién le gusta Jon Secada?
5. ¿Adónde van a ir Isabel y Miguel?

¡ADELANTE!

 ¿Qué te gusta hacer los fines de semana?
Work in pairs and 1) tell your partner the things that you like to do on weekends. 2) Find out if there are activities that you both like. 3) Then, report your likes and dislikes to the class. Follow the model.

MODELO	Compañera(o):	¿Qué te gusta hacer los fines de semana?
	Tú:	*A mí me gusta hablar por teléfono con mis amigos.*
	Compañera(o):	*A mí también me gusta hablar por teléfono con mis amigos.*
	Tú:	*A nosotros(as) nos gusta hablar por teléfono con nuestros amigos.*

 Un diálogo de contrarios Imagine that you and another student are completely opposite in every way. The two of you are friends, despite great differences in likes, dislikes, interests, and possessions. With a partner, make up some details about your two lives and write a dialogue together of about twelve sentences in length, that is, about six to eight comments from each of you.

Capítulo 16 Vamos al centro comercial **383**

ETAPA SYNTHESIS

¿Qué te gusta hacer los fines de semana?

VARIATION
Guide the discussion so students talk about what they like to do for fun or relaxation; where they like to eat; and where they like to go. Have partners comment on one another's activities and record the gist of their discussions in four-column charts, labeled as follows: **Los gustos de mi compañero(a), Mi opinión, Mis gustos, Su opinión.**

 Categorizing

EXPANSION
Use visual reinforcement so students can conceptualize **gustar**. First, name categories from previous chapters, asking **¿A quiénes les gusta...?** Then, have students stand up and confirm, **Sí. A mí me gusta... .**

Un diálogo de contrarios

FYI

ATAJO ATAJO WRITING ASSISTANT SOFTWARE

You might want to have students use this software program when doing this activity.

Individual Needs

More-prepared Students
Have more-prepared students memorize and present their dialogues, using props, music, etc.

Additional Practice and Recycling

FYI

WORKBOOK, PP. 206-210

For recycling and additional practice of the vocabulary, structures, and language functions presented throughout this **etapa**, you can assign the workbook activities as in-class work and/or homework.

TEACH/MODEL

En la papelería

PRESENTATION

 TRANSPARENCY 58

TEXTBOOK CASSETTE/CD CASSETTE 2, SIDE B; CD 3, TRACK 17

TAPESCRIPT P. 213

Introduce the topic by asking the following questions: Where do you go to buy materials for school? What other stationery stores are in the area? What kinds of goods do you find in a stationery store other than paper? Do you think that the rising popularity of computers at home and at school has hurt sales of paper and pens?

Then, have students listen to the dialogue on the Textbook Cassette/CD (with books closed). Proceed by asking students whether they can give the names of some of the items men-tioned. Emphasize the use of **¿En qué puedo servirles?** Then have students practice reading the dialogue with their partners.

VOCABULARY EXPANSION

Explain that **tarjeta postal** is the Spanish term for postcard; **tarjeta** = card; **postal** = [of the] post.

Linguistic Comparisons 4.1

SEGUNDA ETAPA

Preparación

- What are some of the items that you will find at a stationery store or in the paper goods section of a department store?
- What are some of the questions that a person who works in a store usually asks a customer?

En la papelería

Mario y Andrés van de compras a la **papelería** *(stationery store).*

Señora:	Buenos días, muchachos. ¿En qué puedo servirles?
Mario:	Necesitamos **papel para escribir a máquina.** ¿Tiene?
Señora:	¡Cómo no! ¿Cuántas **hojas** quieren?
Mario:	Diez, por favor. ¿Y **papel de avión?**
Señora:	Aquí tienen. **¿Algo más?**
Andrés:	Sí, yo necesito tres **tarjetas de cumpleaños** y una tarjeta del Día de la Madre.
Señora:	Acabamos de recibir unas muy bonitas. Mira aquí.
Andrés:	Mm... Sí, son muy bonitas. ¿Vienen con **sobres?**
Señora:	¡Pues, claro!
Mario:	Bien. **Es todo por hoy.**

papel para escribir a máquina *typewriter paper*   hojas *sheets*   papel de avión *airmail paper*   ¿Algo más? *Anything else?*
Tarjetas de cumpleaños *birthday cards*   sobres *envelopes*   Es todo por hoy. *That's all for today.*

384   *Sexta unidad* Vamos de compras

Etapa Support Materials

- Workbook: pp. 211-215
- Textbook Cassettes/CDs: Cassette 2, Side B; CD 3, Track 17
- Tapescript: Textbook Cassettes/CDs p. 213
- Overhead Transparency: 58
- Middle School Activities: pp. 139
- Lesson Plan Book: pp. 93-94

- Testing Program: Quiz pp. 187,188; Answer Key & Testing Cassettes/CDs Tapescript pp. T73, T74
- Testing Cassettes: Cassette Side B
- Computerized Testing Program: Windows™; Macintosh®
- **Atajo** Writing Assistant Software: Student Text p. 389

¡Te toca a ti!

A. ¿Qué compraron en la papelería?
Mira las fotos que siguen y di qué compró la persona indicada. Sigue el modelo.

MODELO Estela
Estela compró una tarjeta de felicitación.

Estela

1. La Srta. Balboa

2. Ignacio

3. Inés

4. Cristina

6. Roberto

5. el Sr. Rodríguez

Capítulo 16 Vamos al centro comercial **385**

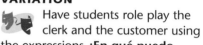

A. ¿Qué compraron en la papelería?

ANSWERS

Answers may vary in some cases.

1. La Srta. Balboa compró sobre de avión.
2. Ignacio... unos sobres.
3. Inés... un cuaderno.
4. Cristina... unas hojas de papel.
5. El Sr. Rodríguez... papel para escribir a máquina.
6. Roberto... un bolígrafo.

VARIATION

Have students role play the clerk and the customer using the expressions **¿En qué puedo servirles?/Yo quisiera...** .

Presentational Communication 1.3

MULTIPLE INTELLIGENCES

- Linguistic: All activities
- Logical-Mathematical: E, F
- Visual-Spatial: A, B
- Bodily-Kinesthetic: **Estructura**
- Auditory-Musical: **Pronunciación,** D, **Aquí escuchamos**
- Interpersonal: C, **Ve a la papelería**
- Intrapersonal: G, **Consejos**

B. ¿Adónde vas para comprar... ?

ANSWERS

 TRANSPARENCY 58

1. ... papelería... un bolígrafo y papel de avión
2. ... tienda de música... discos compactos
3. ... papelería... una tarjeta de cumpleaños
4. ... papelería... lápices
5. ... tienda de música... cintas
6. ... papelería... sobres
7. ... papelería... una goma de borrar

C. En la tienda de música

B. ¿Adónde vas para comprar... ? Mira los dibujos y di adónde vas para comprar cada cosa. Sigue el modelo.

MODELO *Voy a la tienda de música para comprar discos compactos.*

1.   2.   3.

4.   5.   6.   7.

Repaso

C. En la tienda de música
You are shopping for presents for three of your friends at "La Nueva Onda." Together with another student, 1) alternate playing the roles of the clerk and the customer at a record store. 2) Tell the clerk the music your friends like. The clerk will make suggestions for each gift. 3) Buy two CDs and a tape. 4) Pay and leave. Follow the model.

MODELO Tú: *¿En qué puedo servirle?*
Compañero(a): *A mi amiga Claudia le gusta la música clásica. Quiero comprar un disco compacto para ella. ¿Qué tiene Ud.?*

PRONUNCIACIÓN THE CONSONANT **rr**

An **rr** (called a trilled *r*), within a word is pronounced by flapping or trilling the tip of the tongue against the gum ridge behind the upper front teeth. When an **r** is the first letter of a Spanish word, it also has this sound.

386 *Sexta unidad* Vamos de compras

Práctica

D. Escucha a tu maestro(a) cuando lee las siguientes palabras. Después repítelas para practicar la pronunciación.

1. borrador	4. barrio	7. Roberto	9. río
2. perro	5. aburrido	8. rubio	10. música rock
3. correo	6. radio		

ESTRUCTURA

The imperative with **tú**: Affirmative familiar commands

—Raquel, **mira** las tarjetas de cumpleaños. *Raquel, look at the birthday cards.*

—Son muy bonitas. **Compra** dos. *They are very pretty. Buy two.*

1. Regular affirmative **tú** commands have the same form as the present-tense form for **él, ella,** and **usted.**

El **escucha** el disco compacto.	*He is listening to the CD.*
¡Escucha!	*Listen!*
Ella **corre** todos los días.	*She runs every day.*
¡Corre!	*Run!*
Usted **escribe** muy bien.	*You write very well.*
¡Escribe la carta ahora!	*Write the letter now!*

2. The verbs **decir** *(to say, tell),* **hacer, ir, poner** *(to put, place),* **salir, ser, tener,** and **venir** *(to come, to go)* have irregular affirmative **tú** commands.

decir	**di**	ir	**ve**	salir	**sal**	tener	**ten**
hacer	**haz**	poner	**pon**	ser	**sé**	venir	**ven**

Aquí practicamos

E. Tú lo debes... Da la forma del mandato *(command)* con **tú,** de los siguientes verbos.

1. hablar	6. salir	11. descansar
2. comer	7. doblar	12. ser
3. hacer	8. comprar	13. escuchar
4. mirar	9. decir	14. escribir
5. leer	10. correr	15. tener

Pronunciación

PRESENTATION

TEXTBOOK CASSETTE/CD CASSETTE 2, SIDE B; CD 3, TRACK 18

TAPESCRIPT P. 213

Since many students find it difficult to produce the trilled **r**, point out that it is usually easier for a native English speaker to produce a trilled **r** after the letter **p**. Have them invent little phrases in English with **pr** words and encourage them to practice them until they can produce the trilled **r** sound. (*The princess is pretty.*)

Have students listen to the explanation for the trilled **r** on the Textbook Cassette/CD and complete **Práctica D** along with the recording.

Auditory-Musical

Estructura

PRESENTATION

To introduce the command form you could use Total Physical Response (TPR). For example, you might say: **Ven aquí, María, por favor. Escribe en la pizarra, Juan. Mira este libro, Ramón. Sal de la clase, Estela.** Then bring students to the board, miming what they should do if they don't already understand, and having them mime their tasks as well. Continue by writing a few verbs on the board and calling on more students; then, explain how the commands are formed. Point out the irregular command forms.

Bodily-Kinesthetic

FYI

Note that the formation of the negative **tú** command will be presented in the next **etapa.**

PRACTICE/APPLY

E. Tú lo debes...

ANSWERS

1. habla	6. sal	11. descansa
2. come	7. dobla	12. sé
3. haz	8. compra	13. escucha
4. mira	9. di	14. escribe
5. lee	10. corre	15. ten

F. A tu hermano

ANSWERS

1. ven
2. sé
3. haz
4. pon
5. sal
6. ve
7. compra
8. usa
9. ten
10. di

G. Consejos

SUGGESTION

Tell students to be creative in their advice. Have volunteers give some creative advice to their partners in front of the class.

Aquí escuchamos

TEXTBOOK CASSETTE/CD CASSETTE 2, SIDE B; CD 3, TRACK 19

TAPESCRIPT PP. 213-214

Antes de esuchar

POSSIBLE ANSWERS

Hojas, sobres, discos compactos

Después de esuchar

ANSWERS

1. disquetes y una cinta
2. en paquetes de cinco o diez disquetes
3. dos cintas
4. papel
5. "No gracias. Ya tengo mucho papel."
6. sobres

F. A tu hermano Use the command form to get your younger brother to do what you want. Follow the model.

> **MODELO** caminar al quiosco de la esquina
> *Camina al quiosco de la esquina.*

1. venir aquí
2. ser bueno
3. hacer la tarea
4. poner la radio
5. salir de mi cuarto
6. ir al quiosco de periódicos
7. comprar mi revista favorita
8. usar tu dinero
9. tener paciencia
10. decir la verdad

G. Consejos Your best friend has problems at school. Give him (her) some advice on what to do to improve the situation. Use these verbs in the **tú** command form in complete sentences. Follow the models.

> **MODELOS** *Haz la tarea todos los días.*
> *Llega a clase temprano.*

decir	escuchar	hablar	ir	llegar	salir	venir
escribir	estudiar	hacer	leer	practicar	trabajar	

Aquí escuchamos

Para mi computadora... *A clerk helps a customer in a store.*

Antes de escuchar Think about some of the items you might buy to use with a computer. Some of the same vocabulary that you already know in Spanish applies. Can you think of examples?

A escuchar Listen twice to the conversation between the clerk and the customer before answering the questions about it that follow.

Después de escuchar Responde a las siguientes preguntas sobre la conversación entre la empleada y el señor.

1. ¿Qué necesita el señor que va a la papelería?
2. ¿En paquetes de cuántos se venden los disquetes para la computadora?
3. ¿Qúe le pregunta la empleada si necesita el señor?
4. ¿Qué dice él cuando ella le pregunta eso?
5. ¿Qué recuerda el señor que necesita comprar para su esposa?

☀ Spanish for Spanish Speakers

Más consejos

Have Spanish speakers and/or more-prepared students make several cards in Spanish, presenting easy, but creative, scenarios that call for advice. All scenarios should be in the present tense, but allow new vocabulary if it can be easily illustrated or mimed. For example: **No tengo dinero para comprar los regalos de Navidad ¿qué hago?**; No duermo bien, el perro de mi **hermana ladra** (mime barking) **toda la noche ¿qué hago?** Check finished cards for student accessibility. Then, have Spanish speakers present the situations to class teams; teams cooperate to respond in Spanish.

🔍 Analyzing

⊕ Presentational Communication 1.3

¡ADELANTE!

 Ve a la papelería You need computer disks from the stationery store, but you have to stay home to prepare for a major test.

1. Call your friend and explain the situation.
3. Tell him (her) one other thing that you need from the stationery store.
4. After your friend agrees to do this errand, tell him (her) when and where to meet you to deliver the purchases.
5. Thank your friend for the help.

Use informal commands as needed to make your requests. Follow the model for the beginning of your conversation. Work with a partner and finish the conversation

MODELO

Tú: *¡Hola, Estela!*
Estela: *¡Hola! ¿Qué tal?*
Tú: *Bien, pero tengo mucho que hacer.*
Estela: *¿Qué tienes que hacer?*
Tú: *…*

 Consejos One of your friends has some problems with school work. He (she) has asked you what to do in order to be more successful. Try to help by writing a list of eight suggestions for improving the situation. Use the informal command forms of the following verbs in the sentences you write: **estudiar, trabajar, hablar, hacer, practicar, escribir, decir, tener, salir, ver.** Then arrange your sentences in order of priority, starting with the three most useful suggestions for ensuring your friend's success.

Capítulo 16 Vamos al centro comercial **389**

ETAPA SYNTHESIS

Ve a la papelería
SUGGESTION

 Have your Spanish-speaking students model a dialogue for the class before students begin to work in pairs. Then ask 2-3 pairs to present their dialogues in front of the class.

Presentational Communication 1.3

Consejos
FYI

ATAJO ATAJO WRITING ASSISTANT SOFTWARE

You might want to have students use this software program when doing this activity.

Individual Needs

Less-prepared Students
Less-prepared students may need more practice with familiar commands. Give them a list of choices an indecisive person has to make: Shall I stay home tonight and study or shall I go to the baseball game for an hour? Students should respond by selecting one option and forming the **tú** command with it: Go to the baseball game and study in the morning.

Additional Practice and Recycling
FYI

WORKBOOK, PP. 211-215

For recycling and additional practice of the vocabulary, structures, and language functions presented throughout this **etapa**, you can assign the workbook activities as in-class work and/or homework. Answers to the activities are overprinted on each page of the Teacher's Edition of the Workbook.

TERCERA ETAPA

TEACH/MODEL

La tienda de deportes

PRESENTATION

TEXTBOOK CASSETTE/CD CASSETTE 2, SIDE B; CD 3, TRACK 20

TAPESCRIPT P. 214

Get students thinking about this topic by asking: What are some examples of sports equipment? Where do you go to shop for sports equipment of all kinds? What items do you usually buy in a sporting goods store? What sports require the most expensive equipment? the least expensive equipment? Have you ever been to a store that sells used equipment?

☼ Analyzing

Then, play the Textbook Cassette/CD twice (with books closed) to introduce the dialogue. Ask simple comprehension questions: **¿Qué compró la chica en la tienda de deportes? ¿Está en oferta la raqueta en el escaparate? ¿Tienen esquíes para vender?** Then, have pairs take turns reading the dialogue.

◢ Auditory-Musical

FYI

Students should learn the question **¿Cuánto cuesta/cuestan... ?** Point out that **costar** is a stem-changing verb (**o–ue**) in the same way as the verb **poder**.

However, they do not need to know the complete conjugation because they are only going to use the third-person forms of the verb.

VOCABULARY EXPANSION

Help students remember the Spanish word **balón (de baloncesto, de fútbol)** by associating it with the English word *balloon.* You might also want to introduce its synonym **pelota** at this time.

🌐 Linguistic Comparisons 4.1

Preparación

- Where do you go to shop for sports equipment?
- What are some examples of sports equipment?
- What items do you usually buy when you go to a sporting goods store?
- Which sports require the most expensive equipment, and which require the least expensive?

La tienda de deportes

Elsa y Norma **entran** *(enter) en una tienda de deportes.*

Empleado:	Sí, señoritas, ¿qué necesitan?
Elsa:	Quisiera saber cuánto **cuesta** la **raqueta** en el **escaparate.**
Empleado:	¡Ah! **Buen ojo.** Es una raqueta muy buena y cuesta 120 dólares.
Elsa:	¿Cómo? ¿No está **en oferta?**
Empleado:	No, señorita. La oferta **terminó** ayer.
Elsa:	¡Qué pena! Bueno. Y las **pelotas de tenis, ¿qué precio tienen?**
Empleado:	Mm... tres dólares.
Elsa:	Bueno, **voy a llevar** tres. ¿Puedo ver los **zapatos de tenis** también, por favor?
Empleado:	Por supuesto. ¿Algo más?
Norma:	Sí. ¿Venden **esquíes?**
Empleado:	Sí, pero no hay más. Vendimos todos los esquíes en la oferta.
Norma:	Mm... bueno. Gracias.
Empleado:	**A sus órdenes.**

cuesta *costs* **raqueta** *racket* **escaparate** *display window* **Buen ojo.** *Good eye.* **en oferta** *on sale* **terminó** *ended* **pelotas de tenis** *tennis balls* **¿qué precio tienen?** *What do they cost?* **Voy a llevar** *I'll take* **zapatos de tenis** *tennis shoes* **esquíes** *skis* **A sus órdenes.** *At your service.*

390 *Sexta unidad* Vamos de compras

Etapa Support Materials

- Workbook: pp. 216-219
- TRB: Textbook Activity Masters: pp. 112, 113
- Textbook Cassettes/CDs: Cassette 2, Side B; CD 3, Track 20
- Tapescript: Textbook Cassettes/CDs p. 214
- Overhead Transparencies: 59, 60
- Middle School Activities: pp. 140, 141
- Lesson Plan Book: pp. 95-96

- Testing Program: Quiz pp. 189, 190; Answer Key & Testing Cassettes Tapescript p. T74
- Testing Cassettes: Cassette Side B
- Computerized Testing Program: Windows™; Macintosh ®
- Atajo Writing Assistant Software: Student Text p. 304, Workbook p. 219

¡Te toca a ti!

A. Necesito comprar... You are in a sporting goods store and you want to examine the following items before you buy. Ask to see them. Follow the model.

> **MODELO**   pelotas de tenis
> *Quisiera ver las pelotas de tenis, por favor.*

1.

2.

3.

4.

5.

6.

B. ¿Cuánto cuesta...? You want to know the price of different items in the sporting goods store. Ask the clerk. In pairs, play the roles of the customer and clerk. The person playing the clerk should make up reasonable prices for each item from Activity A. Follow the model.

> **MODELO**   (pelotas de tenis)
>   **Tú:** *Buenos días. ¿Cuánto cuestan las pelotas de tenis en el escaparate?*
> **Compañera(o):** *Cuestan 3 dólares por tres.*
>   **Tú:** *Mm... bien. Voy a llevar seis. Aquí tiene 6 dólares.*

❓ ¿Qué crees?

The site of the 1992 Olympic summer Games was:

a) Spain
b) Korea
c) Mexico
d) U.S.A.

respuesta 🖝

Repaso ♻

C. Mis libros favoritos You need to buy a present for a friend. You have decided to get something from a bookstore, but you need some advice. Ask a classmate to suggest three books that you could buy as a present. He (she) should use the **tú** command to make the suggestions.

Capítulo 16 Vamos al centro comercial   **391**

MULTIPLE INTELLIGENCES

- Linguistic: All activities
- Logical-Mathematical: D, E
- Visual-Spatial: A, F, **Aquí escuchamos**
- Auditory-Musical: **Estructura**
- Interpersonal: B, C, **¿Qué deporte?**
- Intrapersonal: **Mi deporte preferido**

The Standards

- Interpersonal Communication 1.1: B, C, E, F, **Adelante** activities
- Interpretive Communication 1.2: A, D, E, F, **Aquí escuchamos**

TEACH/MODEL

Estructura

PRESENTATION

Tell students that you will ask them to do something, but that you may change your mind in the middle of the action so they need to listen carefully. Ask two students to do something and then ask one of them not to do it. For example: **María y Juan, vengan aquí.** (Students get up.) **No, Juan, no vengas. María, ven aquí. José y Alicia, vayan afuera. No, José, no vayas afuera.**

Write the **yo** form of several verbs (include spelling change verbs) on the board and show students how the negative familiar commands are formed. Point out the irregular commands for **ir** and **ser.**

🔊 Auditory-Musical

PRACTICE/APPLY

D. ¡No hagas eso!

ANSWERS

1. no esquíes
2. no lleves
3. no vayas
4. no comas
5. no seas
6. no vendas
7. no compres
8. no salgas
9. no cruces
10. no tengas

ESTRUCTURA

The imperative with tú: Negative familiar commands

¡No **lleves** tus esquíes!	*Don't take your skis!*
¡No **vendas** tu raqueta!	*Don't sell your racket!*
¡No **compartas** tu comida con el perro!	*Don't share your food with the dog!*

1. To form regular negative **tú** commands, drop the -o from the yo form of the present tense and add -es for -ar verbs and -as for -er and -ir verbs.

bailar	yo	bailo	bail-	no **bailes**
beber	yo	bebo	beb-	no **bebas**
escribir	yo	escribo	escrib-	no **escribas**

2. Verbs ending in -car, -gar, and -zar have the same spelling change in the negative **tú** command as they do in the Ud. and Uds. commands. In verbs ending in -car, the c in the -car ending changes to qu (no **practiques**). Verbs that end in -gar, add a u after the g of the ending (no **llegues**). In verbs ending in -zar, the z of the ending changes to c (no **cruces**).

3. Here are the negative **tú** commands of the eight verbs with irregular affirmative **tú** commands you saw in the previous **etapa:**

decir	no **digas**	ir	no **vayas**
hacer	no **hagas**	poner	no **pongas**
salir	no **salgas**	tener	no **tengas**
ser	no **seas**	venir	no **vengas**

Aquí practicamos

☞ a

D. ¡No hagas eso (that)! Da la forma negativa del mandato con **tú** de los siguientes verbos.

1. esquiar aquí
2. llevar los libros
3. ir al parque
4. comer en tu casa
5. ser antipático
6. vender tus pelotas de tenis
7. comprar los zapatos allí
8. salir de la tienda
9. cruzar la calle
10. tener miedo *(to be afraid)*

☀ Spanish for Spanish Speakers

Children's Literature

Have Spanish speakers research Spanish-language children's literature. Students can find information at the library, on the internet, through friends or relatives, or at foreign-language and some larger bookstores. Have students share information on the books they read, compiling a cooperative list with a short summary of titles, authors, accessibility (location) of books, and what they are about.

🔗 Connections with Distinctive Viewpoints 3.2

E. Consejos
Tell your friend not to do these things. Work in pairs. Then reverse roles and repeat.

1. ser malo
2. llegar tarde
3. tener problemas
4. doblar a la derecha
5. escribir en el libro
6. buscar tus cuadernos
7. mirar mucho la TV
8. venir solo(a) a la fiesta
9. poner la radio en clase
10. decir malas palabras

F. Recomendaciones
You are new in the neighborhood and don't know where to go for the best buys. Your friend will direct you to various shops in town to get good prices and good quality. Work with a partner and follow the model.

MODELO
Tú: *Compro carne en la Carnicería Montoya.*
Compañero: *No compres allí. Compra en la Carnicería Martín. Es mejor (better).*

1. Como en el restaurante La Estancia.
2. Hago compras en la Frutería la Sevillana.
3. Voy a la Panadería López.
4. Escucho discos compactos en la tienda de música Cantar y Bailar.
5. Busco lápices y borradores en la Papelería Mollar.
6. Miro las flores en la Florería La Rosa Roja.

Aquí escuchamos

El tenista *A customer is looking for a special item at a sporting goods store.*

Antes de escuchar Based on what you have learned in this **etapa,** what are some of the phrases and expressions that you expect the customer and the saleswoman to use in their conversation?

Capítulo 16 Vamos al centro comercial **393**

E. Consejos
ANSWERS

1. no seas
2. no llegues
3. no tengas
4. no dobles
5. no escribas
6. no busques
7. no mires
8. no vengas
9. no pongas
10. no digas

VARIATION
 Have students write a list of do's and don'ts for new students. They can then rank suggestions from most to least important.

Comparing and Contrasting Prioritizing

F. Recomendaciones
VARIATION
TRANSPARENCY 60

Using vocabulary from previous chapters, read to the class bits of conversations that could be overheard in a variety of places: in science class, at the beach, etc. Include a familiar command in each example: "**¡Alicia, dame ese disco compacto!** Students write the location: **en la tienda de música.**

 Auditory-Musical

ANSWERS
1. No comas... . Come en el Restaurante La Cabaña.
2. No hagas... . Haz compras en el Mercado Popular.
3. No vayas... . Ve a la Panadería la Oriental.
4. No escuches... . Escucha discos compactos en la Tienda de Música.
5. No busques... . Busca... en la Papelería los Amigos.
6. No mires... . Mira las flores en la Florería Arónica.

Aquí escuchamos
  TEXTBOOK CASSETTE/CD CASSETTE 2, SIDE B; CD 3, TRACK 21

TAPESCRIPT

 TRB: ACTIVITY MASTER, P. 112

Antes de escuchar
ANSWERS
Saleswoman: ¿Qué necesita Ud.? / Cuesta ... dólares. / A sus órdenes.
Customer: ¿Cuánto cuesta... ? / ¿Está en oferta? / ¿Qué precio tienen...?

Después de escuchar

ANSWERS

1. F, tennis racket
2. T
3. T
4. F, but they are not very expensive
5. F, $99
6. T
7. F

ETAPA SYNTHESIS

¿Qué deporte?

SUGGESTIONS

Give students time to prepare, practice, and then reverse roles before presenting their mini-situations to the class. Ask follow-up questions in the third person to test listening comprehension. Let those with no involvement in sports select another hobby or interest they enjoy and modify this activity accordingly.

Mi deporte preferido

FYI

 ATAJO WRITING ASSISTANT SOFTWARE

You might want to have students use this software program when doing this activity.

SUGGESTION

As suggested above, modify the activity for those uninterested in sports. Instead they can write about a friend or relative who likes sports, or choose another interest entirely.

Additional Practice and Recycling

FYI

WORKBOOK, PP. 216-219

For recycling and additional practice of the vocabulary, structures, and language functions presented throughout this **etapa**, you can assign the workbook activities as in-class work and/or homework. Answers to the activities are overprinted on each page of the Teacher's Edition of the Workbook.

 A escuchar Listen twice to the conversation between the saleswoman and the customer before answering the true-or-false questions about it on your activity master.

Después de escuchar On your activity master, indicate whether the following statements are true or false. If a statement is false, provide the correct information.

1. The customer wants to buy some tennis shoes.
2. The customer indicates that he already has a tennis racket.
3. The customer wants a larger tennis racket.
4. The saleswoman says that the large rackets are still on sale.
5. The price of the racket is $199.
6. The offer comes with a free can of tennis balls.
7. The man decides not to buy the racket because it is too expensive.

¡ADELANTE!

 ¿Qué deporte? Your friend wants to take up a new sport and asks you for advice because you are familiar with a number of sports.

1. Ask your friend about his (her) preferences for season, team, or individual sports.
2. Find out if your friend likes to play sports for competition or pleasure, and about any equipment to which she (he) has access.
3. Choose a sport and advise your friend to take it up.
4. Explain why, basing your decisions on your friend's talents and preferences.
5. Tell her (him) what to buy in order to start practicing.

 Mi deporte preferido Write six to eight sentences about your favorite sport, indicating why you like it, how often you participate in that sport, where, and with whom.

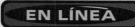 **EN LÍNEA**

Connect with the Spanish-speaking world! Access the **¡Ya verás!** *Gold* home page for Internet activities related to this chapter.

http://yaveras.heinle.com

394 *Sexta unidad* Vamos de compras

Additional Etapa Resources

Refer to the **Etapa** Support Materials list on the opening page of this **etapa** for detailed cross-references to these assessment options.

VOCABULARIO

Para charlar

Para expresar gustos
me / te / le / nos / les encanta(n)
me / te / le / nos / les gusta(n)

Lugares para comprar
una papelería
una tienda de deportes
una tienda de música

Expresiones para comprar o vender
¿En qué puedo servirle(s)?
¿Qué necesita(n)?
No hay más.
Voy a llevar...
Aquí tiene(n).
¿Algo más?
Es todo por hoy.
A sus órdenes.

Para preguntar el precio
¿Cuánto cuesta(n)?
¿Qué precio tiene(n)?
¿No está(n) en oferta?

Temas y contextos

En la tienda de música
una cinta
un disco compacto
un vídeo

En la papelería
una hoja
papel de avión
papel para escribir a máquina
un sobre
una tarjeta de cumpleaños

En la tienda de deportes
unos esquíes
una pelota de tenis
una raqueta
unos zapatos de tenis

Vocabulario general

Sustantivos
un centro comercial
un escaparate
la música latina
el precio

Verbos
decir
poner

Adjetivos
barato(a)
bonito(a)
caro(a)
favorito(a)
suficiente

Otras expresiones
A ver.
Buen ojo.
fueron
por eso
¡Qué pena!
¡Super!

CHAPTER WRAP-UP

SUGGESTION

 Have students write advice on how to maintain a healthy lifestyle.

Individual Needs

 More-prepared students can debate the issue of eliminating school-sponsored sports programs. Less-prepared students could participate in the debate voluntarily, as if at an open forum.

Improvised Conversation

SUGGESTION

 TEXTBOOK CASSETTE/CD CASSETTE 2, SIDE B; CD 3, TRACK 22

 TAPESCRIPT PP. 214-215

 TRB: ACTIVITY MASTER, P. 113

 Have students listen to this dialogue in which two women shop for a gift for their brother. Refer to the TRB for student Activity Masters.

Listening Skills Development

FYI

 LAB MANUAL PP. 107-112

 CASSETTE SIDE A; CD 8, TRACKS 8-15

 TAPESCRIPT: LAB PROGRAM PP.157-167

It is now appropriate to work through the lab manual activities and their accompanying recordings in class or in the language laboratory.

Resource for Spanish-Speaking Students

FYI

 WORKBOOK FOR SPANISH-SPEAKING STUDENTS: PP. 101-106

 ANSWER KEY TO SSS WORKBOOK PP. 29-30

Activities specially written to meet the needs of Spanish-speaking students are available in these workbooks for the reinforcement and extension of the topics and language presented in this chapter.

Additional Chapter Resources

Refer to the Chapter Support Materials list on the opening page of this chapter for detailed cross-references to *¡Ya verás! Gold*'s student-centered technology components and various assessment options.

Spanish for Spanish Speakers

Keeping a Vocabulary Notebook
Remind Spanish-speaking students to add words and expressions from this vocabulary section to the problematic spelling combination categories and personal new vocabulary lists in their notebooks.

Ritos importantes para los jóvenes hispanohablantes

Antes de Leer

POSSIBLE ANSWERS

1. Possible answers:
   Celebra—celebrate
   Sociedad—society
   Elegante—elegant
   Perlas—pearls
   Tradicional—traditional
2. pantalones cortos; pantalones largos; frac
3. Answers will vary. Students might describe a sweet sixteen celebration in the United States or other rites of passage they might know about.

ENCUENTROS CULTURALES

◆

Ritos importantes para los jóvenes hispanohablantes

Reading Strategies

- Activating background knowledge
- Recognizing cognates
- Scanning for specific information

Social rites of passage are important in every society because they can mark a transition from one stage of life to another. In the following reading you will learn about some rites of passage for 15-year-old girls and 13-year-old boys in some Spanish-speaking countries.

Antes de leer

1. Scan the first paragraph and find at least five cognates. Then, guess what kind of celebration is being described.

2. Scan the second paragraph and find three articles of clothing mentioned.

3. Can you describe a rite of passage that you, or someone you know, has experienced?

• •

La quinceañera es una fiesta que se celebra en diversas partes del mundo hispanohablante cuando una chica cumple los quince años. Este día la adolescente es presentada en sociedad. La joven, que también se llama quinceañera, lleva para la ocasión un elegante traje largo, zapatos de tacón y muchas veces aretes, anillo, pulsera y collar de perlas. Esta fiesta tradicional se celebra en un salón de uno de los mejores hoteles de la ciudad en compañía de otras quinceañeras. Para preparar la fiesta, la familia pasa mucho tiempo en las tiendas y los centros comerciales y, claro, gasta mucho dinero. Las familias con menos dinero tienen la fiesta en casa. Hoy en día, algunas quinceañeras prefieren no tener fiesta y gastar el dinero en un largo viaje al extranjero o en comprar un coche.

396 *Sexta unidad* Vamos de compras

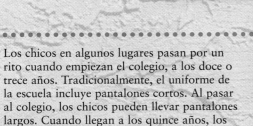

Los chicos en algunos lugares pasan por un rito cuando empiezan el colegio, a los doce o trece años. Tradicionalmente, el uniforme de la escuela incluye pantalones cortos. Al pasar al colegio, los chicos pueden llevar pantalones largos. Cuando llegan a los quince años, los chicos empiezan a asistir a las fiestas de quinceañeras, como acompañantes, donde generalmente llevan frac.

Guía para la lectura

1. Here are some words and expressions to keep in mind as you read.

cumple	*turns (a certain age)*
zapatos de tacón	*high heels*
aretes	*earrings*
anillo	*ring*
pulsera	*bracelet*
collar	*necklace*
al extranjero	*abroad*
frac	*coat and tails*

Después de leer

1. What are the rites of passage between childhood, the teenage years, and adulthood in your culture? How are the rites similar to those mentioned in the reading? How are they different?

2. What other social rites do you know about that may affect you directly or that may affect your friends?

3. Does clothing play an important role in rites of passage in your culture? Explain why or why not.

Capítulo 16 Vamos al centro comercial **397**

Después de leer
ANSWERS

1. Answers will vary according to students culture. One example; in Japanese culture, young girls are celebrated on their twentieth birthday as a sign that they have become adult women.
2. Answers will vary. One example: For some Catholics being baptized, having their first communion and getting married are events that mark the difference between a child, a teenager and an adult.
3. Answers will vary. One example: The white wedding dress used in Catholic and other religious weddings.

CAPÍTULO 17

OBJECTIVES

Functions
- Making purchases and choices
- Expressing quantity
- Asking for prices

Contexts
- Open-air markets
- Supermarkets

Accuracy
- Demonstrative adjectives and pronouns
- Expressions of quantity
- The interrogative words **cuál/cuáles**

Pronunciation
- The consonant **f**

CHAPTER WARM-UP

Setting the Context

In preparation for their learning about making purchases in food markets, have students study the photo on this page. Ask them where Alicia Sánchez is and what she is doing. Ask them to consider whether or not one could take a similar photo in the places they shop for fresh produce. How many items are similar to the produce they see in their local supermarkets? How many are different? Help students identify as many of the different items as possible.

Comparing and Contrasting

Cultural Comparisons 4.2

CORNERS GAME

Have students do a corners activity. Designate the corners of the room as follows: (1) green vegetables, (2) non-green vegetables, (3) red fruits, and (4) other fruits. Tell students to go to the corner for their favorite kind of fruit and vegetable, and have them discuss with another student all of the vegetables or fruits that might fit their category. Then have each pair team up with another pair and paraphrase what they discussed together as a pair. Ask one student at random from each team of four to report to the class.

Categorizing

¿Cuánto cuesta... ?

—Quisiera medio kilo, por favor.
—Bueno. Son 500 pesos.

Objectives

- making purchases and choices
- expressing quantity
- asking for prices

398 *Sexta unidad* Vamos de compras

Chapter Support Materials

- Lab Manual: pp. 113-118
- Lab Program: Cassette Side B; CD 9, Tracks 1-8
- TRB: Textbook Activity Masters: pp. 114-116
- Textbook Cassettes/CDs: Cassette 2, Side B; CD 3, Track 27
- Tapescript: Lab Program pp.168-175 ; Textbook Cassettes/CDs p. 217
- Middle School Activities: pp. 142-145
- Workbook for Spanish-Speaking Students: pp. 107-112
- Answer Key to SSS Workbook: pp. 31-33

- Practice Software: Windows™; Macintosh®
- Testing Program: Chapter Test pp. 201-204; Answer Key & Testing Cassettes Tapescript pp. T79, T80; Oral Assessment p. T80
- Testing Cassettes: Cassette Side B
- Computerized Testing Program: Windows™; Macintosh®
- Video Program: Cassette 2, 1:12:49-1:21:35
- Video Guide: Videoscript pp. 74-77; Activities pp. 141-143
- **Mundos hispanos 1**
- Internet Activities: Student Text p. 415

PRIMERA ETAPA

- Have you ever been to an open-air market? If so, where? when?
- What kinds of products can you buy in a market?
- How is the shopping experience in an outdoor market different from going to a regular grocery store?

Día de feria

*La Sra. Fernández va de compras al **mercado** (market).*

Ayer jueves fue **día de feria** en Oaxaca. La señora Fernández caminó **hasta** la plaza cerca de su casa donde cada semana hay un **mercado al aire libre.** A la señora Fernández le gusta comprar las **frutas** y los **vegetales** que **ofrecen** los **vendedores** porque son productos **frescos** y baratos. **Además** a ella le encanta **regatear.** Hoy, piensa comprar vegetales para una **ensalada.**

Sra. Fernández:	¿Cuánto cuesta el **atado** de zanahorias?
Vendedora:	1.300 pesos.
Sra. Fernández:	Bueno, 2.000 pesos por **estos** dos atados.
Vendedora:	Tenga, 2.100.
Sra. Fernández:	Está bien.

Unas frutas y unos vegetales:

unas fresas   unos limones   unas manzanas

una naranja   unas peras   unas uvas   unas cebollas   unos guisantes

una lechuga   el maíz   unas papas   unos tomates   unas zanahorias

día de feria *market day* **hasta** *as far as* **mercado al aire libre** *open-air market* **frutas** *fruit* **vegetales** *vegetables* **ofrecen** *offer* **vendedores** *sellers* **frescos** *fresh* **Además** *Besides* **regatear** *to bargain* **ensalada** *salad* **atado** *bunch* **estos** *these*

Capítulo 17 ¿Cuánto cuesta...? **399**

Día de feria

PRESENTATION

 TRANSPARENCY 62

 TEXTBOOK CASSETTE/CD CASSETTE 2, SIDE B; CD 3, TRACK 23

 TAPESCRIPT P. 215

Begin with the **Comentarios culturales** on page 400 and present additional descriptions of open-air markets. Explain **el regateo,** or *the bargaining,* typical to such markets. Then use the transparency to present the new vocabulary of fruits and vegetables. Ask students what they like and dislike.

Play the recording on the Cassette/CD and have students summarize, to the best of their abilities, what is being said. Ask them to listen for a form of **el regateo** and other new vocabulary and play the recording again.

☼ Activating Prior Knowledge

◣ Visual-Spatial

VOCABULARY EXPANSION

Maíz is the generic word for corn and is used in such expressions as **tortillas de maíz**, etc.; **choclo** refers to whole kernels of corn (in Chile, Argentina, Uruguay, and Paraguay); **elote** is widely used for an ear of corn; **chícharos** (peas in Mexico); **arvejas** (peas in South America); **ejotes** (green beans) or **judías verdes** (in Spain); **plátanos** (bananas in Spain and Mexico); **cerezas** (cherries); **duraznos** or **melocotones** (peaches); **piña** (pineapple); **jitomate** (tomato in Mexico).

 Linguistic Comparisons 4.1

PRACTICE / APPLY

A. ¿Qué son?

SUGGESTION

 TRANSPARENCY 62

Use the transparency with books closed. You might want to ask students if they like the fruits or vegetables after they identify them.

Determining Preferences

ANSWERS

1. guisantes/chícharos
2. cebollas
3. zanahorias
4. manzanas
5. uvas
6. naranja
7. maíz/elote
8. peras
9. limones
10. tomates/jitomates
11. lechuga
12. papas/patatas

Comentarios CULTURALES

Los mercados al aire libre

Open-air markets are characteristic of many Spanish-speaking countries. In rural areas, these markets are particularly important since they offer a place where people from the surrounding communities can meet to buy, sell, and socialize. Once a week, vendors and shoppers gather in a designated location, often the main **plaza** of a small town. Farmers come from all over the local countryside, bringing vegetables and fruit they have grown on small plots of land. One can also buy pots, pans, brooms, soap, and other household items at the markets, as well as regional handicrafts such as hand woven cloth, colorful shirts, embroidered dresses, musical instruments, and wooden carvings. More and more commonly, there are manufactured goods and high-tech equipment such as radios and televisions for sale.

¡Te toca a ti!

A. ¿Qué son? Identifica las frutas y los vegetales que siguen.

1.

2.

3.

4.

5.

6.

7.

8.

400 *Sexta unidad* Vamos de compras

MULTIPLE INTELLIGENCES

- Linguistic: All activities
- Logical-Mathematical: C, E, F, G
- Visual-Spatial: A, B, H
- Auditory-Musical: **Pronunciación** D, **Aquí escuchamos**
- Interpersonal: I, **El postre, ¿Te gusta más...?**
- Intrapersonal: **¿Qué comemos?**

9. **10.** **11.** **12.**

B. Preparar una ensalada You and a classmate are making a salad for a class party. Decide whether you will make a fruit salad or a green salad. Then, as you examine the contents of the refrigerator (shown in the following drawings), take turns identifying what you see. Together make a list of the items that you want for your salad and a list of those that you don't. Follow the model.

> **MODELO** Compañero(a): *Hay maíz. ¿Quieres maíz?*
> Tú: *Sí, quiero maíz. Me gusta el maíz.* o:
> *No, no me gusta mucho el maíz.* o:
> *¡Claro que no! ¡Es una ensalada de frutas!*

1. **2.** **3.** **4.**

5. **6.** **7.** **8.**

9. **10.**

Capítulo 17 ¿Cuánto cuesta...? **401**

B. Preparar una ensalada

ANSWERS

TRANSPARENCY 63

1. peras
2. cebollas
3. lechuga
4. manzanas
5. uvas
6. guisantes/chícharos
7. tomates/jitomates
8. naranja
9. zanahorias
10. fresas

EXPANSION

Write the words from the Vocabulary Expansion from page T400 on the board. Then, ask personalized questions so students can use new vocabulary. For example: **¿Qué fruta te gusta más? ¿Qué ingredientes te gusta poner en una ensalada?**, etc. Or ask questions using the **pregúntale** format.

Interpretive Communication 1.2

The Standards

• Interpersonal Communication 1.1: B, C, F, I,
  Adelante activities
• Interpretive Communication 1.2: A, E, F, G, H, I,
  Aquí escuchamos
• Cultural Practices and Perspectives 2.1:
  Comentarios culturales
• Linguistic Comparisons 4.1: **Pronunciación,
  Estructura**

C. La oferta

SUGGESTION

After looking at the directions and model (and possibly using the above Expansion) for this activity, ask why students might accept or reject their friend's advice. Brainstorm with them to help them integrate familiar vocabulary into this context. Some examples include: **Sí, es verdad, y yo no tengo mucho dinero./...y yo necesito pelotas de tenis./...y quiero comprar otras cosas también./Sí, y las pelotas de tenis son buenas también./Pero no quiero las pelotas de tenis; quiero la pelota de fútbol./Pero no me gustan las pelotas de tenis./Pero ya tengo pelotas de tenis.**

TEACH / MODEL

Pronunciación

PRESENTATION

TEXTBOOK CASSETTE/CD CASSETTE 2, SIDE B; CD 3, TRACK 24

TAPESCRIPT P. 216

Point out that the consonant combination ph does not exist in Spanish. Therefore, cognates that have a ph in English will have an **f** in Spanish. For example: **filosofía, farmacia, fotografía.**

 Linguistic Comparisons 4.1

PRACTICE / APPLY

SUGGESTION

Have students listen to the explanation for **f** and on the Textbook Cassette/CD and/or pronounce the list of words in **Práctica C** clearly and slowly for students and have them repeat after you. For additional practice, call on random students, or have students call on one another.

Auditory-Musical

Repaso

C. La oferta You and a friend have saved some money to shop for sporting goods at a flea market. One of you is interested in newer, more expensive items. The other is always looking for bargains. Take turns trying to persuade each other, following the model. The first item in each pair is the more expensive one.

> **MODELO**
> **Tú:** *Voy a comprar la pelota de fútbol.* o: *Mira la pelota de fútbol.* o: *¡Qué buena pelota de fútbol!*
> **Amiga(o):** *Pero no compres la pelota de fútbol. Compra las pelotas de tenis. Son más baratas.*
> **Tú:** *Tienes razón* (You're right). *Voy a llevar las pelotas de tenis.* o: *No, yo prefiero la pelota de fútbol.*

1. raqueta grande / pequeña
2. zapatos nuevos / usados
3. esquíes para la nieve / esquíes para el agua
4. fútbol nuevo / viejo
5. bicicleta Cinelli / Sprint
6. pelota de básquetbol / pelota de fútbol

PRONUNCIACIÓN THE CONSONANT **f**

The consonant **f** in Spanish is pronounced exactly like the *f* in English.

Práctica

D. Escucha a tu maestro(a) cuando lee las siguientes palabras. Después repítelas para practicar la pronunciación.

1. fútbol
2. flor
3. ficción
4. frente
5. final

6. farmacia
7. favorito
8. fresco
9. alfombra
10. suficiente

402 *Sexta unidad* Vamos de compras

Focus on Culture

Markets in Latin America

You might also want to have students look again at the photo on the chapter opener. This is a picture of a typical indoor market. Another typical indoor market is La Merced in Mexico City. It is one of the largest markets in the Americas and is over 400 years old. It extends over several city blocks and offers the widest selection of produce at very low prices. Like other markets, it also offers a wide array of other household articles, such as clothing.

Cultural Products and Perspectives 2.2

ESTRUCTURA

Demonstrative adjectives

—¿Quieres **estas** manzanas verdes o
  esas manzanas rojas?

—Quiero **aquellas** manzanas de allá.

*Do you want **these** green apples
or **those** red apples?*

*I want **those** apples over there.*

The Demonstrative Adjectives

	next to the speaker	near the speaker	far from the speaker
	this	*that*	*that*
Masc. sing.	**este** limón	**ese** limón	**aquel** limón
Fem. sing.	**esta** manzana	**esa** manzana	**aquella** manzana
	these	*those*	*those (over there)*
Masc. plural	**estos** limones	**esos** limones	**aquellos** limones
Fem. plural	**estas** uvas	**esas** uvas	**aquellas** uvas

1. Demonstrative adjectives are used to point out specific people or things. In Spanish, there are three sets of demonstrative adjectives. Each one specifies people or things in relation to their distance from the speaker.

2. Like all adjectives in Spanish, demonstrative adjectives agree in number and gender with the noun they modify. They are always placed before the noun.

Aquí practicamos

E. **¿Esta, esa o aquella?** Replace each definite article with the correct demonstrative adjective, according to its column heading. Follow the models.

> **MODELOS** la papa, *near the speaker:*
> *esta papa*
>
> el croissant, *near the listener:*
> *ese croissant*
>
> los bocadillos, *far from listener and speaker:*
> *aquellos bocadillos*

next to the speaker	*near the speaker*	*far from the speaker*
1. la manzana	4. el limón	7. el maíz
2. el limón	5. los tomates	8. las peras
3. los pasteles	6. las fresas	9. el queso

Capítulo 17 ¿Cuánto cuesta...? **403**

TEACH/MODEL

Estructura

PRESENTATION

Use classroom objects to introduce the demonstrative adjectives. Point to objects and say: **Este cuaderno es de Juan. Ese libro es de Estela. Aquel libro es de José.** etc. Do this with both singular and plural demonstratives; then, write them on the board and explain their differences. Teach students: "This and these have the t's" as a memory aid. Explain that these adjectives are often clarified by **aquí, ahí,** and **allá** (**este aquí, ese ahí, aquel allá**). Also, associate **allá** with yonder in English to stress the distance from the speaker. Remind students that demonstratives are adjectives that must agree in both gender and number with the nouns they modify.

 Visual-Spatial

Linguistic Comparisons 4.1

PRACTICE/APPLY

E. ¿Esta, esa o aquella?
SUGGESTIONS

 Have students write out the activity and then edit their partners' work. Write **aquí, ahí,** and **allá** on the board. Then say the cues from the book and add one of the adverbs. The students will repeat the noun with its corresponding demonstrative adjective.

ANSWERS
1. esta manzana
2. este limón
3. estos pasteles
4. ese limón
5. esos tomates
6. esas fresas
7. aquel maíz
8. aquellas peras
9. aquel queso

F. ¿Prefiere estas manzanas o esos tomates?

ANSWERS

Answers will vary according to students' preferences, but they will be using the demonstrative adjectives in one or the other of the following forms:

1. estas naranjas/esas manzanas/estas manzanas
2. esta banana/esa pera/esta pera
3. este limón/esas papas/estas papas
4. este maíz/esos guisantes/estos guisantes
5. estos tomates/esa lechuga/esta echuga
6. estas cebollas/esas bananas/estas bananas
7. estas uvas/esas fresas/estas fresas
8. estas zanahorias/esas naranjas/estas naranjas

TEACH/MODEL

Palabras útiles

PRESENTATION

Introduce the expressions by indicating the quantity of food that would be required for different numbers of people. You could do this by presenting a monologue about a party you are going to have. For example: **Voy a tener una fiesta el sábado y 16 personas van a asistir. Necesito comprar 10 litros de refrescos y 4 botellas de sidra para tomar. Para los bocadillos necesito dos kilos de queso y un kilo de jamón.** etc.

EXPANSION

Point out that the metric system is used all over the world, including those countries where Spanish is spoken.

One liter is approximately equivalent to one quart. (1 liter = 1.057 quarts).

One kilogram is a little more than two pounds. (1 kilogram = 2.205 pounds).

One gram is 0.035 ounce. (1,000 grams = 1 kilogram.

▲▲ Logical-Mathematical

F. ¿Prefiere estas manzanas o esos tomates?

You are the checkout person at a grocery store. Your customer is undecided about what to buy. Offer him (her) choices according to the cues. Work with a partner and follow the model.

> **MODELO** fresas / uvas
> **Tú:** *¿Prefiere Ud. estas fresas o esas uvas?*
> **Compañero(a):** *Prefiero estas uvas, por favor.*

1. naranjas / manzanas	5. tomates / lechuga
2. banana / pera	6. cebollas / bananas
3. limón / papas	7. uvas / fresas
4. maíz / guisantes	8. zanahorias / naranjas

PALABRAS ÚTILES

Expressions of specific quantity

¿Cuánto cuesta **un litro** de leche?	*How much is a liter of milk?*
Quisiera **medio kilo** de uvas.	*I would like a half kilo of grapes.*

The following expressions are used to indicate quantities.

un kilo de	*a kilogram of*
medio kilo de	*a half kilogram of*
una libra de	*a pound of*
50 gramos de	*50 grams of*
un litro de	*a liter of*
una botella de	*a bottle of*
una docena de	*a dozen of*
un pedazo de	*a piece of*
un atado de	*a bunch of*
un paquete de	*a package of*

Aquí practicamos

G. ¿En qué puedo servirle?

Usa la información entre paréntesis para contestar las preguntas de los vendedores. Sigue el modelo.

> **MODELO** ¿Qué desea? (2 kilos de tomates / 1 kilo de uvas)
> *Deseo dos kilos de tomates y un kilo de uvas.*

1. ¿Qué necesita hoy? (1/2 kilo de lechuga / un atado de zanahorias)
2. ¿Qué quisiera? (200 gramos de jamón / 2 docenas de peras)
3. ¿Qué desea? (1/2 litro de leche / 1 botella de agua mineral)
4. ¿En qué puedo servirle? (1/2 docena de naranjas / 2 kilos de uvas)
5. ¿Necesita algo? (3 botellas de limonada / 1 paquete de mantequilla)

☀ Spanish for Spanish Speakers

Shopping Receipts

Have Spanish speakers work with less-advanced students in this expansion-realia activity. Have students bring in a parent or guardian's shopping receipt, or bring in one of your own and photocopy it. Then have pairs of students translate the receipt into Spanish. This activity will help less-prepared students recycle numbers (with purchase prices) and practice and expand their quantity and shopping vocabularies (with the list of items bought). Spanish speakers can share synonyms, spelling, pronunciation, and new vocabulary with the rest of the class.

⊕ Interpretive Communication 1.2

H. ¿Cuánto compraron?

H. ¿Cuánto compraron? Mira los dibujos que siguen y di cuánto de cada cosa compró la persona indicada. Sigue el modelo.

MODELO   ¿Qué compró Juanita?
Ella compró cincuenta gramos de queso.

1. ¿Qué compró Mercedes?   2. ¿Qué compró el señor González?   3. ¿Qué compró Antonio?

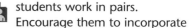

4. ¿Qué compró Maribel?   5. ¿Qué compró la señora Ruiz?   6. ¿Qué compró Francisco?

I. En el mercado

I. En el mercado You are shopping in an open-air market in Caguas, Puerto Rico. Ask the seller the price of each item, and then say how much you want to buy. Work with a partner, alternating the roles of customer (**cliente**) and seller (**vendedor[a]**). Use the cues provided and follow the model.

MODELO   zanahorias: 2 dólares el atado / 2 atados
Cliente: *¿Cuánto cuestan estas zanahorias?*
Vendedor(a):   *Dos dólares el atado.*
Cliente: *Quiero dos atados, por favor.*
Vendedor(a):   *Aquí tiene. Cuatro dólares, por favor.*

1. leche: 2 dólares la botella / 3 botellas
2. naranjas: 3 dólares la docena / 1/2 docena
3. papas: 2 dólares el kilo / 500 gramos
4. cebollas: 1.50 dólares el kilo / 1/2 kilo
5. mantequilla: 2.50 dólares el paquete / 2 paquetes
6. pastel: 1 dólar el pedazo / 2 pedazos

Capítulo 17 ¿Cuánto cuesta...?   **405**

G. ¿En qué puedo servirle?

SUGGESTION

Have students read their answers aloud to practice the pronunciation of new words and phrases.

Auditory-Musical

H. ¿Cuánto compraron?

ANSWERS

1. dos litros de leche
2. un kilo de azúcar
3. un kilo de jamón
4. una docena de naranjas
5. un kilo de plátanos/bananas
6. una libra de manzanas

I. En el mercado

SUGGESTION

Do one or two examples with the class before having students work in pairs.
Encourage them to incorporate greetings and leave-taking expressions into their mini-dialogues.

Interpretive Communication 1.2

ANSWERS

Students substitute the cues, following the model and adding expressions of their choice. They will use **cuesta** in numbers 1, 5, and 6. They will use **cuestan** in 2, 3, and 4.

Aquí escuchamos

 TEXTBOOK CASSETTE/CD CASSETTE 2,
SIDE B; CD 3, TRACK 25

 TAPESCRIPT P. 216

 TRB: ACTIVITY MASTER, P. 114

Antes de escuchar
POSSIBLE ANSWERS
¿Qué necesita?
¿Qué quisiera?
¿Qué desea?
¿Cuánto cuesta(n)… ?

Después de escuchar
ANSWERS
papas, cebollas, mangos, lechuga,
tomates

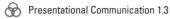
ETAPA SYNTHESIS

El postre
SUGGESTION

 Do the activity first with the whole class. Play the role of the salesperson; the class is the customer. After they see how the activity works, have students work in pairs.

 Presentational Communication 1.3

EXPANSION

Additional role playing situation: You've been sent to the market to buy a variety of things. However, as you're doing the shopping, you buy only things you like. Tell the vendor what you want to buy and how much. Be sure to ask for the price, to thank the vendor, and to give an appropriate leave-taking expression.

Presentational Communication 1.3

¿Te gusta más...?
FYI
This activity requires that students bring magazine pictures to class. Unless you can supply these props at class time, students will need to be aware of this assignment in advance.

Visual-Spatial

Aquí escuchamos

De compras en el mercado *Mr. Estévez has a conversation with a vendor at the market.*

Antes de escuchar Based on what you have learned in this **etapa,** what are some of the questions that you think Mr. Estévez and the vendor might ask each other?

 A escuchar Listen twice to the conversation between Mr. Estévez and the vendor. Pay special attention to the products that Mr. Estévez actually buys.

Después de escuchar En tu hoja reproducible, haz una marca junto a las cosas que compró el Sr. Estévez.

_aguacates	_lechuga	_melón	_zanahorias
_cebollas	_maíz	_papas	_plátanos
_fresas	_mangos	_tomates	
_guisantes	_manzanas	_uvas	

406 *Sexta unidad* Vamos de compras

¡ADELANTE!

 El postre (dessert) Your mother has put you in charge of buying some fruit for dessert. Work in pairs and follow the directions.

Salesperson	Customer
1. Greet the customer.	Greet the salesperson.
2. Ask what he (she) needs.	Say that you need some fruit to buy for dessert **(para el postre)**.
3. Offer a choice of fruits.	Decide what you are going to buy. Ask how much the fruit(s) cost(s).
4. Tell him (her) the price(s).	Bargain over the price.
5. Agree on the price. Ask if he (she) needs something else.	Answer.
6. Respond if necessary, then end the conversation.	End the conversation.

 ¿Te gusta más...? You and a friend have just won the lottery and you want to buy a number of things. 1) Bring to class pairs of magazine pictures of five objects (two different versions of each) whose names you know in Spanish and that you would like to own. Catalogs will be a good source for finding multiple pictures of objects. 2) Following the model, get each other's opinion about which items you each like better, using the appropriate forms of **este** and **ese.** 3) Make a list of the first five things you plan to buy together with your winnings. Follow the model.

MODELO	
Tú:	*¿Te gusta más esta bicicleta americana o esta bicicleta italiana?*
Amiga(o):	*Prefiero esa bicicleta italiana. Y tú, ¿prefieres este viaje a Panamá o este viaje a Costa Rica?*
Tú:	*A mí me gusta más ese viaje a Panamá.*

 ¿Qué comemos? Your family has invited an exchange student from Venezuela, who is your friend at school, to join you for dinner. His parents are in town and are also invited. Work with a classmate to write up a shopping list of eight food items that you need to buy for the dinner, indicating the quantity or amount of each. Consider drinks, salads, vegetables, meat, and desserts.

Capítulo 17 ¿Cuánto cuesta...? **407**

¿Qué comemos?

FYI

ATAJO WRITING ASSISTANT SOFTWARE

You might want to have students use this software program when doing this activity.

SUGGESTION

Have students brainstorm a list of food before they begin writing. If they need additional help, have students review the vocabulary for fruits and vegetables from pages 399 and 400.

Activating Prior Knowledge

Additional Practice and Recycling

FYI

WORKBOOK, PP. 220-226

For recycling and additional practice of the vocabulary, structures, and language functions presented throughout this **etapa,** you can assign the workbook activities as in-class work and/or homework. Answers to the activities are overprinted on each page of the Teacher's Edition of the Workbook.

Additional Etapa Resources

Refer to the **Etapa** Support Materials list on the opening page of this **etapa** for detailed cross-references to these assessment options.

TEACH/MODEL

En el supermercado

PRESENTATION

TRANSPARENCY 64

Use the transparency to introduce the new vocabulary. Have students close their books while you describe Roberto's and Ricardo's shopping schedule. As you narrate, use the transparency to illustrate new vocabulary. Then have students open their books and read the passage together, or ask for a volunteer or volunteers to read it to the class. Continue by asking general questions: **¿Dónde están Roberto y Ricardo? ¿Qué compran?**, etc. The whole class can make the list of items mentioned.

Visual-Spatial

VOCABULARY EXPANSION

Introduce students to *hamburger language*. Have students guess the meanings of the following words; if necessary, help them with less *transparent* translations: **carne picada, catsup, mostaza, mayonesa, pepinillos.** Also point out that Spanish-speakers say **galletas** when the meaning would be understood from context, but that they would specify galletas **saladas** (crackers) and **galletas dulces** (cookies) for clarification.

Linguistic Comparisons 4.1

SEGUNDA ETAPA

Preparación

- What are some of the differences between shopping at a supermarket and at an open-air market?
- What products can you find at a supermarket that you could not get at an open-air market?
- When you go shopping for food, where do you prefer to go? Why?

En el supermercado

Ricardo y Roberto van de compras al supermercado.

Una vez por semana Ricardo hace las compras en el supermercado **para** su mamá. Hoy Roberto también tiene que ir al supermercado para comprar **alimentos** para su familia. Los dos amigos van **juntos.** Primero, van a la sección de los **productos lácteos** porque Ricardo tiene que comprar mantequilla, leche, yogur, crema y queso.

También van a la sección de las **conservas** porque necesitan tres **latas** de **sopa** y una lata de **atún**, una botella de **aceite** y un paquete de **galletas.**

Una vez *Once* **para** *for* **alimentos** *food* **juntos** *together* **productos lácteos** *dairy products* **conservas** *packaged goods* **latas** *cans* **sopa** *soup* **atún** *tuna* **aceite** *oil* **galletas** *cookies*

408 *Sexta unidad* Vamos de compras

Etapa Support Materials

- Workbook: pp. 227-234
- TRB: Textbook Activity Masters: pp. 115, 116
- Textbook Cassettes/CDs: Cassette 2, Side B; CD 3, Track 26
- Tapescript: Textbook Cassettes/CDs p. 216
- Overhead Transparencies: 64, 65, 66
- Middle School Activities: pp. 148-150
- Lesson Plan Book: pp. 100-101

- Testing Program: Quiz pp. 198-200; Answer Key & Testing Cassettes Tapescript pp. T78
- Testing Cassettes: Cassette Side B
- Computerized Testing Program: Windows™; Macintosh®
- **Atajo** Writing Assistant Software: Student Text p. 415. Workbook p. 233

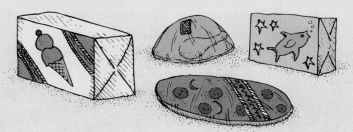

Luego pasan por la sección de los produc-tos **congelados** porque Roberto tiene que comprar **pescado**, una pizza, un **pollo** y también: ¡**helado** de chocolate, por su-puesto! A Roberto le encanta el helado.

Para terminar, ellos compran pastas, **hari-na**, azúcar, **sal**, **pimienta**, arroz y mayone-sa. El **carrito** de Roberto está muy **lleno**.

Luego pasan por *Then they go by* **congelados** *frozen* **pescado** *fish* **pollo** *chicken* **helado** *ice cream* **harina** *flour* **sal** *salt* **pimienta** *pepper* **carrito** *shopping cart* **lleno** *full*

Comentarios CULTURALES

Las frutas y los vegetales tropicales

In the tropical parts of Central and South America, Mexico, and the Caribbean, many kinds of delicious vegetables and fruits are commonly available for everyday con-sumption. You may be familiar with the **agua-cate** *(avocado)* and the chile. Fruits such as **papayas** (small melon-like fruit) and **man-gos** (peach-like fruit) can be found fresh as well as in fruit juices in many supermarkets in the U.S. The **plátano** (a large green banana) is eaten frequently with meals in a number of Caribbean coun-tries. It is generally served fried or boiled. The **mamey** (coconut-like fruit) and the **zapote** (fruit shaped like an apple with green skin and black pulp inside) can often be found on the Mexican table as a much-appreciated dessert. Another popular dessert is guava paste, served with fruit or cheese.

Capítulo 17 ¿Cuánto cuesta...? **409**

Comentarios culturales

VOCABULARY EXPANSION

After reading the **Comentarios culturales**, ask students which fruits and vegetables they have tasted. Remind them that **plátano** means banana in Mexico and Spain. The banana that is usually eaten fried with rice is called a **plátano macho** in Mexico. Explain that the **mamey**, while having a coconut-like flavor, is a soft fruit (unlike the coconut) and its pulp is used to make a delicious **licuado** with milk or to make a favorite Mexican dessert: **dulce de mamey** (made with sugar, milk, mamey pulp, and vanilla). The **zapote** is also used to make another Mexican dessert favorite: **dulce de zapote**. It is made with the **zapote** pulp, orange juice, and sugar. It has a creamy texture and a tangy fla-vor. They enjoy it much the way we do applesauce. **Pasta de guayaba** has a firm texture that can be cut into pieces, and it is almost always served with a fresh white cheese.

Connections with Distinctive Viewpoints 3.2
Linguistic Comparisons 4.1

MULTIPLE INTELLIGENCES

- Linguistic: All activities
- Logical-Mathematical: D, E, F, **Un picnic**
- Visual-Spatial: A
- Auditory-Musical: **Aquí escuchamos**
- Interpersonal: B, C, F, **¿Cuánto cuesta todo esto?**

PRACTICE/APPLY

A. En el carrito de Lidia hay...

ANSWERS

Students follow the model, substituting the following cues:

1. pizza   4. helado
2. sal   5. leche
3. pescado   6. atún

B. Preferencias personales

EXPANSION

Continue practicing the vocabulary by asking additional personalized questions. **¿Prefieres sándwiches de pollo o de atún? ¿Pones mayonesa en tus sándwiches de atún? ¿Qué te gusta poner en las hamburguesas?** etc. You might prefer to ask questions using the **pregúntale** format.

SUGGESTION

Review days of the week by having students fill out a calendar for a typical week of dinners at their house—**Los lunes, tenemos una cena grande con... porque todos están en casa.** They could also predict what meals each family member would cook on various days if they could make anything they wanted.

🔍 Hypothesizing

Individual Needs

More-prepared Students

Give students an opportunity to review **tú** commands, chapter vocabulary, and pronunciation by creating commercials for grocery items. Perhaps more-prepared students would be interested in writing and producing (and videotaping) these commercials.

🔍 Creating

Less-prepared Students

Less-prepared students could act as at-home TV viewers making (constructive) comments about the commercials.

¡Te toca a ti!

A. En el carrito de Lidia hay... Lidia's mother sent her to the store. But since Lidia forgot the shopping list, the supermarket employee helps her to remember by mentioning some items. Work with a partner, alternating the roles of the employee and Lidia. Look at the drawings that follow and indicate what Lidia is buying. Follow the model.

MODELO   Empleado(a):   ¿Necesitas arroz?
                Lidia: *No, pero necesito pasta.*

1. ¿Necesitas harina?   2. ¿Necesitas pimienta?   3. ¿Necesitas pollo?

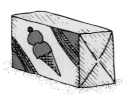   

4. ¿Necesitas galletas?   5. ¿Necesitas yogur?   6. ¿Necesitas mayonesa?

B. Preferencias personales Your father always likes to give you a choice when he prepares meals. He is preparing this week's menu. Tell him what you would like each day from the choices given. Then, with a partner, set up a different menu for the following week, agreeing on what to serve each day. Follow the model.

MODELO   ¿Quisieras carne o pescado hoy?
              Quisiera carne, por favor.

1. ¿Quisieras pollo o atún el lunes?
2. ¿Quisieras yogur o helado el martes?
3. ¿Quisieras pizza o pescado el miércoles?
4. ¿Quisieras pasta o papas el jueves?
5. ¿Quisieras pollo o sopa el viernes?
6. ¿Quisieras mayonesa o aceite en la ensalada el sábado?
7. ¿Quisieras fruta o helado el domingo?

🔵 The Standards 🔵

- Interpersonal Communication 1.1: C, E, G, **Adelante** activities
- Interpretive Communication 1.2: A, B, D, F, G, **Aquí escuchamos**
- Presentational Communication 1.3: **¿Cuánto cuesta todo esto?**
- Cultural Products and Perspectives 2.2: **Comentarios culturales**

Repaso ↻

C. ¿Preparamos una sopa de vegetales? Your favorite aunt and uncle are coming to your house for dinner tonight. They are strict vegetarians, so you have to plan the meal carefully. You have decided to serve vegetable soup and fruit salad. With a classmate, write a shopping list; one for fruits and one for vegetables. Include at least five items on each list. Then, since your budget may not allow you to purchase all the items, organize the fruits and vegetables in the order in which you would prefer to include them in the menu.

MODELO *En la sopa podemos poner _____.*
En la ensalada de frutas podemos poner _____.

ESTRUCTURA

The interrogative words cuál and cuáles

¿**Cuáles** prefieres, las manzanas verdes o las manzanas rojas?   *Which (ones) do you prefer, the green apples or the red apples?*

1. To express *which* or *which one(s)* in questions, the interrogative word ¿**cuál?** is used when asking about a singular noun. ¿**Cuáles?** is used when asking about a plural noun.

2. Like the interrogative word ¿**qué?**, ¿**cuál?** and ¿**cuáles?** can also mean *what?* ¿**Qué?** is used to ask for an explanation or a definition, while ¿**cuál?** and ¿**cuáles?** are used to indicate a choice within a group of nouns.

¿**Qué** es un plátano?	*What is a plantain?*
¿**Qué** hizo Marcos anoche?	*What did Marcos do last night?*
¿**Cuál** es tu dirección?	*What is your address?*
¿**Cuál** es tu número de teléfono?	*What is your phone number?*

Aquí practicamos

D. ¿Cuál quieres? You are babysitting for a young child who doesn't speak very clearly yet. You are trying to guess what he wants by offering him some choices. Follow the model.

MODELO este libro grande / aquel libro pequeño
¿Cuál quieres; este libro grande o aquel libro pequeño?

1. el vídeo de Mickey Mouse / el vídeo de Blanca Nieves (*Snow White*)
2. esta fruta / ese pan dulce
3. este sándwich de queso / aquél de jamón
4. este chocolate / ese jugo
5. estas uvas / esas fresas
6. este helado de chocolate / esa botella de leche

❓ ¿Qué crees?

Chocolate is a product that originally came from:

a) Switzerland
b) Europe
c) Mexico
d) South America

respuesta ☞

Capítulo 17 ¿Cuánto cuesta...?   **411**

C. ¿Preparamos una sopa de vegetales?

SUGGESTION

Have a few students give the ingredients of their soup or salad. Ask follow-up questions to see if other students were listening carefully.

🔊🔊 Auditory-Musical

TEACH / MODEL

Estructura

PRESENTATION

Since students have already seen and used these interrogative words, you might want to introduce them simply by asking questions such as, **¿Cuál es tu apellido? ¿Cuál es tu número de teléfono?** Point out that **cuál/cuáles** is usually followed by a verb rather than a noun, and it is generally used with the verb **ser**, except when asking for a definition: **¿Qué es el mamey?**

🔊🔊 Linguistic

PRACTICE / APPLY

D. ¿Cuál quieres?

ANSWERS

1. ¿Cuál quieres; el vídeo de Mickey Mouse o el vídeo de Blanca Nieves?
2. ¿Cuál quieres; esta fruta o ese pan dulce?
3. ¿Cuál quieres; este sándwich de queso o aquél de jamón?
4. ¿Cuál quieres; este chocolate o ese jugo?
5. ¿Cuáles quieres; estas uvas o eses fresas?
6. ¿Cuál quieres; este helado de chocolate o esa botella de leche?

E. Preguntas personales

ANSWERS

Students add **¿Cuál es...?** each time, substituting the cues. Their partners' responses will vary.

EXPANSION

Have a few students tell the class what they found out about their classmates.

 Interpersonal Communication 1.1

TEACH/MODEL

Nota gramatical

PRESENTATION

Since students have already used the demonstrative adjectives, they will understand when you introduce the pronouns inductively. Make statements using students' possessions and classroom objects. Then write a statement on the board and have students point out the difference between the adjectives and the pronouns (the written accent).

✎ Comparing and Contrasting

🔺 Visual-Spatial

E. Preguntas personales When you are applying for a part-time job in the local grocery store, the manager asks you a series of personal questions. With a partner, role-play the interview, switching roles after completing the first interview. Use **cuál** and **cuáles** in your questions. Follow the model.

MODELO   tu nombre
                ¿Cuál es tu nombre?

1. tu nombre
2. tu dirección
3. tu número de teléfono
4. tus días preferidos para trabajar
5. tu modo de transporte

NOTA GRAMATICAL

Demonstrative pronouns

Ese yogur no es muy bueno.
Éste de es mejor.

That yogurt (there) is not very good.
This one (here) is better.

Estas manzanas son rojas, **ésas** amarillas y **aquéllas** verdes.

These apples (here) are red, those (there) yellow, and those (over there) green.

The Demonstrative Pronouns

	next to the speaker	near the speaker	far from the speaker
	this one	*that one*	*that one (over there)*
Masc. sing.	**éste**	**ése**	**aquél**
Fem. sing.	**ésta**	**ésa**	**aquélla**
Neuter. sing.	**esto**	**eso**	**aquello**
	these ones	*those ones (there)*	*those ones (over there)*
Masc. plural	**éstos**	**ésos**	**aquéllos**
Fem. plural	**éstas**	**ésas**	**aquéllas**

1. Used to point out specific people or things, demonstrative pronouns replace the nouns to which they refer. They have the same forms as the demonstrative adjectives, but they add a written accent in most forms to differentiate them from adjectives. They also reflect the number and gender of the nouns they replace.

☞ C

2. The neuter singular form (**esto, eso, aquello**) is used to refer to ideas, situations, or objects in a general way. These are equivalent to the English *this, that*. These forms do not have an accent because there are no adjectives to differentiate them from.

Esto es muy interesante.
Eso pasa.
Aquello no me gustó.

This is very interesting.
That happens.
I didn't like that.

☀ Spanish for Spanish Speakers

Más preguntas personales

Have students write in their notebooks a list of the most outrageous and ridiculous questions that they'd like to ask the president, famous authors, fictional characters, rock stars, historical figures, or international personalities.

Sample questions might include: To the Queen of England—What do you put in your handbag?; To Superman—Where did you store your street clothes?

✎ Creating

3. You can use adverbs of location with demonstrative pronouns to clarify or emphasize the distance of the nouns from the speaker. You already know **aquí**, and **allí**. The adverb **allá** means *over there*. Use the preposition **de** before the adverb when emphasizing a pronoun.

¿Quiere Ud. **esta** lechuga de **aquí**, **ésa** de **allí** o **aquélla** de **allá**?	*Do you want this lettuce here, that one there, or that one over there?*

Aquí practicamos

F. ¿Cuál? You are doing some shopping with a friend. Because there are so many items to choose from, you have to explain which objects you are discussing. Use **éste(a)**, **ése(a)**, or **aquél(la)** in your answer, according to the cues in parentheses. Follow the model.

> **MODELO** ¿Qué libros vas a comprar? *(those ones there)*
> *Voy a comprar ésos.*

1. ¿Qué calculadora vas a comprar? (this one)
2. ¿Qué frutas vas a comprar? (those ones over there)
3. ¿Qué galletas quieres? (those ones there)
4. ¿Qué paquete de arroz quieres? (this one)
5. ¿Qué pescado vas a comprar? (that one there)
6. ¿Qué jamón quieres? *(that one over there)*

G. ¿Cuál prefieres? Use the cues that follow to tell what you prefer. Remember to make the pronoun agree with the noun provided. Work with a partner and follow the model.

> **MODELO** queso / allí
> **Compañero(a):** ¿Qué queso prefieres?
> **Tú:** Prefiero ése de allí.

1. paquete de mantequilla / allí
2. botella de aceite / allá
3. paquete de arroz / aquí
4. lata de sopa / allá
5. paquete de galletas / allí
6. lata de atún / allá
7. paquete de harina / aquí

Capítulo 17 ¿Cuánto cuesta...? **413**

PRACTICE / APPLY

F. ¿Cuál?
ANSWERS
1. ésta
2. aquéllas
3. ésas
4. éste
5. ése
6. aquél

G. ¿Cuál prefieres?
ANSWERS
1. ése
2. aquélla
3. éste
4. aquélla
5. ése
6. aquélla
7. éste

Focus on Culture

More About Shopping
Although supermarkets are becoming ever more popular in the large cities of Latin America, many people still prefer to buy their produce, meats, eggs, and poultry at the markets, for reasons of freshness and selection. Some might go to supermarkets to stock up on staple articles such as cooking oil, rice, etc., because they often find lower prices there.

Cultural Practices and Perspectives 2.1

Aquí escuchamos

TEXTBOOK CASSETTE/CD CASSETTE 2, SIDE B; CD 3, TRACK 26

TAPESCRIPT P. 216

TRB: ACTIVITY MASTER, P. 115

Antes de escuchar

POSSIBLE ANSWERS

arroz, harina, pollo, pimienta, ensalada, papas

Después de escuchar

ANSWERS
1. Teresa
2. the supermarket
3. chicken, rice, black beans, oil, ice cream
4. chicken
5. mangos, papaya, bananas
6. ice cream

Aquí escuchamos

Por favor, compra... *Teresa and her mother talk about the groceries they need.*

Antes de escuchar Based on what you have learned in this **etapa,** what types of food do you think Teresa and her mother might need for a dinner party?

 A escuchar Listen twice to the conversation between Teresa and her mother before answering the questions about it on your activity master.

Después de escuchar On your activity master, complete the following sentences in English, based on what you heard.

1. The person who is going to do the shopping is . . .
2. The shopping will be done at . . .
3. Three of the items on the shopping list are . . .
4. Some of the fruit to be bought is . . .

¡ADELANTE!

 Un picnic You and a friend are planning a picnic. At the delicatessen you have to decide what you want to buy, but you do not always agree with each other. For each suggestion you make, your friend disagrees and tells you to buy something else. Work with a partner. Use the cues provided and follow the model. Finally, decide on five items that you both are willing to take to the picnic.

MODELO estos sándwiches de atún / esos sándwiches de pollo

Tú: *¿Vamos a llevar estos sándwiches de atún?*

Compañero(a): *No, no lleves ésos de atún. Lleva ésos de pollo.*

1. esa ensalada de frutas / aquella ensalada verde
2. esos tacos de carne / aquellos tacos de queso
3. estos licuados de banana / esos licuados de fresa
4. este helado de fresas / ese yogur de fresas
5. aquella tortilla de jamón / esa tortilla de papas
6. este pastel de fresas / aquel pastel de manzanas
7. esa salsa de tomate / esta salsa de chile
8. esa sopa de pollo / esta sopa de pescado

414 *Sexta unidad* Vamos de compras

☀ Spanish for Spanish Speakers

Spoken Spanish

Ask Spanish speakers to listen to the Spanish used in the **Aquí escuchamos** recording and to compare it to the Spanish they use in their communities. Encourage student to focus, for example, on the consonant **s**: Does it sound similar to the *s* in English? Is it barely audible (as is often the case in Spanish spoken in the Caribbean)? Is it similar to the *th* sound in English? How does it contrast with their spoken Spanish? You might want to have the rest of the class participate in this activity.

🔍 Comparing and Contrasting

🎵 Auditory-Musical

⊕ Linguistic Comparisons 4.1

¿Cuánto cuesta todo esto? You and two friends are planning a dinner for some classmates. You are on a tight food budget. You have only $16 to spend—$3 for beverages, $3 for dessert, and $10 for the main course (**el plato principal**). Compare the prices on the lists and decide how much you can buy of each thing without going over the limit. After you decide, write down what you will buy and how much you will have spent. Work with two classmates and follow the model. Be prepared to report to the class your final menu and its cost.

MODELO	Tú:	*¿Qué vamos a servir?*
	Compañero(a) 1:	*Bueno, para el plato principal, ¿por qué no preparamos pollo con papas fritas y vegetales?*
	Compañero(a) 2:	*A ver. El pollo cuesta…*

PRODUCTOS CONGELADOS
Pescado ....1 kilo/**$5**
Pizza **$5**
Papas fritas (fried) ..**$2**
Pollo ....2/**$5**
Vegetales **$2**
Helado **$4**

PRODUCTOS LÁCTEOS
Yogur ....3/**$2**
Leche ....1 litro/**$1**
Mantequilla **$1**
Crema ....2/**$1**
Queso **$2**

OTROS PRODUCTOS
Pan **$1**
Galletas **$2**
Arroz **$2**
Pastas **$2**
Lechuga **$1**
Tomates ......1 kilo/**$2**

BEBIDAS
Café ....1 kilo/**$5**
Refrescos ......2 litros/**$2**
Agua mineral .....1 litro/**$2**
Limonada ....2 litros/**$3**

CONSERVAS
Sopa ....2/**$1**
Atún ....2/**$2.50**
Salsa de tomate ...2/**$1.50**
Aceitunas ....2/**$1.50**

Capítulo 17 ¿Cuánto cuesta...? **415**

SEGUNDA ETAPA

ETAPA SYNTHESIS

Un picnic

EXPANSION

 TRANSPARENCY 66

 Have a few students present their dialogues, telling the class what they will serve. Then ask follow-up questions to see if the other students were listening carefully.

Presentational Communication 1.3

VARIATION

 Ask students if they ever go on picnics with friends or family members. If so, find out their top three places to picnic.

¿Cuánto cuesta todo esto?

FYI

 ATAJO WRITING ASSISTANT SOFTWARE

You might want to have students use this software program when doing this activity.

SUGGESTION

 Have groups discuss the cost of the items in this activity. Do students think these prices are high or low? Have them correct the prices according to their conclusions. Have students present their revised prices in class for additional number practice. Follow up by comparing the prices each group arrived at. Which group priced items most accurately?

Activating Prior Knowledge

Additional Practice and Recycling

FYI

 WORKBOOK, PP. 227-234

For recycling and additional practice of the vocabulary, structures, and language functions presented throughout this etapa, you can assign the workbook activities as in-class work and/or homework.

Vocabulario

SUGGESTION

Since this chapter is heavily oriented toward useful vocabulary, this would be a good time to assign student projects. Individuals or groups of students could be asked to prepare bulletin board displays of bakery products, meats, delicatessen items, etc. They can use pictures cut out of magazines and then write their own labels in Spanish.

▲▲ Visual-Spatial

TRANSLATION GAME

Divide the class into teams. Then, alternating turns between individuals on each team, give a student ten seconds to translate one of the chapter vocabulary words into Spanish. For every correct answer, assign 1 point. Then ask a member of the next team to translate. Continue until you've exhausted the key vocabulary words. The team with the most points wins.

▲▲ Linguistic

Resource for Spanish-speaking Students

FYI

 WORKBOOK FOR SPANISH-SPEAKING STUDENTS: PP. 107-112

 ANSWER KEY TO SSS WORKBOOK: PP. 31-33

Activities specially written to meet the needs of Spanish-speaking students are available in these workbooks for the reinforcement and extension of the topics and language presented in this chapter.

VOCABULARIO

Para charlar

Para preguntar sobre las preferencias

¿Cuál prefieres...?
¿Cuál quieres...?

Temas y contextos

Cantidades

un atado de
una botella de
una docena de
50 gramos de
un kilo de
una libra de
una lata de
un litro de
medio kilo de
un paquete de
un pedazo de

Conservas

el aceite
el atún
la sopa

Frutas

un aguacate
una ensalada de
  frutas
una fresa
un limón
una manzana
una naranja
una pera
un plátano
una uva

Productos congelados

el helado
el pescado
el pollo

Productos lácteos

la crema
un yogur

Productos varios

el azúcar
una galleta
el harina
la mayonesa
la pasta
la pimienta
la sal

Vegetales

una cebolla
una ensalada de
  vegetales
una ensalada (verde)
unos guisantes
una lechuga
el maíz
una papa
un tomate
una zanahoria

Spanish for Spanish Speakers

Keeping a Vocabulary Notebook

Remind Spanish-speaking students to add words and expressions from this vocabulary section to the problematic spelling combination categories and personal new vocabulary lists they started in their notebooks in Chapter 1. Reinforce that they should continue to do this each time a chapter in the textbook is completed.

Vocabulario general

Sustantivos

los alimentos
un carrito
una feria
un(a) cliente
un mercado al
   aire libre
un(a) vendedor(a)

Verbos

ofrecer
pasar
regatear

Adjetivos

este(a) / estos(as)
ese(a) / esos(as)
aquel(la) / aquellos(as)
amarillo(a)
fresco(a)
lleno(a)
rojo(a)
verde

Otras palabras y expresiones

éste(a) / éstos(as)
ése(a) / ésos(as)
aquél(la) / aquéllos(as)
además
allá
allí
hasta
juntos
luego
una vez

Improvised Conversation

SUGGESTION

 TEXTBOOK CASSETTE/CD CASSETTE 2, SIDE B; CD 3, TRACK 27

 TAPESCRIPT P. 217

 TRB: ACTIVITY MASTER, P. 116

 Have students listen to this conversation in which a woman bargains for fruits and vegetables with a vendor. Refer to the TRB for student activities.

 Auditory-Musical

Listening Skills Development

FYI

LAB MANUAL PP. 113-118

 LAB CASSETTE SIDE B; CD 9, TRACKS 1-8

TAPESCRIPT: LAB PROGRAM PP. 168-175

It is now appropriate to work through the lab manual activities and their accompanying recordings in class or in the language laboratory. These materials provide reinforcement of the pronunciation points, vocabulary, structures, and language functions presented throughout the etapas and continue the development of listening comprehension skills provided in the **Aquí escuchamos** sections and the Improvised Conversation.

Additional Chapter Resources

Refer to the Chapter Support Materials list on the opening page of this chapter for detailed cross-references to *¡Ya verás! Gold's* student-centered technology components and various assessment options.

El Centro Sambil
Antes de leer
POSSIBLE ANSWERS

1. a. The largest mall in the United States is the Mall of America located in Minneapolis, MN.

b. Answers will vary. For example, students may point out that young adults consider the mall as a *home away from home* because they like to get together with their friends and have a good time. They can shop or get something to eat at the same place.

c. Answers will vary.

2. Students may count up to 336 **locales comerciales**.

3. Answers may vary. Students may define **locales comerciales** as local stores or commercial stores.

SUGGESTION

Have students categorize the different types of establishments found in the Centro Sambil. Possible categories include: Stores (clothing, jewelry, music, etc.), Eating establishments (restaurants, fast food, cafes), Entertainment (movie theaters, amusement park), Recreation (ice skating), Services (convention center).

 Categorizing

ENCUENTROS CULTURALES
◆

El Centro Sambil

Antes de leer

Reading Strategies
- Using the title to predict meaning
- Activating background knowledge
- Scanning for specific information

1. Centro Sambil, in Caracas, Venezuela, is advertised as **el centro comercial más grande de Sudamérica.**

  a. Do you or any of your classmates know which shopping center is the largest in the United States? In the world?

  b. Talk about your "shopping center experience." Nowadays, the mall has become a kind of "home away from home" for many people. Why? What kinds of things are there to do in a mall? Do you spend a lot of time at the mall?

  c. What are the positive and negative aspects of large, multipurpose shopping malls?

2. What do you think **locales comerciales** means? Scan the five paragraphs and try to find how many **locales comerciales** there are in the entire **Centro Sambil.**

PRIMER NIVEL	SEGUNDO NIVEL	TERCER NIVEL	CUARTO NIVEL
Autopista	**Acuario**	**Libertador**	**Feria**
Este, nuestro primer nivel comercial, se encuentra al nivel de la autopista Francisco Fajardo. Está distribuido alrededor de cinco plazas o puntos de encuentro que facilita su recorrido. Las cinco plazas son Plaza Jardín, Plaza de la Fuente, Plaza Central, Plaza de la Música y Plaza del Arte. Disfrute aquí de más de 31 locales comerciales y de seis salas de cine.	En este segundo nivel puede usted disfrutar de un acuario marino de más de 120.000 litros de capacidad. Aquí puede usted ver una gran variedad de especies marinas del Océano Pacífico. Encuentre aquí además nuestra joyería, 31 minitiendas y una cafetería, junto a más de 131 diferentes locales comerciales.	Este nivel se encuentra a nivel de la avenida Libertador, a la que tiene acceso peatonal directo. En este nivel puede encontrar usted locales comerciales organizados alrededor de cuatro plazas. Visite aquí 92 diferentes locales comerciales o cualquiera de nuestros restaurantes y cafés al aire libre.	En este nivel puede disfrutar de muchas actividades variadas y servicios diferentes. Encuentre aquí la Feria, nuestro centro de comida rápida, donde hay trece diferentes puntos de venta y capacidad para aproximadamente 1.200 personas. Puede contar con acceso a las terrazas, para que pueda disfrutar de las más variadas vistas y espacios recreativos. Va a encontrar en este nivel 82 locales comerciales, tres plazas y cinco salas de cine.

Guía para la lectura

Here are some words and expressions to keep in mind as you read.

autopista	*highway*
nivel	*level*
puntos de venta	*points of sale*
facilita	*will make easier*
salón de festejos	*party and convention center*
recorrido	*stroll, journey*
patinaje sobre hielo	*ice-skating*
disfrute	*enjoy*
Parque de Diversiones	*Amusement Park*
acceso peatonal	*pedestrian access*
pies cuadrados	*square feet*
al aire libre	*outdoors*

QUINTO NIVEL

Diversión

En este, el quinto y más alto nivel comercial del Centro Sambil, hay toda clase de espectaculares atracciones. Aquí usted puede hacer uso de nuestros 20 diferentes locales comerciales, de nuestro salón de usos múltiples y de nuestro salón de festejos. Distrute junto a su familia de un día de patinaje sobre hielo o diviértanse en nuestro gigantesco Parque de Diversiones, que cubre un área de 7.989,59 metros cuadrados.

Después de leer

1. Where can you eat at the **Centro Sambil**? Where can you go to a café? To a fast-food restaurant?

2. There are **plazas** or "squares" on two different levels of the shopping center; which levels are they?

3. What is your opinion of having a skating rink, an aquarium and an amusement park in a shopping mall? Which of these areas would you go to the most?

4. Is this shopping center similar to ones you have been to in the United States? How is it different?

Capítulo 17 ¿Cuánto cuesta...? **419**

Después de leer

ANSWERS

1. Eat: third level—**Libertador**
   Go to a café: second level—**Acuario**, and third level—**Libertador**
   Fast-food restaurant: fourth level, **Feria**

2. First level—**Autopista** and third level—**Libertador**

3. Answers will vary.

4. Answers will vary.

Focus on Culture

General Stores and Malls

Students' only acquaintance with a "general store" may be through television. The general store, which has a little of everything, is vanishing in favor of the mall, a massive establishment with dozens of specialty stores. Have students discuss how the growth of the mall has affected the culture. What effect has it had on personal relationships, or on the way we spend/save money? While teenagers today spend free time hanging out in the mall, what did their counterparts one hundred years ago do? What do their counterparts in less-developed cultures do today?

Analyzing

Cultural Comparisons 4.2

CAPÍTULO 18

OBJECTIVES

Functions
- Making purchases and choices
- Comparing things

Context
- Various shops (clothing and shoes)

Accuracy
- Expressions of comparison
- Expressing Equality

Pronunciation
- The consonant l

CHAPTER WARM-UP

Setting the Context

In preparation for their learning about making purchases and comparing items, have students look at the photograph on page 420 and read the caption. Ask them if they have ever bought shoes at an outdoor sale or flea market. If any students have shopped for shoes in a different country, discuss the similarities and differences in their expereiences there and in the United States. Has anyone ever engaged in bartering for an item, either in another country or in the United States? If so, have students discuss their sales transactions.

◢ Comparing and Contrasting

◯ Cultural Comparisons 4.2

¿Qué quieres comprar?

—Quiero comprar zapatos nuevos.
—Pues, éstos son bonitos y no son caros.

Objectives

- making purchases and choices
- comparing things

420 *Sexta unidad* Vamos de compras

Chapter Support Materials

- Lab Manual: pp. 119-123
- Lab Program: Cassette Side A, B; CD 9, Tracks 9-14
- TRB: Textbook Activity Masters: pp. 117-119
- Textbook Cassettes/CDs: Cassette 2, Side B; CD 3, Track 32
- Tapescript: Lab Program pp.176-182 ; Textbook Cassettes/CDs p. 218
- Middle School Activities: pp. 151-153
- Workbook for Spanish-Speaking Students
- Practice Software: Windows ™; Macintosh ®

- Testing Program: Chapter Test pp. 210-213; Answer Key & Testing Cassettes Tapescript pp. T82, T83; Oral Assessment p. T83
- Testing Cassettes: Cassette Side B
- Computerized Testing Program: Windows ™; Macintosh ®
- Video Program: Cassette 2, 1:21;44-1:28:39
- Video Guide: Videoscript pp. 78-81; Activities pp. 145-147
- **Mundos hispanos 1**
- Internet Activities: Student Text p. 434

PRIMERA ETAPA

Preparación

- What do you think the name of the store below means?
- What are some of the clothing items that are missing in the drawings?
- Do you know how to say *hat* in Spanish?
- What kinds of things do you say when you make comparisons?

"La Alta Moda"

chaqueta   camisa   blusa   vestido   abrigo

pantalones   suéter

impermeable   falda   camiseta

Hay muchas tiendas en el centro comercial.

Hoy sábado Mercedes y Sarita van de compras al centro comercial en El Paso, Texas. Ellas necesitan comprar un **regalo** para el cumpleaños de Rosa. También a ellas les gusta **ir de escaparates.**

Mercedes:	Aquí tienen **ropa** muy moderna.
Sarita:	¡Mira esta **falda azul**! ¡Qué linda!
Mercedes:	A Rosa le va a gustar ese color. Con este **cinturón negro** es muy **bonita. Creo** que le va a gustar.
Sarita:	Sí, **tienes razón.** Perfecto. Ahora yo necesito un **vestido** para mí.
Mercedes:	Aquí al frente hay una boutique muy elegante.
Sarita:	Mm… entonces, **seguro** que es cara.
Mercedes:	Vamos a ir de escaparates.

regalo *gift*   **ir de escaparates** *go window-shopping*   **ropa** *clothes*   **falda azul** *blue skirt*   **cinturón negro** *black belt*
bonita *pretty*   **creo** *I think*   **tienes razón** *you are right*   **vestido** *dress*   **seguro** *surely*

Capítulo 18 ¿Qué quieres comprar?   **421**

TEACH/MODEL

"La Alta Moda"
PRESENTATION

 TRANSPARENCIES 67 AND 67A

TEXTBOOK CASSETTE/CD CASSETTE 2, SIDE B; CD 3, TRACK 28

TAPESCRIPT P. 217

Use the transparency to present the vocabulary. Ask students about their favorite articles of clothing. Have students listen to the dialogue on the Textbook Cassettes/CDs while looking at the clothing articles shown on the transparency and on page 421. Ask a volunteer to summarize what the dialogue is about. Then have students listen to the dialogue again with their books closed. Afterwards, ask them what new vocabulary they recognized and the words and/or phrases that they do not understand.

🔺🔺 Auditory-Musical

VOCABULARY EXPANSION
Jeans are usually just called **jeans** in most Spanish-speaking countries. Other words still in use are **pantalones de vaquero, vaqueros, pantalones de mezclilla,** or **mahones.** Other useful words that students may ask about are **traje de baño, pantalones cortos, corbata, chaleco, traje,** and **traje deportivo.**

 Linguistic Comparisons 4.1

Etapa Support Materials

- Workbook: pp. 235-241
- TRB: Textbook Activity Masters: p. 117
- Textbook Cassettes/CDs: Cassette 2, Side B; CD 3, Track 28
- Tapescript: Textbook Cassettes/CDs p. 217
- Overhead Transparencies: 67, 67a, 68, 69
- Middle School Activities: pp. 154, 155
- Lesson Plan Book: pp. 103-104

- Testing Program: Quiz pp. 205-207; Answer Key & Testing Cassettes Tapescript p. T81
- Testing Cassettes: Cassette Side B
- Computerized Testing Program: Windows ™; Macintosh ®
- Atajo Writing Assistant Software: Student Text p. 427, Workbook, p. 241

Los colores

PRESENTATION

 TRANSPARENCY 68

Briefly remind students about noun-adjective agreement in Spanish before introducing the color words. Write a noun-adjective pair, such as **la casa bonita**, on the board. Have students give the plural, then change from **casa** to **libro**, then to **libros**, making the necessary agreement adjustments. Use this as a lead-in to the colors. Point out that the color words are also adjectives. Use the transparency or drawings in the text to illustrate the point.

Ask **¿De qué color es la camisa?** and answer your own question according to the color on the transparency. Then have students answer the same question as you point to different items. Continue by asking students about the colors they're wearing. Emphasize the correct noun-adjective agreements, for example, **Roberto lleva una camisa blanca.**

 Presentational Communication 1.3

VOCABULARY EXPANSION

Write the other colors on the board for classroom use: **anaranjado, violeta, rosa (rosado), gris, café (marrón).** Add the adjectives **claro** and **oscuro** and give examples of their use. Another useful color is **azul marino** (navy blue). Write the verb **llevar** on the board and tell students this is the most common one to use with clothing, but that **tener** or **usar** are also acceptable.

 Linguistic

PRACTICE / APPLY

A. ¿Qué llevan hoy?

SUGGESTION

 TRANSPARENCY 69

Play **¿Quién es?** Have students write out descriptions of their classmates based on what they're wearing. Then have them read the descriptions to the class and have the class guess who it is.

Los colores

una camisa roja

un suéter azul

una chaqueta verde

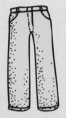

pantalones amarillos

una falda blanca

un impermeable negro

¡Te toca a ti!

A. ¿Qué llevan hoy? In your job as fashion reporter for the school newspaper, you need to know what everyone is wearing. Describe each person's outfit in the drawings that follow. Follow the model.

MODELO Luis lleva una camisa roja con unos pantalones blancos.

Luis

1. Roberta

2. Nadia

3. Alfonso

MULTIPLE INTELLIGENCES

- Linguistic: All activities
- Logical-Mathematical: I
- Bodily-Kinesthetic: A, C, G
- Auditory-Musical: **Pronunciación**, E, **Aquí escuchamos**
- Interpersonal: D

4. Arturo   5. Olga   6. Esteban

B. ¿Dónde trabajas durante las vacaciones?

You have decided to get a sales job this summer at a store in the local shopping center. Explain where you are going to work and what you are going to sell. Follow the model.

MODELO   tienda de música
Voy a trabajar en la tienda de música, y voy a vender discos compactos y cintas.

1. papelería
2. tienda de deportes
3. tienda de música
4. tienda de ropa para mujeres *(women)*
5. tienda de ropa para hombres *(men)*
6. tienda de ropa para niños *(children)*

C. ¿Qué ropa llevas a la fiesta?

You are trying to decide what to wear to a party tonight. Using the items of clothing on page 421 and your favorite colors, put together your outfit. Work with a partner and ask each other what you will be wearing. Be prepared to report back to the class. Follow the model.

MODELO   Compañero(a): *¿Qué vas a llevar a la fiesta?*
              Tú: *Voy a llevar unos pantalones negros y un suéter rojo.*

Repaso

D. En el mercado

For dinner, you need to get fruits and vegetables at the grocery store. In pairs, play the roles of the shopkeeper and the customer. Remember that all the produce is not available all year round. Before you begin, 1) make a list of what you want to buy. 2) Your partner will make a list of what is available. 3) Then make up your own conversation, following the model.

MODELO   Vendedor(a): *Buenos días, señorita (señor). ¿Qué desea?*
              Cliente: *¿Tiene fresas?*
              Vendedor(a): *Sí, ¿cuánto quiere?*
              Cliente: *Medio kilo, por favor.*
              Vendedor(a): *Aquí tiene. ¿Algo más?*

Capítulo 18 ¿Qué quieres comprar?   **423**

The Standards

- Interpersonal Communication 1.1: A, F, **Adelante** activites
- Interpretive Communication 1.2: B, C, D, E, **Aquí escuchamos**
- Cultural Practices and Perspectives 2.1: B
- Cultural Products and Perspectives 2.2: **Comentarios culturales**

POSSIBLE ANSWERS
1. Roberta lleva un vestido blanco y negro.
2. Nadia lleva una blusa azul y unos pantalones amarillos.
3. Alfonso lleva una camisa blanca, un suéter amarillo y unos pantalones verdes.
4. Arturo lleva una camiseta azul (claro) y unos jeans/pantalones azul marino.
5. Olga lleva una blusa amarilla y una falda verde.
6. Esteban lleva un traje deportivo rojo.

B. ¿Dónde trabajas durante las vacaciones?
POSSIBLE ANSWERS
1. Voy a trabajar en la papelería y voy a vender papel y lápices.
2. Voy a trabajar en la tienda de deportes y voy a vender artículos deportivos.
3. ...instrumentos musicales.
4. ...vestidos.
5. ...trajes y corbatas.
6. ...pantalones y camisetas.

C. ¿Qué ropa llevas a la fiesta?
VARIATION
Have students explain what they wear according to the weather conditions: **Está lloviendo** (*it's raining*). **Voy a llevar mi impermeable.**

 Evaluating

D. En el mercado
SUGGESTIONS

 Encourage students to use other appropriate greetings or goodbyes. Ask them to buy at least four different items and to alternate roles. Then have a few pairs of students present their mini-dialogues to the class.

 Presentational Communication 1.3

Pronunciación

SUGGESTION

 TEXTBOOK CASSETTE/CD CASSETTE 2, SIDE B; CD 3, TRACK 29

TAPESCRIPT P. 217

Have students listen to the explanation for the consonant **l** on the Textbook Cassette/CD. The speaker will model the correct pronunciation and enunciate words from **Práctica E**.

Auditory-Musical

Estructura

PRESENTATION

Begin by giving students different numbers of objects (pencils, pens, etc.) to illustrate the comparative with quantity. Then make statements such as, **Julia tiene más lápices que Felipe. Felipe tiene menos lápices que Julia.** To make the meaning clear, first count the number of objects each student has. Continue by using adjectives to compare different people. For example: **Mi mamá es más simpática que mi tía. Mi papá es más alto que sus hermanos. Mis hermanas son más altas que yo.** etc. Then present the irregular comparatives by making sentences that illustrate their use. For example: **Mi abuelo tiene 78 años y mi abuela tiene 75 años. Mi abuelo es mayor que mi abuela. Mi abuela es menor que mi abuelo. El equipo de baloncesto de Duke es mejor que el equipo de Yale.** etc. Then write a few examples on the board and point out that the adjectives must agree with the noun/person to which they refer.

Comparing and Contrasting

Visual-Spatial

PRONUNCIACIÓN THE CONSONANT **l**

The consonant **l** in Spanish is pronounced like the *l* in the English word *leak*.

Práctica

E. Escucha a tu maestro(a) cuando lee las siguientes palabras. Después repítelas para practicar la pronunciación.

1. lápiz
2. leche
3. listo
4. inteligente
5. papel
6. libro
7. luego
8. malo
9. abuela
10. fútbol

ESTRUCTURA

Expressions of comparison

Estas cintas son **más** caras **que** ésas.
These tapes are more expensive than those.

Hoy hay **menos** clientes **que** ayer.
Today there are fewer customers than yesterday.

1. The following constructions are used in Spanish to express the comparisons *more than* and *less/fewer than*, respectively:

más + *noun or adjective* + **que**	**menos** + *noun or adjective* + **que**

2. A few adjectives have an irregular comparative form and do not make comparisons using **más** or **menos**.

bueno, buen	*good*	**mejor(es)**	*better*
malo, mal	*bad, sick*	**peor(es)**	*worse*
joven	*young*	**menor(es)**	*younger*
viejo	*old*	**mayor(es)**	*older*

Estos vestidos son **mejores que** esas blusas.
These dresses are better than those blouses.

Yo soy **menor que** mi hermano.
I am younger than my brother.

Focus on Culture

Describing Seniors

In some Spanish-speaking countries, the word **viejo** is not commonly used when referring an older person because it is considered derogatory or harsh. It is often more common to hear the expression **(una persona) de edad**. In Mexico, the word **grande** is used when describing a senior citizen.

 Linguistic Comparisons 4.1

Aquí practicamos

F. ¿Qué tienes? You are in a bad mood today and disagree with everyone. Say the opposite of what you hear. Follow the model.

> **MODELO** Pedro tiene más cintas que Juan.
> *No, Pedro tiene menos cintas que Juan.*

1. Rafael tiene más dinero que José.
2. Anita tiene menos amigas que Pilar.
3. Yo tengo más paciencia que tú.
4. Tomás tiene menos camisas que Alfonso.
5. Tú tienes más faldas que yo.
6. Mi familia tiene más niños que tu familia.

G. ¿Cuál es mejor? Express which one of the two items shown in the drawings would be a better addition to your wardrobe. Follow the model.

> **MODELO** falda blanca / chaqueta verde
> *Para mí, una falda blanca es mejor que una chaqueta verde.*

1.

2.

3.

4.

5.

6.

7.

8.

Capítulo 18 ¿Qué quieres comprar? **425**

PRACTICE/APPLY

F. ¿Qué tienes?

ANSWERS

1. No, Rafael tiene menos dinero....
2. No, Anita tiene más amigas....
3. No, yo tengo menos paciencia....
4. No, Tomás tiene más camisas....
5. No, tú tienes menos faldas....
6. No, mi familia tiene menos niños....

G. ¿Cuál es mejor?

ANSWERS

Students' preferences will vary but they will be using the following articles of clothing and colors

1. una blusa/chaqueta verde, unos pantalones azules
2. una falda negra, un suéter amarillo
3. una chaqueta verde, un impermeable rojo
4. una camisa blanca, una camiseta azul
5. una blusa verde, una camiseta blanca
6. un vestido blanco y negro, unos pantalones negros
7. un cinturón rojo, un cinturón azul
8. un suéter negro, una blusa amarilla

Individual Needs

More-prepared Students
Have students give a reason for their choices. For example, **Para mí, una falda roja es mejor que una chaqueta negra porque no me gusta el negro, porque no tengo mucha ropa negra, porque nunca llevo chaqueta, porque ya tengo una chaqueta negra.**

☀ Spanish for Spanish Speakers

Idioms

Have Spanish speakers read the following expressions and ask if they are familiar with them: **Más pesado que una mosca** (Pesky as a fly)/ **Más vale tarde que nunca** (Better late than never)/ **Peor que peor** (That is even worse). Encourage students to come up with English equivalents and to use the expressions in sentences in English and Spanish.

⊕ Linguistic Comparisons 4.1

H. Mis amigos y yo

SUGGESTION

Have students work in groups of four. First have them interview each other to find out how many of the items from the activity that each one has, i.e., **¿Cuántos(as) _____ tienes?** Then have them split into pairs and write up their comparisons, e.g., **Yo tengo menos hermanas que mi amiga Ana, pero ella tiene más hermanos que Susana.** Be sure to have different pairs report back to the class with their findings.

 Interpersonal Communication 1.1
Presentational Communication 1.3

Aquí escuchamos

SUGGESTION

	TEXTBOOK CASSETTE/CD CASSETTE 2, SIDE B; CD 3, TRACK 30
	TAPESCRIPT PP. 217–218
	TRB: ACTIVITY MASTER, P. 117

After students listen to the Textbook Cassette/CD, have them prepare some of the comparisons in Spanish. This can provide a quick review and serve as a lead-in to the next activities.

Auditory-Musical

Antes de escuchar

POSSIBLE ANSWERS
color, style, price

Después de escuchar

ANSWERS
1. F. $45
2. T
3. F, the blue one is prettier
4. F. She doesn't have enough money for the blue one and will look for a less expensive one.
5. T
6. F. She likes it.
7. F. She already has one.

H. Mis amigos y yo Use the nouns provided to compare yourself to your friends. Use the expressions **más... que** and **menos... que.** Follow the model.

> **MODELO** hermanas
> Yo *tengo menos hermanas que mi amiga Ana.*

1. hermanos
2. tíos
3. amigos
4. radios
5. cintas
6. libros
7. dinero
8. bicicletas

Aquí escuchamos

¿Más o menos? *Elena and Patricia discuss several items of clothing at the store.*

Antes de escuchar Based on what you have learned in this **etapa,** what clothing qualities do you think Elena and Patricia might compare?

 A escuchar Listen twice to the conversation between Elena and Patricia before answering the true-or-false questions about it on your activity master.

Después de escuchar On your activity master, indicate whether the following statements are true or false. If a statement is false, provide the correct information.

1. Patricia sees a blue blouse that costs $50.
2. The blue blouse is more expensive than the green one.
3. The green blouse is prettier than the blue one.
4. Patricia has a lot of money and doesn't care about the cost of the blouses.
5. Elena sees some blouses on sale that cost less than the other blouses.
6. Patricia doesn't like the white blouse.
7. Patricia says that she is going to buy a black skirt.

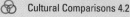

Buying Clothes

Have Spanish speakers or other student that have spent time in a Spanish-speaking country discuss buying clothing in that country. Ask them if it is different in that country/region, and if so, how? Do they think teenagers spend as much time as North American teenagers buying clothes? Is it even possible to generalize for a whole country/group of people? Based on the students' experiences, engage the whole class in a discussion comparing ways that it appears that making purchases is similar and different.

Cultural Comparisons 4.2

¡ADELANTE!

 Mis parientes Using the vocabulary that you have learned in earlier chapters, tell your classmates how many grandparents, aunts, uncles, cousins, brothers, and sisters you have. As you mention the different numbers, a classmate says that he (she) has more or fewer than you. Follow the model.

MODELO

Tú:	*Yo tengo tres hermanos.*
Compañero(a):	*Yo tengo menos hermanos que tú.*
	Tengo un hermano.

La gente (people) famosa You are a reporter for the school paper and are responsible for this month's gossip column. Imagine that you have interviewed several celebrities and are comparing their lifestyles. Choose your own celebrities and write eight comparisons. Be prepared to read them back to the class. Follow the model.

MODELO
Jay Leno tiene más _____ que David Letterman.
Paula Abdul es menos _____ que Diana Ross.

—A mi me gustan estos pantalones. ¿Y a ti?
—Me gustan, pero no quiero comprarlos ahora.

Capítulo 18 ¿Qué quieres comprar? **427**

Mis parientes
SUGGESTION
 Have students total the number of people in their families, then determine who in class has the largest and smallest family. Alternatively, you may want to draw attention to the different generations in families, having students tell how large each generation is in his (her) family, and making class comparisons of these.

 Categorizing
Comparing and Contrasting

La gente famosa
FYI
 ATAJO WRITING ASSISTANT SOFTWARE

You might want to have students use this software program when doing this activity.

Additional Practice and Recycling
FYI
 WORKBOOK, PP. 235-241

For recycling and additional practice of the vocabulary, structures, and language functions presented throughout this **etapa**, you can assign the workbook activities as in-class work and/or homework. Answers to the activities are overprinted on each page of the Teacher's Edition of the Workbook.

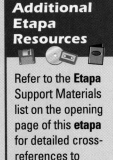

Additional Etapa Resources

Refer to the **Etapa** Support Materials list on the opening page of this **etapa** for detailed cross-references to these assessment options.

TEACH/MODEL

Zapatería "El Tacón"

PRESENTATION

 TRANSPARENCIES 70 AND 70A

Use the transparency to point out the different items in the zapatería. Ask questions such as, **¿Qué llevas hoy—zapatos o botas? ¿Zapatos de tenis o sandalias? ¿Zapatos de tacón o botas? ¿Calcetines o medias? ¿Una bolsa de cuero o una mochila?**

Interpersonal Communication 1.1
Interpretive Communication 1.2

EXPANSION

Reinforce new vocabulary by pointing to what different students are wearing. Then ask general questions using the new words.

SEGUNDA ETAPA

Preparación

- Where do you usually go to buy shoes?
- What kind of shoes do you like to wear most?
- What questions do you usually ask at a shoe store?

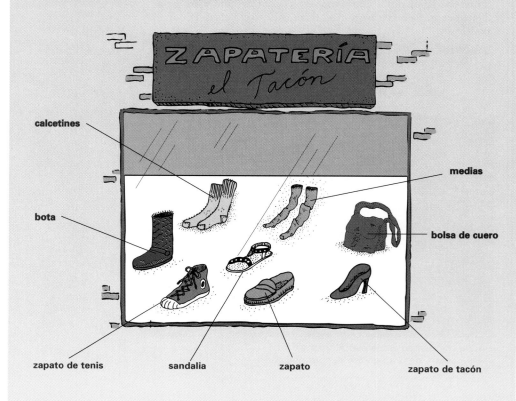

Zapatería "El Tacón"

*¿Qué puedes comprar en una **zapatería** (shoe store)?*

calcetines

medias

bota

bolsa de cuero

zapato de tenis   sandalia   zapato   zapato de tacón

428 *Sexta unidad* Vamos de compras

Etapa Support Materials

- Workbook: pp. 242-246
- TRB: Textbook Activity Masters: pp. 118, 119
- Textbook Cassettes/CDs: Cassette 2, Side B; CD 3, Track 31
- Tapescript: Textbook Cassettes/CDs p. 218
- Overhead Transparencies: 70, 70a, 71
- Middle School Activities: pp. 156, 157
- Lesson Plan Book: pp. 105-106

- Testing Program: Quiz pp. 208, 209; Answer Key & Testing Cassettes Tapescript pp. T81, T82
- Testing Cassettes: Cassette Side B
- Computerized Testing Program: Windows ™; Macintosh ®
- Atajo Writing Assistant Software: Student Text p. 434

¡Te toca a ti!

A. En la zapatería You need to get some new shoes. When the clerk asks you, tell him (her) what you want to see. Take turns with a partner in playing the role of the clerk. Follow the model.

> **MODELO**
>
> Empleado(a): *¿En qué puedo servirle?*
> Cliente: *Quisiera ver unos zapatos de tacón.*

B. ¿Qué número? Now repeat Activity A and give your shoe size to the clerk. Use your European size. Refer to the chart on page 431 for sizes. Follow the model.

> **MODELO**
>
> Empleado(a): *¿En qué puedo servirle?*
> Cliente: *Quisiera ver unos zapatos de tenis.*
> Empleado(a): *¿Qué número?*
> Cliente: *Cuarenta y tres, por favor.*

Repaso

C. La ropa de María y de Marta Use the information in the following chart to make comparisons between María's and Marta's clothes. Use the expressions for comparison **más... que** and **menos... que.** Follow the model.

> **MODELO** *María tiene menos camisetas que Marta.*

	María	Marta
Camisetas	5	6
Faldas	2 faldas cortas 1 falda larga 2 faldas negras	1 falda azul 1 falda amarilla
Vestidos	1 vestido de fiesta 1 vestido rojo 1 vestido verde	1 vestido de fiesta 4 vestidos rojos 1 vestido verde
Suéteres	5	4
Cinturones	1	3
Pantalones	4	2

Capítulo 18 ¿Qué quieres comprar? **429**

PRACTICE/APPLY

A. En la zapatería
VOCABULARY EXPANSION
Point out that in some countries, **medias** is the word most frequently used for all kinds of *socks*, and in other countries it is more common to hear **calcetines**.

 Linguistic Comparisons 4.1

B. ¿Qué número?
SUGGESTION
Quickly review numbers 10-100, counting by 10s and then by 5s, before doing Activity B.

Activating Prior Knowledge

Individual Needs

Less-prepared Students
After students have done both Activities A and B separately, have them combine the activities, asking for at least two items.

C. La ropa de María y de Marta

SUGGESTION
Tell each student to think independently of the conclusions that could be drawn about María's and Marta's clothes. Direct students to form pairs. Then tell the pairs to compare their conclusions until they agree. Tell them to take turns answering first. Ask different students at random to make statements about which person has more or less than the other.

Comparing and Contrasting

VARIATION
After students have made all possible comparisons, have them work with a partner to reach conclusions about each of the girls, e.g., **A Marta no le gustan los pantalones, le gustan los vestidos, especialmente los vestidos rojos.**

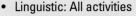

MULTIPLE INTELLIGENCES

- Linguistic: All activities
- Logical-Mathematical: C, G
- Visual-Spatial: A
- Auditory-Musical: **Aquí escucamos**
- Interpersonal: A, F, H

 The Standards

- Interpersonal Communication 1.1: C, D, **Mis parientes**
- Interpretive Communication 1.2: a, B, F, G, H, **Aquí escuchamos**
- Presentational Communication 1.3: **La vida de la gente famosa**

Estructura

PRESENTATION

Begin by making statements and asking questions comparing different students and objects in the classroom. For example: **José es alto. Enrique es alto también. José es tan alto como Enrique. María tiene tres cuadernos y Alicia tiene tres cuadernos. María tiene tantos cuadernos como Alicia.** Then write a few examples on the board and point out agreement between **tantos/tantas** and the nouns they modify.

Interpersonal Communication 1.1

PRACTICE/APPLY

D. Los gemelos

SUGGESTION

Remind students of noun-adjective agreement (especially because all examples in the activity are masculine singular) and ask personal follow-up questions illustrating different agreement possibilities: **¿Las enchiladas son tan buenas como las hamburguesas? ¿Gloria Estefan es tan guapa como Paula Abdul? ¿Los estudiantes de esta clase son tan inteligentes como los estudiantes de la otra clase de español?**

Linguistic

E. Nicolás come tanta comida como Andrés

Individual Needs

Less-prepared Students

Have students scan the activity and note whether items are masculine or feminine, singular or plural and make a note of what form of **tanto** to use in each case. Then have them do the activity.

More-prepared Students

When students have completed the activity, have them create personalized comparison questions to ask each other or the class.

Comparing and Contrasting

ESTRUCTURA

Expressing equality

El carrito de Roberto está **tan lleno como** el de Ricardo.	*Roberto's shopping cart is as full as Ricardo's.*
Margarita compra **tan frecuentemente como** Linda.	*Margarita shops as frequently as Linda.*
Este señor compró **tanta ropa como** esa señora.	*This man bought as much clothing as that woman.*
Laura alquiló **tantos vídeos como** Sonia.	*Laura rented as many videos as Sonia.*

1. To express equality in Spanish, you can use the phrase **tan... como** *(as...as)* with an adjective or an adverb.

| **tan** | + | *adjective or adverb* | + | **como** |

2. The phrase **tanto... como** *(as much/as many...as)* is used with nouns to express equality. Tanto agrees with the nouns to which it refers in gender and number.

| **tanto(a)** | + | *noun* | + | **como** |
| **tantos(as)** | + | *noun* | + | **como** |

Aquí practicamos

D. Los gemelos Because they are identical twins, Nicolás and Andrés are the same in almost every way. Compare them using the cues given. Follow the model.

> **MODELO**   alto
> *Nicolás es tan alto como Andrés.*

1. inteligente	5. interesante
2. gordo	6. simpático
3. bueno	7. guapo
4. energético	8. divertido

E. Nicolás come tanta comida como Andrés The twins' mother is always careful to serve them exactly the same amount of food. Describe what they have on their plates, using the cues that follow. Make sure to use the correct form of **tanto**. Follow the model.

430   *Sexta unidad* Vamos de compras

☀ Spanish for Spanish Speakers

Gender and Number agreement

Have Spanish speakers work on more challenging expressions of equality. Provide them with a list of nouns (including, for example, **problema/s, artista/s, idioma/s,** and **día/s**) and have them use them in sentences expressing equality: **Hablo tantos idiomas como tú.** Then ask students to come up with some of their own words that might provide a challenge. Have students engage in peer-editing and then share with the class.

Interpersonal Communication 1.1

MODELO   helado
            Nicolás tiene tanto helado como Andrés.

1. papas fritas   5. queso
2. pescado   6. fruta
3. carne   7. pastas
4. galletas   8. pollo

F. ¡Yo soy mejor que tú! Some people always think that they are the best. With a classmate, have a bragging contest. Use the cues and your imagination. Follow the model.

MODELO   mi casa / bonita
                    Tú: *Mi casa es tan bonita como la casa del presidente.*
        Compañera(o):   *No importa.* (That doesn't matter.) *Mi casa es más bonita que la casa del presidente.*

1. mis notas / altas   4. mi padre / importante
2. mi madre / inteligente   5. mi tío / rico
3. mi hermana / bonita   6. mi hermano / divertido

? ¿Qué crees?

If you went shopping in Mexico City, in which place would you bargain?

a) supermarket
b) drug store
c) open-air market
d) department store

respuesta

Comentarios CULTURALES

Tallas internacionales

Shoe sizes (**tallas**) are different in Spain and in most of Latin America from those in the United States.

Men's shoes						
U.S.	8	9	10	11	12	13
Spain	41	42	43	44	45,5	47
Women's shoes						
U.S.	4½	5½	6½	7½	8½	9½
Spain	35,5	36,5	38,5	39,5	40,5	42

Capítulo 18 ¿Qué quieres comprar?   **431**

ANSWERS
1. tantas papas fritas como
2. tanto pescado como
3. tanta carne como
4. tantas galletas como
5. tanto queso como
6. tanta fruta como
7. tantas pastas como
8. tanto pollo como

F. ¡Yo soy mejor que tú!

Individual Needs

Less-prepared Students
Help students establish the terms of comparison for each item before beginning the activity.

More-prepared Students
Have more-prepared students create at least three additional situations and compare them.

  Comparing and Contrasting

POSSIBLE ANSWERS
1. ...tan altas como las de Juan
2. ...tan inteligente como la directora
3. ...tan bonita como Cindy Crawford...
4. ...tan importante como un ministro.
5. ...tan rico como tu padre.
6. ...tan divertido como Tom Hanks

☀ Spanish for Spanish Speakers

Idioms

Have Spanish speakers and more-prepared students give the meanings of the following expressions: **Tan pronto como** (as soon as)/ **Tanto mejor** (So much the better)/ **Tanto peor** (So much the worse). Point that **mejor** and **peor** are used as nouns in these expressions and elicit from students how knowing this might help with the English equivalent. If Spanish speakers are familiar with the idioms, ask them to come up with complete sentences using them. Have the rest of the class do the same for their English equivalents.

  Linguistic Comparisons 4.1

Aquí escuchamos

TEXTBOOK CASSETTE/CD CASSETTE 2, SIDE B; CD 3, TRACK 31

TAPESCRIPT P. 218

TRB: ACTIVITY MASTER, P. 118

Antes de escuchar

POSSIBLE ANSWERS

Más cómodos, tan cómodo como, tan elegante como, tan caro (barato) como, más cara (barato), menos caro (barato), cuestan más que, cuestan menos que

Después de escuchar

ANSWERS

1. b
2. b
3. a
4. c
5. a

☞ **c**

Aquí escuchamos

¿De qué talla? *Francisco goes to the shoe store, where a clerk helps him with his requests.*

Antes de escuchar Review the expressions of comparison that you learned in this **etapa.** What kinds of comparisons do you expect Francisco and the sales clerk might make when talking about different shoes?

 A escuchar Listen twice to the conversation between Francisco and the clerk. Pay special attention to the characteristics of the shoes they are discussing, including color, price, and size.

LOS COMPAÑEROS EN EL INTERIOR

432 *Sexta unidad* Vamos de compras

Después de escuchar On your activity master, circle the letter of the correct statements, based on what you heard.

1. Francisco wants to buy . . . **a.** a pair of brown shoes. **b.** a pair of black shoes. **c.** a pair of white shoes.	4. The second pair of shoes costs . . . **a.** more than the first pair. **b.** the same as the first pair. **c.** less than the first pair.
2. The price of the first pair of shoes that the salesman brings out is . . . **a.** $85. **b.** $65. **c.** $75.	5. Francisco is most concerned about . . . **a.** the price of the shoes. **b.** the style of the shoes. **c.** the color of the shoes.
3. Francisco's shoe size is . . . **a.** 10 to 10 1/2. **b.** 9 to 9 1/2. **c.** 11 to 11 1/2.	

¡ADELANTE!

 ¿Cuánto cuesta todo esto (all this)? Work with a partner. You need new shoes, socks, and a bag for this season. You have $40 to spend. Following are the ads for two different shoe stores. Compare their prices and decide where you can get the best deals and what you can buy without going over the limit. Follow the models.

MODELOS   *Los zapatos de tacón son más caros en "La Casa del Zapato".*
Los zapatos de fiesta cuestan tanto en "La Casa del Zapato" como en la zapatería "El Tacón".

¿Cuánto cuesta todo esto?

SUGGESTION

 TRANSPARENCY 71

Before students do this activity, ask them to come up with factors they consider in making purchases and write them on the board, such as: price (**el precio**); color (**los colores**); size (**la talla**); quality (**la calidad**); brand name (**la marca de fábrica**); style (**la moda**); current possessions (**lo que ya tengo**); condition of current possessions (**condición de lo que ya tengo**); fashion (**lo que está de moda**).

VARIATION

After students have done the activity with their partner, create a *tick mark* graph on the board. Enter the two most important factors from each pair to determine the overall most important factors to students in the class when making purchases.

Categorizing
Evaluating

Comparaciones

FYI

 ATAJO WRITING ASSISTANT SOFTWARE

You might want to have students use this software program when doing this activity.

Individual Needs

More-prepared Students
Have students include their reasons for making purchases. For example, **Compro/voy a comprar pantalones vaqueros en (nombre de la tienda) porque hay más tallas y modas que en (nombre de la tienda).**

☼ Creating

Additional Practice and Recycling

FYI

📖 WORKBOOK, PP. 242-246

For recycling and additional practice of the vocabulary, structures, and language functions presented throughout this **etapa**, you can assign the workbook activities as in-class work and/or homework. Answers to the activities are overprinted on each page of the Teacher's Edition of the Workbook.

Listening Skills Development

FYI

📖 LAB MANUAL, PP. 119-123

 LAB CASSETTE SIDE A, B; CD 9, TRACKS 9-14

 TAPESCRIPT: LAB PROGRAM PP. 176-182

It is now appropriate to work through the lab manual activities and their accompanying recordings in class or in the language laboratory.

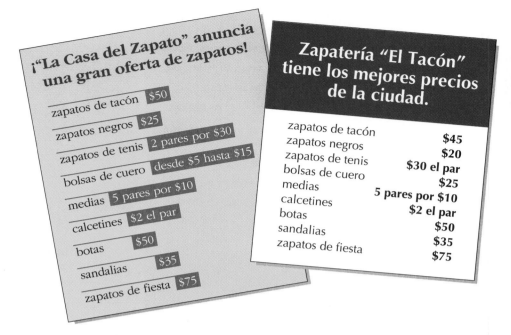

¡"La Casa del Zapato" anuncia una gran oferta de zapatos!

zapatos de tacón $50
zapatos negros $25
zapatos de tenis 2 pares por $30
bolsas de cuero desde $5 hasta $15
medias 5 pares por $10
calcetines $2 el par
botas $50
sandalias $35
zapatos de fiesta $75

Zapatería "El Tacón" tiene los mejores precios de la ciudad.

zapatos de tacón	$45
zapatos negros	$20
zapatos de tenis	$30 el par
bolsas de cuero	$25
medias	5 pares por $10
calcetines	$2 el par
botas	$50
sandalias	$35
zapatos de fiesta	$75

 Comparaciones With a partner, 1) discuss the differences between two quite different stores with which you are both familiar. Consider such factors as location (**la localización**), prices (**los precios**), service (**el servicio**), merchandise quality (**la calidad**), brand names (**las marcas**), sizes (**las tallas**), variety of departments or offerings (**la variedad disponible**), customers (**la clientela**), and background music (**la música de fondo**). 2) Make a list of at least four differences between the two stores. Use the expressions of comparison you have learned. 3) Then, decide on three items that you would prefer to purchase in each store.

EN LÍNEA

Connect with the Spanish-speaking world! Access the **¡Ya verás!** *Gold* home page for Internet activities related to this chapter.

http://yaveras.heinle.com

434 *Sexta unidad* Vamos de compras

Additional Etapa Resources

Refer to the **Etapa** Support Materials list on the opening page of this **etapa** for detailed cross-references to these assessment options.

VOCABULARIO

Para charlar	Temas y contextos	Vocabulario general
Para hacer comparaciones	**Una tienda de ropa**	**Sustantivos**
más... que	un abrigo	una boutique
menos... que	una blusa	la moda
mayor	una camisa	un regalo
mejor	una camiseta	la ropa
menor	una chaqueta	
peor	un cinturón	**Verbos**
	una falda	llevar
Para establecer igualdad	un impermeable	
tan... como	unos pantalones	**Adjetivos**
tanto(a)... como	un suéter	azul
tantos(as)... como	las tallas	blanco(a)
	un vestido	moderno(a)
		negro(a)
	Una zapatería	seguro(a)
	una bolsa de cuero	
	una bota	**Otras palabras y expresiones**
	unos calcetines	ir de escaparates
	unas medias	No importa.
	unas sandalias	
	un zapato	
	un zapato de tacón	
	un zapato de tenis	

Capítulo 18 ¿ Qué quieres comprar? **435**

CHAPTER WRAP-UP

Vocabulario

SUGGESTION

Set up a *shopping extravaganza* in the classroom. Choose several students to be salespersons in different stores (clothing store, shoe store, stationery store, sporting goods, etc.); give each salesperson a list of items and prices. These students set up the stores around the rim of the classroom; other students then go shopping. Everyone is required to make a certain number of purchases or, if you prefer, each person starts out with a specific amount of money. After a certain time for shopping, students report to the class (or to small groups) on what they bought where.

Improvised Conversation

SUGGESTION

 TEXTBOOK CASSETTE/CD CASSETTE 2, SIDE B; CD 3, TRACK 32

 TAPESCRIPT P. 218

 TRB: ACTIVITY MASTER, P. 119

 Have students listen to this conversation between two young women who are looking at dresses in a store. Ask them to listen to find out for what special occasion they need new clothes, and to try to identify words and expressions they use to express their approval or disapproval of the clothes they see.

Resource for Spanish-speaking Students

FYI

 WOKBOOK FOR SPANISH SPEAKING STUDENTS: PP. 113-118

 ANSWER KEY TO SSS WORKBOOK: PP. 33-35

Activities specially written to meet the needs of Spanish-speaking students are available in this workbook for the reinforcement and extension of the topics and language presented in this chapter.

☀ Spanish for Spanish Speakers

Keeping a Vocabulary Notebook

Remind Spanish-speaking students to add words and expressions from this vocabulary section to the problematic spelling combination categories and personal new vocabulary lists they started in their notebooks in Chapter 1. Reinforce that they should continue to do this each time a chapter in the textbook is completed.

Additional Chapter Resources

Refer to the Chapter Support Materials list on the opening page of this chapter for detailed cross-references to *¡Ya verás! Gold*'s student-centered technology components and various assessment options.

Los trajes de Guatemala

Antes de leer

POSSIBLE ANSWERS
1. Suit; bright vibrant colors
2. Answers may vary. Possible answer may be that the reading is about the typical clothing of Guatemala.

SUGGESTION

Have students learn more about the *Popol-vuh*, the sacred epic of the Mayan people, often compared to the *Odyssey* of Greece in its scope and sophistication. How have the beliefs presented there affected the development of the culture down through the ages?

Analyzing

Cultural Practices and Perspectives 2.1

ENCUENTROS CULTURALES

Los trajes de Guatemala

Reading Strategy
• Using the title and the photos to predict meaning

Antes de leer

1. Look at the title and photos. Can you guess the meaning of the word **traje**? What do you notice immediately about Guatemalan weaving?

2. Skim the first paragraph of the reading to get its gist. What do you think the reading will be about?

En los Estados Unidos la mayoría de la gente va a la tienda para comprar su ropa, pero hay muchos lugares donde la gente hace su propia ropa. Guatemala es uno de los pocos países donde la población indígena todavía usa su ropa tradicional—los típicos *trajes*—a diario. Los colores y diseños son espectaculares; representan los diferentes pueblos y más de 21 grupos lingüísticos del país. Visitar la región es como caminar entre un arcoiris humano.

El *Popol-vuh*, el libro más importante de la cultura maya, cuenta la historia de la creación de los indios Maya-Quiché. Una de las leyendas dice que cuatro dioses mantienen las esquinas del cielo. Cada esquina está identificada con un color. Para los descendientes de los antiguos Mayas los colores tienen también gran importancia, como demuestran los trajes típicos. Entre los más hermosos están los trajes de las mujeres del Nebaj, que consisten de un corte (o falda) roja y amarilla, una faja bordada, un huipil—la tradicional blusa—y un colorido adorno de cabeza.

A diferencia de la ropa masculina occidental, tradicionalmente de colores oscuros, los hombres guatemaltecos todavía usan frecuentemente sus coloridos trajes típicos. A veces es más práctico para ellos combinar los trajes con ropas modernas. Las mujeres normalmente siguen la tradición; así, podemos disfrutar de los huipiles de Santiago

436 *Sexta unidad* Vamos de compras

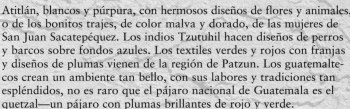

Atitlán, blancos y púrpura, con hermosos diseños de flores y animales, o de los bonitos trajes, de color malva y dorado, de las mujeres de San Juan Sacatepéquez. Los indios Tzutuhil hacen diseños de perros y barcos sobre fondos azules. Los textiles verdes y rojos con franjas y diseños de plumas vienen de la región de Patzun. Los guatemaltecos crean un ambiente tan bello, con sus labores y tradiciones tan espléndidos, no es raro que el pájaro nacional de Guatemala es el quetzal—un pájaro con plumas brillantes de rojo y verde.

Guía para la lectura

Here are some words and expressions to keep in mind as you read.

diseños	designs
arcoiris humano	human rainbow
faja bordada	embroidered sash
adorno de cabeza	headdress
oscuros	dark
tejidas	woven
malva y dorado	mauve and gold
fondos	backgrounds
franjas	fringes
plumas	feathers
ambiente	environment
labores	handiwork, needlework

Después de leer

1. What is the *Popol-vuh*? Explain how it relates to the reading.

2. How do you decide what colors to wear, and what brand of clothing to buy? Does your taste vary, or do you dress the way you did a few years ago?

3. Do you agree that western male clothing tends to be conservative? Would you like to see men wear more colorful clothing? If you are a male, would you wear a more colorful clothing? Why or why not?

4. Think of ways that people identify themselves through clothing. In Guatemala, there has sometimes been pressure for the indigenous people to abandon their traditional dress. To what extent do you think clothing is a form of self-expression? Do you feel pressure to look or dress a certain way? Do you develop opinions about people you don't know based on their clothing?

Capítulo 18 ¿Qué quieres comprar? **437**

Después de leer
POSSIBLE ANSWERS

1. Answers may vary slightly, but might include the following: Popul-vuh is the most important book in Mayan culture. It tells the creation story of the Maya-Quiche Indians. One of the legends tells about the four gods that maintain the four corners of the sky. Each corner is identified with one color. This the reason behind the importance of colors in the Mayan clothing.
2. Answers will vary.
3. Answers will vary.
4. Answers will vary.

☀ Spanish for Spanish Speakers

Typical Guatemalan Clothing

Have Spanish speakers help other students with the vocabulary and constructions in this reading, which may prove challenging for less proficient readers. Making a rough outline of traditional Guatemalan clothing might help clarify the reading. Possible headings include: Women of Nebaj; Guatemalan men; Women of Santiago Atitlán, Women of San Juan Sacatepéquez; Tzutuhil Indians; Patzun region. Under each heading write a few phrases describing the clothing of that group

🔍 Categorizing

⊛ Cultural Practices and Perspectives 2.1

¡Sigamos adelante! Resource

FYI

 LESSON PLAN BOOK P. 108

You might find it helpful to refer to the Lesson Plan Book before you and your students begin the end-of-unit materials.

 PRACTICE/APPLY

A. De compras

EXPANSION

Have students come up with their own shopping situation, using a format similar to the ones provided. Challenge students to look up new vocabulary and use it in their role plays. Ask the class to guess the vocabulary based on the context.

 Making Inferences

Auditory-Musical
Bodily-Kinesthetic

Presentational Communication 1.3

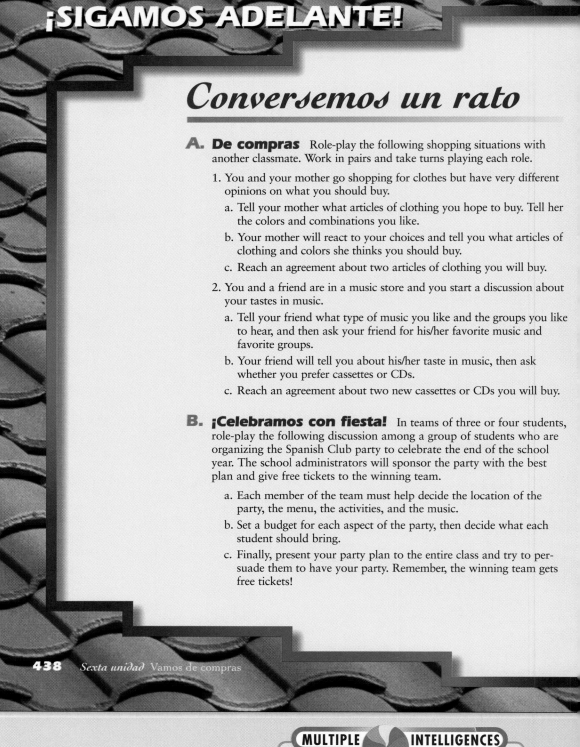

¡SIGAMOS ADELANTE!

Conversemos un rato

A. De compras Role-play the following shopping situations with another classmate. Work in pairs and take turns playing each role.

1. You and your mother go shopping for clothes but have very different opinions on what you should buy.

   a. Tell your mother what articles of clothing you hope to buy. Tell her the colors and combinations you like.

   b. Your mother will react to your choices and tell you what articles of clothing and colors she thinks you should buy.

   c. Reach an agreement about two articles of clothing you will buy.

2. You and a friend are in a music store and you start a discussion about your tastes in music.

   a. Tell your friend what type of music you like and the groups you like to hear, and then ask your friend for his/her favorite music and favorite groups.

   b. Your friend will tell you about his/her taste in music, then ask whether you prefer cassettes or CDs.

   c. Reach an agreement about two new cassettes or CDs you will buy.

B. ¡Celebramos con fiesta! In teams of three or four students, role-play the following discussion among a group of students who are organizing the Spanish Club party to celebrate the end of the school year. The school administrators will sponsor the party with the best plan and give free tickets to the winning team.

   a. Each member of the team must help decide the location of the party, the menu, the activities, and the music.

   b. Set a budget for each aspect of the party, then decide what each student should bring.

   c. Finally, present your party plan to the entire class and try to persuade them to have your party. Remember, the winning team gets free tickets!

MULTIPLE **INTELLIGENCES**

- Auditory-Musical
- Bodily-Kinesthetic
- Interpersonal

 The Standards

- Presentational Communication 1.3

Taller de escritores

Writing a composition

In this unit you will write two to three paragraphs about a purchase you have made (for yourself or as a gift), without revealing the name of the item. You will present your composition to your classmates who will try to guess the item.

> ### La compra que hice para mi abuela
>
> Mañana es el cumpleaños de mi abuela y tuve que comprar un regalo. Pensé mucho antes de decidir comprar esta cosa. A mi abuela le gustan muchas cosas pero es difícil saber exactamente lo que quiere. Hablé con ella y me dijo que tiene mucho tiempo libre. La mayoría de su familia vive lejos y lo más importante para ella es comunicarse con su familia y sus amigas. No le gusta hablar por teléfono pero le gusta recibir cartas. Por fin tuve una idea para un regalo para mi abuela. Tomé el autobús al centro comercial y fui a una papelería. ¿Sabes qué decidí comprarle?

Writing Strategy
- Asking who? what? why? when? where?

A. Reflexión Choose a purchase to describe, then ask yourself ¿quién? ¿qué? ¿por qué? ¿cuándo? ¿dónde? Try to answer these questions as you write.

B. Primer borrador Write a first draft of the composition.

C. Revisión con un(a) compañero(a) Exchange compositions with a classmate. Read each other's work and comment on it, based on these questions. What aspect of the description is the most interesting? What part is the clearest? Is the writing appropriate for its audience? Does the writing reflect the task assigned? What aspect of the composition would you like to have clarified or made more complete?

D. Versión final Revise your first draft at home, based on the feedback you received. Check grammar, spelling, punctuation, and accent marks. Bring your final draft to class.

E. Carpeta Your teacher may choose to place your work in your portfolio, display it on a bulletin board, or use it to evaluate your progress.

¡Sigamos adelante! **439**

MULTIPLE INTELLIGENCES
- Linguistic

The Standards
- Interpretive Communication 1.2

Taller de escritores Resource

FYI
 ATAJO WRITING ASSISTANT SOFTWARE

You might want to have students use this software program when writing the first draft and final version of their writing assignment. Tell them that the following language references in **Atajo** are directly related to and will be helpful to their work.

Phrases: Comparing & distinguishing; Describing objects; Describing people; Talking about past events
Vocabulary: Stores; Stores & products
Grammar: Comparisons: Adjectives; Possession with **de**; Prepositions: **para**; Verbs: Preterite

A. Reflexión
SUGGESTION
Remind students to refer for help in writing to **Vocabulario** list at the end of each chapter, as well as to the **Estructura** and **Nota gramatical** sections in the **etapas**.

B. Primer borrador
SUGGESTION
Have students discuss why it is important to keep the audience in mind when writing captions.

C. Revisión con un(a) compañero(a)
SUGGESTION
Model a peer review by showing some sample captions on a transparency and answering the six revision questions together. Remind students to include some constructive suggestions to improve the captions.

D. Versión final
SUGGESTION
Make students aware that they do not have to incorporate all the suggestions given by their classmates.

Para empezar

SUGGESTION

Ask your class if any of them have ever had to exchange currency in another country or in an international airport. Have students share their experiences with the class. If you have your own experiences or anecdotes about exchanging money in a Spanish-speaking country, share it with the class at this time.

 Connections with Distinctive Viewpoints 3.2

Conexión con la economía

El tipo de cambio

Para empezar Shopping in another country requires knowledge of that country's currency, or monetary system. The following passage discusses **el tipo de cambio**, or the exchange rate.

Before you read the passage and the accompanying chart, try to recall what you already know about exchange rates.

The basic monetary unit in the United States is the dollar. What is the basic monetary unit of England? Spain? France? Germany? Japan? For whom are exchange rates important? When do we need to know about exchange rates?

Cuando la gente quiere comprar algo en otros países es necesario cambiar la **moneda** de su país por la moneda del otro. El tipo de cambio determina el valor de la moneda de un país respecto a la moneda del otro, indicando la cantidad que se puede comprar. Por ejemplo, si se pueden cambiar 125 pesetas españolas (125 pp) por un dólar ($1) estadounidense, un español que viaja a Nueva York con 400 pesetas tiene tres dólares estadounidenses para **gastar** durante su visita. También el norteamericano que llega a Madrid con $3 sale de la casa de cambio con 400 pesetas.

El tipo de cambio varia de día en día, **basándose en** la demanda internacional de las monedas. El siguiente **esquema** indica el tipo de cambio en dólares estadounidenses del 15 de enero de 1998. Se multiplica la cantidad de moneda extranjera por el tipo de cambio del mismo país para determinar el valor en dólares (U.S.).

tipo de cambio *exchange rate*   moneda *money, currency*
gastar *to spend*   basándose en *based on*   esquema *chart*

440   *Sexta unidad* Vamos de compras

El tipo de cambio

País (moneda)	Cantidad		Tipo de cambio		Valor en dólares (U.S.)
Argentina (el peso):	100	X	1,002	=	$100,20
Canadá (el dólar):	100	X	0,696	=	$69,60
Chile (el peso):	100	X	0,0021	=	$00,21
Colombia (el peso):	100	X	0,000755	=	$00,075
Ecuador (el sucre):	100	X	0,000222	=	$00,02
España (la peseta):	100	X	0,00645	=	$00,64
Japón (el yen):	100	X	0,0076	=	$00,76
México (el peso):	100	X	0,1209	=	$12,09
Perú (el sol):	100	X	0,3675	=	$36,75
Venezuela (el bolívar):	100	X	0,0019	=	$00,19

A. La moneda Answer the following questions based on the reading.

1. ¿Cuándo es necesario cambiar la moneda de un país a otro?
2. ¿Qué determina el valor de la moneda de un país?
3. ¿Con cuánta frecuencia cambia el tipo de cambio?
4. ¿Cuál es el título del esquema?
5. ¿Cuáles son las monedas que están en más demanda?

B. ¿Cuánto valen? Reading a chart is not difficult if you approach the task in an organized way. Refer to the exchange rate chart to answer the questions.

1. ¿Qué hay en la primera columna de la izquierda del esquema? ¿la segunda? ¿la tercera? ¿la cuarta?
2. ¿Es importante el orden de las columnas del esquema? ¿Por qué?
3. ¿Cuánto valen 100 dólares canadienses en los Estados Unidos?
4. ¿Cuánto valen 100 soles peruanos en los Estados Unidos?
5. ¿Cuánto valen $12,09 (U.S.) en México?
6. ¿Cuánto valen 64 centavos (U.S.) en España?
7. Jaime tiene 200 bolívares. ¿En qué país puede gastarlos? ¿Qué monedas necesita si va a la Argentina? ¿a Chile? ¿a Colombia? ¿al Ecuador? ¿al Japón?

¡Sigamos adelante! **441**

A. La moneda
POSSIBLE ANSWERS
1. Cuando la gente quiere comparar algo en otros países es necesario cambiar la moneda de su país por la moneda del otro.
2. El tipo de cambio determina el valor de la moneda en un país respecto a la moneda del otro.
3. El tipo de cambio varia día a día, basándose en la demanda internacional de las monedas.
4. El tipo de cambio
5. El yen de Japón, el marco Alemán, el dolar de los Estados Unidos, el franco de Francia

B. ¿Cuánto valen?
ANSWERS
1. País (moneda), Cantidad, Tipo de cambio, Valor en dólares
2. Sí, es importante porque ayuda al lector a determinar fácilmente cómo se multiplica la cantidad de moneda extranjera, por el tipo de cambio del mismo país para determinar el valor en dólares (U.S).
3. $69,60
4. $36,75
5. $100 pesos
6. $100 peseta
7. Jaime puede gastarse los 200 bolívares en Ecuador o en Chile. Si va a la Argentina necesita pesos, en Chile se necesitan pesos, en Colombia se necesitan pesos, en el Ecuador se necesitan sucres, y en el Japón se necesitan yens.

The Standards

• Connections with Other Disciplines 3.1

Venezuela

FYI

To learn more about Venezuela, students can use the internet and go to *http://yaveras.heinle.com*.

TEACH/MODEL

PRESENTATION

Tell students that Venezuela is a country with a varied topography and whose rain forests are home to monkeys, anacondas, alligators, dolphins, as well as mahogany and rubber trees. It is a country rich in mineral resources, and has a great many petroleum reserves. Valuable petroleum exports have generally meant a positive trade balance for Venezuela.

Connections with Distinctive Viewpoints 3.2

Vistas
de los países hispanos

Venezuela

Capital: Caracas

Ciudades principales: Maracay, Valencia, Maracaibo, Barquisimeto

Población: 21.051.000

Idiomas: español, dialectos indígenas

Área territorial: 912.050 km^2

Clima: El clima es variado, según la altitud; con zonas de tempatura caliente y fría, varia de 18º a 29ºC

Moneda: bolívar

442 *Sexta unidad* Vamos de compras

MULTIPLE INTELLIGENCES

• Visual-Spatial

 The Standards

• Connections with Distinctive Viewpoints 3.2

El Salvador

Capital: San Salvador

Ciudades principales: Santa Ana, San Miguel

Población: 5.640.000

Idiomas: español

Área territorial: 20,752 km^2

Clima: En la meseta el clima es templado, en la costa, cálido. La temperatura media es de 24°C

Moneda: colón

meseta *plateau, tableland*

EXPLORA

Find out more about Venezuela and El Salvador! Access the **Nuestros vecinos** page on the **¡Ya verás!** *Gold* web site for a list of URLs.

http://yaveras.heinle.com/vecinos.htm

¡Sigamos adelante! **443**

 MULTIPLE **INTELLIGENCES**

• Visual-Spatial

The Standards

• Connections with Distinctive Viewpoints 3.2

El Salvador

SUGGESTION

Have students look at the photograph and discuss what they see. Tell them that this small country can be divided into three major physical regions: a tropical coastal region along the Pacific Ocean, a central upland area consisting of plateaus and valleys, and a northern mountainous region. Students might be surprised to learn that El Salvador is the most densely populated of the Latin American countries. Its most important crop is coffee, and it is one of Central America's largest producers of the crop.

Connections with Other Disciplines 3.1

New Mexico

PRESENTATION

New Mexico, nicknamed *The Land of Enchantment*, has a rich cultural history and has long been an important cultural contact point for Native Americans, Spanish, Mexican, and Anglo-American peoples. Hispanics comprise about 40% of the State's population, while Native Americans make up around 9%. Initially explored and settled by Spaniards, the area was a Spanish, and later a Mexican, territory until it was annexed by the United States in 1846.

Connections with Other Disciplines 3.1

Arizona

PRESENTATION

New Mexico's neighbor to the east, Arizona is known for its natural beauty and geological sites of interest, including the Grand Canyon and the Petrified Forest. Like New Mexico, it is also known for its rich cultural history and diverse population, as well as for its important educational and cultural institutions.

PRACTICE / APPLY

SUGGESTION

Have students work together to find out more about these Southwestern states. Suggest that they take an area of interest that they share, such as geology or art, and conduct research. Then have them present what they have learned to the class. You might want to have one section or wall of your room reserved for research so that students can learn from each other about the countries and states that are presented in the **Vistas** sections.

Presentational Communication 1.3

Vistas de los hispanos en los Estados Unidos

Arizona

Capital: Phoenix

Ciudades principales: Tucson, Mesa, Scottsdale

Población: 3.677.985

Idiomas: inglés y español

Área territorial: 295.260 km^2

Clima: árido, con una temperatura media anual de 21° C.

New Mexico

Capital: Santa Fe

Ciudades principales: Albuquerque, Las Cruces

Población: 1.515.069

Idiomas: inglés y español

Área territorial: 314.939 km^2

Clima: clima templado y semiárido, temperatura anual de 44° C (40° F) en las montañas, 18° C (64° F) en el sur.

EXPLORA

Find out more about Arizona and New Mexico! Access the **Nuestros vecinos** page on the *¡Ya verás! Gold* web site for a list of URLs.

http://yaveras.heinle.com/vecinos.htm

444 *Sexta unidad* Vamos de compras

MULTIPLE INTELLIGENCES

• Visual-Spatial

The Standards

• Connections with Distinctive Viewpoints 3.2

En la comunidad

Yolanda Miller: representante de tus derechos

"*When you go into a department store or a supermarket, you're probably thinking about what you're about to buy rather than how it came to be in the store in the first place. In my job, however, I'm focused on what's behind the scenes—who worked to make the dress you're buying or who stocked the shelves in the grocery store. I'm a union lawyer for the National Labor Relations Board, or NLRB, and it's my job to protect people's rights.*

I work out of Newark, New Jersey, where there's a large Spanish-speaking population. Because I speak Spanish, most of my caseload is Hispanic. My clients work in many different settings; from the clothing construction factories to the theater district of New York. It's my responsibility to enforce federal laws and help these workers be informed of their rights. That includes everything from the hours they work and the benefits they receive to their right to unionize. I also see to the environment in which they work. I ensure that their working conditions are safe and healthy.

My work is challenging and at times frustrating, but also deeply satisfying. Everything I studied in law school has now come to life in the faces of the people I represent."

¡Ahora te toca a ti!

Take a simple food or object you use on a daily basis. Try to trace its origins. For example, if you chose a loaf of bread, try to find out what went into getting that bread to your table. Who put the bread on the shelf in the store? Who delivered the bread to the store? Who made the bread? Where did the flour come from? Where did the other ingredients come from? Do as much research as you can on your one item, then draw a diagram showing sequence of events which resulted in your being able to use the product you chose. In Spanish, explain your diagram to the class.

Investigate volunteer organizations in your community. Write a brief paragraph in Spanish describing a volunteer activity that interests you. If you wish, do some volunteer work for the organization you have chosen.

MULTIPLE INTELLIGENCES

• Interpersonal

The Standards

• Connections In and Beyond School 5.1

En la comunidad

SUGGESTION

Have students discuss other kinds of jobs involving the law where a second language is necessary or useful. Examples might include: court interpreter, guard, paralegal, or public safety officer.

¡Ahora te toca a ti!

SUGGESTION

Have two students work on the same kind of food or item, but have them choose two different brands (for example, shoe brands). When they have finished their project, have the two students come together and compare and contrast what they discovered.

Comparing and Contrasting

Reading Strategies

The chapter references in parentheses indicate the **Encuentros culturales** sections in which the strategies are used.

Predicting/Previewing

When you predict, you draw on what you already know about a topic, person, or event. Using what you already know helps you make a logical prediction which, in turn, helps you to focus on the material you are reading. You make a prediction, and then you read to check if your prediction is correct. Previewing is looking over the whole reading before you start to read it. This will help you get a sense of what the reading may be about before you begin to read it. The following reading strategies covered in your textbook are related to predicting and previewing.

Activating background and/or prior knowledge

Recalling what you already know or have personally experienced about the reading's topic (Chapters 6-14, Chapters 16-18)

Examining format for content clues

Looking closely at the shape, size, general makeup, and organization of the reading to determine the kind of text it is (for example, an advertisement, a brochure, or a calendar or a description, a comparison, or a narration) and using that knowledge to predict the kinds of information it will include (Chapters 1 & 2, Chapter 8, Chapter 14, Chapter 18)

Scanning for specific information

Searching quickly for some particular piece(s) of information in the reading such as names, dates, and numbers (Chapters 1 & 2, Chapter 5, Chapter 7, Chapter 9, Chapter 12, Chapters 14-18)

Skimming for the gist

Rapidly running your eyes over the reading to see what the overall topic and ideas are and to determine what kind of text it is (Chapters 1-3, Chapter 11, Chapter 18)

Using photos, artwork, and/or illustrations to predict meaning and/or content

Examining the pictures and graphic elements that accompany or make up the reading and making logical guesses about what the text will be about (Chapters 4-6, Chapter 10, Chapter 13, Chapters 15 and 16)

Using the title and the photos, artwork, and/or illustrations to predict meaning and/or content

In combination with the title, examining the pictures and/or graphic elements that accompany or make up the reading to make logical guesses about what the text will be about (Chapter 3, Chapter 9, Chapter 18)

Using the title to predict meaning and/or content

Looking at the reading's title and making logical guesses about what the text will be about (Chapters 12 & 13, Chapter 15, Chapter 17)

Cognate Recognition

Cognates are words that are spelled similarly in two languages and share the same meaning. For example, the Spanish words **hospital, universidad,** and **moderno** are cognates of the English words hospital, university, and modern. There are cognates, however, whose meanings are not what they at first appear to be. For instance, **lectura** in Spanish means reading, not lecture. This type of word is called a false cognate. Looking for cognates and being aware of false cognates will help you understand more easily what you read.

Recognizing cognates

Purposely searching the reading for Spanish words that look like English words and using them to guess at meaning (Chapters 1 & 2, Chapter 5, Chapters 15 & 16)

Writing Strategies

The unit references in parentheses indicate the **Taller de escritores** *section in which the strategy is used.*

Asking who? what? why? *(Unit 6)*

Group brainstorming using clusters *(Unit 3)*

Individual brainstorming using clusters *(Unit 4)*

List writing *(Unit 1, Unit 2)*

Making an outline *(Unit 5)*

Glossary of functions

The numbers in parentheses refer to the chapter in which the word or phrase may be found.

Greeting / taking leave of someone

¡Hola! *(1)*
Buenos días. *(1,2)*
Buenas tardes. *(1)*
Buenas noches. *(1)*
¿Cómo estás? *(1)*
¿Cómo está(n) Ud(s).? *(2)*
¿Cómo te va? *(1)*
¿Qué tal? *(1)*
Muy bien, gracias. *(1,2)*
Bien gracias. ¿Y tú? *(1)*
(Estoy) bien, gracias. ¿Y Ud.? *(2)*
Más o menos. *(1)*
Adiós. *(1)*
Chao. *(1)*
Hasta luego. *(1)*
Saludos a tus padres. *(2)*

Introducing someone

Te presento a… *(1)*
Quisiera presentarle(les) a… *(2)*
Mucho gusto. *(1)*
Encantado(a). *(2)*
Me llamo… *(4)*
Se llama… *(6)*

Being polite

Por favor… *(1)*
(Muchas) gracias. *(1)*
De nada. *(1)*
Sea(n) Ud(s). … *(8)*
Vaya(n) Ud(s). … *(8)*

Talking about preferences

(No) me / te / le / les / nos gusta(n). *(1,16)*
Me / te / le / les / nos encanta(n). *(16)*
¿Cuál quieres? *(17)*
¿Cuál prefieres? *(17)*
¿Qué te gusta más? *(5)*
Me gusta más… *(5)*
Prefiero… *(11)*
Sí, tengo ganas de… *(10,15)*

Ordering / taking orders for food or drink

Vamos al café. *(1)*
Vamos a tomar algo. *(1)*
¿Qué van a pedir? *(3)*
¿Qué desea(n) tomar? *(1)*
¿Y Ud.? *(1)*
Yo quisiera… *(1)*
Voy a comer… *(1)*
Para mí… *(1)*
Aquí tiene(n). *(1)*
¡Un refresco, por favor! *(1)*

Commenting about food

¡Qué bueno(a)! *(3)*
¡Qué comida más rica! *(3)*
¡Qué picante! *(3)*
¡Es riquísimo(a)! *(3)*
¡Es delicioso(a)! *(3)*

Identifying personal possessions

¿De quién es / son? *(4)*
Es / Son de… *(4)*

Getting information about other people

¿De dónde eres / es? *(3)*
¿Dónde vive? *(6)*
¿Cuántos(as)… ? *(6)*
¿Por qué… ? *(6)*
¿Qué… ? *(6)*
¿Quién… ? *(3,6)*
¿Cómo es / son? *(6)*
Está casado(a) con… *(6)*
¿Cuántos años tienes? *(7)*
Tiene… años. *(7)*
Vive en… *(4)*
Es de… *(3)*
Pregúntales a los otros. *(12)*

Expressing frequency / time

a menudo *(7)*
de vez en cuando *(7)*
en otra oportunidad *(7)*

nunca (7)
rara vez (7)
una vez al año (9)
algún día (12)
como de costumbre (11)
una vez (17)
cada domingo (6)
todos los días (6)
la semana entera (11)
por unos minutos (13)
　　una hora (13)
　　un día (13)
　　dos meses (13)
　　tres años (13)

Telling time

¿Qué hora es? (9)
¿A qué hora? (9)
¿Cuándo? (9)
a las cinco de la mañana (9)
a la una de la tarde (9)
desde... hasta... (9)
entre... y... (9)
al mediodía (9)
a la medianoche (9)
ahora (9)

Asking for / giving directions

¿Cómo llego a... ? (8)
¿Dónde está... ? (8)
¿Está lejos / cerca de aquí? (8)
Allí está... (3)
Cruce la calle... (8)
Doble a la derecha. (8)
　　a la izquierda. (8)
Está al final de... (8)
　　al lado de... (8)
　　cerca de... (8)
　　delante de... (8)
　　detrás de... (8)
　　entre... y... (8)
　　en la esquina de... (8)
　　frente a... (8)
　　lejos de... (8)
Tome la calle... (8)
Siga derecho por... (8)

Making plans to go out / to go into town

¿Quieres ir conmigo? (10)
¿Para qué? (10)
Tengo que... (10)
¿Cuándo vamos? (10)
¿Cómo vamos? (12)
¿Adónde vamos? (7)
Vamos a dar un paseo. (10)
　　hacer un mandado. (10)
　　ir de compras. (10)
　　ver a un amigo. (10)
Vamos en autobús. (10)
　　a pie. (10)
　　en bicicleta. (10)
　　en coche. (10)
　　en metro. (10)
　　en taxi. (10)
Vamos hoy. (10)
　　esta mañana / tarde / noche. (10)
　　mañana. (10)
　　mañana por la mañana. (10, 11)
　　el sábado por la noche. (10, 11)
¿Cuánto tarda en llegar a... ? (12)
Tarda diez minutos, como máximo. (12)

Taking the subway

Por favor, un billete sencillo. (11)
　　un billete de diez viajes. (11)
　　un metrotour de tres días. (11)
　　un metrotour de cinco días. (11)
　　una tarjeta de abono transportes. (11)
　　un plano del metro. (11)
¿Dónde hay una estación de metro? (11)
¿Dónde bajamos del tren? (11)
Bajamos en... (11)
Cambiamos en... (11)
¿En qué dirección... ? (11)
¿Qué dirección tomamos? (11)
una línea (11)

Making travel plans

Quiero planear un viaje. (12)
Aquí estoy para servirles. (12)
¿En qué puedo servirles? (12)
¿Cuánto cuesta un viaje de ida y vuelta? (12)
　　　　　　en avión? (12)
Es mucho—sólo tengo... pesetas. (12)
Tengo que hacer las maletas. (13)

Glossary of functions　　**449**

Talking about the past

el año pasado (13)
el mes pasado (13)
la semana pasada (13)
el fin de semana pasado (13)
el jueves pasado (13)
ayer por la mañana (13)
    por la tarde (13)
ayer (13)
anoche (13)
anteayer (13)
¿Cuánto hace que (no te veo)? (14)
Hace (5 años) que (no te veo). (14)
(José,) (no te veo) hace (5 años). (14)

Talking about the present

Nos vamos ahora. (15)
    ahora mismo. (15)
    en este momento. (15)
Estoy comiendo (estudiando, etc.). (15)

Talking about the future

Pienso ir a... (11, 15)
Espero hacer un viaje a... (13)
Quiero... (15)
Quisiera... (15)
Tengo ganas de... (15)
Voy a... (7)
Vamos a ir de viaje esta semana. (11)
    este año. (11)
    este mes. (11)
    la semana próxima. (11)
    el mes próximo. (11)
    el año próximo. (11)
    mañana por la tarde. (10, 11)

Expressing wishes and desires

Quiero... (11, 15)
Tengo ganas de... (10, 15)
Espero... (12, 15)
Quisiera... (15)

Making purchases

¿Cuánto cuesta(n)? (16)
¿Qué precio tiene(n)? (16)
¿No está en oferta? (16)
A ver. (16)
¡Super! (16)
A sus órdenes. (16)
Aquí tiene(n). (16)

¿Cuántos hay? (4)
¿Dónde hay... ? (4)
Aquí hay otro(a)... (3)
No hay más. (16)
¡Qué pena! (16)
Voy a llevar... (16)
(Tiene Ud.) buen ojo. (17)
¿Qué necesita(n)? (16)
Necesito(amos) un atado de... (17)
    una botella de... (17)
    una docena de... (17)
    50 gramos de... (17)
    un (medio) kilo de... (17)
    una libra de... (17)
    un litro de... (17)
    un paquete de... (17)
    un pedazo de... (17)
¿Algo más? (16)
Es todo por hoy. (16)

Making comparisons

mayor que... (18)
peor que... (18)
mejor que... (18)
menor que... (18)
menos... que... (18)
más... que... (18)
tan / tanto... como... (18)

Expressing disbelief

¿Verdad? (2)
¿No? (2)

Making plans to meet

¿Dónde nos encontramos? (9)
¿A qué hora nos encontramos? (9)
De acuerdo. (9)
¡Claro (que sí)! (5, 10)
Sí, puedo. (10)
No, no puedo. (10)
Lo siento. (7)
Es imposible. (10)

Answering the telephone

¡Bueno! (7)
¡Hola! (7)
¡Diga! (7)
¡Dígame! (7)

Regular Verbs

SIMPLE TENSES

Infinitive	Present Indicative	Preterite	Commands	Infinitive	Present Indicative	Preterite	Commands
hablar	hablo	hablé		**aprender**	aprendo	aprendí	aprende
to speak	hablas	hablaste	habla	to learn	aprendes	aprendiste	(no aprendas)
	habla	habló	(no hables)		aprende	aprendió	aprenda
	hablamos	hablamos	hable		aprendemos	aprendimos	aprendan
	habláis	hablasteis	hablen		aprendéis	aprendisteis	
	hablan	hablaron			aprenden	aprendieron	
vivir	vivo	viví	vive				
to live	vives	viviste	(no vivas)				
	vive	vivió	viva				
	vivimos	vivimos	vivan				
	vivís	vivisteis					
	viven	vivieron					

COMPOUND TENSES

Present progressive	estoy estás está estamos estáis están }	hablando aprendiendo viviendo	

Stem-Changing Verbs

SIMPLE TENSES

Infinitive Present Participle Past Participle	Present Indicative	Commands
pensar *to think* e → ie pensando pensado	**pienso** **piensas** **piensa** pensamos pensáis **piensan**	**piensa** **no pienses** **piense** **no penséis** **piensen**

Change of Spelling Verbs

SIMPLE TENSES

Infinitive Present Participle Past Participle	Present Indicative	Preterite
comenzar (e → ie) *to begin* z → c **before e** comenzando comenzado	comienzo comienzas comienza comenzamos comenzáis comienzan	**comencé** comenzaste comenzó comenzamos comenzasteis comenzaron

Infinitive Present Participle Past Participle	Present Indicative	Preterite
pagar *to pay* g → gu **before e** pagando pagado	pago pagas paga pagamos pagáis pagan	**pagué** pagaste pagó pagamos pagasteis pagaron

Infinitive Present Participle Past Participle	Preterite
tocar *to play* c → que **before e** tocando tocado	**toqué** tocaste tocó tocamos tocasteis tocaron

SIMPLE TENSES

Infinitive / Present Participle / Past Participle	Present Indicative	Preterite	Commands
andar *to walk* andando andado		anduve anduviste anduvo anduvimos anduvisteis anduvieron	
estar *to be* estando estado	estoy estás está estamos estáis están	estuve estuviste estuvo estuvimos estuvisteis estuvieron	está (no estés) esté estén
hacer *to make, do* haciendo hecho	hago haces hace hacemos hacéis hacen	hice hiciste hizo hicimos hicisteis hicieron	haz (no hagas) haga hagan
ir *to go* yendo ido	voy vas va vamos vais van	fui fuiste fue fuimos fuisteis fueron	ve (no vayas) vaya id (no vayáis) vayan
poder *can, to be able* pudiendo podido	puedo puedes puede podemos podéis pueden		
ser *to be* siendo sido	soy eres es somos sois son		sé (no seas) sea sean
tener *to have* teniendo tenido	tengo tienes tiene tenemos tenéis tienen	tuve tuviste tuvo tuvimos tuvisteis tuvieron	ten (no tengas) tenga tened (no tengáis) tengan
querer *to like* queriendo querido	quiero quieres quiere queremos queréis quieren		

Glossary

Spanish-English

The numbers in parentheses refer to the chapters in which active words or phrases may be found.

A

a to (1)
  a menudo frequently, often (7)
  a pesar de in spite of
  a pie on foot, walking (10)
  ¿A qué hora? At what time? (9)
  a veces sometimes (1)
  A ver. Let's see. (16)
  al final de at the end of (8)
  al lado de beside, next to (8)
abrazo *m.* embrace, hug (1)
abrigo *m.* coat (18)
abogado(a) *m. (f.)* lawyer (3)
abuela *f.* grandmother (6)
abuelo *m.* grandfather (6)
aburrido(a) bored, boring (6)
acabar de... to have just . . . (2)
acción *f.* action (9)
aceite *m.* oil (17)
aceite de oliva *m.* olive oil
aceituna *f.* olive (2)
acontecimiento *m.* event
¡adelante! go ahead!
además besides (17)
adiós good-bye (1)
adivino(a) *m. (f.)* fortune-teller
¿adónde? where? (7)
adverbio *m.* adverb (1)
aeropuerto *m.* airport (7)
aficionado(a) *m. (f.)* (sports) fan
agua *f.* water (1)
aguacate *m.* avocado (17)
ahora now (9)
  ahora mismo right now (15)
al contraction of **a + el** (7)
alcanzar to reach
alemán (alemana) *m. (f.)* German (3)
Alemania Germany (3)
alfombra *f.* rug, carpet (4)
algo something (1)
alguno(a) some, any
  algún día someday (12)
alimento *m.* food (17)
almorzar to have lunch (12)
alpinismo *m.* mountain climbing; hiking (14)
alquilar un vídeo to rent a video (13)

alrededor around
alto(a) tall (6)
alumno(a) *m. (f.)* student (4)
allá over there (17)
allí there (4)
amarillo(a) yellow (17)
americano(a) *m. (f.)* American (3)
amigo(a) *m. (f.)* friend (1)
andar to go along, walk (13)
animal *m.* animal (5)
anoche last night (13)
anteayer the day before yesterday (13)
antes before (12)
antipático(a) disagreeable (6)
anunciar to announce (9)
anuncio *m.* advertisement
año *m.* year (11)
apartamento *m.* apartment (4)
apellido *m.* last name (6)
aprender to learn (5)
aquel(la) that (17)
aquél(la) *m. (f.)* that one (17)
aquí here (1)
  aquí hay here is/are (2)
Argentina Argentina (3)
argentino(a) *m. (f.)* Argentine (3)
arquitecto(a) *m. (f.)* architect (3)
arroz *m.* rice (3)
arte *m.* or *f.* art (5)
asistir a to attend (13)
atado *m.* bunch (17)
atún *m.* tuna (17)
aunque although
autobús *m.* bus (4)
  estación de autobuses *m.* bus terminal (7)
ave *f.* bird, fowl
avión *m.* plane (12)
ayer yesterday (13)
ayuda *f.* help (8)
ayudar to help
azúcar *m.* sugar (17)
azul blue (18)

B

bailar to dance (1)
baile *m.* dance (9)
  baile folklórico *m.* folk dance (9)

  baile popular *m.* popular dance (9)
bajar to go down, to lower, to get off a train (11)
bajo(a) short (6), *prep.* under
banana *f.* banana (11)
banco *m.* bank (7)
barato(a) cheap (11)
barco *m.* boat
barrio *m.* neighborhood (7)
barro *m.* clay
básquetbol *m.* basketball (5)
bastante enough (1)
  Bastante bien. Pretty good. (1)
batalla *f.* battle
beber to drink (5)
bebida *f.* drink (1)
béisbol *m.* baseball (5)
belleza *f.* beauty
beso *m.* kiss (5)
biblioteca *f.* library (7)
bicicleta *f.* bicycle (4)
bien well, fine; very (1)
bienvenido(a) welcome (3)
billete *m.* ticket (11)
  billete de diez viajes *m.* ten-trip ticket (11)
  billete de ida y vuelta *m.* round-trip ticket (12)
  billete sencillo *m.* one-way ticket (11)
biología *f.* biology (5)
blanco white (18)
blusa *f.* blouse (18)
bocadillo *m.* sandwich (French bread) (1)
bocina *f.* speaker (4)
bolígrafo *m.* ball-point pen (4)
Bolivia Bolivia (3)
boliviano(a) *m. (f.)* Bolivian (3)
bolsa *f.* purse (18)
bonito(a) pretty (6)
borrador *m.* eraser (4)
bota *f.* boot (18)
botella *f.* bottle (1)
boutique *f.* boutique (18)
bucear to snorkel, dive (14)
buceo *m.* snorkeling, diving (14)
bueno(a) good (3)
  Buenas noches. Good evening. / Good night. (1)
  Buenas tardes. Good afternoon. (1)

¡Bueno! Hello? (answering the phone) (7)

Buenos días. Good morning. (1)

burbuja *f.* bubble

buscar to look for (8)

C

caballo *m.* horse

cacahuete *m.* peanut (2)

cada each, every (6)

caer to fall

café *m.* café, coffee (1)

calamares *m.* squid (2)

calcetín *m.* sock (18)

calculadora *f.* calculator (4)

calidad *f.* quality

caliente hot (1)

calle *f.* street (8)

cama *f.* bed (4)

cámara *f.* camera (4)

camarero(a) *m. (f.)* waiter (waitress) (1)

cambiar to change (11)

cambio *m.* change, alteration (12)

caminar to walk (13)

caminar en la playa to walk on the beach (14)

camisa *f.* shirt (18)

camiseta *f.* T-shirt (18)

campaña *f.* campaign

campo *m.* country (vs. city)

Canadá Canada (3)

canadiense *m.* or *f.* Canadian (3)

canción *f.* song

cansado(a) tired (9)

cantante *m.* or *f.* singer

cantar to sing (1)

cantidad *f.* quantity (17)

carne *f.* meat (3)

carnicería *f.* butcher shop (7)

caro(a) expensive (16)

carrera *f.* career

carrito *m.* shopping cart (17)

carta *f.* letter

cartera *f.* wallet (4)

casa *f.* house (4)

casado(a) married (6)

casi almost†

catedral *f.* cathedral (7)

catorce fourteen (4)

cazar to hunt

cebolla *f.* onion (17)

celebrar to celebrate (9)

cenar to have supper (13)

centro *m.* center, downtown (4)

centro comercial shopping center (16)

cerca (de) near, close to (7)

cerrar to close

¡Chao! Bye! (1)

chaqueta *f.* jacket (18)

charlar to chat (1)

chico(a) *m. (f.)* boy (girl)

chile *m.* hot pepper (3)

Chile Chile (3)

chileno(a) *m. (f.)* Chilean (3)

China China (3)

chino(a) *m. (f.)* Chinese (3)

chocolate *m.* chocolate (1)

chorizo *m.* sausage (2)

ciclismo *m.* cycling (14)

cien one hundred (7)

ciencia *f.* science (5)

ciento one hundred (12)

cinco five (4)

cincuenta fifty (7)

cine *m.* movie theater (7)

cinta *f.* tape (cassette) (4)

cinturón *m.* belt (18)

cita *f.* date, appointment (10)

ciudad *f.* city (6)

¡Claro! Of course! (5)

¡Claro que sí! Of course! (reaffirmed) (10)

cliente *m.* customer (17)

club *m.* club (7)

coche *m.* car (4)

cola *f.* tail

colegio *m.* school (7)

Colombia Colombia (3)

colombiano(a) *m. (f.)* Colombian (3)

comedor *m.* dining room

comentar to comment (3)

comentario *m.* commentary

comer to eat (1)

comida *f.* food, meal (1)

comida mexicana Mexican food (3)

como how, as, like (11)

como de costumbre as usual (11)

¿cómo? how?, what? (3)

¿Cómo es? / son? How is it / are they? (6)

¿Cómo está Ud.? How are you? (formal) (2)

¿Cómo estás? How are you? (informal) (1)

¿Cómo te llamas? What's your name? (4)

¿Cómo te va? How is it going? (1)

cómoda *f.* dresser (4)

compañía *f.* company (3)

comparación *f.* comparison (18)

compartir to share (5)

comprar to buy (13)

comprender to understand (5)

computadora *f.* computer (4)

con with (1)

concierto *m.* concert (13)

concurso de poesía *m.* poetry contest (9)

congelado(a) frozen (17)

conmigo with me (10)

conserva *f.* preserve, canned good (17)

construir to build

contador(a) *m. (f.)* accountant (3)

contar to tell, to count (4)

contento(a) happy (9)

contestar to answer (1)

continuar to continue (9)

contra against

conversación telefónica *f.* telephone conversation (7)

corazón *m.* heart

correr to run (5)

corto short (in length)

cosa *f.* thing (4)

Costa Rica Costa Rica (3)

costarricense *m.* or *f.* Costa Rican (3)

costumbre *f.* custom

crema *f.* cream (17)

croissant *m.* croissant (1)

cruzar to cross (8)

cuaderno *m.* notebook (4)

cuadrado *m.* square

¿cuál? which? (17)

cualquier any (13)

¿cuándo? when? (9)

¿cuántos(as)? how many? (6)

¿Cuántos años tienes? How old are you? (7)

¿Cuánto cuesta(n)? How much is it (are they)? (16)

¿Cuántos hay? How many are there? (4)

cuarenta forty (7)

cuarto *m.* room (4)

cuatro four (4)

cuatrocientos(as) four hundred (12)

Cuba Cuba (3)

cubano(a) *m. (f.)* Cuban (3)

cuero *m.* leather (18)

cuerpo *m.* body

D

dar to give (8)
de of (3)
    de acuerdo OK (we are in agreement) (9)
    de costumbre usually (15)
    ¿De dónde es (eres)? Where are you from? (3)
    De nada You're welcome. (1)
    ¿De quién es... ? Whose is it? (4)
    de vez en cuando from time to time (7)
deber to owe, must, should (10)
decir to say (10)
dejar to leave, to relinquish
del contraction of **de + el** (8)
delante de in front of (8)
delgado(a) thin (6)
delicioso(a) delicious (3)
demás rest, remaining
dentista *m.* or *f.* dentist (3)
dentro inside
deporte *m.* sport (5)
deportista sportsman, sportswoman
derecha right (8)
derecho(a) straight (8)
desahogar to ease pain
desayunar to eat breakfast (13)
desayuno *m.* breakfast (1)
descansar to rest (9)
desconocido(a) unknown
desde from (9)
desear to want, wish for (1)
desempleo *m.* unemployment
desfile *m.* parade (9)
desierto *m.* desert
despacio slow (8)
despedirse to say good-bye (1)
después de after (1)
detrás de behind (8)
día *m.* day (10)
    Día de la Independencia *m.* Independence Day (9)
dibujo *m.* drawing
    dibujos animados animated film, cartoon
dieciseis sixteen (4)
diecisiete seventeen (4)
dieciocho eighteen (4)
diecinueve nineteen (4)
diez ten (4)
¡Diga! / ¡Dígame! Hello? (answering the phone) (7)

dinero *m.* money (2)
dirección *f.* direction, address (7)
disco compacto *m.* compact disc (4)
discoteca *f.* dance club (7)
disculparse to apologize (7)
discutir to argue (12)
disfrutar to enjoy
divertido(a) fun, amusing (6)
divorciado(a) divorced (6)
doblar to turn (8)
doce twelve (4)
docena *f.* dozen (17)
doctor(a) *m. (f.)* doctor (3)
domingo *m.* Sunday (10)
dominicano(a) *m. (f.)* Dominican (3)
¿dónde? where? (3)
    ¿Dónde está... ? Where is . . . ? (8)
    ¿Dónde hay... ? Where is / are there . . . ? (4)
dormir to sleep (15)
dos two (4)
doscientos(as) two hundred (12)
dueño(a) *m. (f.)* owner
durante during (15)

E

Ecuador Ecuador (3)
ecuatoriano(a) *m. (f.)* Ecuadoran (3)
edad *f.* age (7)
edificio *m.* building (7)
ejemplo *m.* example
    por ejemplo for example
el *m.* the (2)
él he (2)
El Salvador El Salvador (3)
ella she (2)
ellos(as) *m. (f.)* they (2)
embajador(a) *m. (f.)* ambassador, ambassadress
empezar to begin
en in (1)
    en este momento at this moment (15)
    en otra oportunidad at some other time (7)
    ¿En qué dirección? In which direction? (11)
    ¿En qué puedo servirle(s)? How can I help you (plural)? (12)
encantado(a) delighted (2)
enchilada *f.* soft, corn tortilla filled with cheese, meat, or chicken (3)
encontrar to find (9)

encontrarse (con) to meet (9)
encuesta *f.* survey (12)
enemigo(a) *m. (f.)* enemy
enfermero(a) *m. (f.)* nurse (3)
enfermo(a) sick (9)
enojado(a) angry, mad (9)
ensalada *f.* salad (17)
    ensalada de frutas *f.* fruit salad (17)
    ensalada de vegetales (verduras) *f.* vegetable salad (17)
entero whole (11)
entonces then (9)
entrada *f.* entrance ticket (11)
entre between (8)
equipo *m.* team (13)
escaparate *m.* shop window (16)
escribir to write (5)
escrito written
escritorio *m.* desk (4)
escuchar to listen (to) (1)
escuela *f.* school (4)
    escuela secundaria *f.* high school (7)
escultura *f.* sculpture (5)
ese(a) that (17)
ése(a) *m. (f.)* that one (17)
espacio *m.* space
España Spain (3)
español(a) *m. (f.)* Spaniard, Spanish (1)
especia *f.* spice
especial special (11)
especie *f.* species
esperar to hope, to wait (12)
espíritu *m.* spirit
esposa *f.* wife (6)
esposo *m.* husband (6)
esquema *m.* chart, diagram
esquí *m.* ski (16)
    esquí acuático *m.* water ski (14)
esquina *f.* corner (8)
    en la esquina de on the corner of (8)
establecer to establish (18)
estación *f.* station (7)
estacionamiento *m.* parking lot (8)
estadio *m.* stadium (7)
Estados Unidos United States (3)
estadounidense *m.* or *f.* American, from the United States (3)
estante *m.* book shelf (4)
estar to be (8)
    Está al final de... It's at the end of . . . (8)
    estar en forma to be in shape
este(a) this (17)

éste(a)   *m. (f.)*   this one   (17)
estéreo   *m.*   stereo   (4)
estrella   *f.*   star
estudiante   *m.* or *f.*   student   (3)
estudiar   to study   (1)
etapa   *f.*   stage, phase
éxito   *m.*   success
expresar   to express   (1)
expresión   *f.*   expression   (1)

F

fácil   easy
falda   *f.*   skirt   (18)
familia   *f.*   family   (6)
famoso(a)   famous   (12)
farmacia   *f.*   pharmacy, drugstore   (7)
favorito(a)   favorite   (16)
feo(a)   ugly, plain   (6)
feria   *f.*   fair   (9)
fiesta   *f.*   party   (9)
   Fiesta del pueblo   *f.*   religious festival
      honoring a town's patron saint   (9)
fin de semana   *m.*   weekend   (13)
finalmente   finally   (14)
firmar   to sign
flan   *m.*   caramel custard   (3)
flecha   *f.*   arrow
florería   *f.*   flower shop   (7)
francés (francesa)   *m. (f.)*   French   (3)
Francia   France   (3)
frecuentemente   frequently   (10)
frente a   across from, facing   (8)
fresa   *f.*   strawberry   (1)
fresco(a)   cool   (17)
frío(a)   cold   (1)
frijoles   *m.*   beans   (3)
fruta   *f.*   fruit   (17)
fuegos artificiales   *m.*   fireworks   (9)
fuerza   *f.*   strength
fútbol   *m.*   soccer   (5)
   fútbol americano   *m.*   football   (5)
futuro   *m.*   future   (15)

G

gafas   *f. pl.*   eyeglasses
galleta   *f.*   biscuit, cookie   (17)
ganar   to earn   (2)
garaje   *m.*   garage   (3)
gastar   to spend, to waste
gato   *m.*   cat   (5)
gente   *f.*   people
gimnasio   *m.*   gym   (13)

globo   *m.*   globe, sphere, balloon   (1)
gordo(a)   fat   (6)
grabadora   *f.*   tape recorder   (4)
gracia   *f.*   grace
gracias   thank you   (1)
   la misa de Acción de Gracias   *f.*
      Thanksgiving Day mass   (9)
gramo   *m.*   gram   (17)
granadina   *f.*   grenadine   (1)
grande   large, big   (6)
gratis   free
grupo   *m.*   group   (1)
guapo(a)   handsome   (6)
Guatemala   Guatemala   (3)
guatemalteco(a)   *m. (f.)*   Guatemalan   (3)
guisante   *m.*   pea   (17)
guitarra   *f.*   guitar   (14)
gustar   to like   (1)
gusto   *m.*   taste   (5)

H

habilidad   *f.*   ability
hablar   to talk   (1)
hacer   to do, to make   (10)
   hacer la cama   to make the bed   (13)
   hacer ejercicio   to exercise   (13)
   hacer las maletas   to pack   (13)
   hacer un mandado   to do an errand
      (10)
   hacer un viaje   to take a trip   (13)
hamburguesa   *f.*   hamburger   (3)
harina   *f.*   flour   (17)
hasta   until   (9)
   Hasta luego.   See you later.   (1)
hay   there is / are   (4)
helado   *m.*   ice cream   (17)
hermana   *f.*   sister   (6)
hermano   *m.*   brother   (6)
hermoso(a)   beautiful   (12)
hija   *f.*   daughter   (6)
hijo   *m.*   son   (6)
hispano(a)   *m. (f.)*   Hispanic   (9)
historia   *f.*   history, story
hoja   *f.*   leaf, piece of paper   (16)
¡Hola!   Hello!   (1)
hombre   *m.*   man   (3)
Honduras   Honduras   (3)
hondureño(a)   *m. (f.)*   Honduran   (3)
hora   *f.*   hour   (9)
horario   *m.*   schedule   (11)
horrible   horrible   (3)
hospital   *m.*   hospital   (7)
hotel   *m.*   hotel   (7)
hoy   today   (10)

I

ida y vuelta   round trip
idea   *f.*   idea   (9)
iglesia   *f.*   church   (7)
igual   equal
igualdad   *f.*   equality   (18)
Igualmente.   Likewise.   (2)
impermeable   *m.*   raincoat   (18)
imposible   impossible   (10)
indígena   native
ingeniero(a)   *m. (f.)*   engineer   (3)
Inglaterra   England   (3)
inglés (inglesa)   *m. (f.)*   Englishman
   (Englishwoman), English   (3)
inteligente   intelligent   (6)
intercambio   *m.*   exchange   (3)
interesante   interesting   (6)
invierno   *m.*   winter
invitar   to invite   (13)
ir   to go   (7)
   ir a…   to be going to . . .   (10)
   ir de camping   to go camping   (14)
   ir de compras   to go shopping   (10)
   ir de pesca   to go fishing   (14)
   Vamos a…   Let's (go) . . .   (1)
Italia   Italy   (3)
italiano(a)   *m. (f.)*   Italian   (3)
izquierda   left   (8)

J

jamón   *m.*   ham   (1)
Japón   Japan   (3)
japonés (japonesa)   *m. (f.)*   Japanese   (3)
jazz   *m.*   jazz   (5)
joven   young person   (11)
joya   *f.*   jewel
jueves   *m.*   Thursday   (10)
jugador(a)   *m. (f.)*   player
jugar   to play (a sport or game)   (11)
   jugar al baloncesto   to play basketball
      (14)
   jugar al hockey   to play hockey   (14)
   jugar al hockey sobre hierba   to play
      field hockey   (14)
   jugar al golf   to play golf   (14)
jugo   *m.*   juice   (1)
juguete   *m.*   toy
junto   together   (17)
juventud   *f.*   youth

K

kilo *m.* kilogram (17)
   medio kilo half kilo (17)
kilómetro *m.* kilometer (12)

L

la *f.* the (2)
lácteo(a) dairy (17)
   producto lácteo *m.* dairy product (17)
lápiz *m.* pencil (4)
largo long
las *f.* the (plural) (4)
lata *f.* can, tin (17)
leche *f.* milk (1)
lechuga *f.* lettuce (17)
leer to read (5)
lejos (de) far (from) (8)
lengua *f.* language; tongue (5)
levantar pesas to lift weights (14)
leyenda *f.* legend
libra *f.* pound (17)
librería *f.* bookstore (7)
libro *m.* book (4)
licuado *m.* milkshake (1)
limón *m.* lemon (1)
limonada *f.* lemonade (1)
línea *f.* line (11)
listo(a) ready (9)
litro *m.* liter (17)
llamar to call (7)
llamarse to be called (4)
   Me llamo... My name is ... (4)
   Se llama... His or her name is ... (6)
llave *f.* key (4)
llegar to arrive (8)
lleno(a) full (17)
llevar to take, carry (4)
llover to rain
los *m.* the (plural) (4)
luchar to fight
luego then, afterwards (14)
lugar *m.* place, location (7)
lunes *m.* Monday (10)
luz *f.* light

M

madre *f.* mother (6)
maíz *m.* corn (17)
mal poorly (1)

malo(a) bad (3)
mamá mother, mom (2)
mantener to maintain
mantequilla *f.* butter (1)
manzana *f.* apple (17)
mañana *f.* morning; tomorrow (10)
martes *m.* Tuesday (10)
máquina *f.* machine (4)
   máquina de escribir *f.* typewriter (4)
más more (2)
   más o menos so-so (1)
   más... que more ... than (18)
mayonesa *f.* mayonnaise (17)
mayor older (18)
mayoría *f.* majority
mecánico(a) *m. (f.)* mechanic (3)
media *f.* stocking (18)
medianoche *f.* midnight (9)
médico *m.* doctor (3)
medio(a) half (17)
medio *m.* middle, means (4)
   medio de transporte *m.* means of transportation (4)
mediodía *m.* midday, noon (9)
mejor better, best (9)
melocotón *m.* peach (1)
menor younger (18)
menos less; minus (4)
menos... que less ... than (18)
mercado *m.* market (7)
   mercado al aire libre *m.* open-air market (17)
merienda *f.* snack (1)
mermelada *f.* jelly (1)
mes *m.* month (11)
metro *m.* subway (10)
   estación de metro *f.* subway station (11)
mexicano(a) *m. (f.)* Mexican (3)
México Mexico (3)
mi(s) my (plural) (4)
mí me (1)
mientras in the meantime
miércoles *m.* Wednesday (10)
mil one thousand (12)
milla *f.* mile (12)
millón *m.* million (12)
minuto *m.* minute (14)
mirar to look at, to watch (2)
   ¡Mira! Look! (3)
mismo(a) same
mitad *f.* half
mochila *f.* knapsack (4)
moda *f.* style, fashion (18)

moderno(a) modern (18)
montar en bicicleta to ride a bicycle (13)
moreno(a) *m. (f.)* dark-haired, brunet(te) (6)
morir to die
motocicleta *f.* motorcycle (4)
muchacha *f.* young woman (4)
muchacho *m.* young man (4)
muchísimo very much (1)
mucho(a) a lot (1)
   Muchas gracias. Thank you very much. (1)
   Mucho gusto. Nice to meet you. (1)
muerte *f.* death
mujer *f.* woman (3)
mundo *m.* world
museo *m.* museum (7)
música *f.* music (1)
   música clásica *f.* classical music (5)
   música rock *f.* rock music (5)
muy very (1)
   Muy bien, gracias. Very well, thank you. (1)

N

nacer to be born
nacionalidad *f.* nationality (3)
nada nothing (13)
nadar to swim (13)
nadie nobody
naranja *f.* orange (1)
natación *f.* swimming (14)
naturaleza *f.* nature (5)
necesitar to need (2)
negocio *m. (f.)* business (3)
   hombre (mujer) de negocios *m. (f.)* businessman (businesswoman) (3)
negro black (18)
Nicaragua Nicaragua (3)
nicaragüense *m. or f.* Nicaraguan (3)
niña *f.* girl, baby
niño *m.* boy, baby
nivel *m.* level
no no; not (1)
noche *f.* night (9)
   esta noche tonight (7)
nombre *m.* name (6)
norte *m.* north
norteamericano(a) *m. (f.)* North American (3)
nosotros(as) *m. (f.)* we (1)
novecientos(as) nine hundred (12)

noventa ninety (7)
novia *f.* girlfriend (5)
novio *m.* boyfriend (5)
nuestro(a) our (4)
nueve nine (4)
nuevo(a) new (12)
número *m.* number (7)
nunca never (7)

O

o or (12)
ocho eight (4)
ochenta eighty (7)
ochocientos(as) eight hundred (12)
oferta *f.* sale (16)
  ¿No está(n) en oferta? It's not on
  sale? (16)
oficina de correos *f.* post office (7)
ofrecer to offer (17)
ojo *m.* eye
once eleven (4)
orden *m.* order (12)
  a sus órdenes at your service (12)
oreja *f.* ear
oro *m.* gold
otro(a) other, another (11)
  otra cosa *f.* another thing (11)

P

padre *m.* father (6)
  padres *m.* parents (2)
pagar to pay (12)
país *m.* country (8)
paisaje *m.* landscape
pájaro *m.* bird (5)
palabra *f.* word (1)
pan *m.* bread (1)
  pan dulce *m.* any kind of sweet roll
  (1)
  pan tostado *m.* toast (1)
panadería *f.* bakery (7)
Panamá Panama (3)
panameño(a) *m. (f.)* Panamanian (3)
pantalones *m.* trousers (18)
papa *f.* potato (17)
papel *m.* paper (16)
  papel de avión *m.* air mail stationery
  (16)
  papel para escribir a máquina *m.*
  typing paper (16)
papelería *f.* stationery store (16)
paquete *m.* package (17)

para for, in order to (1)
  para que in order that
Paraguay Paraguay (3)
paraguayo(a) *m. (f.)* Paraguayan (3)
pariente *m.* relative (6)
parque *m.* park (7)
  parque zoológico *m.* zoo (13)
pasado past, last (13)
pasar to pass (2)
  pasar tiempo to spend time (13)
paseo *m.* walk (10)
  dar un paseo to take a walk (10)
pasta *f.* pasta (17)
pastel *m.* pastry, pie (1)
patata *f.* potato (2)
  patatas bravas *f.* cooked potatoes
  diced and served in spicy sauce (2)
patinar to skate (14)
  patinar sobre hielo to ice skate (14)
pedazo *m.* piece (17)
pedir to ask for (something), to request (8)
peine *m.* comb
película *f.* film, movie (5)
  película cómica *f.* comedy movie
  (5)
  película de aventura *f.* adventure
  movie (5)
  película de ciencia ficción *f.* science
  fiction movie (5)
  película de horror *f.* horror movie
  (5)
peligro *m.* danger
peligroso(a) dangerous
pelirrojo(a) redheaded (6)
pelota *f.* ball (16)
  pelota de tenis *f.* tennis ball (16)
pendiente *m.* earring
pensar to think (11)
peor worse, worst (18)
pequeño(a) small (6)
pera *f.* pear (17)
perder to lose (13)
perdón excuse me (1)
periodista *m. or f.* journalist (3)
pero but (2)
perro *m.* dog (5)
perseguir to persecute, to pursue
persona *f.* person (6)
Perú Peru (3)
peruano(a) *m. (f.)* Peruvian (3)
a pesar de in spite of
pescado *m.* fish (17)
picante spicy (3)
piedra *f.* stone
pimienta *f.* pepper (17)

pintura *f.* painting (5)
piscina *f.* swimming pool (7)
planear to plan (12)
plano del metro *m.* subway map (11)
planta *f.* plant; floor (4)
plata *f.* silver
plátano *m.* banana, plantain (17)
plato *m.* dish
playa *f.* beach (12)
plaza *f.* plaza, square (7)
pluma *f.* fountain pen, feather (4),
poco little (1)
poder to be able to (10)
policía *f.* police, *m. or f.* police officer
  (7)
  estación de policía *f.* police station
  (7)
política *f.* politics (5)
pollo *m.* chicken (3)
poner to put, place (16)
por for (11)
  por eso that is why (16)
  por favor please (1)
  por fin finally (14)
  por la mañana in the morning (11)
  por la noche at night (11)
  por la tarde in the afternoon (11)
  por supuesto of course (9)
¿por qué? why? (6)
porque because (6)
portafolio *m.* briefcase (4)
posesión *f.* possession (4)
póster *m.* poster (4)
practicar to practice (1)
  practicar el surfing to surf (14)
  practicar la vela to sail (14)
precio *m.* price (16)
preferencia *f.* preference (17)
preferir to prefer (7)
pregunta *f.* qustion (2)
preguntar to ask a question (9)
premio *m.* prize (9)
preocupar to preoccupy, to worry
preparar to prepare (9)
presentación *f.* presentation, introduction
  (2)
presentar to present, introduce (1)
primero first (7)
primo(a) *m. (f.)* cousin (6)
producto *m.* product (17)
profesión *f.* profession (3)
profesor(a) *m. (f.)* professor, teacher (3)
pronombre *m.* pronoun (1)
pronto soon
propina *f.* tip (12)

proteger to protect
próximo(a) next (10)
prueba *f.* test
público(a) public (7)
pueblo *m.* town, a people
Puerto Rico Puerto Rico (3)
puertorriqueño(a) *m. (f.)* Puerto Rican (3)
pues then (1)

Q

que that (1)
¿qué? what? (6)
    ¿Qué día es hoy? What day is today? (10)
    ¿Qué hay? What's new? (1)
    ¿Qué hora es? What time is it? (9)
    ¿Qué pasa? What's going on? (1)
    ¿Qué tal? How are you? (1)
¡Qué... ! How ...! (3)
    ¡Qué bueno(a)! Great! (3)
    ¡Qué comida más rica! What delicious food! (3)
    ¡Qué hambre! I'm starving! (2)
    ¡Qué horrible! How terrible! (3)
    ¡Qué pena! What a pity! (16)
quemado(a) burned
quemar to burn
quedar to stay (8)
querer to want (7)
    Yo quisiera... I would like ... (1)
queso *m.* cheese (1)
¿quién? who? (3)
química *f.* chemistry (5)
quince fifteen (4)
quinientos(as) five hundred (12)
quiosco de periódicos *m.* newspaper kiosk (8)

R

radio despertador *m.* clock radio (4)
raqueta *f.* racket (16)
rara vez rarely (7)
razón *f.* reason
rebanada de pan *f.* slice of bread (1)
receta *f.* recipe
recibir to receive (5)
recordar to remember
recuerdo *m.* memory (3)
refresco *m.* soft drink (1)
regalo *m.* gift (18)
regatear to bargain (17)

regresar to return
regular regular; so-so (in response to greeting) (1)
reina *f.* queen
repaso *m.* review (3)
repetir to repeat (13)
República Dominicana Dominican Republic (3)
restaurante *m.* restaurant (1)
revista *f.* magazine
rey *m.* king
riquísimo(a) delicious (3)
rojo(a) red (17)
ropa *f.* clothes (18)
    ropa de marca *f.* designer clothes
rubio(a) blond(e) (6)
ruido *m.* noise
Rusia Russia (3)
ruso(a) *m. (f.)* Russian (3)

S

sábado *m.* Saturday (10)
sacapuntas *m.* pencil sharpener (4)
sacar to obtain, to get out (something) (14)
sal *f.* salt (17)
salir (de) to go out, leave (13)
salir con to go out with (13)
salsa *f.* sauce; type of music (3)
salud *f.* health
saludar to greet (1)
saludo *m.* greeting (2)
salvadoreño(a) *m. (f.)* Salvadoran (3)
sandalia *f.* sandal (18)
sándwich *m.* sandwich (1)
secretario(a) *m. (f.)* secretary (3)
seguir to follow, to continue
segundo(a) second
seguro(a) sure (18)
seis six (4)
seiscientos(as) six hundred (12)
semana *f.* week (11)
sentido *m.* sense
sentir to feel
    Lo siento. I'm sorry. (7)
señor Mr. (1)
señora Mrs. (1)
señorita Miss (1)
ser to be (3)
    Es de... Is from ..., It belongs to ... (3)
    Es la una y media. It is 1:30. (9)
    Son de... They are from ..., They belong to ... (3)

    Son las tres. It is 3 o'clock. (9)
serie *f.* series, sequence (14)
serio(a) serious (6)
servir to serve (12)
sesenta sixty (7)
setecientos(as) seven hundred (12)
setenta seventy (7)
si if (12)
sí yes (1)
siempre always (1)
siete seven (4)
silla *f.* chair (4)
simpático(a) nice (6)
sin without
sin límite unlimited (11)
sino but
sobre *m.* envelope (16)
sobre *prep., adv.* above
soda *f.* soda water (1)
sol *m.* sun
sólo only (12)
sopa *f.* soup (17)
su(s) his, her, your, their (4)
subir to raise
Sudamerica *f.* South America (2)
suerte *f.* fortune, luck
suéter *m.* sweater (18)
suficiente enough (16)
¡Super! Super! (16)
sur *m.* south
suroeste *m.* southwest
sustantivo *m.* noun (1)

T

taco *m.* taco, corn tortilla filled with meat and other things (3)
talla *f.* (clothing) size (18)
también also (2)
tampoco neither (2)
tan so (8)
    tan / tanto... como as / as much ... as (18)
tapa española *f.* Spanish snack (2)
taquilla *f.* booth (11)
tardar to take (an amount of time) (12)
tarde *f.* afternoon, late (7)
tarea *f.* task; homework (9)
tarjeta *f.* card (11)
    tarjeta de abono transportes *f.* commuter pass (11)
    tarjeta de cumpleaños *f.* birthday card (16)
    tarjeta del Día de la Madre *f.*

Mother's Day card (16)
taxi *m.* taxi (10)
té *m.* tea (1)
teatro *m.* theatre (7)
teléfono *m.* telephone (7)
telenovela *f.* soap opera (4)
televisor (a colores) *m.* (color) television set (4)
temer to fear
temporada *f.* (sports) season
tener to have (6)
    tener... años to be . . . years old (7)
    tener ganas de... to feel like . . . (10)
    tener hambre to be hungry (7)
    tener que to have to (6)
    tener sed to be thirsty (7)
tenis *m.* tennis (5)
tercero(a) third
terminar to end (13)
terremoto *m.* earthquake
tía *f.* aunt (6)
tiempo *m.* time (14)
    tiempo libre *m.* free time
tienda *f.* store (7)
    tienda de deportes *f.* sporting goods store (16)
    tienda de música *f.* music store (16)
    tienda de ropa *f.* clothing store (18)
tierra *f.* earth
tío *m.* uncle (6)
tocar to touch, to play an instrument (2)
    te toca a ti it's your turn
todavía still
todo(a) all (9)
    todos los días *m.* every day (1)
tomar to drink, to take (1)
    tomar el sol to sunbathe (14)
tomate *m.* tomato (17)
tonto(a) silly, stupid, foolish (6)
torre *f.* tower
tortilla *f.* omelette (Spain) or cornmeal pancake (Mexico) (2)
trabajador(a) *m. (f.)* worker
trabajar to work (1)
trabajo *m.* work
traer to bring
transporte *m.* transportation (4)
tratar de to try, to endeavor
trece thirteen (4)
treinta thirty (7)
tren *m.* train (7)
    estación de trenes train station (7)
tres three (4)
trescientos(as) three hundred (12)

triste sad (9)
tú you (familiar) (1)
tu(s) your (plural) (4)
turista *m. or f.* tourist (11)

U

un(a) a, an (1)
universidad *f.* university (7)
uno one (4)
uno(as) some (1)
Uruguay Uruguay (3)
uruguayo(a) *m. (f.)* Uruguayan (3)
usar to use (13)
usted (Ud.) you (formal) (1)
ustedes (Uds.) you (formal plural) (1)
usualmente usually (10)
útil useful
uva *f.* grape (17)

V

valiente brave
valor *m.* value
vaqueros *m.* jeans
varios(as) various (17)
vaso *m.* glass (1)
vegetal *m.* vegetable (17)
veinte twenty (4)
vendedor(a) *m. (f.)* salesman (woman) (17)
vender to sell (5)
venezolano(a) *m. (f.)* Venezuelan (3)
Venezuela Venezuela (3)
venir to come (9)
venta *f.* sale
ver to see (9)
    Nos vemos. See you. (farewell) (1)
verbo *m.* verb (1)
¿verdad? right? (2)
verdadero(a) true, real
verde green (17)
vestido *m.* dress (18)
vestir to dress
vez *f.* time, instance (9)
    una vez once (17)
    una vez al año once a year (9)
vía *f.* (railway) track
viajar to travel (1)
viaje *m.* trip (12)
    agencia de viajes *f.* travel agency (12)
vida *f.* life (13)
vídeo *m.* video (4)
videocasetera *f.* videocassette player (4)

viejo(a) old (6)
viernes *m.* Friday (10)
Vietnam Vietnam (3)
vietnamita *m. or f.* Vietnamese (3)
visitar to visit (7)
vista *f.* sight
vivienda *f.* housing (4)
vivir to live (5)
vólibol *m.* volleyball (5)
volver to go back (13)
vosotros(as) *m. (f.)* you (familiar plural) (1)
voz *f.* voice

W

waterpolo *m.* waterpolo (14)
windsurf *m.* windsurfing (14)

Y

y and (1)
yo I (1)
yogur *m.* yogurt (17)

Z

zanahoria *f.* carrot (17)
zapatería *f.* shoe store (18)
zapato *m.* shoe (18)
    zapato de tacón *m.* high-heeled shoe (18)
    zapato de tenis *m.* tennis shoe (16)

T461

Glossary

English-Spanish

The numbers in parentheses refer to the chapters in which active words or phrases may be found.

A

ability **habilildad** *f.*
(to be) able to **poder** (10)
above **sobre**
accountant **contador(a)** *m. (f.)* (3)
across from **frente a** (8)
action **acción** *f.* (9)
address **dirección** *f.* (7)
adventure movie **película de aventura** *f.* (5)
adverb **adverbio** *m.* (1)
advertisement **anuncio** *m.*
after **después de** (1)
afternoon **tarde** *f.* (7)
afterwards **luego** (14)
against **contra**
age **edad** *f.* (7)
air mail stationery **papel de avión** *m.* (16)
airport **aeropuerto** *m.* (7)
all **todo(a)** (9)
almost **casi**
also **también** (2)
alteration **cambio** *m.* (12)
although **aunque**
always **siempre** (1)
ambassador **embajador** *m.*
American **americano(a)** *m. (f.)* (3), (from the United States) **estadounidense** *m. or f.* (3)
amusing **divertido(a)** (6)
and **y** (1)
angry **enojado(a)** (9)
animal **animal** *m.* (5)
(to) announce **anunciar** (9)
another **otro(a)** (11)
    another thing **otra cosa** *f.* (11)
(to) answer **contestar** (1)
any **cualquier** (13)
apartment **apartamento** *m.* (4)
(to) apologize **disculparse** (7)
apple **manzana** *f.* (17)
appointment **cita** *f.* (10)
architect **arquitecto(a)** *m. (f.)* (3)
Argentina **Argentina** (3)
Argentine **argentino(a)** *m. (f.)* (3)
(to) argue **discutir** (12)
around **alrededor**

A (cont.)

(to) arrive **llegar** (8)
arrow **flecha** *f.*
art **arte** *m. or f.* (5)
as **como** (11)
    as / as much … as **tan / tanto… como** (18)
    as usual **como de costumbre** (11)
(to) ask a question **preguntar** (6)
(to) ask for (something) **pedir** (8)
at **a** (1)
    at night **por la noche** (11)
    at some other time **en otra oportunidad** (7)
    at the end of **al final de** (8)
at this moment **en este momento** (15)
    At what time? **¿A qué hora?** (9)
    at your service **a sus órdenes** (12)
(to) attend **asistir a** (13)
aunt **tía** *f.* (6)
avocado **aguacate** *m.* (17)

B

bad **malo(a)** (6)
bakery **panadería** *f.* (7)
ball **pelota** *f.* (16)
balloon **globo** *m.* (1)
banana **banana** *f.,* **plátano** *m.* (1)
bank **banco** *m.*
(to) bargain **regatear** (17)
baseball **béisbol** *m.* (5)
basketball **básquetbol** *m.* (5); **baloncesto** *m. (14)*
battle **batalla** *f.*
(to) be **estar** (8), **ser** (3)
    to be in shape **estar en forma**
beach **playa** *f.* (12)
beans **frijoles** *m.* (3)
beautiful **hermoso(a)** (12)
beauty **belleza** *f.*
because **porque** (6)
bed **cama** *f.* (4)
before **antes** (12)
(to) begin **empezar**
behind **detrás de** (8)
belt **cinturón** *m.* (18)
beside **al lado de** (8)
besides **además** (17)

B (cont.)

better **mejor** (9)
between **entre** (8)
big **grande** (6)
bicycle **bicicleta** *f.* (4)
biology **biología** *f.* (5)
bird **pájaro** *m.* (5), **ave** *f.*
birthday card **tarjeta de cumpleaños** *f.* (16)
biscuit **galleta** *f.* (17)
black **negro** (18)
blond(e) **rubio(a)** (6)
blouse **blusa** *f.* (18)
blue **azul** (18)
boat **barco** *m.*
body **cuerpo** *m.*
Bolivia **Bolivia** (3)
Bolivian **boliviano(a)** *m. (f.)* (3)
book **libro** *m.* (4)
bookshelf **estante** *m.* (4)
bookstore **librería** *f.* (7)
boot **bota** *f.* (18)
booth **taquilla** *f.* (11)
bored, boring **aburrido(a)** (6)
(to) be born **nacer**
bottle **botella** *f.* (17)
boutique **boutique** *f.* (18)
boy **chico** *m.,* **niño** *f.*
boyfriend **novio** *m.* (5)
brave **valiente**
bread **pan** *m.* (1)
    bread, slice of **rebanada de pan** *f.* (1)
breakfast **desayuno** *m.* (1)
briefcase **portafolio** *m.* (4)
(to) bring **traer**
brother **hermano** *m.* (6)
brunet(te) **moreno(a)** (6)
(to) build **construir**
building **edificio** *m.* (7)
bunch **atado** *m.* (17)
(to) burn **quemar**
burned **quemado(a)**
bus **autobús** *m.* (4)
    bus terminal **estación de autobuses** *m.* (7)
business **negocio** *m.* (3)
businessman(woman) **hombre (mujer) de negocios** (3)
but **pero** (2)
butcher shop **carnicería** *f.* (7)

butter **mantequilla** *f.* (1)
(to) buy **comprar** (13)

C

café **café** *m.* (1)
(to) call **llamar** (7)
calculator **calculadora** *f.* (4)
(to be) called **llamarse** (4)
camera **cámara** *f.* (4)
can **lata** *f.* (17)
Canada **Canadá** (3)
Canadian **canadiense** *m.* or *f.* (3)
canned goods **preservas** *f. pl.* (17)
car **coche** *m.* (4)
card **tarjeta** *f.* (11)
career **carrera** *f.*
carpet **alfombra** *f.* (4)
carrot **zanahoria** *f.* (17)
(to) carry **llevar** (4)
cat **gato** *m.* (5)
cathedral **catedral** *f.* (7)
(to) celebrate **celebrar** (9)
center **centro** *m.* (16)
chair **silla** *f.* (4)
change **cambio** *m.* (12)
(to) change **cambiar** (11)
chart **esquema** *m.*
(to) chat **charlar** (1)
cheap **barato(a)** (11)
cheese **queso** *m.* (2)
chemistry **química** *f.* (5)
chicken **pollo** *m.* (3)
Chile **Chile** (3)
Chilean **chileno(a)** *m. (f.)* (3)
China **China** (3)
Chinese **chino(a)** *m. (f.)* (3)
chocolate **chocolate** *m.* (1)
church **iglesia** *f.* (7)
city **ciudad** *f.* (6)
classical music **música clásica** *f.* (5)
clay **barro** *m.*
clock radio **radio despertador** *m.* (4)
close (to) **cerca (de)** (7)
(to) close **cerrar**
clothes **ropa** *f.* (18)
    designer clothes **ropa de marca**
clothing store **tienda de ropa** *f.* (18)
club **club** *m.* (7)
coat **abrigo** *m.* (18)
coffee **café** *m.* (1)
cold **frío(a)** (1)
Colombia **Colombia** (3)
Colombian **colombiano(a)**

m. (f.) (3)
comb **peine** *m.*
(to) come **venir** (9)
(to) comment **comentar** (3)
commentary **comentario** *m.*
commuter pass **tarjeta de abono transportes**
    f. (11)
compact disc **disco compacto** *m.* (4)
company **compañía** *f.* (3)
comparison **comparación** *f.* (18)
computer **computadora** *f.* (4)
concert **concierto** *m.* (13)
(to) cook **cocinar** (13)
(to) continue **continuar** (9), **seguir**
cookie **galleta** *f.* (17)
cool **fresco(a)** (17)
corn **maíz** *m.* (17)
corner **esquina** *f.* (8)
Costa Rica **Costa Rica** (3)
Costa Rican **costarricense** *m.* or *f.* (3)
country **país** *m.* (8), (vs. city) **campo**
    m.
cousin **primo(a)** *m. (f.)* (6)
cream **crema** *f.* (17)
croissant **croissant** *m.* (1)
(to) cross **cruzar** (8)
Cuba **Cuba** (3)
Cuban **cubano(a)** *m. (f.)* (3)
custard, caramel **flan** *m.* (3)
customer **cliente** (17)
custom **costumbre** *f.*
cycling **ciclismo** *m.* (14)

D

dairy **lácteo(a)** (17)
    dairy product **producto lácteo** *m.* (17)
dance **baile** *m.* (9)
(to) dance **bailar** (1)
dance club **discoteca** (7)
danger **peligro** *m.*
dangerous **peligroso(a)**
date **cita** *f.* (10)
daughter **hija** *f.* (6)
day **día** *m.* (10)
death **muerte** *f.*
delicious **delicioso(a), riquísimo** (3)
delighted **encantado(a)** (2)
dentist **dentista** *m.* or *f.* (3)
desert **desierto** *m.*
desk **escritorio** *m.* (4)
(to) die **morir**
dining room **comedor** *m.*
direction **dirección** *f.* (7)

disagreeable **antipático(a)** (6)
dish **plato** *m.*
divorced **divorciado(a)** (6)
(to) do **hacer** (10)
    (to) do an errand **hacer un mandado**
    (10)
doctor **médico** *m.,* **doctor(a)** *m. (f.)* (3)
dog **perro** *m.* (5)
Dominican **dominicano(a)**
    m. (f.) (3)
Dominican Republic **República Dominicana**
    (3)
downtown **centro** *m.* (4)
dozen **docena** *f.* (17)
drawing **dibujo** *m.*
dress **vestido** *m.* (18)
(to) dress **vestir**
dresser **cómoda** *f.* (4)
drink **bebida** *f.* (1)
(to) drink **tomar** (1), **beber** (5)
drugstore **farmacia** *f.* (7)
during **durante** (15)

E

each **cada** (6)
ear **oreja** *f.*
(to) earn **ganar** (2)
earring **pendiente** *m.*
earth **tierra** *f.*
earthquake **terremoto** *m.*
(to) ease pain **desahogar**
easy **fácil**
(to) eat **comer** (1)
    (to) eat breakfast **desayunar**
Ecuador **Ecuador** (3)
Ecuadoran **ecuatoriano(a)**
    m. (f.) (3)
eight **ocho** (4)
eight hundred **ochocientos(as)** (12)
eighteen **dieciocho** (4)
eighty **ochenta** (7)
El Salvador **El Salvador** (3)
eleven **once** (4)
(to) end **terminar** (13)
enemy **enemigo(a)** *m. (f.)*
engineer **ingeniero(a)** *m. (f.)* (3)
England **Inglaterra** (3)
English **inglés (inglesa)** (3)
Englishman **inglés** *m.* (3)
Englishwoman **inglesa** *f.* (3)
(to) enjoy **disfrutar**
enough **suficiente** (16), **bastante** (1)
entrance ticket **entrada** *f.* (11)

envelope **sobre** *m.* (16)
equal **igual**
equality **igualdad** *f.* (18)
eraser **borrador** *m.* (4)
(to) establish **establecer** (18)
event **acontecimiento** *m.*
every **cada** (6)
  every day **todos los días** *m.* (1)
example **ejemplo** *m.*
  for example **por ejemplo**
exchange **intercambio** *m.* (3)
excuse me **perdón** (1)
to exercise **hacer ejercicio** (13)
expensive **caro(a)** (16)
(to) express **expresar** (1)
expression **expresión** *f.* (1)
eye **ojo** *m.*
eyeglasses **gafas** *f. pl.*

F

facing **frente a** (8)
fair **feria** *f.* (9)
to fall **caer**
family **familia** *f.* (6)
famous **famoso(a)** (12)
fan (person) **aficionado(a)** *m. (f.)*
far (from) **lejos (de)** (8)
fat **gordo(a)** (6)
father **padre** *m.* (6)
favorite **favorito(a)** (16)
(to) fear **temer**
(to) feel **sentir**
  (to) feel like . . . **tener ganas de...** (10)
festival (religious) honoring a town's patron
  saint **Fiesta del pueblo** *f.* (9)
field hockey **hockey sobre hierba** *m.* (14)
fifteen **quince** (4)
fifty **cincuenta** (7)
(to) fight **luchar**
film **película** *f.* (5)
finally **finalmente, por fin** (14)
(to) find **encontrar** (9)
fine **bien** (1)
fireworks **fuegos artificiales** *m.* (9)
first **primero** (7)
fish **pescado** *m.* (17)
five **cinco** (4)
five hundred **quinientos(as)** (12)
flour **harina** *f.* (17)
flower shop **florería** *f.* (7)
folk dance **baile folklórico** *m.* (9)
food **alimento** *m.* (17), **comida** *f.* (3)
foolish **tonto(a)** (6)

football **fútbol americano** *m.* (5)
for **para** (1), **por** (11)
fortune **suerte** *f.*
fortune-teller **adivino(a)** *m. (f.)*
forty **cuarenta** (7)
four **cuatro** (4)
four hundred **cuatrocientos(as)** (12)
fourteen **catorce** (4)
France **Francia** (3)
free **gratis**
French **francés (francesa)** *m. (f.)*
  (3)
frequently **a menudo** (7),
  frecuentemente (10)
Friday **viernes** *m.* (10)
friend **amigo(a)** *m. (f.)* (1)
from **de, desde** (9)
  from time to time **de vez en cuando** (7)
frozen **congelado(a)** (17)
fruit **fruta** *f.* (17)
  fruit salad **ensalada de**
  frutas *f.* (17)
full **lleno(a)** (17)
fun **divertido(a)** (6)
future **futuro** *m.* (15)

G

garage **garaje** *m.* (3)
German **alemán (alemana)**
  m. (f.) (3)
Germany **Alemania** (3)
(to) get out (something) **sacar** (14)
gift **regalo** *m.* (18)
girl **chica** *f.,* **niña** *f.*
girlfriend **novia** *f.* (5)
(to) give **dar** (8)
glass **vaso** *m.* (1)
globe **globo** *m.* (1)
(to) go **ir** (7)
  go ahead! **¡adelante!**
  (to) go along **andar** (13)
  (to) go back **volver** (13)
  (to) go camping **ir de camping** (14)
  (to) go down **bajar** (11)
  (to) go fishing **ir de pesca** (14)
  (to) go out **salir (de)** (13)
  (to) go shopping **ir de compras** (10)
  (to be) going to . . . **ir a...** (10)
gold **oro** *m.*
good **bueno(a)** (3)
  Good afternoon. **Buenas tardes.** (1)
  Good evening. **Buenas noches.** (1)
  Good morning. **Buenos días.** (1)

  Good night. **Buenas noches.** (1)
good-bye **adiós, chao** (1)
grace **gracia** *f.*
gram **gramo** *m.* (17)
grandfather **abuelo** *m.* (6)
grandmother **abuela** *f.* (6)
grape **uva** *f.* (17)
Great! **¡Qué bueno(a)!** (3)
green **verde** (17)
(to) greet **saludar** (1)
greeting **saludo** *m.* (2)
grenadine **granadina** *f.* (1)
group **grupo** *m.* (1)
Guatemala **Guatemala** (3)
Guatemalan **guatemalteco(a)** *m. (f.)* (3)
guitar **guitarra** *f.* (14)
gym **gimnasio** *m.* (13)

H

half **medio(a)** (17), **mitad** *f.*
  half kilo **medio kilo** (17)
ham **jamón** *m.* (1)
hamburger **hamburguesa** *f.* (3)
handsome **guapo(a)** (6)
happy **contento(a)** (9)
(to) have **tener** (6)
  (to) have just . . . **acabar de...** (2)
  (to) have lunch **almorzar** (12)
  (to) have supper **cenar** (13)
  (to) have to **tener que** (6)
he **él** (2)
health **salud** *f.*
heart **corazón** *m.*
Hello! **¡Hola!** (1)
  Hello? (answering the phone) **¡Bueno!,**
  ¡Diga! / ¡Dígame! (7)
help **ayuda** *f.* (8)
(to) help **ayudar**
her **su(s)** (4)
here **aquí** (4)
here is/are **aquí hay** (2)
high-heeled shoe **zapato de tacón** *m.* (18)
high school **escuela secundaria** *f.* (7)
his **su(s)** (4)
Hispanic **hispano(a)** *m. (f.)* (9)
homework **tarea** *f.* (9)
Honduran **hondureño(a)**
  m. (f.) (3)
Honduras **Honduras** (3)
(to) hope **esperar** (12)
horrible **horrible** (3)
horse **caballo** *m.*
hospital **hospital** *m.* (7)
hot **caliente** (1)

hot pepper **chile** m. (3)
hotel **hotel** m. (7)
hour **hora** f. (14)
house **casa** f. (4)
how **como** (11)
   how? **¿cómo?** (3)
   How are you? **¿Qué tal?** (1)
   How are you? (formal) **¿Cómo está Ud.?**
   (2), (informal) **¿Cómo estás?** (1)
   How can I help you (plural)? **¿En qué**
   puedo servirle(s)? (12)
   How is it / are they? **¿Cómo es / son?**
   (6)
   How is it going? **¿Cómo te va?** (1)
   how many? **¿cuántos(as)?** (6)
   How many are there? **¿Cuántos hay?**
   (4)
   How much is it (are they)? **¿Cuánto**
   cuesta(n)? (16)
   How old are you? **¿Cuántos años**
   tienes? (7)
   How . . . ! **¡Qué . . . !** (3)
   How terrible! **¡Qué horrible!** (3)
hug **abrazo** (1)
hundred **cien** (7), **ciento** (12)
(to be) hungry **tener hambre** (7)
(to) hunt **cazar**
husband **esposo** m. (6)

I

I **yo** (1)
ice cream **helado** m. (17)
(to) ice skate **patinar sobre hielo** (14)
idea **idea** f. (9)
if **si** (12)
impossible **imposible** (10)
in **en** (1)
   in front of **delante de** (8)
   in order to **para** (9)
   in order that **para que**
   in the afternoon **por la tarde** (11)
   in the meantime **mientras**
   in the morning **por la mañana** (11)
   In which direction? **¿En qué dirección?**
   (11)
Independence Day **Día de la Independencia**
   m. (9)
inside **dentro**
instance **vez** (7)
intelligent **inteligente** (6)
interesting **interesante** (6)
(to) introduce **presentar** (1)
introduction **presentación** f. (2)

(to) invite **invitar** (13)
It belongs to . . . **Es de...** (4)
It is 3 o'clock. **Son las tres.** (9)
It is 1:30. **Es la una y media.** (9)
It's at the end of . . . **Está a(l) final de...** (8)
It's not on sale? **¿No está(n) en oferta?** (16)
Italian **italiano(a)** m. (f.) (3)
Italy **Italia** (3)

J

jacket **chaqueta** f. (18)
Japan **Japón** (3)
Japanese **japonés (japonesa)** m. (f.) (3)
jazz **jazz** m. (5)
jeans **vaqueros** m.
jelly **mermelada** f. (1)
jewel **joya** f.
journalist **periodista** m. or f. (3)
juice **jugo** m. (1)

K

key **llave** f. (4)
kilogram **kilo** m. (17)
kilometer **kilómetro** m. (12)
king **rey** m.
kiss **beso** m. (5)
knapsack **mochila** f. (4)

L

landscape **paisaje** m.
language **lengua** f. (5)
large **grande** (6)
late **tarde** (9)
lawyer **abogado(a)** m. (f.) (3)
leaf **hoja** f. (16)
(to) learn **aprender** (5)
leather **cuero** m. (18)
(to) leave **salir (de)** (13)
leave (something) **dejar**
left **izquierda** (8)
legend **leyenda** f.
lemon **limón** m. (17)
lemonade **limonada** f. (1)
less . . . than **menos... que** (18)
Let's go . . . **Vamos ...** (1)
Let's see. **A ver.** (16)
letter **carta** f.
lettuce **lechuga** f. (17)
level **nivel** m.
library **biblioteca** f. (7)

life **vida** f. (13)
(to) lift weights **levantar pesas** (14)
like **como** (11)
(to) like **gustar** (5)
Likewise. **Igualmente.** (2)
line **línea** f. (11)
(to) listen **escuchar** (1)
liter **litro** m. (17)
little, a **poco(a)** (1)
(to) live **vivir** (5)
location **lugar** m. (7)
long **largo**
Look! **¡Mira!** (3)
   (to) look at **mirar** (2)
   (to) look for **buscar** (8)
(to) lose **perder** (13)
lot, a **mucho(a)** (1)
(to) lower **bajar** (11)
luck **suerte)** f.

M

machine **máquina** f. (4)
mad **enojado(a)** (9)
magazine **revista** f.
(to) maintain **mantener**
majority **mayoría** f.
(to) make **hacer** (10)
   (to) make the bed **hacer la cama** (13)
man **hombre** m. (3)
market **mercado** m. (7)
married **casado(a)** (6)
mayonnaise **mayonesa** f. (17)
me **mí** (1)
meal **comida** f. (1)
means of transportation **medio de transporte**
   m. (4)
meat **carne** f. (3)
mechanic **mecánico(a)** m. (f.) (3)
(to) meet **encontrar, encontrarse (con)** (9)
memory **recuerdo** m.
Mexican **mexicano(a)** m. (f.) (3)
   Mexican food **comida mexicana** (3)
Mexico **México** (3)
midday **mediodía** m. (9)
middle **medio** m. (4)
midnight **medianoche** f. (9)
mile **milla** f. (12)
milk **leche** f. (1)
milkshake **licuado** m. (1)
million **millón** (12)
minus **menos** (4)
minute **minuto** m. (14)
Miss **señorita** f. (1)

modern **moderno(a)** (18)
Monday **lunes** *m.* (10)
money **dinero** *m.* (2)
month **mes** *m.* (11)
more **más** (2)
more . . . than **más . . . que** (18)
morning **mañana** *f.* (10)
mother **madre** *f.* (6)
   Mother's Day card **tarjeta del Día de la Madre** *f.* (16)
motorcycle **motocicleta** *f.* (4)
mountain **montaña** *f.*
   mountain climbing **alpinismo** *m.* *(14)*
movie **película** *f.* (5)
   movie, comedy **película cómica** *f.* (5)
   movie, horror **película de horror** *f.* (5)
   movie theater **cine** *m.* (7)
Mr. **señor** *m.* (1)
Mrs. **señora** *f.* (1)
much **mucho** (1)
   very much **muchísimo** (1)
museum **museo** *m.* (7)
music **música** *f.* (5)
music store **tienda de música** (16)
must **deber** (10)
my **mi(s)** (4)

N

name **nombre** *m.* (6)
   last name **apellido** *m.* (6)
(to be) named **llamarse** (4)
nationality **nacionalidad** *f.* (3)
native **indígena**
nature **naturaleza** *f.* (5)
near **cerca (de)** (7)
(to) need **necesitar** (2)
neighborhood **barrio** *m.* (7)
neither **tampoco** (2)
never **nunca** (7)
new **nuevo(a)** (12)
newspaper kiosk **quiosco de periódicos** *m.* (8)
next **próximo(a)** (10)
   next to **al lado de** (8)
Nicaragua **Nicaragua** (3)
Nicaraguan **nicaragüense** *m. or f.* (3)
nice **simpático(a)** (6)
   Nice to meet you. **Mucho gusto.** (1)
night **noche** *f.* (9)
   last night **anoche** (13)
nine hundred **novecientos(as)** (12)

nine **nueve** (4)
nineteen **diecinueve** (4)
ninety **noventa** (7)
no **no** (1)
nobody **nadie**
noise **ruido** *m.*
noon **mediodía** (9)
north **norte** *m.*
North American **norteamericano(a)** *m. (f.)* (3)
notebook **cuaderno** *m.* (4)
nothing **nada** (13)
noun **sustantivo** *m.* (1)
now **ahora** (9)
number **número** *m.* (7)
nurse **enfermero(a)** *m. (f.)* (3)

O

(to) obtain **sacar** (14)
of **de** (3)
   of course **por supuesto** (9)
   Of course! **¡Claro!** (5)
   Of course! (reaffirmed) **¡Claro que sí!** (10)
(to) offer **ofrecer** (17)
often **a menudo** (7)
oil **aceite** *m.* (17)
OK **de acuerdo** (9)
old **viejo(a)** (6)
older **mayor** (18)
olive **aceituna** *f.* (2)
   olive oil **aceite de oliva** *m.*
omelette (Spain) **tortilla** *f.* (2)
on **en** (1)
   on foot **a pie** (10)
   on the corner of **en la esquina de** (8)
once **una vez** (17)
   once a year **una vez al año** (9)
one **uno** (4)
one hundred **ciento** (12)
onion **cebolla** *f.* (17)
only **sólo, solamente** (12)
open-air market **mercado al aire libre** *m.* (17)
or **o** (12)
orange **naranja** *f.* (1)
order **orden** *m.* (12)
other **otro(a)** (11)
our **nuestro(a)** (4)
over there **allá** (17)
(to) owe **deber** (10)
owner **dueño(a)** *m. (f.)*

P

(to) pack **hacer las maletas** (13)
package **paquete** *m.* (17)
painting **pintura** *f.* (5)
Panama **Panamá** (3)
Panamanian **panameño(a)** *m. (f.)* (3)
pants **pantalones** *m.* (18)
paper **papel** *m.* (16)
   piece of paper **hoja** *f.* (16)
parade **desfile** *m.* (9)
Paraguay **Paraguay** (3)
Paraguayan **paraguayo(a)** *m. (f.)* (3)
(to) pardon **disculpar** (7)
parents **padres** *m.* (2)
park **parque** *m.* (7)
parking lot **estacionamiento** *m.* (8)
party **fiesta** *f.* (9)
(to) pass **pasar** (17)
   pasta **pasta** *f.* (2)
pastry **pastel** *m.* (1)
(to) pay **pagar** (12)
pea **guisante** *m.* (17)
peach **melocotón** *m.* (1)
peanut **cacahuete** *m.* (2)
pear **pera** *f.* (17)
pen, ball-point **bolígrafo** *m.* (4)
pen, fountain **pluma** *f.* (4)
pencil **lápiz** *m.* (4)
   pencil sharpener **sacapuntas** *m.* (4)
people **gente** *f.*
pepper **pimienta** *f.* (17)
to persecute **perseguir**
person **persona** *f.* (6)
Peru **Perú** (3)
Peruvian **peruano(a)** *m. (f.)* (3)
pharmacy **farmacia** *f.* (7)
pie **pastel** *m.* (1)
piece **pedazo** *m.* (17)
place **lugar** *m.* (7)
plain **feo(a)** (6)
(to) plan **planear** (12)
plane **avión** *m.* (1)
plant **planta** *f.* (4)
(to) play (a sport or game) **jugar** (11)
   (to) play basketball **jugar al baloncesto** (14)
   (to) play field hockey **jugar al hockey sobre hierba** (14)
   (to) play golf **jugar al golf** (14)
   (to) play hockey **jugar al hockey** (14)
(to) play (an instrument) **tocar** (2)
player **jugador(a)** *m. (f.)*
plaza **plaza** *f.* (7)

please **por favor** (1)
poetry contest **concurso de poesía** *m.* (9)
police **policía** *f.* (7)
  police officer **policía** *m.* or *f.* (7)
  police station **estación de policía** *f.* (7)
politics **política** *f.* (5)
pool **piscina** *f.* (7)
poorly **mal** (1)
popular dance **baile popular** *m.* (9)
possession **posesión** *f.* (4)
post office **oficina de correos** *f.* (7)
poster **póster** *m.* (4)
potato **papa** *f.* (17), **patata** *f.* (2)
  potatoes: cooked, diced, and served in spicy sauce **patatas bravas** *f.* (2)
pound **libra** *f.* (17)
(to) practice **practicar** (1)
(to) prefer **preferir** (7)
preference **preferencia** *f.* (17)
(to) prepare **preparar** (9)
(to) present **presentar** (1)
presentation **presentación** *f.* (2)
preserve **conserva** *f.* (17)
pretty **bonito(a)** (6)
Pretty good. **Bastante bien.** (1)
price **precio** *m.* (16)
prize **premio** *m.* (9)
product **producto** *m.* (17)
profession **profesión** *f.* (3)
professor **profesor(a)** *m. (f.)* (3)
(to) protect **proteger**
public **público** (7)
Puerto Rican **puertorriqueño(a)** *m. (f.)* (3)
Puerto Rico **Puerto Rico** (3)
purse **bolsa** *f.* (4)
(to) put **poner** (16)

Q

quality **calidad** *f.* (3)
quantity **cantidad** *f.* (17)
queen **reina** *f.*
question **pregunta** *f.* (2)

R

racket **raqueta** *f.* (16)
(to) rain **llover**
raincoat **impermeable** *m.* (18)
(to) raise **subir**
rarely **rara vez** (7)
(to) reach **alcanzar**
(to) read **leer** (5)

ready **listo(a)** (9)
reason **razón** *f.*
(to) receive **recibir** (5)
recipe **receta** *f.*
red **rojo(a)** (17)
redhead **pelirrojo(a)** (6)
relative **pariente** *m.* (6)
remember **recordar**
(to) rent a video **alquilar un vídeo** (13)
(to) repeat **repetir** (13)
(to) request **pedir** (8)
(to) rest **descansar** (9)
restaurant **restaurante** *m.* (1)
(to) return **regresar**
review **repaso** *m.*
rice **arroz** *m.* (3)
(to) ride a bicycle **montar en bicicleta** (13)
right **derecha** (8)
  right? **¿verdad?** (2)
  right now **ahora mismo** (15)
rock music **música rock** *f.* (5)
(to) roller-skate **patinar** (14)
room **cuarto** *m.* (4)
round-trip ticket **billete de ida y vuelta** *m.* (12)
rug **alfombra** *f.* (4)
(to) run **correr** (5)
Russia **Rusia** (3)
Russian **ruso(a)** *m. (f.)* (3)

S

sad **triste** (9)
(to) sail **practicar la vela** (14)
salad **ensalada** *f.* (17)
sale **oferta** *f.* (16), **venta** *f.*
salesman(woman) **vendedor(a)** *m. (f.)* (17)
salt **sal** *f.* (17)
Salvadoran **salvadoreño(a)** *m. (f.)* (3)
same **mismo(a)**
sandal **sandalia** *f.* (18)
sandwich **sándwich** *m.* (1), (French bread) **bocadillo** *m.* (1)
Saturday **sábado** *m.* (10)
sauce **salsa** *f.* (3)
sausage **chorizo** *m.* (2)
(to) say **decir** (10)
  (to) say good-bye **despedirse** (1)
schedule **horario** *m.* (11)
school **colegio** *m.* (7), **escuela** *f.* (4)
science **ciencia** *f.* (5)
science fiction movie **película de ciencia ficción** *f.* (5)
sculpture **escultura** *f.* (5)

season (sports) **temporada** *f.*
secretary **secretario(a)** *m. (f.)* (3)
(to) see **ver** (9)
  See you. **Nos vemos.** (1)
  See you later. **Hasta luego.** (1)
(to) sell **vender** (5)
sense **sentido** *m.*
sequence, series **serie** *f.* (14)
serious **serio(a)** (6)
seven **siete** (4)
seven hundred **setecientos(as)** (12)
seventeen **diecisiete** (4)
seventy **setenta** (7)
(to) share **compartir** (5)
she **ella** (2)
shirt **camisa** *f.* (18)
shoe **zapato** *m.* (18)
shoe store **zapatería** *f.* (18)
(to) shop **ir de compras** (10)
shopping cart **carrito** *m.* (17)
shopping center **centro comercial** (16)
short **bajo(a)**, (in length) **corto(a)** (6)
should **deber** (10)
sick **enfermo(a)** (9)
sight **vista** *f.*
(to) sign **firmar**
silly **tonto(a)** (6)
silver **plata** *f.*
(to) sing **cantar** (1)
singer **cantante** *m.* or *f.*
sister **hermana** *f.* (6)
six **seis** (4)
six hundred **seiscientos(as)** (12)
sixteen **dieciseis** (4)
sixty **sesenta** (7)
size (clothing) **talla** (18)
(to) skate **patinar** (14)
ski **esquí** *m.* (16)
skirt **falda** *f.* (18)
(to) sleep **dormir** (15)
slice of bread **rebanada de pan** *f.* (1)
slow **despacio** (8)
small **pequeño(a)** (6)
snack **merienda** *f.* (1)
  snack, Spanish **tapa española** *f.* (2)
(to) snorkel **bucear** (14)
snorkeling **buceo** *m.*
so **tan** (8)
  so-so **más o menos** (1)
soccer **fútbol** *m.* (5)
sock **calcetín** *m.* (18)
soda **soda** *f.* (1)
soft drink **refresco** *m.* (1)
some **alguno(a)**

English-Spanish Glossary **467**

someday **algún día** (12)
something **algo** (1)
sometimes **a veces** (1)
son **hijo** m. (6)
song **canción** f.
soon **pronto**
I'm sorry. **Lo siento.** (7)
soup **sopa** f. (17)
south **sur** m.
southwest **suroeste** m.
space **espacio** m.
Spain **España** (3)
Spaniard **español(a)** m. (f.) (3)
Spanish **español(a)** (1)
speaker **bocina** (4)
special **especial** (11)
species **especie** f.
(to) spend **gastar**
(to) spend time **pasar tiempo** (13)
sphere **globo** m. (1)
spice **especia** f.
spicy **picante** (3)
spirit **espíritu** m.
sport **deporte** m. (5)
sporting goods store **tienda de deportes** f. (16)
sportsman (sportswoman) **deportista** m. or f.
square **plaza** f. (7), (geometry) **cuadrado** m.
squid **calamares** m. (2)
stadium **estadio** m. (7)
stage (phase) **etapa**
star **estrella** f.
station **estación** f. (7)
stationery store **papelería** f. (16)
(to) stay **quedar** (8)
stereo **estéreo** m. (4)
still **todavía**
stocking **media** f. (18)
stone **piedra** f.
store **tienda** f. (7)
story **cuento** m., **historia** f.
strawberry **fresa** f. (1)
street **calle** f. (8)
strength **fuerza** f.
student **alumno(a)** m. (f.) (4), **estudiante** m. or f. (3)
(to) study **estudiar** (1)
stupid **tonto(a)** (6)
style **moda** f. (18)
subway **metro** m. (11)
    subway map **plano del metro** m. (11)
    subway station **estación de metro**

f. (11)
success **éxito** m.
sugar **azúcar** m. (17)
sun **sol** m.
(to) sunbathe **tomar el sol** (14)
Sunday **domingo** m. (10)
Super! **¡Super!** (16)
sure **seguro(a)** (18)
(to) surf **practicar el surfing** (14)
survey **encuesta** f. (12)
sweater **suéter** m. (18)
sweet roll, any kind **pan dulce** m. (1)
(to) swim **nadar** (13)
swimming **natación** f. (14)
swimming pool **piscina** f. (7)

T

T-shirt **camiseta** f. (18)
tail **cola** f.
(to) take **tomar** (1), **llevar** (4)
    (to) take a trip **hacer un viaje** (13)
    (to) take a walk **dar un paseo** (10)
(to) talk **hablar** (1)
tall **alto(a)** (6)
tape (cassette) **cinta** f. (4)
    tape recorder **grabadora** f. (4)
taste **gusto** m. (5)
taxi **taxi** m. (11)
tea **té** m. (1)
teacher **profesor(a)** m. (f.) (3)
team **equipo** m. (13)
telephone **teléfono** m. (7)
    telephone conversation **conversación telefónica** f. (7)
television set, (color) **televisor (a colores)** m. (4)
(to) tell (a story) **contar**
ten **diez** (4)
tennis **tenis** m. (5)
    tennis ball **pelota de tenis** f. (16)
    tennis shoe **zapato de tenis** m. (16)
thank you **gracias** (1)
    Thank you very much. **Muchas gracias.** (1)
Thanksgiving Day mass **la misa de Acción de Gracias** f. (9)
that **aquel(la)**, **ese(a)** (17), **que** (1)
    that is why **por eso** (16)
    that one **ése(a)** m. (f.) (17)
    that one over there **aquél(la)** m. (f.) (17)
the **el** m., **la** f., (plural) **los** m., **las**

f. (2)
theater **teatro** m. (7)
    movie theater **cine** m. (7)
their **su(s)** (4)
then **entonces** (9), **luego** (14), **pues** (1)
there **allí** (4)
there is / are **hay** (4)
they **ellos(as)** m. (f.) (2)
thin **delgado(a)** (6)
thing **cosa** f. (4)
    another thing **otra cosa** f. (11)
(to) think **pensar** (11)
(to be) thirsty **tener sed** (7)
thirteen **trece** (4)
thirty **treinta** (4)
this **este(a)** (17)
this one **éste(a)** m. (f.) (17)
thousand **mil** (12)
three **tres** (4)
three hundred **trescientos(as)** (12)
Thursday **jueves** m. (10)
ticket **billete** m. (11)
    ticket, ten-trip **billete de diez viajes** m. (11)
    ticket, one-way **billete sencillo** m. (11)
time **tiempo** m. (14), **vez** f. (9)
tin **lata** f. (17)
tip **propina** f. (12)
tired **cansado(a)** (9)
to **a** (1)
    toast **pan tostado** m. (1)
today **hoy** (10)
together **junto(a)** (17)
tomato **tomate** m. (17)
tomorrow **mañana** (10)
tongue **lengua** f. (5)
tonight **esta noche** (7)
(to) touch **tocar** (2)
tourist **turista** m. or f. (11)
tower **torre** f.
town **pueblo** m.
toy **juguete** m.
track (railway.) **vía** f.
train **tren** m. (7)
    train station **estación de trenes** (7)
transportation **transporte** m. (4)
(to) travel **viajar** (1)
travel agency **agencia de viajes** f. (12)
trip **viaje** m. (12)
trousers **pantalones** m. (18)
true **verdadero(a)**
(to) try (endeavor) **tratar de**
Tuesday **martes** m. (10)

tuna **atún** *m.* (17)
(to) turn **doblar** (8)
twelve **doce** (4)
twenty **veinte** (4)
two hundred **doscientos(as)** (12)
typewriter **máquina de escribir** *f.* (4)
typing paper **papel para escribir a máquina** *m.* (16)

U

ugly **feo(a)** (6)
uncle **tío** *m.* (6)
(to) understand **comprender** (5)
unemployment **desempleo** *m.*
United States **Estados Unidos** (3)
university **universidad** *f.* (7)
unknown **desconocido(a)**
unlimited **sin límite** (11)
until **hasta** (9)
Uruguay **Uruguay** (3)
Uruguayan **uruguayo(a)** *m. (f.)* (3)
(to) use **usar** (13)
useful **útil**
usually **usualmente** (10), **de costumbre** (15)

V

value **valor** *m.*
various **varios(as)** (17)
vegetable **vegetal** *m.* (17)
vegetable salad **ensalada de vegetales (verduras)** *f.* (17)
Venezuela **Venezuela** (3)
Venezuelan **venezolano(a)** *m. (f.)* (3)
verb **verbo** (1)
very **muy, bien** (1)
very much **muchísimo** (1)
Very well, thank you. **Muy bien, gracias.** (1)
video **vídeo** *m.* (4)
videocassette player **videocasetera** *f.* (4)
Vietnam **Vietnam** (3)
Vietnamese **vietnamita** *m. or f.* (3)
(to) visit **visitar** (13)
voice **voz** *f.*
volleyball **vólibol** *m.* (5)

W

(to) wait **esperar** (12)
waiter (waitress) **camarero(a)** *m. (f.)* (1)

(to) walk **caminar, andar** (13)
(to) walk on the beach **caminar en la playa** (14).
a walk **paseo** *m.* (10)
walking **a pie** (10)
wallet **cartera** *f.* (4)
(to) want **desear** (1), **querer** (7)
I would like . . . **Yo quisiera. . .** (1)
(to) watch **mirar** (2)
water **agua** *f.* (1)
water ski **esquí acuático** *m.* (14)
we **nosotros(as)** *m. (f.)* (1)
Wednesday **miércoles** *m.* (10)
week **semana** *f.* (11)
weekend **fin de semana** *m.* (13)
welcome **bienvenido(a)** (3)
well **bien** (1)
what? **¿qué?, ¿cómo?** (1)
What a pity! **¡Qué pena!** (16)
What day is today? **¿Qué día es hoy?** (10)
What delicious food! **¡Qué comida más rica!** (3)
What's going on? **¿Qué pasó?** (1)
What's new? **¿Qué hay (de nuevo)?** (1)
What time is it? **¿Qué hora es?** (9)
What's your name? **¿Cómo te llamas?** (4)
when? **¿cuándo?** (9)
where? **¿adónde?** (7), **¿dónde?** (6)
Where are you from? **¿De dónde es (eres)?** (3)
Where is / are there . . . ? **¿Dónde hay. . . ?** (4)
Where is . . . ? **¿Dónde está. . . ?** (8)
which? **¿cuál?** (17)
white **blanco** (18)
who? **¿quién?** (3)
whole **entero** (11)
Whose is it? **¿De quién es. . . ?** (4)
why? **¿por qué?** (6)
wife **esposa** *f.* (6)
store window **escaparate** *m.* (16)
winter **invierno** *m.*
(to) wish for **desear** (1)
with **con** (1)
with me **conmigo** (10)
with pleasure **con mucho gusto** (1)
without **sin** *m.* (11)
woman **mujer** *f.* (3)
word **palabra** *f.* (1)
(to) work **trabajar** (1)
work **trabajo** *m.*
worker **trabajador(a)** *m. (f.)*

world **mundo** *m.*
(to) worry **preocupar**
worse, worst **peor** (18)
(to) write **escribir** (5)
written **escrito**

Y

year **año** *m.* (11)
(to be) . . . years old **tener. . . años** (7)
yellow **amarillo(a)** (17)
yes **sí** (1)
yesterday **ayer** (13)
yogurt **yogur** *m.* (17)
you (familiar) **tú,** (familiar plural) **vosotros (as)** *m. (f.),* (formal) **usted (Ud.),** (formal plural) **ustedes (Uds.)** (1)
you're welcome **de nada** (1)
young **joven** (11)
younger **menor** (18)
your **su(s)** (18), **tu(s)** (4)
youth **juventud** *f.*

Z

zoo **parque zoológico** *m.* (13)

Index

a
+ **el**, 160, 189
+ pronoun, 381
a, an, 12
¿a qué hora?, 208
able to do something, 251
abrazo, 5
activities
able to do something, 251
going to do something, 235, 361
hoping to do something, 285
imperatives, 196-198, 387, 392
past, 304, 310-311
planning to do something, 269, 361
wanting to do something, 169, 237, 285, 301-302, 361, 380-381
wishing to do something, 361
addresses, 176
directions, 185, 193, 258
adjectives
agreement with nouns, 57-58, 94, 138-139
of condition, **estar** and, 214
demonstrative, 403
descriptive, 138-139
expressing comparison, 424
nationality, 57-58
possessive, 94, 216
ser + adjective, 138
tan + adjective + **como**, 430
¿adónde?, 310
adverbs
expressing frequency, 162
expressing series of actions, 344
expressing the past, 322
gustar and, 7
frequency, 19
interrogative words, 411
for present and future tenses, 261-262
tan + adverb + **como**, 430
affirmative familiar commands, 387
afternoon, 207, 241-242, 261
age, 178
agreement
demonstrative adjectives, 403
nouns and adjectives, 57-58, 94, 138-139
nouns and indefinite articles, 12
al, 160, 189
alphabet, Spanish, 5
also, 39
andar, preterite tense, 322
animals, 113
anoche, 305
answering the telephone, 165
aquél, aquéllo(a), aquéllos(as), 412-413
aquel, aquella, aquellos(as), 403
-ar verbs
imperatives, 196-198

present tense, 17-18, 30-31
preterite tense, 304
art, 113
articles
definite, 79-80
indefinite, 12
asking. *See* questions

bar de tapas, 29
baseball, 351-352
be (**estar**), 190
+ adjectives of condition, 214
expressing present progressive, 353-354, 361
preterite tense, 322
be (**ser**)
+ **de**, 108
imperatives, 198, 387, 392
present tense, 52
belonging. *See* possession
beverages, 9-10
expressing hunger or thirst, 178
billetes, 266-268
buildings, 157-158, 164, 173-174
directions to, 185, 193
buying, 173-174, 379
clothes and shoes, 421-422, 428
open-air markets, 399-400
ordering food and beverages, 9-10, 47-48, 56
stationery, 384
tickets, 266-268

cabs, 276
cafés, 13
ordering food and beverages, 9-10, 47-48, 56
can do something, 251
-car verbs
negative **tú** imperatives, 392
preterite tense, 343
cien, ciento, 280
cities, 158
clothing stores, 421-422, 428
collective nouns, 80
colors, 422
come (**venir**), 209
commands, 196-198, 387, 392
comparisons, 424
conditions, adjectives of, 214
countries, 53
adjectives of nationality, 57-58
¿cuál?, ¿cuáles?, 411
¿cuándo?, 208
¿cuántos?, ¿cuántas?, 135-136
culture
addresses, 176

American sports, 351-352
cities, 158
holidays, 205
introducing and meeting people, 36-37
La Puerta del Sol, 279
metro, 260
open-air markets, 400
public transportation, 268
Spanish-speaking countries, 53
speaking Spanish, 194
stores, 174
supermarkets, 409
tallas (shoe sizes), 431
tapas, 29
telephone conversations, 165
telephone numbers, 176

days
days of the week, 241-242, 244, 318
time of day, 207, 241-242, 261
de
del, 189
indicating possession, 81, 108
in names, 127
decir, imperative forms, 387, 392
definite articles, 79-80
del, 189
demonstrative adjectives, 403
demonstrative pronouns, 412-413
descriptive adjectives, 138-139
desire
encantar, 380
gustar, 6-7, 105, 380-381
past, present, and future, 361
preferir, 169, 361
querer, 169, 361
to do something, 237, 285, 301-302, 361
Día de la Independencia, 204
directions, 185, 193, 258
dislikes. *See* likes and dislikes
do (**hacer**), 245
expressing how long ago, 332
imperative forms, 387, 392
preterite tense, 306
+ **que**, 332
¿dónde?, 135-136, 185, 193
¿adónde?, 310
drinking beverages, 9-10

eating
beverages, 9-10
expressing hunger or thirst, 178
foods, 15
meals, 20
either, 39
el, 79-80
a +, 160, 189

de +, 189
él, ella, ellos(as), 31
embraces, 5
encantar, 380
entonces, 344
equality, 430
-er verbs
    imperatives, 196-198
    present tense, 116
    preterite tense, 314
ese, esa, esos(as), 403
ése, ésa, eso, ésos(as), 412-413
esperar + infinitive, 361
estar, 190
    + adjectives of condition, 214
    expressing present progressive, 353-354, 361
    preterite tense, 322
este, esta, estos(as), 403
éste, esta, esto, éstos(as), 412-413
evening, 207, 242, 261
extended family, 132, 134

familiar commands, 387, 392
family, 124, 132, 134
fewer, 424
finally, 344
finalmente, 344
first, 344
food, 9, 15, 47-48, 56
    beverages, 9-10
    expressing hunger or thirst, 178
    fruits and vegetables, 409
    meals, 20
    open-air markets for, 399-400
    ordering, 9-10, 47-48, 56
    snacks, 27
    supermarkets for, 408-409
for what reason?, 231-232
formal introductions, 36-37
frequency, 19, 162, 178
fruits, 409
furnishings, 84-85, 91
future tense, 361
    adverbs for, 261-262
    ir a + infinitive, 235, 361

-gar verbs
    negative **tú** imperatives, 392
    preterite tense, 335
gender
    demonstrative adjectives, 403
    indefinite articles, 12
    noun-adjective agreement, 57-58, 94, 138
    nouns and, 12
    possessive adjectives, 216
    profession nouns, 60

third person pronouns, 31
giving directions, 185, 193, 258
go (**ir**), 160
    imperatives, 198, 387, 392
    ir a + infinitive, 235, 361
    preterite tense, 310-312
going to do something, 235, 361
greetings and goodbyes, 3-5, 36-37
    on telephone, 165
gustar, 105, 380-381
    adverbs for, 7
    + infinitive, 6

hacer, 245
    expressing how long ago, 332
    imperative forms, 387, 392
    preterite tense, 306
    + **que**, 332
hambre, 178
have (**tener**)
    asking person's age, 178
    expressing hunger or thirst, 178
    preterite tense, 322
hay, 87
her, his, 216
holidays, 204-205, 212
home furnishings, 84-85, 91
hoping to do something, 285
hours, 207
how many?, 135
hoy, 241-242, 261
hunger, 178

imperatives, 196-198, 387, 392
indefinite articles, 12
informal introductions, 36-37
information questions, 135-136
interrogative words, 411
introducing people, 3, 36-37
ir, 160
    imperatives, 198, 387, 392
    ir a + infinitive, 235, 361
    preterite tense, 310-312
-ir verbs
    imperatives, 196-198
    present tense, 116
    preterite tense, 314
irregular second-person commands, 198
its, 216

job names, 60

la, las, 79-80
last names, 125
leavetaking. *See* greetings and goodbyes
less, 424
likes and dislikes, 103-104

encantar, 380
gustar, 6-7, 105, 380-381
    past, present, and future, 361
    preferir, 169, 361
    querer, 169, 361
    sports, 331
    wanting to do something, 237, 285, 301-302, 361
location
    addresses, 176
    asking where something is, 135
    asking where something is from, 52
    directions to, 185, 193, 258
    time to travel to, 276-277, 279, 283
los, 79-80
love to do something, 169, 381

making plans. *See* planning
mañana, 207, 241-242, 261
markets, 399-400, 408-409
más, 424
meals, 20
meeting people, 3-5, 36-37
menos, 424
mercados, 399-400
metro, 258, 260
more, 424
morning, 207, 241-242, 261
movies, 112
music, 113

names
    countries, 52
    de in, 127
    last names, 125
nationality, 57-58
-ndo form of verbs, 353-354, 361
negative familiar commands, 392
neither, 39
night, 207, 242, 261
noche, 207, 242, 261
nosotros, nosotras, 17
nouns
    agreement with adjectives, 57-58, 94, 138-139
    collective, 80
    gender and, 12
    professions, 60
    specific, 80
numbers
    0 to 20, 86-87
    20 to 100, 176
    100 to 1,000,000, 279-280
    age, 178
    asking how many, 135
    expressing specific quantity, 404
    frequency, 19, 162, 178

open-air markets, 399-400
ordering food and beverages, 9-10, 47-48, 56

papelerías, 384
paper stores, 384
¿para qué?, 231-232
past
    activities, 304, 310-311
    adverbs for, 320
    expressing how long ago, 332
pensar, 269, 361
people
    ages, 178
    expressing condition of, 214
    family, 124, 132, 134
    meeting, 3-5, 36-37
    professions, 60
    talking on telephone, 165
    titles for, 80
place (**poner**), imperative forms, 387, 392
plan (**pensar**), 269, 361
planning
    going to do something, 235, 361
    hoping to do something, 285
    pensar, 269, 361
    wanting to do something, 169, 237, 285,
        301-302, 361, 380-381
playing sports, 113, 329-331, 338-339, 351-352,
    358-359
plaza, 158
plurals, formation of, 58, 60, 138-139
poder, 251
poner, imperative forms, 387, 392
por fin, 344
¿por qué?, 135-136
possession, 216
    adjectives for, 94
    expressing with **de**, 81, 108
    expressing with **tener**, 127
    pronouns for, 216
    talking about, 77-78, 82-86, 89, 94-96
preferences. *See* likes and dislikes
preferir, 169, 361
prepositions expressing the past, 322
present progressive, 353-354, 361
present tense, 361
    adverbs for, 261-262
    -ar verbs, 17-18, 30-31
    -er and **-ir** verbs, 116
    ser, 52
preterite tense, 361
    andar, estar, tener, 322
    -ar verbs, 304
    -car verbs, 343
    -er and **-ir** verbs, 314
    -gar verbs, 335
    hacer, 306

ir, 310-312
primero, 344
professions, 60
progressives, 353-354, 361
pronouns
    a +, 381
    demonstrative, 412-413
    expressing possession, 216
    subject pronouns, 17
    third person, 31
pronunciation
    a, 126, 133
    /b/ sound, 93
    c, 195, 260
    ch, 107, 114
    d, 402
    f, 160, 167
    g, 234
    h, 93
    i, 278
    j, 206
    /k/ sound, 213
    l, 38
    ll, 79
    m and **n**, 93
    ñ, 380
    o, 187
    p, 86
    qu, 126, 133
    r, 187
    s, 11
    /s/ sound, 28
    Spanish alphabet, 175
    t, 424
    u, 187, 185
    v, 5
    z, 50
public buildings, 157-158, 164, 173-174
    directions to, 185, 193
public transportation, 266, 268
Puerta del Sol, 279
put (**poner**), imperative forms, 387, 392

quantity. *See* number
¿qué hora es?, 207
querer, 169, 361
questions
    about location, 135-136, 185, 193, 310
    about time, 207-208
    asking for directions, 185, 193, 258
    ¿cuál?, ¿cuáles?, 411
    ¿cuántos?, ¿cuántas?, 135-136
    greetings and goodbyes, 3-5
    for information, 135-136
    for what reason?, 231-232
    who?, 135-136
    why?, 135-136

yes/no, 33
¿quién?, 135-136
quisiera + infinitive, 361

restaurants, 13
    bar de tapas, 29
    ordering food and beverages, 9-10, 47-48,
        56
room furnishings, 84-85, 91

salir, imperative forms, 387, 392
say (**decir**), imperative forms, 387, 392
school supplies, 77
second person imperatives, 196-198
sed, 178
ser
    + adjective, 138
    + **de**, 108
    imperatives, 198, 387, 392
    present tense, 52
series of actions, 344
shoe sizes, 431
shoe stores, 428
shopping, 173-174, 379
    for clothing and shoes, 421-422, 428
    open-air markets, 384
    for stationery, 384
    supermarkets, 408-409
    for tickets, 266-268
snacks, 27
some, 12
Spanish alphabet, 5
Spanish-speaking countries, 53
sports, 113, 329-331
    baseball, 351-352
    in summer, 338-339
    tennis, 358-359
stationery stores, 384
stores, 173-174, 379
    for clothing and shoes, 421-422, 428
    open-air markets, 384
    for stationery, 384
    supermarkets, 408-409
    for tickets, 266-268
su, sus, 216
subject pronouns, 17
    third person, 31
subways, 258, 266
    La Puerta del Sol, 279
summer sports, 338-339
supermarkets, 408-409

tallas, 431
también, 39
tampoco, 39
tan + adjective + **como**, 430
tan + adverb + **como**, 430

tanto(a) + noun + **como**, 430
tantos(as) + noun + **como**, 430
tapas, 27, 29
taquilla, 266
tarde, 207, 241-242, 261
taxis, 276
telephone conversations, 165
telephone numbers, 176
tell (**decir**), imperative forms, 387, 392
telling time, 207
tener, 127
    asking about someone's age, 178
    expressing hunger or thirst, 178
    imperative forms, 387, 392
    preterite tense, 322
    + **que** + infinitive, 129
    tener ganas de + infinitive, 237, 361
tennis, 358-359
that, 403
that one, 412-413
the, 80
their, 216
then, 344
there is, *there are*, 87
these, 403
these ones, 412-413
think (**pensar**), 269, 361
third person pronouns, 31
    expressing possession, 216
thirst, 178
this, 403
this one, 412-413
those, 403
those ones, 412-413
tickets, 266-268
time
    adverbs for, 261-262
    asking about, 208
    days of the week, 241-242, 244, 318
    expressing how long ago, 332
    expressing series of actions, 344
    expressing with verbs, 361
    how to tell, 207
    in the past, 304
    summer, 338-339
    time of day, 241-242
    to travel to a destination, 276-277, 279, 283
titles for people, 80
today, 241-242, 261
tomorrow, 241-242, 261
trains. *See* subways
transportation, 248-249
    directions, 185, 193, 258
    La Puerta del Sol, 279
    public transportation, 266, 268
    subways, 258, 266
    taxis, 276

    time to travel, 266-267, 279, 283
    travel agencies, 283
    vehicles, 91, 283
travel agencies, 283
trips, 283
tú, 17
    imperatives with, 387, 392

Ud., Uds., 17, 31
    imperatives with, 196-198
un, una, unos, unas, 12
usted, ustedes, 17, 31
    imperatives with, 196-198

vacations, 283
vegetables, 409
vehicles, 91, 283
venir, 209
    imperative forms, 387, 392
verbs
    conjugated, followed by infinitive, 39
    ending in **-ar**. *See* **-ar** verbs
    ending in **-er**. *See* **-er** verbs
    ending in **-ir**. *See* **-ir** verbs
    expressing time and, 361
    imperatives, 196-198, 387, 392
    -ndo form, 353-354, 361
vosotros, vosotras, 17

walk (**andar**), preterite tense, 322
wanting
    encantar, 380
    gustar, 6-7, 105, 380-381
    past, present, and future, 361
    planning to do something, 269, 361
    preferir, 169, 361
    querer, 169, 361
    to do something, 237, 285, 301-302, 361
weekdays, 241-242, 244
weeks, activities of, 318
what?, 135, 411
what time?, 207
when?, 208
where?, 135, 185, 193, 310
which?, *which ones?*, 411
who?, 135
why?, 136, 231-232
wish (**esperar**), 361

yes/no questions, 33
yo, 17

-zar verbs, negative imperative forms, 392